CAMBRIDGE LIBRARY COLLECTION

Books of enduring scholarly value

Religion

For centuries, scripture and theology were the focus of prodigious amounts of scholarship and publishing, dominated in the English-speaking world by the work of Protestant Christians. Enlightenment philosophy and science, anthropology, ethnology and the colonial experience all brought new perspectives, lively debates and heated controversies to the study of religion and its role in the world, many of which continue to this day. This series explores the editing and interpretation of religious texts, the history of religious ideas and institutions, and not least the encounter between religion and science.

Adversaria Critica Sacra

Published posthumously in 1893, Frederick Scrivener's Adversaria Critica Sacra remains a volume of key importance to biblical scholars today, representing Scrivener's remarkable accuracy in his study and collation of manuscripts. During an age when many manuscripts were being newly discovered, and New Testament textual criticism was a rapidly developing field, Scrivener's collations played an important role in highlighting and making available the many different readings in existence. The book presents sixty-three manuscripts containing all or part of the Greek New Testament, including twenty which contain the Gospels in whole or in part, fifteen Lectionaries (Greek Church Lesson-books), five copies of Acts and the Catholic Epistles, and ten which are collations of the earliest printed editions of the Greek New Testament. Scrivener provides an informative general account of each manuscript, and an estimate of their respective critical values.

Cambridge University Press has long been a pioneer in the reissuing of out-of-print titles from its own backlist, producing digital reprints of books that are still sought after by scholars and students but could not be reprinted economically using traditional technology. The Cambridge Library Collection extends this activity to a wider range of books which are still of importance to researchers and professionals, either for the source material they contain, or as landmarks in the history of their academic discipline.

Drawing from the world-renowned collections in the Cambridge University Library, and guided by the advice of experts in each subject area, Cambridge University Press is using state-of-the-art scanning machines in its own Printing House to capture the content of each book selected for inclusion. The files are processed to give a consistently clear, crisp image, and the books finished to the high quality standard for which the Press is recognised around the world. The latest print-on-demand technology ensures that the books will remain available indefinitely, and that orders for single or multiple copies can quickly be supplied.

The Cambridge Library Collection will bring back to life books of enduring scholarly value (including out-of-copyright works originally issued by other publishers) across a wide range of disciplines in the humanities and social sciences and in science and technology.

Adversaria
Critica Sacra

With a Short Explanatory Introduction

FREDERICK HENRY AMBROSE SCRIVENER

CAMBRIDGE UNIVERSITY PRESS

Cambridge, New York, Melbourne, Madrid, Cape Town, Singapore,
São Paolo, Delhi, Dubai, Tokyo

Published in the United States of America by Cambridge University Press, New York

www.cambridge.org
Information on this title: www.cambridge.org/9781108007481

© in this compilation Cambridge University Press 2009

This edition first published 1893
This digitally printed version 2009

ISBN 978-1-108-00748-1 Paperback

ADVERSARIA CRITICA SACRA.

London: C. J. CLAY AND SONS,
CAMBRIDGE UNIVERSITY PRESS WAREHOUSE,
AVE MARIA LANE.

Cambridge: DEIGHTON, BELL AND CO.
Leipzig: F. A. BROCKHAUS.
New York: MACMILLAN AND CO.

ADVERSARIA CRITICA

SACRA

WITH A SHORT EXPLANATORY INTRODUCTION

BY

FREDERICK H. A. SCRIVENER, M.A., D.C.L., LL.D.,

PREBENDARY OF EXETER, VICAR OF HENDON,
SOMETIME SCHOLAR OF TRINITY COLLEGE, CAMBRIDGE,
ONE OF THE COMPANY OF THE REVISERS OF THE NEW TESTAMENT.

QUOD POTUI.

CAMBRIDGE:
AT THE UNIVERSITY PRESS.
1893

𝕮𝖆𝖒𝖇𝖗𝖎𝖉𝖌𝖊

PRINTED BY C. J. CLAY, M.A. AND SONS,
AT THE UNIVERSITY PRESS.

ADVERTISEMENT.

The editor begs leave to return his grateful thanks to the Syndics of the Cambridge University Press for their most liberal aid in publishing the present and not a few of his earlier works. The arrangement of the critical matter here presented for the first time is unusual, but he trusts that it will not prove very inconvenient to the reader : it was unavoidable, in consequence of a dimness of sight which grew upon him during the time these sheets were laboriously passing through the press.

TABLE OF CONTENTS.

INTRODUCTION.

1. No phase in the ordinary experience of human life is more melancholy, than the spectacle of a scholar's breaking off abruptly work undertaken on a large scale and with a high purpose, by reason of the stroke of death, often of sudden death. It was thus that the historian Thucydides was hindered from completing his "possession for ever," by closing his narrative at the end of the twenty-first year of the Peloponnesian war, although that struggle was protracted for six years longer; nay more, by leaving his eighth book a mere rude sketch, after he had wrought the preceding seven to the most elaborate perfection. It was thus that Lord Macaulay, who had projected and made copious preparations for the History of England for a period of some hundred and twenty years, was taken from us before he had achieved more than a third part of his ambitious design. This calamity, one of the saddest incidents of our mortal lot, has fallen especially heavy upon the students of the Textual Criticism of the New Testament, whose field embraces labour so wide and varied, that no single life can hope to cover more than a small portion of it. Tischendorf, for example, was stricken down, almost in late middle age, in the midst of his zealous and happy researches, hardly leaving behind him an unpublished vestige of what he had discovered and expected to make known to the world. Tregelles left his pious work little better than a fragment, to be supplemented, so far as it could be at all, by the charitable toil of strangers who honoured him for the disinterested devotion of his whole existence to the illustration of Holy Scripture. Matthaei was forced to bequeath his painful collations of no less than twenty-four manuscripts, to a German bookseller, who probably lacked the means rather than the will to print them. But the most afflicting instance of all is that of Bentley, the prince of English scholars, the fruit of whose efforts in this

S.   b

divine study, spread over at least twenty years, is now contained in a few manuscript collations, in a state too crude
for publication, preserved in the Library of Trinity College,
Cambridge, a foundation of which its humblest member may
well be proud, since the Mastership of the College did honour
even to him. When it pleased God to smite me with what
I believed to be deadly sickness, the like fate (if I might
venture to compare great things with very small) seemed
reserved for my own literary collections. I had accumulated
them during the broken and scanty leisure of forty years, and
seemed now called upon to leave them, without having contri-
buted whatever light they might be able to afford to the solu-
tion of the hitherto uncertain problem of settling the sacred
text of the New Testament. In this instance, however, the
Divine mercy has proved better than my faithless fears. Life
and intellectual vigour have been in some measure restored
to me. The Syndics of the Cambridge University Press have
been pleased to aid me in presenting to the publick my latest
contribution to this branch of learning, as thirty-five years ago
they printed for me one of my earliest. Other friends[1] too have
volunteered such help as will enable me to commence in hope
a task which I can hardly expect adequately to complete.

2. Of the sixty-three manuscripts of the Greek New
Testament and other like documents which this volume
is designed to illustrate, twenty contain the Gospels in
whole or in part, five the Acts and Catholic Epistles,

[1] Chiefly the venerated J. W. Burgon, B.D., Dean of Chichester, whose
death (4th Aug. 1888), while these lines were in press, is destined to add
another name to the above melancholy list of unfinished work. He had been
engaged day and night for years, in making a complete index or view of the
manuscripts used by the Nicene (and ante-Nicene) Fathers, by way of shewing
that they were not identical with those copied in Codd. ℵ and B, and, inasmuch as they were older, they must needs be purer and more authentic than
these overvalued uncials. The enterprise is now a fragment, but its effect
on the stability of the opposite system is direct and cannot be shaken. Such
failures remind us of Wordsworth's lines,

> Things incomplete, and purposes destroyed,
> Make sadder transits o'er Truth's mystic glass
> Than nobler objects utterly decayed.

(Sir Henry Taylor, *Notes from Life*, p. 162.)

five S. Paul's Epistles, four the Apocalypse, fifteen are Lectionaries, or Greek Church Lesson-books, six contain palimpsest and other fragments of the Septuagint Greek Version of the Old Testament, ten are collations of the earliest printed editions of the Greek New Testament. Of each of these I will first submit to the reader some general account and estimate of their respective critical values, and then subjoin a comparison of the text of the chief of them with that of my own most recent edition (Editio Major 1887) of Stephen's standard N.T. of 1550. To avoid the inconvenience of employing many Arabic numerals in almost every line, I have indicated the respective codices by the small letters of the English alphabet, arranging them on the list, as nearly as possible, in the order of their relative merit. A table is prefixed to the several divisions of the N.T., which shall identify each codex with the number assigned to it in my own *Plain Introduction* (3rd edition). It is anticipated that such a plan will prove acceptable to the reader, and involve no confusion or difficulty in applying to his use the results here exhibited. The numbers which follow the letters in our lists, therefore, are those of Scrivener's *Plain Introduction*. To them succeed the proper class-marks of the manuscripts in the Libraries wherein they are deposited, their apparent dates, and the initials of the persons who have collated them: F. H. A. S. being those of the present editor; F. G. S. those of his eldest son, Frederick George Scrivener, B.A., of Exeter College, Oxford, Vicar of Lakenheath, Suffolk; H.C.H. those of an amateur student, who has freely bestowed on us his most friendly help, H. C. Hoskier, Esq., of Hayes, Kent.

LIST OF GREEK CODICES AND EDITIONS, COLLATED FOR THE PRESENT VOLUME.

EVANGELIA (20 MSS.).

W^D Uncial fragment (Mark vii. viii.), Trinity College, Cambridge [VIII or IX century]. F.H.A.S. *Described below, p. xi.*

a Evan. 556. Burdett-Coutts III. 5 [XII century]. F.H.A.S., p. xvi.

b Evan. 604. British Museum, Egerton 2610 [XI or XII]. H.C.H., p. xxv.

c Evan. 59. Gonville and Caius Coll. Cambr. 403 [XII]. F.H.A.S., p. xxviii.

d Evan. 66. Trin. Coll. Cambr. O. VIII. 3 [XII]. F.H.A.S., p. xxxi.

e Evan. 492. Wake 12. Christ Church, Oxford [XI]. F.H.A.S. (Act. 193, Paul. 277, Apoc. 26), p. xxxiv.

f Evan. 503. Wake 34. Christ Church, Oxford [XI or XII]. F.H.A.S. (Act. 190, Paul. 244, Apoc. 27), p. xxxvi.

g Evan. 547. Burdett-Coutts I. 7 [XIII]. F.G.S., p. xxxvii.

h Evan. 548. Burdett-Coutts I. 9 [XII]. F.G.S., p. xli.

i Evan. 549. Burdett-Coutts II. 7 [XIII]. F.G.S. (Act. 219), p. xlii.

j Evan. 618. Hoskier, [XII]. H.C.H., p. xliii.

k Evan. 550. Burdett-Coutts II. 13 [XII]. F.G.S., p. xliii.

l Evan. 552. Burdett-Coutts II. 18 [XII]. p. xlv.

m Evan. 553. Burdett-Coutts II. 26^1 [XIII]. F.H.A.S., p. xlvi.

n Evan. 554. Burdett-Coutts II. 26^2 [XIV]. F.H.A.S., p. xlvii.

o Evan. 555. Burdett-Coutts III. 4 [XIII]. F.G.S., p. xlix.

p Evan. 557. Burdett-Coutts III. 9 [XIII]. F.G.S., p. l.

q Evan. 558. Burdett-Coutts III. 10 [dated 1430]. F.H.A.S., p. liv.

r Evan. 559. Burdett-Coutts III. 41 [XII or XIII]. F.H.A.S., p. lviii.

s Evan. 612. Burdett-Coutts I. 1 [XII]. F.H.A.S., p. lxiii.

EVANGELISTARIA (8 MSS.).

t Evst. 221. Trin. Coll. Camb. O. IV. 22 [XII]. F.H.A.S., p. lxiv.

u Evst. 251. Burdett-Coutts I. 10 [XII]. F.H.A.S. (Apost. 64), p. lxvi.

v Evst. 252. Burdett-Coutts III. 29 [XIV]. F.H.A.S. (Apost. 66), p. lxvii.

w   Evst. 253.   Burdett-Coutts III. 42 [XIV].   F.H.A.S.
     (Apost. 67), p. lxviii.

x   Evst. 290.   Burdett-Coutts III. 44 [XIV].   F.H.A.S.
     (Apost. 78), p. lxxi.

y   Evst. 249.   Burdett-Coutts III. 46 [XIII or XIV].   F.G.S.
     (Apost. 82), p. lxxi.

z   Evst. 250.   Burdett-Coutts III. 52 [XIII].   F.G.S., p. lxxii.

zz   Evst. 253².   Burdett-Coutts III. 53 [XV].   F.H.A.S.
     (Apost. 68), p. lxxii.

ACT., EPP. CATHOLICÆ (5 MSS.).

a   Act. 220.   Burdett-Coutts III. 1 [XI or XII] (Paul. 264),
     p. lxxiii.

e   Act. 193.   Wake 12.   Christ Church, Oxford (Evan.
     492, Paul. 277, Apoc. 26 [XI]).   F.H.A.S., p. lxxiv.

f   Act. 190.   Wake 34.   Christ Church, Oxford (Evan.
     503, Paul. 244, Apoc. 27 [XI or XII]).   F.H.A.S.,
     p. lxxv.

i   Act. 219.   Burdett-Coutts II. 7 [XIII].   F.G.S. (Evan.
     549), p. lxxv.

β   Act. 221.   Burdett-Coutts III. 37 [XII].   F.H.A.S. (Paul.
     265, Apoc. 8), p. lxxv.

EPP. PAULINÆ (5 MSS.).

a   Paul. 264.   Burdett-Coutts III. 1 [XI or XII]. (Act. 220),
     p. lxxvii.

e   Paul. 277.   Wake 12.   Christ Church, Oxford [XI].
     F.H.A.S. (Evan. 492, Act. 193, Apoc. 26), p. lxxvii.

f   Paul. 244.   Wake 34.   Christ Church, Oxford [XI or
     XII]. F.H.A.S. (Evan. 503, Act. 190, Apoc. 27), p. lxxx.

β   Paul. 265.   Burdett-Coutts III. 37 [XII].   F.H.A.S. (Act.
     221, Apoc. 8), p. lxxxiii.

δ   Paul. 266.   Burdett-Coutts II. 4 [X or XI].   F.H.A.S.
     (Apoc. 89), p. lxxxiv.

APOCALYPSIS (4 MSS.).

e   Apoc. 26.   Wake 12.   Christ Church, Oxford [XI].
     F.H.A.S. (Evan. 492, Act. 193, Paul. 277), p. lxxxvii.

f Apoc. 27. Wake 34. Christ Church, Oxford [xi or xii].
   F.H.A.S. (Evan. 503, Act. 190, Paul. 244), p. lxxxviii.

η Apoc. 15. Basil. A. N. iii. 12 [xv]. H.C.H. (Evan. E
   uncial), fragment (cf. Hoskier, *Collation*, Appendix F).

δ Apoc. 89. Burdett-Coutts ii. 4 [x or xi]. F.H.A.S.
   (Paul. 266), p. lxxxviii.

APOSTOLOS (7 MSS.).

u Apost. 64. Burdett-Coutts i. 10 [xii]. F.H.A.S. (Evst.
   251), p. lxxxix.

i Apost. 65. Burdett-Coutts iii. 24 [xii or xiii]. F.G.S.,
   p. lxxxix.

v Apost. 66. Burdett-Coutts iii. 29 [xiv]. F.H.A.S. (Evst.
   252), p. xc.

w Apost. 67. Burdett-Coutts iii. 42 [xiv]. F.H.A.S.
   (Evst. 253), p. xc.

y Apost. 82. Burdett-Coutts iii. 46 [xiii or xiv]. F.G.S.
   (Evst. 249), p. xc.

zz Apost. 68. Burdett-Coutts iii. 53 [xv]. F.H.A.S. (Evst.
   253^2), p. xc.

x Apost. 78. Burdett-Coutts iii. 44 [xiv]. F.H.A.S. (Evst.
   290), p. xc.

PALIMPSEST AND OTHER FRAGMENTS OF THE SEPTUAGINT (6 MSS.).

κ Burdett-Coutts iii. 6. F.H.A.S.

λ Burdett-Coutts iii. 46 [xi or xii]. F.H.A.S. (Evst. 249),
   p. lxxi.

μ Burdett-Coutts iii. 52. F.H.A.S. (Evst. 250^2), p. lxxii.

ν Burdett-Coutts iii. 42. F.H.A.S. (Evst. 253), p. lxviii.

o Burdett Coutts iii. 44. F.H.A.S. (Evst. 290), p. lxxi.

zz Burdett-Coutts iii. 53. F.H.A.S. (Evst. 253^2), p. lxxii.

EDITIONS OF N.T.

C. Complutensian 1514. p. xci.

E. Erasmi editiones. p. xciii.

E. 1. Erasmi 1516. p. xciii.

E. 2. Erasmi 1519. p. xciii.

E. 5.   Erasmi 1535.   p. xciii.
St. 1.   Stephani 1546.   p. xcv.
St. 2.   Stephani 1549.   p. xcv.
B.   Bezae 1565, 1598.   p. xcviii.
Elz. 1 and 2.   p. c.

ADVERSARIA CRITICA SACRA.

The uncial W^D, a fragment of S. Mark, of the VIIIth or IXth century.

W^D was discovered in 1862 by the late H. Bradshaw (Fellow of King's College, Cambridge, and University Librarian), in the Library of Trinity College, Cambridge, its slips (27 in number) being worked into the binding of a volume of Gregory Nazianzen: they are now carefully arranged between sheets of glass. They comprise portions of two sheets or four leaves (*Folia* 1, 4, 5, 8, the two inner sheets of an octavo quire being quite lost), containing fragments of Marc. vii. 3—4; 6—8; 30—36; 36—viii. 4; 4—10; 11—16; ix. 2; 7—9 in uncial letters of the ninth century (perhaps a little earlier) slightly leaning to the right. Each perfect column is 6 inches high by 3½ broad, and has 24 lines in single column on a page: the letters average about a quarter of an inch high. The ink is a yellowish brown. The (so-called) Ammonian sections stand in the margin, without the Eusebian canons, but a kind of harmony of the Gospels is given at the foot of the perfect columns, an arrangement which occurs also in Codd. E at Basle, T^b at S. Petersburg, M (partially), 262, 264 at Paris. The τίτλοι in red stand at the top of the pages (in Mark viii. 16, they are read off on the opposite page), and their corresponding numerals in the margin. The breathings and accents are often very faint: marks of lessons and their ends (T̂), musical notes and crosses serving for stops in red (turned by time deep black), sometimes cover the original notes of punctuation. The large *phi*, and cross-like *psi*, with the crowding of letters (θ &c.) at the end of lines, are indications of the late date which is assigned by us to W^D.

xii ADVERSARIA

Evangelii S. Marci Fragmenta Cantabrigiensia
(W^D). Trin. Coll. B. VIII. 5.

Folium 1 recto.
S. Marci vii. 3, 4.

και παντεσ οι ιουδαιο ν
μὴ πυγμη νιψοντα α^σ
θί υσιν Τ̄
ὁυντεσ την παραδοσ
τῶν πρεσβυτέρων· ι

ξθ λε ω ρνγ

Fol. 4 recto.
S. Marc. vii. 30—36.

ογ
οδ

Π̄ Τ̄ ΜΟΓΓΙΛΑΛΟΥ
δαιμόνιον ἐξεληλυθοσ
αι παλιν ἐξελθὼν ἀπ ω̄
ὁρίων τῦρου κὰι σὶδ οσ·
ἦλθεν εισ την θάλα ὴ
τῆσ γαλιλαίασ ἀῦα μέ ν
των οριων τῆσ ʹ
ωσ + και φερουσιν 'αυτῶ
κωφον και μογγιλαλον;
κ̇ὰι παρεκάλουν ἀυτοϋ̈
ϊ επι χεῖρα + κ̧
επιλαβομενοσ υτον ἀῖο
τοῦ ὀχλου κατιδίαν ἐπτυ
σεν εἰσ τουσ δακτύλουσ ἀυ
τοῦ· και εβαλεν εἰσ τὰ ὠτα
τοῦ κωφοῦ· κ̇αι ἤψατο
τῆσ γλωσσασ του μογγιλά
λου + και ἀναβλέψασ ε τον
ὀυν̄ον̄· νεστέναξεν· και
λέγει ἀυ ω + ἐφφάθα· ο εσ
τιν δια ητι + κα̧ι ˸ δι ᾽ευθεωσ
ηνοίχθησαν ἀυτοῦ̈ ἀι ἀκο
αί; κ̇ὰι τοῦ μογγιλάλου ἐλυ
θ
ἐλάλη ὀρθῶσ + και διεστείλατο

Μ̇ Λ̇ ᛁ̇ Μ̇
οε ϛγ μθ ρξ
οϛ

Folium 1 *verso.*
S. Marci vii. 6—8.

ρρω απεχει απ εμου· μα
ιν δὲ σέβονται με διδάσ
ντεσ διδασκα ιασ εν
ατα ανων· βαπτισμου
στῶν και ποτηρίων

Λ

Fol. 4 *verso.*
S. Marc. vii. 36–viii. 4.

o͞e
η

TA AP

Ὀσον ἐ αὐτοῖσ διεστέλλετο·
'αν οἶσ ἵνα μηδένι λέγωσιν
'αν οἱ μάλλον π ρισσοτέ ͞
ρ κηρυσσον; καὶ πάν

o͞s
η

τε ιεπλήσσοντ λεγοντεσ
ῶσ πάντα ποιεῖ· τοὺσ
κωφοὺσ ποιεί ἀκουεῖν·
κ̈αὶ τοὺσ ἀλαλοὺσ λαλεῖν· ͞†

κ͞α

Ἐν ε ἔιναισ ταῖσ ἡμέραισ
παμπολλ
θεντοσ· μη εχοντω
τι ἀγωσιν ' προσκαλεσά
με οσ τοὺσ μαθητασ. λέ
γει υτοῖσ· σπλ χνίζο
μ πι τον ὄχλον ὅτη ἤδη
ἡμ ' ραι τρεῖσ προ μένου
σί μ ι· καὶ οὐκ έ σιν τί
φ ωσιν· κάι ν ἀπολύ
σω τοὺσ νηστ ισ εἰσ οι
κ 'υτι σον
ται ἐν τῆ ὁδῶ· τινὲσ γὰρ
αὐτῶν μακρόθεν ἤκου
σιν και ἀπεκρίθη ν ἀυ
τῶ οἱ μαθηται · αυτου·

- - ̆ , ͻ

πόθεν τούτουσ δυνήση
ταί τισ χορτάσαι ὦ ε ἄρτῶ
επ ερημίασ · και επηρώτα
᾽αυτουσ ποσουσ ἔχετε ἄρτ υσ·
οἱ δὲ εἶπον · ει   +
ρήγγειλεν τω οχλω ἀναι ε
σεῖν ἐπι τῆσ γῆσ· κὰι λα
βὸν τοὺσ ἑπτὰ ἄρτουσ· ἐ
χαριστήσασ· ἔκλασεν κὰι
εδ᾽δου τοῖσ μαθηταῖσ ἀι
του ινα παραθῶσιν· και
παρέθηκαν τῶ ὀχλω·
και εἴχον ἰχθύδια ὀλιγα ϛ
ἀυτὰ ευλογήσασ· εἶπεν πα
ραθηναι· ἔφαγον δὲ κὰι
εχορ ασθησαν· κὰι ἦραν
περισ ευματα κλασματῶ
ἑπτὰ σπυρίδασ· ἦσαν δὲ
ὁι φαγόντεσ ωσ τετρακισ
χίλιοι· κὰι ἀπέλυσεν ἀυ
τοῖσ·   κὰι ἐμβᾶσ ἐυ
Θεως εἰσ το πλοίον μετὰ τῶ
μαθητῶν αυτ ῦ ἦλθ
ἐισ τὰ μέρη δαλμανουθα·

$\frac{4}{OZ}$

M̄	Λ	⫶	M̄
OZ		ΚΓΜΓ	ρξα
			ρξβ

Μ   μβανει ο ισ
τον πετ ον κὰι ἰάκωβō
κὰι ἰωαννην κὰι ἀνα
γει ἀυτου ε οροσ ὑψηλο
κατιδιαν μόνουσ· κὰι
μεταμορφοῦται ἔμπροσ

M̄	Λ	↓
πϛ	Ϛζ	ρυ
πz	Ϛη	ρυβ

Π ΤΗ ΖΥΜΗС ΤѠΝ ΦΑΡΙϹ ΙѠΝ
καὶ ἐξηλθον οἱ φαρισαίοι.
καὶ ἡ ξαντο συζητεῖν
αυτω· ζητοῦντεσ παρ αυ
τοῦ σημεῖον απο τοῦ ουνου
πειρα οντε αὐτόν· κὰι
αναστεναξασ τῷ πνι αυ
τοῦ λέγει· τί ἡ γενεα
ΟΗ Αὐτη σημεῖον ἐπιζητεῖ
ἀμήν λέγω ὑμὶν. εἰ δο
θήσεται τῇ γενεὰ ἄυτη
ημειον· και αφ σ ἀυ
κδ Τουσ ἐμβὰσ παλιν εἰσ το
πλοίον· ἀπῆλθεν εἰσ το
πέραν· καὶ ἐπελάθοντο
οἱ μαθηταὶ ἀυτου λαβεῖν
ἄρτουσ· και εἰ μη να ἄρ
τον ουκ εἶχον μεθ εαυτῶ
οθ ἐν τῷ πλοίω· και διε
Cτέλλετο ἀυτοῖσ λέγων· ὁ
ρᾶτε κὰι βλέπετε ἀπο τῆσ
ζύμησ τῶν φαρισαίων.
καὶ τῆσ ζύμησ ἡρώδου·
π   γιζο
λουσ λεγοντεσ, οτι αρτουσ

M   Λ   Ϊ   M̃
ΟΗ   ρξγ
οθ   ρμθ   ρξδ
π   ρξε

. . . . . .
μου ο ἀγαπητοσ ὸν εξελε
ξάμην , ἀκου τε ἀυτοῦ·
και ἐνθεωσ π ριβλεψάμε
νοι· ουκετ ο
εἰ μη ν̄ μόνον· και κα

M̃

Various readings of Cod. W^D, *collated with Stephen's text (Scrivener's Editio Major* 1887).

Mark vii. 3 νιψονται. εσθιουσιν. 6 ματιν. 30 − και την θυγατερα βεβλημενην επι της κλινης. 31 απ (*pro* εκ). ηλθεν. εις (*pro* προς). + της (*ante* [Δεκαπολε]ως). 32 + και (*ante* μογγιλαλον). παρεκαλουν. − αυτω την χειρα. 33 επιλαβομενος. + επτυσεν εις τους δακτυλους αυτου και (*post* κατιδιαν). του κωφου (*pro* αυτου *prim.*). −πτυσας. γλωσσας. του μογγιλαλου (*pro* αυτου *secund.*). 34 [αν]εστεναξεν. εστιν. 35 −ευθεως (*habet* margo). +του μογγιλαλου (*ante* ελυθη). ελαλη. 36 λεγωσιν (*pro* ειπωσιν). −αυτος. +αυτοι (*ante* μαλλον). παντες (*pro* υπερπερισσως). 37 ποιει (*pro* πεποιηκε). −και (*post* ποιει). [τους αλαλους]. CAP. viii. 1 θεντος (*pro* οντος). −και. − ο ιησους. −αυτου. 2 ο τη. ημεραι. εχουσιν. φαγωσιν. ηκουσιν. ηκοισιν. 4 χορτασαι ωδε. 5 [επηρωτα]. [ειπον]. 6 παρηγγειλεν. λαβον. εκλασεν. παραθωσιν. 7 [ειχον]. +αυτα (*ante* ευλογησας). ειπεν παραθηναι. − και (*ante* αυτα). 10 εμβας ευθεως. 12 αυτη (*pro* ταυτη). 14 +οι μαθηται αυτου (*ante* λαβειν). 16 [λεγοντες]. CAP. ix. 2 M μβανει (*pro* παραλαμβανει). −τον *bis.* [Ιωαννην]. μεταμορφουται. 7 +ον εξελεξαμην (*post* αγαπητος). ακουετε αυτου. 8 ευθεως (*pro* εξαπινα). − μεθ εαυτων.

N.B. Mark vii. 33 contains readings which seem absolutely unique. Mark vii. 36 + αυτοι (*ante* μαλλον) is supported by אBDLΔ 33 and by several versions.

a. Evan. 556. BURDETT-COUTTS III. 5.

N.B. A full Collation of this manuscript, compared with Codd. 13.69.124.346, is given below, Part I., pp. 1—59.

This document, which claims a post of honour among the codices of the Greek New Testament, was brought to England in 1870 for the Baroness Burdett-Coutts from Janina through the agency of the (late) Rev. Reginald H. Barnes, M.A., Prebendary of Exeter (died 1889), whose account of the transaction is subjoined (below, pp. xxi—xxv). Its high importance as an instrument of criticism arises from the fact that it forms one of a small class of cursive manuscripts which must have been derived (whether directly or indirectly) from a venerable original now lost, older than themselves. The close affinity subsisting between three copies (Cod. 13 at Paris, Cod. 69 at

Leicester[1], Cod. 124 at Vienna) had long been observed, but the credit of having undertaken the detailed and laborious comparison necessary to prove that they actually represent a single archetype is due to W. H. Ferrar, Fellow and Professor of Latin in Trinity College, Dublin, who died young in 1871. A fourth copy had also become known to him through Scholz's N. T. (Cod. 346 at Milan) which, since Ferrar was unable to examine it through ill-health, was collated for him through the learned and ever gracious Dr Ceriani, the Librarian of the Ambrosian Library at Milan. After Professor Ferrar's death, his unfinished papers happily fell into the very capable hands of T. K. Abbott, Fellow of Trinity College and Professor of Biblical Greek in the University of Dublin. The latter scholar published in 1877 *"A Collation of Four important Manuscripts of the Gospels:* with a view to prove their common origin and to restore the text of their archetype;" and if the success of the latter portion of his design must be regarded as somewhat doubtful or premature, the materials accumulated by him have their separate and distinctive value.

The manuscript now before us (Evan. 556) was announced in 1883 in my *" Plain Introduction"* (p. 236) as pertaining to the same class, and the collation given in this volume (pp. 1— 59) is a very minute one, made with the best care I could bestow upon it. Subsequently this curious and interesting subject has attracted the busy mind of the Abbé J. P. P. Martin, Professor at the École Supérieure of Theology at Paris, in whose *"Quatre Manuscrits Importants du Nouveau Testament, auxquels on peut en ajouter un cinquième"* Paris 1886, the

---

[1] Much light has recently (1887) been thrown on "The Origin of the Leicester Codex" by J. Rendel Harris of Haverford College, Pennsylvania, and Fellow of Clare College, Cambridge, such as may hereafter lead to more exact knowledge of its date and country. Dr Swete and Mr Harris had found in Caius College Library a vellum Psalter written in what seems the same very peculiar hand as Cod. 69, with signatures resembling Cod. 69, the fragments of which in my edition of Cod. 69 I had stupidly overlooked. He shews that both it and the Caius Gospels were in the possession of the Cambridge Minorites about 1366, and that in Cod. 69 the Acts originally stood first and the Gospels last.

matter is discussed in his usual exhaustive style. We must state, however, that Martin's fifth codex is not our Evan. 556 (which had only been noticed by him as he corrected his proofs and is mentioned only in his Postscript), but another copy (Cod. 348) also at Milan and dated 29 December, A.D. 1023, which, though a native of the same region (Calabria) as Cod. 346 (which Cod. 69 does not seem to be), and resembling it in general appearance, can hardly be referred to the same class as Codd. 13, 69, 124, 346, 556, inasmuch as it does not agree with them in transposing Joan. vii. 53—viii. 11 to Luc. xxi. 38, or Luc. xxii. 43, 44 to Matth. xxvi. 39 (the verses are found in *both* Gospels), which are the CHARAC-TERISTIC variations from the common text exhibited by the other five. Mr R. Harris (*Journal of Exegetical Society*, pp. 81—89, 1887) would fain add to this company Cod. Peckover = Ev. 561, which resembles the other five in Matth. xxvi. 39 (by insertion); Luc. xxii. 43, 44 (by complete omission); Matth. xiii. 35 (+ ἠσαΐου); Marc. xii. 7; xiv. 41; Luc. xii. 7; xxii. 47 and in many other characteristic places, but while omitting the *pericope adulteræ* in S. John, does not insert it at the end of Luke xxi. Cod. 561 by its marginal notes plainly shews that it was written at Constantinople. There is however no question as to the right of our Cod. 556 to rank with the other four; in fact it is more constant to Codd. 13, 346 than are Codd. 69, 124, especially the latter. It is a quarto volume written on coarse thick vellum eleven inches high, eight and a half broad, in old binding, set off with six brass knobs, on 183 leaves, in two columns on a page, 26 lines in a column, in fair condition, but the ink is faint at parts and ten leaves are quite lost: viz. Matth. xii. 11—xiii. 10 (two leaves); Table of κεφάλαια to S. Mark (κ to μη); Marc. viii. 4—28 (one); Luc. xv. 20—xvi. 9 (one); Johan. ii. 22—iv. 6 (two leaves); iv. 52—v. 43 (two leaves); xi. 21—47 (one). Three or four leaves also are loose. Slight illuminations occur at the head of books: modern ink retraces letters now and then. It contains the larger Κεφ. (sometimes subdivided by rubric numerals), Ammonian sections, Eusebian canons in the margin, many rubrical directions, τίτλοι in red

at the head of columns, and may date from the eleventh or
twelfth century. A second hand (Matth. xi. 7; xiii. 41; xv.
4, 26) has more than once gone over the manuscript, yet not
systematically. Some changes look *primâ manu* (e.g. margin
of Matth. iv. 10; v. 19). Others are noted by s above, yet not
corrected. Others are rude erasures, or else quite modern (e.g.
Matth. vi.; Luc. iii.; x. 35). Iota *ascript* (never *subscript*)
occurs very often, especially in S. Mark, even with verbs
(Marc. iv. 31; vii. 8). Ὁμοιοτέλευτα rather too often: Marc.
ii. 18; iv. 24; xii. 26; xiv. 70; xv. 14; Luc. xii. 22, 47;
xiii. 28, 29; Johan. iv. 14. Ν ἐφελκυστικὸν is found often
(416 times) especially with εἶπεν, ἐστιν: in Matth. xii. 7;
Luc. viii. 10; Johan. v. 46; vii. 7; viii. 27 there is a hiatus
for lack of it. Breathings and accents are very regular, but
on some sort of system, if not according to modern use: e.g.
frequent, but not constant, αὑτοῦ, αὑτῶν, &c., with Evan. 575
(kˢᶜʳ) about 20 times in S. Matthew, much oftener in S. Luke;
βασιλεῖα, δυνηθῆναι, ἐπιχειρῶν, περὶ επάτει, ἐξ᾽, ὀλίγον, οὐδ᾽
ἐν, πιλᾶτος (about Joan. xviii, xix). Of itacisms, 358 occur
in S. John alone, 259 in SS. Matt. and Mark: viz. ει (for ι)
16; ι (for ει) 35; ο (for ω) 40; ω (for ο) 33; αι (for ε) 13; ε
(for αι) 31; ει (for η) 23; η (for ει) 19; η (for ι) 11; ι (for η)
7; ε (for η) 11; η (for ε) 2; οι (for ι) 3; ου (for ω) 3; ω (for
ου) 20; η (for υ) 3 (also in pronouns 3); υ (for η) 5 (also in
pronouns 3); υ (for οι) 1; υ (for ει) 1; η (for οι) 1; οι (for η) 1;
ι (for υ) 1; οι (for ει) 2. Unusual forms are ἀνέπεσαν Johan.
vi. 10: δραγμὴ *bis* Luc. xv. 8: εἶπαν Johan. vi. 34; xviii.
34; xix. 7: ἐθεώρων Johan. vi. 28: ἔμελλεν Johan. xii. 6:
ἔμπροσθε Johan. i. 15, 27: εὐσπλαγχνίσθη (so Wake 12)
Matth. xiv. 14; Marc. vi. 34; Luc. vii. 13; x. 33: ἴδαμεν
Luc. v. 26: ἴδεν *sæpe*; οὕτω (usually οὕτως) Matth. iii. 15:
νύκταν Luc. ii. 37: σάρκαν Johan. vi. 53 (not 54, 56): συνε-
τίθεντο Johan. ix. 22: χεῖραν Matth. xii. 9. For punctuation
+ is a full stop; + (Matth. vi. 25, 26; vii. 9, 10; viii. 29)
or ; (Marc. vi. 13) is an interrogation. With the Bodleian
Genesis: ⸓ in margin represents the citations from the Old
Testament. This codex is full of lectionary rubrics, which
(as in Cod. 69 although it has none) will sometimes affect

the sense so that particles are often omitted at the beginning
of lessons : e.g. Luc. ix. 28; xxi. 20, &c. For more see p. 9.
After the subscription to S. John follow eight leaves
(under slight illumination) of a Synaxarion from Easter
Day to εὐαγγέλια ἑωθινὰ ῑα. Then under illumination τῇ
β τοῦ νέου ἔτους 7 leaves (one loose). Then a Menology,
12 leaves. See Collation, p. 57. Then κ͒. + ἀκολου⁰ εἰς
διαφόρους ἡμ. εἰς ἐγκαίνια ναοῦ, εἰς παν͒ rubro. On fol. 183
Limits of Five Patriarchates (cf. Cod. 69). See p. 59.
Mr J. Rendel Harris has printed in his "Leicester Codex,"
pp. 64, 65, the Patriarchates from Cod. 69 under the title
in our MS. (a) of Γνῶσις καὶ ἐπίγνωσις, τῶν πατριαρχῶν
θρόνων. He will find his collation, like those of the rest
of us, not quite faultless. Fol. 183 b, second column, with
illumination Αἱ τάξεις τῶν κλιμάτων τῆς ἀφρικῆς. πρῶτον
κλῖμα ἡ λιβύη καλουμένη λούβια καὶ μαιά δι (videtur : not
μαίρακι κτέ., as in Harris) Δεύτερον κλῖμα ἡ μαυρουσία ἤτοι
αἰθιοπία μέλεδι. ἐς σε ουδ | Τρίτον κλῖμα ἡμίβακ ἤγουν
σέχελ. | Τέταρτον κλῖμα ἡ μουμέδα. ἤγουν ζέβ | Πέμπτον
κλῖμα ἀφρική ἤν. Of one leaf only a few letters remain.

While the position of Johan. vii. 53—viii. 11 in our five
manuscripts readily places them in a distinct class by themselves, we must not dissemble that they present frequent
divergencies from each other, thus proving that one or more
transcripts have intervened between the lost original and the
copies actually before us. In recording the variations between
the several copies we have not taken account of ordinary
itacisms, such as abound more or less in all manuscripts,
but only of those of an unusual or peculiar character. The
various readings proper (including these few itacisms) common
to all five codices amount in the Gospels of S. Luke and
S. John to 1041 : to which we must add 83 in places
where the four agree, one being lost: in all 1124. In the
passages wherein they differ from each other, our Evan.
556 agrees most with Cod. 13 [1] : *proximus, longo sed proxi-*

---

[1] In the following places, the close connection between Codd. 13, 556,
where they stand alone, cannot well be mistaken. Matth. iii. 4 τρυχῶν. 7 om.
ἐρχομένους. v. 31 ὑποστάσιον. ix. 27 +κε (before υἱὲ). xxii. 4 *primâ manu*

mus intervallo with Cod. 346 : next with Cod. 69, least of all with Cod. 124, especially in S. Mark : yet we have no great cause to suspect that any of them has been carelessly collated by critics, rather the contrary. Where the five are divided in the two above named Gospels (SS. Luke, John), Evan. 556 is with Cod. 13 no less than 534 times (in 60 places with it alone): with Cod. 346, 531 times (38 being alone): with Cod. 69, 386 times (28 being alone): but with Cod. 124, only 322 times (14 being alone). The favourite combinations, of four complete copies out of the five are Codd. 13, 69, 346, 246 times: Codd. 13, 124, 346, 118 times: but Codd. 13, 69, 124 only 39 times. Codd. 13, 346[1] combine with our MS. 103 times, and these three are the most cognate. The divergencies of Cod. 69, and especially of 124, complicate the problem without disproving it, at least until more codices of this class shall be found among the host yet unknown or uncollated. Recent students of the text of the N. T. begin to see that it is by this method of tracing out affinities between existing authorities that a consistent theory of the origin of various readings can most safely help us to estimate their respective values. I am thankful so far as I have been able to contribute, however little, to promote this great end.

The subjoined communication is from the pen of the late Rev. Reginald Barnes, Prebendary of Exeter.

The Editor, who is the writer's fellow Prebendary in the Cathedral of Exeter, permits him to state some circumstances connected with these MSS. They were bought by him at Janina

---

τιθημένα. 46 λόγων 13, λόγου 556 (*pro* λόγον). Marc. viii. 38 μοιχαλλίδι. ix. 11 διελθεῖν. 21 om. ὁ δὲ εἶπε. xiii. 2 λίθων. xiv. 69 καὶ οὕτως (for οὗτος). Luc. viii. 6 ἠκμάδα. ix. 31 ὠφθέντες. x. 7 ἐξ᾽ οἰκίαν (with 69.346). 35 om. δύο. xii. 29 φάγησθε. xvi. 16 om. εἰς. 20 ἐβέβλυτο. xix. 2 om. ὀνόματι. xx. 46 ταῖς δείπνοις. xxi. 19 κτήσεσθε. 24 + οὖν (after ἄχρι). xxii. 59 om. ἦν. Johan. iv. 12 om. οἱ. 14 + ζῶντος (before ἀλλομένου). vii. 28 om. ὁ ἰησοῦς. 52 σὺ erased. x. 22 χιμῶν. xi. 1 ἑαυτῆς (for αὐτῆς). 12 αὐτῶ (for αὐτοῦ). xii. 7 + ὅτι (before εἰς). xiii. 24 πύθεσθε *p. m.* To prove direct transcription, the more minute these variations from the common text the better.

[1] In Matth. i. 16 Codd. 346, 556 agree with Cureton's Syriac version alone.

S.   c

in 1864 from a dealer, who parted with all his store. All the due forms of complete and public barter were observed. It was a strange medley and miscellaneous heap. The writer had the advantage of the supervision of Major R. Stuart, at that time H. M. Consul at Janina, and by his advice he gave a sum of some hundreds of pounds which Miss Burdett-Coutts (now the Baroness Burdett-Coutts) had entrusted to him for such purchases.

With the MSS. there were many other objects which the dealer valued more highly—all of which apparently belonged to a private collection augmented from time to time down to the commencement of the 18th century, but one of which the nucleus and bulk dates far back in our Christian era. They may be taken in this order. 1. The coins. 2. A bronze figure of a Roman with a tunic. 3. A golden winged Victory.

I. Of the coins, the Roman Imperial series extends over a period reaching from Augustus to Constantine; none of them are rare. The Byzantine series consists of 16 gold coins ranging in date from Nicephorus II. (Phocas) A.D. 969 to Isaac II. A.D. 1195. Among these may be noted a rare solidus of Theodora 1055–56. There are also rare silver coins of Theophilus and Michael III., of Michael III. (alone), and of Leo VI. and Constantine X.

The small series of *Mediæval and Modern* coins includes gold ducats of Sigismund and Mathias Corvinus, Kings of Hungary; a gold Osella of A. Mocenigo II., Doge of Venice 1700–1709, rare in this metal; an interesting gold sequin of P. D'Aubusson, Grandmaster of the Knights of Malta, 1476–1503; and 17 silver coins of the Princes of Achaia and Dukes of Athens, all belonging to a somewhat rare class.

II. The bronze figure is valued by Mr Murray and Mr Francks of the British Museum very highly. It is probably of the Flavian era, and represents a man kneeling on one knee, the left, and shading with his right hand his face as though a strong light were shining down on him from above. The tunic has a space over both shoulders, which was originally filled in by a silver clavus angustus.

III. The golden winged Victory. The writer is able to give an account of this very remarkable jewel from the pen of Mr J. Theodore Bent.

13, GREAT CUMBERLAND PLACE,
W. LONDON,
21 *July*, 1888.

A GOLDEN "WINGED VICTORY."

"The small figure of a winged Victory before us is in the possession of the Baroness Burdett-Coutts and was brought from Janina some years ago by Mr Reginald H. Barnes.

"It is one of a pair of earrings, and a specimen of the finest workmanship of the period immediately following the conquests of Alexander the Great when subjects of a similar motive were greatly in vogue both for sculpture and for decoration.

"The gold in which it is cast is, as is usually the case in ornamental specimens of this period, 32 carats, being therefore excessively pliable. The body of the Victory has been made on a foundation of cement—a process used to prevent the metal doubling up when hammered. The cement was burnt out when the figure was completed to the goldsmith's taste and then the drapery was soldered on. The details of the hair, face, feet with sandals, and arms are very fine, the hands however exhibit a certain want of finish, which may be accounted for by the fact that there are obvious traces of their each having held something which by comparison with other figures of a similar nature we may suppose to have been a wreath and a trophy or palm-branch. The height of the body from head to foot is $1\frac{1}{4}$ inches, and the wings, which are fixed on behind, though not so widespread as is the case with most of these figures, are most minutely engraved and bear close scrutiny with a magnifying glass; at their fullest expansion they correspond exactly to the height of the body, namely, $1\frac{1}{4}$ inches.

"Above the head is fixed on a circular disc $\frac{11}{16}$ of an inch in diameter, and upon it is a representation of the chariot of Helios, drawn by four horses, issuing from the sun's rays and driven by Eos. The goldsmith obtained this admirable effect by soldering together very minute portions of gold, of which the horses' legs are composed of three. The object of the disc was to hide the hole in the lobe of the ear, and is found in all similar specimens of earrings. The straight sort of wand which we see behind the body was originally bent back and formed the hook by which the ornament was suspended from the ear. The minutely-decorated

c 2

disc is the most curious portion of the ornament before us, and is almost without parallel. Earrings of winged Victories, of which we find specimens in most Museums, have, all of them, these discs, but they are of much inferior workmanship : those, for example, in the British Museum, which were found in Ithaca, and those in the Hermitage at St Petersburg, have merely the representation of the sun's face or of a conventional flower on the disc, effects obtained with infinitely less trouble.

"We can however advantageously compare the subject of this disc with a large pendant in the Louvre [No. 112 in the old catalogue of the Museum of Napoleon III.], in which a chariot of Helios similarly treated, and so minute that it could be covered by the wing of a fly, is being driven over a half crescent which is supported by two small winged Victories, each with a trophy in one hand and a flower in the other. Exquisite however as this pendant is in its detail, its general effect is spoilt by the lower portion being composed of heavy chains with amphoræ hung to them, giving to the whole a confused appearance which detracts from the value of the work.

"We may also compare our earring with many late works found at Kertch, but they are much less carefully executed and are much heavier; so heavy that as time went on women named *auriculæ ornatrices* were employed to heal the wounds in the earlobes caused by the weight of the ornaments.

"Again, a gold necklace pendant in the Cabinet of Antiquities at Athens represents a winged Victory very similar in workman-ship to the one before us, but of course without the disc above, which was not required in this case : her wings are of great fine-ness, and in the left hand she holds a crown of laurel, whilst with the right she holds back the drapery from her right leg.

"The connection of ideas between the Sun and Victory seems pretty general in most of the specimens of ornaments of this nature. Where the disc is necessary as a decoration for a small circular basis, the sun's face and the rays, πανόπτης · κύκλος · ἡλίου, naturally suggested itself; and the brilliancy of the subject, the golden team (χρυσόζυγον), was one which was likely to be em-ployed by the goldsmith. From the above-mentioned pendant in the Louvre we see the motive well expressed. The victory of the sun over night and darkness is represented by the chariot driving over the crescent of the moon supported by winged Victories, and later Greek mythology is replete with instances of the sun as an emblem of Victory and Strength. In Roman times Hercules Victor was a sun-god pure and simple. This small figure of Victory is especially interesting as being one of the most perfect specimens of that art which the Greeks invented and taught, namely, that of treating gold with the chisel, which became a distinct advance in the working and production of gold ornaments.

(Signed) J. THEODORE BENT."

Thus far extends the communication of the Reverend Prebendary Barnes. It is inserted here, at his special desire, in respect for his honoured memory.

b. Evan. 604. British Museum, Egerton 604.

For this valuable manuscript we are indebted to a zealous amateur in this branch of study, H. C. Hoskier, Esq., of Hayes, Kent. The collation is entirely his: the following description is abridged from a wonderfully full and exhaustive one which he has furnished to me, of much critical value, but too long to suit the scale of the present volume. It is now (1890) published by Mr Hoskier, a rare monument of industry and critical skill. Other contributions from Mr Hoskier will be noticed in their proper places hereafter, but the present is the most considerable, and for it I owe to him my best thanks. Cod. 604 is a small quarto, only $5\frac{13}{16}$ high by $4\frac{1}{4}$ broad, of 297 vellum leaves, with 19 lines to a page, about 30 letters in a line, and was apparently written in the twelfth century. It was bought in London in 1882, having previously been located somewhere in Germany. Dean Burgon's attention was soon drawn to it. He describes it as "a genuine and charming little copy, in xvth century binding": adding that "it calls aloud for collation," being full of readings which resemble Cod. B, some of them almost unique (e.g. Luc. xi. 2)[1]. It contains Eusebius' epistle to Carpianus, the Eusebian

[1] Luc. xi. 2 τὸ πνά σου τὸ ἅγιον ἐφ' ἡμᾶς καὶ καθαρισάτω ἡμᾶς (pro ἡ βασιλεία σου, only with Gregory of Nyssa, teste Burgon). Hort, N. T. ii. p. 60;

canons (very small and beautifully written in gold), tables of the larger κεφάλαια prefixed to the first three Gospels, τίτλοι at the head of the pages, the numerals of the Ammonian sections and the Eusebian canons in the margin, but these last three quite partially. 'Αρχαὶ and τέλη of lessons are also noted sometimes *p. m.*, sometimes later, and pictures of the four Evangelists are much superior to the style that prevails in most codices, the faces in particular being full of expression. The text of this copy is broken up into paragraphs (as in k^scr = Brit. Mus. Addit. 11,300 and others), not corresponding with the Ammonian sections (in Matth. the paragraphs are 397, Marc. 209, Luc. 368, Johan. 349), each beginning with a capital letter in gold. Three blank paper leaves commence the volume and four end it: in the last of these is a note *s. m.* partly erased, dated A.D. 1338 or 1335. The original signatures are still usually legible at the top of each page, some are cut away : others, now missing, are supplied by a later hand, but these at the foot of the page. Quotations from the Old Test. are occasionally set in gold in the margin (⸖), iota subscript is never found by the first hand, but iota ascript occurs 149 times, not seldom with verbs or even with adverbs (ἐπανωι, εξωι) ; (80 times in S. Matthew), 17 of them being with Ἡρώιδης (the form adopted by Dr Hort in his N. T.), but not uniformly (e.g. Matth. ii. 12). *Compendia scribendi* are somewhat numerous, e.g. ⸖ η for δέη Matth. xxvi. 35; μηῖνὶ (> for δε) Luc. viii. 56, here in the middle of a word; ᾽Λ for ἐστι Luc. v. 39 : Johan. viii. 54; and most often at the end of a line. *Homoeoteleuta* are rare (Marc. ii. 19 ; xv. 8 ; Luc. vii. 39 ; ix. 19 ; xv. 27) ; a whole line seems lost in Johan. xv. 4. Corrections (by later hands for the most part) are not at all many. The original scribe was much his own διορθωτής, but three correctors at least were subsequently engaged

from whom, *Notes on select readings*, I suppose, Hoskier cites Gregory Nys., Maximus the Confessor, and Tertullian. Hoskier (*Introduction*, p. xxxv) adds the two last authorities. Conf. Cod. 582 and Cod. r below, B.-C. III. 41 (p. lviii). It is in parts (e.g. Mark i. and subsequent chapters) much akin to Cod. f, Wake 34.

on the text or margin: one of them wrote the date (1338) on the paper page. Breathings and accents are correct as a rule, yet πιλᾶτος, ὀσφῦν, ἄρον, πνεύμασι at places : in punctuation we find … for full stop,, for comma, ; for interrogation. The apostrophe in ἐξ᾽, οὐχ᾽, ὅτ᾽ ἂν, not in κατιδίαν ἀπαρτι, καθεῖς. Of itacisms we have only 206: e.g. ο (for ω) 70 times; ω (for ο) 26; η (for ει) 15; ει (for η) 7; ι (for η) 27; η (for ι) 10; and others less frequent αι (for ε) 11 times; ε (for αι) 8; ι (for ει) 9; ει (for ι) 5; η (for υ) 1; υ (for η) 1; η (for ε) 1; ι (for υ) 2; ε (for ει) 1; οι (for ι) 2. Ν ἐφελκυστικὸν occurs 373 times, often erased (p. m), the hiatus for lack of it only in Luc. xxii. 25. Οὕτως before a consonant 33 times. We have εἶπαν in Luc. i. 61; v. 33; vii. 20; ix. 13.

The variations from the common or Stephen's text are many and of deep interest. Mr Hoskier has counted them, and makes them amount to 2724 in all, whereof 791 are omissions, 353 additions, 1288 substitutions, 292 transpositions. He also subjoins a formidable list of places in which Evan. 604 stands, so far as he knows, absolutely alone. In S. Matthew they number 79: such are Cap. i. 6, 24; vii. 14; x. 13; xvi. 21; xxi. 5; xxii. 18; xxv. 32, 45. Some are nearly alone, as Mark ii. 27 ἐκτίσθη (pro ἐγένετο) with Codd. 1.131.209. This list is followed by an analysis of the authorities accessible to Mr Hoskier for the various readings supported by Evan. 604, a monument of patient labour, beyond any praise of ours. No less than 436 passages are examined in detail, and all the Greek manuscripts, whether uncial or cursive, which support the readings of this codex, pass severally under review. The evidence of versions and ecclesiastical writers however is missing, at times doubtless to our loss, though we may believe they would rather complicate the general result than materially modify it. Mr Hoskier's conclusion shall be given in his own words : "I defy any one, after having carefully perused the foregoing lists, and after having noted the almost incomprehensible combinations and permutations of both the uncial and cursive manuscripts, to go back again to the teaching of Dr Hort with any degree of confidence. How useless and superfluous to talk of Evan. 604 having *a large western element*, or of its *siding in many places with the neutral text*. The whole question of families and recensions is thus brought prominently before the eye, and with space we could largely comment upon the deeply interesting combinations which thus present themselves to the critic. But *do* let us realise that we are in the infancy of this part of the science,...and not imagine that we have successfully laid certain immutable foundation stones, and can safely continue to build thereon. It is not so: much, if not all, of these foundations must be demolished....It has cost me a vast amount of labour and trouble to prepare this statement of evidence with any degree of accuracy; but I am sure it is worth while, and I trust that it may stimulate others to come to our aid, and also help to annul much of Dr Hort's erroneous theories[1]."

The next two manuscripts Evan. 59 and 66 have been loosely collated by Mill for his great edition of the N. T. 1707.

c. Evan. 59. Gonville and Caius College (No. 403).

This important copy of the Gospels has been shown by Mr J. Rendel Harris ("*Origin of the Leicester Codex,*" p. 18) to have once belonged to the Oxford Minorites, as appears from an inscription on p. 1, "Iste liber est de con[ventu] fratrum minorum omissus (concessus) et accomodatus fri Ric. Brynkley Magistro." Then within a square on first page of S. Matthew we read "Nov. Test. Gr. quod Collegio de Gonville et Caius dono dedit Thomas Hatcher Artium Magister A.M. 1567." Brynkley was Warden of

---

[1] And to the same effect writes Mr J. Rendel Harris in his *Origin of the Codex Leicestrensis*, p. 1. "It is not a little curious to the person who commences the critical study of the documents of the N. T., to find that he can discover no settled proportion between the age of a manuscript and the [critical] weight attached to it...A little study soon convinces the tyro of the impossibility of determining any law by which the value of a codex can be determined in terms of its age only without reference to its history."

the Grey Friars (now Sidney Sussex College), Cambridge,
and died in 1369, without having returned the manuscript
to Oxford. It may have come into the hands of Hatcher
when the Friars' House was dissolved in 1538. The Caius
Psalter, written in the same handwriting as Cod. 69 (above
p. xvii, note), also belonged to Brynkley, and was bound
at Grey Friars (as appears from vellum cases used in binding)
(Harris pp. 23—27) not earlier than 1366. This manuscript
was first used for Walton's Polyglott, but only very imperfectly:
better, though defectively, by Mill, who complains bitterly of
its numberless inaccuracies (Proleg. 1372), those of transcription being especially gross. This defect cannot but
somewhat impair the critical value of a Codex, in other
respects of great interest and importance. It was seen
by Wetstein in 1716, and minutely collated in 1860 by
Scrivener, who, with the manuscript before him, compared
it with the various readings of Mill and Wetstein. It is a
vellum copy in small quarto size on 472 pages, of the
twelfth century, with rude pictures of SS. Mark and Luke
only. There are 23 or 24 lines on each page, and clearly
written in what seems to be Indian ink, black and glossy,
so that the corrections, whether by the first or second hand,
are rather effected by washing out (as often in Cod. D) than
by erasing. It contains no prefatory matter or tables of
κεφάλαια prefixed to the several Gospels, yet we find
their numerals and τίτλοι in red, at the head (sometimes
at the foot) of the several pages. Also in margin κεφάλαια
minora (Ammonian sections) but no Eusebian canons below
them. The *compendia scribendi* are many and rare (e.g.
ϊ for εστι, Λ´ for ειαν, σ· for ὅτι Luc. xxii. 70). Breathings
and accents are often false and capricious, often in the middle
of a word and differing in same verse : η and ο usually
aspirated : not so ρρ or initial ρ. Itacisms quite numerous :
(some unusual) but unequally distributed[1] : in some places
almost none : ω (for ο) 259 ; ο (for ω) 318 ; η (for ει) 292 ;
ει (for η) 155 ; αι (for ε) 212 ; ε (for αι) 123 ; η (for ι) 253 ;

---

[1] They are given in full once or twice in our Collation (e.g. Mark vi.;
Luke viii., ix.) where they are very frequent.

ι (for η) 173; ι (for ει) 84; ει (for ι) 30; η (for ε) 11;
ε (for η) 16; ει (for ε) 2; ε (for ει) 8; η (for υ; pronouns
&c.) 92; υ (for η) 39; οι (for η) 25; η (for οι) 36; οι (for ει)
10; ει (for οι) 12; ι (for οι) 20; ι (for υ) 10; υ (for ι) 7;
οι (for υ) 3; υ (for οι) 5; ου (for ω) 11; ω (for ου) 5; ο (for
οι e.g. ποεῖν) 5; ο (for ου) 2; ο (for η) 1; ει (for ου) 1;
ε (for ι) 1; υ (for ει) 3; ει (for υ) 4; ω (for οι) 1;
υ (for ε) 1; υι (for υ) 1. TOTAL 2243. We find N ἐφελκυστικὸν (εἶπεν oftenest) 410: the hiatus for the lack of
it 53 times especially about Johan. iv. 25; vi.—xiii. Ὁμοιοτέλευτα 81 omissions (as frequent as in any extant MS.).
From same beginnings 8: repetitions from same causes 8.
No ι subscript or ascript.   Punctuation ; interrogation, and
, comma rare, . very often, even if no stop is needed.

As usual (e.g. Cod. 65) prepositions in composition are accentuated, as also a preposition before its case. A grave
accent will sometimes end a sentence.   We read *passim*
πλήρωμα, καὶ νὸς σῶμα μου, ὅτ'ἀν, ὅτ' ἂν and ὅταν, ἐὰν, ναὶ,
μὲ᾽ν, δὲ᾽, μὴ᾽, ἐπεὶ᾽, μηδὲ, ἐξ᾽ (often inserted by a later hand),
σκύλεις, κλαθμὸς, ἔχθος (for -ρος), χείρους (for χοίρους),
μέλλει (for μέλει), κρῖμα, διατί, διατοῦτο, ὧδε ὧδε, οὕτως (often
οὕτω Matth. iii. 15).   There is a tendency to doubling conso-
nants, λαμβάννω often (not Luke xi. 10, 26), νοσσος, ἐλλέγχω,
κρεμμασθὲν, κατάλυμμα, μϊ for μὴ often, η and ν confounded:
β for υ, 17 times, almost always at beginning of a line: μβ for
ββ in σάββατον e.g. Johan. xx. 1; 19 (often corrected *s. m.*).
Various readings sometimes *rubro* (Matth. xv. 14; Luc. viii.
35, 38; xiii. 34; Johan. ii. 17; xvi. 23; xviii. 3).   Red marks
in margin (Marc. ix. 17—19; xiii. 3, 9), as if they were
citations.   This copy is much with Cod. D: Matth. viii. 28,
32; ix. 8, 15; xiii. 27; xxi. 24, 28; xxvi. 3; Marc. xiii. 16;
Luc. viii. 48; xiv. 17; xxii. 10, 52; Joan. viii. 6.   Also with
Cod. 61; Matth. xxi. 19; xv. 20.   A few out of many specimens
of rare readings: Matth. i. 5; iv. 18; v. 1—25, 28; viii. 10, 24;
ix. 4, 18; Luc. xii. 56; xvi. 16; xx. 11; Johan. xviii. 32; lastly
Matth. xxiii. 35—υἱοῦ βαραχίου omitted by the first hand[1],
though Walton and Mill do not record the fact. *In grammar*

---

[1] The two words are supplied *s. m.* at the foot of the page.

dative stands for accusative (10 times): Marc. viii. 11; x. 34,
49; xv. 20; Luc. xi. 46; xiv. 31; xv. 2; xix. 11; Johan. iv. 34;
viii. 51. So accusative for dative (25 times): Matth. ix. 24,
p. m.; xi. 25; xii. 4, 47; xiv. 33; xvii. 14; xx. 31; Marc. ii. 32;
vi. 19, 36; ix. 25; x. 32; xii. 13; Luc. v. 7; vi. 34; ix. 60;
x. 40; xii. 1; xiv. 29; xix. 39; xx. 15; xxiii. 36; Joan. vi.
31; xii. 23; xviii. 16. Augment omitted (9 times): Matth.
x. 25; xiii. 2; xiv. 11; Luc. vi. 13; xiii. 34; xvi. 8; xxiv.
27; Joan. vi. 18, 26. Thus also the so-called Alexandrine
forms: χεῖραν Matth. ix. 18; xii. 10, 13 (so Cod. Wake 12);
Luc. xv. 22; Joan. xx. 25, 27 only: τρίχαν Matth. v. 36 (so
Cod. 66): ἄνδραν Joan. iv. 16: ἔναν Marc. xi. 29: πόδαν Luc.
iv. 11: τιναν Joan. xviii. 4: χεῖρα (pro χήραν) Luc. xviii. 5:
χειρῶν Luc. xx. 47; xxi. 2, 3: πενθέρα (pro -αν) Matth. viii.
14: τὸν ἄμμον Matth. vii. 26: τὸν κλεῖδα Luc. xi. 52. Especially in verbs: προσέπεσαν Matth. vii. 25: ἀνέπεσαν Marc. vi.
40: ἐξήλθατε Luc. xxii. 52: ἔλαβα Joan. x. 18: σαρεῖ Luc.
xv. 8: ἐπιγνοῦντες Matth. xiv. 35: ηὐλισθῆ (3rd pers.) Matth.
xxi. 17: ἐκατέκλασε Luc. ix. 16: ἐκαθέρισε sæpe. Some
additional clauses are interpolated in the body of the text:
e.g. Matth. xii. 33; xxvi. 43; Johan. i. 36. The readings of
Cod. c are incorporated with the Collation of other manuscripts, below, p. 60.

d. Evan. 66, Gal. Trinity College, Cambridge, O. viii. 3.

This copy, written on paper and in good condition, once
belonged to Thomas Gale (1636—1702), formerly Fellow of
Trinity College and High Master of S. Paul's School. He is
reputed to have written the Latin inscription on the Monument in London, and became Dean of York in 1697. He gave
Arabic books that year to his College, and probably bequeathed
to it this copy, together with the Evangelistarium (O. iv.
22) to be described below p. lxiv. The fineness and thinness
of the paper (though somewhat worm-eaten) led Bradshaw
to refer this MS. to the 13th century, but the general style
and handwriting would rather lead us to assign it to a century

earlier, which is the same date as Gonville Cod. 59. Mill tells us
(Proleg. & 1469) that Gale shewed him this copy in London.
He shortly describes it (citing it 364 times, or about one
variation in three) and indicates its readings by the notation
of *Gal.* Although inserted in the great printed Catalogue
of Manuscripts Oxford 1697, it was once lost sight of, and its
location was discovered by Bradshaw in 1862, when Scrivener
borrowed and collated it afresh. The volume is a quarto,
8¾ in. long, by 6 broad, 294 leaves in all (including foreign
matter, or 564 pages); 35 quires (last of five sheets) with
signatures, 21 lines on a page. There are rude pictures
of the four Evangelists (S. John in a meditating attitude),
with Synaxarion prefixed and Epistola Carpiano, followed
by 11 blank pages for Canons of Eusebius; tables (*rubro*)
of the larger κεφάλαια to the last three Gospels. In
margins Ammonian sections in black, over Eusebian canons
in red, τίτλοι and numerals of larger κεφάλαια. In Luke only
to τίτλοι *rubro* are subjoined as a harmony the corresponding κεφάλαια in the other three Gospels. Much rubrical
matter in marg.; ἀρχαὶ and τέλη in text *rubro*. Citations
in marg. >. Short scholia and various readings occasionally[1]
occur in the margin, one set earlier, but chiefly in later hands.
We find 77 ν ἐφελκυστικά, with verbs (εἶπεν &c.), no ι ascript
or subscript *p. m.*; but the hiatus is frequent about Luke xii.;
with breathings and accents full, but somewhat careless *p. m.*;
semicolon (not interrog.) Luc. ix. 6, 52; xiii. 9. Stops often
added *s. m.* Margin *s. m.* in same state as when Mill collated
Gal. e.g. Luc. xiii. 25; xiv. 5; xvii. 2; xxii. 30; xxiii. 8; except
xiv. 5 from Cod. 69. In this copy ει is awkwardly written, υ for
β Matth. xxvi. 4; Luc. x. 1; but β for υ Luc. iii. 35; xi. 46 *p. m.*?
† for ες often. ὁμοιοτέλευτα are only 11. It contains 508 itacisms, whereof 250 of first hand are corrected later. These are

---

[1] They are always noted in our Collation, see Matth. vii. 6; ix. 30; xii. 33;
xvi. 20; xvii. 11; xxi. 9, 33; xxii. 12; xxiii. 15; xxvii. 32. Johan. i. 28; iv.
52; vi. 9, 12; vii. 4, 29, 34, 38, 53; viii. 2, 4, 9, 20, 43; x. 21, 22, 25, 29, 33,
39; xi. 41, 43, 44; xii. 6, 13, 19, 37, 40, 41, 47, 48; xviii. 14, 20; xx. 11, 18;
xxi. 1, 7, 15. These specimens (chiefly of marginal various readings) may
suffice. Glosses stand thick about Luke i.

ει (for η) 57; η (for ει) 55; ω (for ο) 119; ο (for ω) 62; ι (for
η) 17 : η (for ι) 31 ; ι (for ει) 10 ; ει (for ι) 13 ; η (for ε) 2 ;
ε (for η) 12 ; αι (for ε) 57 ; ε (for αι) 29 ; υ (for η) 12 ; η (for
υ) 10 (chiefly pronouns); ι (for υ) 3; υ (for ι) 4; υ (for οι)
3 ; υ (for ει) 1 ; η (for οι) 2 ; ι (for οι) 1 ; οι (for ι) 2 ; οι (for
υ) 1 ; ου (for ω) 3; ω (for ου) 1. Rarer forms are ἐκβάλατε
Matth. xxii. 13 ; κοσμημένον Luc. xi. 25 : γραμμένα Luc.
xviii. 31 p. m.: accusative in -αν Matth. v. 36 (τρίχαν, so
Cod. 69); Marc. vii. 30 p. m. (θυγατεραν), as also Luc. xiii.
16 p. m.; πενθερὰ (accus.) Luc. xii. 53. Mostly οὐκ ἔτι,
but οὐκέτι Marc. xii. 34 ; Luc. xx. 40 ; Johan. xiv. 19 ; xvii.
11; xxi. 6. σκαδαλίζω mostly so written, p. m. This manuscript is not on the whole very peculiar in its text, although
much with Codd. D. 69 in rare readings; e.g. Matth. xxiii. 35
(with 69) ; xxvii. 2, 8 ; Marc. xv. 32 ; Luc. v. 10 ; viii. 17 ;
xiv. 2 ; xvii. 24 ; xxii. 53 ; xxiii. 1, 2, 5 ; Johan. vi. 7 ; vii. 12 ;
xiii. 26 ; xiv. 16 ; xv. 19 (with D) ; xviii. 7 (with D).
Simples and compounds are sometimes interchanged, e.g.
Matth. xii. 45, 49 ; Marc. xiii. 22 ; Luc. xix. 1, 23; xxi. 2.
Notice also peculiarities of punctuation in Matth. x. 40, 42 ;
xx. 12 ; xxvii. 42 ; Marc. xi. 32 ; xii. 28 ; xiii. 9 ; xv. 23, 31 ;
xvi. 6; Luc. iv. 18, 34; vi. 9; ix. 27; xii. 1; xxi. 30; Johan. viii.
13; xii. 27; xiii. 30, 31 ; xiv. 9, 24 ; xx. 28. We find also
μή` as negative Johan. iii. 18. οὕτως mostly (19 times), ὁ μὲ`ν
p. m., ὧδε p. m., also ἐξ', ἐν' Marc. ii. 19 ; Luc. vii. 16: even
εἰς' in two places. The readings of Cod. d are incorporated
with the collation of other manuscripts, below, Part II. p. 60.

We next pass on to Oxford, where a large body of Greek
manuscripts, not a few of them already collated, have not
been yet made available for use. The little I have been able
to accomplish here has only made me desire to publish the
whole collection, which task I must now leave to some fortunate scholar who enjoys more leisure than I ever ventured to
aspire to. They consist of fourteen copies of the Gospels
only. They were brought from Constantinople by Thomas
Payne, Archdeacon of Brecon, once Chaplain of our Embassy
there, to Archbishop Wake in 1731, and have been described

by G. W. Kitchin, now Dean of Winchester, in his "*Catalogue of the Manuscripts in Christ Church Library*" (1867). To that Library Archbishop Wake (d. 1735), who had been a Canon there, had bequeathed them, and they are kept apart with his other manuscripts in a cedar closet at Christ Church Library. Th. Mangey (1684—1755), the editor of Philo, states on the fly-leaves that he had collated six of them in 1749; Caspar Wetstein collated two for his relative's great New Testament (1751—2); while in the margin of a 4to Greek Testament (Geneva, 1620) is inserted a most laborious collation and full description of eight of the Wake manuscripts, by John Walker, the diligent and most faithful assistant of the great Bentley in his critical studies. Of these several collations only one (Wake 12) was collated by more than one person, and Wake 12, 34 for the Apocalypse alone. Dean Gaisford catalogued the whole of them in 1837, and Scrivener, by the aid of the learned and amiable W. Jacobson, D.D., late Bishop of Chester, was permitted to inspect them in 1861 (seen afterwards also in 1883). Two of the principal copies I was permitted to borrow and to scrutinize at home (1863—4) with the following result.

e.   Evan. 492, Wake 12, Christ Church, Oxford (Act. 193, Paul. 277, Apoc. 26).

Called also Codex Dionysii, from the name of its scribe. Scholz, on the mistaken information of Dean Gaisford, calls this copy Evangelistarium 181, Apost. 57; but the manuscript contains the Gospels in their proper order, with unusually full liturgical matter. They are followed by the Acts, Catholic, and Pauline Epistles in their usual order; last of all comes the Apocalypse. The following leaves are lost (see also below, p. xxxv): Act. i. 1—vii. 49; x. 19—xiv. 10; xv. 15—xvi. 11; xviii. 1—xxi. 25; xxiii. 18—James iii. 17; 1 Cor. xii. 11— xv. 12; xvi. 13—15; Gal. v. 16—vi. 8. Some illuminations have been wantonly cut out. In the Gospels, besides much liturgical matter *rubro*, we have Prologues, the Epistle to Carpianus, the Eusebian tables, the larger κεφάλαια with their τίτλοι, the Ammonian sections (black) and Eusebian canons (red). This copy contains much foreign matter and scholia. Codex Dionysii is a large folio (12⅛ inches high by 9 broad) of the eleventh century, of 240 vellum leaves, fine clear hand, 36 lines on a page. In the Gospels the itacisms amount to 658 ; viz. ι (for ει) 15 ; ει (for ι) 15 ; ι (for η) 98 ; η (for ι) 36 ; ε (for αι) 42 ; αι (for ε) 104 ; η (for ει) 56 ; ει (for η) 74 ; ο (for ω) 83 ; ω (for ο) 76 ; ε (for η) 14 ; η (for ε) 6 ; η (for υ) 2 ; υ (for η) 9 ; ου (for ω) 3 ; ω (for ου) 1 ; η (for οι) 5 ; οι (for η) 1 ; ι (for οι) 4 ; οι (for ι) 5 ; υ (for οι) 1 ; υ (for ι) 1 ; ει (for υ) 1 ; ει (for οι) 1 ; οι (for ει) 1. There are in the Gospels 12 omissions by ὁμοιοτέλευτα, e.g. in Marc. iii. 8 ; Johan. xiv. 26. The augment is omitted, Matth. ix. 9 ; xiii. 17 ; Marc. xv. 10 ; Luc. i. 17 ; vi. 13 ; viii. 1 ; xiii. 13 ; xvii. 10 ; xxi. 38 ; Johan. xx. 8 ; xiv. 14. Reduplication is omitted, Luc. xi. 21 ; xii. 52 ; xxii. 22. Unusual forms are εὐσπλαγνίσθη (so Evan. 556) Matth. ix. 36 ; xiv. 14 ; Marc. vi. 34 ; Luc. vii. 13 ; x. 33 ; xv. 20. εὐρεύνησον Johan. vii. 52. ἐκαθερίσθη Matth. viii. 13 ; Luc. iv. 27. ἀπεκατεστάθη Matth. xii. 13 ; Marc. iii. 5 ; Luc. vi. 10. ἔμελλεν (for ἔμελεν) Johan. xii. 6 ; 1 Pet. v. 7. ἐδώκει Luc. xix. 15. σαρεῖ Luc. xv. 8. εἰδόντες Matth. xxii. 29. εἴδαμεν Marc. ix. 38. γυναῖκαν Luc. vii. 34. θυγατέραν Luc. xiii. 16. χεῖραν Matth. xii. 13 ; Marc. iii. 1. ἀρχιερέα Johan. xviii. 24. χήρα (accus.) Luc. xxi. 2. τὴν θύρα Johan. xviii. 16. δεῖπνον μέγαν Luc. xiii. 19 (non xiv. 15). Dative put for accusative, Marc. x. 33, 49 ; Luc. i. 65 : also accusative for dative, Matth. xv. 35 ; xvii. 14 ; xviii. 26 ; xx. 4 ; xxvii. 44 ; so Act. xxi. 40 ; James v. 6. Ν ἐφελκυστικὸν with εἶπεν occurs 190 times, elsewhere 332 times in the Gospels. Hiatus (5) for lack of ν Matth. xii. 6 ; xiii. 52 ; Marc. x. 24 ; Luc. v. 33 ; Johan. xviii. 31. ι ascript very often, subscript never. In S. Luke about 10 verses are lost, through wanton mutilation of the manuscript for the sake of illuminations, in S. John 489 out of 880 verses have perished : mut. John i. 1—vii. 39 (8 leaves) ; viii. 31—ix. 11 (second leaf of ιζ quaternion) ; x. 10—xi. 54 (two leaves) ; xii. 36—xiii. 27 (one leaf). For account of other parts of the manuscript see below, Acts

p. lxxiv, Paul. p. lxxvii, Apocalypse p. lxxxvii. This copy stands nearly alone in MATTH. v. 30 τῶν μελῶν σου ἀπόληται. xii. 1 καὶ οἱ μαθηταὶ [– δὲ]. xvii. 20 – καὶ οὐδὲν ἀδυνατήσει ὑμῖν. xviii. 26 αὐτὸν (pro αὐτῷ). xix. 8 ἔγραψεν (pro ἐπέτρεψεν). xx. 27 πρῶτος εἶναι; xxi. 9 – εὐλογημένος ad fin. versûs. 32 – αἱ. xxiii. 6 δὲ (pro τε). xxvi. 18 + αὐτοῖς (post εἶπεν). 46 + ἰούδας (post ἤγγικεν). xxvii. 43 – νῦν. MARC. ii. 27 λέγει (pro ἔλεγεν). vi. 3 – ἐν. 13 ἐξέβαλον. εἴληφον. x. 5 ἐπιστολὴν (pro ἐντολὴν). xii. 43 fin. + τὰ δῶρα (post γαζοφυλάκιον). LUC. xiv. 5 [ὄνος]. xx. 19 – τὸν λαὸν. xxiii. 15 ἀνέπεμψα γὰρ αὐτὸν πρὸς ἡμᾶς. JOHAN. vii. 53—viii. 11 habet, nullo omissionis vestigio. Cod. e also contains a large number of transcriptural errors. See Marc. ii. 8; v. 31; xi. 13, &c. Punctuation often worth notice, e.g. Matth. ix. 5.

f.   Evan. 503, Wake 34, Christ Church, Oxford (Act. 190, Paul. 244, Apoc. 27. See p. xxxiv.).

This manuscript exhibits more numerous and more interesting variations than Wake 12, and often resembles Cod. b (Evan. 604). It is of about the same date (eleventh or twelfth century) as the preceding and is even more mutilated. It measures 10 inches long by 7½ broad, a quarto on vellum of 201 leaves, 31 (in Gospels 29 lines) on a page, the ink being a reddish brown. The fragments occur in the following order. Fol. 1 begins with the ὑπόθεσις of Œcumenius to 2 Peter. Fol. 2 contains Act. xvii. 24—xviii. 13: then follows 1 Johan. with Œcumenius' ὑπόθεσις without tables of κεφάλαια, 1 John iii. 9—iv. 9 (one leaf) being lost. Then 2, 3 John, Jude, Œcumenius' hypotheses with tables of κεφάλαια; the Apocalypse (without ὑπόθεσις or tables of κεφ.) continuing on the page on which Jude ends. On the same page whereon the Apocalypse ends, is written ὑπόθεσις Œcumenii to Romans, and Euthalii table of κεφάλαια. Then follow S. Paul's Epistles complete, except Heb. vii. 26—ix. 28 (two leaves). All these Epistles

have prologues, table of κεφάλαια (not the larger of Euthalius, but of Œcumenius) with notes of Church readings by
the first hand, and a Synaxarion later. The Gospels follow
Hebrews on fol. 131 b, and so perhaps they did originally.
Mut. Luc. ii. 15—47, ending Luc. vi. 42.

The Four Gospels, apparently relegated to the last place
by the binder, as Mr Harris (p. xvii, note ¹) believes to be the
case with Cod. 69. Certainly the same hand wrote the whole
codex, Wake 34. The Gospels, ending at Luc. vi. 42, have
τίτλοι and Church lessons in the margin; the larger κεφάλαια
and Ammonian sections, but not the Eusebian canons. Re-
serving notices of other portions of the New Testament for
their proper places, we find in the portions of the Gospels
which survive, 10 ὁμοιοτέλευτα, ν ἐφελκυστικὰ (often with
nouns) 196 times, but only 106 itacisms: ω (for ου) 2; ου
(for ω) 1; υ (for η) 1; η (for υ) 2; ε (for αι) 3; αι (for ε) 10;
ι (for ει) 2; ει (for ι) 7; ει (for η) 14; η (for ει) 8; οι (for υ)
3; υ (for οι) 2; ω (for ο) 12; ο (for ω) 15; η (for ι) 10; ι (for
η) 3; ε (for η) 6; η (for ε) 3: also ευ for Attic ηυ passim. A
few unusual forms occur, for this copy does not contain many:
ἀνέπεσαν Marc. vi. 40; ἐνεβριμοῦντο Marc. xiv. 5; ἀπάγγειλαν
Matth. xxviii. 11. Very peculiar is ὑποδημάτων for ποδῶν,
Marc. vi. 11. The present volume (pp. 60 sqq.) contains a
full collation of Cod. f with Codd. cde, with select readings
of Codd. bj and the chief editions, frequently suppressing mere
itacisms, ν ἐφελκυστικά, breathings and accents, and transcriptural errors, unless they have some special suggestiveness.

g. Evan. 547. B.-C. I. 7.

This small quarto volume, measuring 6 inches high by
4 wide, is of paper and about the thirteenth century in date.
It contains 267 leaves and 22 lines on a page. It is clearly
and correctly written (but ὁμοιοτέλευτον John xiv. 27 *p. m.* and
elsewhere), itacisms being comparatively rare, breathings and
accents sufficiently accurate. The first six leaves consist of a

S.   d brief synaxarion and menology. There are comely pictures of S. Mark and S. Luke, and the two earlier Gospels are preceded by tables of κεφάλαια. Slight illuminations stand at the head of each Gospel, τίτλοι and notes of Church lessons (John vii. 53 εἰς τὴν πελαγίαν) at the head and foot of pages, all in very pale red, but no numerals of κεφάλαια, Ammonian sections or Eusebian canons in the margin. The text of Luc. i. 26—42 and of Luc. xx. 37—xxi. 24 is lost. The copy being in bad condition, the leaves have been repaired and the decayed letters sometimes retraced by a recent hand. After the subscription to S. John (τέλος εἴληφεν τοῦ χυ μου ἡ βίβλος | ἡ τέτρας ὧδε τῶν μαθητῶν τοῦ χυ | δόξα τῶ ἁγίω θῶ ἀμην) is added p. m. ξθΘπλ; I know not the meaning of the letters. In the cover of the binding is inserted a small brass plate, with three figures (that in the centre being the Lord in the act of blessing). See Cod. B.-C. ii. 7, below p. xlii, where a similar plate is described.

Notable readings are few and of little consequence: so closely does this copy agree with the Received text; but compare MATTH. ii. 13. τῶν μάγων (pro αὐτῶν). iv. 20. + αὐτῶν εὐθέως (post δίκτυα). vii. 8. εὑρήσει (pro εὑρίσκει). viii. 27. ὑπακούουσιν αὐτοῦ. ix. 18. ἄρχων τις εἰσελθὼν. x. 27. ἠκούσατε. 29. + τοῦ ἐν οὐρανοῖς (post πρσ ὑμῶν). xi. 21. + καθήμεναι (post σποδῷ). xii. 21. - ἐν. 32. ἐὰν (pro ἂν). 45. + καὶ (ante τότε). λαμβάνει. γίνονται. xiii. 27. - ἐν τῶ σῶ ἀγρῶ. - τά. 29. + καὶ (ante τὸν σῖτον). 32. λαχάνων et σπερμάτων transfert. xv. 18. ἐξέρχονται. xvi. 3. συνίετε (pro δύνασθε). 21. διδάσκειν (pro δεικνύειν). 27. τὰ ἔργα (pro τὴν πρᾶξιν). xvii. 27. ἀναβαίνοντα. xviii. 11. + ζητῆσαι καὶ (ante σῶσαι). xxi. 18. ἐπὶ (pro εἰς). xxii. 41. αὐτοῖς (pro αὐτούς). 45. + ἐν πνι (post δαδ). xxiii. 26. αὐτοῦ (pro αὐτῶν). xxv. 29. δοκεῖ ἔχειν (pro ἔχει). xxvi. 39. προσελθὼν. 56. - τότε οἱ μαθηταὶ usque ad ἔφυγον. xxvii. 35. - ἵνα πληρωθῇ ad fin. vers.

MARC. ii. 14. + ὁ ιϲ (post παράγων). 26. - τοῦ. iii. 4. ἀπολέσαι (pro ἀποκτεῖναι). 32. + καὶ αἱ ἀδελφαί σου (ante ἔξω). iv. 3. + καὶ συνίετε (post ἀκούετε). v. 11. πρὸς τῶ

ὄρει. vi. 20. ἀκούων. 25. δὸς (pro δῷς). 35. – ὅτι.
ix. 40. καθ᾽ ἡμῶν ὑπὲρ ἡμῶν. x. 31. – οἱ. xi. 8. τοὺς
χιτῶνας (pro τὰ ἱμάτια). 25. ἡμῶν (pro ὑμῶν). 26. +ὑμῶν
(post ἀφήσει). 32. –ἐὰν. πάντες. xii. 2. ἀπήγγειλε p. m.?
ἀπέστειλε s. m. xiii. 28. μάνθανε (pro μάθετε). xiv. 1. +ἐν
(ante δόλω). Luc. i. 55. τὸν ἀβραὰμ καὶ τὸ σπέρμα αὐτοῦ ἕως τοῦ αἰῶνος.
ii. 14. [εὐδοκία]. 22. [αὐτῶν]. 28. αὐτὸν (pro αὐτὸ). iii. 33.
+τοῦ ἰωρὰμ (ante τοῦ ἐσρὼμ). iv. 42. ἐπεζήτουν. v. 19. πῶς
(pro διὰ ποίας). vi. 9. ἀποκτεῖναι (pro ἀπολέσαι). 18. ἀπὸ
(pro ὑπὸ). viii. 3. +καὶ (post ἀφ᾽ ἧς). 22. ἀνέβη καὶ ἀνέβησαν
(pro καὶ ἀνήχθησαν s. m.). 24. +σωσον (ante ἀπολύμεθα
sic). 33. θάλασσαν (pro λίμνην). 45. – καὶ λέγεις τίς ὁ
ἁψάμενός μου. xii. 21. fin. +ταῦτα λέγων ἐφώνει ὁ ἔχων
ὦτα ἀκούειν ἀκουέτω. 54. – καὶ prim. xiii. 10. – δὲ.
15. ὑποκριταὶ. 20. – καὶ (ante πάλιν). 29. – ἀπὸ secund.
32. +τὰ (ante δαιμόνια). 33. ἐρχομένη (pro ἐχ.). xiv. 1.
εἰσελθεῖν. 5. υἱὸς (pro ὄνος). 12. –καὶ. ποιεῖς. xv. 2. –οἱ
secund. 21. +ποίησόν με ὡς ἕνα τῶν μισθίων σου. 29.
– ἐντολήν σου παρῆλθον· καὶ ἐμοί. xvi. 4. μεταθῶ (pro
μετασταθῶ). 24. +ἐλέησόν με (ante πέρ ἀβραὰμ) bis scriptum. xvii. 4. – ἐπὶ σε. 36. Habet δύο ἔσονται ἐν τῷ ἀγρῷ
εἷς (– ὁ) κ.τ.λ. 37. πτῶμα (pro σῶμα). +καὶ (ante οἱ
ἀετοί). xviii. 5. ὑποπιάζη. 32. Transfert ὑβρισθήσεται and
ἐμπτυσθήσεται. xix. 43. συνάξουσι. xx. 14. διελογίσαντο.
23. +οἱ δὲ ἔδειξαν καὶ εἶπε (post δηνάριον). 33. ἔσται (pro
γίνεται). xxi. 25. ἤχους. 30. + δὲ (post βλέποντας).
36. – ταῦτα. xxii. 4. – τοῖς secund. 10. ἐν τῇ πόλει.
25. κατακυριεύουσιν. 36. πωλήσει (pro πωλησάτω). 47. fin.
+τοῦτο γὰρ σημείόνει αὐτοῖς· ὃν ἂν φιλήσω αὐτός ἐστι.
51. – δὲ. 66. – τε. fin. αὐτῶν. xxiii. 1. ἤγαγον. 7. εἰς
(pro πρὸς). 9. αὐτῷ (pro αὐτὸν). 17. +δέσμιον (post ἕνα).
25. – αὐτοῖς. 26. – τοῦ. 29. +αἱ (ante κοιλίαι). 53. fin.
+καὶ προσεκύλισε λίθον μέγαν ἐπὶ τὴν θύραν τοῦ μνημείου.
54. – καὶ secund. xxiv. 18. – ἐν prim. 47. μου (pro αὐτοῦ
retraced s. m.).

Johan. i. 26. – ὁ. 27. – ἐγώ. 40. + οὖν (post ἦλθον).
– δὲ. 42. – ὁ. 49. – ὁ. ii. 5. + δὲ (post λέγει). ἂν λέγει.

17. καταφάγεται. 19. – ὁ. 22. – αὐτοῖς. iii. 3. – ὁ.
10. – ὁ. 23. παρεγένοντο. 28. – μοι. iv. 3. – πάλιν.
31. + αὐτοῦ (post μαθηταὶ). 53. + ἰάθη (post ὥρα). v. 1.
+ ἡ (ante ἑορτὴ). – ὁ. 4. ἐγένετο. 24. πρὸς (pro εἰς).
44. ζητοῦντες (pro ζητεῖτε). vi. 15. – πάλιν. 22. συνῆλθε.
24. – καὶ prim. 45. – τοῦ. ἀκούων. 54. + ἐν (ante τῇ ἑ.).
70. – ὁ ἴσ. vii. 41. ἄλλοι δὲ ἔλεγον ὅτι. vii. 53—viii.
11. Nullo dubitationis vestigio, ut plurimae lectiones oc-
current variae, e. g. viii. 4. ταύτην εὕρομεν ἐπαυτοφόρω
μοιχευομένην. 5. ἡμῶν (pro ἡμῖν). λιθάζειν. fin. περὶ
αὐτῆς. 6. κατηγορίαν κατ᾽ αὐτοῦ. fin. + μὴ προσποι-
ούμενος. 7. ἀναβλέψας (pro ἀνακύψας). πρῶτος, [τὸν
λίθον]. 9. εἷς καθείς. κατελήφθη. οὖσα (pro ἑστῶσα).
10. γύναι (pro ἡ γυνὴ). – ἐκεῖνοι. 14. + ἀπὸ τοῦ νῦν (ante
μηκέτι). 12. initial Π. 57. αὐτῶ οἱ ἰουδαῖοι (– πρὸς αὐ.).
58. ἤμην (pro εἰμι). xi. 14. – ὁ ἴσ. 42. παρεστῶσα.
47. + κατὰ τοῦ ἰυ (post συνέδριον). xii. 13. – ὁ. 17. ὅτι.
18. ἀπήντησεν. 28. + ἅγιε (post πάτερ). xiii. 2. βεβλημένου
(pro βεβληκότος). xiv. 10. + ἐν (ante ὑμῖν). xvi. 7. + ἐγὼ
(ante μὴ). 10. πορεύομαι (pro ὑπάγω). 15. λαμβάνει.
xvii. 2. δώσει. 26. + καὶ (post ἵνα). xviii. 2. – τὸν.
20. – τῇ. 25. + οὖν (post ἠρνήσατο). 40. – πάλιν. xix. 4.
ὁ πιλάτος. 6. εἶδεν αὐτοῦ ὁ ὄχλος καὶ οἱ ἀρχιερεῖς καὶ οἱ
ὑπηρέται. 17. + καὶ ἤγαγον εἰς τὸ πραιτώριον (pro ἀπήγαγον). 23. εἰς τέσσαρα μέρη. 35. + αὐτοῦ (post μαρτυρία).
38. – δὲ. – ὁ. 40. + ἐν (ante ὀθονίοις). xx. 19. δὲ (pro
οὖν). 28. – ὁ. – αὐτῷ. xxi. 4. γενομένης ἤδη. ἐπὶ (pro
εἰς). 15. – ὁ ἰησοῦς. 18. εἰ σὺ (pro οἴσει).

Many of these are small glosses; we have not usually set
down examples in the above list where the current of evidence is decidedly against the Received text (e.g. Johan.
iii. 25).

Yet notice moreover the following readings. It will be
seen, however, that this codex seldom, if ever, countenances
the oldest uncials (‎אBC, &c.), even when they are supported
by a scanty list of later copies. The pericope adulterae John
vii. 53—viii. 11 has every line obelized in the margin (⌐⌐).

Matth. xvi. 20. – *ἰησοῦς*. Luke xiv. 5. [ὄνος]. Acts viii.
37. *Deest versus*. xiii. 6. +ὅλην (*ante τὴν νῆσον*). xiv.
18, 19. *fin.* 18 + ἀλλὰ πορεύεσθαι ἕκαστον εἰς τὰ ἴδια.
(v. 19) διατριβόντων δὲ αὐτῶν καὶ διδασκόντων ἐπῆλθον
ἀπὸ ἀντιοχείας καὶ ἰκονίου ἰουδαῖοι· καὶ διαλεγομένων αὐτῶν
παρρησία, ἀνέπεισαν τοὺς ὄχλους ἀποστῆναι ἀπ' αὐτῶν
λέγοντες οὐδὲν ἀληθὲς λέγουσιν ἀλλὰ πάντα ψεύδονται.
λιθάσαντες δὲ τὸν παῦλον κ.τ.λ.
but not the other ordinary additions found in many manuscripts of this book. xvi. 7. – καὶ οὐκ εἴασεν αυτοὺς τὸ
πνεῦμα.

h. Evan. 548. B.-C. I. 9.

This neat fragment is one of the Baroness Burdett-Coutts'
collection (above pp. xxi, xxii) containing S. Matthew and
S. Mark 125 leaves 4to. scarcely 7 inches by 5, preceded by
6 leaves of a Synaxarion. It is an elegant specimen of the
twelfth century, having 18 lines on a page. The following
portions are lost : Matth. xi. 28—xiii. 33 ; xviii. 13—xxi. 15;
33—xxii. 10 ; xxiv. 46—xxv. 21 ; Marc. iii. 11—v. 31 ; ix. 18—
xii. 6, 34—44. It ends Marc. xvi. 20 πανταχοῦ. Many capitals,
lectionary marks in margin. Ammonian sections and Eusebian
canons in margin, all these in red, but no numerals for
κεφάλαια, though τίτλοι at head of pages. Itacisms not
very many, chiefly ι for η, η for ι, ι for ει, ω for ο, ε for αι :
ἀνεπέσαν Marc. vi. 40. No ι subscript, but ascript e.g.
Matth. ii. 9, 19, but very rarely (yet even ζημιωθῆι Marc.
viii. 36). Ν ἐφελκυστικὸν almost constant. Not a few changes
by a second hand, especially in correcting itacisms, or by in-
sertions in margin of words or capitals omitted in text. This
MS. is carefully written ('Ομοιοτέλευτον Matth. vii. 9 only)
and a few breathings misplaced, e.g. ἤρξατο *semel*, but real
various readings of any consequence are not frequent.
Yet see Matth. viii. 18; xv. 6; xvi. 20 *s.m.*; xxiv. 6 ;
xxvi. 27, 73; xxviii. 6. Marc. vi. 3; vii. 19; viii. 7 ; xvi.
2, 19.

i. Evan. 549 (Act. 219). B.-C. II. 7.

This remarkable copy, consisting altogether of 172 leaves, is a small duodecimo of 5 inches long and 3 broad, in a very minute hand of the twelfth or thirteenth century, containing from 26 to 31 lines on a page, the writing being not only very small, but full of abridgements, so as to become very painful to read, especially towards the last five pages of the Acts, where the scribe seems to change. On the blue silk cover is fixed a brass tablet more elaborate than that just described (B.-C. I. 7, g p. xxxviii), also consisting of three figures, whereof the Lord sits in the centre. On the other leaf of the binding the superscription runs ι͞σ κ͞σ. This copy contains the four Gospels, with slight illuminations at their heads, followed by the Acts, which breaks off at cap. xxvi. 24 μαίνη παῦλε, some leaves having been cut out. There is much foreign matter in this interesting little book. Besides two leaves used in binding, we find *rubro* (7 leaves) Τοῦ ἐν ἁγίοις π͞ρσ ἡμῶν γρηγορίου ἀρχιεπισκόπου κωσταντῖνουπόλεως τοῦ θεολόγου, διὰ στίχων ἡρωικῶν περὶ γενεαλογίας χ͞υ· where every hexameter line in black has under it a prose paraphrase in red. Then follow χ͞υ θαύματα παρὰ ματθαίω ἰωάννῃ τὲ καὶ λουκᾶ καὶ μάρκω· οὐ μὴν ἀλλὰ καὶ παραβολαὶ δϊαφόραι· ἐν οἷς διὰ ἰαμβῶν καὶ ἐπῶν : with black verses and red paraphrases as before. Then follow παραβολαὶ marg. rubro. Then tables of κεφάλαια of S. Matthew, with numerals in margin and τίτλοι at head and foot of pages. In the margin of Matth. v. only are very minute scholia in black and red. Like verses of Gregory precede SS. Mark and Luke, but follow S. John : tables of κεφάλαια precede SS. Luke and John, but there are no rubrical notes, and the Ammonian sections and Eusebian canons occur only on one open leaf containing Luke xii. (ρ͞μα to ρ͞ζ). The ι subscript is found twice only on the page of heroics before S. Luke's Gospel. Before the Acts stands a ὑπόθεσις, but no chapter divisions, except a few capitals in red. The variations from the common text are not many or remarkable (but τοῦ κ͞υ Acts xx. 28), the itacisms quite rare.

j. Evan. 618 (Hoskier).

Mr H. C. Hoskier, of whose persevering labours we have spoken above (p. xxv), bought of Quaritch, the London bookseller, in 1886, a beautiful copy of the Gospels, whose previous history is unknown to me, written on thickish (occasionally thinner) vellum. It contains 352 leaves, the first and last blank. On the last is the date of the owner (α‚ψκθ′, i.e. 1729). In size it is 9⅜ in. by 6⅝, in old leathern binding, with leather clasps, quite complete. Its specialty is five sumptuous miniatures, on a gold ground, Moses, the Evangelists, each before their several Gospels, at the heading of each of which are beautiful pictures of birds, beasts, &c., exquisitely painted. It is rare to see so fine a copy, which may date from the twelfth century, or perhaps a little earlier. The manuscript contains also κεφ. b, τίτλοι, Am., Eus. (not given regularly), marks of O. T. quotations in the margin. A few Church lessons at the end of each Gospel are invariably given. Even the sacred name of *Jesus* and *Jerusalem* are sometimes given in full. N ἐφελκυστικὸν is quite rare, but οὕτως *always*. Mr Hoskier enumerates 13 cases of *iota subscript*, but two only of *ascript* (Marc. xvi. 9; Johan. i. 25), and both those at the end of a line. Itacisms occur but rarely. A second hand has been busy throughout the manuscript making corrections, always adding the aspirate to ο ωδε. But, after all, the scribe himself may have been the corrector (διορθωτής). Of the real various readings there are a fair number of some interest, but in general they approach very near to the Received text. Many readings are given by us in Appendix I. Mr Hoskier has published (1889) the readings in full in his edition of Egerton 2610, Appendix A (pp. 1—25).

k. Evan. 550. B.-C. ii. 13.

A poor looking copy of the Gospels complete, 7 in. long by 5 wide, containing 143 leaves, with slight Arabesques and 29 lines on a page. It is of about the twelfth century in date,

with many numbers of Ammonian sections (yet more often
without Ammonian sections) and Eusebian canons in margin:
some rubrical notes and a few τίτλοι (rubro) in a later hand.
Somewhat carelessly written (ὁμοιοτέλευτα e.g. Luc. vii. 20 ;
Joan. ix. 35), especially in regard to breathings and accents
(e.g. αὕτη for αὔτη, ὅδος, ὄνομα). Itacisms are very common
(983 in all), especially ε for αι, ο for ω, οι for η, η for ει, &c.
The genealogy in Luke iii. presents many variations from
the common text (vv. 19, 26, 29, 30 ; 26—34 confusè), and
Johan. vii. 53—viii. 12 is omitted with no vestige left, while
Matth. xxvii. 35 is given in full. There are many corrections
s. m. in margin (and in Matth., Luke ii. 34 s. m. in the text),
but Matth. ix. 35 ; Luke ii. 34 ; Johan. xviii. 39 ; xxi. 1 the
marginal corrections seem p. m. The only foreign matter is
1½ pages at end of S. John, s. m. αρ τῆς φύσεως τῶν ζωών καὶ
ἑρμηνείας τοῦ ἐν ἁγίοις π̅ρ̅σ̅ ἡμῶν ιω̅ τοῦ χρυσοστόμου περὶ
φυσιολογίας· Ὁ φυσιολόγος καλὸς ἐλέγξει περὶ τοῦ λέοντος
κ.τ.λ. Compare also
MATTH. i. 6. – τὸν secund. 7. ἱεροβοάμ. 10. ἀμμὼν.
11. + ἐγέννησε τὸν Ἰωακεὶμ· Ἰωακεὶμ δὲ (ante τὸν Ἰεχ.).
iii. 8. καρπὸν ἄξιον. iv. 20. + αὐτῶν (post δίκτυα). v. 39.
ῥαπίζει ἐπὶ τὴν δεξίαν (– σου). 45. ὅμοιοι (pro υἱοὶ).
47. οἱ ἐθνικοὶ ὡσαύτως. vi. 31. περιβαλλώμεθα. vii. 6. δότε.
14. τί (pro ὅτι). 16. μήτε (pro μήτι). 25. προσέκοψαν
(pro προσέπεσον). viii. 4. + σου (post δῶρον). 12. γεννη-
θήτω. 13. fin. + καὶ ὑποστρέψας ὁ ἐκατοντάρχος εἰς τὸν
οἶκον αὐτοῦ ἐν αὐτῇ τῇ ὥρα εὗρεν τὸν παῖδα ὑγιαίνοντα.
ix. 16. ῥάκκους. – ἀγνάφου. 22. αὐτῇ εἶπεν. x. 8. – νεκροὺς
ἐγείρετε. 11. – ἕως ἂν ἐξέλθητε. 15. + τῇ (ante γῇ). 23.
ἔλθοι. xi. 17. εὔξασθε (sic, pro ἐκόψασθε). xii. 5. – καὶ
ἀναίτιοί εἰσι. 22. κωφὸν καὶ τυφλὸν. 50. ποιήσει. xiii. 22.
ἀγάπη (pro ἀπάτη). 30. + οὖν (post ἄφετε). 33. + ὁ ι̅σ̅
(post αὐτοῖς). xiv. 6. γινομένων (pro ἀγομένων). 11. + αὐτὴν
(post ἤνεγκεν). 30. ἐκραύγαζεν. xv. 1. – οἱ. 13. – αὐτοῖς
(post εἶπεν). 14. τυφλοί εἰσιν ὁδηγοὶ. 25. προσεκύνησεν.
βοήθη μοι. xxvii. 20. ἐποίησαν (pro ἔπεισαν). 49. Deest
versus. xxviii. 9. – καὶ. – ὁ. 13. ὑμῶν (pro ἡμῶν).

MARC. ii. 26. − τοῦ secund. vii. 19. καθαρίζων. 33. +εἰς
τὰ ὦτα αὐτοῦ (post πτυσασ). ix. 5. + ἐθέλεις (ante ποιή-
σωμεν). xvi. 9—20. Habet. LUC. ii. 25. εὐσεβὴς (pro εὐλαβὴς). xiv. 5. [ὄνος]. ἀνα-
στήσει (pro ἀνασπάσει). xviii. 2. τόπω (pro πόλει). xx. 19.
− τὸν λαὸν. 41. + τινὲς (post λέγουσι). xxiii. 26. − καὶ ώς.
−τοῦ (ante ἐρχομένου). JOHAN. i. 19. + πρὸς αὐτὸν (post λευΐτας). 51. μεῖζον.
iv. 3. − πάλιν. 9. ἰουδαίοις σαμαρείται. 46. πάλιν ὁ ι̅σ̅.
47. ἀνῆλθεν (pro ἀπῆλθε). v. 30. − πατρὸς p. m. 41. παρὰ
α̅νου. vi. 3. − ὁ ι̅σ̅. 14. τὸ σημεῖον ὃ ἐποίησεν ὁ ι̅σ̅. 19.
ὡσεὶ. 22. ἄλλον (pro ἄλλο). 40. γὰρ (pro δὲ). τῶ πατρός
p. m. 43. οὖν αὐτοῖς ὁ ι̅σ̅. 45. ἀκούων. 52. τὴν σάρκα
δοῦναι φαγεῖν. 57. − ζων. 61. οἱ μαθηταὶ αὐτοῦ περὶ τούτου.
65. + αὐτοῖς (post ἔλεγεν). 70. εἰς ἐξ ὑμῶν. vii. 8. [οὔπω].
12. πολὺς ἦν περὶ αὐτοῦ. 32. ὑπηρέτας οἱ ἀρχιερεῖς καὶ οἱ
φαρισαῖοι. 40. τῶν λόγων. 50. ὁ ἐλθὼν πρὸς αὐτὸν νυκτός.
51. πρῶτον (pro πρότερον). viii. 21. αὐτοῖς πάλιν ὁ ι̅σ̅.
38. νοεῖτε (pro ποιεῖτε). 44. ἐκ τοῦ πατρὸς. ix. 25. − οὖν.
31. ποιεῖ. xi. 29. − δὲ (post ἐκείνη). 50. − ἡμῖν. xii. 13. − ὁ
prim. 24. − ἀμὴν secund. 26. τις διακονῆ. xiii. 11. ἤδη.
+ ἐξ ἀρχῆς (post γὰρ). 21. − καὶ ἐμαρτύρησε. 33. ἐγὼ
ὑπάγω. xiv. 11. ταῦτα (pro αὐτὰ). xvi. 4. ἡμῶν (pro ὑμῶν).
xviii. 1. [κέδρων]. 28. − οὖν. xix. 17. − καὶ ἀπήγαγον.
19. ὁ ι̅σ̅ ὁ ναζ. 39. − ὡσεὶ. xx. 9. − ἐκ νεκρῶν. xxi. 1. − ὁ
ι̅σ̅ τοῖς μαθηταῖς p. m., habet marg. s. m. 15. ὁ ι̅σ̅. 16. − λέγει
αὐτῶ secund. (ante ναὶ κε̅).

Few of these variations are very notable (yet see Matth.
xi. 17; xiii. 22; xxvii. 49; Luc. xviii. 2; Johan. vi. 57; viii.
38). N ἐφελκυστικὸν occurs 578 times, a hiatus 6 times.
Omission by ὁμοιοτέλευτον 16 times (with same beginning
twice), ι ascript twice, subscript 52 times.

l. Evan. 552. B.-C. II. 18.

A very neat copy of the Gospels in bad condition [XII],
24⁰, on 212 leaves, 6 inches long by 3½ broad. A picture of

S. Mark (partly washed out) is on the reverse of leaf 1. Leaf 2 contains John i. 1, 1—15 misplaced by binder. Leaf 3 begins Matth. xii. 41 ἰωνᾶ ὧδε, and continuously to end of Gospels. Arabesques in pale red at the heads of books. Much lectionary in scarlet. Also Am. (not Eus.) κεφ. .t. and τίτλοι, κεφ. At end, about ten leaves of fragments of a synaxarium and menology.

m. and n.   Evan. 553 and 554.   B.-C. II. 26¹ and 26².

B.-C. II. is a mere bundle of vellum fragments, not of the same size, whereof one (B.-C.¹) comprises 27 leaves of S. Mark, the other (B.-C.²) 47 larger leaves of SS. Matthew and Mark. We will describe them separately, for their juxtaposition is only accidental.

m.   Evan. 553.   B.-C. II. 26¹.

This poor fragment of 27 leaves dates from the end of the twelfth century. It measures 7½ inches long by 5½ broad, and contains on 27 leaves (three torn) Marc. iii. 21— iv. 13; 37—vii. 29; viii. 15—27; ix. 9—x. 5; 29—xi. 32, neatly written on good vellum, from 19 to 21 lines on a page, but the margin disfigured with a wretched modern scribble. There are τίτλοι, the Ammonian sections and Eusebian canons are in the margin. We find ι subscript mostly, even with verbs (ποιῷ). Corrections by erasure, whether by first hand (capp. viii. 25; ix. 22; xii. 9, 19, 23) or by a later (ix. 28, 38 ; x. 3 ; xi. 24). Ὁμοιοτέλευτον in cap. ix. 38, and ν ἐφελκυστικὸν 25 times, mostly with εἶπεν, or after a pause. We note only 20 itacisms : η (for ει) 4 ; ει (for η) 1 ; η (for ι) 1 ; ι (for η) 1 ; ω (for ο) 4 ; ο (for ω) 4 ; ε (for αι) 2 ; αι (for ε) 1 ; ἡμεῖς and ὑμεῖς twice interchanged. Breathings and accents are fairly regular, but initial η and ο are often aspirated (ἡγέρθη, ἡνάγκασε, ὁλίγον, ὄψε). Compare for readings MARC. iii. 22. − ὅτι secund. v. 4. διασπᾶσθαι. 16. διηγήσαντο δὲ (− καὶ). vi. 2. − ὅτι. 15. − ἦ. 16. − ὁ.

27. ἐνεχθῆναι. 32. ἀπῆλθεν. 33. – οἱ ὄχλοι. ἐπέγνωσαν αὐτούς. 34. ὁ ἶσ̄ εἶδεν. 44. – ὡσεὶ. 47. ἦν (post μόνος). 53. ἦλθεν ἐπὶ τὴν γεννησαρὲθ (γ supra, s. m.). vii. 4. εἰσὶν (pro ἐστιν). 17. εἰσῆλθον. 19. [καθαρίζον]. ix. 25. συντρέχει ὄχλος. 28. ὅτι διατί ὑμεῖς (η supra, s. m.). 34. διελέγχθησαν p. m. 38. – καὶ ἐκωλύσαμεν ad fin. versús p. m. 50. + τὸ (ante ἅλας tert.). xi. 3. ἀποστελεῖ αὐτὸν. 28. δέδωκεν. xii. 26. τοῦ (pro τῆς). + εἰμϊ (post ἐγὼ). 28. ἐστὶν ἐντολὴ πρώτη πάντων. 30. Αὕτη πρώτη πάντων ἐντολή. 31. ἑαυτόν (pro σεαυτόν). xvi. 8. ἐλθοῦσαι. – ταχύ : and the interpolation after cap. xi. 26 from Matth. vii. 7, 8. Ends Marc. xii. 32 ἐπ' ἀληθείας.

n. Evan. 554. B.-C. II. 26².

This fragment contains, on 47 leaves of coarse vellum, 8½ inches long by 5½ broad, Matth. xviii. 32—xxiv. 10 ; xxvi. 28—xxviii. 20 ; Marc. i. 16—xiii. 9 ; xiv. 9—27. It is in bad condition through damp and dirt, and the writing exhibits many abridgements. It might be referred to the thirteenth century, but that a date which looks p. m. at the end of the list of the 48 κεφάλαια of S. Mark has ἔτους ϛωλα [A.D. 1323] μὴν τῶ αὐτῶ .... φερουαρίου εἰς τὴν ιγ ἡμέραν παρασκευῆ...., but then in 1323, the 13th of February fell on a Sunday, not on a Friday. The τίτλοι and numbers of κεφάλαια at the top and foot of the pages are pale red in S. Matthew, black in S. Mark. The Ammonian sections also are red in S. Matthew, with the numeral of the Eusebian canons subjoined, in Mark they are often in black, the canons mostly omitted. The rubrical directions in margin are both in black and red. Some corrections seem p. m., others plainly s. m. (Matth. xx. 13, 20 ; xxi. 42 ; xxvii. 64 ; Marc. i. 22 ; v. 19 ; vi. 15 ; x. 32 ; xi. 3). There are too many (14) omissions by ὁμοιοτέλευτον : Matth. xxi. 32 ; xxii. 2, 3 ; xxiii. 3, 12 ; Marc. ii. 22 ; iv. 24 ; vii. 20 ; viii. 11, 37 ; ix. 5 ; x. 19, 32 ; xi. 15, 28. There is found no ι ascript, subscript but once (ᾐτήσατο Marc. vi. 25). Ν ἐφελκυστικὸν is seen only seven times, a hiatus for the lack of it thrice. This copy is not incorrect as a whole, but with a tendency to omit words. Not a few itacisms (115) occur: ι (for η) 8; η (for ι) 8; ο (for ω) 19; ω (for ο) 14; η (for ει) 22; ει (for η) 6; ε (for αι) 4; αι (for ε) 8; ι (for ει) only 1; ει (for ι) 3; ε (for η) 1; ου (for ω) 2 with verbs; ω (for ου) 1; υ (for ι) 3; οι (for ι) 2; ει (for οι) 1; συ (for σοι) 2; η and υ interchanged Matth. xxii. 4; xxvi. 40; Marc. vi. 34. Notice also the following readings :

MATTH. xix. 19. – σου prim. 21. – ὕπαγε. xx. 24. δώδεκα (pro δέκα). 25. κατακυριεύσουσιν. xxi. 14. χολοὶ καὶ τυφλοὶ. 21. οὐ (pro μὴ). 26. –δὲ. 34. –δὲ. 36. –δούλους. xxii. 1. –λέγων. 13. χεῖρας καὶ πόδας. 29. –δὲ. 37. ι͞σ ἔφη. –τῇ prim. et sec. 45. +ἐν π͞νι (ante καλεῖ). xxvi. 40. –οὕτως. 42. –οὐ. 43. οἱ ὀφθαλμοὶ αὐτῶν. 45. παραδοθήσεται. 48. ἐὰν (pro ἂν). 52. fin. ἀποθανοῦνται. 59. θανατώσ᾽ αὐτόν. 63. εἴπῃς ἡμῖν. 69. ναζαραίου (pro γαλιλαίου). 71. γαλιλαίου (pro ναζαραίου). 73. –οἱ ἑστῶτες. xxvii. 5. +τριάκοντα (ante ἀργύρια). 6. κωβονᾶν. 31. –αὐτὸν. 48. –καὶ (ante περιθεὶς). 55. +καὶ (ante γυναῖκες). 63. ὁ πλάνος ἐκεῖνος. 64. +ἡμῶν κοιμωμένων (ante καὶ εἴπωσι). xxviii. 2. +τοῦ μνημείου (post θύρας). 4. ὡς οἱ (pro ὡσεὶ). 8. ἐλθοῦσαι. –ταχύ.

MARC. i. 23. ἀνέκραζε. 33. συνηγμένη. 35. +ὁ ι͞σ (post ἀπῆλθεν). ii. 10. –δὲ. iii. 4. ἀγαθὸν ποιῆσαι. 5. –σου. 6. ἐλθόντες. 30. +ὅτι (ante π͞να). iv. 11. –τὰ. 17. αὐτοῖς (pro ἑαυτοῖς). 18. –οὗτοί εἰσιν secund. 19. –αἱ (ante περὶ). 21. οὐχὶ (pro οὐχ ἵνα). 25. ἔχει (pro ἂν ἔχῃ). v. 1. ἦλθεν. 7. μοι (pro με). 9. λεγεὼν (pro λέγων). 16. διηγήσαντο δὲ (– καὶ). vi. 13. ἐξέβαλον. 14. αἱ δυνάμεις ἐνεργοῦσιν. 17. ἔθετο (pro ἔδησεν). –τῇ. 18. –τῷ ἡρώδῃ. 20. ἀκούων. 29. –αὐτοῦ secund. –τῷ. vii. 17. εἰσῆλθον. 25. –αὐτῆς. 36. διεστείλατο. viii. 13. –πάλιν εἰς τὸ. 22. αὐτὸν (pro αὐτοῦ). 24. –ὁρῶ. 31. – πολλὰ. 34. ἀκολουθεῖν (pro ἐλθεῖν). ix. 1. –ὅτι. 16. ζητεῖτε. 18. –ἂν. 22. αὐτὸν εἰς τὸ πῦρ (–καὶ). 25. σύντρέχει ὄχλος. 28. ὅτι (τί p. m.?). 33. λογίζεσθε.

42. ἐὰν (pro ἂν). x. 1. – ὄχλοι. 14. ὁ δὲ ι̅σ̅ ἰδών. – καὶ
(ante μὴ). 15. fin. ἐν αὐτῇ (pro εἰς αὐ.). 17. ἰδοὺ τίς
πλούσιος προσδραμὼν (pro προσδραμὼν εἰς). 24. – τοῖς
secund. 33. – ἰδού. – τοῖς secund. 35. – ἵνα. xi. 11. πάντας
s. m. 14. – αὐτοῦ. 19. ἐπορεύοντο. xii. 8. καὶ ἐκβάλλοντες
αὐτὸν ἔξω τοῦ ἀμπελῶνος ἀπέκτειναν. 27. ὁ θ̅σ̅ θ̅σ̅ νεκρῶν
ἀλλὰ ζώντων. 32. ἐστὶ θ̅σ̅ πλὴν αὐτοῦ ἄλλος. 42. ἔβαλλε
p. m. 43. – ὅτι. 44. ἔβαλλον. xiv. 15. – μέγα. 22. +τὸν
(ante ἄρτον).
This copy ends καὶ λέγει αὐτοῖς Marc. xiv. 27.

o. Evan. 555. B.-C. III. 4.

This is a small neat quarto (7 inches high by 5 broad) on
264 leaves of vellum of 24 lines on a page, neatly written in
the thirteenth century. At the end are annexed six leaves
of an imperfect synaxarion and menology, possibly by the
first hand. This codex has tables of κεφάλαια (three of them
in red), a πρόλογος or ὑπόθεσις with a rude portrait of the
Evangelist prefixed to each Gospel (Johan. xix. 25—xxi. 2
being lost), and the eight leaves containing Matth. vii. 1—x.
18 being misplaced by the binder at Matth. xxvi. 26. The
numerals of the κεφάλαια are marked and τίτλοι in red at
the head and foot of the pages. The Ammonian sections
stand in the margin, and the Eusebian canons under them
very partially. The Church lessons stand also in the margin
in red. Breathings, accents &c. are correct, and the scribe
seldom trips into mere error. There are not many itacisms
(except o for ω) in the copy, ι subscript is rare (Johan. vii. 37
τῇ ἐσχάτῃ ἡμέρᾳ), the characteristic readings of Cod. a &c. in
Luke xxii. 43, 44 and John vii. 53—viii. 12 do not appear in
it, and the text closely resembles that of the Textus Receptus.
Yet a few rather minute variations may be noted, e. g.
MATTH. xii. 37. κατακριθηση (pro καταδικασθηση). xiii. 32.
πάντων supra, p. m. λαχάνων. xxi. 46. – αὐτόν. xxiii. 25.
+τοῦ πίνακος (post παροψίδος). MARC. ix. 28. – αὐτὸν.
x. 1. +πολλοὶ (post ὄχλοι). 17. +ἰδού τις πλούσιος (post

1 ADVERSARIA

ὁδόν). xiii. 11. μεριμνατε (pro προμερ.). xiv. 12. τῇ πρώτη τῶν ἀζ. ἡμέρᾳ. LUC. i. 27. +καὶ πατρέας (ante δαδ). viii. 14. πεσὼν. xii. 21. fin. +ταῦτα λέγων ἐφώνει ὁ ἔχων ὦτα ἀκούειν ἀκουέτω. xxiii. 1. ἀναστὰς. JOHAN. ii. 22. αὐτοῦ. + αὐτοῖς (post λόγω). xii. 40. τετύφλοκεν. 42. ὁμολόγουν. xv. 10. – ἐντολὰς secund. xix. 17. + καὶ ἤγαγον εἰς τὸ πραιτώριον (post ἰν). The few corrections appear to me to be made by the original scribe. The subscription at the end of the fourth Gospel stands rubro Κατὰ χάριν κ͞ε νικανδρὸν σῶσον.

p. Evan. 557. B.-C. iii. 9.

This neat little codex (measuring only 5½ inches high by 3½ broad) in general style of writing much resembles Cod. 555, and is of the same date, the thirteenth century. It contains 256 leaves, of 22 lines on each page. Tables of κεφάλαια precede the last three Gospels, and rough pictures of the Evangelists, all but S. Luke's. Slight illuminations stand at the head of each Gospel. Τίτλοι in red are found at the top and bottom of the several pages. Numerals of κεφάλαια and Ammonian sections with capitals (without the Eusebian canons) are in the margin in red, but often wrongly put, in a very unusual fashion. This copy is quite free from references to Church lessons. The omissions through ὁμοιοτέλευτον are frequent (e.g. Matth. x. 37; Marc. ix. 43—46; x. 27, 42; xii. 39; xiv. 19; xv. 14; Luc. x. 27; Joan. iii. 31; iv. 5; v. 32; vi. 11, 32, 42; viii. 14; ix. 7; xii. 34; xiii. 34; xiv. 17; xvii. 21. Itacisms (especially ει or ι for η, ο for ω, and vice versâ) are rare in the first two Gospels, but more frequent afterwards: ν ἐφελκυστικὸν is very common, and though the punctuation is accurate, the sign of interrogation never occurs. This book must have been transcribed from an older copy which was defective in S. Luke, inasmuch as from cap. xi. 30 τῇ γενεᾷ ταύτη the Gospel goes on with no break in the text to cap. xiii. 1 παρῆσαν δέ τινες; from cap. xiii. 14 καὶ

οὐκ ἰσχύσουσιν to xiv. 2 καὶ ἰδοὺ ἄνος τίς: from cap.
xiv. 12—16 (ἔλεγε δὲ ἄνος τίς), xvi. 1—13 ἔλεγε δὲ πρὸς
τοὺς μαθητὰς αὐτοῦ οὐδεὶς οἰκέτης δύναται. But indeed this
copy contains an unusual number of variations from the
ordinary text, though none of first rate importance: e.g.
MATTH. ii. 19. – ἐν αἰγύπτω. 22. – ἐπὶ τῆς ἰουδαίας.
vii. 1. κρίνατε. 13. – ἡ ὁδός. ἐρχόμενοι. 14. – ἡ πύλη.
x. 29. τοῦ ἐν οὐνοῖς (pro ὑμῶν). xi. 1. τοὺς λόγους (pro
διατάσσων). xii. 15. – γνούς. 40. κοιλία (pro καρδία).
44. – καὶ κεκοσμημένον. xiii. 33. ἔκρυψεν. 39. + οἱ (ante
ἄγγελοι). – εἰσιν. xiv. 19. – τοὺς ἄρτους. xv. 23. Deest
versus. xvi. 9. + συνίετε καὶ (ante μνημονεύετε). 21. παρὰ
(pro ἀπό). xvii. 21. ἐξ ἔρχεται (pro ἐκπορεύεται). 22.
+ ἁμαρτωλῶν (post ἀνθρώπων). 27. – αὐτοῖς. xxiii. 25.
ἀδικίας (pro ἀκρασίας). 28. ἀδικίας (pro ἀνομίας).
MARC. i. 1. ἐν βίβλω λόγων ἡσαίου τοῦ προφήτου. ii. 9.
+ σου (post ἁμαρτίας). – καὶ ἀρόν σου τὸν κράββατον.
26. – τοῦ. vii. 19. – αὐτοῦ. καθαρίζων. viii. 19. – τοὺς.
+ καὶ. + καὶ (ante πόσους). x. 40. + παρὰ τοῦ πρς (post
ἡτοίμασται). 47. παράγεται (post ἔστιν). – ἰησοῦ. xi. 14.
μηκέτι ἐκ σοῦ καρπὸς γένηται εἰς τὸν αἰῶνα. ἤκουσαν.
32. φοβούμεθα (– τὸν λαὸν). xii. 6. – πρὸς αὐτοὺς ἔσχατον.
7. init. ἐκεῖνοι ἰδόντες αὐτὸν εἶπον πρὸς ἑαυτοὺς (– ὅτι).
24. – οὐ διὰ τοῦτο. xiii. 8. ἀρχὴ. 14. ἐν τόπω ἁγνῶ (pro
ὅπου οὐ δεῖ). 20. ἐκολοβόθησαν αἱ ἡμέραι ἐκεῖναι. 24. τῶν
ἡμερῶν ἐκείνων (pro ἐκείνην). xiv. 3. – τῇ. μυστικῆς
(pro πιστικῆς). 12. φαγεῖν (pro ἵνα φάγης). 41. ἀπάρχει?
(pro ἀπέχει). 45. – ἐλθών. + αὐτῷ (post λέγει). 71. – ὃν
λέγετε. xv. 8. τὸν βαραββᾶν (pro καθὼς ἀεὶ ἐποίει αὐτοῖς).
47. Deest versus. xvi. 19. τοῦ πρσ (pro τοῦ θυ).
LUC. i. 24. ζαχαρίου (pro αὐτοῦ). 48. τοῦ δούλου (pro
τῆς δούλης). 66. ἀκούοντες. 74. – ἐκ χειρός. ii. 17. προσ-
εκύνησαν καὶ ἐγνώρισαν. – τούτου. 25. εὐσεβὴς (pro
εὐλαβής). 29. – κατὰ τὸ ῥῆμά σου. iii. 12. + ὑπ᾽ αὐτοῦ
(post βαπτισθῆναι). 18. λέγων (pro παρακαλῶν). 25. – τοῦ
μααὰθ τοῦ ματταθίου. 38. σὴμ (pro σὴθ). iv. 1. ἐγενετο
(pro ἤγετο). 10. + ἐν πάσαις ταῖς ὁδοῖς σου (post σε).

30. ἐν μέσω (pro διὰ μέσου). 42. – τοῦ μὴ πορεύεσθαι ἀπ'
αὐτῶν. v. 14. αὐτον (pro αὐτῷ). 21. – οὗτος. 35. + μετ'
ἐξουσίας (post τότε). 36. fin. καὶ τῷ παλαίω συμφωνεῖ τὸ
ἀπὸ τοῦ καινοῦ. vi. 4. – ἔλαβε καὶ. 8. ἐξηρραμένην (pro
ξηρὰν). 9. πρὸς αὐτοὺς ὁ ῑ͞σ. 23. χάρητε. – γὰρ prim.
28. – εὐλογεῖτε τοὺς καταρωμένους ὑμῖν καὶ. 45. προσφέρει
(pro προφέρει) bis. vii. 5. + ἡμῶν (post συναγωγὴν). 6. – οὐ
prim. 21. πολλοῖς τυφλοῖς. – τὸ. 25. διάγοντες (pro
ὑπάρχοντες). 29. ὑπὸ (pro τὸ βάπτισμα). 45. ἦλθον (pro
εἰσῆλθον). 49. – καὶ (ante ἁμαρτίας). viii. 2. πολλὰ (pro
ἑπτὰ). 14. ἀκούοντες. 24. ἐπαύσατε. + μεγάλη (post
γαλήνη). 28. + πολλὰ (ante βασανίσης). 31. ἐπιτάξει.
39. εἴληφε (pro ἤλειφε). 45. – καὶ οἱ μετ' αὐτοῦ, ἐπιστάτα.
52. αὐτῇ (pro αὐτὴν). 53. ἰδόντες (pro εἰδότες). 55. ἐξανέστη.
ix. 4. – ἂν. 5. δέξονται. 11. + τὰ (ante περὶ). 35. + ἐν ᾧ
ηὐδόκησα (post ἀγαπητὸς). 42. ἔρριψεν (pro ἔρρηξεν).
+ αὐτὸν (post συνεσπάραξεν). 44. τὰς καρδίας (pro τὰ ὦτα).
x. 22. ἐπιγινώσκει τὸν υἱὸν τίς ἐστιν εἰ μὴ. 23. + πάλιν
(post στραφεὶς). 34. – προσελθὼν. – αὐτὸν secund. xi. 18.
ἐμερίσθη. xiii. 18. ἔλεγε δὲ τίνι ὁμοιώσω τὴν βασίλειαν τοῦ
θ͞υ· ὁμοία ἐστὶ κόκκω· (sic). 21. – καὶ prim. xiv. 4. – καὶ
ἀπέλυσε. 5. βοῦς ἢ υἱὸς. 21. ἐπὶ (pro εἶπε). 24. fin. + πολλοὶ
γὰρ εἰσι κλητοὶ ὀλίγοι δὲ ἐκλεκτοί. 31. – ἑτέρω βασιλεῖ.
xv. 7. ὅτι χαίρει ἐπ' αὐτῷ μᾶλλον ἢ ἐπὶ τοῖς ἐνενήκονταεννέα
τοῖς μὴ πεπλανημένοις οὕτως ἔσται χαρὰ ἐν τῷ οὐ͞νω κ.τ.λ.
+ πεπλανημένοις (ante οἵτινες). xvi. 16. βιάζεται (pro
εὐαγγελ.). εἰς ἑαυτὴν. 24. + μοι (post πέμψον). xvii. 6.
ἔχετε. ἐπήκουσεν· 37. πτῶμα. xix. 4. προσδραμὼν.
26. + καὶ περισσευθήσεται (post δοθήσεται). xx. 19. ἐπὶ
τὸν ι͞ν (pro ἐπ' αὐτὸν). xxi. 10. καὶ (pro τότε). 21. ἐκ μέσου
(pro ἐν μέσω). 25. καὶ σημεῖα ἐν ἄστροις (pro καὶ σελήνη
καὶ ἄστροις). 30. – ἤδη. 38. – πρὸς αὐτὸν. xxii. 47. +
πολὺς (post ὄχλος). 54. ἦγον. + ἀπὸ (ante μακρόθεν).
61. – καὶ στραφεὶς ὁ κ͞σ ἐνέβλεψε τῷ πέτρω. 65. – εἰς.
70. Deest versus. 71. + πρὸς αὐτὸν (ante εἶπον). xxiii. 3.
– αὐτῷ. 15. + ἐν (ante αὐτῷ). 23. + τοῦ (ante σταυρ.).
25. – αὐτοῖς. διὰ φόνον καὶ στάσιν. 28. ἐπ' ἐμοὶ. 35.

– σὺν. 40. οὐδὲν φοβεῖ σύ. 48. + ἐξεπλήσσοντο (post ταύτην). 53. ἐν σινδόνι καὶ. μνημείῳ (pro μνήματι). xxiv. 12. – μόνα. 24. – οὕτω. JOAN. i. 10. – ἐν τῷ κόσμῳ ἦν p. m. 29. – ὁ ἰωάννης. 35. – πάλιν. 42. – ὁ. 46. μωσῆς καὶ οἱ προφῆται ἐν τῶ νόμω. iii. 28. αὐτοῦ (pro ἐκείνου). iv. 23. ὅτι (pro ὅτε). 27. ἐθαύμαζον. 35. – ἔτι. 40. + καὶ (ante ἠρώτων). 52. γὰρ (pro οὖν). v. 1. + ἡ (ante ἑορτὴ). 2. – ἐπὶ τῇ. 3. ταύτη γὰρ (pro ταύταις). 4. + κυ (post ἄγγελος). κατέβαινε κατὰ καιρὸν ἐν τῇ προβατικῇ κολυμβήθρα. 7. προλαμβάνημαι (pro πρὸ ἐμοῦ καταβαίνει). 44. ἀνων (pro ἀλλήλων). vi. 15. – πάλιν. 22. – ἐκεῖνο. ἀνέβησαν. 23. ἦλθον. ιυ (pro κυ). 24. – καὶ prim. 27. – ὁ πηρ. 30. καὶ πιστεύσωμεν. 31. ὑμῶν (pro ἡμῶν). 42. – ἰησοῦς. – οὗτος. 55. – γὰρ. vii. 2. – ἐγγὺς. 8. – ταύτην prim. οὐκ (pro οὔπω). 26. – ἀληθῶς. 31. μὴ (pro μήτι). – τούτων. 32. + οὖν (post ἤκουσαν). 46. + καὶ εἶπον (post ὑπηρέται). ἐλάλησεν οὕτως. Pericope adult. sine signo habet. viii. 2. – πρὸς αὐτὸν. 3. fin. + πειραζοντες. 3. [κατελήφθη]. 9. – ἕως τῶν ἐσχάτων. οὖσα (pro ἑστῶσα). 10. – ἡ γυνὴ. 11. κρινῶ. 44. οὐκ ἕστηκεν. ix. 7. λέγεται (pro ἑρμηνεύεται). 11. – καὶ νίψαι. 15. ἀνέῳξεν αὐτοῦ τοὺς ὀφθαλμοὺς (pro ἀνέβλεψεν). 30. ἁμαρτωλὸν ανον (pro ἁμαρτωλῶν). 34. ὅλως. 39. – τοῦτον. 41. – ἂν. xi. 1. – ἀπὸ βηθανίας. 16. σὺν αὐτῶ (pro μετ᾽ αὐτοῦ). 22. δώη (pro δώσει). – ὁ θσ. 41. – ὁ τεθνηκὼς κείμενος. 48. – καὶ prim. 52. – τὰ διεσκορπισμένα. 56. + ποῦ ἐστιν ἐκεῖνος (post ἑστηκότες). xii. 3. βυστικῆς (pro πιστικῆς). (Cf. Marc. xiv. 3.) xiii. 2. – ἤδη. 4. ἀπὸ (pro ἐκ). 20. ἀποστείλαντά (pro πέμψαντά). xiv. 9. ἔχεις μεθ᾽ ἡμῶν (pro μεθ᾽ ὑμῶν εἰμι). 13. + τὸν πρα (post αἰτήσητε). 30. – τούτου. εὑρήσει (pro οὐκ ἔχει). xv. 6. ξηρανθήσεται (pro ἐξηράνθη). 26. + μου (ante τὸ πνεῦμα). xvi. 3. τὸν πέμψαντά με (pro τὸν πρα). 4. – ὑμῖν secund. 13. – τὸ πνα τῆς ἀληθείας. xvii. 21. fin. + καὶ ἠγάπησας αὐτοὺς καθὼς ἐμὲ ἠγάπησας. 24. + πεπληρωμένην

S.   e

ἐν αὐτοῖς (post τὴν ἐμὴν). xviii. 3. ἀρχόντων (pro ἀρχιερέων).
16. τὴν θύραν. 19. ὡς οὖν (pro ὁ οὖν). 28. –οὖν. 39. –ὑμῖν.
–οὖν. 40. –πάλιν. xix. 3. ἤρξαντο λέγειν αὐτῶ (pro
ἔλεγον). 12. ἐζήτει ἀπολῦσαι αὐτὸν ὁ πιλάτος. 21. – τῶν
ἰουδαίων prim. 30. δὲ (pro οὖν). 36. + ἀπ' (ante αὐτοῦ).
38. τοῦ κυ̅ (pro τοῦ ἰυ̅). xx. 13. +τίνα ζητεῖς (post κλαίεις).
xxi. 1. + αὐτοῦ (post μαθηταῖς). 7. – πέτρος. 18. ἑαυτὸν
(pro σεαυτὸν).

We have designedly omitted, from this long list, variations
for which there is much authority elsewhere, and it would
be curious to discover which of the peculiarities of this codex
(mere errors excluded) may be countenanced by other codices
yet unexamined.

q. Evan. 558. B.-C. iii. 10.

This manuscript (dated in the fifteenth century) is written
on thick paper, measuring 8 inches high by 5½ broad on
374 leaves (or 424, including in same hand 16 prefatory
and 34 supplemental leaves), with 16 lines on a page. It is
boldly but clearly written, Joan. viii. 3—12; xi. 44—xii. 6
being supplied by a later hand. The signatures stand at the
foot of the page for every sheet of eight leaves, but the
leaves are much misplaced in binding. Its old wooden cover
is overlaid with embroidery work. Its prefatory matter consists of tables of Eusebian canons rubro, Eusebius Carpiano,
table of κεφάλαια and Prologue to S. Matthew, followed by
18 verses of rude senarii Τὸν ἐκ τελώνου θαυμαστὸν θεηγόρον
κ.τ.λ. There are fair pictures of the Lord in the act of
blessing, of the Virgin and Child, of S. Matthew in inferior
style. Before each of the other Gospels are tables of κεφάλαια,
Prologues and pictures of each Evangelist. Slight illuminations at the head of the Gospels. There are no τίτλοι in
S. Matthew but the Ammonian sections and number of the
Eusebian canons, the ἀρχαὶ and τέλη, down to Matth. xv. 12,
with a few Church lessons are set in the margin. The supplemental leaves comprise short theological questions and answers,

and on their first page an inscription *rubro* states that the
book was written παρ' ἐμοὶ (*sic*) τοῦ εὐτελοῦς καὶ ἀβρωτίμου
πάντων μερόπων καὶ χωρικοῦ γράφεως θεοδώρου τοῦ κοτζᾶ·
ἐκ χώρας μεθώνης τελειωθὲν ἐν ἔτει συστάσεως κόσμου ⑵ ᾽λη.
ιν. η. ἀπὸ δὲ τῆς ἐνσάρκου οἰκονομίας αὐλ μηνὶ μαϊώ λᾶ : the
year of the world 6938 (Indiction 8), being equivalent to A.D.
1430. The first hand must have revised the MS. throughout,
but a later scribe corrects Marc. ix. 32; x. 41; xiv. 3; Luc.
xxiii. 31; Joan. vii. 47; x. 11, and the margin of Matth.
xi. 23, 25; xxiv. 15; Luc. viii. 49; xx. 31. Nine clauses are
lost by ὁμοιότελευτον (Matth. xiii. 12; Luc. x. 27; xi. 10; xvii.
33; xxii. 30; Joan. iv. 14; viii. 24; xiv. 7, 27), also by the
same beginning (Luc. x. 22). There is no reduplication, Marc.
v. 4, nor augment in Matth. xix. 13; xxv. 7, 35; Marc. v. 13;
ix. 32; Luc. xxiv. 21; Joan. vii. 47. Ν ἐφελκυστικὸν 17
times (thrice corrected), but an hiatus left, Luc. i. 56, 57; vii.
17; xvi. 26. The ι ascript 17 times up to Luc. i. 75, then
ceases, but ι subscript first in Luc. i. 77 (in the same hand and
on same page as the last ascript) thence found 85 times, mostly
with article after the preposition ἐν. The itacisms (98) by
first hand (which sometimes corrects them) are 398 : viz. ω
(for ο) 64; ο (for ω) 56; ει (for η) 43; η (for ει) 75; η (for ι)
18; ι (for η) 22; αι (for ε) 30; ει (for ι) 9; ι (for ει) 11; η
and υ (pronouns interchanged) 25; other η (for υ) 6; υ (for η)
6; ει (for υ) 2; υ (for ει) Matth. xii. 48; υ (for ι) 3; ι (for υ) 2;
ου (for ο) 1; ω (for ου) 4; ου (for ω) 7; η (for ευ?) Luc. v. 7;
υ (for ου) 1; ι (for οι) 1; οι (for ι) 7; η (for οι) 3. The only
Alexandrine form is χεῖραν Joan. xx. 25. οὕτω only Matth.
v. 47; vii. 17; xvii. 12; Luc. xxi. 31, elsewhere οὕτως. Breathing and accents fairly regular, with usual licence of non-
accenting, or double accent with prepositions. ὧδε only Luc.
xxiv. 6; Joan. vi. 9. Unusual readings are Marc. vi. 22.
αὐτοῦ (*pro* αὐτῆς). Luc. ii. 22. αὐτοῦ (*pro* αὐτῆς). xiv. 4.
υἱὸς (*pro* ὄνος). xv. 21. *fin.* +ποιησόν με ὡς ἕνα τῶν μισθίων
σου. Joan. vii. 8. οὐκ (*pro* οὔπω *prim.*). x. 11. ὁ τιθεὶς
τὴν ψυχὴν p. m. (αὐτοῦ τίθησιν *erased*). But the following
also are more or less remarkable :

MATTH. ii. 8. ἔλθω. 12. ἀνακαλύψαι. iv. 8. αὐτὸν (*pro*

e 2

αὐτῷ). 21. δύο ἄλλους. 22. τῷ ῑῡ (pro αὐτῷ). v. 13. ἐν ἰσχύει. 16. ἡμῶν (pro ὑμῶν tert.). 18. ἀμὴν (pro γὰρ). 36. — μίαν. 46. — γὰρ. vi. 7. — οἱ. 14. — γὰρ. — ὑμῖν. vii. 19. τέμνεται (pro ἐκκόπτεται). viii. 13. fin. + καὶ ὑποστρέψας ὁ ἑκατον. (ν eras.) εἰς τὸν οἶκον αὐτοῦ εὗρε τὸν παῖδα ὑγιαίνοντα. 20. — καὶ. ix. 5. — εἰπεῖν prim. 6. — δὲ. 8. — τοῖς. 11. + καὶ πίνει (post ἐσθίει). 14. — λέγοντες. 15. + χρόνον (post ὅσον). 18. — ἰδοὺ. 32. — δὲ. x. 2. — δὲ. 8. — νεκροὺς ἐγείρετε. 33. — ἂν secund. 34. + οὖν (ante νομίσητε). xi. 8. — μαλακοῖς. xii. 10. ἦν ἐκεῖ τὴν χ. 35. — θησαυροῦ secund. 37. κατακριθήσῃ. + καὶ (ante κεκοσμημένον. xiii. 3. ἐν παραβολαῖς πολλά. 4. ἦλθον τὰ πετεινὰ τοῦ οὐρανοῦ. 19. διαρπάζει. 30. — τὰ. 32. + πάντων (post μεῖζον). 33. ἔκρυψεν. 40. συνάγεται. καίεται. xiv. 6. τελουμένων (pro ἀγομένων). 13. — ἐκεῖθεν. xv. 2. + τὸν (ante ἄρτον). 13. + αὐτοῖς (post εἶπεν). 18. διὰ (pro ἐκ prim.). xvi. 1. σαδδουκαῖοι καὶ φαρισαῖοι. 11. + τοῦ (ante προσέχειν). 21. — καὶ ἀρχιερέων. 24. ἀκολουθεῖν (pro ἐλθεῖν). 28. ἑστῶτες. xvii. 12. — ἐν. 25. τίνος. xviii. 10. — ἐν οὐρανοῖς prim. 16. — ἔτι. 24. — εἷς. xix. 6. οὐκ (pro οὐκέτι). 8. — οὐ γέγονεν. 28. Jungit ἐν τῇ παλ. cum sequentibus. θρόνων. xx. 6. εἶδεν (pro εὗρεν). 23. τοῦτο οὐκ ἐστιν δοῦναι. xxi. 14. χωλοὶ καὶ τυφλοὶ. 16. καὶ εἶπε (pro ὁ δὲ ῑσ λέγει). 19. μίαν ἐν τῇ ὁδῳ. 34. — δὲ. xxiii. 8. διδάσκαλος (pro ὁ καθηγητὴς). 37. ἰελὴμ ἰλὴμ (sic). xxiv. 7. λοιμοὶ καὶ λιμοὶ. 45. — τὴν. xxvi. 26. εὐχαριστήσας (pro εὐλογήσας). 40. ἀγρυπνῆσαι (pro γρηγορῆσαι). 56. — πάντες. xxvii. 45. ἐγένετο σκότος. 50. — πάλιν. 54. + δὲ (post ἰδόντες). xxviii. 2. + τοῦ μνημείου (post θύρας).

Nor are there fewer variations (minute as some are) in the three remaining Gospels, especially in small omissions and additions.

MARC. i. 38. ἐλήλυθα. ii. 10. ἔχει ἐξουσίαν ἐπὶ τῆς γῆς ἀφιέναι. 18. μαθηταί σου (pro σοὶ μ.). 26. — τοῦ secund. iii. 7. ἠκολούθησεν αὐτῷ ἀπὸ τῆς γαλιλαίας. 23. + αὐτὸς (ante προσκαλ.). iv. 3. fin. + τὸν σπόρον αὐτοῦ. 13. τὰς παραβολὰς πάσας. 22. ὃ οὐ (pro ἐὰν μὴ). v. 6. — ἀπὸ.

CRITICA SACRA. lvii

12. – πάντες. 28. + ἐν ἑαυτη (post γὰρ). vi. 2. + αἰ (ante δυνάμεις). 6. ὅσον ἐὰν μὴ δέξονται. 20. ἀκούων. 33. αὐτοὺς (pro αὐτὸν). 56. εἰς πόλεις ἢ κώμας ἢ ἀγροὺς. vii. 17. εἰσῆλθον. viii. 1. ἐλθόντος (pro ὄντος). 15. fin. τῶν ἡροδιανῶν. 23. – αὐτὸν prim. 31. – τρεῖς ἡμέρας ἀναστῆναι καὶ. 38. τῶν ἁγίων ἀγγέλων. ix. 28. + διατί (post ὅτι). 38. + ἐπὶ (post τινὰ). x. 6. ἀπ᾽ ἀρχῆς δὲ. 17. – εἷς. 30. π͞ρα ἢ μ͞ρα (pro μητέρας). xi. 28. δέδωκεν. 32. ἀλλ᾽ (– ἐὰν). xii. 36. δ͞α͞δ ἐν π͞νι ἁγίῳ εἶπε. 39. + φιλούντων (ante ἀσπασμοὺς). xiii. 3. καὶ ἰωάννης καὶ ἰάκωβος. 23. ἅπαντα. 28. ὁ κλάδος αὐτῆς (– ἤδη). 32. – τῆς secund. τῶν οὐρανῶν (pro οἱ ἐν οὐρανῷ). xiv. 36. ἀλλ᾽ εἴτι συ (pro ἀλλὰ τί συ). xv. 3. fin. + ὁ δὲ οὐδὲν ἀπεκρίνατο. 4. – πάλιν. 34. – μου prim.

LUC. i. 34. + μοι (ante τοῦτο). 50. καὶ γενεὰν (pro γενεῶν). 63. ἔσται (pro ἐστὶ). 65. – πάντα. 66. ἀκούοντες. ii. 9. – κ͞υ prim. 12. – ὑμῖν. 25. – ἦν secund. 39. – αὐτῶν. 43. – τὰς. iii. 1. – ἐν. 13. – ὑμῖν. 15. ἢ (pro εἴη). 16. βαπτίζω ὑμᾶς ἐν ὕδατι. 17. καταπαύσει p.m. 33. + τοῦ ἰωράμ. (ante τοῦ ἐσρώμ). iv. 11. – ὅτι. 27. + ἐξ (ante αὐτῶν). 43. ἐν (pro ταῖς). v. 2. ἀπέπλυνον. 11. δίκτυα (pro πλοῖα). 33. – σοὶ. 36. καὶ τὸ παλαιὸν οὐ συμφωνεῖ τῶ ἀπὸ τοῦ καινοῦ (– ἐπίβλημα secund.). vi. 1. – αὐτὸν. 9. ἀποκτεῖναι (pro ἀπολέσαι). 26. – ὑμῖν. – πάντες. vii. 24. εὐαγγέλων (pro ἀγγέλων). viii. 3. αὐτοῖς (pro αὐτῷ). 4. + τοῦ (ante ὄχλου). 16. – δὲ. 18. – καὶ (ante ὃ δοκεῖ). 21. + οἱ (ante ἀδελφοὶ). fin. – αὐτὸν. 26. ἦν (pro ἐστὶν). 38. – δὲ. 39. θ͞σ (pro ι͞σ). 44. + δὲ (ante ὄπισθεν). ix. 12. τοὺς ὄχλους. 21. αὐτῶ (pro αὐτοῖς). 23. – καθ᾽ ἡμέραν. 33. – καὶ (ante ποιήσωμεν). 42. ἐπέδωκεν. 56. – γὰρ. x. 2. – τοῦ (ante κ͞υ). 4. βαλλάντια μηδὲ. 8. – τὰ. 27. – καὶ ἐξ ὅλης τῆς ἰσχύος σου. 35. – δύο. xi. 5. ἐρεῖ (pro εἴπῃ). 6. – μου. 9. ἀνοιχθήσεται (sic v. 10). 11. + ἐξ (ante ὑμῶν). 12. ὠὸν αἰτήσῃ. 17. τὸ διανόημα. 25. – καὶ (ante κεκοσμ.). 26. ἐλθόντα. 34. ἔσται (pro ἐστίν secund.). xii. 5. μετὰ τοῦ (pro μετὰ τὸ). 15. αὐτῶ (pro αὐτοῦ prim.). 16. ἐφόρησεν. xiii. 12. ὁ ι͞σ αὐτὴν. 20. init. – καὶ

34. ἐπισυναγαγεῖν. xiv. 5. υἱὸς (pro ὄνος). 16. – αὐτῷ. xv. 1. – οἱ secund. 4. ἔχων ἐξ ὑμῶν. 6. + αὐτοῦ (post γείτονας). 9. – εὑροῦσα. 21. fin. + ποίησόν με ὡς ἕνα τῶν μισθίων σου. 30. τὸν μόσχον σιτευτόν. xvi. 14. ἐμυκτήριζον. 15. βδέλυγμά ἐστιν ἐνώπιον τοῦ θεοῦ. 18. μοιχᾶται (pro μοιχεύει prim.). 28. – τοῦτον. xvii. 23. + ὁ χσ (ante μή). 25. ἐκ (pro ἀπό). 33. – αὐτὴν prim. 34. – ὁ prim. xviii. 17. ἀμην bis scriptum. 37. προέρχεται. xix. 15. – καὶ (ante εἶπε). 31. – αὐτοῦ. 37. ἤρξατο. 48. ἀκούειν. xx. 19. ὄχλον (pro λαόν). 22. φόρους. 24. οἱ δὲ ἔδειξαν καὶ εἶπε (post δηνάριον). 40. – δὲ. xxi. 16. καὶ συγγενῶν καὶ φίλων καὶ ἀδελφῶν. 23. + τότε (ante ἀνάγκη). 24. + ἐν (ante στόματι). 36. – ταῦτα. 38. – πρὸς αὐτόν. xxii. 3. τοῖς ἱερεῦσι καὶ στρατηγοῖς. 5. συνεχάρησαν. 15. σφαγεῖν. 23. ἐξ αὐτῶν εἴη. 36. πωλήσει, ἀγοράσει. 37. ἐπ' (pro ἐν). 47. προῆγεν αὐτούς. 60. τί (pro ὅ). – ὁ secund. xxiii. 1. ἀναστάντες. ἤγαγον. 25. + τὸν βαραββᾶν (ante τὸν διά). 33. λεγόμενον (pro καλούμενον). 56. – καὶ (ante τὸ μὲν). xxiv. 6. σὺν ὑμῖν (pro ἐν τῇ γαλιλαίᾳ λέγων). 21. ἐλπίζομεν. JOAN. i. 13, 19, 26, 34, 51 ; ii. 3, 12, 13, 16, 18; iii. 20, 21, 28, 36 ; iv. 1, 2, 3, 14, 33, 46 ; v. 1, 44; vi. 10, 11, 17, 21, 30, 49, 51, 55, 61, 64, 71 ; vii. 4, 8, 31, 46, 47; viii. 36, 41, 43, 52; ix. 9, 20, 41 ; x. 11, 25, 33, 35, 39, 40, 41 ; xi. 2, 3, 33 ; xii. 13, 20, 28 ; xiii. 8, 26, 34, 37 ; xiv. 5, 23, 26, 30 ; xvi. 15, 21, 25 ; xvii. 20 ; xviii. 6, 21, 40 ; xix. 2, 3, 4, 5, 7, 8, 12, 13, 17, 19, 26, 36, 37, 40 ; xx. 26 ; xxi. 3, 4.

r. Evan. 559. B.-C. III. 41.

This well-written codex, of the twelfth or thirteenth century, is mutilated, without covers, and otherwise in bad condition. It measures 6½ inches by 4½, and consists of 275 leaves of thick vellum, with 22 lines on a page. It begins with the 52nd κεφάλαιον or table of S. Matthew. The tables are complete before the other Evangelists; with τίτλοι at heads of pages, but no corresponding numerals or Ammonian sections in margin or reference to Church lessons. A picture of S. John is defaced; the others probably cut out: slight illuminations are at the head of each Gospel. The MS. breaks off at John xviii. 30 εἰ μὴ ἦν οὗτος κακοποι. Many leaves are misplaced in binding to the reader's perplexity. Thus the leaf Matth. viii. 3—15 follows cap. v. 37; and in five or six other places the same heedlessness occurs. We find no sign of ι subscript or ascript. Ν ἐφελκυστικὸν is met with 63 times, an hiatus for lack of it 13 times. Though on the whole the scribe is not inaccurate, omissions by ὁμοιοτέλευτον are found 21 times (Matth. i. 12; v. 22; vii. 10, 19; x. 33; xii. 31; xviii. 18; xix. 9. Marc. x. 34; xi. 28; xiii. 20; xiv. 46; xv. 41. Luc. vii. 20; xxii. 30. Johan. vii. 28; ix. 32; xii. 34, 45; xvii. 18; xviii. 7). There is much correction throughout, especially of itacisms, by a somewhat later hand. The red letters also were inserted in a later stage, when breathings and accents were sometimes added. Itacisms number 387 in all: viz. η (for ι) 28; ι (for η) 17; ε (for αι) 15; αι (for ε) 22; η (for ει) 54; ει (for η) 37; ι (for ει) 43; ει (for ι) 10; ω (for ο) 62; ο (for ω) 52; η (for ε) 4; ε (for η) 16; η (for υ) 5; υ (for η) 4, besides ἡμεῖς and ὑμεῖς interchanged 24 times: ω (for ου) 5; ου (for ω) 1; η (for οι) 10; οι (for η) 5; οι (for υ) 2; ι (for υ) 4; ει (for υ) 1; οι (for ι) 4. The augment is omitted five times (Matth. xviii. 23, 28; xxvii. 44; Luc. v. 13; vii. 41; Johan. i. 20). Alexandrine forms are only τρίχαν Matth. v. 36; καθήκουν Luc. v. 19; οὕτω is found 13 times, elsewhere οὕτως: μέλλει for μέλει twice, κυλὸς always. For unusual readings see

MATTH. ii. 22. —ἐπὶ. iii. 11. —καὶ πυρί. 13. πρὸς (*pro* ἐπὶ). 15. —ἡμῖν. vi. 1. +δὲ (*post* προσέχετε). 8. ἡμῶν (*pro* ὑμῶν), viii. 10. ἀμὴν ἀμὴν. x. 21. ἐπαναστήσεται. 25. ἀπεκάλεσαν. *fin.* αὐτῷ (*pro* αὐτοῦ). xi. 16. παιδίοις. 19. τέκνων αὐτοῖς (cf. x. 25). xii. 29. τὰ σκεύη (*pro* τὴν οἰκίαν). xiii. 10. λαλεῖ. 11. δίδοται *p. m.* 14. —ἐπ'. —ἡ *secund.* xiv. 5. ἐφοβεῖτο. 16. ὑμεῖς αὐτοῖς. 25. —δὲ. 31. καὶ εὐθέως (—δὲ). 33. —ἐλθόντες. xv. 11. —τοῦτο κοινοῖ τὸν ἄνθρωπον. 13. +αὐτοῖς (*post* εἶπεν). 14. ἐμπεσοῦνται. 18. —ἐκ (*ante* τοῦ στ.). 27. +καὶ (*post* καὶ γὰρ). 28. —ισ̄. 32. ἡμέραι ἤδη. 39. ἀνέβη. ὄρη.

lx ADVERSARIA

xvi. 3. συνίετε (pro δύνασθε). 4. αὐτῇ οὐ δοθήσεται. 11. σαδδουκαίων καὶ φαρισαίων. 20. –ĩσ. 21. – αὐτόν. 26. ζημιωθῇ ἡ ψυχὴ αὐτοῦ (– δὲ). xvii. 2. ἐγένοντο. 5. + δὲ (post ἔτι). 14. +τις (post ἄνθρωπος). αὐτὸν (pro αὐτῷ). 21. ἐξέρχεται. 27. ἀναβαίνοντα ἰχθὺν. xviii. 3. – ἀμὴν λέγω ὑμῖν. 7. – ἐστιν. 8. – ἐστιν. ἐλθεῖν (pro εἰσελθεῖν). 15. –καὶ (post ὕπαγε). 16. δύο ἢ τριῶν μαρτύρων. 25. ἔχει. xix. 3. – αὐτῷ. – ἀνθρώπῳ. 6. – ὁ p. m. 9. – εἰ. 16. τίς (pro εἷς). 17. init. ὁ δὲ ĩσ. 20. – ἔτι. 28. μοι ἐν τῇ παλιγγενεσία ὅταν (sic). 30. +οἱ (ante ἔσχατοι secund.). xx. 7. – ὅτι. 21. αὐτοὶ (pro οὗτοι). 22. πίνω (pro μέλλω πίνειν). 29. ἐκπορευομένου αὐτοῦ. xxi. 16. +οὐκ (ante ἀκούεις). 21. ἀμὴν ἀμὴν. 22. ἐὰν (pro ἂν). 23. τί (pro τίσ). 24. κἀγὼ ὑμᾶς. 25. – οὖν. 42. οὕτως (pro οὗτος). xxii. 9. + δ' (ante οὖν). 30. – ἐν οὐρανῷ (ante εἰσὶ). 37. ἔφη (pro εἶπεν). –τῇ bis. 45. +ἐν πνι (post δάδ). xxiii. 8. – ὁ. διδάσκαλος (pro καθηγητὴς). 14. τοῦ θυ (pro τῶν οὐρανῶν). 30. +ὅτι (ante εἰ). xxiv. 2. – οὐ. 6. μελήσετε. 8. ἀρχαὶ p. m. 9. –τῶν ἐθνῶν. 14. –τοῦτο. 18. –ὀπίσω. 20. σαββάτου (–ἐν). 32. μάθε. fin. +αὐτῆς. 34. +δὲ (post ἀμὴν). 36. –δὲ. –τῆς secund. –μου. xxv. 6. +τῆς (ante νυκτὸς). 20. ἐν (pro ἐπ'). 29. fin. +ὁ ἔχων ὦτα ἀκούειν, ἀκουέτω. xxvi. 4. ἀπολέσωσιν (pro ἀποκτείνωσιν). 9. πολλοῦ πραθῆναι p. m. 21. + δὲ (post ἀμὴν). 42. + δὲ (post πάλιν). 52. ἀποθανοῦνται (pro ἀπολοῦνται). 65. ἀκούσατε. xxvii. 58. ὁ δὲ πίλατος (– τότε). 65. – δὲ. xxviii. 6. – γὰρ. 11. – ἅπαντα. 15. + τοῖς (ante ἰουδαίοις).

Marc. i. 17. –γενέσθαι. 22. +πάντες (ante ἐπὶ). 34. fin. ἠίδεισαν. fin. χν αὐτὸν εἶναι. 35. +ὁ ĩσ (post ἀπῆλθεν). 45. +τὴν (ante πόλιν). ii. 21. κε καὶ. ἐπιβάλλει (pro ἐπιρράπτει). iii. 4. +τί (ante ἔξεστιν). ἀπολέσαι (pro ἀποκτεῖναι). 5. – ὑγιὴς. 11. προσέπιπτον. ἔκραζον. 17. αὐτοῦ (post ἰακώβου). iv. 3. ἀκούετε. 13. +πάντα (post πάσας τὰς παραβολὰς). 24. ἀντιμετρήθησεται. 26. +καὶ (ante ὡς ἐὰν). 31. ὡς (pro ὃς). 39. ἐκοπίασεν p. m. v. 1. ἦλθεν. 11. τῷ ὄρει. 27. Jungit ὄπισθεν ἥψατο. 29. ἴατο. vi. 7. – τοὺς. +μαθητὰς αὐτοῦ (post δώδεκα).

30. ἀνήγγειλαν. 31. οἱ ὑπάγοντες ᾽καὶ οἱ ἐρχόμενοι. 35. λέγοντες αὐτῶ (pro λέγουσιν). 39. — αὐτοῖς. 43. + τὸ περισ-
σεῦον (post ἦραν). 45. + ὁ ἶσ (post ἠνάγκασεν). 47. + δὲ
(post ὀψίας). 48. ἐναντίος ὁ ἄνεμος. vii. 15. — εἰς. 21. δὲ
(pro γὰρ). 28. ἀποκριθεῖσα (— καὶ). 32. παρεκάλουν.
viii. 3. οἴκους. ἤκουσι. 14. + οἱ μαθηταὶ αὐτοῦ (ante
λαβεῖν). 15. + ὁ ἶσ (ante λέγων). 17. τὴν καρδίαν ὑμῶν
ἔχετε. 19. — τοὺς secund. 24. — ὅτι. — ὁρῶ. ix. 18. — ἀν.
35. ἔστω (pro ἔσται). 42. ἐπὶ (pro περὶ). 43. — τὰς.
50. ἀρτύετε. x. 1. διὰ τοῦ. 14. — καὶ. 21. + ἔτι (ante ἐν).
30. πρα καὶ μρα (pro μητέρας). 35. — οἱ. 38. βαπτίσομαι
p. m. 39. — ἶσ. 41. ιυ καὶ ἰακώβου. 42. — ὅτι. xi. 4.
— πρὸς τὴν θύραν. 6. + αὐτοῖς (post ἐνετείλατο). 7. ἐκάθισαν.
21. ἐξηράνθη. xii. 9. — τοῦ ἀμπελῶνος. 22. ἀφῆκε. 28.
εἰπὼν (pro αὐτὸν). xiii. 17. — ταῖς. 19. — τοιαύτη. 29. — ἐπὶ
θύραις. 36. ἐξελθών. xiv. 21. — τοῦ ἀνθρώπου secund.
25. + δὲ (post ἀμὴν). 27. — ἐν τῇ νυκτὶ ταύτῃ. 31. + πέτρος
(ante ἐκ). 62. ἐκ δεξιῶν καθήμενον. ἐπὶ (pro μετὰ). 67. — ιυ.
69. ἠρνήσατο. 70. — πάλιν μετὰ μικρὸν. xv. 7. — ὁ. συστα-
σιωτῶν p. m. 11. ἀνέπεισαν. 27. αὐτῶ (pro αὐτοῦ). 28. Deest
versus. 42. γενομένης ὀψίας. 43. — ὁ.

Luc. i. 6. + τοῖς (ante δικαιώ-). 12. ἔπεσεν. 27. + καὶ
πατριᾶς (ante δᾱδ). 39. — εἰς πόλιν ἰούδα. 53. ἀγαθὰ.
63. ἔσται τὸ ὄν. 75. — τῆς ζωῆς. 77. ἐν αὐτῶ (pro αὐτῶν).
ii. 1. + τοῦ (ante ἀπογράφεσθαι). 3. εἰς τὴν ἰδίαν πόλιν
ἕκαστος. 15. + τί (post ἴδωμεν). 17. ἐπὶ (pro περὶ prim.).
22. αὐτοῦ (pro αὐτῶν) [cum Codd. D. 61. &c.]. 25. ἦν ἅγιον.
28. — καὶ εὐλόγησε τὸν θν. 44. ἐν τῇ συνοδία αὐτὸν εἶναι.
iii. 2. ἐπὶ ἀρχιερέως. — τοῦ. 12. + ὑπ᾽ αὐτοῦ (ante καὶ
εἶπον). 18. τῶ λαῶ. 33. + τοῦ ἰωράμ (post ἀράμ). iv. 40.
δύναντος. ἤγον. v. 13. ἀπῆλθεν ἀπ᾽ αὐτοῦ ἡ λέπρα.
16. — καὶ. 19. πῶς (pro διὰ ποίας). 22. — ἀποκριθεὶς.
34. ἕως (pro ἐν ᾧ). 35. νηστεύουσιν. 36. + σχίσας (ante
ἐπιβάλλει). — ἐπίβλημα secund. vi. 10. + ἐν ἀρχῇ (ante
εἶπε). 26. — ὑμῖν. — πάντες. 32. αὐτῶν (pro αὐτοὺς).
34. ὀφείλετε (pro ἐλπίζετε). ἶσα. 35. κύριος (pro χρηστὸς).

lxii ADVERSARIA

vii. 11. τῶ (pro τῇ). 28. − προφήτης. 38. τοῦ ῑυ̅ (pro αὐτοῦ prim.). 43. + ῑσ̅ (ante εἶπεν 2°). viii. 22. ἀνέβη. 24. − ἐπιστάτα semel. 39. − καὶ. 55. αὐτὴν (pro αὐτῇ). ix. 10. παραγαγὼν. 13. ἰχθύες δύο. 45. ἐπερωτῆσαι. 46. τοῦ (pro τὸ). 52. πόλιν (pro κώμην). 55, 56. − καὶ εἶπεν usque ad σῶσαι. 57. − ἐν τῇ ὁδῷ. x. 6. μὲν εἰ (pro ᾖ). xi. 2. (cf. Cod. 69) − ἡμῶν ἐν τοῖς οὐρανοῖς. − γενηθήτω usque ad τῆς γῆς. 4. ὀφείλομεν (pro ἀφίεμεν). − ἀλλὰ ῥῦσαι ἡμᾶς ἀπὸ τοῦ πονηροῦ. 13. ὄντες (pro ὑπάρχοντες). 21. φυλάττῃ. 25. + σχολάζοντα (ante σεσ-). 33. − οὐδὲ ὑπὸ τὸν μόδιον. xii. 1. καταπίπτειν (pro καταπατεῖν). 13. fin. + μου. 46. ὑποκριτῶν (pro ἀπίστων). 55. πλέοντα. xiii. 4. − ἀνθρώπους. 20. − καὶ. 34. − ὄρνις. τὰ ἑαυτῆς νοσσία. xiv. 1. εἰσελθεῖν. 5. υἱὸς (pro ὄνος). 15. ἄριστον (pro ἄρτον). 21. πάντα (pro ταῦτα). 24. fin. πολλοὶ γὰρ εἰσὶ κλητοὶ ὀλίγοι δὲ ἐκλεκτοί. xv. 8. δραγμὴν. 14. + ἀσώτως (ante πάντα). 32. ὅτε (pro ὅτι). xvi. 8. − οἱ. xvii. 7. ἐλθόντι. 21. − ᾖ. 27. ἦλθεν νῶε. ἅπαντα. xix. 2. − καλούμενος. 8. ῑν̅ (pro κύριον). 13. πραγματεύεσθε. xx. 8. − ἐγὼ. 15. − αὐτοῖς. 23. fin. + οἱ δὲ ἔδειξαν καὶ εἶπε. 29. + παρ᾽ ἡμῖν (post ἦσαν). 31. + ὡσαύτως (ante ὡσαύτως). xxi. 3. + ἡ πτωχὴ ἡ χήρα αὕτη. 16. καὶ συγγενῶν καὶ φίλων καὶ ἀδελφῶν. 23. − ταῖς secund. 37. τῶν (pro τὸ καλούμενον). xxii. 5. ἀργύρια. 18. + ἀπὸ τοῦ νῦν (post πίω). 27. − οὐχὶ ὁ ἀνακείμενος. 30. − ἐν τῇ βασιλείᾳ μου. xxiii. 19. γινομένην. 24. ἀπέκρινε. 53. − αὐτὸ secund. 54. − καὶ secund. xxiv. 16. − μὴ. 19. − ἐναντίον τοῦ θυ̅ καὶ παντὸς τοῦ λαοῦ. 26. αὐτῶ p. m.

JOAN. i. 3, 4. · ὁ γέγονεν·. 15. + τοῦ (ante αὐτοῦ). 32. ὡς (pro ὡσεὶ). 49. − ὁ. + σε (post ὄντα). ii. 6. τὸν (pro τῶν). 15. + ὡς (rubro, ante φραγέλλιον). 22. − αὐτοῖς. 24. πάντα. iii. 9. + καὶ (ante πῶς). iv. 1. − ὁ κσ̅. 2. αὐτὸς ῑσ̅. 3. − πάλιν. 8. τροφὴν. 9. παρ᾽ ἐμοῦ ποιεῖν. 35. τετράμηνός. 36. ἐνάγει (pro συνάγει). 38. − ὑμεῖς. 47. οὕτως (pro οὗτος). 49. − μου. ˙ 53. + αὐτοῦ (post πη̅ρ). v. 20. αὐτοῦ (pro αὐτῷ prim.). 36. − αὐτὰ (prim.). vi. 15. − πάλιν.

19. γενόμενον. 39. αὐτὸν (pro αὐτὸ ἐν). 41. ὁ ἐκ τοῦ
οὐρανοῦ καταβάς. 57. ἀπέσταλκέ. 61. γογγύσουσι.
69. – ἡμεῖς. 70. εἷς ἐξ ὑμῶν. vii. 26. – ὁ. 32. ὑπηρέτας
οἱ φαρισαῖοι καὶ οἱ ἱερεῖς. 51. κρινεῖ. 53. usque ad viii. 12.
deest nullo vestigio. viii. 16. ἐὰν δὲ κρίνω. 36. – ὁ υἱὸς.
53. +καὶ (ante ἀπέθανε). ix. 16. οὕτως (pro οὗτος). 26. πάλιν
αὐτῷ. 27. μαθηταὶ αὐτοῦ. x. 8. – πρὸ ἐμοῦ. 18. – ἔχω
secund. 19. – ἐν. 24. ἔρρεις (pro αἴρεις). 41. – ἰωάννης
secund. xi. 48. πιστεύουσιν. xii. 18. – καὶ. ἤκουσαν.
31. – τούτου p. m. 34. – ὅτι (ante δεῖ). 47. init. – καὶ.
xiii. 13. ὁ κσ̄ καὶ ὁ διδάσκαλος. 18. – τὴν. 25. + οὕτως
(post ἐκεῖνος). xiv. 21. – με secund. xvi. 25. παρὰ (pro
περὶ). xviii. 2. +καὶ (ante ὁ ισ̄). 25. + οὖν (post ἠρνήσατο).
28. – ἵνα 2°. Ends at v. 30 κακοποι.

Notice especially the abridged form (p. lxii) of the Lord's
Prayer, Luke xi. 2—4, of which variation Burgon speaks somewhat too strongly in The Revision Revised, pp. 34—36.

s.　Evan. 612.　B.-C. I. 1.

This is not so much a MS. of the Gospels as an Ὠδεῖον,
containing only the Magnificat[1] and Benedictus[1] (Luc. i. 46—
55; 68—79) of the N. T., and is here given as a specimen
of a class, which includes the uncial books under the notation
of O (Plain Introduction, p. 137) and Muralt's dated 5ᵖᵉ (ib.
p. 227). It is an exquisite little vellum book, of the twelfth
century, 3½ inches by 2½, in a very elegant minute hand (in
places hard to read), on 112 leaves, from 25 to 28 lines on a
page, the titles and initial letters being rubro. It contains
cli Psalms from LXX.; Song of Moses (Ex. xv. 1—14); also
that in Deut. xxxii. 14—43; Song of Hannah (1 Sam. ii.); of
Habakkuk (cap. iii.); of Isaiah (cap. xxvi.); of Jonah (cap.
ii.); of the Three Holy Children in LXX.; ᾠδὴ τῆς ὑπεραγίας
θκ̄ου (Magnificat)[1]: ᾠδῶν σφράγισμα τοῦ ζαχαρίου μέγας
(Benedictus)[1]. Since the verso of the last leaf is blank, this

[1] The variations are: Luc. i. 30. γενεασ (forsan γενεὰν) καὶ γενεὰν.
55. ἕωσ αἰῶνος (pro εἰς τὸν αἰῶνα). 74. ἐκ χειρὸς. 76. προπορευσει (ευ dub.).
79. ἐπιφάναι. – ὁδὸν εἰρήνης.

Odeum could not have contained the *Nunc dimittis*, as do
O^{b}O^{d}O^e.

N.B. A portion of these Lessons from the Gospels, as
Cod. t, and many others contain the Church lessons for the
whole year as set forth in the ordinary synaxaria and meno-
logies of festival, but many are extracted from Euchologies,
Liturgical service books of various kinds, and Ritual or Typica
(Suicer, *Thesaurus Ecclesiasticus*, Tom. II. 1335) and a single
MS. will contain only a small part of the sacred text, the
Gospels and other portions of the N. T. (see below, p. lxxxix,
Apostolus) occurring promiscuously (Codd. uvw). We here
exhibit descriptions of

EVANGELISTARIA.

t. Evst. 221. Gale's Evangelistarium, Trin. Coll., Cambridge. O. iv. 22.

The history of this manuscript has been given when
describing Evan. 66, d. p. Few copies extant come so near
to the *textus receptus*, and thus exhibit so few various readings. It is a folio of 12⅓ inches long and nine broad, written
in a fine bold hand of the twelfth century, with illuminated
capitals and gold, and red musical notes, on 249 leaves, in two
columns and 17 or 18 or 20 lines on each page. Like many
other Evangelistaria it does not go through the whole year,
but contains the daily lessons only from Easter to Pentecost
and the Holy week in full, afterwards those only for Saturdays and Sundays (σαββατοκυριακαί) with full lessons for
Saints' days. This copy has been unexamined hitherto, and
was shown to me by Mr Bradshaw. It is correctly (ὁμοιο-
τέλ. only nine times) as well as beautifully written. N ἐφελκυστικὸν (often with εἶπεν) is found 179 times; but a
hiatus for the lack of it in Joan. v. 45; Marc. xvi. 18.

The itacisms are as many as 902, of a very ordinary type; viz. ω (for ο) 104; ο (for ω) 125; η (for ει) 122; ει (for η) 125; ι (for ει) 45; ει (for ι) 25; ι (for η) 83; η (for ι) 87; ε (for η) 9; η (for ε) 4; αι (for ε) 76; ε (for αι) 70; οι (for υ) 6; υ (for οι) 8; η (for υ) 5; υ (for η) 8 (for pronouns); ω (for ου) 4; ου (for ω) 3. The augment is wanting, Joan. i. 20; vi. 26; Luc. xxiv. 51; Matth. ix. 9; xiv. 14; xxv. 7; Luc. v. 26; xiii. 13; xvii. 10; ii. 15 *p. m.*; ii. 38; xxii. 6; Marc. xvi. 14. So the reduplication. An accusative for dative, Joan. vii. 45; xx. 17; Matth. ii. 2, 8, 11; xxviii. 17; Marc. vi. 28; Luc. i. 17; xxii. 22: dative for accusative, Marc. xv. 22; Joan. viii. 7. Other rarer forms are, παραδιδουντες Luc. xxii. 21; ἀπεκατεστάθη Luc. vi. 10; ἐκαθερίσθησαν Luc. xvii. 14, 17; ἀνέπεσαν Joan. vi. 10; ἑοράκατε Joan. vi. 36; ἔμπροσθε Joan. i. 15, 17, 30; Matth. xi. 10; Luc. x. 21 *fin.*; Marc. i. 2; ἔξωθε Matth. xxiii. 27; μέλλει (for μέλει) *passim*, χεῖραν Joan. xx. 27; θυγατέραν Luc. xiii. 16; ἀρχιερέαν Matth. xxvi. 57; τὴν θύρα Joan. xviii. 16; οὕτω Matth. xxiv. 33, rarely. The variations from the common text are chiefly at the latter part of MS. especially Joan. xii. For rarer readings see Joan. v. 18; vi. 10, 22, 28, 39; vii. 6, 40, 41; viii. 39, 43, 44; ix. 15; x. 25; xi. 3, 34, 47; xii. 18, 19, 26, 28, 29, 30, 35, 47, 50, 49; xv. 4; xvi. 4, 20, 21, 25; xxi. 20; xviii. 10, 11, 36, 37; xix. 28, 11 (*bis*); Matth. iii. 9; iv. 4; vi. 16; viii. 25; xii. 20; xv. 23; xxi. 1, 2, 3, 32; xxii. 28; xxiii. 23, 28, 34; xxiv. 6, 9; xxv. 6, 16; xxvi. 28, 59; xviii. 14, 15, 16, 20; x. 42; xv. 37 *p. m.*; xix. 18; xxii. 16; xxiv. 6; xxv. 10, 20; xxvii. 63; Luc. i. 1—30, 59; v. 6, 7; vi. 34; vii. 9; viii. 35, 39, 52, 54; ix. 38, 41, 62; x. 34; xiii. 25; xiv. 6; xviii. 43; xvii. 3, 4, 7, 8; xv. 14, 17, 20; xxi. 8, 34, 35; xxiii. 38, 46, 47; ii. 11, 31, 25, 26, 28; iii. 14; iv. 28; ix. 31, 33, 34, 35; xxiv. 10; xxii. 4, 23, 24, 26. We cite the above texts in the order in which they stand in Evangelistaria.

Breathings are erroneous at times, prepositions often lacking them: grave for acute often. A second hand makes many corrections in a paler ink, yet contemporaneous; some of them look almost *primâ manu*, e.g. Matth. xv. 37; Marc. x.

30, even Matth. xxi. 27; Luc. ii. 15. No ι ascript or subscript, only ι ascr. seems erased, Matth. ix. 2. Rubric capitals are often omitted in mere carelessness, e.g. Joan. xix. 32; xxi. 8. Rubric often rejects words by putting points around. *Lessons in the Menology,* compared with Scrivener, *Plain Introduction,* pp. 85—6, third edition: June 25, εἰς τὴν ἐπανάστασιν τῶν ἀθέων σαρακεινῶν. Other uncommon feasts are SEPT. 4, Babylas. 6, Eudoxius. 9, Joakim et Anna. 16, Euphemia. 20, τοῦ μεγαλομάρτυρος εὐσταθίου καὶ τῆς συνοδίας αὐτοῦ. 26, ἡ μετάστασις τοῦ ἁγιόυ ἰῶ τοῦ θεολόγου. 30, τοῦ ἁγιόυ γρηγορίου τῆς μεγάλης ἀρμεν. OCT. 1, τοῦ ἁγίου ἀποστόλου ἀνανίου. 2, τῶν ἁγίων μαρ^τ κυπρ^ι καὶ ἰούστ. 7, τῶν ἁγί μαρ^τ σεργίου καὶ βακ^χ. 11, τῶν ἐν ἁγιόις πρων ἡμῶν καὶ πατριαρ^χ νεκταρίου· ἀρσακίου· ἀττικοῦ· καὶ σιγινίου. 21, τ^ν ὁσίου πρσ ἡμῶν ἱλαρί. 25, τοῦ ἁγίου μαρ^τ δημητρίου καὶ εἰς τὸν μέγαν σεισμόν. 30, τοῦ ἐν ἁγί κυριακοῦ καὶ τοῦ ἁγι ζηνοβίου καὶ εἰς τὸν χρυσοστο καὶ ἐπιφανίου κύπρου. NOV. 1, τῶν ἁγιων ἀναργύρων. 2, τῶν ἁγί μάρ ἀκινδύνου καὶ τοῦ συμ. 25, τῶν ἁγίων μαρ^τ κλήμεντος ρώμης καὶ πέτρου ἀλεξαν^δ. DEC. 4, τῆς ἁγιάς μεγαλομάρτυρος βαρβάρας. These specimens may perhaps suffice, and the divergencies from the conventional type are more numerous than usual. It is from noting the peculiarities of a given menology that we may best conjecture the country or diocese in which the manuscript before us was written, which may perhaps in this case be some eastern region of the patriarchate of Constantinople. The service against the incursions of the Saracens (June 25) will fix the date of the composition of this liturgy as not earlier than the seventh or eighth century.

u. Evst. 251. B.-C. I. 10 (Apost. 64).

This is a shabby looking codex of about the twelfth or thirteenth century 7⅜ high by 4⅜ wide, 12°, 60 leaves with 17 lines on a page. It has been used by the late Dr Swainson, Master of Christ's College, Cambridge, for his valuable treatise on the *Greek Liturgies* (Introduction, p. xxi) and "contains the Liturgies of S. Chrysostom, S. Basil and the Presanctified, the quires being sewn together very roughly, and two or three being lost." The Biblical portions are in the same hand, only somewhat smaller than the Liturgical. They consist of 19 lessons, viz. Matth. x. 1—8; xiv. 14—22; xvii. 1—10; Marc. viii. 34—ix. 1; Luc. i. 24—38; 27, 28; x. 15—21; 16—21; 38—42, 38, 39; Joan. i. 29—33; Act. xix. 1—8; Rom. v. 18—23; 1 Cor. iv. 9—16; Gal. vi. 11—17; Phil. ii. 5—11; 1 Thess. iv. 13—17; Heb. ii. 2—10; 11—18; 2 Pet. i. 10—19. No ι ascript or subscript is found. There is no very special critical value in the readings. Not incorrectly written. Slight illuminations at beginning of several parts. At foot of fol. 57 b (τῇ ά τῶν ἀσωμάτων) is a fair picture of an angel with golden glory: on fol. 59 one of S. John ὁ πρόδρομος in the same style.

v. Evst. 252. B.-C. iii. 29 (Apost. 66).

This is a small folio on coarse paper of the fourteenth century, 8½ inches long by 6 broad, on 172 leaves, in bad condition, full of the grossest itacisms, poor illuminations and careless errors (e.g. 2 Tim. ii. 6). No ι subscript or ascript. It contains only 28 lessons from the N. T. (viz. Matth. x. 2—15; Luc. i. 39—54; ii. 29—32; vi. 17—23; 21; ix. 1—6; x. 16—21; 38—42; xxiv. 12—35; Joan. i. 1—17; 18—28; iii. 13—17; Act. i. 12—26; ii. 14—20; iii. 11—16; Rom. xiii. 11—xiv. 4; 1 Cor. i. 18—25; iv. 9—16; Phil. ii. 5—11; Heb. ii. 2—10; iii. 17—21; 2 Tim. ii. 1—10, 9. Too incorrect to be of much value. The rest of the volume consists of matter of very varied character, the Liturgies of Chrysostom, Basil, and the Presanctified, prayers for Saints' days, a menology, a table of lunar days with curious notes both biblical and astronomical, Ps. cxxxv, LXX. (fol. 85), and other miscellaneous pieces, liturgical or secular. A strange volume indeed. Notice Luc. xxiv. 21. - ταύτην. 32. ἐκάλη (*pro* ἐλάλει). 41. - αὐτῶν. 42. ὑπέδωκαν. 45. ἤνοιξεν. Act.

i. 9. — ἤ (*ante* νεφέλη). 11. οὕτως (*pro* οὗτος). 12. + οἱ ἀπόστολοι (*post* ὑπέστρεψαν). 15, 16. ἄνδρες ἀδελφοὶ ἤν ται ὄχλος ὀνομάτων ἐπὶ τὸ αὐτῶ ὡς ἑκατὸν ἤκωσι. 26. συνεγκατεψηφεῖσθη. ii. 2. ὁ λαὸς (*pro* ὅλον). 3. καὶ ἐκάθησέν τε. 5. τὸν ἀνῶν (*pro* τῶν ὑπὸ τὸν οὐρανὸν). 7. — πάντες.

w. Evst. 253. B.-C. III. 42 (Apoc. 67).

This Euchology also has been used by Dr Swainson, *Greek Liturgies* (Introduction, p. xxi) and, being perfect, the liturgies "more expanded" and the Bible lessons far more numerous[1], has proved to him, as to us, far more useful than B.-C. I. 10 (u). It measures six inches long by four broad, and is full three inches in thickness: of 310 leaves of stout glazed paper (20 or 24 lines on a page), dating from the fourteenth

---

[1] The codex contains as many as 154 lessons, whereof 23 are duplicates, and three from Isaiah (xii. 3—6; xxxv. 1—10; lv. 1—13). Of the rest 102 are from the Gospels, 49 from the Apostles. The kind of passages used in Euchologies may appear from the following list of those in B.-C. III. 42, in the order in which they occur. *Burial:* 1 Thess. iv. 13—17 (twice); Joan. v. 24—30 (twice); Eph. vi. 10—17 (thrice); Matth. x. 37, 38 (twice); xi. 28 —30; Col. iii. 12—16 (twice); Luc. ix. 23—27; Jac. v. 10—20; 1 Joan. v. 1—15 (twice); Rom. xv. 1—7; Luc. xix. 1—10; 1 Cor. xii. 27—xiii. 8 (twice); Matth. x. 5—8 (twice); Rom. viii. 14—21; Luc. x. 25—37; Gal. ii. 16—20; Marc. vi. 7—12; Luc. vii. 36—50; Matth. vi. 14—21 (twice); Heb. ii. 2—10, 11—18; 9; Luc. x. 16—21; Act. xix. 1—8; Matth. xi. 2—14; Phil. ii. 5—11; Luc. x. 38—42; xi. 27, 28; 1 Cor. iv. 9, 16; i. 18—24; Joan. xix. 25—35 (twice); Rom. vi. 18—23; Marc. viii. 34—ix. 1; Matth. vi. 22—33; Luc. vi. 31—36; 1 Cor. xiv. 20—25; Luc. xi. 47—51; Heb. xiii. 7—16; Matth. v. 14 —19; Heb. vii. 26—viii. 2; Joan. x. 9—16; Phil. iii. 20—iv. 3; Matth. xii. 1—8; x. 16—22; 2 Tim. ii. 1—10; Joan. xv. 17—xvi. 2 (twice); 2 Cor. v. 1—10; Marc. v. 24—34; Gal. v. 22—vi. 2; Heb. xiii. 17—21; Matth. xi. 27—30; Heb. x. 32—38; Luc. xii. 8—12; Eph. v. 8—19; Matth. xxv. 1—13 (twice); xvi. 24—28. In the *Menology:* Luc. i. 39—49, 56; Joan. xii. 28 —36; xix. 6—35 (twice); Luc. i. 24, 25; 57—80; vi. 17—23; Matth. xviii. 10—20; Joan. x. 1—9; Heb. ix. 1—7; Matth. i. 18—25; Gal. iv. 4—7; Matth. ii. 1—12; Marc. i. 9—11; Tit. ii. 11—14; iii. 4—7; Matth. iii. 13— 17; Luc. ii. 25—32 (twice); Heb. vii. 7—17; Luc. ii. 22—40; vii. 17—30; i. 24—38; Marc. viii. 9—13; Luc. ix. 28—36; 2 Pet. i. 10—19; Matth. xvii. 1—9; xiv. 1—13; Act. xiii. 25—32; Matth. vi. 14—30. *Lent Lessons:* 2 Tim. iii. 10—15; Luc. xviii. 9—14; 1 Cor. vi. 12—30; Luc. xv. 11—32; 2 Cor. viii. 8—ix. 2; Matth. xxv. 31—46 (twice); Rom. xiii. 11—xiv. 4;

or fifteenth century. We find here no ι subscript or ascript, also ν ἐφελκυστικὸν 22 times (once corrected) and hiatus for lack of it 4 times. Omission by ὁμοιοτέλευτον occurs nine times: Matth. xviii. 18; xxv. 3, 4, 36; xxvii. 33; Johan. x. 3, 4; xxi. 23; 1 Cor. i. 27; xi. 25; Isai. xii. 5. Of itacisms there are 151: ι (for η) 8; η (for ι) 8; υ (for η) 2; η (for υ) 1; ήμ- (for ὑμ-) 7; ὑμ- (for ήμ-) 2; ε (for αι) 12; αι (for ε) 16; ω (for ο) 19; ο (for ω) 26; ι (for ει) 5; ει (for ι) 5; ει (for η) 18; η (for ει) 12; ε (for η) 4; η (for ε) 1; ω (for ου) 2; ι (for υ) 1; η (for οι) 1; ι (for οι) 1. We read ὧδε nine times, οὕτως 13 times only. Breathings and accents pretty well put, yet μὴ` interrogative, οὐ μὴ`, οἱ δε`, μέλει interchanged with μέλλει, η three times aspirated wrongly (ἡγέρθη). A few titles and slight illuminations, rubro. Changes are usually p. m., but a few later. For notable readings compare Matth. vi. 14; xiv. 8; xvi. 28; xxiv. 39; xxv. 24, 25, 40; xxvi. 1, 21, 26, 28, 29, 57, 65; xxvii. 37, 43, 63; xxviii. 8; Marc. v. 28; vi. 13; ix. 1; xv. 18; Luc. vi. 20; vii. 42; xxiv. 10; Johan. v. 4; vii. 50; ix. 28; xiii. 12, 15; xiv. 20; xv. 19; xviii. 3, 25, 40; xix. 12, 28; 1 Cor. vi. 15; xi. 25; Phil. iv. 3. The contents are given generally by Dr Swainson. As we seldom meet with so complete a copy, we will

Joan. i. 44—52; Marc. viii. 34; Heb. xii. 28—xiii. 8; Joan. xi. 1—45. *Holy Week:* Matth. xxi. 1—11; 15—17; Phil. iv. 4—9; Matth. xxiv. 3—35; xxiv. 36—xxvi. 2; xxvi. 6—16 (twice); 1 Cor. xi. 23—32; Matth. xxvi. 1—20; Joan. xiii. 3—17; Matth. xxvi. 21—39; Luc. xxii. 43, 45; Matth. xxvi. 40—xxvii. 2. *Gospels* τῶν ἁγίων παθῶν: Joan. xiii. 31—xviii. 1; xviii. 1—28; Matth. xxvi. 37—75 (twice); Joan. xviii. 28—xix. 16; Matth. xxvii. 3 —32 (twice); Marc. xv. 16—32; Matth. xxvii. 33—54; Luc. xxiii. 32—49; Joan. xix. 25—37 (twice); Joan. xix. 38—42; Matth. xxvii. 62—66. *Good Friday:* 1 Cor. i. 18—ii. 2; Matth. xxvii. 1—38; Luc. xxiii. 39—44; Matth. xxvi. 39—54; xxvi. 1—20; xxvi. 55—61; Rom. vi. 3—11; Matth. xxviii. 1 —28. *Easter to All Saints:* Act. i. 1—8; Joan. i. 1—17; Marc. xv. 43— xvi. 8; Joan. v. 14—30; v. 5—42; ix. 1—38; xvii. 1—13 (twice); Act. ii. 1—11; Joan. vii. 27—viii. 12; Rom. vii. 52—viii. 12; Heb. xi. 33—xii. 2; Matth. x. 32, 33, 37, 38; xix. 27—30. Εὐαγγέλια ἑωθινὰ ῑα. Matth. xxvii. 16—20 (twice); Marc. xvi. 1—8, 9—20; Luc. xxiv. 1—12, 12—35, 36—53; Joan. xx. 1—10, 11—18, 19—31; xxi. 1—14, 15—35. *Baptism:* [Isaiah xii. 3—65; xxxv. 1—10; lv. 1—13]; 1 Cor. x. 1—4; Marc. i. 9—11. Εὐχαὶ: Luc. x. 19—21; Fol. 297; 1 Joan. iv. 12—19; xix. 25—27 (twice); xxi. 24, 25; 2 Cor. xi. 21—xii. 9; Matth. xvi. 13—19.

S.   *f*

enumerate its contents in detail. It is arranged in quires of
8 leaves each : last is λή, or 304 leaves. Foll. 1—33 Νεοκα-
νονον σὺν θῶ ὠμώ. Foll. 33—47 συνόδου ϛ τῆς τρούλλης
[A.D. 692] with subscription † ὁ ἐνὶ ἱερομονάχοις ἐλάχιστος
καὶ πνῖκος ὅ^{δης} ὑπέγραψε. Foll. 48—67 ἐξοδιαστϊκόν : rubro
(Burial Service). Fol. 124 a Liturgy of S. Chrysostom.
Fol. 127, also of S. Basil. Fol. 156b, also of the Presanctified. Foll. 164—178 ἀποστόλου εὐαγγέλια τῆς ὅλης ἐβδό-
μαδος καὶ εἰς διαφόρους ἁγίους. Foll. 179—195, Menology,
from Sept. 8 : this menology gives most fully the days sacred
to the Baptist. Fol. 195, Sunday Lessons in Lent. Then,
Lessons for Holy Week : εὐαγγελία ιβ τῶν ἁγίων παθῶν :
Good Friday Lessons. Fol. 244, Lessons from Easter to All
Saints' Day. Fol. 255, ιᾱ εὐαγγέλια ἑωθινά. Fol. 264,
ἀκολουθία τῶν φώτων (Lessons from Isaiah : Baptism). Fol.
271, ἀκολουθία τῆς γοννκλισίας. Fol. 282, special εὐχαὶ ἐπὶ
τοὺς μέλλοντας μεταλαμβάνειν τῶν ἀχράντων μυστηρίων : for
plenary Absolution, for rash swearing, for drought, for laying
a foundation of a Church or house, or on going to war, for
persons under penalties or in prison, for field or vineyard or
garden hurt by rain or locusts, and the like. Prayer of the
holy martyr Trypho of Lampsacus—exorcisms of noxious
creatures, or whatever unclean thing had fallen into the wine
or oil press—for a polluted vessel—to bless the vintage or
wine or oil—for success in fishing. This strange miscellany
ends in Fol. 296, it may be p. m. Δόξα σοι ἁγιά τριάς· ὁ ἐν
οὐνοῖς ἐμὸς θσ΄· ὁ πηρ καὶ ὁ υἱὸς καὶ τὸ παράκλητον πνα, ἡ ἐμὴ
λατρεία καὶ τὸ σεβας· ὅτι πεπεράωταί μοι καὶ τὸ παρὸν
πυκτίον ἤγουν εὐχολόγϊον καὶ οἱ ἐντευξόμενοι εὔχεσθέ μοι· ὁ
δὲ γράψας ματθαῖος ἦν ὁ τάλας καὶ σκαιώτατος πάντων ἀνῶν
καὶ μοναχός τάχα. The same hand has on next page the
signature λή and 8 or 9 leaves. Foll. 297—299 has 5
lessons (1 Johan. iv. 12—19; Johan. xix. 25—27; 2 Cor. xi.
21—xii. 9; Matth. xvi. 13—19). In Foll. 300—305 in same
minute hand ἀκολουθία εἰς μνημόσυνον. Then 3 blank
leaves disfigured by some modern scrawl; then lastly in a
much later hand than MS., a table in red and black, τὰ μετ᾽
ὀνομασθέντα ὀνόματα τῶν μοναχῶν καὶ γυναικῶν and τὰ τῶν

γυναικῶν μετ' ὀνομασθέντα, the names of monks and women
being in separate tables in alphabetical order.

x.   Evst. 290.   B.-C. III. 44 (Apost. 78).

This copy is a Typicum (see p. lxiv) 4to, on paper 8½
inches long, 5½ wide, of the fourteenth century. Its sur-
viving leaves are 339 and six are lost (fol. 210 is cut out).
The signatures of the quaternions are put at the head of the
pages, not (as usual) at the foot, down to p 8, whereof one
leaf is missing. There are in it two separate hands, used
promiscuously (compare fol. 256—263), of which one may be
of the fifteenth century. This codex contains only 29 lessons,
eleven being LXX. of the Old Testament (Gen. i. 1—13;
xiv. 14—20; Num. xxiv. 3—9, 17, I8; Deut. i. 8—17; x.
14—21; Prov. x. 31—xi. 12; Isai. vii. 10—16; ix. 6, 7;
xi. 1—10; Dan. ii. 31—36, 44, 45; Micah iv. 6, 7; v. 2—4);
five of the Apocrypha (Wisd. iii. 1—9; iv. 7—15, twice;
v. 15—vi. 3; Baruch iii. 35—iv. 4): two of the Gospels
(Matth. xi. 27—30; Marc. viii. 34—ix. 1): ten of S. Paul's
Epistles (Gal. iii. 8—12, 23—29; iv. 4—7; v. 22—vi. 2;
Col. iii. 4—11; Heb. i. 1—12; ix. 1—7; xiii. 17—21; xi. 9,
10, 32—40, 33—xii. 2). There are in this Typicum some
interesting variations from common text: e.g. Gal. iii. 23,
29; Col. iii. 54. The itacisms are few, chiefly o and ω interchanged, less often ι and η, ε and αι.

y.   Evst. 249.   B.-C. III. 46 (Apost. 82).

This interesting copy is in quarto, 9½ inches long by
7 inches broad, of the 13th or 14th century, containing 205
leaves (much mutilated) of one column in a page of 21 lines,
then 15 pages of palimpsest in two columns of 25 lines each,
yet they may be in the same hand. The under writing
seems some two centuries older, and consists of LXX. lessons from Genesis, Isaiah and Proverbs (the collation is
given below: the readings are closer to the Roman 1587

f 2

than to Cod. Alex.). The lectionary is partly from the
Gospels, partly from the Epistles. This copy is very careless
in parts and itacisms very thick in parts. Ν ἐφελκυστικὸν
and ι ascript often erased. The MS. begins Johan vi.
53, σάρ|κα τοῦ υἱοῦ τοῦ ἀνόν, in the lesson for preparation
in second week after Easter, at first the lessons are given
for every day in the week, then after the eleventh week
of S. Luke, Saturday and Sunday lessons only are given.
Many rubrical and musical notes in red. The 15 palimpsest leaves contain portions of a Menology about Christmas
time. The writing is clear, bold and legible throughout.

z. Evst. 250. B.-C. III. 52.

This fragment (9½ inches high by 7½ broad) contains
lessons from the Gospels only on 84 pages in one column of
25 lines each, bearing date about the thirteenth century.
The lessons for every day in the week immediately before
Pentecost are given, beginning Saturday after Ascension Day
(Johan. xiv. 13), then only on Saturday and Sunday for each
week. Many leaves are lost. The last twenty-two leaves
contain an abridged menology from the new year in September
to March 13: viz. τοῦ ὁσίου νικηφόρου ἀρχεπισκόπου.

zz. Evst. 253². B.-C. III. 53 (Apost. 68).

A Euchology on paper, 9 inches by 5½, rudely written in
the fifteenth century, with capitals rubro, very coarse, on 227
leaves, 26 lines on a page, but several leaves are lost. Begins
in the Baptismal service: καὶ ζωὴν αἰώνιον· καὶ ἀξιώσον
ἡμᾶς. Accents and breathings are too inaccurate to be
worth notice. The readings in Matth. i. 1—25 (e.g. Matth.
i. 5. −ἐκ τῆς ῥαχὰβ et ἐκ τῆς ῥούθ. 16. −ματθὰν δὲ ἐγέννησε
τὸν ἰακὼβ ἰακὼβ δὲ. Luke ii. 3. − ἔκαστος. 5. ἐγγύω.
14. [εὐδοκία]; Luke ii. 1—20, 21, 40—52, are remarkable.
So Johan. v. 3, 4. Itacisms are perpetual especially the

interchange of *o* and *ω*. Lessons from Epistles and Gospels about in equal numbers. From the LXX. occur as lessons Isai. xii. 3—6; xxxv. 1—10; lv. 1—13; with Ps. cxxxviii. 1—6.

ACT.: CATH. EPP.

a. Act. 220 (Paul. 264). B.-C. III. 1.

A noble specimen of calligraphy in a bold hand, large 4to, 11½ inches long, 8 inches wide, yet in critical value very inferior to the copy described below p. lxxv. Here the Epistle to the Hebrews stands last of S. Paul's Epistles, which, however, precede the Catholic. It contains 375 leaves of the finest vellum with broad margins, with 22 lines on each page, richly illuminated, but 2 Cor. i. 1—3; Eph. i. 1—4; Heb. i. 1—6 have been shamefully mutilated for the sake of the illuminations. The titles, subscriptions and capitals are in gold and colours, very rich and fresh, though the date may be of the eleventh or perhaps the twelfth century. Full directions in red stand at the top and bottom and in the margin of each page: there are no tables of κεφάλαια, but their numerals and τίτλοι occur throughout. To each book are prefixed hexameter lines, and the ordinary ὑπόθεσις, and to eight of them Theodoret's also. The subscription on the last page, at the end of Jude is in gold: κέ ἰϋ χὲ υἱὲ τοῦ θϋ, ἐλέησόν με τὸν πολιαμάρτητον ἀντώνϊον τάχα καὶ μονα-χὸν τὸν μαλεύκην [μηλεύκην?]. At the beginning are set 20 pages comprising a Synaxarion of the whole Apostolos, ὑπόθεσις to the Acts, ἀποδημία παύλου, εὐθαλίου τοῦ δια-κόνου περὶ τῶν χρόνων τοῦ κηρύγματος τοῦ ἁγίου παύλου· ἔκθεσις κεφαλαίων τῶν πράξαιων τῶν ἁγίων ἀποστόλων: at the end a menology. All these apparently are the work of the original scribe: 3 or 4 leaves of foreign matter are cut out after the menology. Few itacisms occur (chiefly *ω* for *o*, *ει* for *η*, *η* for *ι*) in this carefully written manuscript, which closely lxxiv ADVERSARIA

agrees with common text (but see ACTS xii. 25. + εἰς ἀντιό-
χειαν (post ἴλημ). xiii. 41. + καὶ ἐπιβλέψατε (post θαυμά-
σατε). xiv. 12. ἐλάλουν (pro ἐκάλουν). xv. 29. καὶ ὅσα μὴ
θέλετε ἑαυτοῖς γίνεσθαι, ἑτέροις μὴ ποιεῖτε (post πορνείας).
xx. 7. ἄχρι (pro μέχρι). xxi. 4. – τούς. xxii. 20. πρωτο-
μάρτυρος. Rom. v. 1 ἔχομεν, but 1 Cor. xv. 49 φορέσωμεν.

e. Act. 193. Wake 12 (Evan. 492, Paul. 277, Apoc. 26).
See above, p. xxxiv.

This copy in the Acts is but a fragment (only 273 verses
out of 1007), beginning with cap. vii. 49 (two quires lost),
breaking off in middle of ὑπόθεσις to Act. Also mutilated
cap. x. 19—xiv. 10 (two leaves lost); xv. 15—xvi. 11; xviii.
1—xxi. 25; xxiii. 18—James iii. 17 (one quire). This portion
of the MS. contains κεφάλαια and Œcumenius' prologues with
scholia. This copy is sometimes with Codd. ℵAB e.g. James
iv. 5. – κατωκισεν. 7. + δε (post ἀντίστητε): with Cod. D,
e.g. Act. xvi. 12. αὐτῇ (pro ταύτῃ). 13. δὲ (pro τὲ). 19. –τὸν
secund. xvii. 8. ἀκούσαντες. And it is found yet oftener
with GH and ordinary cursives. It stands alone, or
nearly so, in Act. vii. 58. εἰ βάλλοντες. – αὐτῶν. viii. 2.
συνεκομίσαντο. 16. – κυρίου. 24. – ὁ. ix. 2. – ὄντας.
3. + αὐτὸν (post πορεύεσθαι). 10. αὐτῷ (pro πρὸς αὐτὸν).
24. βουλῇ (pro ἐπιβουλὴ). x. 9. +αὐτῶν (ante ἐκείνων with
eˢᶜʳ only). xv. 5. + καὶ (ante παραγγέλλειν τὲ). 7. ζητήσεως
(pro συζητ.). xvi. 14. ἤκουσεν. 17. τῷ σίλα (pro ἡμῖν).
19. – τὸν secund. xvii. 16. τὸν σίλαν καὶ τιμόθεον (– αὐτοὺς). 27. καί γε (– τοι). xxi. 33. ἐγγίσας δὲ (– τότε).
xxii. 12. εὐλαβὴς (pro εὐσεβὴς). 14. τὴν φωνὴν τὴν.
24. αὐτὸν ἀνετάζεσθαι. 28. – τε. JAMES iv. 8. ἡμῖν (pro
ὑμῖν). 11. νόμον (pro νόμου 1°). 1 JOHAN. iii. 6. οὐχ᾽
ἁμαρτήσεν. 15. οἶδαᵘ (pro οἴδατε). 16. γινώσκομεν (pro
ἐγνώκαμεν). 17. δ᾽ ἂν ἔχει. iv. 2. γινώσκεται πνα. – ἐκ.
v. 10. μαρτυρίαν ἐν αὐτῷ. ἑαυτὸν (pro αὐτὸν). 15. ἐὰν
(pro ἂν). 16. ἐπερωτήσῃ. JUDE 4. – γὰρ. 5. τῆς (pro

γῆς). 8. μὲν (pro μέντοι). 9. ἐξενεγκεῖν. 12. + καὶ (ante ἐκριζωθέντα). 23. — τῆς. 25. + πρὸ παντὸς τοῦ αἰῶνος (post ἐξουσία).

f. Act. 190. Wake 34 (Evan. 503, Paul. 244, Apoc. 27). See above, p. xxxvi. We have stated above how little this MS. contains of this portion of the N. T. ι ascript occurs very often (24 times) in the fragment which remains of the Acts (cap. xvii. 24—xviii. 13), less frequently elsewhere. Verbs never seem to take the ι.

i. Act. 219 (Evan. 549). B.-C. II. 7. See above, p. xlii.

β. Act. 221 (Paul. 265). B.-C. III. 37.

Next only to Cod. a or Evan. 556, this is doubtless the most valuable of the Baroness Burdett-Coutts' collection of manuscripts, whether we regard the number or the rarity of the various readings it exhibits. In the Acts it agrees so much with Tischendorf's lo^ti (Cod. 61 Brit. Mus. Addit. 20,003) as to be specially useful in the 297 verses wherein that prime cursive is defective: in the Catholic Epistles it closely resembles Cod. 184 (Lambeth 1184 or c^scr) in the most remarkable variations (e. g. James i. 17, 18), so that the connection between them cannot be accidental[1]. The Philoxenian Syriac *cum asterisco* is next to this pair, then Cod. 100 (Matthaei d, or Mosc. Syn. 334), Lambeth (Cod. 182 a^scr, Cod. 185 d^scr) and the second hand of Cod. 66 at Vienna. The text of the Pauline Epistles may be less notable, but that also contains quite as many unique readings (below, p. lxxxiii), and

[1] These variations of reading, of the nature of glosses, are at end of ver. 17. + τροπὴ· (ante ἢ τροπῆς [not e^scr]). *fin.* + οὐδὲ μέχρη (μέχρι c^scr) ὑπονοίας τινὸς ὑποβολὴ. ver. 18. + πρώτους καὶ τιμιωτάτους τῆς ὁρωμένης κτίσεως (ante ἀπαρχήν).

sometimes agrees with the first hand of Cod. Sinaiticus (‏א‎)
almost alone. This manuscript is 6 inches long, 4 wide, being
a thick quarto (270 leaves) vellum, of the twelfth century,
very neatly written, with 20 lines on a page, and full Church
lessons in red at top and foot of the pages. There is not one
Alexandrine form. The itacisms, however, amount to 198:
viz. ι (pro η) 9; η (pro ι) 20; ι (pro ει) 12; ει (pro ι) 5; ε
(pro αι) 3; αι (pro ε) 3; ω (pro ο) 29; ο (pro ω) 36; ει (pro
η) 20; η (pro ει) 10; οι (pro ει) once; οι (pro η) twice; ε (pro
η) 2; υ (interchanged with η) 3 times; and in the plural of
personal pronouns no less than 43 times: Ν ἐφελκυστικὸν
only Acts xiii. 32, but a hiatus for want of ν Acts xii. 19;
1 Cor. vi. 16. We find ι subscript in about 112 verses (or the
MS. might be thought earlier than the twelfth century), often
several in the same verse. No augment 2 Tim. i. 16, no reduplication 2 Cor. ix. 3. It is pretty accurately written,
though breathings and accents are overlooked now and then,
but omissions by ὁμοιοτέλευτον are as many as twenty (cf.
Act. vii. 55; James iv. 17). Οὕτω for οὕτως only in Rom. vi.
19; 2 Cor. vii. 14; Phil. iii. 17, and κατεπώθη thrice (1 Cor.
xv. 54). This copy has been corrected and retouched by
late hands. Besides the 270 leaves of the book itself, there
are 14 leaves on vellum and paper at beginning and end. (1)
On paper, 8 leaves. Fragment of menology of Apostolos,
xvth century, from Sept. till near end of July. (2) Two
vellum leaves [XIV or later] transposed and one page blank,
scribbled. Matth. vii. 3 ὀφθαλμῷ τοῦ ἀδ.—26 ἄμμον (given
in B.-C. I. 9 or h). (3) On reverse of last leaf of Hebrews
and on seven following vellum leaves with title rubro οἱ εἰς
τὴν ὑπεραγίαν θ̄κ̄ο̄ν̄ τοῦ σεργίου οἶκοι a thanksgiving to
the Blessed Virgin. (4) On wooden cover, Fable of Dog and
Flesh τ̓ φερον ποταμοῦ πλησίων κύ[ων] κρέας | κύψας
ἑαυτὸν ἄλλον εἰς ὕδωρ βλέπει | χάνων δὲ λοιπὸν τῷ κάτο
λαβεῖν κρέας | ἀπεστερ... This MS. contains no ὑπόθεσις
or like matter, and only nine of the Pauline Epistles have
subscriptions. In this MS. again the Catholic Epistles precede
the Pauline, whereof the Hebrews stands last (cf. p. lxxiii).
    The following remarkable readings may be seen in the

Acts and Catholic Epistles, itacisms and other ordinary forms being neglected, as sufficiently stated above. (For peculiar readings in the Pauline Epistles p. lxxxiii). Act. xiv. 10. + σοι λέγω· ἐν τῷ ονοματι του κ͞υ ι͞υ χ͞υ (post φωνῇ syrᵖᵐᵍ CDE ae oˢᶜʳ). 19. *init.* διατριβόντων δὲ αὐτῶν καὶ διδασκόντων ἐπῆλθον δὲ CDE syrᵖᵐᵍ. xviii. 27. προπεμψάμενοι (pro προτρεψάμενοι) A. 1. 4 gˢᶜʳ. xix. 36. τούτων ὄντων A. 1. boˢᶜʳ. xx. 18. ἐπέβημεν solus. 22. συναντήσαντα (– μοι). xxii. 10. *fin.* τί σε δεῖ ποιῆσαι (pro ὧν τ. σ. π.) (H. 100). 15. + τε (post ὧν) E. 100. bcoˢᶜʳ. xxiii. 6. – δὲ. 7. λαλοῦντος B. 100. xxviii. 25. διὰ τοῦ προφήτου ἡσαίου 100. James i. 17, 18 (see p. lxxv, note). iii. 17. εὐδιάκριτος (pro ἀδιακ.) καὶ 100. v. 3. + ταῖς (ante ἐσχάταις) 29. 100. jˢᶜʳ. 9. – ἀδελφοὶ 100. 1 Pet. i. 1. – καὶ (ante βἴθυνίας) 100. ii. 21. + ἵνα κληρονομίαν κληρονομήσητε (ante ἵνα) solus. iv. 3. πορευομένους ℵ. 100. 6. ἄνον gˢᶜʳ 100. 2 Pet. ii. 10. + τὰς θείας δυνάμεις ἢ τὰς ἐκκλησιαστικὰς ἀρχὰς (ante δόξας) solus. 18. ὄντως ὀλίγον ἀποφυγόντας (sic). iii. 11. δὲ οὕτως (pro οὖν) (29. 100). 18. αὐξάνοιτε 100. boˢᶜʳ. 1 John. iv. 9. – ὁ θ͞σ. 17. + πρὸς τὸν ἀνθρωποσαντα (post κρίσεως) solus. v. 6. + καὶ πνεύματος (post αἵματος) AP. 4. aˢᶜʳ. 66**. 2 John. v. 3. + ὑμῖν (post χάρις). καὶ (pro ἔλεος) solus. 3 John. v. 3. – γὰρ ℵ 100. cdˢᶜʳ. 6. ἀληθείᾳ καὶ (ante ἀγάπη) 10. 10. – ἐκ ℵ 100. bhˢᶜʳ. Jude v. 7. σαρκὸς ὀπίσω ἐπέχουσαι solus.

PAUL. EPP.

a. Paul. 264. B.-C. III. 1 (Act. 220), p. lxxiii.

e. Paul. 277, Wake 12 (Evan. 492, Act 193, Apoc. 26). See above, pp. xxxiv, lxxiv.

In the Pauline Epistles (*mutil.* in 1 Cor. xii. 11—xv. 12; xvi. 13—15; Gal. v. 16—vi. 8) each is preceded by the Prologue, ascribed to Œcumenius, and a table of κεφάλαια.

These last are subdivided into μερικαὶ ὑποδιαιρέσεις in Rom., 1, 2 Cor., Eph., Col. (in part), 2 Thess., 1, 2 Tim., Hebr. (in part). Marginal glosses are very numerous in this part of the MS., and in S. Paul's Epistles their value is considerable. We see ι subscript only in gloss on Phil. iv. 18, and in Pauline Epistles there occur ν ἐφελκυστικὸν 111 times, but an hiatus for lack of it 1 Cor. x. 19; 2 Cor. ii. 3. The scribe is a little careless, for there are no less than 26 omissions by ὁμοιοτέλευτον (Rom. i. 25, 30; iv. 10; vi. 15; vii. 3, 8; viii. 31; ix. 33; xi. 19, 20; xii. 1; xiii. 9; 1 Cor. ix. 5; xii. 10; xv. 17, 36; 2 Cor. xii. 14; Eph. iii. 18; 2 Thess. iii. 12; 2 Tim. iv. 10; Tit. i. 11; Heb. iii. 11; iv. 3, 12; vii. 6; ix. 19). Omission from the same beginning 2 Cor. x. 2, 3; Eph. ii. 6. A line or two is lost Eph. iv. 12. The itacisms are 388: viz. η (for ει) 32; ει (for η) 53; η (for ι) 26; ι (for η) 21; αι (for ε) 44; ε (for αι) 19; ο (for ω) 74; ω (for ο) 55; ει (for ι) 12; ι (for ει) 8; η (for ε) 3; ε (for η) 10; η (for υ) 14; υ (for η) 10; η (for οι) 1; οι (for ι) 1 Cor. iv. 10; οι (for ει) Gal. i. 19; οι (for υ) 1 Tim. v. 23; ου (for ω) Tit. i. 13; ii. 4; Heb. viii. 11. One augment is lost 2 Cor. xi. 4: also the reduplication Rom. i. 1; 2 Cor. ix. 3; Gal. ii. 12; iii. 1; Heb. xi. 3, 5: also the usual augment, Rom. iii. 7; xv. 20; 1 Cor. ix. 12; Gal. ii. 13, 14; 1 Tim. vi. 16; 2 Tim. i. 16. We find also the following forms: οὐχ for οὐκ Gal. ii. 14 (most ουκ' and οὐχ' Rom. v. 15 before aspirates): γυναῖκαν 1 Cor. ix. 5; μετετέθηκαν (cf. Cod. ℵ) Heb. xi. 5; ἔπεσαν Heb. iii. 17; παράγγελε 1 Tim. iv. 11; v. 7 p. m.: οὕτω is read only in Gal. iv. 3, 29; Heb. vi. 9. Breathings and accents are somewhat irregular, e.g. ἀβρααμ et ἁβρααμ, ἄγγελος, ὀπίσω 1 Tim. v. 15, ἄρα Gal. iv. 31 (ἆρα ferè), καθῶς 28 times, καθὼς 58 times. So ὅτ'ἀν 1 Cor. xv. 24 or ὅταν, μὴ`, ἂν, μὲ`ν, δὲ`, ἐπεὶ` (12 times). Some changes are plainly s. m. 1 Cor. v. 4; vii. 22, 31, 39; viii. 7, 10; xvi. 10, 19; 2 Cor. ii. 7; viii. 11; ix. 6; xi. 7; Gal. v. 1; 1 Thess. v. 21; Heb. iv. 4; vii. 2. For various readings compare ROM. i. 5. – ἐν. 17. θ͞ω (pro θ͞υ). ii. 5. + καὶ (ante δικαιοκρισίας) (ℵᶜ). iii. 29. μόνων (B). v. 9. – δι' αὐτοῦ. 14. – ἐπὶ secund. 16. παραπτώσεων (pro παραπτωμάτων). vi. 14. οὐκ ἔτι

CRITICA SACRA. lxxix

(*pro* οὐ *prim.*) (א). vii. 5. – τῇ. viii. 16. ὑμῶν (*pro* ἡμῶν).
19. πίστεως (*pro* κτίσεως). ix. 20. – οὕτως. x. 10. στόμα.
xi. 15. – ἡ *prim.* 18. βλαστάνεις (*pro* βαστάζεις). 26. ἀσε-
βεῖς (*pro* ἀσεβείας). xv. 16. – ἁγίῳ. 26. διακονίαν (*pro*
κοινωνίαν). 1 COR. ii. 12. + τὸ ἐκ (*ante* τοῦ κόσμου). λαλοῦμεν
(*pro* ἐλάβομεν). iii. 7. – τι. 21. εἰσίν (*pro* ἐστίν). vi. 5. ἔνι
(*pro* ἐστιν) (אBC). vii. 17. περιπατεῖτε. 20. + ἐν (*ante* ᾗ).
viii. 1. + δὲ (*ante* γνῶσις). 4. + δὲ (*post* περὶ). 7. εἰς (*pro*
ὡς). ix. 5. – ἐξουσίαν, 14. διετάξατο. x. 18. θυσίαν
(– τὰς). 19. – τι *bis.* – ἤ. 20. ὅτι ἂν (*pro* ἃ) θύει.
xv. 31. ὑμετέραν (אλ). xvi. 12. – πρὸς ὑμᾶς. 17. + καὶ
(*post* δὲ). 2 COR. i. 4. ᾗ (*pro* ἧσ). 14. ἐπεγνώσατε.
ii. 1. – τοῦτο. iii. 3. ἐγγεγραμμένοι. iv. 13. – καὶ *secund.*
17. – ἡμῖν. v. 15. κρίνοντας. – εἰ (אB). vi. 10. καὶ ἀεὶ
(*pro* ἀεὶ δὲ). vii. 4. – μοι *secund.* 7. – με. 12. φανερωθέντος.
viii. 11. – τὸ (*ante* ἐπιτελέσαι). 12. – ἤ. ix. 3. κενωθὲν.
x. 7. αὐτῷ (*pro* ἑαυτῷ). 8. – καὶ *prim.* (אcscr). xi. 4. καθῶς
(*pro* καλῶς). xiii. 7. ἡμᾶς (*pro* ὑμᾶς), ἵνα μὴ ἡμεῖς (*pro* οὐχ
ἵνα). 12. – ἁγίῳ. GAL. i. 14. πάντας (*pro* πολλοὺς).
ii. 15. – οὐκ ἐξ ἐθνῶν. iii. 17. – εἰς χν (אB). iv. 29. ποτὲ
(*pro* τότε). v. 2. γράφω (*pro* λέγω). 6. τίς (*pro* τι).
EPH. iv. 28. κλέπτης (*pro* κλέπτων). PHIL. i. 7. ὑμῶν (*pro*
ὑμᾶς). ii. 4. τῶν (*pro* τὰ *secund.*). iii. 2. καταμονήν. 4. καὶ
γε (*pro* καίπερ). iv. 10. δη ποτε (*pro* ἤδη ποτὲ). COL. i. 22.
ἡμᾶς (*pro* ὑμᾶς). 24. – μου (אB). 25. – μοι. ii. 12. συνερ-
γείας (*pro* ἐνεργείας). iii. 15. πνι (*pro* σώματι). 21. παροργ-
ίζετε (*pro* ἐρεθίζετε) (א). 23. + μετ' εὐνοίας (*ante* ἐργάζεσθε).
iv. 12. πεπληροφορημένοι (אB). 1 THESS. i. 1. ὑμῶν (*pro*
ἡμῶν). ii. 8. ὁμηρόμενοι (אB). 15. – ιν. ἡμᾶς (*pro* ὑμᾶς).
19. ὑμῶν (*pro* ἡμῶν). iii. 5. ποτε (*pro* πῶς). 9. χαίρωμεν
δι' ὑμῶν. v. 23. – καὶ *prim.* 2 THESS. i. 6. + καὶ (*post*
εἴπερ). 10. πιστεύσωσιν. ii. 14. ὑμῶν (*pro* ἡμῶν *prim.*).
iii. 4. πρὸς (*pro* ἐφ'). 1 TIM. i. 4. + τῇ (*ante* πίστει).
18. αὐτοῖς (*pro* αὐταῖς). ii. 10. θεοσεβεῖν. 14. + ὁ (*ante*
ἀδὰμ). iii. 2. – σώφρονα. v. 18. μὴ (*pro* οὐ) (oscr). 19. κατα-
δέχου (oscr). 24. – καὶ. vi. 3. προσέρχεσθε. 16. – ἀθα-
νασίαν. 2 TIM. ii. 5. ἀθλητὴς ἀθλήσει (– τις). 16. – δὲ.

19. κ̄ῡ (pro χ̄ῡ) (‫א‬). iii. 13. — τό. iv. 21. εὔουλος. TITUS
i. 6. ἔχοντες. 11. — ὅλους. 14. ἐντολάς. iii. 10. αἱρετικῶν
ἀνῶν. 12. πρὸς σὲ ᾿Αρτεμὸν ἐλθεῖν. PHILEM. 3. + ἡμῶν
(post κυρίου). HEB. i. 13. σου (pro μου). ii. 11. οὐ καταισχύ-
νεται. 17. ἁμαρτήμασι. iv. 1. — οὖν. 12. — πᾶσαν. v. 3.
+ καὶ (post καθὼς) (eˢᶜʳ). — καὶ (post οὕτως). vi. 8. ἀτάραχος
(pro κατάρας). 11. ἐνδείξασθαι. vii. 1. Αὐτὸς (pro οὗτος).
ix. 14. ἡμῶν (pro ὑμῶν) (ADK complut.). 15. παραβάντων
(pro -άσεων). — τῇ. x. 33. + ὡς (pro δὲ). 34. — ἐν (‫א‬).
xi. 2. αὐτῇ (pro ταύτη). 13. λαμβάνοντες. — καὶ πεισθέντες.
28. ἐποίησε. xii. 11. — μὲν. 24. τοῦ (pro τὸν). ῎Αβελ
(Chrys.). xiii. 5. εἶπεν (pro εἴρηκεν). 9. παραφέρεσθε (‫א‬).
— ἐν.
Many glosses occur about 2 Cor., Gal., Phil., &c.

f. Paul. 244, Wake 34 (Evan. 503, Act. 190, Apoc. 27).
See above, pp. xxxvi, lxxv.

The Pauline Epistles are complete, except Heb. vii. 26—
ix. 28 (two leaves). The last leaf of the Epistles (131 b) on
the reverse of the end of Hebrews contains thrice over in a
late hand the initial words of S. Matthew, so that the place
of the Gospels (which has only 29 lines in page) seems not
due to a recent binder, though this may not have been its
original position. From Rom. xi. (88 chapters) ν ἐφελκυστικὸν
occurs 81 times, often with nouns: in the Gospels as stated
above (p. xxxvii) it occurs 196 times (also Act. 90 times),
which also contain ten ὁμοιοτέλευτα and 106 itacisms: viz. ω
(for ου) 2 ; ου (for ω) 2 ; υ (for η) 1 ; η (for υ) 2 ; ε (for αι) 4 ;
αι (for ε) 11 ; ι (for ει) 2 ; ει (for ι) 7 ; ει (for η) 14 ; η (for ει)
8 ; οι (for υ) 3 ; υ (for οι) 2 ; ω (for ο) 12 ; ο (for ω) 15 ; η (for
ι) 10 ; ι (for η) 3 ; ε (for η) 6 ; η (for ε) 3. The ευ (for Attic
ηυ) always. Itacisms are quite few, and in the 88 chapters of
S. Paul only 100: viz. αι (for ε) 9 ; ε (for αι) 3 ; ο (for ω) 12 ;
ω (for ο) 16 ; υ (for η) 8 ; η (for υ) 13 ; ι (for ει) 12 ; ει (for ι)
1 ; ε (for η) 6 ; ει (for η) 8 ; η (for ει) 6 ; ου (for ω) 2 ; η (for
ι) 3 ; ι (for η) 1. Prologues of Œcumenius and tables of

κεφάλαια precede each Epistle. With these Euthalian capita
are numerals of shorter capita *p. m.* Corrections, chiefly
p. m., but for breathings and accents *s. m.*, up to 1 Cor.
Breathing and accents much neglected or set wrong: few
compound words are accentuated separately. Few Alexandrine forms, e.g. ἀνηγγέλλη Rom. xv. 21. Rarer readings are
(often with Cod. 69): ROM. xi. 35. παρέδωκεν. xiii. 9. – ἑτέρα.
xv. 18. – τι. – οὐ *secund.* 1 COR. i. 12. ὑμῶν (*pro* ὑμῖν).
ii. 4. ἀνθρωπίνοις (*pro* -ης). 12. ἀπὸ (*pro* ὑπὸ) (Cod. 69).
iv. 6. + μὴ (*ante* φυσιοῦσθε). xi. 6. κειρέσθων. κειρέσθαι.
xiii. 3. καθήσομαι. xv. 42. + τε (*post* σπείρεται). 2 COR. vi.
2. fin. ἡμέραι σωτηρίας. vii. 8. σωτηρίαν (*pro* ὥραν). 13. + δὲ
s. m. (*post* ἐπὶ *prim.*). viii. 14. ὃ (*pro* ὁ) *bis.* xiii. 3. ἀλλ’
ἀδυνατεῖ. GAL. ii. 16. – ἰησοῦν. iii. 17. ὁ μετὰ ἔτη τριακόσια
p. m. τετρακόσια *s. m.* v. 1. – στήκετε *s. m.* τῇ ἐλευθερίᾳ
οὖν χσ ἠλευθέρωσεν· στήκετε καὶ *p. m.* (Cod. 69). vi. 18.
– χριστοῦ. EPH. ii. 16. ἀποκαταλλάξει. – τῷ. iii. 3. προε-
γράψαμεν. – ἐν. iv. 6. καὶ ἐπὶ πᾶσιν ἡμῖν (69). 32. ἑαυτούς.
fin. ἡμῖν. PHIL. i. 26. – πάλιν. ii. 4. τὸ (*pro* τὰ *secund.*).
COL. i. 5. ἡμῖν (*pro* ὑμῖν). 13. ἐκ τοῦ σκότους τῆς ἐξουσίας.
1 THESS. ii. 12. [μαρτυρούμενος] (69). 18. ὑμᾶς (*pro* ἡμᾶς).
iii. 4. fin. ὑμῶν. iv. 13. θέλομεν. κοιμημένων. v. 4. γὰρ
(*pro* δὲ). 2 THESS. i. 9. – τοῦ. iii. 5. + τὴν (*ante* ὑπομονὴν).
7. παρέλαβον. 14. ὑμῶν (*pro* ἡμῶν). 1 TIM. iii. 2. νηφάλειον
(iv. 11 ε *supra s. m.*). 12. γενοῦ. v. 11. ἐθέλουσιν. 2 TIM.
i. 18. ἔλεον. iv. 13. κατέλιπον. TITUS i. 1. χυ ιυ. ii. 7. πᾶσιν.
iii. 8. – τῷ. PHILEM. 6. + ἔργου (*ante* ἀγαθοῦ). HEB. ii. 17.
– τὸν. iv. 5. – εἰ. v. 8. οἰκονομίαν (*pro* ὑπακόην). vi. 2.
κρίσεως (*pro* κρίματος). vii. 13. ἐφ’ ὧν. 21. + εἶ (*post* σὺ).
23. + τῶ (*pro* τὸ). x. 9. τὸ θέλημά σου. ὁ θσ. xii. 5. ὑμῶν
(*pro* ὑμῖν). 7. εἰς (*pro* εἰ). 15. ἐν χολῇ. 17. – καὶ. 27. – μὴ.
xiii. 3. κακοχουμένων (69). 5. ἐγκαταλείπω. 21. – τῶν
αἰώνων (69).

A collation of the Gospels with Codd. 59.66 Wake 12 is
subjoined in this volume, pp. 60 sqq. It is often with Codd.
BCDy^scr. Note especially in the early chapters.

MATTHEW i. 6. – δὲ *secund.* 20. φοβηθεὶς. ii. 4. + τοὺς

(*ante* γραμματεῖς). 13. τῶν μάγων (*pro* αὐτῶν). iii. 5. +πᾶσα (*ante* ἱεροσόλυμα). 12. – αὐτοῦ *tert.* iv. 1. ὑπὸ τοῦ π̅ν̅σ̅ εἰς τὴν ἔρημον. 17. ἐν (*pro* ἐπὶ). 18. – δὲ. 23. ὁ ι̅σ̅ ὅλην τὴν γαλιλαίαν. v. 30. ἀπέλθη (*pro* βληθῇ). 31. – δὲ. αὐτὴν (*pro* αὐτῇ). 32. πᾶς ὁ ἀπολύων (*pro* ὃς ἂν ἀπολύσῃ). 36. ποιῆσαι ἢ μέλαιναν. 40. *fin.* + σου. 47. φίλους (*pro* ἀδελφοὺς). 48. ὡς (*pro* ὥσπερ). vii. 12. καὶ ὑμεῖς οὕτως. 23. + πάντες (*ante* οἱ ἐργαζόμενοι). 24. – οὖν. viii. 17. ὑπὸ (*pro* διὰ). 29. – ἰησοῦ. 31. *fin.* + καὶ ἐπέτρεψεν αὐτοῖς. ix. 6. – τότε. 8. ἐφοβήθησαν (*pro* ἐθαύμασαν). 11. ἔλεγον (*pro* εἶπον). 13. δικαίους καλέσαι. 15. + χρόνον (*post* ὅσον). 16. ἐν (*pro* ἐπὶ). 17. ἀπόλλυνται· ἀλλὰ οἶνον νέον εἰς ἀσκοὺς βάλλουσι καινούς. ἀμφότεροι. 25. ἐλθὼν. ἤγειρε. 33. οὕτως ἐφάνη. 35. *fin.* + καὶ πολλοὶ ἠκολούθησαν αὐτῶι. 36. ἐπ᾽ αὐτοὺς (*pro* περὶ αὐτῶν) (y^scr). x. 1. + ὁ ι̅σ̅ (*post* προσκαλ.). 2. – τὰς. 4. ὃς καὶ παρέδωκεν (*pro* ὁ καὶ π.). 10. *fin.* – ἐστιν. 14. + ἔξω (*post* ἐξερχόμενοι) (y^scr). 25. τῶι δούλωι (*pro* ὁ δοῦλος) (y^scr). 29. τῆς γῆς. 30. ἠρίθμηνται (y^scr). 31. + γὰρ (*post* πολλῶν). 42. + τῶν ἐλαχίστων (*post* τούτων). xii. 36. ἀμὴν δὲ λέγω ὑμῖν. 46. λαλῆσαι αὐτῷ. 47. ἰδεῖν (*pro* σοι λαλῆσαι). 48. λέγοντι (*pro* εἰπόντι). xiii. 51. – κύριε (BD). 52. λέγει (*pro* ὁ δὲ εἶπεν) (D). προφέρει (*pro* ἐκβάλλει). 54. + πᾶσα (*ante* ἡ σοφία) (D). 55. ἰωάννης (*pro* ἰωσῆς). 57. – αὐτοῦ *prim.* (BD). xiv. 3. ἐν τῇ φυλακῇ ἀπέθετο (B). 6. γενομένων (*pro* ἀγομένων (C). 8. θέλω ἵνα μοι δῶς (*pro* δός μοι φησίν). 9. λυπηθεὶς (– καὶ) (BD). 11. + τὸ κοράσιον (*ante* ἤνεγκε). 12. πτῶμα (BD). 16. – ἰησοῦς (א*D). 24. ἦν μέσον τῆς θαλάσσης. 25. ἦλθε. – ὁ ι̅σ̅. 26. – οἱ μαθηταὶ (א). ἐπὶ τὴν θάλασσαν περιπατοῦντα. 28. ὁ πέτρος εἶπεν αὐτῶι (B*). 32. ἀναβάντων (BD). 33. προσελθόντες. 33. ἐπὶ τὴν γῆν εἰς γεννησαρέτ (BD). 36. + κἂν (*ante* μόνον).

These specimens may shew the worth of this copy. In the Gospels it much resembles Cod. D, also Cod. 61. But Cod. א *p. m.* only in Matth. xiv. 16.

β. Paul. 265. B.-C. III. 37 (Act. 221), p. lxxv.

The Pauline Epistles in this remarkable copy present a full century of peculiar and solitary readings which bear emphatic testimony to its singular value. Rom. i. 10. – δεό-μενος. 18. – θῦ p. m. (et cod. 47). ii. 6. ἀνταποδώσει. iii. 10. – ὅτι. 25. αἵματι αὐτοῦ (37 Origen). v. 9. μελλούσης κολάσεως (pro ὀργῆς). 21. θῦ (pro κυ) solus. vii. 8. γὰρ (pro δὲ) solus. 18. καρδία (pro σαρκὶ) solus. viii. 4. θυ (pro νόμου) solus. 32. δέδωκεν (pro παρέδωκεν) solus. ix. 16. τρέχοντος (pro θέλοντος). θέλοντος (pro τρέχοντος) solus. 19. θελήματι (pro βουλήματι) solus. x. 5. + αὐτοῦ (post δικαιοσύνην) solus. 12. – πάντων solus. xi. 11. πταί-σωσι (pro πέσωσι). 17. κοινωνὸς solus. 31. + ἐν (ante τῷ ὑμετέρῳ) solus. xii. 20. – πυρὸς solus. xiii. 9. τῷ λόγῳ τούτῳ (pro τούτῳ τῷ λόγῳ). xiv. 10. – τοῦ (ante χυ). 19. – τὰ secund. solus. 21. σκανδαλίζεται ἢ προσκόπτει (– ἢ ἀσθενεῖ) solus. xvi. 1. – ὑμῖν solus. 18. κοινῆς ἀπάτης (pro καὶ εὐλογίας) solus. 24. – ἀμήν. 25—27. om. hoc loco. 1 Cor. i. 6. – ἐν (ante ὑμῖν) solus. iii. 6. ηὔξησεν solus. iv. 6. + μὴ (ante φυσιοῦσθε) b**ehnˢᶜʳ ¹. vii. 6. οὐκ (pro οὐ κατ᾽) solus. viii. 3. οὕτως (pro οὗτος) solus. x. 12. πέσοι solus. 21. πιεῖν solus. xii. 6. ὁ δὲ αὐτός ἐστιν ὁ θσ solus. xiii. 3. – μου secund. p. m. solus. xiv. 1. – δὲ prim. solus. 5. λέγειν (pro λαλεῖν) solus. 12. πρὸς οἰκοδομὴν τῆς ἐκ-κλησίας, solus. xv. 18. – ἐν χῳ solus. 20. ἐκ νεκρῶν ἐγήγερται. xvi. 18. ἡμῶν (pro ἐμὸν). 2 Cor. i. 12. + τῆς συνειδήσεως (post καύχησις). ii. 6. – τῶν solus. v. 19. + αὐ-τοῖς (post ἡμῖν) solus. ix. 2. παρευεσκεύασε p. m. xii. 12. ἐν σημείοις καὶ τεραϊ (– καὶ δυνάμεσι) cf. bˢᶜʳ. xiii. 13. + καὶ πρσ (post θυ) dn**ˢᶜʳ. Gal. ii. 10. + δὲ (post μόνον) solus. 16. εἰ μὴ (pro ἐὰν μὴ) solus. iii. 17. τριακόσια (pro τετρα-κοσια) (67.69). 19. ἐξετέθη solus. 22. – πάντα (ante ὑπὸ).

Eph. ii. 19. + ἀδελφοὶ (ante οὐκέτι) initio pericopes. iii. 8. θυ

---

¹ These letters refer to the MSS. collated in the Appendix to the Codex Augiensis.

(*pro* χ̄ῡ) *solus.* iv. 2. ἀλλήλους *solus.* v. 6. γὰρ ταῦτα *solus.*
vi. 4. *init.* – καί. 13. στῆναι (*pro* ἀντιστῆναι) *solus.* 21.
– διάκονος ℵ *p. m.* PHIL. i. 4. ἐπὶ (*pro* ἐν) *solus.* 6. + εἰς
(*ante* αὐτὸ) *solus.* 29. αὐτὸ (*pro* αὐτοῦ). ii. 1. εἴτϊς σπλάγχνα
καὶ οἰκτιρμοί· εἴ τις κοινωνία π̄ν̄σ̄ *solus.* iii. 19. – ὁ *solus.*
21. + καὶ (*ante* μετασχηματίσει) *solus.* iv. 3. ναὶ καὶ σὲ
(– γνήσιε) *solus.* COL. i. 5. ἡμῖν (*pro* ὑμῖν) *solus.* 6. ἔγνωτε
solus. 27. τὸ πλάτος *solus.* ii. 14. ἦρεν αὐτῶ (*pro* ἦρκεν
αὐτὸ) *solus.* iv. 3. *init.* καὶ δέομαι ἵνα *solus.* 1 THESS. iii. 9.
+ καὶ (*ante* ἔμπροσθεν). iv. 14. + διὰ (*ante* τοὺς κοιμηθέντας).
2 THESS. i. 7. – τοῖς *solus.* 9. αἰώνιαν ὄλεθρον *solus.* ii. 10.
εὐδοκίας (*pro* ἀδικίας) cf. ver. 12. 1 TIM. ii. 5. καὶ εἰς (*pro*
εἷς καὶ). v. 18. *fin.* + ἐστι. vi. 16. – ὃν εἶδεν οὐδεὶς ἄνων οὐδὲ
ἰδεῖν δύναται *solus.* 2 TIM. iii. 6. ἐκδύνοντες *solus.* αἰχμα-
λωτίζοντες (– τὰ) *solus.* iv. 17. παρέστη μοι *solus.* τὸ κήρυγμα
δι᾽ ἐμοῦ oˢᶜʳ. TITUS iii. 8. τούτου *solus.* PHILEM. 24. λουκᾶς·
καὶ δημᾶς *solus.* HEB. i. 3. + τοῦ θρόνου (*post* δεξιᾷ) dˢᶜʳ.
8. + καὶ εἰς τὸν αἰῶνα (*ante* τοῦ αἰῶνος) *solus.* ii. 1. – ἡμᾶς.
10. ἡμῶν (*pro* αὐτῶν) *solus.* iv. 5. – ἐν τούτῳ *solus.* 16.
προσερχόμεθα P*a*cdgkl*o. vii. 3. – μήτε ἀρχὴν ἡμερῶν
μήτε ζωῆς τέλος *solus.* 9. + διὰ (*ante* λευὶ) *solus.* 11. ἐν
(*pro* ἐπ᾽) *solus.* viii. 7. σκηνὴ (*pro* ἐκείνη) *solus.* x. 11. προσ-
φέρων θυσίας πολλάκις *solus.* xi. 11. + δὲ (*post* πίστει)
solus. xii. 25. παραιτήσασθε *solus.* xiii. 11. – περὶ ἁμαρτίας
solus. A goodly list of solitary various readings truly.

δ. Paul. 266. B.-C. II. 4 [X or XI]. Apoc. 89 (cf. Evan.
603, Act. 231).

The history of this beautiful manuscript is more curious
than pleasant to tell. In 1871 the Baroness Burdett-Coutts imported from Janina (see above pp. xxi, xxii) 67 vellum leaves
in coarse velvet binding, containing S. Paul's Epistles from
Ephesians downwards, followed by the Apocalypse, which,
after I had collated them, she presented to the Library of Sir
Roger Cholmely's School, Highgate, where they remain. In
the same year 1871 Sir Ivor B. Guest sold (with three others)

to the British Museum (Additional MSS. 28,815) a fragment containing the Gospels, Acts, Catholic and Pauline Epistles down to Galatians, the rest of the original volume being evidently torn out of the book, after it had been already sumptuously bound with silver-gilt plates. In 1875 Mr Edward A. Guy, of Miami University, Oxford, Ohio, U.S.A., on comparing my description of B.-C. II. 4 contained in the second edition of *Plain Introduction* with the Museum fragment, concluded that the two portions originally formed one magnificent copy of the whole New Testament, whereof not more than twenty such are known to exist. When I borrowed the Highgate Codex and took it to the Museum, I saw that the illuminated heading and initial capital on the first page (Eph. i.) of B.-C. II. 4 had been worked off through damp on the verso of the last leaf (302) of the Museum book : while on the other hand the red κεφάλαια of Gal. vi. in the Museum book was visible on the top of the first leaf of B.-C. II. 4. The identity of the copies being thus ascertained, it is a pity that the two fragments cannot be brought together, but the Governors of Highgate School prize their portion, at least for the sake of the donor, who cannot very urgently recall her own gift. It is said that Mr Guy collated the Museum portion, as I did B.-C. II. 4, including the Apocalypse, but I have not access to Mr Guy's work or time to recollate it, so that I must leave it to some industrious and more fortunate student. I am told that Mr Guy has now joined one of the obscurer American sects, which is indifferent or averse to these sacred studies. The complete manuscript was a grand folio, on fine vellum, of the tenth or eleventh centuries, 11½ inches long, by 9½ wide, containing 369 leaves, with 30 lines on a page, having two pictures of S. Luke (one before the Acts), one of S. John, with illuminated headings. The Eusebian tables with their preliminary Epistola Carpiano, may have perished, for the margin of the Gospels exhibits both the Ammonian sections and Eusebian numerals, though there is a Gospel Harmony at the foot of leaves 17, 18, and many brief marginal scholia throughout *primâ manu*. The τίτλοι are also found in gold letters. In the Epistles are also τίτλοι at head and foot of pages, and κεφάλαια numbered in margin, but no chapter divisions in the Apocalypse. At the end on three leaves is the unfinished ἐπίγραμμα of Dorotheus, Bishop of Tyre in Julian's reign, on the 70 disciples and the twelve Apostles. This is found in some three other manuscripts, in Erasmus' first edition of the New Testament (1516) and partially in Stephen's 1550. The Hebrews precedes the Pastoral Epistles. In S. Paul's Epistles ι ascript and ν ἐφελκυστικὸν always with verbs (except Heb. i. 14; xii. 8, 11) are frequent, and itacisms in all 49 times : αι (for ε) 5 ; ε (for αι) 2 ; ι (for ει) 5; ει (for ι) 8; ει (for η) 5 ; η (for ει) 3; ω (for ο) 6 ; ο (for ω) 9 ; ι (for η) 2 ; η (for ι) 3 ; ε (for η) 1 ; υ (for οι) 1. υ and η in plurals of pronouns interchanged 13 times. Omissions by ὁμοιοτέλευτον Phil. ii. 20 ; 2 Thess. iii. 4; 1 Tim. i. 9 ; 2 Tim. iv. 10 ; mostly corrected *s. m.* which corrector is met with in about 13 other places : in marg. *p.m.*, Eph. v. 5; Col. iv. 11. Rare or remarkable readings in the portion collated and now buried at Highgate, are PHIL. ii. 4. τὸ ἑτέρου (*pro* τὰ ἑτέρων). 23. ἐξαῦτις. 26. + ἰδεῖν (*post* ὑμᾶς). 30. πληρώσῃ. iii. 7. ἀλλ᾽ ἅτινα ἦν μὴ (*pro* μοι). 8. − γε. COL. i. 20. ἐπὶ (*pro* ἐν). ii. 13. ἡμᾶς (*pro* ὑμᾶς). ἡμῶν (*pro* ὑμῶν). + ἡμᾶς (*post* συνεζωοποίησεν).

iii. 3. − τῷ (ante θ̄ω̄). 1 THESS. i. 5. − ἐν (ante π̄ν̄ῑ). ii. 6. ἀπ᾽ (*pro* ἀπὸ). iv. 6. διεμαρτυρόμεθα. 17. οἱ ζῶντες ἡμεῖς. 2 THESS. i. 4. ὑμᾶς (*pro* ἡμᾶς). iii. 8. ἐλάβομεν (*pro* ἐφάγομεν). HEB. i. 11. αὐτοῦ (*pro* αὐτοὶ). ii. 1. παραρυῶμεν. ix. 11. Ῑσ̄ *p. m.* (*pro* χ̄σ̄). x. 1. − αὐταῖς δύνανται. xii. 1. τρέχομεν. 28. λατρεύομεν. xiii. 17. + δὲ (*post* πείθεσθε). 1 TIM. i. 1. κ̄ῡ χ̄ῡ ῑῡ. ii. 7. − ἐν χ̄ω̄. iii. 3. − μὴ αἰσχροκερδῆ. iv. 8. ἐπαγγελίας. 2 TIM. i. 14. παραθήκην. *fin.* ὑμῖν. 15. − οἱ. φύγελος. 18. ἔλεον (*non ver.* 16). ii. 8. − χ̄ῡ. iii. 6. − τὸ. iv. 16. − μου. 17. − μοι. 20. ἀπέλειπον. TITUS i. 1. − δὲ. ii. 2. πρεσβυτέρους. νηφαλέους. 8. περὶ ἡμῶν λέγειν. 8, 10. [ὑμῶν]. PHILEM. v. 22. + καὶ (*post* ὅτι).

APOCALYPSE.[1]

e. Apoc. 26, Wake 12 (Evan. 492, Act. 193, Paul 277).   See
pp. xxxiv, lxxiv, lxxvii.

On the same page and column as the end of Epistle to
Hebrews stands Oecumenius' prologue to Apocalypse; then
follow Andreas' Preface and a list of the 72 κεφάλαια of Apocalypse, whose numerals *rubro* are set in the margin with rubric
capitals, where κεφ. or lessons begin. This part of Wake 12
contains no marginal glosses such as abound in the Pauline
Epistles (p. lxxviii). It is written in two columns of 36 lines
each, with title *rubro* Ἀποκάλυψις δοθῆσα τῷ θεολόγῳ ἰωάννῃ.
(So Wake 34.) At the end of the volume (Fol. 231 b) are
several (7½) pages περὶ τῶν οἰκουμενικῶν ζʹ συνόδων, including περὶ τοπικῶν συνόδων, not much like Cod. 69. No ν ἐφελκυστικὸν except εἶπεν capp. vii. 14; xvii. 7: a hiatus cap. xiii.
14. No ι ascript, but eleven cases of ι subscript. There are 15
itacisms: η (for ει) 5; ει (for η) 2; ει (for ι) 2; υ (for η) cap.
xx. 2; αι (for ε) 3; η (for ι) 5; ι (for η) 2; ω (for ου) cap.
xi. 10; ω (for ο) 12; ο (for ω) 16, (chiefly μετοπον). There
occur ὁμοιτέλευτα cap. xviii. 23; xxi. 13, and omission from
the same beginning cap. xvi. 13. Breathings are somewhat
careless, e.g. ὅρος, ὧδε semper, ἑστῶτας, οὐ μὴ, οὐχ semel.
For the dialysis .. we often have —, as in Cod. ℵ. Commas are
found when quite needless. In cap. iii. 17 (;) stands for semicolon, mostly for interrogation. Many changes made by *p. m.*
on revising, and original readings look as if washed out (as in
Cod. Evan. D), but cap. xxii. 19 looks *s. m.* This copy has
many rare or even singular readings: e.g. capp. i. 11; ii. 7 *bis*,
17, 20, 25, 26; iii. 1; iv. 3; vi. 14; vii. 1, 12; viii. 2; ix. 5, 20;
xvi. 18, 19; xvii. 8, 16, 17; xviii. 6, 7, 8; xix. 2, 9, 17, 19;
xx. 8, 11, 12; xxi. 5, 7, 13, 22, 25; xxii. 1, 2, 3, 6, 21 (Cod. A).
This is Caspar Wetstein's Cod. 26, who made 87 errors in
collating it, and not much less in representing Cod. 27. We
have corrected his oversight by annexing (*sic*) to the true
reading. See Part III.

---

[1] Full collation of these three MSS. is given in Part III. pp. 143 ff.

f. Apoc. 27, Wake 34 (Evan. 503, Act. 190, Paul. 244).
See above p. xxxvi.

This copy begins in Fol. 12 b in the middle of the page without ὑπόθεσις or table of κεφάλαια. It contains the unusual number of twelve omissions by ὁμοιοτέλευτον : cap. iii. 7 ; iv. 7 ; vi. 6 ; ix. 2 ; xii. 11 ; xiv. 8 ; xv. 7 ; xvii. 6 ; xviii. 16, 19 ; xix. 15 ; xx. 5. Unusual grammatical forms are rare, but ἀπῆλθα Apoc. x. 9. Ν ἐφελκυστικὸν occurs in the whole MS. 349 times : viz. Catholic Epp. 20, Pauline 90, Gospels 196, Apoc. 43. For rare readings compare Apoc. i. 6; ii. 5; iii. 2 ; iv. 6 ; vi. 2, 27 ; vii. 2 ; viii. 6 ; ix. 9 ; xi. 15 ; xix. 12; xx. 12; xxi. 10. Yet after all, our collation (pp. 143 ff.) shews Wake 12, Wake 34, B.-C. ii. 4 (e f δ) very much together : their agreement closely coincides with the Complutensian edition.

δ. Apoc. 89. B.-C. ii. 4 (Evan. 603, Act. 231, Paul. 266).
See p. lxxxiv.

This codex, whose fate has been described above, has no preface except its simple title in gold, Ἀποκάλυψις τοῦ ἁγίου ἀποστόλου· καὶ εὐαγγελιστοῦ ἰῶ. There is no table of κεφάλαια or their numerals in the margin, but small and plain capitals at the beginning of lines, where the sense is broken. The writing is beautifully clear, breathings and accents mostly regular. The ὁμοιοτέλευτα are in cap. xx. 5 ; xxi. 15; xxii. 6. No ι is seen, ascript or subscript : ν ἐφελκυστικὸν appears 12 times, itacisms do not exceed 11 : η (for ι) cap. xvii. 4 ; η (for ει) iii. 7 ; vi. 10 ; ει (for ι) iv. 3; αι (for ε) xviii. 13 ; ο (for ω) xiv. 1; ω (for ο) v. 6; ix. 16; xix. 10; xx. 8 p. m.; xxii. 9. A few corrections in the text look all primâ manu : others also p. m. in the margin are cap. v. 14 ; xi. 15 ; xix. 10. For rarer or interesting readings compare cap. i. 4, 9, 17 ; ii. 8. 10, 18, 22, 25, 27 ; iii. 1, 2, 3, 7, 9, 12, 16, 17, 18; iv. 3, 4, 11 ; v. 8, 9 ; vi. 9, 10 ; vii. 9, 14 ; viii. 8, 12 ; ix. 2, 6, 7, 16,

19 ; xii. 8, 12 ; xiii. 4, 11, 16, 17 ; xiv. 5, 7, 8, 19 ; xv. 2, 4 ;
xvi. 8, 21 ; xvii. 6, 8 ; xviii. 2, 7, 11, 13 ; xix. 1, 17 ; xx. 7, 12,
13 ; xxi. 4, 5, 6, 7, 23, 24 ; xxii. 3, 5. (CH [i.e. *note*] in margin
of cap. iii. 20.)

APOSTOLOS.[1]

u. Apostolos 64, B.-C. I. 10 (Evst. 251). See p. lxvi.

i. Apost. 65. B.-C. III. 24.

This is one of the somewhat few lectionaries proper (as
distinguished from euchologies, liturgical books and Typica)
which furnish lessons from the Apostolos only, not from the
Gospels. It is a vellum folio of the twelfth or thirteenth
century, contains 160 leaves, 10½ inches by 8, written in two
columns of 28 lines on a page. With red musical notes and
much red for lections, and verses from Psalms before the
lessons. The text reaches from the second Sunday after
Easter (the MS. beginning Act. vi. 6 αὐτοῖς τὰς χείρας), through
the Ascension, Pentecost, to the sixteenth week after Pentecost, and the Saturdays and Sundays τῶν νηστειῶν, ending at
Evensong Easter Eve (Rom. vi. 3—11) Fol. 114. The Menology
(Foll. 114 b—160) has almost no lessons given at length (yet
2 Pet. i. 10—19, Fol. 157; Phil. ii. 5.—11, Fol. 158; Act. xiii.
25—39, Fol. 159), but overflows with rubrical directions. It
is very full, and begins with September, ends abruptly Aug.
29, and with some miscellaneous lessons. But all is ill-written,
many lessons are lost, many words are omitted by ὁμοιοτέ-

---

[1] In addition to those Lectionaries here given from the Burdett collection
add the following, now deposited by her in the library of Highgate Grammar
School (*see* p. lxxxiv), awaiting such study as the editor's decaying sight and
advanced age have denied him. May this collation, which he once contem-
plated, reward his more fortunate successor with such a store of critical
novelties as he himself lighted on in 1845 at the British Museum in yᵒʳ
(Burney 22). The manuscripts are B.-C. I. 8; I. 23; I. 24; II. 3; II. 5; III.
21; III. 43.

λευτον, and the itacisms are numberless, and at times quite
monstrous, e.g. *αἰγήροντε* (1 Cor. xv. 32), so that much weight
cannot be attached to its evidence. It apparently belongs to
the Constantinopolitan diocese, many of whose archbishops
are named, and in the menology for May 21 (Fol. 152 b) we
commemorate τῶν ἐν ἁγίοις βασιλέων ἡμῶν κωσταντίνου καὶ
ἐλένης.

v.	Apost. 66.	B.-C. iii. 29 (Evst. 252).	See p. lxvii.
w.	Apost. 67.	B.-C. iii. 42 (Evst. 253).	See p. lxviii.
x.	Apost. 78.	B.-C. iii. 44 (Evst. 290).	See p. lxxi.
y.	Apost. 82.	B.-C. iii. 46 (Evst. 249).	See p. lxxi.
zz.	Apost. 68.	B.-C. iii. 53 (Evst. 253).	See p. lxxii.

EARLY EDITIONS OF THE GREEK TESTAMENT.

In addition to the various readings of the manuscripts of
the Greek Testament previously described in this Introduction, we have added the variations from what we regard as
the received or standard text of the third edition of Stephen
1550 (as represented in Scrivener's editio major 1887) to be
met with in substance in the primary editions of the Complutensian (C), Erasmus (1516—35), Stephen's first and second
editions (St. 1, 2, 1546, 1549), Beza's first and last editions
(B. 1, 5, 1565, 1598), and that of the Elzevirs (Elz. 1, 2, 1624,
1633). Of all these books a collation (as exact as my diligence
will permit) has been made by myself not a few years since,
except those of Erasmus third (1522), and fourth (1527),
which illness has hindered me from attempting. The readings from these two editions I have gathered from Wetstein's
N. T. 1751—2, without absolutely vouching for his accuracy
(but whose accuracy shall we vouch for ?), although in this
portion of his great work Wetstein took especial pains[1]. We

---

[1] Yet Wetstein adopts, rightly or not, all the representations of Mill as to
the readings of the Aldine Bible (1518) except in Luc. xi. 34 ; Acts xii. 25 ;
2 Cor. xi. 1.

confine our description of these early editions to the orthography and grammatical forms which occur in them. Their
history, at least so far as we thought it necessary to trace it,
their miscellaneous contents, and the manuscripts from which
the text is drawn, have been described at length in the fifth
chapter of Scrivener's *Plain Introduction to the Criticism of
the N. T.*, third edition, pp. 422—443.

(1) C. Complutensian edition (1514 printed, 1522 published), fol.

Two Greek Psalters with *Magnificat* and *Benedictus* (what
we have elsewhere called *Odea*, p. lxiii) appeared first at
Milan in 1481, then at Venice in 1486, the first six chapters
of S. John were published at Venice by Aldus Manutius in
1504, John i. 1—14 at Tübingen in 1512, but the first
edition of the whole N. T. bears date Jan. 10, 1514, although
it was not made public before 1522, five years after the
death of its munificent projector and cost-payer, Francis
Ximenes de Cisneros, Regent of Castile and Primate of Spain.
It is a portion of a Polyglott Bible in six folio volumes,
printed at the University he had founded, Alcalá de Henares,
better known by its Latin name *Complutum*. The N. T.
portion contains the Latin Vulgate (in the form then best
known) on the right of each page, and in a parallel column
the Greek text on the left, in very beautiful though peculiar
type, with some idiosyncrasies of Greek accent which were
subsequently laid aside. Breathings are omitted altogether.
Since from the nature of the case, this Greek text must have
been formed from the authority of manuscripts (and those
not early ones) alone, it naturally retains the fashion of
orthography and grammatical inflexion represented by their
prototypes. Thus, as in such manuscripts as we have often
previously described, there occur 224 itacisms (chiefly ω for *o*,
η for ει, ει for ι, η for υ, οι for ει, and *vice versâ*); 32 instances
of ν ἐφελκυστικὸν is the redundant ν before a consonant;
15 cases of the lack of ν before a vowel, οὕτως sometimes

preceding a consonant, but ν 68 times; οὐκ and οὐχ interchanged 12 times. The following peculiarities, found in
many manuscripts, may shew that the grammatical Greek
forms were not yet settled among scholars: παρηγγελεν
Marc. vi. 8; παραγγέλων 1 Cor. vii 10; παράγγελε 1 Tim. iv.
11; v. 7; vi. 17; παραγγέλομεν 2 Thess. iii. 4; διάγγελε
Luc. ix. 60; διαγγέλων Acts xxi. 26; ἀναγγέλων 2 Cor. vii.
7; καταγγέλων 1 Cor. ii. 1. The augment is omitted nine
times (Matth. xi. 17; Act. vii. 42; xxvi. 32; Rom. i. 2 : Gal.
ii. 13; 1 Tim. vi. 10; 2 Tim. i. 16; Rev. iv. 8; xii. 17), the
reduplication twice (Johan. xi. 52; 1 Cor. xi. 5); μέλλει and
μέλει confounded Marc. ix. 38; Act. xviii. 17; Rev. iii. 2;
xii. 4. Other forms, some of which might be called Alexan-
drian, παμπόλου Marc. viii. 1; νηρέαν Rom. xvi. 15; ἐξαίρειτε
1 Cor. v. 13; ἀποκτένει 2 Cor. iii. 6, &c.; στιχούμεν Gal. v.
25; εἶπα Heb. iii. 10; εὑράμενος Heb. ix. 12; ἀπεσχέσθαι
1 Pet. ii. 11; καταλείποντες 2 Pet. ii. 15; περιβαλλεῖται
Rev. iii. 5; δειγνύντος Rev. xxii. 8. The stops in the Greek
(not in the parallel Latin) are careless, being (.), (,), (·), but
never (;). We often find σ at the end of words for ς, ϋ or ῡ
at the beginning of syllables; there is no ι either subscript
or ascript, and no capital letters except at the beginning of a
chapter, where they are often flourished. The following
forms are also derived from the general practice of manuscripts, and occur perpetually: ἀπάρτι, ἀπάρχης, δαν (for δ'
αν) ειμή, εξαυτής, επιτοαυτό, εφόσον, εωσότου, καίτοιγε,
καθημέραν κατιδίαν, κατόναρ, μεθήμων, μέντοι, ουμή, του-
τέστι: and for the most part διαπαντός, διατί, διατούτο,
είτις, ουκέτι. Sometimes the preposition and its case make
but a single word, as παραφύσιν, ευποιήσαι (Vulg. benefacere,
Marc. xiv. 7). Since the Complutensian has been said to be
very inaccurately printed, we may state that we have noted
only 50 errors of the press: but in one place (Heb. vii. 3)
part of the ninth Euthalian κεφάλαιον (εν ω ότι και του
αβρααμ προετιμήθη) has through inadvertence crept into the
text. In this primary edition the Epistle to the Hebrews
stands last of those of S. Paul, and all of them precede the
Acts of the Apostles.

(2)	Desiderii Erasmi editiones (1516, 1519, 1522, 1527, 1535), fol.

Here again, as in the case of the Complutensian Polyglott we need not repeat from ordinary sources of information the personal or literary history of Erasmus himself, the untoward haste wherewith the text of the first edition, undertaken to get the start of Ximenes' rival work, which it did very effectually, was hurried through the Basle press of Froben in the space of less than a year. The only manuscripts he can have used throughout were, and are now, at Basle, Gospel Cod. 2, Acts, Paul. Cod. 2, Paul. Cod. 7 (important), all of no high antiquity, with occasional reference to an older copy Gospels, Acts, Paul. Cod. 1, and Act. Paul. Cod. 4. For the Apocalypse he had but one copy, once John Reuchlin's, long lost, but happily re-discovered in 1861 by Professor Delitsch, in a private library at Mayhingen in Bavaria, and published as edited by him. It is to this book that reference is made in our collation of the Apocalypse under the notation of "Cod. Reuchlin." The last six verses of this book, being lost in Cod. Reuchlin, were boldly translated by Erasmus from the Latin. The first edition of Erasmus', by reason of its hurried publication, is perhaps the most inaccurate volume ever issued from the press, although a theologian of some account, John Hausschein (Oecolampadius) of Basle had undertaken the correction of the press, at end of volume in some hundreds of places. This edition, like the Complutensian, was affected by the peculiarities of the modern manuscripts from which it was printed. No less than 501 itacisms (including those in the second edition) were hence imported into the text[1], ν ἐφελ-κυστικὸν is much (but not constantly) used with verbs before a consonant at the beginning of the next word; but hiatus for the lack of it 23 times, while ι subscript,

---

[1] They consist of o (for ω) 58 times ; ω (for o) 55 ; η (for $\epsilon\iota$) 33 ; $\epsilon\iota$ (for η) 65 ; η (for ι) 25 ; ι (for η) 31; $a\iota$ (for ϵ) 18 ; ϵ (for $a\iota$) 25 ; $\epsilon\iota$ (for ι) 30 ; ι (for $\epsilon\iota$) 49 ; η (for ν) 27 ; ν (for η) 45 ; ι (for ν) 8 ; ν (for ι) 5 ; η (for ϵ) 5 ; ϵ (for η) 13 ; ω (for ov) 2 ; ov (for ω) 6 ; all of the ordinary type of those in later cursive manuscripts.

which in other places is set pretty correctly, is placed under
η in the plural of the subjunctive mood active, but not in
the singular (e.g. James ii. 3 ἐπιβλέψητε, εἴπητε, but ver. 2
εἰσέλθη *bis*). We meet with οὕτως before a consonant usually,
but οὕτω four times. For omission of augments and re-
duplications notice ἐκπορεύοντο Rev. iv. 5; ἐκάθικεν Heb.
xii. 2; ἐπαισχύνθη 2 Tim. i. 16; ἀποκρίθη Rev. vii. 19;
ἐρημωμένην Rev. xvii. 16; περιζωσμένοι Rev. xv. 6; and other
irregularities, συμμαρτυροῖ Rom. viii. 16; λάλον Rev. xiii.
5; ἐκχέετε Rev. xvi. 1. The stops are so loosely (often falsely
placed) that it is useless to record them; the grave and acute
accent are used almost indifferently before the end of a clause
or paragraph; σ is often used for ς not at the end of a word.
For the second edition there was less hurry, and the worst
errata (e.g. the ι subscript) were set right, and one new
manuscript Cod. 3 of Gospels, Act., Paul. consulted. It is of
no great value, and had been borrowed for this purpose from
a Belgian convent. The Annotations were enlarged. Those
employed for the first edition had been compiled and probably
set in type before the Greek text had been arranged, and
some foreign matter[1] added from Greek sources. The letter
to Carpianus, tables of Eusebian canons, and (before each
Gospel) tables of κεφάλαια; τίτλοι, Ammonian sections, and
Eusebian numerals set in their usual places. Yet many of
the worst faults of the first edition are retained in the second[2].
Mill estimates the textual variations of the two editions at
400, but they are obviously too few. The third edition of
1522 first contained the insertion from the Codex Britannicus
(cf. Scrivener, *Plain Introduction*, pp. 648—55, third edition)

[1] Dorotheus of Tyre, *Lives* of the Four Evangelists, Sophronius' Lives,
Prologue or ὑπόθεσις to each Gospel by Theophylact, &c.

[2] E.g. Matth. vi. 26; xxi. 22; Mark xiv. 38, 59; xv. 14; Luc. ii. 22; viii.
1; xv. 13; xxiii. 48; Johan. vi. 4, 34; viii. 44, 48; ix. 21; xiv. 8; xvii. 11;
Act. ii. 4; iii. 6; v. 28; vii. 22, 37, 39; Rom. i. 18, 19; v. 11; xii. 11; xv.
27; xvi. 12; 1 Cor. iv. 5; xii. 21; xiv. 21; 2 Cor. ii. 12; ix. 5; x. 8; xii. 13,
20; xiii. 12; Eph. i. 9; iv. 30; 1 Thess. iii. 8; v. 18, 27; 2 Thess. ii. 13;
iii. 6, 14, 27; 2 Tim. i. 3; ii. 21; Hebr. vii. 5; ix. 12; xi. 34, 37; xiii. 19;
1 Pet. iv. 1, 19; 2 Pet. i. 17; 1 Johan. iv. 15; Jude 15; Rev. iii. 2; iv. 8; vi.
6, 11; vii. 2; ix. 8; xii. 13, 16; xiv. 5, 7; xvi. 20; xviii. 10; xix. 4, 18;
xx. 4.

of 1 Johan. v. 7, but contains according to Mill 118 variations from the second, which Reuss (*Bibliotheca N. T. Gr.*, but his plan of reckoning, however, materially differs from Mill's) reduces to seven. In this year Erasmus obtained his first sight of the Complutensian Polyglott, from which source he made 106 or 113 changes in the text, which Reuss in his system brought down to six, yet 90 are found in the Apocalypse alone. The last edition of Erasmus bears date 1535, the year before he died. Reuss notes only two variations from the fourth (1 Cor. xii. 2 ; Act. ix. 28), Mill only two, but we notice in S. James' Epistle only cap. i. 22 ; ii. 6 ; iii. 12 ; subscriptio. The first three and last editions of Erasmus are printed in two parallel columns (like the Complutensian), the Greek text on the left column, the Latin on the right, but the Latin is not the Vulgate as ordinarily represented, but as revised long since by the editor himself, and keeping rather close to it in tone and literary form. In the fourth edition, however, the Latin Vulgate is inserted between the other two, we presume in the vain hope of silencing the cavillers whom he addresses in an elaborate dissertation prefixed to his fourth and fifth editions "Contra morosos quosdam ac indoctos." This mode of conciliating having proved unsuccessful, Erasmus withdrew in his edition eight years afterwards this unavailing addition to the size and cost of a book sufficiently bulky in itself.

(3) Robert Stephen's editions (1546, 1549, 1550 folio, 1551)[1].

The editions of Robert Stephen (Estienne), mainly by reason of their typographical beauty, have exercised a far

---

[1] Since these descriptions of Stephen's and Elzevir's editions were written Mr Hoskier has published his Collation of Cod. b (above, p. xxv) and has annexed to them ten elaborate Appendices (A to J), containing (among other matters) full and minute lists of the differences between Stephen and the common text, and of the divergences from each other of the Elzevir text in its several forms. It would be unscholarlike to say that these Appendices are hardly worth the trouble of a full collation, for whatsoever is attempted

wider influence over the criticism of the New Testament
than either the Complutensian or those of Erasmus. Indeed
his third or folio edition of 1550, with the earliest supply of
various readings in the margin, is by many, especially in
England, regarded as the standard of the Received text.
Scrivener's Editio Major, 1887, which has been used throughout for our present work, has been reprinted from it with all
possible care and accuracy. In Stephen's first edition (1546)
the Preface makes an obscure reference to manuscript collations as the basis of his Greek text, and in his principal edition
of 1550, in a Graeco-Latin Preface to the Reader, he announces
his authorities to be sixteen in number, whereof the Complutensian Polyglott (a) was one (cited by him in the margin
610 times); another (β) is doubtless the great Codex Bezae,
which did not reach Cambridge University Library, whose
glory it now is, before 1581; eight other manuscripts procured
from the Royal Library at Paris, the other six from other
quarters ἃ αὐτοὶ πανταχόθεν συνηθροίσαμεν (in the parallel
Latin it is rendered "quæ undique corrogare licuit.") Codex
Bezae itself indeed, though it had been in Italy τὸ δὲ β΄ ἐστὶ
τὸ ἐν Ἰταλίᾳ ὑπὸ τῶν ἡμετέρων ἀντιβληθὲν φίλων (St. 3
Preface) in 1546, was returned to its proper owners at Lyons,
and remained there until 1562. The recognition of the
aforesaid codices has gathered around it a perfect critical
literature of its own, and by the researches of Le Long,
Bishop Marsh and other scholars, with one or two small
exceptions, the question may be regarded as settled. On
comparing the codices themselves with the margin of 1550
we come to see how very negligently Stephen represents the
authorities he cites; as indeed well he may, since we now
know that at least a portion of the collations are the work of
his yet more illustrious son Henry Stephen, who in 1546 was
only eighteen years old. The two editions which preceded
that of 1550 contained no critical apparatus. The books

---

in these studies should be done, once and for all, thoroughly and well. It is
enough to say that we have not felt it incumbent on us to produce Mr Hoskier's
labours in full, but rather to employ his *tentamina* to the review and correction
of our own.

of 1546 and 1549 are in a small 12mo form, most elegantly
printed with type cast at the expense of Francis I.: the open-
ing words of the Preface common to both "*O mirificam* Regis
nostri optimi et praestantissimi principis liberalitatem" has
given them the name by which they are known to book-
worms. The two books correspond page by page, line by
line: also in Preface and title-page. St. 1 and St. 2 differ
from each other in text 139 times, in punctuation 28 times,
in accents 214 (St. 2 being almost always right), in breathings
74 (chiefly ἀβραὰμ St. 1, ἀβρ. St. 2, 3). The *errata* (really
such) are in St. 1, 126; in St. 2, 102; very seldom the
same, and in St. 2 a table of them at the end. St. 2 was
set up from St. 1, and apparently St. 2 was the usual exemplar
of St. 3, although in Rom. xvi. 11 ἠροδίωνα, 12 κοπιῶσας are
from St. 1. More important is the fact that the main edition
of 1550, with its critical apparatus, perhaps more showy than
useful, differs from the smaller books of 1546, 1549 jointly
334 times (St. 1 alone 372) in text, 27 in punctuation. In
the Apocalypse, St. 1 and 2 are close to the text of Erasmus
(departing from it only in eleven places), of whose labours
Stephen takes no notice, while admitting his obligations to
the Complutensian Polyglott, which he follows against St. 1
in no less than 61 places. But, in truth, the men of
Stephen's generation had yet to learn how much care and
toil their work needed, if it was to be even tolerably
executed. St. 1 often follows manuscripts cited in St. 3,
where St. 3 records no variation in text: π (i.e. πάντες)
perpetually stands in the margin of St. 3, when *all* his copies
certainly do not favour the variation. Nor did he always
employ all the readings he had at hand[1]. But it was much
to have made a first essay in Biblical criticism: our obligations to this learned man far exceed, by way of example to

---

[1] In his dedication to Queen Elizabeth (N. T. 1565), Beza speaks clearly
of a copy of R. Stephen's "cum viginti quinque plus minus manuscriptis...
ab Henrico Stephano, ejus filio, et paternæ sedulitatis hærede, quam diligen-
tissime collatum." Indeed Beza, in whose possession Cod. D then was,
cites from it, as Wetstein points out, three readings under the name
of "quidam codex" and several others from other Stephanic copies, which
Robert Stephen had neglected to use.

others, what he actually achieved. St. 4 1551 is the small
edition (16°) which he published without his name on the
title-page the next year after his third at Geneva, which has
become to him the land of exile for conscience' sake. It is
chiefly notable for first representing our modern verses breaking up the continuous text, a convenient, yet in many respects,
a misleading experiment : " triste lumen," as Reuss puts it,
"nec posthac extinguendum." This fourth edition contains
the Greek text, set between the Latin Vulgate and Erasmus'
revision thereof. Reuss names only six instances in which
Stephen's third and fourth editions differ: we can name at
least nine more. Finally, besides the bilingual epistle to
the Reader, quoted above, the great standard volume contains
Chrysostom's Homily I. to S. Matthew (then first published),
Epistola Carpiano and tables of Eusebian canons, table of
citations of O. T. in N. T., whether literal or virtual, 72
Hexameter lines, headed Ερρικος ο Ρωβερτου Στεφανου
φιλοθεω παντι, Prologue by Theophylact, with *Lives* by
Sophronius and Dorotheus of Tyre, and κεφ. before each
Gospel ; in margin of text, τίτλοι, numerals of κεφάλαια
Ammonian sections, Eusebian numerals. Before the Acts
stand 'Αποδημία Παύλου, Euthalius περὶ τῶν χρόνων, tables
of κεφάλαια, Chrysostom's prologue before Pauline Epistles.
Each separate one has a prologue (chiefly Theodoret's) κεφ.
tables. The Acts and Epistles have κεφ. numerals. The
Apocalypse has no κεφ. or prologue, but only Latin chapters
subdivided by numerals.

(4)   Theodore Beza's editions (1556, 1565 [B. 2], 1582,
1589, 1598 [B. 5]) fol.

Reuss and others will not admit the first-named edition
of 1556 to belong to Beza, and indeed it is only the elegant
Latin version which strictly belongs to him, and now first
appears ; the Greek text being that of Stephen's fourth
edition 1551 : so that his editions properly so called are four,
not five [1]. This is not, however, his own mode of reckoning,

---

[1] [We cannot find any trace of a Greek text in or accompanying the
folio Beza of 1556—1557.]

inasmuch as on the title-page of that of 1565 he speaks of
"Annotationes, quas iterum hac secunda editione recognovit,"
and in his latest edition of 1598, in his Epistle to the Reader
he states expressly " Annus agitur quadragesimus secundus,
ex quo N. T. Latinam interpretationem emendare sum
aggressus, Graeco contextu non modo cum novem decim
vetustissimis quam pluribus manuscriptis et multis passim
impressis codicibus, sed etiam cum Syra interpretatione
collato," the forty-two years bringing us back to 1556, not to
1565. If we impute these last cited words to Beza's senile
decay of memory (of which other instances may be alleged),
the title-page of 1565 can hardly be thus accounted for.
Still, no doubt, as regards the Greek text, this is the earliest
with which we are concerned. It is a noble folio, the text
(after the example of Er. 4) arranged in three columns,
Greek text, his own version taken from 1556, the Latin
Vulgate, with an elaborate dedication to Queen Elizabeth,
dated from Geneva (where all his editions were printed) Dec.
19, 1564, being the second anniversary of the battle of
Dreux. This only and his last edition (B. 5) we have fully
and carefully collated, B. 4 (1589) was closely followed in
B. 5, the third (B. 3) is almost identical with B. 2. His
materials were Henry Stephen's collation, of which we have
spoken before (p. xcvi), Cod. D of the Gospels, Cod. D of the
Pauline Epistles, first noticed in his third edition (1582), and
the Peshito Syriac version as translated by Sm. Tremellius in
1569. Add to this a few bold conjectures of Beza's own,
of which Luke ii. 22 τοῦ καθαρισμοῦ αὐτῆς for αὐτοῦ is the
most conspicuous example. Cf. 1 Thess. i. 4; 2 Thess. ii. 4.
Wetstein calculates that Beza's text differs from Stephen's in
some fifty places, his version or Annotationes from Stephen's
Greek in 150. Since Reuss' reckonings are derived not from
a full collation of the whole N. T., but from a selection of
a thousand texts chosen as characteristic, his results must
always prove below the truth, yet they will generally shew
the drift of the editions cited with accuracy sufficient for
most purposes. He states that B. 2 (1565) differs from St.
4 (1551) in only 25 places, whereof it sides with Erasmus

4 times, with the Complutensian 9, 4 times with them both, and 9 are new, whereof Colinaeus in 1534 had already adopted two (Act. xvii. 25; Jac. v. 12). He notes also that B. 3 (1582) withdraws one peculiar reading of B. 3, but adds 14 more. The editions of 1589 (B. 4) and 1598 (B. 5) are notable as being the basis on which the Authorised English translation (1611) was formed. B. 4, according to Reuss, departs from B. 3 only five times, B. 5 from B. 4 but twice. These last statements I regard as somewhat doubtful. We have collated fully B. 2 and B. 5.

(5) Elzevir editions (Elz. 1, 1624, Elz. 2, 1633).

As Stephen 1550 is mostly regarded as the standard of the Received text in England, so Continental critics have assigned that distinction to one of the editions of 1624, 1633 published in 12° at Leyden by the brothers Bonaventure and Abraham Elzevir, chiefly by reason of their supposed exemption from press errors. Πίναξ μαρτυριῶν of citations from the Old Testament stands at the beginning of each edition, abridged from St. 1550. Elz. 1633 has also tables of κεφάλαια prefixed to the Gospels, ἔκθεσις κεφαλαίων of the Acts and all the Epistles. Elz. 1624 has no Preface, but is stated on the title-page to be *ex Regiis, aliisque optimis editionibus cum cura expressum:* by *Regiis* we understand St. 3, and by "editionibus quae maxime ac prae ceteris nunc omnibus probantur," in the Preface to Elz. 1633, as by "aliisque optimis editionibus" on the title-page of Elz. 1624, must refer to the several editions of Beza: Reuss notes but nine variations out of his thousand readings as subsisting between Elz. 1624 and Beza's smaller edition of 1565. Elz. 1633 is easily distinguished from the elder book, by having the verses broken up into separate sentences, instead of their numbers only being indicated in the margin, as in Elz. 1624. The Preface of Elz. 1633, with a confidence which no doubt helped on its own accomplishment, declares "Textum ergo habes nunc ab omnibus receptum, in quo nihil immutatum aut corruptum damus[1]." On comparing the two Elzevir editions we mark that while some of the worst misprints of the elder book are corrected in the younger (Matth. vi. 34; Act. xxvii. 13; 1 Cor. x. 10; Col. ii. 13; 1 Thess. ii. 17; Hebr. viii. 9; 2 Pet. i. 7), others just as gross are retained (Act. ix. 3; Rom. vii. 2; xiii. 5; 1 Cor. xii. 23; xiii. 3; 2 Cor. iv. 4; v. 19; Hebr. xii. 9; Rev. iii. 12; vii. 7; xviii. 16), besides the admission of other *errata* peculiar to itself (Marc. iii. 10; Johan. v. 2; Rom. xv. 3; 1 Cor. ix. 2; 2 Cor. i. 11; vi. 16; Col. iv. 7; Rev. xxii. 3). Of real various readings between the two Elzevirs we observe but seven, in six of which Elz. 1633 follows the Complutensian (Marc. iv. 18; viii. 24; Luc. xi. 33; xii. 20; Johan. iii. 6 *bis*; 2 Tim. i. 12; Rev. xvi. 5)[2]. The editions of the Elzevirs have been found by us to differ from Stephen's third (1550) in about 287 places, whereof Mill detected but 12, Tischendorf gives a catalogue of 150. Mr Hoskier (Appendix C, p. 25) regards 1641 as the most beautiful and correct of the several Elzevir editions.

[1] We have always understood this expression on the part of the unknown editors of 1633 to refer not to themselves but to the older edition of 1624, which had at any rate then stood the test of nine years' use. Hence we cannot speak with Dr Weymouth (*Resultant Gr. Test.* Preface, p. viii) of its "audacious claim to be what it was not or ever has been", or of the Leyden printers of 1633 being guided in their work of that year by the Holy Spirit of God, which was withheld from all other editors before or since, and from themselves in 1624. If indeed it were "*themselves*".

[2] We will make Mr Hoskier a present of Johan. iv. 51 οἱ δοῦλοι. See Hoskier, Appendix C. p. 10.

POSTSCRIPT.

September 29, 1890.

MY lamented friend and fellow student, the late Very Reverend J. W. Burgon, Dean of Chichester, very earnestly requested me, that if I lived to complete the present work, I would publickly testify that my latest labours had in no wise modified my previous critical convictions, namely, that the true text of the New Testament can best and most safely be gathered from a comprehensive acquaintance with every source of information yet open to us, whether they be Manuscripts of the original text, Versions, or Fathers; rather than from a partial representation of three or four authorities which, though in date the more ancient and akin in character, cannot be made even tolerably to agree together.

I saw on my own part no need of such avowal, yet (*neqet quis carmina Gallo?*) I could not deny Dean Burgon's request. The Dean's capital argument arising from the fact that the text used by Patristic writers is often purer than primary manuscripts written one or two centuries younger than they (see p. vi. note 1) needs, of course, much care in its application, and can only be insisted on when the context renders it quite clear what the reading before the elder writer actually was. Such a case (and it is by no means of rare occurrence) as the following seems to me absolutely conclusive. In John III. 13 the clause ὁ ὢν ἐν τῷ οὐρανῷ, omitted by some four manuscripts (Codd. אBC. and 33), three at least of them being the production of an age deeply steeped in Arianism, is vindicated by Hippolytus, who flourished a full century before the date of the most ancient of them ; while the theological inference drawn by him, ἀποσταλεὶς ἵνα δείξῃ τὸν ἐπὶ γῆς ὄντα εἶναι καὶ ἐν οὐρανῷ, leaves no possible doubt as to the reading of the copy which Hippolytus had before him.

Compare Tregelles (*Account of Printed Text*, p. 25) for Marc. xvi. 16, 17.

PART I.

COLLATION

OF

MS. 556. B.–C. III. 5.

TITLE (under slight illumination): *rubro.* Εὐαγγέλιον ἐκ τοῦ κατὰ ματθαίου (*sic*) cf. Marc. title.

MATT. I. 1. δαδ ἀβραὰμ *passim.* 4. ἀμιναδαμ *bis* (– τὸν ἀμιναδαβ, ἀμιναδαβ δε ἐγέννησε 346). 5. ἰωβηδ *bis* 124. 6. – ὁ βασιλεὺς. σολομῶνα 124.346. 7. ἀβιοὺδ *bis* (*non* 346). 7, 8. ἀσὰφ *bis* (*non* 346). 8, 9. ὀζίαν ?². ὀζειαν 346. ὀζιασ. 10. [ἀμών]. ἀμμων *bis* 124. 13, 14. ἐλιακεὶμ *bis.* (– τον ελιακειμ, ελιακειμ δε ἐγεννησε 124.) 14, 15. ἐλιοὺδ *bis.* 14. αχεμ, αχιμ. 16, 17. [ματθὰν]. 16. ἰακὼβ δὲ ἐγέννησε τὸν ἰωσήφ + ῷ μνηστευθῆσα παρθένος μαριὰμ, ἐγέννησεν ἲν τὸν λεγομενον χν. 346. 18. [ἰῦ]. [γέννησις], (μνηστευθησεις 346) [γὰρ]. πρινὴ. ἐγγαστρὶ (*sic* ver. 22) Marc. XIII. 17. 19. [παραδειγ.]. ἀπολύσαι. 20. – κυ. ἐφάνη κατ' ὄναρ. φοβηθεὶς (124). 20. – εστιν 346. 22. – τοῦ 124. [καλεσουσι]. 24. δι' ἐγερθεὶς *prim.* 124. 25. ἔτεκεν [rest as Scr.].

II. 1. + χῦ (*post* ιυ) 346. 2. ἤλθωμεν 346. 3. ὁ βασιλεὺς ἡρώδης 124. γὼν. 4. γεννάται. 5. Βιθλεὲμ *non* ver. 6, 8, 16. – γὰρ. 6. ἰούδα. 7. ἠκρίβωσε. εκρυβωσε 346. 8. εἶπεν 124. ἐξετάσατε ἀκριβῶς 124. ἐπ' ἂν. (ἀναγγειλατε 124). 9. – ὁ 124. 11. εἶδον (*pro* εὗρον) 346, ἰδόντες 124. 12. χῶραν. 13. [φαιν. κατ' ὄναρ]. φεύγε. 14. ἦν. 15. [τοῦ κυ]. ἐξ'. 16. ἐνέπ. ἀποστεῖλας. παίδας. διετοὺς. 17. ῥῥηθὲν [ὑπὸ]. 18. ἠκούσθη. [θρῆνος καὶ] ὀδυρμὸς· εἰσίν 124. 19. ἠρώδου. φαίνεται κατ ὄναρ 124. 21. ὁ δὲ. [ἠλθεν]. 22. – ἐπὶ 124. [ἠρ. τοῦ π. αὐτοῦ]. 23. νάζαρεθ λεγομένην 124. 23. πληρωθὴ *hic.*

III. 1. [νν] *passim.* 2. βασιλεῖα. 3. διὰ ἠσαίου 124. εὐθεῖας. 4. – ὁ 124. τρυχῶν 13. ζωνην. ὀσφὺν. [αὐτοῦ ἦν].

S.   1

5. [*nil additum*]. 7. – ἐρχομένους 13. [αὐτοῦ]. 8. καρπὸν ἄξιον
13.124.346. 9. ἐγείραι. 10. [καὶ]. κεῖται. 11. μὲν οὖν 13.
rubro
ὑμᾶς βαπτίζω 13. 12. + μὲν 13.124, not 346 (*ante σῖτον*) 13.124.
– αὐτοῦ *tert*. 13.124 [not after ἀποθήκην]. 13, 14. -θῆναι.
14. χρεῖαν. 15. εἶπεν αὐτῶι 13.124. [οὕτω]. πληρώσαι. 16. βαπ-
τισθεὶς δὲ (– καὶ) 13.124.346. ἠνεώχθησαν αὐτῶι. ἴδεν. καταβαῖνον
ὡς εἰ. [καὶ ἐρχόμενον].

IV. 1. πειρασθῆναι. 2. [τεσσαρ-]. ἐπείνασεν. 3. – αὐτῷ
prim. 13. + αὐτῶ (*post* εἶπεν) 13.124. οὗτοι. 4. εἶπεν 346.
οὐκ᾽ [-ται ἄνος]. ἐν (*pro* ἐπὶ) 13.124.346. διαστό-. 5. ἵστησιν.
[λέγει]. 6. ἐντελεῖται περισοῦ. ἐπιχειρῶν ἀροῦσίν 13.124. 7. πάλιν·
13.124. πᾶλιν v. 8. οὐκ᾽. 8. πᾶσας. βασιλείας. 9. εἶπεν (*pro*
λέγει) 13. πάντα σοι. 10. marg. ὀπίσω μου (*post* ὕπαγε) 346.
12. Ἀκοῦσας. [ὁ ῑσ̄]. 13. καταλοιπὼν. ναζαρὲθ 13. κατώκισεν
-λῶν so ver. 14. 14. πληρωθῇ. [ἠσ.]. 16. φῶς ἴδεν 13.124.
χώρα. σκιὰ. 17. ἤγγικεν. βασιλεία. 18. – ὁ ῑσ̄. ἴδεν 13.124.
[ἁλιεῖς] ver. 19. [αὐτοῖς· Δεῦτε]. 20. οἱ δὲ᾽. οἱ δὲ ver. 22.
21. ἴδεν. 23. [ὅλην τὴν γαλ. ὁ ῑσ̄] 13.124. βασιλείας. 24. [ἀπ.].
– καὶ (*ante* δαιμον.) 13.

V. 1. -θον αὐτῶ. 3. βασιλεῖα sic v. 10. 4, 5. [no change].
5. πραεῖς. 9. – αὐτοὶ 13.124. 11. ὅτ᾽ ἂν. διώξουσι. [ῥῆμα.
ψευδόμενοι]. 12. οὗτος. 13. ἔν τινι. βληθῆναι. -τείσθαι.
14. ἐστὲ. κρυβῆναι. 16. οὕτως. δοξάσω σοι j (*sic*). 17. νομήσητε 124. καταλύσαι. πληρώσαι. 18. κερέα 13.346. + καὶ τῶν
προφητῶν (*post* νόμου) 13.124. 19. λύσει. 19. τούτων. διδάξει
prim. only (*bis* 346). οὕτως. βασιλεῖα bis. οὗτος. 20. ὑμῶν ἡ
δικαιοσύνη 13.124. -λεῖα. 21. [ἐρρέθη]. 22. εἰκῆι. ῥακκὰ 13.
124. + τῶ ἀδελφῶ αὐτοῦ (*ante* μωρὲ) 13.124. 23. [κακεῖ 13.124
not 346]. τί κατα σοῦ. 24. ἀδελφώ σου. -ρον σου. 25. ἐννοῶν
13.124.346. Τῶι. ἕως οὗ 13.124. μετ᾽ αὐτοῦ ἐν τῇ ὁδῷ 124.
– σε παραδῶ *secund.* 13.124. 26. ἀποδῶς. 27. ἐρρέθη. [τοῖς
ἀρχαίοις] 13.124. 28. ἐπιθυμῆσαι [αὐτὴν] 13.124. [αὐτοῦ].
29. μελών so ver. 30. βληθῇ. 30. ἡ χείρ σου ἡ δεξιὰ 13.124.
30. σῶμα σου. βληθῇ.
31. [ἐρρέθη]. – ὅτι 13.124. ἀπολύσηι. δότω. αὐτῆι. ὑποστάσιον. 32. πᾶς ὁ ἀπολύιον. πορνεῖας. μοιχευθῆναι 13.124, ὃς

COLLATION OF COD. 556 WITH CODD. 13.69.124.346.   3

ἂν ἀπολελυμένην γαμήσῃ μοιχᾶται. 33. [ἐρρέθη]. οὐκ'. 34. ὁμόσε.
ὅλος 346. ver. 35 semel. μῆτε. ἐστιν so ver. 35 bis.
36. μὴ δὲ 13.124. ποιῆσαι λευκὴν ἢ μέλαιναν 13.124.
37. [ἔστω]. 38. [ἐρρέθη] – καὶ 13. ὀδόντα, ὀδόντος. 39. ἀντιστῆναι. [ῥαπίσει ἐπὶ]. [σου σιαγ.]. 40. κριθῆναι. -να
σου. 41. ἀγγαρεύσῃ 13. μήλιον 13.124. 42. [δίδου 346. δος
13.124]. δανίσασθαι 13.124. ἀποστράφῇς. 43. [ἐρρέθη]. 44. [nil
omissum] τοῖς pro οὖσιν 13.124.346. 45. ἔπιπον. + τοις (ante
οὖνοις) α (13.124.346). 46. ἔξετε 13.124. τελώναι. [τὸ αὐτὸ].
47. οἱ τελώναι τὸ αὐτὸ (pro οὕτω) 13.124.346. 48. ὡς (pro ὥσπερ)
13.124. οὐράνιος (pro ἐν τοῖς οὐρανοῖς) 13.124.346. ἐστιν.

VI. 1. [as Scr.] μῆγε. 2. Ὅταν ποιεῖς 13. 4. [ἢ σου ἡ ἐλεη.]
τῶι bis –αὐτὸς 13.124. [ἐν τῶν φ.]. 5. ὅτ' ἂν [ver. 6 as Scr.]
–ἂν 13.124. –ὅτι 13.124. 6. -μίεϊόν. κλεῖσας. πρι σου (– τῶ) ἐν
13.124. [ἐν τῶ φανερῶ]. 7. [βαττο-]. 8. οἶδε [no add.]. χρείαν
ἔχεται προτοῦ 13. 10. [ἐλθέτω]. βασιλεία σου. οὖνωι. ἐπι τῆς.
13. π ο ν η ρ οῦ (widely) rescript. βασιλεῖα [Doxologiam habet].
15. [no omission]. 16. ὅτ' ἂν. [ὥσπερ]. [αὐτῶν]. [ὅτι].
17. ἄλειψαί. 18. [τοῖς ἀνοισ νηστ.]. πρι σου. [κρυπτῶ] πῆρ σου
[habet ἐν τῶ φανερῶ]. 19. ἐπιτῆς. σῆς ver. 20. 20. οὐδε.
21. [as Scr.]. 22. – τος ἐστὶν. ἐὰν prim. [rest as Scr.]. σῶμα
σου bis. 23. ἐστιν. 24. εἰ γὰρ. H supra. καταφρονήσει.
μαμωνᾶ. 25. ἢ τί πίητε (non καὶ) 13.124. μῆδε τὸ σώματι. ἐστιν.
26. οὐχ'. 27. δε ἐξ. 27. προσθῆναι 13.124. ἡλικίαν, πήχυν.
28. περιενδ. [verbs as Scr.]. 29. σολομῶν. πᾶσῃ. αὐτοῦ sic.
30. ὀλιγόπιστοι. 32. ταῦτα γὰρ πάντα 13.124. ἐπιζητοῦσιν 13.124.
33. βασιλείαν τοῦ θῦ· καὶ τὴν δικ. 34. [-σητε]. – αὔριον secund.
μεριμνήσῃ (– τὰ) ἑαυτῆς εἰς τὴν αὔριον 124. fin. ἑαυτής (pro αὐτῆς)
13.124.

VII. 2. ἀντιμετριθήσεται 13.124. 3. ἀδελφού σου ver. 5.
4. -φώ σου. ἐκ (pro ἀπὸ) 13.124. -μού σου. -μώ σου ver. 5.
5. [ordo as Scr.]. ἀπὸ (pro ἐκ) 13.124. 6. δότε 13. κυσίν 124.
καταπάτησουσιν 13.124. 7. εὑρήσεται 13. 8. [ἀνοιγήσεται].
9. ἐστιν ἐξ'. ὃ (pro ὃν) 13.124. [αἰτήσῃ] ver. 10. 10. ἢ 13.346.
καὶ ἐὰν. 12. ἐὰν (pro ἂν) 346. οὕτως. οὕτως (pro οὗτος) 13.124.
προφῆται. 13. εἰσελθάτε δια τῆς 13.124. [ἡ πύλη] so ver. 14.

1—2

εὐρούχωρος. ἐρχόμενοι (pro εἰσερχόμενοι) 13.124. 14. τί (pro ὅτι) 13.124. τεθλημμένη 13.346. ὀλίγοι. 15. [δὲ]. εἰσι. 16. γνώσεσθε (pro ἐπιγν. not ver. 20). μήτινες (pro μήτι) 13. [σταφυλὴν]: ἀποτρι. σύκα. 17. οὕτως. [as Scr. ordo]. 18. [ποιεῖν]. 19. + οὖν (post πᾶν) 13. 20. ἀράγε [ἀπὸ]. 21. -λεῖαν. [ἐν οὐνοῖς]. 22. ἐροῦσίν. σῶ prim. ἐπροφητεύσαμεν 13.124. 23. + πάντες (ante οἱ ἐργ.) 13.124. 24. [τούτους]. ὁμοιωθήσεται [– αὐτὸν] 13. 124. [τὴν οἰκίαν αὐτοῦ] so ver. 26. 25. [ἦλθον] ver. 27. προσέπεσαν 13.124.346. οὐκ᾽. 26. ὅστις ἀκούει (pro ὁ ἀκούων) 13.124. ποιεῖ (pro ποιῶν) 13.124. οἰκοδόμησε 13.124, ver. 24 dub. οι. 27. προσέκρουσαν (pro προσέκοψαν) 13.124. ἐκείνη. ἔπεσεν. fin. + σφόδρα 13.124. 28. συνετ.]. ἐπιτῆ. 29. οὐχ᾽. fin. + αὐτῶν only 13.124.

VIII. 1. καταβάντος δὲ αὐτοῦ 13.124. 2. προσελθὼν 13.346. [-ρίσαι]. 3. ἐκτεῖνας. ἤψατο. – ὁ ἶσ 13.124. [θερ-]. μωϋσῆς 13.124. [rest as Scr.]. 5. εἰσελθόντος δὲ αὐτοῦ (– τοῦ ἰῦ) 13.124. [καπερ-]. [-χος]. παρακαλὸν 346. 6. δεινὸς 124.346. 7, 8. [as Scr.]. 8. ἄξιος (pro ἱκανὸς) μόνω 346. λόγω 13.124.346. παῖς μου (so ver. 6). 9. [no add.]. στρατιώτας. 10. θσ (pro ἰσ). + αὐτῶ (post ἀκολ.) 346. ἀμὴν 13.124 bis scriptum [rest as Scr.]. 11. ἀνακληθήσονται 13.124. -λεῖα. 12. -λεῖας. ὀδόντων. 13. ἑκατοντάρχη hic [non ver. 8] 13.124.346. [rest as Scr. no add.]. ὥρα ἐκείνη. 14. ἴδεν passim 13.124.346. 15. + εὐθέως (ante ἀφῆκεν) 13.124.346. διεικόνει [αὐτοῖς]. 17. [ἦσ.] 18. πολλοὺς ὄχλους. 20. ἀλώπεκες. κλίνει 13.124.346. 21. [αὐτοῦ]. πρα μου. 22. [ἶσ εἶπεν]. ἀκολούθη ἴ. 23. – τὸ 13.124.346. 24. ἐκάθευδεν 13.124.346. 25. οἱ μαθηταῖ (– αὐτοῦ 13.124.346). – ἡμᾶς 13.346. 26. ὀλιγόπιστοι. 27. τῶ ἀνέμω 13.124.346. [ὅτι καὶ]. [ὑπ. αὐτῶ]. 28. ἐλθόντος αὐτοῦ 13.124.346. γεργεσινῶν 13. 124. ἐκείνησ. 29. σὺ (pro σοι) 124.346. 31. [as Scr.]. 32. [as Scr.] only – τῶν χοίρων secund. 13.124. 34. [as Scr.].

IX. 1. + ὁ ἶσ (post ἐμβὰς) 13.346. – τὸ 13.124.346. διεπέρασεν. 2. προσέφερον. [rest as Scr.] so ver. 5. 3. [εἶπον]. 4. [ἰδὼν]. + αὐτοῖς (post εἶπεν) 13.124.346. ἵνα τί. [ὑμεῖς]. 5. ἔγειρε 13.124.346. 6. ἐγερθεὶς ἄρόν. 8. [ἐθαύμασων]. 9. ἐκεῖθεν ὁ ἶσ 13.124.346. ἴδεν. τελωνεῖον 13.124.346. [ματθ-]. ἀναστὰς.

COLLATION OF COD. 556 WITH CODD. 13.69.124.346. 5

[-θησεν]. 10. [αὐτοῦ ἀνακ.] τελώναι. 11. -σαίοι [εἶπον] so ver. 14.
Διὰ τί. 12. [ῑσ]. ἀκοῦσας. [αὐτοῖς]. χρεῖαν. [ἀλλ']. 13. [ἔλεον].
ἀλλὰ [εἰς μετ.]. 14. αὐτῶι. [νν]. διὰ τί. νηστεύουσιν. 15. – οἱ
13.124.346. ἐφ̄όσον fin., + ὅτᾱν. 16. ῥάκκους 13.124.346. 17. ἐκ-
χεῖται. ἀπόλλυνται 13.124. ἀμφότεροι 13.124.346. -ούνται.
18. ἄρχων τίς προσελθὼν τῶ ῑῡ 13.346. –Ὅτι 13.124.346. ἀλλ'.
ἐπεῖθεσ 13.124.346. ἐπαυτῆς. 19. [-ησεν]. ει ἔλεγεν. 21. κρα-
σπέδου (pro ἱματίου) 13.124.346. 22. ῑσ στραφεὶς 13.124. εῑπεν.
ὥρας ἐκείνησ. 23. αὐλιτὰς 13.124. ἔλεγεν (pro λέγει αὐτοῖς) 13.
124.(346). 24. καταγέλων ἱ. 25. ἤγειρεν (pro ἠγέρθη) 13.124.346.
26. [αὐτη]. -είνην. 27. [αὐτῶ]. – καὶ λέγοντες 13.124.346. + κε
(ante υἱὲ δᾱδ) 13. 28. προσῆλθον αὐτῶι. τ. ποιῆσαι, +. 30. [as
Scr.]. 31. διεφήμησαν 13.346. [-εῑνη]. 32. [ᾱνον] not 124.
33. –Ὅτι 13.124.346. 34. [habet]. 35. πᾶσας. κώμας. -λείας.
[ἐν τῶ λαῶ]. fin. + καὶ πολλοὶ ἠκολούθησαν αὐτῶ 13.346. 36. + ὁ ῑσ
(post ὄχλους) 13.346. εὔσπλα. 13.124.346. ἐσκυλμένοι καὶ ἐρριμ-
μένοι ὡσεὶ 13.124.346. 37. ὀλίγοι.

X. 1. + ὁ ῑσ (post προσκ.) 13.346. 2. εἰσὶν 13.346. [νν].
3. [τθ.]. τελῶνης. ἀλφαίου. θαδδαῖος et λεββαῖος change places
13.346. 4. [κανανίτης]. ἰούδασ ἰσκ. παρέδωκεν (pro παραδοὺς)
13.124.346. 5. [-ρειτῶν]. 7. βασιλεῖα passim. 8. νεκροὺς ἐγείρετε (placed before λεπρ.) 13.346. 9. μῆτε (pro μηδὲ prim.)
13.124.346. μῆτε secund. 10. μὴ πῆραν. μῆτε (pro μηδὲ) bis.
[μῆτε ῥάβδους] 13.124.346. [ἐστίν]. 11. εἰσέλθητε ἢ κώμην
13.124.346. -τέ τισ. ἐστιν. 13. ἦ ἡ bis. ἐλθάτω 13.124.346.
14. ἂν (pro ἐὰν). μηδὲ. + ἢ κώμης (ante ἐκείνης). ἐκτεινάξατε
13.124.346. [no ἐκ]. 15. [γομορρων]. 18. ἐπι. 19. Οτ' ἂν.
παραδίδωσιν 13. fin. λαλήσητε [rest as Scr.] 13.124.346. 21. ἐπ-
αναστήσονται. 22. ὑπομείνας. 23. ὅτᾱν. διώκουσιν 13.124.346.
ταυτη. ἑτέραν (pro τὴν ἄλλην). + κᾱν ἐκ ταύτης διώκουσιν ὑμᾶς
φεύγετε εἰς τὴν ἄλλην (ante ἀμὴν) 13.124.346. [τοῦ]. ιηλ.
24. οὐκ ἔστιν. μαθητῆς. + αὐτοῦ (post διδάσκαλον) 13.346.
25. ἐπεκάλεσαν 13.346. [rest as Scr.]. 26. ἐστιν συγκεκαλυμμένον
13.124.346. 28. φοβεῖσθε (pro -θῆτε), -θαι 13.346. ἀποκτενόντων
13.124.346. -κτεῖναι. [φοβήθητε] 13.346. – καὶ ante τὴν ψυχὴν
καὶ τὸ σῶμα 13.124.346 (τῶ 346). 29. ἐξ'. πεσεῖται. fin. , +.
30. εἰσίν. 31. + αὐτοὺς (post φοβηθῆτε) 13.346. 32. + τοῖς (ante

οὐνοῖς) 13.346 *non* ver. 33.   33. ἂν ἀπαρνησητέ με 13.124.346.
34. νομήσητε 13.   — ἐπὶ τὴν γῆν 13.   35. πενθερὰς.   38. οὐκ' *bis*
[rest as Scr.].   41. [λήψεται].

XI. 2. [νν *passim*]. ἀκούσας. δεσμοτηρίω [δύο] 13.346. αὐτῶ.
4. + τῶ (*ante* ἰωάννη) 13.346.   5. [καὶ χ.] περιπατοῦσιν. [καὶ κωφ.].
[καὶ] πτ. εὐαγγελίζονται καὶ νεκροὶ ἐγείρουνται *ordo* 13.124.346.
6. [ἐὰν]. 7. [-θετε] so ver. 8, 9 not 124. ἀνέμω *p. m.* and *s. m.*
fin. , + so ver. 8. 9. ἰδεῖν· προφήτην,. 10. γάρ ἐστιν. προπροσ.
[ὃς]. 11. βασιλεῖα so ver. 12 *passim.* [αὐτοῦ ἐστιν]. 13. προφῆται.
ἐπροφήτευσαν 13.124.346. 14. [ἠλίας]. 16. ταύτην. ἐστιν παιδίοις.
καθημένοις ἐν ἀγοραῖς. ἃ προσφωνοῦντα τοῖς ἑτέροισ 13.124.346.
17. λέγουσιν (− καὶ) ηὐλίσαμεν 346. οὐχ'. [ὑμῖν]. οὐκεκό-.
18. ἦλθεν. + πρὸς ὑμᾶς (*post* γὰρ) 13.124.346. λέγουσιν.
19. φίλος τελωνῶν 13.346. πάντων τῶν τέκνων 13.124.346. 20. +ὁ
ι̑σ (*ante* ὀνειδ.) 13.124.346. πλείσται. 21. χῶραζείν 13.124.346.
[βηθσαϊδάν]. 21. − εἰ. 22. + οὖν (*post* πλὴν). 23. [καπερ.].
ἡ ἕωστοῦ 124. ὑψώθης 13.346. [ᾅδου. καταβιβ. rest as Scr.] 346.
25. [ἀπέκρυψας]. 26. [ἐγένετο εὐδοκία]. 27. τίσ. βούλητε. [rest
as Scr.]. 29. πρᾶός. εὑρήσεται 13.346.

Henceforth only note special cases of accents, breathings, ι
ascript, but note all itacisms.

XII. 1. σάββασιν so ver. 10. 2. +αὐτοὺς (*post* ἰδόντες)
13.124.346. οὐκ' ἔξεστιν. 3. δᾱδ. [ν αὐτὸς]. 4. ἔφαγεν ὃ (*pro*
οὓς) 13.124. 5. +τοῖς ἐν τῶ ἱερῶ (*post* ὅτι) 13.346. [rest as Scr.].
βεβηλοῦσιν. εἰσίν 124. 6. [-ζων] 346. 7. τι ἐστὶ ἔλεον. 8. ἐστὶν.
− καὶ 13.124.346. 10. + ἐκεῖ (*post* ἦν) 13.124.346. [τὴν]. χεῖραν
13.124. ἔξεστιν. [-εύειν. -σωσιν]. 11. *Post* τοῖς *hiat usque ad*
cap. XIII. 10. καὶ προσελθόντες. [Two leaves.]

XIII. 10. εἶπαν. διὰ τί. 11. [αὐτοῖς]. 13. λαλῶ αὐτοῖς
13.124.346. 13. + ἵνα (*ante* βλέποντες). βλέπωσιν. (*non* οὐ).
μη (not οὐ) ἀκούσωσιν καὶ μὴ συνιῶσιν 13.124.346. *fin.* + μήποτε
ἐπιστρέψωσιν 13.124.346, cf. ver. 15. 14. − ἐπ' 13.124.346. -τεία
[ἠσ.]. ἀκοῇ ἀκούσητε 13.124.346. 15. ὦσὶν. ἴδωσιν. ἀκούσωσιν.
συνῶσιν. ἰάσωμαι 13.124.346. 16. βλέπουσιν. ἀκούωσιν 13.124.
346. 17. [γὰρ] οὐχ' εἶδον. 18. [σπείροντοσ] 13.346. 19. σπαρεῖς
(so ver. 20, 22). 21. ἐστιν. 22. [τούτου]. συνπνίγει. 23. − τὴν
secund. 13. συνιῶν. [ὁ *ter.*]. 24. Ὁμοιώθη. σπείραντι 13.346.

25. ἔσπειρεν. ἀναμέσον. 26. ἐποίησεν. – καὶ (ante τὰ ζιζ.)
13.124.346. 27. δοῦλος. εἶπαν 13.346. [ἔσπειρας]. [τὰ ζιζ.].
28. [δούλοι]. εἶπαν αὐτῶ 13.124.346. ἐλθόντες 13.346. συλ-
λέξομεν 13.346. 29. [ἔφη]. οὐχὶ (pro οὔ) 13.124.346. 30. [μέχρι].
– τῷ 13.124.346. δήσαντες αὐτὰ [εἰς]. [συναγάγετε]. 31. ἐλάλησεν
(pro παρέθηκεν) 13.124.346. 32. μείζων 13.346. ἐστίν. [-νοῦν].
33. + λέγων (post αὐτοῖς) 13.124.346. 34. οὐδὲν (pro οὐκ) 13.346.
35. + ἠσαΐου (post διὰ) 13.124.346.361. [λῆς κόσμου]. 36. [as
Scr.]. 37. [αὐτοῖς]. 38. οὗτοι. 39. [ὁ σπ. αὐ. ἐστὶν]. – τοῦ (ante
αἰῶνος) 13.124.346. 40. καίεται 13.124. 40. [τούτου]. 41. σκάνδαλα. 42. ὀδόντων so ver. 50. 43. τῶν (pro τοῦ) cf. 124. [ἀκούειν].
44. [πάλιν]. ἔκρυψεν. [ordo as Scr.]. 45. [ἄνω]. εἶχεν. ἠγόρασεν.
47. βληθήσει 13. 48. ἦν. ἐπὶ τὸν αἰγιαλὸν (– καὶ). [ἀγγεῖα].
51. [λέγει αὐτ. ὁ ῑσ̄.] 13.124.346. – κ̄ε̄. 52. [εἶπεν]. θεὶς τῇ
βασιλεία (– εἰς) 13.124.346. 53. ταύτας. 54. ἐκπλήσσεσθαι
13.124.346. 55. οὐχ᾽. οὐχ (pro οὐχὶ) 13.124.346. [ἰωσῆς].
ἰούδας. πάσαι. εἰσίν·, +. 57. ἔστιν. + ἰδία (ante πατρίδι) 13.
124.346. αὐτοῦ prim. 13.124.346.

XIV. 1. [ἠρῶ] pass. εἶπεν. 2. [νν] pass. 3. + τότε (ante
κρατήσας) 13.124.346. [αὐτὸν]. ἐν φυλακῇ ἀπέθετο. [ἤμων].
[φιλίππου]. 4. [as Scr.]. 6. Γενέσιον δὲ ἀγ. 13.346. -νων.
ὠρχίσατο. 7. ὤμωσεν (pro ὡμολόγησεν) 13.124.346. ἂν αἰτήσεται.
8. προβιβασθίσα. [ὦδε]. 9. λυπηθεὶς (– δὲ) (13).124.(346).
δωθήναι. 11. ἠνέχθη. ἐν (pro ἐπὶ). ἤνεγκεν. 12. πτῶμα (pro
σῶμα) 13.124.346. [αὐτὸ]. 13. ἀκούσας δὲ 13.124.346. κατιδίαν
v. 23. πεζῇ. 14. [ὁ ῑσ̄] ἴδεν. εὐσπλαγχνίσθη ἐπ᾽ αὐτοῖς 13.124.
15. ὀψίασ not v. 23. κῶμας [rest as Scr.]. 16. [ῑσ̄]. 18. εἶπεν.
[αὐτοὺς ὦδε]. 19. – καὶ (ante λαβὼν 13.124.346. [εὐλ.]. 20. πε-
ρισσεύων 13.124. 21. [γ. καὶ π.]. 22. εὐθέως ἠνάγκασεν ὁ ῑσ̄.
[αὐτοῦ]. [τὸ πλ.]. 23. προσεύξασθε. 24. σταδίους πολλοὺς ἀπὸ
τῆς γῆς ἀπῆχε 346 (pro μέσον τῆς θαλάσσης ἦν) 13.124.346.
25. ἦλθεν. [ὁ ῑσ̄]. τὴν θάλασσαν. 26. οἱ δε μαθηταὶ ἰδόντες αὐτὸν
περιπατοῦντα ἐπὶ τῆς θαλάσσης 13.124.346. 27. εὐθὺς. [ordo as
Scr.] so ver. 28. 28. εἶπεν. εἰ σὺ εἶ. ἐλθεῖν πρὸσ σὲ 13.124.
29. [as Scr.]. 30. βλέπον. [ἰσχυρὸν]. σῶσόν με. 31. ὀλιγόπιστε.
33. προσελθόντες 13.124.346. 34. ἦλθον, ἐπὶ τὴν γῆν 13.124.346.
γεννήσαρεθ. 35. ἐπιγνῶντες 13.124. ἐκείνου τοῦ τόπου 13.124.346.
36. [αὐτὸν]. + κἂν (ante μόνον) 13.346.

8   MATT. XV. 1—XVIII. 31.

XV. 1. – οἱ. φαρισαῖοι καὶ γραμμ. 2. διὰ τί ver. 3. νίπτωνται.
ὅτ᾽ ἄν. 3. διατὴν. 4. λέγον. πρα͞ σου. 5. δᾶν (pro ἄν). [καὶ].
τιμήσει 13.124.346. – αὐτοῦ secund. 13.124.346. 6. τὸν νόμον
(pro τὴν ἐντολὴν) 13.124.346. παράδωσιν not ver. 2. 7. [προε.]
346. 8. [nil omissum] 13.346. 9. σέβοντέ 13. διδασκαλείασ 13.
11. κοινοὶ bis ver. 17, 20. 12. – αὐτοῦ 13.124.346. λέγουσιν
(pro εἶπον) 13.124.346. οἴδας. 13. εἶπεν. 14. τυφλοί εἰσιν
ὁδηγοὶ τυφλῶν. τυφλὸς δὲ τυφλὸν ὁδηγὸν σφαλήσεται. καὶ ἀμφότεροι πεσοῦνται εἰς τὸν βόθυνον 13.124.346. 15. ταύτην τὴν
παραβολήν 13.124.346. 16. [ἰσ]. ἔσται, +. 17. [οὔπω] 13.124.
346. καὶ ἐκεῖνα. 22. ἔκραξεν (– αὐτῶ) 13.124.346. [υἱὲ δᾶδ].
23. λόγω 13. [rest as Scr.]. 24. οὐκ᾽. 25. προσεκύνη 346.
βοήθη 13. 26. οὐκ᾽ ἔστι κ. 27. εἶπεν. [γὰρ]. ἐσθίειν. ψῦχίων.
αὐτῶν. 28. θέλης 346. 29. ἦλθεν. + ὁ ἰσ (post ὄρος) 346.
30. αὐτοῦ (pro τοῦ ἰῦ) 13.124.346. [rest as Scr.]. 31. τὸν ὄχλον
13.124.346. βλέποντες. + καὶ (ante κυλλ.) 346. + καὶ (ante
χωλοὺς) 13.124. [ἐδόξασαν]. ἰσραήλ plene hic. 32. εἶπεν. [ἤδη
ἡμέρας]. 33. [αὐτοῦ]. – ἐν (supra see manus.). 34. εἶπαν 346.
35. παραγγείλας τῶ ὄχλω 13.124.346. 36. ἔλαβε (– καὶ) 13.124.346.
+ καὶ (ante εὐχαρ.) 13.124. ἐδίδου 13.124.346. – αὐτοῦ 13.124.346.
τοῖς ὄχλοις 13.124.346. 37. [ordo as Scr.]. 38. + ὡς (ante τετρ.)
13.124.346. [γ. καὶ π.]. 39. ἀνέβη 13.346. – τὸ 13.124.346.
[μάγδαλά].

XVI. 1. ἐπηρώτων 13.124.346. 2. – ὀψίασ ad fin. ver. 3
13.124. 4. μοιχαλεῖς 13.124.346. [τοῦ πρ.]. ἀπῆλθεν. 5. ἐξελ-
θόντες 13.124.346. – αὐτοῦ [ἄρ. λαβ.]. 8. [αὐτοῖς]. ὀλιγόπιστοι.
οὐκέχετε (not ἐλάβετε hic) 13.124.346. 10. [σπυ.]. 11. ἄρτων
13.124.346. προσέχετε (not δὲ). 12. εἶπεν [τοῦ ἄρτου] ἀλλὰ.
13. [-ρείας]. ἠρῶτα. [με]. 14. [as Scr.]. 15. [nil additum].
16. εἶπεν. 17. ἀποκριθεὶς δὲ 13.124.346. [βαρἰωνᾶ]. ἀπεκάλυψεν.
οὐνιος (pro ἐν τοῖς οὐνοις) 13.124.346. 18. [ἅδου]. κατ᾽ ἰσχύ-.
19. [καὶ]. [κλεῖσ]. [ὃ ἐὰν bis]. [-νον]. 20. [αὐτοῦ]. μηδενὶ.
[ἰσ ἡ χσ] 13.346. – ἰσ 124. 21. [ὁ]. εἰσ ἱεροσόλυμα 13.124.346.
ἀπελθεῖν. ἀρχιερέων καὶ πρεσβυτέρων 13.124.346. + τοῦ λαοῦ
(post γραμματέων) 13.124.346. 22. αὐτῶ ἐπιτιμᾶν 13.124.346.
[λέγων]. 23. ἐπιστραφεὶς εἶπεν 13.346. εἰ ἐμοῦ. Leaf loose from
ver. 24 to cap. XVII. 18. 24. [ὁ ἰσ] εἶπεν. 25. [ἄν]. αὐτοῦ prim.
(so ver. 26 fin., ver. 27 prim. et sec.). 26. ὠφεληθήσεται 13.124.346.

27. αὐτοῦ *prim. et sec.* 28. ὅτι 13.124.346 εἰσίν τινες τῶν ὧδε
ἑστώτων 13.124.346. γεύσονται. ἴδωσιν.

XVII. 1. [καὶ Ἰακ. νν]. κατ᾽ ἰδίαν ver. 19. 2. ἔλλαμψε.
ἐγένοντο 13.346. 3. ὤφθη 13.124.346. μωυσῆς. [μετ᾽ αὐτοῦ
συλλ.]. 4. εἶπεν. [-σωμεν ὧδε τρ. σκ.]. μωυσῆ μίαν καὶ ἠλία μίαν
13.124. 5. φωτὸς (*pro* φωτεινῆ) 13.124.346. [εὐδ.]. [αὐτ. ἀκ.].
6. [ἔπεσον]. 7. [προσελ.]. καὶ ἁψάμενος 13.124.346. – καὶ (*ante*
εἶπεν). 8. οὐδ᾽ ἕνα. ἴδων. 9. ἐκ (*pro* ἀπὸ) 13.124.346. μηδ᾽ ἐνὶ.
[ἀναστῇ]. 10. [αὐτοῦ...ἠλ.] (– αυτοῦ 124). 11. [ἴσ αὐτοῖς ἠλ.].
[πρῶτον]. + τὰ (*ante* πάντα) 124.346. 12. ἦλθεν. [ἀλλ᾽]. οὕτως.
15. γονυπετὸν αὐτὸν (*pro* αὐτῷ) 13.124.346. [rest as Scr.].
[πάσχει]. οὐκ ἠδ. ver. 19. 17. [ἀποκριθεὶς δὲ]. ἕως πότε ἀνέξομαι
ὑμων· 13.346. ἕως πότε μεθ᾽ ὑμῶν ἔσομαι· 18. ὥρασ. 19. [εἶπον].
20. ὁ δὲ ἴσ λέγει. ὀλιγοπιστίαν (*pro* απ.) 13.124.346. μετάβα
ἐντεῦθεν καταβήσεται (*pro* μεταβ.) 13.124.346. 21. [*Habet*
versum]. 22. [ἀναστρ.]. 23. ἀναστήσεται (*pro* ἐγερ-) 13.124.346.
24. [καπερ-]. [εἶπον]. 25. εἰσελθόντων (*pro* ὅτε εἰσ.) 13.124.346.
προ ἐφθ. λαμβάνουσιν 13. 26. [as Scr.]. ἀράγε. 27. ἀναβαίνοντα
346. [rest as Scr.].

XVIII. 1. [ὥρα προσ] ἆρα. 2. [ὁ ἴσ]. 4. ταπεινώσει
13.124.346. 5. [ἐὰν]. ἐν παιδίον τοιοῦτον 13.124.346. 6. σκαν-
δαλίσει. εἰς (*pro* ἐπὶ) 13.124.346. 7. [ἐστιν]. τὰ σκάνδαλα
secund. 13.124.346. 8. αὐτὸν (*pro* αὐτὰ) 13.124.346. [χ. ἢ κ.].
9. ἐστιν. ἔχειν καὶ (*pro* ἔχοντα) 13.124.346. 10. ἐν οὐνοῖς].
11. *deest versus* 13 only. 12. γένωνται 13.124. ἀφήσει. ἐνενήκοντα ἐννέα so ver. 13. + πρόβατα 13.346. + καὶ (*ante* πορ.)
13.124.346. ζητήσει. πλανόμενον. 13. + τοῦ (*ante* εὑρεῖν) 13.
124.346. ἐν (*pro* ἐπ᾽) 13.124.346. 14. μου (*pro* ὑμῶν) 13.124.346.
[εἷς]. 15. – δὲ 13.124. – καὶ (*ante* ἔλ.). 16. μετὰ σεαυτοῦ 13.69.
17. [εἰπὲ]. 18. ἂν (*pro* ἐὰν) *bis* 13.69.124.346. [τῷ] *bis non* 124.
19. πάλιν + ἀμὴν 13.69.124.346. + ἐξ (*ante* ὑμῶν). [-σωσιν].
αἰτήσονται 13.124.346. 20. ὅπου (*pro* οὗ) 13.69.124.346. 21. προσ.
αὐτῷ ὁ π. εἶπεν. ἁμαρτήσῃ. ὁ ἀδελφός μου εἰς ἐμὲ 13.69.124.346.
23. Διὰ τούτω ὠμ. ἠθέλησεν. συνάραι. *fin.* αὐτοῦ. 24, 25. [as
Scr.]. 26. ἀποδώσω σοι 13.69.124. [rest as Scr.]. 27. [ἐκείνου].
δάνιον 13.69.124.346. *fin.* αὐτοῦ (*pro* αὐτῷ). 28. [ἐκεῖνος]. εἴ τι
ὀφείλῃς 13.69.124.346. 29. ἅπαντα σοι ἀποδώσω 69.124.346.
[rest as Scr.]. 30. ἠθέλησεν. [ἀλλὰ...οὗ]. 31. ἀπελθόντες

13.69.124.346. [as Scr.]. 33, 34. [καὶ ἐγώ]. 34. ἕως. 35. οὕτωσ.
ἐπ᾽ουνιος. [τὰ παραπτώματα αὐτῶν].

XIX. 1. [τῆς]. 3, 4. [as Scr.]. 4. ἀπαρχῆς ver. 8. 5. [ἕνεκεν].
+ αὐτοῦ (post πρα). κολληθήσεται 13.69.346. fin. αὐτοῦ. 6. ὁ
(pro ὅ). 7. [μωσῆς] cf. ver. 8. [αὐτήν]. 8. μωϋσῆς. οὕτως.
9. παρεκτὸς λόγου πορνείας 13.69.124.346. γαμῶν (pro γαμήσας)
13.69.124.346. [rest as Scr.]. 10. αὐτοῦ. 11. [τοῦτον].
12. οὕτως. 13. προσηνέχθησαν. [-πεν ἄφ.]. κωλύσητε 13.124.
[πρόσ με]. 15. τὰς χεῖρασ αὐτοῖσ 13.69.124.346. 16. αὐτῶ εἶπεν
13.69.346. [ἀγαθὲ]. [ἔχει·]. 17. [as Scr.]. 18. ἔφη (pro ἰσ
εἶπε) 13.124.346. [rest as Scr.]. 19. πρα σου. 20. ταῦτα πάντα
13.69.124.346. [rest as Scr.]. 21. λέγει (pro ἔφη) 13.69.124.346.
[δὸς πτ.]. [ἐν οὐνῶ]. δεύρω ἀκολούθη μοι 124. 22. [τὸν λόγον].
ἀπῆλθεν. 23. εἶπεν. πλούσιος δυσκόλως. 24. ἐστιν. εἰσελθεῖν
(pro διελθεῖν) 13.69.346. [rest as Scr.]. πλούσιος 13.69.346.
25. – αὐτοῦ ἆρα 13.69.124. 26. ἐστιν prim. – ἐστι secund.
13.69.124.346. [π. δ.]. 27. ἆρα. 28. ὅτ᾽ ἂν. καθήσεσθε
13.69.124. [ὑμεῖς]. 29. ὅστις (pro ὅς) 13.62.124.346. [rest as
Scr.]. 30. + οἱ (ante ἔσχατοι secund.) 13.69.346.

XX. 3. – τὴν 13.69.124.346. ἴδεν 13.124. 4. καὶ ἐκείνοισ
13.69.346. + μου (post ἀμπελῶνα) 13.69.346.124. 5. [πάλιν ἐξ-].
ἐνάτην 13.69.124. ὡσαύτως. 6, 7, 8, 13. [as Scr.]. 9. ἐλθόντες
οὖν (– καὶ). 10. init. καὶ ἐλθόντες (– δὲ) 13.69.124.346. ἐνόμησαν.
πλεῖον [λήψ-] 13.69.124.346. – καὶ secund. 13.346. 11. [ὅτι].
ὧραν passim. – αὐτοὺς. καύσωνα +. 14. [δὲ]. 15. [ἤ]. ὃ θέλω
ποιῆσαι 13.69.124.346. [εἰ]. 16. [nil omissum]. ὀλίγοι. 17. – ὁ
ἰσ 346. παρέλαβεν. + αὐτοῦ (post μαθητὰς) 13.346. καὶ ἐν τῇ
ὁδῷ εἶπεν 13.69.124.346. 18. ἀρχιερεῦσιν. γραμματεῦσιν. κατα-
κρίνουσιν. [θανάτῳ]. 19. ἐμπέξαι. [ἀναστ.]. 20. [παρ᾽]. 21. + σου
(post εὐωνύμων). [rest as Scr.]. 22. ἢ (pro καὶ ante τὸ βάπτισμα).
23. καὶ λέγει αὐτοῖς ὁ ἰσ 13.69.124.346. [nil om.]. καὶ ἐξευωνύμων
(– μου) 13.69.124.346. [ἐμὸν δοῦναι]. ἡτοίμασται. 24. ἀκούσαντες
(– καὶ) 13.69.124*. 25. οὐχ᾽. – δὲ 13.69.124. [ἔσται]. [ἐὰν].
[ἐν ὑμῖν εἶναι]. ἔσται (pro ἔστω) 13.69.124.346. 28. ἦλθεν.
αὐτοῦ. 29. ἱεριχῶ. 30. ἰῦ (pro κε) 69.(124). [rest as Scr.].
31. μείζων? ἐκραύγαζον 13.69.124.346. κε ἐλέησον ἡμᾶς, υἱὸς δᾱδ
13.69.346. 32. [ὁ ἰσ]. εἶπεν. [θέλετε π.]. 33. ἀνοιγῶσιν 13.69.

124.346. [ἥμ. οἱ ὀρθ.]. 34. ὀμμάτων (*pro* ὀρθ.) 13.69.124.346.
[αὐτων οἱ ὁ.].

XXI. 1. βηθσφαγὴ καὶ βηθανίαν πρὸς 13.69.124.346. [ὁ ισ̅].
τῶν μαθητῶν αὐτοῦ (*pro* μαθητὰς) 13.69.124.346. 2. πορεύεσθε all
four. ἀπέναντι. [rest as Scr.]. 3. εἴπῃ· τί. αὐτῶν *male*. [εὐθέως].
ἀποστέλλει. 4. ὅλον. ὑπὸ (*pro* διὰ) four. 5. [καὶ πῶλον].
6. [προσ.]. 7. αὐτῶ (*pro* ἐπάνω *prim.*). αὐτῶν. [-σεν]. 8. [-νvον].
9. +αὐτὸν (*post* προάγοντες) 69.124. ὡσ ἀννὰ bis. 11. - ισ̅
13.124. [-ἐτ]. 12. [ὁ ισ̅]. - τοῦ θεοῦ· κατέστρεψεν 13. 13. [-ήσα
τε]. 14. - ἐν τῷ ἱερῷ 13.69. 15. οἱ γραμματεῖς καὶ οἱ ἀρχιερεῖς
four. ἐποίησεν. [-δας κρά-]. ὡσάννά. 16. [εἶπον]. κατ᾽ ἠρτίσω.
18. [as Scr.]. ἐπείνασεν. 19. [not οὐ]. 22. [as Scr.]. 23. ἐλθόντος αὐτοῦ four. [-θον]. ἔδωκεν. 24. [ὁ]. 25, 26. [as Scr.].
27. [εἶπον] ὑμῖν λέγω 13.69.346. 28. - δὲ four. εἶπεν. - μου
13.124.346. 29. ὑπάγω κε̅· καὶ οὐκ ἀπῆλθεν· (*pro* οὐ θέλω κ.τ.λ.)
four. 30. προσελθὼν δὲ. ἑτέρω (*pro* δευτέρω) four. οὐ θέλω·
ὕστερον δὲ μεταμεληθεὶς ἀπῆλθεν (*pro* ἐγὼ κε̅ κ.τ.λ.). 34. - αὐτῶ
four. ἔσχοντος (*pro* πρῶτος) four. 32. ἦλθεν. [προσ ὑμ. ἰω].
οὐδὲ (*pro* οὐ) 13.69.124. 33. [τις]. περιέθηκεν. πῦργον. [-δοτο].
36. τῶν πρῶτον. 37. ἀπέστειλεν. 38. κατασχῶμεν. 40. ὅτ᾽ ἂν.
41. [ἐκδόσεται]. 42. *fin.* ὑμῶν 13.69.124. 43. Διὰ τοῦτο. [ὅτι].
44. [*habet*] four. ἂν (*pro* δὰν) 13.124.346. πέσει η *supra*.
45. [καὶ ἀκ.]. 46. ποιάσαι (*pro* κρατῆσαι) 13.346. ἐπιδὴ. [rest
as Scr.].

XXIII. 1. ἐλάλησεν ὁ ισ̅ 13.69.124.346. αὐτοῦ. 2. καθέ-
δρας μωϋσέως four. 3. ἐὰν four. [rest as Scr.]. 4. αὐτῶν᾽.
θέλωσι. [rest as Scr.]. 5. γὰρ (*pro* δὲ *secund.*) four. [rest as
Scr.]. 6. δὲ (*pro* τε) four. 7. ῥαββεῖ bis four. 8. ῥαββεί.
[rest as Scr.]. 9. οὐνιος (*pro* ἐν τοῖς οὐνοις) 13.69.124. 10. ἐστιν
ὁ καθηγητὴς ὑμῶν four. 13 (verse 14). ὅτι κλείετε four. *init.* οὐαὶ
δὲ both verses. [ver. 13 follows ὅτι κατεσθ. *fin.* κρῖμα] four.
15. +τοῦ (*ante* ποιῆσαι) four. 16. ὁμόσῃ bis not ver. 18, 20—22.
ὀφείλει not v. 18. 17. [as Scr.]. 18. ἂν (*pro* ἐὰν) four.
19. [μωροὶ καὶ]. + ἐστιν (*ante* μείζων). 22. [-κοῦντι]. 23. καὶ
τὴν κρίσιν καὶ τὸν ἔλεον four. [rest as Scr.]. 24. [οἱ]. 25. ἐξαρπ.
26. [τῆς π.]. αὐτοῦ (*pro* αὐτῶν) four. 27. [παρ-]. μὲν ἔξωθεν
four. 28. οὕτως. ἐστὲ μεστοὶ four. 29. οἰκοδομεῖται. 30. ἤμεθα

prim. 13.69.346. ἦμεν αὐτῶν κοινωνοὶ four. 31. αὐτοῖς (pro
ἑαυτοῖς). ἔσται ε supra. 32. [-σατε]. 33. ὄφις 346. 34. – ἰδού.
– καὶ (ante ἐξ prim.). 35. + ἄν (ante ἔλθη) four. [-χυν-]. [ἄβελ].
[υἱοῦ βαρ.]. 36. [ταῦτα π.]. 37. ἱερουσαλεὶμ Ἰλῆμ. ἀποκτένουσα
four. ὄρνεις ἐπισυνάγει four. [ἑαυτῆς]. [-γας καὶ]. 38. ἀφίετε.
[ἔρημος]. 39. + ὅτι (ante οὐ μή) four.

XXIV. 1. ἀπὸ τοῦ ἱεροῦ ἐπορεύετο four. 2. ἀποκριθεὶσ (pro
ἶσ) four. [οὐ]. ταῦτα πάντα four. – μὴ 13.69.124. 3. -τὰς
κατ'ἰδίαν. [εἰπὲ]. [τῆσσυν-]. 5. σουσ-. 6. [πάντα]. ἐστὶν.
7. [ἐπὶ]. [καὶ λοιμοὶ]. 8. ταῦτα δὲ πάντα four. 9. θλίψιν ver.
21, 29. [τῶν ἐθ.]. 10. παραδώσουσιν. 15. ἑστὼς 13. 16. [ἐπι] τὰ.
17. [-βαινέτω]. ἄραι τὰ four. 18. [τὸ ἱμάτιον] four. 19. ἐγγαστρὶ
cap. I. 18. 20. γένητε. – ἐν four. 21. οἶα. [οὐ γέγονεν].
ἀπαρχῆσ'. 23. [-σητε]. 24. πλανῆσαι. 27. [καὶ ἡ]. 28. [γὰρ]
ἐὰν. 29. [ἀπὸ]. 30. [τῶ οὐνῶ]. κόψονται τότε four. 31. [φωνῆς].
τῶν οὐνῶν ἕως τῶν ἄκρων four. 32. ὄτ'ἂν. ἐκφύη. 33. οὕτως.
ὅτἂν. ταῦτα πάντα four. 34. + ὅτι (ante οὐ μὴ) four. [ἂν].
ταῦτα πάντας four. 35. [-σονται]. παρέλθωσιν. 36. – τῆς (ante
ὥρας) four. + οὐδὲ 13.124.346. ὁ υἱὸς (ante εἰ μὴ). – μου 13.69.
346. 37. [as Scr.]. 38. [-ραις ταῖς]. ἐγγαμίζοντες. ἄχρισ (– ἦσ)
four. εἰσῆλθεν. οὐκ'. [καὶ ἡ]. 40. [as Scr.]. 41. μύλωνι.
fin. + δύο ἐπικλίνης μιᾶς· εἷς παραλαμβάνεται καὶ εἷς ἀφίεται 13.124.
346. 42. ἡμέρα (pro ὥρᾳ) 13.69.124. 43. ὥρα (pro φυλακῇ) four.
[-ρυγῆναι]. 44. [ὥρα οὐ δοκεῖτε]. 45. [αὐτοῦ prim.]. οἰκετίας
(pro θεραπείας) 13.346. οἰκίας א 69.561. δοῦναι four. 46. οὕτως
ποιοῦντα. 48. [as Scr.]. 49. + αὐτοῦ (post συνδ.)? 13.69.124.
ἐσθίει 13.346. πίνει 13.(69).124.346. 51. ὀδόντων.

XXV. 1. [αυτων]. ἀπάν ver. 6. 2. [as Scr.]. 3. [αἵτινες].
αὐτῶν (pro ἑαυτῶν prim.) four. 4. ἀγγίοισ 13.124.69*. [αὐτῶν
bis]. 6. ἐξέρχεσθαι. [rest as Scr.]. ἐκόσμισαν 13. [αὐτῶν].
8. [εἶπον]. 9. [οὐκ']. [δὲ]. 10. αἵτοιμοι (– αἰ) 69. 11. [καὶ].
13. [no omission]. 15. ἔδωκεν. fin. +. 16. [δὲ]. ἠργασατο
13.69.124. ἐκέρδησεν (pro ἐποίησεν) 69.124. [τάλαντα]. 17. ὡσ-
αὕτως [καὶ]. ἐκέρδησεν [καὶ αὐτὸς]. 18. fin. αὐτοῦ ver. 21, 23, 26.
[rest as Scr.]. 19. πολὺν χρόνον four. [μετ' αὐτῶν λόγον].
20. [as Scr.]. 21. [δὲ]. ὀλίγα ἦσ ver. 23. 22. εἶπεν [as Scr.]
ver. 24. 26. [πον. δ.]. ὀκνηρὲ. συνάγων. 27, 29. [as Scr.].

30. ἄχρειον ἐκβάλετε four. 30. ὀδόντων. *fin.* + ταῦτα λέγων ἐφώνει·
ὁ ἔχων ὦτα ἀκούειν, ἀκουέτω four. 31. Ὅτ᾽ ἂν αὐτοῦ *bis* so ver. 33.
[ἅγιοι]. καθίσῃ. 28. συναχθήσονται four. [ἀφοριεῖ]. 36. ἤλθατε
four. 37. ἴδωμεν (so ver. 38) 346. 39. ἴδομεν four. [ἀσθενῇ].
40. [as Scr.]. 41. ἐξεν. [οἱ]. 44. – αὐτῷ four. ἴδομεν 13.69.124.
45. ἐφόσον. 46. οὗτοι.

XXVI. 1. εἶπεν. 2. παραδίδοτε. 3. – καὶ οἱ γραμματεῖς
13.69.346. 4. δόλῳ κρατήσωσιν four. 6. σίμων° (*sic*). 7. ἔχουσα
ἀλάβαστρον μύρου βαρυτίμου four. τῆς κεφαλῆς 13.69. 8. [αὐτοῦ].
αὕτη. 9. [as Scr.]. 10. – γὰρ. ἠργάσατο 13. 14. εἰς *evanuit.*
ἰούδας ver. 25, 47. ἀρχί- εἶπεν. 15. καγὼ. 17. [αὐτῷ]. + ἀπελθόντες (*ante* ἑτοιμ.) 13.346. 18. + ἰσ (*post* δὲ) four. 18. ἐστιν.
20. [no addit.]. 22. – αὐτῷ four. εἰς ἕκαστος αὐτῶν. 23. [as
Scr.]. 24. οὐκεγ. 25. εἶπεν ver. 26. [ῥαββί] ver. 49. 26. αὐτῶν
δὲ ἐσθιόντων 13.69.346. [τὸν ἄρ.]. εὐχαριστήσας (*pro* εὐλογήσας) four. δοὺς – καὶ (*ante* εἶπεν) 13.69. 27, 28. [as Scr.].
29. – ὅτι 13.69. ἀπάρτι *passim* 69 ver. 64. γενήματος 13.124.346.
ὅτ᾽ἂν. [μεθ᾽ ὑμ. κ.]. 31. διασκορπισθήσονται four. 33. – καὶ four.
34. ἀλέκτωρα 346. τρὶς. 35. Ἐὰν (*pro* κἂν) *rubro.* + δὲ (*post*
ὁμοίως) 124. εἶπαν. 36. γεθσημανεῖ 13.69.346. αὐτοῖς (*pro* τοῖς
μαθηταῖς) four. ἂν (*pro* οὖ) 13.69.346. ἐκεῖ. προσεύξομαι (four).
38. + ὁ ἰσ (*ante* περίλυπός). 39. προσελθὼν 13.69.124. So 561.
[μου]. ἐστιν. παρελθάτω 13.124.346. οὐχ᾽. *fin.* + Luc. XXII. 43,
44, 13.69.124.(346). (43. ἀπὸ τοῦ οὐνοῦ 346. 44. [δὲ]. ἱδρὸς.
θρόμβῃ). 40. αὐτοῖς (*pro* τῷ πέτρω) 13.69.346. 42. ὁ ἰσ (*post*
λέγων) four. τὸ ποτήριον τοῦτο 69.346. [ἀπ᾽ ἐμοῦ]. 43. πάλιν
εὗρεν αὐτοὺς 13.124.346. βεβαρυμένοι 69.124. 44. *init.* – καὶ.
πάλιν ἀπελθὼν (four). [ἐκ τρίτου]. [No 2nd πάλιν]. 45. [αὐτοῦ].
– τὸ. 47. ἦλθεν. 48. [ἂν]. 49. εἶπεν. 50. ὃ (*pro* ᾧ) four.
51. τὴν μάχαιρα. 52. ἀποθανοῦνται (*pro* ἀπολοῦνται) 13.69.346.
[rest as Scr.]. 53. λεγεόνων (13 -ωνων). [rest as Scr.]. 54. οὕτως.
55. ἐξήλθατε four. [rest as Scr.]. 56. [as Scr.]. 57. ἀρχιερεαν
ς *supra.* 58. [as Scr.]. ἠκολουθὴ *p.m.* ει *s.m.* 13.124. 59. [as
Scr.]. 60. οὐχ᾽ *bis.* [as Scr.]. 61. -μάρτυρεσ *errore.* – αὐτὸν
69. 62. ἀποκρίνει Η *supra.* , + 63. – ἀποκριθεὶς 13.69. 65. [ὅτι]
ἐβλασφήμησεν. [αὐτοῦ]. 66. ἐστίν. 67. ἐκολάφησαν 13.124.346.
[ρρ]. 69. ἐκάθητο ἔξω 13.124.346. 71. [αὐτὸν *prim.*]. ἴδεν four.
[rest as Scr.]. 72. [μεθ᾽]. 74. καταθεματίζειν four. [εὐθέως].
ἐφώνησεν. 75. [as Scr.]. τρὶς.

14 MATT. XXVII. 2—MARK II. 3.

XXVII. 2. [αὐτὸν secund. πιλ.] passim. ἡγεμώνῃ. 3. εἰδὼν.
[rest as Scr.]. 4. [ἀθῶον]. εἶπαν 13 not ver. 6. τίς (pro τί).
ὄψη 13.124. 5. εἰς τὸν ναὸν four. ἀνεχώρησεν. 6. ἔξεστιν.
κορβονᾶν four. ἔστιν. 8. δι᾽ ὅ. 9. ἱερεμίου 13. 11. [ἔστη].
[αὐτῶ]. 12. –τῶν secund. four. 15. εἰωθῇ 13.69.346. τῶ ὄχλω
ἕνα four. εἴθελον 13. 16. fin. + ὅστις διαφόνον ἦν βεβλημένος
εἰς φυλακήν 13.124.(346). 17. δὲ (pro οὖν) four. [rest as Scr.].
20. αἰτήσωνται. 21, 22, 23, 24. [as Scr.]. 25. εἶπεν. 28. [ἐκ δ.].
χλαμύδα κοκκίνην περιέθηκαν αὐτῶ 69.124.346. 29. ἔθηκαν 69.124.
τῆσ κεφαλῆς 69.124.346. ἐν τῇ δεξιᾶ 13.124.346. ἐνέπαιζον αὐτόν
ὦ supra. [ὁ β.]. 31. [as Scr.]. 32. κυριναῖον 69.124.346.
33. [γολγοθᾶ] ὅ (pro ὅς) 69.346. [rest as Scr.]. 34. [πιεῖν bis].
οἶνον (pro ὄξος) 69. ἠθέλησε 69.346. 35. [as Scr.]. 36. –αὐτον.
40. [as Scr.]. 41. –δὲ 69.346. ἐμπέζοντες hic 69. σῶσαι 69.
, +. 42. πιστεύσωμεν 69.124.(346). [rest as Scr.]. 43. εἶπεν.
[rest as Scr.]. εἰμὶ. 44. σὺν 5ρω. fin. αὐτόν (pro αὐτῶ) 69.124.
346. 45. ἐνάτης 124.346. 46. ἐνάτην. λιμᾶσάβ. ἐγκατέλιπας
346. [rest as Scr.]. 47. [ἑστώτων]. [ἠλίαν] ver. 49. φωνῇ
οὕτως. 49. εἶπαν (pro ἔλεγον) 124.346. σῶσων. 51. καταπαίτασμα
ς supra. εἰς δύο ἐπάνωθεν 69. 52. ἠγέρθησαν 69.124. 53. ἐνέφ.
54. [-ταρχοσ]. ἦν [rest as Scr.]. 55. ἀπομακρόθεν 69. 56. μαγ-
δάλινὴ 124.346. [ἰωσῇ]. 57. [ἐμαθήτευσε]. 58. [τὸ σῶμα].
59. ἰωσῆφ ἐνείλισεν (pro ἐνετ.) 124 cf. 69. [no ἐν]. 60. –αὐτὸ
69. [no ἐπὶ]. 61. [μαρία] μαγδαλινὴ ver. 56. 63. ὁ πλάνος
ἐκεῖνος 69.124.346. 64. [αὐτοῦ]. –νυκτὸς 124.346. 65. –δὲ
69.124.346.

XXVIII. 1. Ὀψὲ [δὲ]. [μαρία] ἡ μαγδαλινὴ 124.346.
2. [not +καὶ]. +τοῦ μνημείου (post θύρας) 346. 3. [ἰδέα] ὡσεὶ
(so ver. 4). 4. ἐσίσθησαν. [ἐγένοντο]. 5. εἶπεν. γυναιξὶν.
6. εἶπεν. [ὁ κσ]. 8. ἀπελθούσαι 69.124.346. –αὐτοῦ. 9. [no
omission] only 69. ὁ ισ ὑπήντησεν 124.346. 10. ὑπάγεται. καὶ
ἐκεῖ 13. 11. [ἀπήγγ-]. 14. [ἐπὶ]. [αὐτὸν]. ποιήσωμεν 13.69.
124.346. 15. [διεφ.]. 17. [αὐτῶ]. 18. μι (pro μοι) 13. ἐπιγῆσ.
19. [as Scr.]. 20. εἰμὶ. [ἀμήν]. Subscription Τέλοσ τοῦ κατὰ
ματθαίου εὐαγγελίου | sic: vid title. Ἐκ τοῦ κατὰ ματθαῖον sic 124
εὐαγγελίου ἐγράφη ἑβραϊστὶ ἐν παλαιστείνι μετὰ ἢ ἔτη τῆς ἀναλήψεως
τοῦ κυ̅· ἔχει δὲ ῥήματα β̅φκβ̅+ ἔχει δὲ στείχους β̅ φ̅ξ̅. 2nd loose leaf
from cap. XXVIII. 7 to end κεφ. of Marc. Τοῦ κατ᾽ μάρκον εὐ̅ᾱ τὰ
κεφαλ̅ rubro.

Collation of κεφ. to Mark, 4th column of loose leaf: rest on a lost
leaf. Collated with Mill's N. T. and with 69. β'. −τοῦ. ς'. −τοῦ
69. θ'. περὶ παραβολῆς τοῦ σπόρου 69. ια'. τοῦ ἔχοντος τὸν λεγεῶνα
69. ις'. [περὶ] τῶν νε ἄρτων (−καὶ τῶν δύο ἰχθύων). ιθ'. φοινικήσσης.
Title to Mark (illuminated) Εὐαγγέλιον cf. 69 ἐκ^τ κ^τ Μάρκον rubro.
MARC. I. 1, 2, 4. [as Scr.]. 3. [ἐρήμωι Ἐτ.]. 4. [νν].
5. − ἡ four. ἱεροσολυμεῖται 13.69.124.346. καὶ πάντες ἐβαπτίζοντο
four. [ποτάμωι ὑπ' αὐτοῦ]. 6. [ἦν δε ἰω.]. [ἐσθίων]. 8. μὲν ὑμᾶς
ἐβάπτισα ἐν ὕδ. four. − δὲ four. [ἐν πν.]. 9. [καὶ]. + ὁ (ante ἰσ)
four. ναζαρὲθ 69*. εἰς τὸν ἰορδάνην ὑπὸ ἰωάννου four. 10. [εὐθέως].
ἐκ (pro ἀπὸ) four. ἴδε. [ὥσει]. καταβαίνων p.m. (ω eras.). εἰς
(pro ἐπ') four. 11. [ἐγένετο]. σοὶ (pro ὦ) four. 12. [εὐθὺς].
ἐκβάλλει αὐτὸν 13.69.346. 13. − ἐκεῖ 13.346. + ἐπὶ (ante ἡμέρασ)
four. [τεσσαρ.-]. + καὶ τεσσαράκοντα νύκτας (ante πειρ.) 13.346.
14. [Μετὰ δὲ : rest as Scr.]. 16. καὶ παράγων (pro περιπ. δὲ) four.
ἴδεν 13.124.346. + τοῦ (ante σίμωνος). τοῦ σίμωνος (pro αὐτοῦ)
four. ἀμφιβάλλοντας four. τὰ δίκτυα (pro ἀμφίβλησατρον) four.
εἰς τὴν θάλασσαν four. 18. [εὐθέως] ver. 19. − αὐτῶν 13.69.346.
19. [ἐκεῖθεν]. ἴδεν four. 20. + εὐθὺς (ante ἀφέντες) 13.69.346.
21. [καπ.]. − εἰσελθὼν. ἐδίδασκεν εἰς τὴν συναγωγήν 13.69.346.
22. οὐχ'. [no αὐτῶν]. 23. [καὶ ἦν]. 24. [ἔα]. ναζαρινὲ. [οἶδα].
25. [λέγων]. 26. κράξαν ἔ supra s. m. [ἐξ]. 27. ἑαυτοὺς (pro
αὐτοὺς) four. λέγοντες 346. ἐστὶν supra. ἡ καινὴ διδαχὴ αὕτη
four. ὅτι κατεξουσίαν. 28. ἐξῆλθεν. [εὐθὺς]. + πανταχοῦ four.
29. εὐθὺς 13.69.346. ἐξελθὼν ἦλθεν four. 30. + τοῦ (ante σίμωνος)
four. 31. [εὐθέως]. 32. [ἔδυ]. + πάντες (post ἔφερον) 69.124.(346).
33. ἡ πόλις ὅλη ἦν συνηγμένη 69.124.346. 34. ἐθεράπευσεν.
ποικίλοις 69.346. ἐξέβαλεν. οὐκ' ἤφιεν. fin. + τὸν χν εἶναι 69.
124.346. 35. [ἔννυχον] + καὶ (post λίαν) 69.346. ἐξῆλθεν. [κακεῖ].
36. ὅτι (pro ὁ) 69.124. 37. σε ζητοῦσιν 69.124.346 [rest as Scr.].
38. κομοπόλεις 124 [no ἀλλαχοῦ]. καὶ ἐκεῖ. ἐλήλυθα 69.124.346.
39. [ἦν]. εἰς τὰς συναγωγὰς 69.124.346. 40. − αὐτὸν prim.
γονυπετον^s αὐτὸν. [ὅτι]. 41. λέγων (pro καὶ λεγει) 69.124.346
[rest as Scr.]. 42. − εἰπόντος αὐτοῦ [εὐθέωσ] so ver. 45. [·θαρίσθη].
44. − μηδὲν 69.124. [ἀλλ']. ἀρχιερεῖ (pro ἱερεῖ) 69.346. μωϋσῆς.
45. [as Scr.].

II. 1. εἰσῆλθεν πάλιν 13.(69).124.346. [καπερ.]. [εἰς οἶκόν]
ἐστιν. 2. [εὐθέως] ver. 8, 12. 3. πρὸς αὐτόν, φέροντες παραλυτικόν

four.   4. [προσέγγισαι]. κράβαττον four. − ἐφ᾽ οὗ (pro ἐφ᾽ ᾧ)
13.69.346.   5. [καὶ ἰδὼν]. σου (pro σοι) αἱ ἁμαρτίαι 13.346.
7. [τί]. οὕτως.   8. + αὐτοὶ (post οὕτως) 13.69.346- [εἶπεν].
9. σου αἱ ἁμαρτίαι (pro σοι). ἔγειρε [καὶ] 69.124. κράβαττόν.
10. ἀφ᾽. ἐπὶ. 11. ἔγειρε [καὶ] 69.124 ver. 12. κράβαττόν (so ver.
12). 12. ἐναντίων (o s. m.) 13.346. ἐξίστασθε. ἴδωμεν [rest as
Scr.] 13.346. 13. ἐξῆλθεν ὁ ῑσ [πάλιν παρὰ] 13.69.346. 14. Παράγων
δὲ 13.69.346. ἰάκωβον (pro λευεὶν) ν...ον (mut. ?) 13.69.124* text.
15. [ἐγένετο]. − ἐν τῷ four. [ἠκολούθησαν]. 16. [as Scr.].
17. η (pro οἱ prim.) 346. [rest as Scr.]. 18. φαρισαῖοι (pro τῶν
φαρισαίων) 13.69.346. διὰ τί. [οἱ τῶν]. −οἱ δὲ σοὶ μαθηταὶ οὐ νηστεύουσιν (ὁμοιοτ.). 19. ἐστιν. ἔχουσιν. [ordo as Scr.]. − οὐ errore.
20. ὅτ᾽ἀν ἐκείνη τῇ ἡμέραι 13.69.346. 21. init. − καὶ 13.69.346.
ῥάκκους four. ἐπιράπτει four. − ἐπὶ. − αὐτοῦ four. + ἀπὸ (post
καινὸν) four. 22. − ὁ νέοσ 13.69. [rest as Scr.]. 23. πάλιν
ἐγένετο αὐτὸν four. πορεύεσθαι 13.69.124. οἱ μαθηταὶ αὐτοῦ
ἤρξαντο ὁδοιποροῦντες [τίλλοντες] four. 24. + οἱ μαθηταί four σου
(post ποιοῦσιν) four. − ἐν. 25. λέγει (pro αὐτὸς ἔλεγεν) four. δᾱδ
passim. 26. [πῶς]. [τοῦ ἀρχ.]. − τοῦ 124. + μόνοις (ante τοῖς
ϕ
ἱερεῦσι) four. οὖσιν. 27. οὐχ [no καὶ]. (Modern scrawl illegible
at foot of page.)

III. 1. εἰσῆλθεν. 2. σάββασιν [rest as Scr.]. 3. ἔγειρε [rest
as Scr.] 13.69.124.346. 4. ἔξεστιν + ἐν four. οἱ δὲ̈ [rest as Scr.].
5. [συλλ-]. ἐξέτεινεν. ἀπεκατεστάθη 13.124.346. [no omission].
6. [εὐθέως]. ἐδίδουν κατ᾽ (pro ἐποίουν) ἀπολέσωσιν four. 7. μετὰ
                                                                    ς
τῶν μαθητῶν αὐτοῦ ἀνεχώρησεν παρὰ [rest as Scr.] four. 8. τύρων.
σιδόνα. ἀκούοντες four. [rest as Scr.]. 9. εἶπεν. προσκαρτερεῖ.
fin. + οἱ ὄχλοι four. 10. αὐτῶι (pro αὐτοῦ). 11. − τὰ bis four.
π̄ν̄α sic. ὅτ᾽ἀν. ἐθεώρουν four. πρόσέπιπτον four. ἔκραζον four.
[λέγοντα]. 12. ποιῶσιν four. 13. + ὁ ῑσ (post ὄρος). ἠθέλησεν
four. 14. + οὓς καὶ four ἀποστόλους ὀνόμασεν (post δώδεκα) 13.346.
ὦσιν. 15. [as Scr.]. 16. init. + πρῶτον σίμωνα καὶ ἐπέθηκεν four.
[rest as Scr.]. 17. − τοῦ (ante ἰακ.) four. [rest as Scr.]. 18. + τὸν
                                                            ν
τελώνην (post Ματθ.) four. σίμω (sic). [κανανίτην]. 19. [as Scr.].
20. μηδὲ (pro μήτε) 13.124.346. [rest as Scr.]. 21. ἐξέσταται
13.69. 23. [-νασ -νὰν]. ἐκβαλεῖν four. 25. ἐφ᾽ ἑαυτῇ 13 not ver.
26. [rest as Scr.]. 26. [as Scr.]. 27. ἀλλ᾽ οὐδεὶς δύναται four,

αὐτοῦ. ἁρπάσαι four. διαοπάσει [rest as Scr.]. 28. + αἱ (ante
βλασφ.) four. ὅσα [ἂν: rest as Scr.] four. 29. ἁμαρτίας (pro
κρίσεωσ) 13.69.346. 31. καὶ ἔρχονται (- οὖν) 13.69.346. καλοῦντες
(pro φωνοῦντες) four. 32. ἐκάθητο περὶ αὐτὸν ὄχλος four. [rest
as Scr.]. καὶ λέγουσιν (pro εἶπον δὲ) four. [nil additum] only
in 124. ζητοῦσίν. 33. καὶ λέγει (pro λέγων) 13.69.346. καὶ
(pro ἤ). [μου]. 34. τοὺς κύκλωι περὶ αὐτὸν μαθητὰς καθ. four.
εἶπεν (pro λέγει). ἰδοὺ. 35. – μου secund. 13.69.346. ἐστίν.

IV. 1. Πάλιν δὲ (– καὶ) four. συνάγεται 13.69.124. [πολὺς].
ἐμβάντα καθῆσθαι εἰς τὸ πλοῖον four. [ἦν]. 3. [τοῦ]. 4. [ὃ].
ἔπεσεν. ἦλθεν. – τοῦ οὐρανοῦ four. 5. [ἄλλο δὲ]. [πετρῶδες·
ὅπου]. εἶχεν. [εὐθέως] ἐξεβλάστησεν (pro ἐξαν.) four. [βάθος
γῆς]. 6. [as Scr.]. 7. [εἰς]. ἔδωκεν. 8. [ἄλλο]. [αὐξάνοντα]
[ἐν] ter. 9. – αὐτοῖς four. [ὁ ἔχων]. 10. ἐπηρώτησαν. οἱ μαθηταὶ
αὐτοῦ· τίς ἡ παραβολὴ αὕτη (post αὐτὸν ad fin. vers.) four. 11. [as
Scr.]. 12. βλέπωσιν. ἴδωσιν. ἀκούσωσιν. συνιῶσιν. ἐπιστρέψωσιν.
[τὰ ἁμαρ.]. 15. ὅτ ἂν. [εὐθέως]. [-νὰς]. εἰς αὐτούς (pro ἐν ταῖς
καρδίαις αὐτῶν) 13.69. 16. – ὁμοίως 13.69. ἀκούσωσιν. εὐθὺς.
17. λαμβάνουσιν. – αὐτὸν. ἔχουσιν. θλήψεως. [εὐθέως]. 18. καὶ
οἱ (pro καὶ οὗτοί εἰσιν οἱ). ἀκούσαντες four. [τούτου]. 19. [συμπν.].
20. οὗτοι. ἀκούουσιν. ἐν ter. 13, but ἓν ver. 8. 21. + ἴδετε (ante
μή τι) four. λύχνος (13.69.124 – ὁ) καίεται (pro ἔρχεται) four.
ἢ ἵνα ὑπὸ τὴν κλίνην τεθῆι. four. τεθῇ (pro ἐπιτεθῇ) four. 22. ἐστιν.
– τι four. εἰ μὴ ἵνα φανερωθῇ· (pro ὁ ἐὰν κ.τ.λ.). [rest as Scr.].
24. – ἐν ᾧ μέτρω μετρεῖτε μετρηθήσεται ὑμῖν (ὅμοιοτ.). [τοῖς ἀκ.].
25. ἔχει γὰρ (pro γὰρ ἂν ἔχῃ) four. fin. + ἐν ᾧ μέτρω μετρεῖτε
13.69.346 μετριθήσεται 124 ὑμῖν καὶ προστεθήσεται ὑμῖν. 26. οὗτος
(pro οὕτως) 13.346. ὥσπερ (pro ὡς ἐὰν) four. – τὸν four.
27. ἐγείρεται (346). [rest as Scr.]. 28. [as Scr.]. 29. ὅτ’ ἂν.
ἐξαποστέλλει 13.69.346. [rest as Scr.]. 30. πῶς (pro τίνι) ὁμοιώσω
four. τίνι (pro ποίᾳ) 13.69.346. αὐτὴν θῶμεν (pro παραβ. αὐτήν)
13.69.346. 31. init. + παραβάλομεν αὐτὴν ὡς κόκκον 13.69.346.
σπαρῆ. ἐστὶν [rest as Scr.]. 32. ὅτ’ ἂν. σπαρεῖ. – τὰ. 33. [πολ-
λαῖς]. ἐδύναντο. 34. κατ’ ἰδίαν. ἀπέλυεν 124.346. [rest as Scr.].
35. ἔλεγεν. 36. ἀφίουσιν 69. + καὶ (ante παραλαμ-) four. καὶ
ἄλλα δὲ πλοῖα ἦν four. 37. λέλαψ’ μεγάλη ἀνέμου 13.69.346. καὶ
τὰ (pro τὰ δὲ) 13.69.346: [rest as Scr.]. 38. καὶ ἦν αὐτός. ἐν
(pro ἐπὶ) four. ἐγείραντες four. – καὶ (ante λέγουσιν) four.
39. ἐγερθεὶς four. ἐπετίμησεν. εἶπεν. 40. οὕτως δηλοί ἐστε

s,   2

13.346. οὔπω (pro πῶσ οὐχ) 13.69.346. εχετων. 41. ἆρα. αὐτῶ ὑπακούει 13.69.346.

V. 1. ἦλθεν four. — τῆς θαλάσσης 13.69. 2. ἐξελθόντος αὐτοῦ four. [so ver. 13, 29, 30, 35, 36, 42, εὐθεωσ] ὑπήντησεν 13.69.346. 3. μνήμασιν 13.(69).124.346. οὔτε. + οὐκ ἔτι (ante οὐδεὶς) four. ἐδύνατο four. 4. πολλάκης· πεδημ alt. (ϛ supra). ἀλύσεσιν. ἀλύσις. ἴσχυεν αὐτὸν four. 5. διὰ παντὸς. μνημείοις καὶ ἐν τοῖς ὄρεσιν 13.69.346. κραυγάζων four. 6. καὶ ἰδὼν (– δὲ) 13.69.346. ἀπομακρόθεν. ἔδραμεν. [αὐτῶι]. 7. εἶπεν. ὁρκίζω. 8. ἔλεγεν. 9. ὄνομά σοι 13.69.346. λέγει αὐτῶι (pro ἀπεκρίθη λέγων) λεγεῶν ὄνομά μοι ἐστὶν four. 10. παρεκάλη p. m. (ϛ supra) [rest as Scr.]. 11. ἀγέλη χοίρων βοσκομένη μεγάλη πρὸς τὸ ὄρει (τὸ four). 12. παρακαλέσαντες four. αὐτὸν εἶπον (pro πάντες οἱ δαίμονες λέγοντες) 13.69. 346. 13. τὰ πνα τά. [rest as Scr.]. 14. καὶ οἱ (pro οἱ δὲ) four. αὐτοὺς (pro τοὺς χοίρους) four. ἐστιν [rest as Scr.]. 15. θεωροῦσιν. – καὶ tert. 13.69.346. [λεγεῶνα]. 18. [ἐμβάντος]. μετ᾽ αὐτοῦ ἦ four. 19. καὶ (pro ὁ δὲ) four. διάγγειλον four. σοι ὁ κσ πεποίηκεν four. ἠλέησέν. 20. ἀπῆλθεν. 21. + ἦλθεν (post πάλιν) 13.69.346. [no καὶ]. ἐπ᾽ (pro πρὸς) four. 22. [ἰδοὺ]. πρὸς πίπτει [πρὸς] four. 23. [παρεκάλει]. – ὅτι. ἐσχάτος (ϛ supra). χεῖρα αὐτῆι. four. ἵνα (pro ὅπως) 13.69.346. ζήσῃ 13.69.124. 24. ἀπῆλθεν. ἠκολούθη. 25. τίς οὖσα. ῥήσει. δώδεκα ἔτη four. 26. αὐτῆς (pro ἑαυτῆς) four. 27. [-σα περὶ]. εἰς τὸν ὄχλον (pro ἐν τῳ ὄχλῳ) four. 28. [as Scr.]. 29. ἰᾶται. 30. ἐξ. ἔλεγεν. 33. φοβηθίσα. [ἐπ᾽]. ἦλθεν. + ἔμπροσθεν πάντων (ante πᾶσαν) four. αἰτίαν αὐτῆς (pro τὴν ἀλήθειαν) 13.69.346. 34. + ισ (post ὁ δὲ) four. [θύγατερ]. σέσωκεν 124.346. ἴσθη (ϛ supra). 35. ἀπέθανεν. σκύλλης 13.69. 346. 36. ἀκούσας. 37. [as Scr.]. οὐκ᾽. 38. [ἔρχεται]. + καὶ (ante κλαίοντας) four. 39. fin. + εἰδότες ὅτι ἀπέθανεν four. 40. [ὁ δὲ] πάντας ἔξω (pro ἅπαντας) 13.346. κατακεκλιμένον (pro ἀνακ.) 13.69.(346). 41. τὰ λειθὰ κουμεῖ. ἔγειρε. 42. [no add.]. 43. [γνῶ].

VI. 1. [ἦλθεν]. 2. + οἱ (ante πολλοὶ) 13.69.346. ἀκούσαντες four. τοῦτο (pro -ῳ) 13.69.346. καὶ (– ὅτι) four. [rest as Scr.]. 3. τέκτος, sic. + (ὁ erased) υἱὸς καὶ τῆς μαρίας. [ἀδ. δὲ]. ἰώσητος four. 4. ἔλεγεν. – αὐτοῖς 13.69.346. ἐστὶν. ἑαυτοῦ (pro αὐτοῦ prim.) four. συγγενεῦσιν 13.(69).124.346. [rest as Scr.]. 5. ἐδύνατο not ver. 19. ἐθεράπευσεν. [rest as Scr.]. 6. ἐθαύμαζεν. περιῆγεν

ὁ ἰσ. τὰς κύκλῳ κώμας. 7. – τῶν bis four. 8. παρήγγελλεν 346.
[rest as Scr.]. 9, 10, 12, 19. [as Scr.]. 11. ὃς ἂν τόπος μὴ δέξηται
four. [no omission]. 13. [λλ]. ἥλιφον 13. fin. + αὐτούς four.
14. + τὴν ἀκοὴν ἰῦ (post ἡρῴδης) 13.69.346. [rest as Scr.].
15. + δὲ (post ἄλλοι prim.) four. [ἠλίας]. [ἐστὶν]. – ἢ four.
16. ἀπεκεφάλησα 346. οὗτος ἐκ νεκρῶν ἠγέρθη (– ἐστιν· αὐτὸς) four.
17. – ὁ 13.346. καὶ ἔβαλεν εἰς φυλακὴν (pro ἐν τῇ φυλακῇ) four.
20. + ἃ (ante ἐποίει) four. ἤκουεν. 21. [ὅτε]. ἐποίεισε (ς supra).
22. [αὐτῆς]. ἂν (pro ἐὰν). [rest as Scr.]. 24. εἶπεν bis [rest as
Scr.]. 25. [εὐθέως] ver. 27, 45, 50, not 54. ἰωάννου (ν supra).
[rest as Scr.]. 26. [as Scr.]. 27. σπεκουλάτορα four. [rest as
Scr.] 28. [ὁ δὲ]. 29. – αὐτὸ. τωι μνιμείω. 30. [as Scr.].
31. εἶπεν αὐτοῖς ὁ ἰσ four. κατ᾽ ἰδίαν ver. 32. ἀναπαύσασθε 13.69.
346. εὐκαίρουν. 32. ἀπῆλθεν ἐν τῷ πλοίωι (four). εἰς ἔρημον τόπον.
33. ἴδων (pro εἶδον). – πολλοὶ 13.69.346. fin. συνεισῆλθον πρὸς
αὐτούς 13.69.346. [rest as Scr.]. 34. ἴδεν. – ὁ ἰσ four. πολὺν.
εὐσπλαγχνίσθη 13.346. [ἐπ᾽ αὐτοῖς]. 35. – αὐτοῦ. + αὐτῷ (post
λέγουσιν). 36. ἑαυτοῖς ras. Cf. 69. [ἄρτους]. – γὰρ. [οὐκ ἔχ.].
37. δηναρίων διακοσίων four. δώσωμεν. 38. γνῶντες λέγουσιν αὐτῷ
13.346. [rest as Scr.]. 39. ἀνακλιθῆναι 69. χλορῷ. 40. [as
Scr.]. 41. εὐλόγησεν. κατέκλασεν. ἐμέρισεν. [rest as Scr.].
43. [κλασμάτων]. κοφίνων πληρώματα four. + δύο (ante ἰχθύων)
four. 44. – ὡσεὶ four. 45. ἠνάγκασεν ὁ ἰσ 13.346. + αὐτὸν (post
προάγειν) four. ἀπολύσει. 48. ἴδεν. + σφόδρα (post αὐτοῖς) four.
[καὶ περὶ]. ἤθελεν. 49. οἱ δὲ. [as Scr.]. 50. ἴδον. ἐλάλησεν.
51. [ἐκ περισσοῦ]. [καὶ ἔθαν.]. 52. ἦν γὰρ αὐτῶν ἡ καρδία 13.124.
346. 53. εἰς γῆν γεννησαρέθ (– τὴν) 13.346. 54. εὐθὺσ 13.69.346.
55. + οἱ ἄνδρες τοῦ τόπου ἐκείνου (ante ἔδραμον) four. εἰς ὅλην τὴν
περίχωρον ἐκ. + καὶ (ante ἤρξαντο). κραβάττοις. [ἐκεῖ]. ἐστιν.
56. ἤψαντο (pro ἥπτοντο) 13.346. [rest as Scr.]. δ ιεσωζοντο
four.

VII. 2. χερσὶν. [-οντας]. + τοὺς (ante ἄρτους) four. [ἐμέμ-
ψαντο]. 3. [πυγμῇ]. ἐσθίουσιν ver. 4, 5. παράδωσιν 13.124.346 :
so ver. 5, 8, not ver. 9, 13. 4. [ἀπὸ]. [καὶ κλινῶν]. 5. + λέγοντες
(ante Διὰ τί) four. περιπατοῦσιν [ordo as Scr.] κοιναῖς χερσὶν
ἀνίπτοις four. 6. ἐπροφήτευσεν 13.124.346. χείλεσιν. [rest as
Scr.]. 7. διδασκαλείας 124. 8. [as Scr.]. 10. μωϋσῆς 13.69.346.
εἶπεν. – σου secund. τελευτάτωι. 11. ἐστιν. – ὃ secund. 13.69.
346. 12. init. – καὶ. οὐκ ἔτι 346. – αὐτοῦ bis. 13. παραδώσει

2—2

13.69.346.   πολλὰ τοιαῦτα four.   14, 15, 16, 19. [as Scr.].
15. ἐστιν.   17. – καὶ (init. lect.).   [rest as Scr.].   18. οὕτως.
19. ἀλλὰ.   καθαρίζων four.   20. ἔλεγεν.   21. μοιχίαι.   πορνίαι
φον. κλοπ.   22. ἀσελγία.   24. ὅρια [rest as Scr.].   – τὴν four.
ἠθέλησεν.   25. εἶχεν τὸ θυγάτριον (– αὐτῆς) ἐν πνι ἀκαθάρτωι 13.69.
346.   ἐλθοῦσα προσέπεσεν αὐτῶ.   – πρὸς τοὺς πόδας αὐτοῦ.   26. συραφοινίκισσα four.   τῆς θυγατρὸς αὐτῆς ἐκβάλη 13.69.346.
(– ἐκ).   27. ἐστιν. [as Scr.].   28. λέγουσα (pro καὶ λέγει αὐτῇ)
13.69.   – ναὶ.   [καὶ γάρ].   ἐσθίουσιν.   29. ἐξελήλυθεν. [as Scr.].
30. εὗρεν.   -θὼς p. m.   -ο s. m.   [rest as Scr.].   31. + ὁ ισ (post
ἐξελθὼν) 69.124.346.   [καὶ σιδῶνος].   ἦλθεν εἰς (pro πρὸς).   ἀναμέσον 69.   32. [as Scr.].   33. κατιδίαν.   ἐπέβαλε four.   + πτύσας
(post αὐτοῦ prim.) four.   – πτύσας sequens.   34. ἀνεστέναξεν
13.346.   35. [as Scr.].   36. ε (pro δὲ).   [rest as Scr.].   37. ὑπὲρ
περισσῶς 69*.   πεποίηκεν.   [τοὺς ἀλάλους].

VIII. 1.   πάλιν πολλοῦ (pro παμπ.) 13.69.(124).346.   φάγωσιν.
[rest as Scr.].   2. σπαχνίζομαι.   [ἡμέρας].   -ραι 124.   προσμένουσίν
μοι.   ἔχουσιν.   φάγωσιν.   3. νήστεις εἰς τὸν ο. four.   τινὲς γὰρ.
ἀπομακρόθεν.   ἤκουσιν 13.   Deest unum folium ab αὐτοῦ ver. 4
usque ad ver. 28 τὸν βαπτιστήν.   28. ἄλλοι δὲ ἠλ.   καὶ ἄλλοι four.
29. fin. + ὁ υἱὸς τοῦ θῦ τοῦ ζῶντος [rest as Scr.] four.   30. [λέγωσι].
31. + ἀπο τότε (ante ἤρξατο) four.   ἀπὸ τῶν ἀρχιερέων καὶ πρεσβυτέρων
καὶ τῶν γραμματέων four.   τῆ τρίτη ἡμέρα (pro μετὰ τρεῖς ἡμ.) four.
ἐλάλη.   32. [as Scr.].   33. ἐπετίμησεν [τῶι Πέτρω].   [λέγων].   λλὰ.
34. Εἴτις four.   [ἐλθεῖν].   αὐτοῦ so ver. 35, 36, 37.   ἀκολουθήτω.
35. θέλῃ ἀπολέσει (pro -σῃ) τὴν ἑαυτοῦ ψυχὴν four.   [rest as Scr.]
36. ὠφελήσει ἅνος 13.69.346.   κερδήσῃ.   37. [as Scr.].   38. ᾿Αν
ἐπεσχυνθῇ 13.69.346.   μοιχαλλίδι 13.   ἐπεσχ.   ὅτ᾿ ἄν.

IX. 1.   γεύσονται four.   ἐληλυθυῖα [rest as Scr.] 346.
2. + καὶ ἐν τωι προσεύχεσθαι αὐτοὺς (ante μετεμορφώθη ὁ ισ sic)
four.   3. ἐγένοντο four.   [ὡς χιὼν].   + οὕτως (ante λευκάναι) four.
4. + ἰδοὺ (ante ὤφθη) 13.69.346.   μωσῆ (ς supra).   σύνλα-.
5. ἔλεγεν (pro λέγει) 69.   θέλεις ποιήσωμεν (– καὶ) four.   μωϋσῆ
[rest as Scr.].   6. λαλήσει four.   [ἦσαν γὰρ ἐκφ.].   7. + ἰδοὺ (ante
ἐγενετο) four.   φωνὴ ἦλθεν four.   [rest as Scr.].   8. οὐκ ἔτι.   ἴδον.
[ἀλλὰ].   9. ἃ ἴδων 13.69.346 ἐξηγησωνται 346.   10. οἱ δὲ (pro καὶ).
συνζ- ἐστιν (τὸ illegible spaces: forsan ὅταν cum 13.69.124.346).
11. ἐπηρώτησαν four.   πῶς οὖν (pro ὅτι) four.   διελθεῖν (pro δεῖ

ἐλθεῖν) 13. 12. + τὰ (ante πάντα) 13.346. [rest as Scr.].
13. – καὶ prim. ἐλήλυθεν. [ἠθέλησαν]. 14. + αὐτοῦ (post
μαθητὰς) 13.69.346. ἴδεν 13.346. + τοὺς (ante γραμματεῖς)
13.346. συνζητ. [αὐτοῖς]. 15. εὐθὺς 13.69.346. ἰδόντες four.
ἐξεθαμβήθησαν four. 16. ἐπηρώτησεν. συνζ- [αὐτούς]. 17. ἐκ τοῦ
ὄχλου εἷς four. εἶπεν αὐτῷ. 18. – αὐτοῦ. ξηρένεται 13.124.346.
[rest as Scr.]. 19. καὶ ἀποκριθεὶς ὁ ιϲ four. – αὐτῷ + διεστραμένη
(ante ἕως prim.) four. 20. ἐσπάραξε τὸ παιδίον (– αὐτὸν) four.
21. + λέγων (ante πόσος) four. ἀφ' οὗ (pro ὡς) 13.124.346. – ὁ
δὲ εἶπε 13. 22. – καὶ secund. 13.69.346. [rest as Scr.]. 23. – Τὸ
four. 24. εἶπεν (pro ἔλεγε) 13.69.346. μοι (pro μου). [rest as
Scr.]. 25. + ὁ (ante ὄχλος) four. ἐπετίμησεν. [rest as Scr.].
26. ἐξῆλθεν. ὡσ εἰ. [rest as Scr.]. 27. τῆς χειρὸς αὐτοῦ (– αὐτὸν)
13.69.346. 28. εἰσελθόντος αὐτοῦ 13.69.346. 28. προσῆλθον
αὐτῶι οἱ μαθηταὶ αὐτοῦ κατ' ἰδίαν· καὶ ἐπηρώτησαν αὐτὸν λέγοντες ὅτι.
29. νηστεία. 30. [as Scr.]. 31. [αὐτοῖς]. παραδοθήσεται four.
ἀποκτενοῦσιν [τῇ τρ. ἡμ.] ἐγερθήσεται (pro ἀναστήσεται) 13.69.346.
32. ἠγνώουν. ἐρωτῆσαι 13.69.346. 33. εἰσῆλθεν 13.69. καφάρναουμ
hic tantum p. m. διελογίζεσθε πρὸς ἑαυτούς 13.69.346. 34. τίς
αὐτῶν μείζων εἴη 13.69.346. 35. καθήσας. 37. ἂν (pro ἐὰν prim.)
13.69.346. μόνον ἀλλὰ καὶ (post δέξηται) 13.69.(346). [rest as
Scr.]. 38. καὶ ἀποκριθεὶς αὐτῶ ἰωάννης εἶπεν διδάσκαλε. + ἐν (post
τινὰ). – ὅτι οὐκ ἀκολουθεῖ ἡμῖν four. 39. – ιϲ εἶπεν 13.69.346.
39. ἐν (pro ἐπὶ). 40. ἔστιν (prim.). ἡμῶν bis (pro ὑμῶν bis)
13.69.346. 41. ἐπὶ τῶ (pro ἐν) 13.69.346. [rest as Scr.].
42. μυλωνικὸς λίθος 13.69.124.(346). [rest as Scr.]. 43. ἐστίν
σοι. [rest as Scr.]. 44. [habet]. 45. ἐστίν σε (pro σοι). – τὴν
(ante γέενναν) 13.69. [rest as Scr.]. 46. [Habet]. 47. – σοὶ
13.69.346. + σε (post εἰσελθεῖν) 13.69.346. 48. [τοῦ πυρὸς].
49. [as Scr.]. 50. + γὰρ (post καλὸν) four. γὰρ (pro δὲ)
13.69.346. ἀρτύσητε 13.69.346. – ὑμεῖς οὖν (ante ἔχετε) 13.
69.346.

X. 1. καὶ ἐκεῖθεν four. – διὰ τοῦ four. σὺν πορεύεται four.
– πάλιν. ὄχλος. 2, 6, 13, 20. [as Scr.]. 3. μωϋσῆς. 4. οἱ δὲ
[μωσῆς]. ἐπέτρεψεν. 5. ἔγραψεν (– ὑμῖν) four. 7. init. + καὶ
εἶπεν [rest as Scr.] four. 8. οὐκ ἔτι εἰσὶν. σὰρξ μία four.
10. [as Scr.]. 11. ἐὰν ἀνὴρ (– ὃς) four. 12. γυνὴ ἐὰν ἐξέλθη
(pro ἀπολύσῃ) ἀπὸ ανδ. four. – αὐτῆς. γαμήσῃ ἄλλον four.
14. ἠγανάκτησεν καὶ ἐπιτιμήσας αὐτοῖς εἶπεν four. – καὶ (ante μὴ)

four.   15. ἂν (pro ἐὰν) 13.   16. ἐνεγκαλισάμενος four.   τίθων
13.69.(124).346.   εὐλόγει four.   17. + ἰδοὺ τίς πλούσιος (ante
προσδραμὼν, −εἶς) four.   γονυπετῶν four.   + λέγων (ante διδάσκαλε)
four.   − ἵνα.   19. [ordo as Scr.].   ἀποστερίσῃς 346.   21. λέγει
(pro εἶπεν) four.   + εἰ θέλεις τέλειος εἶναι (ante ἕν) four.   διάδος
13.69.346.   − τοῖς four.   καὶ ἄρας τὸν στρον σου δεύρω ἀκολούθη μοι
four.   22. + τούτωι four.   ἀπῆλθεν.   24. ἐστιν.   εἰσελθεῖν εἰς τὴν
βασιλείαν τοῦ θῦ four.   25. εὐκοποτερόν ἐστιν 13.124.346.   κάμιλον
13.   διατρυπήματος βελόνης 13.69.(124).346.   διελθεῖν 13.124.346.
26. οἱ δὲ.   [rest as Scr.].   27. + μὲν (post παρα) four.   + τοῦτο
(ante ἀδύνατον) four.   − τῷ prim. 69.124.346.   ἐστιν.   28. (init.
lect.) − καὶ four.   [rest as Scr.].   29. καὶ ἀποκριθεὶς four.   + ἕνεκεν
(ante τοῦ εὐ-) four.   [rest as Scr.].   30. [as Scr.].   31. [οἱ].
32. + αὐτὸν (ante ἐφοβοῦντο) four.   33. [as Scr.].   34. ἐμπέξουσιν
13.69.   [rest as Scr.].   35. + σε (post ἐάν) four.   36. ποιήσω
(− με) 13.69.346.   37. οἱ δὲ ver. 39.   ἐν τῇ βασιλείᾳ τῆς δόξησ
four.   [rest as Scr.].   38. + ἀποκριθεὶς (post ἰσ) four.   ἢ (pro καὶ)
four.   39. [μὲν].   40. [καὶ].   − μοῦ secund. four.   42. [as Scr.].
43. οὐχ οὗτος.   ἂν (pro ἐὰν) 13.69.346.   μέγας γενέσθαι four.
ὑμῶν διάκονος four.   44. ἐὰν (pro ἂν) 13.69.124.   [rest as Scr.].
46. ἱεριχῶ bis.   + ἰδοὺ ὁ (ante υἰὸς) four.   [rest as Scr.].   47. ιυ
υἱὸς δᾱδ.   48. ιυ υἱὲ δᾱδ.   49. φωνοῦσιν.   [αὐτὸν φων.] θαρσῶν
ἐγείρου 13.69.346.   50. [as Scr.].   51. ραβουνί.   [rest as Scr.].
52. σέσωκέν.   [εὐθέως].   ἀνέβλεψεν.   αὐτῶι (pro τῷ ιυ) four.

XI.   1. ἤγγισαν four.   ἱεροσόλυμα four.   βηθσφαγὴ.   [ἀπο-
στέλλει], λέγων (pro καὶ λέγει) 13.69.346.   2, 3. [εὐθέως].
+ οὔπω (ante κεκάθικεν) four.   + καὶ (ante λύσαντες) 13.69.346.
3. λύετε τὸν πῶλον (pro ποιεῖτε τοῦτο).   [ὅτι].   αὐτοῦ.   ἀποστέλλει.
4. δὲ (pro οὖν) four.   − τὸν four.   [τὴν].   5. τινὲς δὲ (− καὶ)
13.69.124.   [−ἐστηκοτων.]   6. [as Scr.].   7. ἄγουσιν four.   [rest as
Scr.].   8. στιβάδας 13.69.346.   [rest as Scr.].   9. τῶι ὑψίστωι
(post ὡς ἀννὰ) so ver. 10 four.   10. − ἐν ὀνόματι κυ four.   11. − καὶ
secund.   ἡμέρας (pro ὥρας) four.   12. ἐπ᾽ αὔριον.   − αὐτῶν
13.69.346.   ἐπείνασεν.   13. ἀπομακρόθεν four.   + εἰς αὐτὴν (post
ἦλθεν) four.   τί ἐν.   + μόνον (post φύλλα) four.   [rest as Scr.].
14. − ὁ ισ 124.   φάγει (η supra) 13.69.346.   [rest as Scr.].
15. + ἐξέχεεν (post κολλ.) four.   [rest as Scr.].   16. τίς.   17. ἐδίδασκεν.   καὶ ἔλεγεν (pro λέγων) 13.69.346.   [αὐτοῖς].   πᾶσιν.

[rest as Scr.]. 18. ἀπολέσωσιν. πᾶς γὰρ (pro ὅτι πᾶς) 13.69.346. [rest as Scr.]. 19. ἐγίνετο 13.69. [rest as Scr.]. 20. ἴδον. τὴν συκῆ (errore). 20, 21. [as Scr.]. 22. + ὁ (ante ισ̄) four. + εἰ (ante ἔχετε) four. 23. ἐὰν (pro ἂν) 13.69.346. – καὶ βλήθητι none. [rest as Scr.]. 24. [as Scr.]. 25. ῝Οτ᾽ ἂν στήκετε four. 26. [Habet]. + ὑμῖν (post ἀφήσει) 13.69. 28 fin. ποιεῖς. [rest as Scr.]. 29. ἱμᾶς καὶ ἐγώ. [rest as Scr.]. 30. [as Scr.]. 31. διελογίζοντο four. + τί εἴπωμεν (post λέγοντες) four. + ὅτι (ante ἐξ᾽) 69.346. 32. [ἐὰν] φοβούμεθα (pro ἐφοβ.) four. ὄντως ὅτι four. [rest as Scr.]. 33. τῶι ιῡ λέγουσιν four. ἀποκριθεὶς ὁ ισ̄ 13.69.346.

XII. 1. λαλεῖν (pro λέγειν) four. ἄνοστις ἐφεύτευσεν ἀμπελῶνα 13.69.346. περιέθηκεν. οἰκοδόμησε πῦργον 346. [ἐξέδοτο]13.69.346. ὁ̓πεδήμησεν. 2. ἀπέστειλεν ver. 4, 5, 6. [τοῦ καρποῦ]. 3. οἱ δὲ̈. [rest as Scr.]. 5. τοὺς δὲ̈ ἀποκτένοντες four. 6. init. ὕστερον δὲ four. ἔτι ἕνα υἱὸν ἔχων (– οὖν) four. + τὸν (ante ἀγαπητὸν) four. ἔσχατον πρὸς αὐτοὺς four. 7. θεασάμενοι four αὐτὸν 561 ἐρχόμενον πρὸς αὐτοὺς εἶπεν. 8. καὶ ἀπέκτειναν transfert ad fin. vers. four. 11. ἔστιν. 12. εἶπεν. 13. ἀποστέλλουσιν 13.346. + ἐκ (post τινὰς) 13.69.346. ἀγρεύσωσιν. 14. [οἱ δὲ]. + ἤρξαντο ἐρωτᾶν αὐτὸν ἐν δόλωι (ante λέγοντες) four. ἔξεστιν. 15. + ισ̄ (ante εἰδὼς) alt? four. + ὑποκριταί (post πειράζετε) four. ἴδωι. 16. [οἱ δὲ εἶπον]. – αὐτῷ 13.69.346. 17. + οὖν (post ἀπόδοτε) four. [rest as Scr.]. 18. ἀνάστασις οὐκ᾽ ἔστιν four. [-τησαν]. 19. μωϋσῆς. ἐξαναστήσει. [rest as Scr.]. 20. + παρ᾽ ἡμῖν (post ἦσαν) four. ἔλαβεν. ἀφῆκεν. 21. ἀπέθανεν. ἀφῆκεν. ὡσαύτως. 22. – ἔλαβον αὐτὴν 13.69.346. [καὶ] οὐκ᾽. ἔσχατον δὲ πάντων καὶ ἡ γυνὴ ἀπέθανεν 13.69.346. 23. ὅτ᾽ ἂν οὖν ἀναστῶσιν 13.69.346. ἐν τῇ ἀναστάσει. + ἡ (ante γυνή) 13. 24. ἀποκριθεὶς δὲ (– καὶ) four. [rest as Scr.]. μήδε. 25. ὅτ᾽ ἂν. γαμίσκοντε. + θῦ (post ἄγγελοι) 13.69.346. 26. + τῆς ἀναστάσεως (post περὶ δὲ) four. τοῦ (pro τῆς) 13.69.346. [ὡς]. – λέγων Ἐγὼ ὁ θσ̄ (ὁμοιοτ.). ἀβρ. [ὁ ter.]. 27. οὐκ᾽ ἔστιν ὁ θσ̄ θσ̄ four. – θσ̄ (ante ζώντων) four. 28. συνζ. ἰδὼν (pro εἰδὼς) 13.69.346. ἀπεκρίθη αὐτοῖς. ποῖα ἐστὶν. – πασῶν four. 29. εἶπεν (pro ἀπεκρίθη) 13.69.346. πάντων. + ἐστιν (post ἐντολῶν) fin. ἐστιν. 30. – τῆς prim. – σου ult. [rest as Scr.]. 31. [ὁμοία]. αὕτηι 13. fin. ἔστιν. 32. [εἶπας]. ἐστιν ὁ θσ̄. 33. ⌊nil omiss.⌋. ὡς erased s. m. σεαυτόν. πλήον ἐστιν 13. [τῶν θυσ.]. 34. ἰδὼν ὁ

ισ αὐτὸν. ἐτόλμα οὐκέτι four. ἐπερωτᾶν 13.69.346. 35. ἔλεγεν.
δᾱδ ἐστίν. 36. − γὰρ. ἐν π͞νι ἁγίω four. [rest as Scr.]. 37. πῶς
(pro πόθεν) 13.69.346. [rest as Scr.]. ἐστὶν. 38. [as Scr.].
40. Οἳ [κατεσθίοντες]. + καὶ ὀρφανῶν (post χηρῶν) four. οἵτινες
(pro οὗτοι) 13.69.346. [λήψ.]. [κρίμα]. 41. ἑστως (pro καθίσας)
13.69.346. κατενώπιον. ἔβαλλεν τὸν χαλκὸν four. 42. [ἐλθοῦσα].
ἔβαλεν. ἐστιν. 43. βέβληκεν. βαλλόντων. γαζοφυλακεῖον 69.
44. περισσεύοντας errore?

XIII. 1. + ἐκ (post εἷς) 13.69.124. 2. ἀποκριθεὶς ὁ ι͞σ four.
τὰς οἰκοδομὰς τὰς μεγάλας four. + ἀμὴν λέγω σοι (ante οὐ μὴ)
four. + ὧδε (ante λίθος) 13.124.346. λίθων 13. καταλυθήσεται.
3. ἐπηρώτα. κατ᾽ ἰδίαν. καὶ ἰωάννης καὶ ἰάκωβος four. εἶπον.
ταῦτα πάντα 13.69.346. 5. καὶ ἀποκριθεὶς (− δὲ) ὁ ι͞σ. ἤρξατο
αὐτοῖς λέγειν four. 6. [γὰρ]. ὁ χ͞σ (post εἰμι) four. 7. ἀκούετε
13.124. [γὰρ]. 8. ἐπ᾽ ἔθν· [rest as Scr.]; 9. ταῦτα δὲ πάντα
ἀρχὴ ὠδίνων. [γὰρ]. -γὰς δαρίσεσθε. 10. [as Scr.]. 11. ὅτ᾽ ἂν.
ἄγωσιν 13.69.346. + πῶς ἢ (ante τί) four. ἐκεινωι (pro τοῦτο)
346. [rest as Scr.]. 12. − δὲ. 14. ὅτ᾽ ἂν. στήκον (pro ἑστὸς)
13.69.346. [nil omissum]. 15. εἰσελθάτω 69.124.346. [rest as
Scr.]. 16. [ὦν]. 17. ἐγγαστρὶ Matt. i. 22. 18. ταῦτα (pro ἡ
φυγὴ ὑμῶν) 13.69. 19. θλίψεις γέγονεν. ἀπαρχῆς οὐδ᾽ (pro καὶ) οὐ
μὴ 13.69.346. 20. ὁ θ͞σ (pro κ͞σ) 13.69.346. ἐκόλοβωσεν bis.
+ ἐκείνας (post ἡμέρας). διὰ δε (−ἀλλὰ) 13.69.346. 21. −ἢ 13.69.
346. πιστεύετε. [rest as Scr.]. 22. ψευδόχρηστοι 13.69.346.
ποιήσουσιν (pro δώσουσι) 69. [καὶ] τοὺς. 23, 24. [as Scr.].
25. ἀστέραις (ε supra) ἐκ τοῦ οὐ͞νοῦ εσ. ἐκπίπτε 346. 26. νεφέληι
13.69.346. καὶ δόξης πολλῆς four. 27. [αὐτοῦ bis]. ἀπάκρου.
28. ὅτ᾽ ἂν. ἤδη ὁ κλάδος αὐτῆς 13.69.346. ἐκφύη. 29. οὕτως.
ὅτ᾽ ἂν ἴδητε ταῦτα four. [-σκετε]. 30. ἕως ἂν (pro μέχρις οὗ) four.
ταῦτα πάντα four. 31. [-σονται] παρέλθωσιν. 32. καὶ ὥρας
(− τῆς) four. 32 fin. + μόνος 13.124.346. [rest as Scr.]. 33. + δὲ
καὶ (post βλέπετε) four. [καὶ προσ.]. 34. ὥσπερ γὰρ (pro ὡς)
four. [καὶ ἑκάστω]. 36. ἀλεκτροφωνίας four. ἐξέφνης 13.124.346.
37. [ἃ]. πᾶσιν.

XIV. 1. − ἐν 13.69.346. 2. [as Scr.]. 3. εἰς βηθανία errore.
3. προσῆλθεν αὐτῶι (pro ἦλθε) four. πολυτίμου (pro πολυτελοῦς)
four. [rest as Scr.]. 4. + τῶν μαθητῶν (post τινες) four. [rest

as Scr.]. 5. ἥδυν. πραθῆναι τὸ μύρον τοῦτο four. [rest as Scr.].
6. + γὰρ (post καλὸν) four. ἠργάσατο ἐν 69.124 ἐμοί four. 7. ὅτ᾽
ἄν. αὐτοῖς (pro -οὺς) four. 8. – αὕτη 13.69.346. ἐποίησεν.
προέλαβεν. [rest as Scr.]. 9. + ὅτι (ante ὅπου ἂν) 124. – τοῦτο
13.69.346. 10. – ὁ prim. four, et secund. 13.69.346. + ἰδοὺ (ante
ἰούδας) four. αὐτὸν παραδῶ 13.69.346. [rest as Scr.]. 11. εὐκ.
αὐτὸν παραδῶ. 13. τῶν μαθητῶν αὐτοῦ δύο 13.69.346. + εἰσελθόντων
ὑμῶν εἰς τὴν πόλιν (ante ἀπαντήσει) four. + καὶ (ante ἀκολουθ.)
four. 14. [ἐὰν]. ἐστιν. + μου (post κατάλυμά) 13.69.346. φάγομαι 13.69.124.(346). 15. ἀνώγαιον. [rest as Scr.]. 16, 18, 20,
21. [as Scr.]. 17. ὀψ. 19. καθεῖς. + εἰμί (post ἐγὼ prim.) four.
[rest as Scr.]. 22. + καὶ (ante εὐλογῆσας) 13.69.346. ἔκλασεν.
ἐδίδου (pro ἔδωκεν) (13).69.124.346. εἶπεν. [φάγετε]. 23. – τὸ
13.124. 24. [τὸ τῆς καινῆς] ὑπὲρ (pro περὶ) ἐκχυννόμενον four.
fin. + εἰς ἄφεσιν ἁμαρτιῶν four. 25. γενήματος four. ὅτ᾽ ἂν αὐτω
(ὁ supra s. m.). 27. + ὑμεῖς (post πάντες) four. – ἐν secund. 13.69.
346. τὰ πρόβατα διασκορπισθήσεται 13.69.346. 29. ἀποκριθεὶς
λέγει (pro εἶπεν) four. εἰ καὶ four. 30. + σὺ (post ὅτι) four.
– ἐν 13.69.346. πρὶν ἀλέκτορα δὶς φωνήσει 13.69.346. με ἀπαρνήσῃ
(124). 31. ὁ δὲ πέτρος μᾶλλον περισσῶς ἔλεγεν four. + ὅτι (ante
ἐὰν). δέῃ με four. [-σομαι]. 32. [οὗ τὸ] γεθσημανεῖ. + ἂν ἀπελθὼν
13.69.346 (ante προσεύξομαι 13.124.346). 33. [τὸν ἰακ.]. + τὸν
(ante ἰωάννην) four μετ᾽ αὐτοῦ 13.69.346. 34. τότε (pro καὶ
prim.) four. 35. προσελθὼν four. ἔπεσεν ἐπιπρόσωπον four ἐπὶ τὴν
γῆν four. ἐστιν. ἵνα transfert in locum ante παρέλθῃ 13.(124*).346.
36. + μου (post πὴρ) four. σοι δυνατά ἐστιν 13.69.346. τοῦτο
ἀπ᾽ ἐμοῦ four. ἀλλ᾽ οὐχ ὡς four. ὡς (pro τι) σύ 13.69.346.
37. ἰσχύσατε four. 38. ἔλθητε 13.346. 39. εὔξατο. 40. καταβαρυνόμενοι four. ἀποκριθῶσιν. [rest as Scr.]. 41. ἀπέχει sic; τὸ
561 + τέλος four. 42. ἤγγικεν. 43. – εὐθέως 13.69.346. [ὧν].
– πολὺς 13.69. – τῶν (ante γραμ. et πρεσβ.) 13.69.(124).346.
44. ἐστιν. [rest as Scr.]. 45. [εὐθεως]. χαῖρε ῥαββὶ (ῥαβ. once
only) four. 46. – ἐπ᾽ αὐτὸν 13.69.(124)*.346. αὐτῶι (pro αὐτῶν)
13.69.346. 47. ἔπεσεν 13.(69).346. [rest as Scr.]. 48. ἐξήλθατε
four. [-τήσατε]. fin. + τῶν προφητῶν four. 50 init. τότε (– καὶ)
four. οἱ μαθηταὶ four. – πάντες 13.(69).346. 51. ἠκολούθησεν
four. σινδῶνα (1st only) γυμνός (– ἐπὶ) 13.69.346. οἱ δὲ νεανίσκοι
ἐκράτησαν αὐτόν four. [ἀπ᾽ αὐτῶν]. 53. + καϊάφαν (post ἀρχιερέα)
four. – αὐτῷ 13.69.124**.346. [rest as Scr.]. 54. ἀπομακρόθεν
ἠκολούθει. σὺν καθ. + αὐτοῦ (post ὑπηρετῶν) four. – καὶ sequens

26 MARK XIV. 55—XVI. 20.

13.69.346. θερμενόμενος. [τὸ]. 55. – ἐζήτουν errore. [εὕρ.].
56. [ἴσαι]. 57. ἄλλοι δε (pro καί τινες) four. 59. οὐδ' 346.
60. εἰσ μέσων alt. (– τὸ) four. ἐπηρώτησεν. οὐδὲν jungit τι οὗτοι.
61. + ἐκ δεύτερου (post αὐτὸν) four. 62. + ἀποκριθεὶς (post ισ)
four. + αὐτῶ σὺ εἶπας ὅτι (ante ἐγώ εἰμι) four. ἐκ δεξιῶν καθήμενον
four. 63. χειτῶνας. 64. τὴν βλασφημίαν τοῦ στόματος αὐτοῦ four.
καὶ (pro οἱ δὲ) four. [εἶναι ἔνοχον]. 65. – αὐτῷ secund. + νῦν
χε τίς ἐστιν ὁ παίσας σε (post προφήτευσον) four. ἐλάμβανον (pro
ἔβαλλον) 13.69.346. 66. [as Scr.]. 67. αὐτὸν (pro τὸν πέτρον)
θερμενόμενον 13.69.346. ιυ ἦς. 68. οὔτε (pro οὐδὲ) four. εἰς τὴν
ἔξω προαύλιον four. -ωρ ἐφώνησεν. 69. [π. ἤρξ.]. παρεστηκῶσιν.
καὶ οὕτως (pro οὗτος) 13. ἠρνήσατο. 70: – καὶ γὰρ γαλιλαῖος εἶ
(· ὁμοιοτ.). [rest as Scr.]. 71. [ὀμνύειν]. 72. + εὐθέως (ante ἐκ
δευτέρου) four. ἐφώνησεν. ἀναμνησθεὶς four. [τοῦ ῥήματος οὗ].
ἀλέκτωρα. ἔκλαιεν. [rest as Scr.].

XV. 1. [εὐθέως]. ἐπι τὼ (ο supra s. m.). + αὐτὸν (post παρέδωκαν) 13.69.346. [rest as Scr.]. 2. + λέγων (post πιλάτος) sic
passim four. 3. αὐτῶι (pro αὐτοῦ) four. fin. + αὐτὸς δὲ οὐδὲν
ἀπεκρίνατο four. 4. ἐπηρῶτα four. [rest as Scr.]. 5. ἀπεκρίνατο
13.69.346. 6. εἰώθη ὁ ἡγεμὼν ἀπολύειν (pro ἀπέλυεν) four. ὃν ἂν
(pro ὅνπερ) ἤ- four. 7. + τότε (post δὲ) four. βαραββᾶς non
11. στασιαστῶν 13.69.346. 8. ἀνασήσας non ver. 11, 13.
[ἀεὶ]. 10. ᾔδει (pro ἐγίνωσκε) 13.69.346. παρέδωκαν four. ἀπολύσει. 12. –θέλετε 13.69. τὸν (pro ὃν λέγετε) 13.69. 13. ἔκραζον
four. ἀνασειόμενοι ὑπὸ τῶν ἀρχιερέων καὶ ἔλεγον four. 14. Omittit
vers. (ὁμοιοτ.). 15. παρέδωκεν. [rest as Scr.]. 16. εἰς τὴν αὐλὴν
(pro τῆς αὐλῆς) 13.69.346. 17. ἐνδιδύσκουσιν. χλαμύδα κοκκίνην
καὶ πορφύραν four. περιτίθουσιν four. 18. ὁ βασιλεὺς four.
20. τὴν χλαμύδα καὶ τὴν πορφύραν four. [rest as Scr.]. 21. κυριναῖον 13.124.346. [ἀπ']. 22. ἄγουσιν (pro φέρουσιν) 13.69.346.
εἰς τὸν (pro ἐπὶ) four. [-νον]. 23. ἔλαβεν. [rest as Scr.].
24. διεμερίζοντο four. κλήρους 13.346. [rest as Scr.]. 25. ὅτε
(pro καὶ) four. 27. ἐξευω. 28. [Habet]. 29. αὐτῶν τὰς κεφαλὰς.
οὐᾶ. [rest as Scr.]. 31. – δὲ four. fin. +, 13*. 33. – τοῦ
13.69.346. πιστεύσωμεν + αὐτῶ four. 33. καὶ γενομένης (– δὲ)
four. ἐνάτης. 34. τῇ ἐνάτη ὥρα four. λιμὰς ἀβαχθανί. ἐστιν.
– μου prim. 13.69.346. [με ἐγ...λιπες]. 35. ἴδε ἡλίαν four.
36. καὶ δραμόντες ἐγέμισαν (– εἷς καὶ) (13). καὶ περιθέντες (– τε)
four. ἐπότιζον. λέγοντες four. 37. ἐξέπευσεν. 38. ἀπ' ἄνωθεν.

39. ἐξεναντίας. οὕτως. [rest as Scr.].   40. ἦν (– καὶ sequens)
13.69.124. μαγδαλινή 13. – ἡ τοῦ four. ἰώσητος four. σαλώμη.
41. [αἲ καὶ].   42. ἐστιν. πρὸς σάββατον 13.124.346.   43. ἐλθὼν
(pro ἦλθεν) 13.69.346. εἰσῆλθεν. ἠτίσατο 13.   44. τέθνηκεν.
ἀπέθανεν. [πάλαι].   45. [σῶμα].   46. ἐνείλισεν. ἔθηκεν four. ἐν
τῇ πέτρα (pro ἐκ πέτρας) four. [rest as Scr.].   47. μαγδαλινὴ 13.
μαρία ἰακώβου four καὶ ἰώσητος μη̅ρ 13.69.346. [τίθεται].

XVI. 1.   μαγδαλινὴ 13.   – ἡ τοῦ four. ἀλείψωσι τὸν ι̅ν̅
(– αὐτὸν) four.   2. τῆς μιᾶσ τῶν σ. four. [μνημεῖον].   3. ἀπὸ (pro
ἐκ) 13.69.346.   4. [as Scr.].   5. [εἰσελ-].   6. ὁ δὲ̈. ναζαρινὸν
13.346.   7. [ἀλλ'].   vers. 8. ⁀ˢˡᵞ marg. rubro.   8. – ταχὺ four.
εἶχεν δὲ̈. fin. ἀρχ ἑωθ Γ' rubro, no other break.   rubro marg. ⁀ˢˡᵈ η.
New lesson.   9. – δὲ 13.69.124.   μαγδαλινὴ [ἀφ'] 13.   + ὁ ι̅σ̅
(post Ἀναστὰς – δὲ) four.   10. [no δε].   rubro marg. ⁀ˢˡᵉ η. κλαί-
ουσιν.   11. ⁀ˢˡˢ rubro marg.   14. [no δὲ].   + ἐκ νεκρῶν (ante οὐκ)
four.   17. [ταῦτα παρακ.]. ἐκβαλοῦσιν. [καιναισ].   19. [no add.].
βλάψη four.   19. τοὺς οὐνοὺς four. [rest as Scr.].   20. [ἀμήν].

Subs. : Εὐαγγέλιον κατὰ μάρκον· ἐγράφη ῥωμαιστὶ ἐν ῥώμη μετὰ
ιβ' ἔτη τῆς ἀναλήψεως τοῦ κυρίου· ἔχει δὲ ῥήματα χίλια ἑξακόσια
ἑβδομήκοντα πέντε· στιˣˣ α̅ χ̅ ι̅ς̅ (13.346).

Itacisms and dialectic forms in SS. Matth. and Mark continued
from p. 15.   Itacisms ι (pro ει) 37 : ει (pro ι) 6 : ω (pro o) 41: o
(pro ω) 38: ι (pro η) 29: η (pro ι) 20: αι (pro ε) 14: ε (pro αι)
26: η (pro ει) 30: ει (pro η) 26: ε (pro η) 2: η (pro ε) 2: υ (pro
η) 1: η (pro υ) 3: in pron. only Matt. XXI. 22: η (pro οι) 2: οι
(pro η) 2: ι (pro οι) 1: ω (pro ου) 4: ου (pro ω) 7: υ (pro οι) 1.
κατασκευασμένον Luc. I. 17. εἶ (pro εἴη) Luc. I. 29; III. 15 (not
VIII. 9; IX. 47). εἰσελθάτω Mc. XIII. 15: ἐξήλθατε XV. 48. Luc.
VII. 24, 25, 26. ἐλθάτω Luc. XI. 3. εἰσήλθατε Luc. II. 52. τίθων
Mc. IX. 16: περιτίθουσιν XV. 17. ἐπηρώτουν Luc. III. 10. ἀφίομεν
Luc. XI. 4. ἀνορθώθη Luc. XIII. 13. εἴδατε Luc. VII. 22. κατεγέλουν Luc. VIII. 53. παραγενάμενος Luc. XIV. 21. ἐξῆλθατε Luc.
XXII. 52. Ink restored (late) at places, or text very faint, never
quite illegible : ὁ δὲ̈, οἱ δὲ̈ saepe. Leaves lost Matt. XII. 11—XIII.
10 (two): κεφ table Marc. κ' to μη' (one), Marc. VIII. 4—28 (one).

Ἐκ τοῦ κατὰ λν εὐαγγελίου τὰ κε̅ 69. Collated with Mill N. T.
ς̅ ἐρωτησάντων. ζ σρσ (pro χυ̅) 69. θ. – τοῦ 69. ις̅ διαταγῆς (pro
ἐκλογῆς) 69. κα̅ ἀλειψάσης. κδ̅. περὶ τοῦ ἔχοντος τὸν λεγεῶνα 69.
κθ̅. τῶν μαθητῶν (pro τοῦ κυ̅) 69. λθ̅ κοφ̅. μθ. ιν̅ (pro κν̅).
μς̅. ηὐφόρησεν. μὴ ἀσθενίας. ν. – εἰ ὀλίʳ. να̅. τοῦ (pro τῷ) 69.
νβ̅ ὑδροπικοῦ. νγ̅. προτοκλησίας. νδ̅ ἐν τῶι δείπνω 69. νε̅ –παρα-
βολή. νς̅ περὶ περιβολῆς ρ̅ προβάτων 69. νζ̅. ἀποδημίσαντος.
νθ̅. – τοῦ secund. 69 bis. ξβ̅. – τοῦ secund. 69. ξγ̅ τὸν ιν̅ πλουσίου
69. ξς̅. – ἑαυτῷ 69. ξθ̅. περὶ τῶν ἠρωτισάν τὸν κν̅ οἱ ἀρχιερεῖς καὶ
οἱ πρεσβύτεροι 69. ο̅ παραβολὴ ἀμπελῶνος. οα̅ περὶ τῶν σαδδουκαίων καὶ κίνσου. οβ̅ περὶ τοῦ κυ̅ ἐπερωτήσεως 69. ογ̅ περὶ ἐπερωτήσεως πῶς... οδ̅ – βαλούσης. οε̅ – τῆς 69. – ἐρώτησις 69.
οη̅. – καὶ ἀρνήσεως πέτρου 69. οθ. περὶ ἐξουθένησις ἡρώδου.
πβ̅. τοῦ κυριακοῦ σώματος 69. πγ̅. κλεῶπα (– τοῦ) 69. Illumin.
over Εὐαγγέλιον κατὰ Λουκᾶν.

LUKE I. 2. ἀπαρχῆς four. 4. ἀσφαλίαν 13.124.346. 5. [τοῦ
β.]. [rest as Scr.]. 6. [ἐνώπιον]. 7. καθ' ὅτι. καὶ ἐλισάβετ
ver. 13 (not ver. 5) 24, 36, 40, 41 bis, 57, 69. 8. ἐφῆμ. (346).
ἐναντίον four. ἱερατίας 69.346. [-άσαι]. 10. [τοῦ λαοῦ ἦν].
11. +ὁ (ante ἄγγελος). 13. δι' ὅτι. σοι erased. [νν]. 14. ἐν τῇ
γεννήσει 13.69.124. 16. [τοῦ] θυ̅ (pro κυ̅) four. 17. προσελεύσεται
346. ἡλίου. κατασκευασμένον four. 18. εἶπεν. 20. ἀνθ ὧν.
21. – αὐτοῖς 13.69. [rest as Scr.]. 22. διέμεινε 124.346. 24. τὰς
ἡμέρασ ταύτασ 13.69.346. 25. οὗτος. [ὁ κσ̅]. ἐφίδεν four. [τὸ
ὄν]. 26. ἀπὸ (pro ὑπὸ) 13.69.346. – τοῦ 69.346. ναζαρὲθ four.
27. [μεμν.]. τω ὄνομα (ὁ supra p. m.)? 28. [εἰσελθὼν]. εἶπεν.
[nil omiss.]. 29. εἰ (pro εἴη) four. [rest as Scr.]. 30. αὐτῇ ὁ
ἄγγελος 13.69.124. 31. συλλήψει 69.346. ἐνγαστρὶ hic. τέξει
Η supra. 32. δᾱδ passim. 34. +μοι (post ἔσται) four. 35. αὐτῇ
changed. διὸ̇. γεννόμενον [nil add.] four. 36. συγγενίς. γήρει
four. 37. [τῶ θῶ̅]. 38. εἶπεν. 39. [μαριὰμ]. ἰούδα. 40. ἠσπά-
σατο 69. 41. ἤκουσεν four τὸν ἀσπασμὸν τῆς μαρίας ἡ ἐλισάβετ
13.69. 42. ἀνεβόησεν [φωνῇ] four. γυναιξὶν. 43. πρόσ με.
45. +ἡ (ante τελείωσις) 13.346. 46. εἶπεν. ἠγαλλ. 49. [μεγαλεῖα].

50. γενεὰν καὶ γενεὰν four. 52. καθεῖλεν. 55. ἀβραὰμ passim.
ἔωσ αἰῶνος (pro εἰς τὸν αἰῶνα) 13.69.346. 56. ὡς εἰ. 57. Τῆς
(pro τῇ) 13. 59. τῇ ἡμέρα τῇ ὀγδόη. περιτομὴν four. 60. [ἰωάννης]
passim. 61. [εἶπον]. συγγενία 13.346. ὄνομα errore. 62. fin.
αὐτό four. 63. [τὸ ὀν.]. 65. περὶ οἰκ. 66. [-σαντες]. ἆρα. [καὶ
χεὶρ]. fin. αὐτῶν (pro αὐτοῦ) four. 67. ἐπροφήτευσε 13.124.
68. λύτρωσι errore. 69. ἤγειρεν. - τῷ δᾱδ passim. [τοῦ π.].
70. - τῶν secund. four. 73, 74. jungit ἡμῖν ἀφόβως. 74. - τῶν
13.69. - ἡμῶν 13.69. 75 fin. μῶν (ἡ supra). [rest as Scr.].
76. [σὺ παι.]. 77. [αὐτῶν]. 78. [ἐπεσκέψατο]. 79. κατευθῆναι.

II. 1. ἀπογράψασθαι 13.69.346 so ver. 5. 2. - ἡ. [πρ. ἐγ.].
κυρινίου four. 3. [ἰδίαν]. 4. ναζαρὲθ four. δᾱδ. 5. [-ασθαι].
[μεμν-]. 7. ἔτεκεν. δι᾽ ὅτι. [ἐν τῆι φ.]. 9. [ἰδοὺ]. 12. [τὸ
σημ.]. εὑρήσεται 13.69.124. ἐσπαργανόμενον four. [κείμ.]. - τῇ
four. 13. ἐξέφνης 13.346. [οὔνιου]. 14. [εὐδοκία]. 15. οἱ ἄγγελοι
εἰς τὸν οὔνον four. ἑαυτοὺς (pro ἀλλήλους) 13.69.346. [rest as
Scr.]. 16. [ἦλθον]. εὗρον four. 17. [διεγνώρ.]. 19. [as Scr.].
20. ὑπέστρεψαν 13.124.346.(69). ἴδον four. 21. +αἱ (ante ἡμέραι)
13.69.346. [τὸ παιδίον]. - καὶ secund. four. [συλληφ.]. 22. [αὐ-
τῶν]. μωϋσέως four. 24. [as Scr.]. 25. ἦν ἅγιον four. 26. κε-
χριματισμένον 346. - ἦ. 27. ἰθισμένον 13.69. 28. αὐτὸν (pro
αὐτὸ) four. αὐτοῦ. εἶπεν. 30. ἴδον. 33. [as Scr.]. 34. εἶπεν.
μαρίαν. 35. [δὲ]. μετὰ ἀνδρὸς ἔτη ἐπτὰ (ink renewed late).
37. καὶ αὐτῇ χήρα 13.69.124. [ὡς]. τεσσάρων (s supra s. m.). [ἀπό].
νύκταν (modern ink, but seems p. m.) 13.69.346. 38. ἀνθ᾽ ὡμ.
ἐλάλη 13. [rest as Scr.]. 39. ἑαυτῶν 69.124.346. ναζαρέθ four.
[rest as Scr.]. 40. [as Scr.]. 41. κατέτος. 42, 43. [as Scr.].
44. [ἐν τη συν. εἶναι]. ἦλθον. συγγενεῦσιν four. - ἐν tert.
45. [αὐτὸν prim.]. ἀναζητοῦντες four. 46. [μεθ᾽]. 48. εἶπεν.
[ordo, as Scr.]. καὶ ἐγὼ four. ὀδυνόμενοι 13.69.346. 49. εἶπεν
δὲ (- καὶ). ἤδητε 13.346. με εἶναι. 51. ναζαρέθ four. ἡ δε μηρ
(- καὶ) four. [π. τὰ ῥ. τ.]. 52. [σοφ. καὶ] ἡλικία.

III. 1. - δὲ prim. 13.124. [πιλ- τετραρχ. ter.]. 2. [-εων]
13.124. τοῦ erased. 3. [τὴν]. 4. [ἠσ.]. λέγων τος supra (τος
                                                    ει
quite modern) 13. 5. εὐθεῖαν λίας (ει modern) 13.124.346.
7. ἔλεγε δὲ (- οὖν) four. 8. [καρπ. ἀξ.]. ἀβρ. passim. 9. [καλὸν].

10. ἐπηρώτουν 13.69.346 not ver. 14. ποιήσωμεν four. 11. ἔλεγεν.

ποιήτω. 12. [εἶπον]. ποιήσωμεν 346. 13. εἶπεν. 14. τί ποιήσωμεν $\overset{β}{}$ $\overset{α}{}$
καὶ ἡμεῖς (β α modern, supra) four. εἶπεν πρὸς. διασείσηται
(ε supra). [μηδὲ συκοφαντήσ·τε ει] 13.69.124. 15. –τοῦ four. [νν].
εἰ (pro εἴη) 13.69.124*.346. 16. [ordo as Scr.]. ὑμᾶς βαπτίζω ἐν
ὕδατι four. – δὲ (added modern). + κύψασ (ante λῦσαι) four.
ἱμᾶντα. 17. πτύον. σίτον [rest as Scr.]. 19. [τετραρ-]. – Φιλίππου
four. 20. [καὶ τοῦτο]. πᾶσιν. [rest as Scr.]. 21. – δὲ (℣ marg.
modern) 13.69. 22. ὡς εἰ. +πρὸς αὐτὸν (ante λέγουσαν) 13.69.346.
εὐδόκησα. 23. ὁ ισ ἦν 13.346. ἀρχόμενος εἶναι ὡς ἐτῶν τριάκοντα,
four. – ὢν four. 24. ἠλεί 124. ματθάν· 13.69.346. λευεῖ· four.
μελχεῖ· ἰανναῖ· four. [ματτ-]. 25. ἀμῶς. ἐσλαί (pro ἐσλί) 13.
69.346. μαάτ 13.69.346. [ματτ.]. 26. σεμεεῖ 13.124.346.
27. ἰωσήχ· 13.69.346. ἰῶδα 13.69.346. ἰωαννάν. νηρεῖ· four.
μελχεῖ· four. 28. ἀδδ (μή eras). [ἐλμωδάμ ?] 13.124.346. ἰησοῦ
(pro ἰωσή) 13.69.346. 29. ἐλεέζερ 13.124. ἰωρέμ 13.346.(69).
μαθθάτ. λευεῖ· 124. 30. [ἰωνάμ ?] 124. 31. ἐλιακείμ. μελέα· 13.
μεννᾶ· 13.346. νάθαν. 32. ἰωβήδ 13.69.346. σαλμάν 13.69.346.
33. τοῦ ἀδμίν. τοῦ ἀρηΐ (pro ἀράμ.) four. [ἐσρώμ]. 34. ἰοῦδα.
θαρρά. 35. σερούχ four. φαλέγ four. ἔβερ. [καϊνάν]. 37. [ἰαρέδ].
μελελεήλ four. [καϊναν].

IV. 1. [as Scr.]. fin. +. 2. + οὐδὲ ἔπιεν (post οὐδὲν) four.
ἐπείνασεν. [rest as Scr.]. 3. [as Scr.]. 4. ἀπεκρίθη δὲ αὐτῶ ὁ ισ
λέγων four. – ὅτι four. οὐχ' | οὐκ. – ὁ four. [nil omissum].
5. [nil omiss.]. + λίαν (post ὑψηλὸν) four. 6 ἂν (pro ἐὰν) 13.346.
7. προσκυνήσεις 13.346. μου nearly illeg. fin. πᾶσα four. 8. ὁ ισ
εἶπεν αὐτῶ four. [nil omiss.]. κν τὸν θν σου προσκυνήσεις four.
9. – ὁ (ante υἱὸς) four. ἔνθεν (pro ἐντεῦθεν) 13.346. [rest as
Scr.]. 11. ἀροῦσιν. 12. κσ (pro ισ) 13.69. [ordo as Scr.]
14. ἐξῆλθεν. 16. τὴν ναζαρέθ four. ὅπου (pro οὗ) 13.346.
ἀνατεθραμμένος four. 17. ἐπεδώθη 13.346. τοῦ προφήτου ἠσαίου
13.69.346. [rest as Scr.]. 18. εἵνεκεν 13.69.124. εὐαγγελίσασθαι
four. – ἰάσασθαι usque ad καρδίαν 13.69. κηρύξαι (so ver. 19).
20. τὸ ὑπηρέτηι. ἐκάθισεν. [ordo as Scr.]. εἰς αὐτὸν (pro αὐτῷ)
four. 22. οὐχὶ ὁ υἱός ἐστιν 13.69.346. ἰωσήφ οὕτως +, 23. εἶπεν.
εἰς καπερναοὐμ four. 24. εἶπεν. [αὐτοῦ]. 25. ἐπαλ. + ὅτι (ante
πολλαὶ) 13.69.346. ἠλίου. [ἐπί]. ὃς (pro ὡς) 13.69.346. μεγάλη

13.69. 26. ἠλίας. σαρεφθὰ 13.69.346. σιδονίας. 27. ἐν τῶι ιηλ
ἐπὶ ἐλισσαίου τοῦ προφήτου 13.69.346. [-θαρ]. ναιμᾶς. 29. τοῦ
(pro τῆς) ὀφρῦος four. ᾠκοδόμητο αὐτῶν 13.69.346. ὥστε (pro
εἰς τὸ) 13.69.346. κατακρυμνῆσαι. 30. διελθὼν. 31. [καπερ.].
σάββασιν. 33. [λέγων]. 34. ναζαρινὲ 13.69.346. 35. φημώθητι
13.69.124. ἀπ᾽ (pro ἐξ) four. [ῥίψαν]. 38. ἀπὸ (pro ἐκ) four.
38. – ἡ four. συνεχωμένη. ἠρώτησεν. 39. διηκόνει [παραχρῆμα
δε]. 40. [πάντες]. ἐπιτιθεὶς 13.69.124. [-σεν]. 41. [ἐξήρχετο].
κραυγάζοντα four. [ὁ χσ]. αὐτὸν τὸν χν four. 42. ἐπεζήτουν four.
κατεῖχον. 43. ὁ δὲ ισ εἶπεν 13.346. [με δεῖ]. ἐπὶ (pro εἰς) four.
ἀπεστάλην. 44. εἰς τὰς four συναγωγὰς [τῆς γαλιλαίας] four.

V. 1. γεννησαρὲθ four. [rest as Scr.]. 2. ἴδεν four. [rest
as Scr.]. 3. ὀλίγον. [rest as Scr.]. 4. εἶπεν. 5. [as Scr.].
6. πλῆθος ἰχθύων four. [διερρ-]. [τὸ δ.]. 7. [as Scr.]. 8. + ὁ
(ante Σίμων) 13.69. –πέτρος 13.69. πρὸς ἔπε (σε supra modern).
[τοῦ] ιυ. 9. [ἦ]. [νν]. 10. εἶπεν. [ὁ ισ]. 11. [ἅπαντα].
12. – ἐν τῷ 13.69. [καὶ ἰδὼν]. 13. λέγων (pro εἰπών) four.
ἀπῆλθεν ἡ λέπρα 13.69.346. μηδ᾽ ἐνὶ. 14. προσέταξεν μωϋσῆς
four. 15. –δὲ (init. lect.) 13.69.346. –ὑπ᾽ αὐτοῦ 13.69. ἀσθενιῶν
13.346. 17. + ἐν μιᾷ τῶν συναγωγῶν (post διδάσκων) four. [no oi
art.]. συνεληλυθότες. [αὐτούς]. 18. αὐτῶν (pro αὐτοῦ) 13.69.
19. πόθεν (pro διὰ ποίας) four. 20. + ὁ ισ (post ἰδὼν) four.
[αὐτῶι]. 21. [as Scr.]. 22. [ἀποκρ.] εἶπεν. 23. ἔγειρε 13.69.124.
24. εἶπεν. παραλυτικῶι four. ἔγειρε 13.124.346. [rest as Scr.].
25. πάντων (pro αὐτῶν). [ἐφ᾽ ὧ]. 26. ἴδαμεν: 13 i [nil
omiss. as in 13.69.124]. 27. ἐξῆλθεν ὁ ισ 13.69.346. [ἐθεάσατο].
λευὶν. τελωνεῖον 346. 28. [as Scr.]. λέγει (pro εἶπεν) 13.69.346.
29. ἐποίησεν. – ὁ. οἰκεία (ς supra). 29. πολὺς τελωνῶν 13.69.346.
30. διὰ τί, so ver. 33. + τῶν (ante τελωνῶν) four. [rest as Scr.].
ἐσθίετε altered s. m. 31. εἶπεν. ἰσχύοντες (pro ὑγιαιν.) 13.69.346.
[ἀλλ᾽]. 33. Οἱ δὲ᾽. νηστεύουσιν. ἐσθίουσιν (ink renewed, modern).
34. + ισ (post οἱ δὲ) four. εἶπεν. ἐστίν. [νηστεύειν]. 35. – καὶ
(ante ὅταν) four. ἀρθῇ 13. + καὶ (ante τοτε faint) four. νηστεύ-
σωσιν. 36. αὐτοῖς (pro πρὸς αὐτοὺς) 13.69.346. + ἀπὸ (ante
ἱματίου) four. + τὸ (ante ἐπίβλημα secund.) four. [rest as Scr.].
37. [as Scr.]. 38. ἀλλ᾽ four. [rest as Scr.]. 39. πιῶν. [εὐθέως].

32   LUKE VI. 1—VIII. 16.

VI. 1. δευτέρω πρώτω 69.(124)*. [rest as Scr.]. 2 *fin.*
σαββάτωι 13.124. 3. ὁ ισ εἶπεν πρὸς αὐτούς four. [rest as Scr.].
4. πῶς (*pro* ὡς) four. – ἔλαβε καὶ four. 6. - καὶ prim. 13.69.124.
ἦν ἐκεῖ ἀνοσ. 7. καὶ παρετήρουν (– δὲ) four. [rest as Scr.]. *fin.*
+ αὐτὸν four. 8. εἶπε δὲ (– καὶ) 13.69. ἔγειρε four. [ὁ δὲ].
9. εἶπεν δὲ (– οὖν) four. ὑμᾶς τί ἔξεστι· ἀγαθοπ. κακοπ. so ver. 33.
10. + μετ' ὀργῆς (*ante* εἶπεν τῶ ἄνω) four. ἐξέτεινεν (*pro* ἐποίησεν
οὕτω) four. ἀπέκατεστάθη four. [*nil omiss.*]. 11. ποιήσαιεν 69.
13. προσεφώνησεν. ὀνόμασεν 13.346. 14. ὀνόμασεν 13.346. + καὶ
(*ante* ἰάκωβον) four. + καὶ (*ante* ματθ-) 13.346. 15. + καὶ (*ante*
ἰάκωβον) 13.69.346. – τὸν τοῦ 13.69.346. ἀλφαιοῦ. 16. + καὶ
(*ante* ἰοῦδαν prim.) four. [ριώτην]. [ὃς καὶ]. 17. ἔστη. [ὄχλος
μαθητῶν]. σιδόνος 69. 18, 19. [as Scr.]. 20. ἔλεγεν. + τῶ πνι
(*post* πτωχοὶ) four. 22. ὅτ' ἂν secund. [rest as Scr.]. 23. χάρητε
(124).13.69.346.   τοῖς οὐνοῖς 13.69.346.   [ταῦτα] so ver. 26.
25. – ὑμῖν prim. 13.69. + νῦν (*post* ἐμπεπλ-) four. – ὑμῖν secund.
13.69. 26. – ὑμῖν 13.124.346. ὅτ' ἂν. ὑμᾶς εἴπωσιν. – οἱ 13.
27. ἀλλὰ four. ὑμᾶς (*pro* ὑμῖν) four. 28. – καὶ four. [ὑπὲρ].
fin. + καὶ διωκόντων ὑμᾶς 13.346. 29. [ἐπὶ]. στέψον αὐτῶ (*pro*
πάρεχε) four. κωλύσις. 30. δὲ τὸ αἰτ. 31. [as Scr.]. 32. ἐστίν.
ἀγαπῶσιν. 33. [καὶ ἐὰν] ἀγαθοποιεῖτε ver. 9. χάρις ἐστίν. ποιοῦσιν.
34. δανίζετε. [ἀπολ.]. ἐστίν. [γὰρ οἱ]. δανίζουσιν. ἀπολάβουσι.
[ἴσα]. 35. καὶ δανίζετε eras. s. m. [μηδὲν]. ἀπελπιζοντες. [rest
as Scr.]. 36. + ὁ οὔνιος (*post* πηρ) four. ἐστίν. [rest as Scr.].
37. καταδικάζητε. 38. – γὰρ 13.69. [rest as Scr.]. 39. ἔλεγεν
δὲ καὶ four. ἐμπεσοῦνται εἰς βόθυνον (+,) 13.69.346. 40. ἔστιν.
-- αὐτοῦ four. 41. τὴν δὲ ἐν τῶ σῶι four. ὀφθαλμῶ. δοκὸν.
42. [ἢ]. ἐκβαλῶ 69. μὴ (*pro* οὐ) four. *Transferunt* ἐκβαλεῖν ad
fin. vers. four. 43. ἐστιν. + πάλιν (*post* οὐδὲ) four. 44. συλλέ-
γουσιν σύκα. σταφυλὰς τρυγῶσιν 13.69.346. 45. [as Scr.]. 46. – δὲ
(*init. lect.*). 47. ὅμοιός ἐστιν 13.69.346. 48. οἰκοδεσπότη (*pro*
ἄνω). ἔσκαψεν. ἐβάθυνεν. ἔθηκεν. [-μύρας]. πρὸς ἔρρηξεν : so
ver. 49. οὐκ' ἴσχυσεν. 49. οἰκοδομοῦντι 13.69.346. εὐθέως συνέ-
πεσεν four. – τὸ 346.

VII. 1. + αὐτοῦ (*post* ἐπλήρωσεν) 13.69.346. – αὐτοῦ (*post*
ῥήματα). [καπερ-]. 3. – πρὸς αὐτὸν 13.69. διασώσει 13.124.
346. 4. οἱ δὲ. ἠρῶτον (*pro* παρεκ.) 13.346. [παρέξει]. 6. – ἀπὸ
four. ἀπέστειλε (*pro* ἔπεμψε) four. μου ὑπὸ τὴν στέγην 69.124.346.

[rest as Scr.]. 7. δι᾽ ὅ. ἐμ᾽ αὐτὸν. + μόνον (post ἀλλὰ) four. [-θήσεται]. 8. ἐμ᾽ αὐτοῦ. 9. εἶπεν. + ἀμὴν (ante λέγω) four. τὸ σαύτην. 10. [as Scr.]. πεφθέντες (μ p. m. supra). 11. τῶι (pro τῇ) 13.69.346. ἐπορεύθη 13. ναείν 13.124.346. [αὐτῶι]. οἰκανοί 69. 12. ἤγγιζεν 13.124.346. αὐτοῦ : so ver. 15. καὶ αὐτῆι 69.346. χῆρα. [rest as Scr.]. + ἦν (post ἱκανὸς sic) 13.124.346. 13. εὐσπλαγχνίσθη. ἐπ᾽ αὐτὴν 13.69.346. 14. εἶπεν. 15. [ἀνεκαθ-]. [ἔδωκεν]. 16. πάντας four. [ἐγήγ-]. fin.+εἰς ἀγαθόν four. 17. [ἐν bis]. 19. [νν]. ἔπεμψεν. κν (pro ιν) 13.(69). [ἄλλον]. 20. [as Scr.]. 21. ἐκείνη (pro αὐτῇ) four. – δὲ 13.69. ἐθεράπευσεν. [τὸ βλ.]. 22. εἴδατε 13. – ὅτι 13.69. ἀναβλέπουσιν. περὶ πατοῦσιν. + καὶ (ante κωφοὶ) four. ἀκούουσιν. 24. ἐξήλθατε four. 25. ἐξήλθατε four. [rest as Scr.]. 26. ἐξήλθατε four. 27. οὗτος γάρ ἐστιν four. [ἐγώ]. 28. δὲ (pro γὰρ). [προφήτης]. fin. ἐστιν. 30. νομικαὶ (ink renewed—error). 31. – εἶπε δὲ ὁ Κύριος four. 32. εἰσιν. λέγοντες (pro καὶ λέγουσιν) four. ηὐλίσαμεν. –ὑμῖν secund. ἐκόψασθε (pro ἐκλαύσατε) 13.(69).346. 33. ἐληλυθεν. βαπτισθὴς (sic) 13. – ἄρτον 13.69. – οἶνον 13.69. [μήτε bis]. 34. φίλος τελωνῶν four. 35. πάντων τῶν τέκνων αὐτῆς four. 36. Ἡρῶτα. αὐτῶν (pro αὐτὸν) 13.69.346. τὸν οἶκον four. ἀνεκλήθη 124. 37. γυνή τις ἦν ἐν τῇ πόλει ἁμαρτωλός (– ἥτις ἦν) four. + καὶ (ante ἐπιγνοῦσα) four. [ἀνάκειται]. 38. [as Scr.]. 39. [ἦν προφ.]. ἐστιν. 40. εἶπεν. ὁ δὲ φησίν. 41. χρεοφειλέται (13).346. δανιστῇ 13.124.346. 42. [as Scr.]. 43. ὁ δὲ ισ εἶπεν. [rest as Scr.]. 44. εἰς (pro ἐπὶ). θριξὶν [τῆσ κεφαλῆσ]. ἐξέμαξεν. 45. + ἀγάπης (post φίλημά μοι) 13.346. εἰσῆλθεν 13.69.346. διέλειπε 13.69.124 [μοῦ τ. π.] so ver. 47. 47. [αἱ ἁμ. αὐτ.]. 49. ἐστιν οὗτος. 50. σέσωκεν.

VIII. 1. καθ᾽ ἑξῆς. διόδευεν 13.69.346. 2. ἀσθενιῶν 13.346. [-ηνὴ hic]. 3. ἑπτὰ [νν] χουζᾶ. [Σουσ-]. αὐτοῖς (pro -ῷ) four. ἐκ (pro ἀπὸ) four. 4. συνελθόντος four. 5. ἑαυτοῦ (pro αὐτοῦ). [ὃ μὲν] ἔπεσεν. 6. [ἔπεσεν] ἠκμάδα 13. 7. [συμφ-]. 8. εἰς (pro ἐπὶ) 13.69.346. – ταῦτα λέγων ad fin. vers. (cf. ver. 15, 18) 13.69.346. 9. [as Scr.]. 10. ὁ δὲ᾽. + αὐτοῖς (post εἶπεν) four. + λαλῶ (ante ἵνα) 13.346. + ἀκούσωσι (post ἀκούοντες) 13.69.124. συνιῶσι (hiatus). 11. ἔστιν prim. 12. [ἀκούοντες]. 13. [τῆς π.]. ὅτ᾽ ἂν. 14. ἐμπεσὼν 13.346. ἡδωνῶν (ον supra p. m.?). σὺν πνί- τελεσφοροῦσιν. 15. ἀκούοντες four. καρπὸν φέρουσιν 13.69. fin. + πολλή four. + ταῦτα λέγων ἐφώνει ὁ ἔχων ὦτα ἀκούειν ἀκουέτω four. 16. [ἀλλ᾽].

λυχνείας.   τίθησιν (pro ἐπιτ.).   βλέπουσι 124.   17. [as Scr.].
18. + καὶ προστεθήσεται ὑμῖν τοῖς ἀκούουσιν (post ἀκούετε) four.
ἐὰν (pro ἂν prim.) four.   19. [παρέγοντο].   δὲ transfert post αὐτὸν
69. 20. init.—καὶ 13.69. ἀπηγγέλλη 69? [λεγόντων]. [σε θέλ.].
21. ὁ δὲ. εἶπεν πρὸς. [αὐτόν]. 22. ἐγένετο δὲ four. ἀνέβη four.
+ τὸ (ante πλοῖον) four. εἶπεν. 23. ἀφ᾽ ὕπνωσεν. [rest as Scr.].
λέλαψ 13.124.346. 24. διεγερθεὶς 13.124.346. 25. εἶπεν. [ἐστιν
prim.]. ἔστιν οὗτος four. 26. καταπλεύσαντες four. [γαδαρηνῶν].
ἀντίπερα four. 27. [δὲ] εἰς οἰκίαν (pro ἐν οἰκίᾳ) 13.69.346. [rest
as Scr.]. 28. εἶπεν. 29. Videtur (faint) esse παρήγγειλε. [rest
as Scr.]. 30. εἶπεν λεγεῶν. πολλὰ δαιμόνια 13.69.346. 31. παρεκάλουν four. ἐπιτάξει. 32. βοσκομένη 13.69. [παρεκάλουν].
33. εἰσῆλθον 124. 34. γεγονὸς 13.69.346. − ἀπελθόντες four.
35. [as Scr.]. 35. ᵘυ supra modern: nescio quare. lect. cf. ver. 37
supra ἄρξν. 36. − καὶ four. 37. ἠρώτησεν ? videtur, | γεργεσηνῶν
(non ver. 26) 13. [τὸ πλ.]. 38. τὰ δαιμόνια ἐξεληλύθει four. [ὁ
ισ̄]. 39. ἐποίησεν σοι. ἀπῆλθεν. 40. [as Scr.]. 41. οὗτος (pro
αὐτὸς) four. [τοῦ ιῡ]. 42. αὐτῆ 13. [ἐν δὲ τω ὑπάγειν]. συνέθλιβον
13.69.346. 43. ἰατροῖς (− εἰς) four. [rest as Scr.]. 45. σὺν αὐτῶ
(pro μετ᾽ αὐτοῦ) four. [rest as Scr.]. 46. init. modern correction
ωι. No: only through worn leaf. [rest as Scr.]. 47. − αὐτῷ
secund. 13.69. 48. ὁ δὲ. [θάρσει θύγατερ]. 49. ἔρχετε. [rest as
Scr]. 50. [as Scr.]. 51. ἐλθὼν four. ἀφῆκεν τινὰ συνελθεῖν αὐτῶ
13.124.346. καὶ ἰωάννην καὶ ἰάκωβον four. 52. εἶπεν. οὐ γὰρ
(pro οὐκ) four. 53. κατεγέλουν videtur 13.346. [no addition].
54. init. αὐτοῦ (ink renewed) errore. [rest as Scr.]. 54. [αὐτῆ
δοθῆναι].

IX. 1. [συγ·]. ἀποστόλους (pro μαθητὰς αὐτοῦ) four. 2. [as
Scr.]. 3. εἶπεν. ῥάβδον four. [ἀνα]. 5. ἐὰν (pro ἂν) four.
5. + ἀπὸ τῆς οἰκίας ἢ (ante ἀπὸ) four. [rest as Scr.]. 7. [τετραρ-].
γενόμενα 13.69.346. − ὑπ᾽ αὐτοῦ 13.69. [νν passim]. ἠγέρθη
four. ἀπο (pro ἐκ). 8. [ἠλ.]. τίς (pro εἷς) 13.69.346. ἀρχέων
not ver. 19. 9. εἶπεν δὲ (− καὶ) ὁ four. ἀπεκεφάλησα 13.69.346.
[ἐγώ]. 10. τῶ ιῡ (pro αὐτῷ) four. ὑπεχώρησεν κατ᾽ ἰδίαν. [rest
as Scr.]. 11. ἀποδεξάμενος four. ἰάσατο. 12. πορευθέντες (pro
ἀπελθόντες) four. − τοὺς four. καταλύσωσιν. 13. εἶπεν. ἰχθύες
δύο four. [rest as Scr.]. 14. [γὰρ]. ὡσ εἰ. 15. οὕτως κατέκλιναν
four, πάντας 13.346. 16. κατέκλασεν. + αὐτοῦ (post μαθηταῖς) four.
[-τιθέναι]. 17. πάντες καὶ ἐχορτάσθησαν four. περίσσευμα (pro

COLLATION OF COD. 556 WITH CODD. 13.69.124.346. 35

-ευσαν) 13.69.346. 18. κατὰ μόνας. +αὐτοῦ (post μαθ-) four.
[rest as Scr.]. 19. οἱ δὲ [εἶπον]. +ἕτεροι δὲ ἱερεμίαν (post ἠλίαν)
four. 20. εἶπεν bis. —δὲ ὁ 13.69. 21. ὁ δὲ'. παρήγγειλεν μηδ'
ἐνὶ λέγειν (not εἰπεῖν) four. 22. ἀρχιερέων καὶ πρεσβυτέρων four.
fin. ἐγερθήσεται 13.346. 23. ἔλεγεν. ἔρχεσθαι 13.69. [ἀπαρ.].
αὐτοῦ. [καθημέραν]. ἀκολουθήτω 13.124. 24. ἐὰν (pro ἂν prim.)
13.69.346. αὐτοῦ secund. (non prim.). 25. ζημιωθεῖ. 26. ἐπεσχυνθῇ. [λόγουσ]. ἐπεσχυνθήσεται. ὅτ' ἂν. αὐτοῦ. 27. [ὧδε]
ἑστώτων 69.124.346. [rest as Scr.]. 28. —δὲ (init. lect.) ὡς εἰ
13.69.346. —τὸν 13.69.346. 30. μωϋσης. 31. οἱ (four) ὠφθέντες
13. +δὲ (post ἔλεγον) four. [ἔμελλε]. 32. βεβαρυμένοι 13.69.
346. [εἶδον hic]. 33. τρεῖς σκηνᾶς four. μίαν μωσεῖ. 34. [as
Scr.]. 35. [ἀγαπητὸς]. αὐτοῦ. 36. [ὁ]. ἑοράκασιν 13. 37. —ἐν.
38. ἐβόησε 13.69.346. ἐπίβλεψαι. [ἐστίν μοι]. 39. ἐξέφνης
13.346. [μόγις]. -τρίβον. 40. ἐκβάλωσιν 13.124.346. 41. πρὸς
ὑμᾶς ἔσομαι four. προσαγάγετε. τὸν υἱόν σου ὧδε four. 43. ἐποίει
ὁ ισ four. εἶπεν (-η 13). 45. παρ' (pro ἀπ') 13.69.346. αὐτὸν
ἐρωτῆσαι four. 46. εἰσῆλθεν. [εἴη hic]. 47. [ἰδὼν]. +τῆς καρδίας
(ante ἐπιλαβ.) 13.346. [παιδίου]. 48. ἂν (pro ἐὰν) prim. non
secund. 13.69.346. [ἔσται]. 49. —ὁ 13.69.346. ἴδομεν. ἐν (pro
ἐπὶ) four. —τὰ four. [-σαμεν]. 50. [καὶ εἶπεν]. ἐστιν bis.
[ἡμῶν bis]. 51. συνπλ. [-ληψ-]. [αὐτοῦ ἐστήριξεν]. 52. ἑαυτοῦ
(pro αὐτοῦ) 13.124.346.(69 s. m.). εἰσῆλθων. πόλιν (pro κώμην)
four, not ver. 56. [-ρειτῶν]. 54. ἐποίησεν. [rest as Scr.].
55. —ὑμεῖς 13.69.124. [rest as Scr.]. 56. —γὰρ 13.69.124.
ἦλθεν. [rest as Scr.]. 57. καὶ ἐγένετο (—δὲ) four. εἶπεν. ἐὰν
(pro ἂν) four. 59. εἶπεν bis. [κε]. πρῶτον ἀπελθεῖν 13.(69).346.
60. εἶπεν. [ὁ ισ]. 61. εἶπεν. 62. εἶπεν δὲ ὁ ισ πρὸς αὐτὸν four.
αὐτοῦ. [rest as Scr.].

X. 1. ἤμελλεν αὐτὸς διέρχεσθαι 13.69.346. 2. ἔλεγεν. δε
(pro οὖν) four. ὀλίγοι fere. ἐκβάλη ἐργάτας 13.124.346. 3. [ἐγὼ].
4. βαλλάντιον 13.69.346. μῆτε (pro μηδὲ) four. [καὶ] μηδένα. 5. δ'
ἂν πόλιν εἰσέλθητε ἢ οἰκίαν four. +ἐν (post εἰρήνη) four. 6. —μὲν
four. ἢ ἐκεῖ [no ὁ]. ἐπαναπαύσετε ἐπ' αὐτῶ. 7. [-θίοντες]. ἐστιν.
ἐξ οἰκίαν 13.69.346. 8. —δ' four. δέχονται (not ver. 10) four.
10. εἰσέλθητε 13.69.346. 11. ὑμῖν (pro ἡμῖν) 13.69.346. +εἰς
τοὺς πόδας ἡμῶν (ante ἀπομ-) 13.69. [ἐφ' ὑμᾶς]. 12. - δὲ four.
ἀνεκτότερον ἔσται ἐν τῇ ἡμέρα ἐκείνη four. πόλη. 13. χόραζεῖν.
βηθσαϊδάν. ἐγενήθησαν four. [καθήμεναι]. 14. ἡμέρα κρίσεως

3—2

(*pro* τῇ κρίσει) 13.69.346. 15. καταβιβασθήσει. [rest as Scr.].
16. [ἀκ. ὑμ.]. *fin.* + καὶ ὁ ἀκούων ἐμοῦ ἀκούει τοῦ ἀποστείλαντός με
13.124.346. 17. [no δύο, or in ver. 1]. 18. εἶπεν. πεσόντα
(*videtur*). 19. δίδομι. ἀδικήσει. 20. − μᾶλλον four. 21. ὁ ι̅σ̅
τῶ 13.346. π̅ν̅ι̅. [ἐγ. εὐδ.]. 22. − καὶ στραφεὶς πρὸς τοὺς μαθητὰς
εἶπε 13.69. μοι παρεδόθη four. [ἐὰν]. 23. κατ᾽ ἰδίαν εἶπεν.
24. [εἶδον]. 25. [καὶ λέγων]. 26. ὁ δὲ ι̅σ̅ 69.124.346. εἶπεν.
27. ὁ δὲ̈. *fin.* ἑαυτόν 13.124.(346). [rest as Scr.]. 28. εἶπεν.
ἀπεκρίθεις. 29. [-οὖν]. εἶπεν. 30. ἐκδύναντες *errore.* [rest as
Scr.]. 32. ἀντιπαρῆλθεν. [rest as Scr.]. 33. σαμαρείτις (ς *supra*).
[αὐτὸν]. εὐσπλαγχνίσθη 13.346. 34. [as Scr.]. 35. − δύο *p. m.*
13. *Habet* marg., in a modern hand. ὅτ᾽ ἂν (*pro* ὅ τι ἂν). [rest
as Scr.]. 36. [οὖν]. πλησίον δοκῇ σοι (ς *supra*) four. 37. εἶπεν δὲ
(*pro* οὖν) 13.69.346. 38. [as Scr.]. 39. [μαρία]. παρακαθήσασα
13.69.346. ἤκουεν. [rest as Scr.]. 40. περὶ ἐσπάτω. εἶπεν.
[-λιπε *et* εἰπὲ]. 41. ὁ ι̅σ̅ εἶπεν αὐτῇ four. [τυρβάζῃ]. 42. ἐστιν.
[rest as Scr.].

XI. 1. εἶπεν. ἐδίδαξεν. 2. εἶπεν. ὅτ᾽ ἂν προσεύχεσθε four.
ἐλθάτω 13.346. καθήμέραν. [2, 3 rest as Scr.]. 4. ἀφίομεν
13.69.124. [no omission]. 5. εἶπεν. ἐρεῖ 13.69.346. 7. + γὰρ
(*post* ἤδη) four. 8. αὐτοῦ φίλος 13.69.346. ἀνεδείαν 13.346.
ὅσον. 9. ἀνυγήσεται (ver. 10 as Scr.). 11. ἐξ᾽ ὑμῶν four. ἢ
(*pro* εἰ) four. [ἐπιδ. αὐτ.]. 12. − ἐὰν 13.69.346. αἰτήσει 13.
[μή]. 13. δόματα ἀγαθὰ four. + ἡμῶν (*post* π̅η̅ρ̅) 13.(346).
14. [καὶ αὐτὸ ἦν]. καὶ ἐγένετο (− δὲ) 13.69. ἐκβληθέντος four.
15. [εἶπον]. + τῶ (*post* -βοὺλ) four. 16. ἐξ᾽ οὖνοῦ ἐζήτουν παρ᾽
αὐτοῦ four. 17. [as Scr.]. 18. ἡ erased ? *vix.* 19. [οἱ]. ἐκβάλωσιν
13.346. αὐτοὶ κριταὶ ὑμῶν four. 20. + ἐγὼ (*post* θ̅ῦ̅ *prim.*) four. 21.
ὅτ᾽ ἂν καθοπλ. φυλασσ.. *eras.* ἐστὶν. αὐτοῦ. 22. ἐπ᾽ ἂν. [σκύλα].
23. ἐστιν. 24. ὅτ᾽ ἂν. ζητῶν 13.69.346. εὑρίσκων four. 25. ἐλθὼν
four. + σχολάζονται (*ante* σεσαρ.) four. 26. ἕτερα πνεύματα πονη-
ρότερα ἑαυτοῦ ἑπτὰ 13.124.346. 27. [γ. φ.]. 28. εἶπεν. [rest as
Scr.]. 29. + γενεὰ (*ante* πονηρά ἐστιν) four. [ἐπιζητεῖ]. [τοῦ
προφ.]. 30. [as Scr.]. 31. σολομῶνος *bis* four. 32. νινευίται
four. 33. [δὲ]. κρυπτὴν ἀλλὰ 13.69.124. βλέπουσι τὸ φῶς four.
34. + σου (*ante* ὅτ᾽ ἂν) 13.346. [οὖν]. − καὶ (*post* ἢ) 13. φωτινὸν
346. ἐπ᾽ ἂν. *fin.* + ἔσται 13.124.346. 36. ἔχων 13.346 μέρος τί
13.69.346. ὅτ᾽ ἂν. φωτίζει 13.69. 37. + αὐτὸν ταῦτα (*ante* ἐρώτα,
sic) four. − τις 13.69.346. *fin.* καὶ εἰσελθὼν εἰς τὴν οἰκίαν τοῦ

COLLATION OF COD. 556 WITH CODD. 13.69.124.346. 37

φαρισαίου ἀνεκλίθη four. 39. εἶπεν. 40. τὸ ἔξωθεν τὸ ἔσωθεν
(– καὶ) ἐποίησεν. 41. ἅπαντα four. ἔσται (pro ἐστιν) four.
42. ἀλλά. + καὶ τὸ ἄνηθον (post ἡδύοσμον) four. + δὲ (ante ἔδει)
four. παρεῖναι (pro ἀφιέναι) 13.346. 43. + καὶ τὴν πρωτοκλισίαν
ἐν τοῖς δείπνοις (post συναγωγαῖς) four. 44. [no omission, except]
– οἱ (ante περιπ.) four. 45. fin. +, 46. εἶπεν. 47. [οἱ δέ].
48. μαρτυρεῖτε ὅτι (– καὶ) four. τοὺς τάφουσ αὐτῶν οἰκοδομεῖτε
(– τὰ μνη. αὐτ.) four. 49. – καὶ (post ἀποστόλους) 13.69.124.
ἀποκτενοῦσιν. [ἐκδιω.]. 50. ἐκκεχυμένον 13.69.346. 51. [τοῦ]
bis. 52. + καὶ (ante αὐτοὶ) four. εἰσήλθατε four. 53. [nil omiss.]
αὐτῶι (pro αὐτὸν) 13.69.346. 54. αὐτὸν ζητοῦντες (– καὶ) four.
– τοῦ (ante στόματος). [rest as Scr.].

XII. 1. πρῶτον προσέχετε. [rest as Scr.]. 2. – δὲ (init.
lect.) 13.69.346. 3. οὓς. ταμίοις 13. 4. ἀποκτενόντων four. τί
περισσότερον 13.69.346. 5. ἔχοντα ἐξουσίαν four. 6. πωλοῦνται
13.69.346. 7. [οὖν]. fin. + ὑμεῖς four. 8. ἐν αὐτῷ erased?
ἑαυτὸν 13.69.346. 9. [ἐνώπιον]. 10. τὸ π̅ν̅α̅ τὸ ἅγιον four.
11. ὅτ᾿ ἂν. [πρόσφ.]. εἰς (pro ἐπὶ) four. μεριμνήσητε 13.69.346.
[ἢ τί]. 13. εἶπεν (ver. 15) μερίσασθε. 14. κατέστησεν. κριτὴν
(pro δικαστὴν) 13.69.346. 15. πάσης (pro τῆς) 13.69.346. [αὐτοῦ].
16. εἶπεν. ηὐφόρησεν 13.69.346. 17. συνάξαι 13.69.346. 18. εἶπεν.
καθελῶ. τὸν σίτον (pro τὰ γενήματα) four. 20. εἶπεν. [rest as
Scr.]. 21. [ἑαυτῶι]. fin. + ταῦτα λέγων ἐφώνει ὁ ἔχων ὦτα ἀκούειν
ἀκουέτω four. 22. εἶπεν. [αὐτοῦ]. λέγω ὑμῖν four. [ὑμῶν].
+ ὑμῶν (post σώματι) four. 23. + γὰρ (post ἤ) four. ἐστὶν.
24. [οὐ]. – οὐδὲ θερίζουσιν (ὁμοιοτ.) 13. ἐστὶν ταμίον. ὁ δὲ θ̅σ̅
τρέφει (φ supra p. m.?) αὐτὰ 13.69.346. 25. προσθῆναι 13.346.
[rest as Scr.]. 26. [οὔτε]. 27. + ὅτι (ante οὐδὲ Σολομῶν) four.
[rest as Scr.]. 28. σήμερον ἐν ἀγρῷ (– τῷ) ὄντα 13.69.346.
[ἀμφιέννυσιν]. ὀλιγόπιστοι. 29. φάγησθε ἢ 13. 30. ἐπιζητοῦσιν
four. fin. + ἁπάντων four. 31. + πρῶτον (post ζητεῖτε) four. [τοῦ
θ̅ῦ̅ et πάντα]. 33. πωλύσατε. βαλλάντια (videtur?). 35. [ὑμῶν αἱ
ὀσφύες]. 36. αὐτὸν (pro ἑαυτῶν). [ἀναλύσει]. 37. [ἐλθὼν ὁ κ̅σ̅].
38. οὕτως. [rest as Scr.]. 39. – ἂν secund. 13.69. [διορυγῆναι].
fin. αὐτοῦ. 40. [οὖν]. 41. εἶπεν. [δὲ αὐτῷ]. – Κύριε 13.69.124.
42. init. καὶ εἶπεν ὁ ι̅σ̅ 13.69. ἄρα. [καὶ φρ.]. αὐτοῦ so ver. 45,
47. + αὐτοῖς (post διδόναι) four. – τὸ 13.69.346. 43. οὕτως
ποιοῦντα 13.69.346. 44. πᾶσιν. [αὐτοῦ]. 45. + κακὸς (ante
δοῦλος) four. – τε. 47. αὐτοῦ (pro ἑαυτοῦ). – μηδὲ ποιήσας

(ὁμοιοτ.). 49. ἐπὶ (pro εἰς) four. 50. ἔωσ ὅτου 13.69.346.
52. [οἴκωι ἐνὶ]. δυσὶν. τρισίν. 53. πῆρ. fin. αὐτῆς. [rest as
Scr.]. 54. ἔλεγεν. ὅτ᾽ ἂν (so ver. 55). – τὴν four. + ὅτι (ante
ὄμβρος) four. οὕτως. [rest as Scr.]. 55. fin. + οὕτως 13.124.346.
56. [as Scr.]. 57. ἑαυτὸν 124.346. 58. παραδώσει four. πράκτωρι
346. βάλη 13.124.346. 59. [ἔωσ οὗ].

XIII. 1. ὃν (pro ὧν). [-πιλάτος passim]. ἔμιξεν. 2. [ὁ ισ̄].
οὗτοι οἱ γαλιλαῖοι four. τὰ τοιαῦτα four. 3. μετανοήσητε 69.
ὁμοίως (pro ὡσαύτως) 13.69.346. 4. [καὶ ὀκτὼ] πύργος. αὐτοὶ
(pro οὗτοι) four. + τοὺς (ante ἄνους) four. [ἐν ἱλήμ]. 5. – ἀλλ᾽.
μετανοήσετε 13.124.346. 6. ἔλεγεν. συκῆν εἶχεν. αὐτοῦ. [ἐν τῶι
α. α. πεφυτ.]. ἦλθεν ζητῶν καρπὸν four. 7. εἶπεν. + ἀφ᾽ οὗ (ante
ἔρχομαι) four. + οὖν (post ἔκκοψον) four. ἵνα τί. 8. κόπρον
13.69.346. 9. κ᾽ ἂν. ποιήσει 13.346. 10. + τῶν ἡμερῶν καὶ (post
μιᾷ) 13.346. – ἐν 13.69.346. σάββασιν. 11. [ἦν]. [καὶ ὀκτὼ].
[συγκ.]. 12. προσέφωνησεν. [-σαι τῆς]. 13. ἐνορθώθη 13.69.346.
ἐδόξαζεν. 14. αὐταῖς (pro ταύταις) 69. [rest as Scr.]. 15. δὲ
(pro οὖν) four. ισ̄ (pro κσ̄) four. ὑποκριταί four. [ὄνον]. ἀνα-
γαγὼν. 16. + τὴν (ante θυγατέρα ἀβρ.) 13. σατανὰς. 17. κατῖσ-
χύνοντο. 18. Ἔλεγεν οὖν (pro δὲ) 13.69.346. + ὁμοιώματι (ante
ὁμοιώσω) (13).69.124.346. 19. ἐστὶν. [ὃν]. ηὔξησεν. [μέγα].
κατεσκήνουν four. 20. εἶπεν. 21. [ἐνεκρ.]. 22. πορίαν 13.124.346.
23. εἶπεν δὲ αὐτῶ Τίς 13.346. – πρὸς αὐτοὺς 69.124. 24. [πύλης].
25. Ἐὰν (pro ἂν) 13.346.124. εἰσέλθη (pro ἐγερθῇ) 13.69.346.
ἑστάναι. [κε bis]. ἐσταί not ver. 27. 26. ἄρξησθε 13.69.346.
27. [ὑμᾶς]. [οἱ]. [τῆς]. 28. ὀδόντων. ὅτ᾽ ἂν. – ὑμᾶς δε usque
ad τοῦ θῦ (ver. 29. ὁμοιοτ.). 30. εἰσὶν secund. 31. Ἐν αὐτῇ τῇ
ὥρα προσῆλθον four. 32. ἀλώπεκι. [rest as Scr.]. 34. – Ἱερουσαλὴμ
secund. 346. ἀποκτένουσα 13.124.346. ὄρνεις 69.124.346. [rest
as Scr.]. 35. ἀφίετε (ς supra). [ἔρημος]. – ἀμὴν. λέγω δὲ [ὅτι]
four. ἴδετέ με. – ἥξῃ ὅτε 13.69.

XIV. 1. εἰσελθεῖν (pro ἐν τῷ ἐλθεῖν) 13.69.(346). 2. ὑδροπικὸς
69.(346). 3. εἶπεν. [λέγων εἰ]. fin. + ἢ οὐ four. ἡ (pro οἱ)
13.346. 4. + αὐτοῦ (post ἐπιλαβόμενος) four. ἀπέλυσεν. 5. εἶπεν.
[ὄνος]. πεσεῖται four. – καὶ sequens 13.69.346. – ἐν four.
6. [αὐτῷ]. 8. ὅτ᾽ ἂν so ver. 10, 12, 13. πρωτοκλησίαν (non ver. 7).
κεκλιμένος. 9. τοῦτο. μετὰ 13.69.346. 10. ἀνάπεσαι 346. [εἴπῃ].

+ πάντων (*ante* τῶν συν.) four.   12. ἔλεγεν. αὐτῶν (ο *supra*
p. m.).   ποιεῖς 346.   μὴ δὲ *ter.*   συγγενής.   γείτωνάς 13.346.
+ σου τοὺς (*ante* πλουσίους) four.   ἀντικαλέσουσίν σε 69.   γένοιται
(s *supra*).   13.   ποιεῖς 69.   ἀναπείρους 13.346.   14.   δὲ (*pro* γὰρ)
four.   15.   ὅστις (*pro* ὃς) four.   φάγηται 13.346.   ἄριστον (*pro*
ἄρτον) four.   16. [ἐποίησε].   17.   ὅτι ἔρχεσθε· ἤδη 13.346.   ἐστιν π.
18. [as Scr.].   19.   εἶπεν (so ver. 20, 21).   21.   παραγενάμενος four.
αὐτοῦ *bis.*   ἀναπείρους 13.124.346.   τοὺς (*pro* χωλοὺς καὶ) 124.346.
22.   ὡς προσέταξας four.   ἐστιν.   23. [ὁ οἶκός μου].   24. *fin.*+πολλοὶ
γάρ εἰσι κλητοὶ four 561.   ὀλίγοι δὲ ἐκλεκτοί.   25.   εἶπεν.   26.   αὐτοῦ
(*pro* ἑαυτοῦ *prim.*) four.   εἶναι μαθητής four.   [rest as Scr.].
27. [as Scr.].   28. + ὁ (*ante* θέλων) 13.124.346.   πύργον.   τὰ εἰς
(*pro* τὰ πρὸς) four.   29.   μὴ ποτὲ.   θεμελίου *sic* 13.69.   29.   ἐμπέζειν
αὐτῶι.   31.   ἐν (*pro* ἐν).   ὑπαντῆσαι 124.346.   εἴκοσι.   [rest as
Scr.].   32.   εἶδε μήγε.   ὄντως 346.   33.   πᾶσιν.   [μου εἶναι].
34. + οὖν (*post* καλὸν) four.   [rest as Scr.].   35.   βάλλωσιν (346).

XV. 1.   αὐτῶ ἐγγίζοντες four.   2.   οἱ γραμματεῖς καὶ οἱ φαρισαῖοι
four.   3. − λέγων 13.69.   4.   ἐξ᾽ αὐτῶν ἕν.   οὐχὶ four καταλίπει
13.346.   ἐνενήκοντα ἐννέα so ver. 7.   + οὗ (*post* ἕως) four.   6. [ἑαυτοῦ].
συγκαλεῖται so ver. 9, four.   συγχάρηταί so ver. 9.   *fin.* +, so ver. 9.
7.   οὕτως.   8.   δραγμὰς (χ *supra p. m.*) 13.346.(69).   δραγμὴν not
ver. 9.   οὐχ᾽.   οὗ (*pro* ὅτου) 13.346.   9. [τὰς γ.].   10.   χαρὰ ἔσται
13.69.346.   ἐν οὐρανῷ four.   11.   εἶπεν *bis.*   12. + μοι (*ante* μέρος)
13.124.346.   [καὶ διε.].   13. [ἅπαντα].   κακεῖ 13.69.346.   διεσκόρ-
πισεν.   14. [ἰσχυρὸς].   16.   χορτασθῆναι ἐκ (*pro* γεμ. τ. κ. α. ἀπὸ)
four.   17.   ἔφη (*pro* εἶπε) four.   + ὧδε (*ante* λιμῶ) 13.124.346.
[rest as Scr.].   19. [καὶ].   20. *post* π̄ρᾱ leaf lost to cap. XVI.

XVI. 9.   ἐκλείπητε 13.124.346.   [no αὐτῶν].   10.   ἐστιν *bis.*
12.   ἀλλωτρίωι.   ἐγένεσθαι.   [rest as Scr.].   13.   οἰκέτης (s *supra*
-*vix*, but so 13.346).   εἰ (*pro* ἢ *prim.*) 13.346.   14. [καὶ *prim.*].
ὄντες (*pro* ὑπάρχοντες) four.   15. [ἐστίν].   16.   μέχρι (*pro* ἕως)
four.   [νν].   + τις (*post* πᾶς) 13.69.   − εἰς 13.   17.   εὐκοπότερόν
ἐστιν (− δὲ) 346.   κερεὰν 13.69.346.   18. [πᾶς].   20.   ἐβέβλυτο
13.   εἰλκόμενος 13.   [rest as Scr.].   21. [ψιχίων τῶν].   *fin.* + καὶ
οὐδεὶς ἐδίδου αὐτῶι (cap. xv. 17) four.   ἀπέλυχον.   22. − δὲ *prim.*
13.69.   [τοῦ ἀβρ.].   23.   ἄδη.   [τὸν ἀβρ.].   ἀπομακρόθεν. *fin.*
αὐτοῦ.   24.   εἶπεν (so ver. 25, 27, 31).   25. − σὺ 13.69.346.   ὧδε
(*pro* ὅδε) four.   ὀδυνάσαι 346.   26. [ἐπὶ].   ἔνθεν (*pro* ἐντεῦθεν)

13.124. δύνονται 69. μὴ δὲ οἱ. 27. σε οὖν 13.69.346. 29. + δὲ (*post* λέγει) 13.346. [αὐτῶι ἀβρ.]. [μωσέα]. 30. ἀλλά. + τῶν (*ante* νεκρῶν). 31. ἀπὸ τῶν (*pro* ἐκ)· four. πισθήσονται 13.(69). 124.346. [rest as Scr.].

XVII. 1. εἶπεν. ἐστιν. [τοῦ μὴ ἐ. τὰ σ.]. πλὴν four οὐαὶ (—δὲ) 346. 2. λίθος μυλικὸς 13.69.346. [ἔνα τ. μ. τ.]. 3. ἁμαρτήσῃ four. [rest as Scr.]. 4. ἁμαρτήσῃ four. — ἐπὶ σὲ four. 5. [εἶπον]. 6. εἶπεν. ἔχετε four. *fin.* ἡμῖν corrected to ὑμῖν *p. m.* 7. ἐρεῖ αντῶ εὐθέως· [-σαι] (not 124). 8. + καὶ (*ante* σύ) 13.124.346. 9. χάρ. ἔχειν 13.346. πάντα τὰ 69.124.346. διάτεταγ|χθέντα (ss *supra* not ver. 10). [rest as Scr.]. 10. οὕτως. ὅτ᾽ ἂν. ἄχριοι 13.346. [ὅτι *bis*]. 11. ἀναμέσον (*pro* διὰ μ.) four. σαμαρίας 69. [rest as Scr.]. 12. ὑπήντησαν αὐτ. 13.69.346. 14. + αὐτοὺς (*post* ἰδὼν) four. ἱερεῦσιν. 16. [-ρείτης]. 17. [οὐχὶ]. 20. ἐπερωτιθεὶς 13.346. 21. [ἰδοὺ *ter.*] 13.346. 22. εἶπεν. τοῦ ἐπιθυμῆσαι ὑμᾶς (*pro* ὅτε ἐπιθυμήσετε) 13.69.346. 23. — ἰδοὺ *secund.* — ἀπέλθητε μηδὲ 13.69.346. διώξετε 13.69.(346). 24. —ἡ *secund.* 13.69. ὑπὸ τὸν οὐρανῶν. [ὑπ᾽ οὐνὸν] — καὶ four. [rest as Scr.]. 26. — τοῦ *prim.* only, four. — καὶ *secund.* four. 27. ἐγαμίζοντο. εἰσῆλθεν. [ἄπ-] so ver. 29. 28. καθὼς (*pro* καὶ ὡς) 13.69.346. 29. ἐξῆλθεν. ἔβρεξεν θίον καὶ πῦρ four. ἐξ (*pro* ἀπ᾽) four. [ἄπ-]. 30. [ταῦτα]. 31. — τῷ 13.69.346. 32. μνημόνευε. 33. [σώσαι]. δ᾽ ἂν (*pro* ἐὰν *secund.*) 13.69.124. ἀπολέσῃ τὴν ψυχὴν αὐτοῦ (*pro* ἀπ. αὐτὴν) 13.69.124. 34. ἐν ἐκείνῃ τῇ νυκτὶ δύο ἔσονται 13.(346) [rest as Scr.]. 35. [δύο ἐσ.]. ἀλήθουσι. ἡ μία four. ἡ δὲ (*pro* καὶ ἡ) four. 36. (in B. E.) —ὁ (*ante* εἷς) four. ἡ δὲ ἑτέρα (*pro* καὶ ὁ ἕτερος) 124. 37. πτῶμα 13.69.346. οἱ ἀετοὶ συναχθήσονται (no καὶ) 13.69.124.

XVIII 1. ἔλεγεν. — καὶ *prim.* four. + αὐτοὺς (*post* προσεύχεσθαι) 13.69.124. ἐνκακεῖν 13.69.346. 3. [no τις]. 4. ἤθελεν four. [δὲ τ.]. [ἄνον οὐκ]. 5. κόπους 13.69.124. ὑπὸπιάζη four. 7. ἐπ᾽ αὐτούς +,. 8. *init.* + ναὶ four. [ἄρα]. 9. εἶπεν. — καὶ *prim.* 13.69.346. -οῦντες. 10. [ὁ εἷς]. 11, 12. [as Scr.]. 13. ὁ δὲ (*pro* καὶ ὁ) four. [rest as Scr.]. 14. οὗτ (-ως *videtur*) δεδικαιομένος 13.346. αὐτοῦ ἢ γὰρ ἐκεῖνος 13.124.346. [no ὅτι]. 15. ἅπτεται 69.346. ἐπετίμων 13.346. 16. ἔλεγεν (*pro* εἶπεν) 13.346. 17. ἂν (*pro* ἐὰν) 13.69.346. 18. αὐτὸν τίς 13.69.346. 19. [ὁ θσ]. 20. [σου *bis*]. 21. εἶπεν. — πάντα *solus.* [rest as Scr.]. 22, 23.

[as Scr.]. 24. εἶπεν. [rest as Scr.]. 25. εὐκοπότερον 13.346. κάμιλον 13.124. [τρυμαλιὰς]. βελώνης four. διελθεῖν (pro εἰσ. prim.) 13.124.346. 26. [εἶπον]. 27. ὁ δὲ ἴσ 13.124.346. εἶπεν. [παρὰ τῷ θῷ]. 28. [ὁ]. ἀφέντες 13.69.346. πάντα τὰ ἴδια καὶ four. 29. [ὅτι]. [rest as Scr.]. 30. [as Scr.]. 31. εἶπεν. περὶ τοῦ υἱοῦ (pro τῷ υἱῷ) four. 32. ἔθνεσιν. 33. τῇ τρίτῃ ἡμέρα four. 34. αὐτοῖς (pro αὐτοὶ). 35. -ριχῶ. πρὸς αἰτῶν. 36. τί ἂν εἴη four. 39. + ιυ (ante υἱέ) four. [rest as Scr.]. 40. [ὁ ἴσ]. 41. ἐγγίζοντος 13.69.346. + ὁ ισ (ante λέγων) four. εἶπεν. 42. σέσωκεν. 43. ἀνέβλεψεν. ὄχλος (pro λαὸς) four.

XIX. 1. ἱεριχῶ. 2. –ὀνόματι 13. οὗτος (pro αὐτὸς) 69.346. αὐτὸς (pro οὗτος ἦν) 13.69.346. 3. ἐστιν. 4. –δι’ 124. [rest as Scr.]. 5. [εἶδεν αὐτὸν καὶ] εἶπεν. 7. οἱ φαρισαίοι (pro ἅπαντες) 13.69.346. εἰσῆλθεν. 8. εἶπεν. ιν (pro κν) four. [rest as Scr.]. 9. καθ’ ὅτι. 10. ἦλθεν. 11. παραβολὴν εἶπεν 13.69.346. [rest as Scr.]. 13. εἶπεν. [ἕως]. 14. αὐτοῦ. ἀπηστειλαν? πρεσβίαν. θέλωμεν. 15. εἶπεν. [ἔδωκε]. [rest as Scr.]. 16. ἡμνάστου (sic) only σσου cf. ver. 18, 20, 22 προσηργάσατο δ. 13.346. 17. [εὖ]. δοῦλε ἀγαθέ 13.346. 18. κε ἡ μνάσσου 69.346. [γίνου ἐπ-]. 19. + ὁ (ante ἕτερος) four. 20. ἡ μνάσσου. fin. + καὶ συνάγεις ὅθεν οὐ διεσκόρπισας four. 22. – δὲ four. + ὁ κύριος αὐτοῦ (ante ἐκ) four. στόμαστοστε? (vid. ver. 16). fin. + καὶ συνάγων ὃ οὐ διεσκόρπισα four. 23. διὰ τί. –τὴν four. καὶ ἐλθὼν ἐγὼ 13.69.346. [rest as Scr.]. 24. τῷ ἔχοντι τὰς δέκα μνάς 13.69.346. 25. [εἶπον]. 26. γὰρ erased s. m. + καὶ περισσευθήσεται (post δοθήσεται) four. [ἀπ’ αὐτοῦ]. 27. θέλοντας 13.69.346. [rest as Scr.]. 29. βηθσφαγὴ. [-νίαν]. τῷ secund. [-ῶν]. αὐτοῦ. λέγων (pro εἰπών) 13.69.346. 30. εὑρήσεται. ἐκάθισεν λύσαντες. 31. διὰ τί οὔτ..σ eras. s. m. [αὐτῷ]. αὐτοῦ so ver. 34. 33, 34. [εἶπον] so ver. 39. 34. [ὅτι]. 35. [as Scr.]. 36. [αὐτῶν]. 37. [ἤρξαντο]. 38. [πασῶν]. +γινομένων (ante δυνάμεων) 13.69.346. [rest as Scr.]. 40. [as Scr.]. 41. ἐπ’ αὐτήν. 42. σοι (pro σου secund.) 13.69. 43. συνάξουσίν 13.69.346. 44. ἐδαφιοῦσίν. [rest as Scr.]. 45. [π. καὶ ἀ.]. – ἐν αὐτῷ 13.69.346. 46. καὶ ἔσται ̔ οἶκός μου οἶκος προσευχῆς four. 47. καθημέραν. 48. οὐχ’ εὗρ. ἐξεκρέμαντο (videtur) ς supra.

XX. 1. οἱ γραμματεῖς καὶ οἱ ἀρχιερεῖς four. 2. εἶπαν 13.69. [rest as Scr.]. 3. εἶπεν. [ἕνα]. 4. [no τὸ: νν]. 5. διὰ τί. – οὖν

42   LUKE XX. 6—XXII. 24.

13.69.124.   6. πᾶς ὁ λαός. γεγονέναι (pro εἶναι) four.   7. + τὸ
(ante πόθεν) four.   9. πός τις ἐφ. ἀπεδήμησεν. [rest as Scr.].
10. [ἐν]. ἀπέστειλεν. [δῶσιν]. δήραντες? (η erased s. m.) 124 so
ver. 11. [αὐτὸν ἐξ-]. [π. ἔτ-]. 11. οἱ δὲ. δωρ- (erased η) 13.124.
12. [as Scr.].   13. [ἰδόντες]. 14, 16. [as Scr.]. 17. εἶπεν. ἐστὶν.
18. θλασθήσεται solus. 19. [ἐζήτησαν]. οἱ γραμματεῖς καὶ οἱ
ἀρχιερεῖς 13.124.346. εἶπεν τὴν παραβολὴν ταύτην four. 20. [as
Scr.]. ἤγε.. νος erasure s. m. 21. ὀρθῶς. λαμάνεις (β p. m.).
supra. ἐπαληθείας. 22. ἡμᾶς (pro ἡμῖν) 13.69.346. 23. εἶπεν.
[no omission]. δείξατε 13.69. fin. + οἱ δὲ four. ἔδειξαν· καὶ
εἶπεν. 24. [as Scr.]. 25. εἶπεν πρὸς αὐτούς 13.69.346. τοίνυν
ἀπόδοτε 13.69.346. +τῷ (ante καίσαρι) 13.346. 26. [as Scr.].
27. [ἀντιλ]. ἐπηρωτουν four (124). 28. μωϋσῆς 13.69.346. [ἀπο-
θανῃ bis]. ἐξαναστήσει four. 30. [as Scr.]. 31. [ὡσαύτως semel].
+ καὶ (post ἑπτὰ) 13.124.346. 32. – δὲ 13.69.124. ἀπέθανεν καὶ
ἡ γυνή. 33. [ἐν τῇ οὖν]. 34. [ἀποκρ.]. ἐκγαμίζονται (so ver. 35)
13.346. 36. εἰσιν bis. [τοῦ]. 37. [μωσῆς]. [τὸν ter.]. εἰσίν.
39. [εἶπον]. 40. [οὐκ ἔτι δὲ]. 41. εἶπεν. λέγουσιν οἱ γραμματεῖς
ὅτι ὁ χσ υἱὸς δαδ̄ ἐστίν. 42. + τῶν (ante ψαλμῶν) 13.69.346. [rest
as Scr.]. 44. [as Scr.]. 45. εἶπεν [αὐτοῦ]. 46. ἐν στολαῖς περι-
πατεῖν 13.69.346. πρωτοκλησίας 13.69.346. ἐν ταῖς δείπνοις sic 13.
47. προσευχόμενοι four. [rest as Scr.]. [κρίμα].

XXI. 1. εἰς τὸ γαζοφυλάκιον τὰ δῶρα αὐτῶν four. 2. εἶδεν.
τινὰ καὶ four. πενηχρὰν 13.124.346. [δ. λ.]. 3. αὕτη ἡ πτωχὴ
four. [πλεῖον]. 4. [ἀπ·]. περισσεύματος four. αὐτῶν (pro π.
αὐτοῖς). πάντα τὸν βίον αὐτῆς 124.346. ἔβαλεν. fin. +ταῦτα λέγων
ἐφώνει ὁ ἔχων ὦτα ἀκούειν ἀκουέτω four. 5. ἀναθήμασιν. 6. εἶπεν.
+ ὧδε (post λίθω) four. 7. ὅτ᾽ ἂν ver. 9. 8. εἶπεν. [ὅτι] ἤγγικεν.
[οὖν]. 9. πτωηθῆτε. 10. [ἐπὶ bis]. 11. μεγάλα ἀπ᾽ οὐρανοῦ
ἔσονται four. [rest as Scr.]. 12. πάντων 13.69.346. [no τὰς].
[ἀγομένους]. ἡγεμῶνας. 13. [δὲ]. 14. [as Scr.]. 15. ἀντιστῆναι
ἢ ἀντ᾽ ειπεῖν πάντες ὑμεῖν four. 16. – καὶ prim. 13.69.346. 19. κτήσεσθε (13). 20. Ὅτ᾽ ἂν (– δὲ init. lect.) 13. [τὴν]. [γνῶτε].
22. αὐταί εἰσιν four. [πληρωθῆναι]. 23. [δὲ]. [ἐν γ.]. – ἐν (post
ὀργῇ) 13.69.346. 24. + οὖν (sic: post ἄχρι) 13. πληρωθῶσιν.
[rest as Scr.]. 25. ἤχους 13.69.346. [rest as Scr.]. 26. ἀπὸ
ψυχῶν 13.69.346 τῶν. 27. [as Scr.]. 28. γένεσθαι (ἵ supra p. m.?).
δι᾽ ὅτι. 29. εἶπεν. 30. ὅτ᾽ ἂν ver. 31. ἀπ᾽ αὐτῶν (pro ἀφ᾽ ἑαυτ.)
13.69.346. [ἤδη bis]. τὸ θέρος ἐγγύς ἐστιν 13.69.346. 31. οὕτως.
+ πάντα (post ταῦτα) 69.124.346. 32. ἀμὴν bis script. 13.69.

+ ταῦτα (*ante* πάντα) four. 33. [-σονται]. παρέλθωσιν. 34. - δὲ
(*init. lect.*) 13.69.346. βαρηθῶσιν 13.124. αἱ καρδίαι ὑμῶν four.
κρεπάλη 13. αἰφνιδίως. [rest as Scr.]. 35. γὰρ ἀπελεύσεται
solus. 36. ἀγρυπνῆτε οὖν 13.346. [rest as Scr.]. 37. [as Scr.].
38. ὤρθριζεν. JOHAN. VII. 53 *pergit eâdem lineâ vix* αὐτοῦ + καὶ
ἀπῆλθεν ἒ last line in page. No Ammonian numeral between
cap. XXI. 34 σ̅ν̅θ̅ and cap. XXII. 1 σ̅ξ̅. No Ammonian in
Johan. VII. 53 to VIII. 11, but the pericope omitted, *nullo
omissionis vestigio* (passing on in same line from cap. VII. 52 to
VIII. 12. γήγερται+αρ πάλιν^{χ rubro}). S. Luke ends ἁμάρτανε τέ^λ (*then
late ink* τη | ἴε ἒ πρωΐ^λ). JOHAN. VII. 53. ἀπῆλθεν (*pro* ἐπορεύθη)
four. VIII. 1. καὶ ὁ ι̅σ̅ ἐπορεύθη four. 2. ἦλθεν (*pro* παρεγένετο)
four. - εἰς τὸ ἱερὸν *ad fin.* vers. four. 3. καὶ προσήνεγκαν four
αὐτῶι οἱ γρ. καὶ οἱ φαρ. γυναῖκα four. ἐπὶ (*pro* εν) four. + τῶ
(*ante* μέσω) 69.124.346. 4. εἶπον (*pro* λέγουσιν) four. εἴληπται
ἐπ' αὐτῶι φόρω four. 5. ἡμῖν μωσῆς four. λιθάζειν four. *fin.*+περὶ
αὐτῆς four. 6. ἔχωσιν κατηγορίαν κατ' αὐτοῦ four. ἔγραψεν four.
7. ἀναβλέψας (*pro* ἀνακύψας) four. εἶπεν αὐτοῖς four. - τὸν four.
βαλέτω ἐπ' αὐτήν four. 9. - οἱ δὲ *usque ad* ἐλεγχόμενοι 13.69.124.
καὶ ἐξῆλθον (*pro* ἐξήρχοντο) 13.69.124. καθ' εἷς. - μόνος 13.69.124.
οὖσα (*pro* ἑστῶσα) four. 10. ἀναβλέψας (*pro* ἀνακύψας) four.
- καὶ μηδενα *usque ad* γυναικὸς 13.69.124. *Habet* ἴδεν αὐτὴν καὶ
εἶπεν (- αὐτῇ). γύναι four. - ἐκεῖνοι 13.69.124. 11. καὶ ὁ ι̅σ̅
εἶπεν αὐτῇ four. - καὶ (*ante* μὴ) κέτι) four.

XXII. 1. ἤγγιζεν. 2. - τὸ *solus.* 3. εἰσῆλθεν. - ὁ four.
-νὰς. [ἐπικαλ-]. 4. συνελάλησεν. ἀρχιερεῦσιν [καὶ τοῖς στρ.].
ὅπως (*pro* τὸ πῶς) four. [αὐτ. παρ. αὐτοῖς]. 5. ἀργύρια 13.69.346.
6. ἐξωμολόγησεν. [τοῦ παραδ.]. - ἄτερ ὄχλου 13.69. 7. ἦλθεν
- ἡ 13.346. ἐν ᾗ δεῖ 13.69.346. 8. ἀπέστειλεν. ἵνα φάγωμεν
τὸ πάσχα four. 9. εἶπαν 346. + ἵνα (*ante* ἑτοιμ.) 13.69.124.
[no addition]. 10. [οὗ]. 11. οἰκοδεσπότει. 12. + ἕτοιμον (*ante*
ἐκεῖ) 69.124.346. 13. [as Scr.]. 14. ἀνέπεσεν. [δώδεκα]. 15. εἶπεν:
so ver. 17. 16. [οὐκέτι]. ἀπ' (*pro* ἐξ) four. 17. [no τὸ]. *fin.* εἰς
ἑαυτούς four. 18. γενήματος four. [rest as Scr.]. 19. ἔκλασεν.
ὑπὲρ..μῶν *eras.* 13.346. 20. ὡσαύτως καὶ τὸ π. ἐμῶ αἵματι (*pro*
αἵματί μου) four. [ἐκχυνό-]. 21. - ἰδοὺ 13.69. 22. κατὰ τὸ
ὡρισμένον πορεύεται four. [rest as Scr.]. 23. σὺνζ. πράσσειν
μέλλων 13.69. 24. φιλονϊκία 124.346. ἐν ἑαυτοῖς 69.124.346.

25. κατακυριεύουσιν four.   26. [γενέσθω].   27. + ἐστὶν (post μείζων) four.   [rest as Scr.].   29. διατίθεμε.   30. [ἐσθίητε].   + μετ᾽ ἐμοῦ (post πίνητε) four.   καθήσεσθε.   θρόνους (+ δώδεκα) four.   [rest as Scr.].   31. εἶπεν δὲ ὁ κσ. ἐξετήσατο.   32, 33. [as Scr.].   34. ὁ δὲ εἶπεν.   [μή].   ἕως four.   τρεῖς 346.   με ἀπαρνήσει μὴ εἰδέναι.   35. οὔθ᾽ ἑνόσ four.   [rest as Scr.].   36. εἶπεν δὲ (− οὖν) four.   βαλλάντιον (not ver. 35) 13.69.346.   πωλήσει four.   ἀγοράσει four.   37. [as Scr.].   38. οἱ δὲ [εἶπον].   ἐστιν.   39. − αὐτοῦ 69.124.   40. ἐμπεσεῖν (pro εἰσελθεῖν) four.   42. παρενέγκαι four.   42. γινέσθω 13.   [rest as Scr.].   42. Ammonïan σπβ̄.   ver. 45 σπγ̄.   Om. ver. 43, 44, so Cod. 561, with no sign of omission.   Habet ad fin. Matt. XXVI. 39.   45. [no αὐτοῦ].   κοιμωμένους αὐτοὺς four.   47. [δὲ].   αὐτούς (pro αὐτῶν) four.   ἤγγισεν.   fin. + τοῦτο γὰρ four 561 σημεῖον δέδωκεν αὐτοῖς δέδωκει 561 ὃν ἂν φιλήσω αὐτός ἐστιν.   49. [as Scr.].   50. τοῦ ἀρχιερέως τὸν δοῦλον 13.69.346.   ἀφεῖλεν τὸ οὖς αὐτοῦ.   51. ἐάσατε four.   [αὐτοῦ].   52. ἐξήλθατε four.   [rest as Scr.].   53. καθ᾽ ἡμέραν ὄντως 346.   [rest as Scr.].   54. αὐτῶ (four) ἀπομακρόθεν 13.69.346.   [rest as Scr.].   55. συνκαθισ. ἐκάθιτο.   [rest as Scr.].   56. εἶπεν.   57. [as Scr.].   58. ἔφη (pro εἶπεν sec.) four.   59. ὡσ εἰ.   − ἦν 13.   60. − ὁ four.   61. ἀνέβλεψεν 13.124.346.   [λόγου].   ἴυ (pro κῦ) 13.346.   [no ἦ].   + σήμερον (ante φωνῆσαι) four.   62. [ὁ πέτρος].   63. [τὸν ἴν].   64. [as Scr.].   66. πρωὶ (pro ἡμέρα) 13.69.346.   ἀπήγαγον four.   [ἑαυτῶν].   67. [εἰπέ].   68. ἐὰν δὲ καὶ ἐπερωτήσω ὑμᾶς four.   [rest as Scr.].   69. [no δὲ].   70. [εἶπον] so ver. 71.   71. χ. ἔχομεν μ. (ω p. m.).

XXIII. 1. ἤγαγον four.   [πιλάτον] passim.   2. [εὕρομεν].   + ἡμῶν (post ἔθνος) four.   [rest as Scr.].   3. [ἐπηρ.].   4. εἶπεν.   αἴτιον ver. 14, not ver. 22.   5. [no καὶ].   6. − ὁ.   ἐστιν.   7. [no τὸν].   8. ἐχάρι.   ἐξ ἱκανοῦ χρόνου θέλων four.   περὶ αὐτοῦ πολλὰ four.   10. εἱστήκησαν.   11. καὶ (pro ὁ) four.   [rest as Scr.].   12. − ὁ secund. four.   [rest as Scr.].   13. εἶπεν.   14. διαστρέφοντα four.   ἐν αὐτῶ αἴτιον (pro ἐν τ. α. τ.) ver. 4 four.   [οὐδὲν].   15. Ὁ rubro marg. s. m. (abreast: Ἡρώδης).   αὐτὸν πρὸς ὑμᾶς 13.69.   + ἐν (ante αὐτῶ) 13.69.124.   17. ἀνάγκειν δὲ ἔχεν.   18. [ἀνέκραξαν].   − δὲ 124.346.   πᾶν πληθεῖ 13.124.346.   19. [as Scr.].   20. [οὖν] προσεφώνησεν αὐτοῖς four.   21. [as Scr.].   22. + γὰρ (ante αἴτιον) four.   23. [no omission].   24. [ὁ δὲ] ἐπέκρινεν.   25. + τὸν βαραββᾶν (ante τὸν διὰ στάσιν) four.   φώνω.   τὸ θελήματι.   [rest as Scr.].

COLLATION OF COD. 556 WITH CODD. 13.69.124.346. 45

26. σίμωνα τινὰ κυριναῖον ἐρχομένου (videtur: mutat.) four. αὐτὸν
(pro αὐτῷ). [rest as Scr.]. 27. πλῆθος πολὺ four. [αἲ καὶ].
28. [ὁ]. εἶπεν. 29. – ἰδού four. ἐλεύσονται four. ἐροῦσιν. + αἱ
(ante κοιλίαι) four. [ἐθήλασαν]. 30. ἄρξωνται 13.124. [πέσετε].
31. [τῷ]. 33. [ἀπῆλθον]. ὃν μὲν. ὃν δὲ ἐξενωνύμων 13.69.124.
346. 34. [no omiss.]. ἔλεγεν. ποιοῦσιν. ἔβαλλον κλῆρον
124.346. 35. + αὐτὸν (ante καὶ) four. [σὺν αὐτοῖς]. ἔσωσεν. ὁ
υἱὸς τοῦ θεοῦ ὁ ἐκλεκτός four. 36. ἐνέπεζον 69.346. καὶ ὄξως (ς supra).
37. [εἰ]. + ὁ χσ (post εἰ) four. 38. ἐπ᾽ αὐτῶι γεγραμμένη four.
[no omission]. 39, 40, 43, 45. [as Scr.]. 41. ἔπραξεν. 42. ὅτ᾽ ἂν.
[rest as Scr.]. 44. [ἦν δὲ] ὡς ἡ ὥρα (ς supra) 13.69.346. ἐνάτης 124.
346. 46. εἶπεν. [-θήσομαι]. τοῦτο (pro ταῦτα) four. 47. [as Scr.].
48. παραγενόμενοι. – ἐπὶ τὴν θεωρίαν ταύτην four, at καὶ θεωρήσαντες
τὴν θεωρίαν ταύτην· four. θεωροῦντες 69. τὰ γινόμενα 13.69.124.
αὐτῶν (pro ἑαυτῶν) 13.69. 49. [αὐτοῦ μακρόθεν]. 51. συνκατατιθέμενος.
[ὃς καὶ]. – καὶ αὐτὸς 13.69.346. [rest as Scr.]. 53. – αὐτὸ prim.
13.69.346. + καθαρὰ (post σινδόνι) 13.69.346. – αὐτὸ tert. 13.69.
346. οὐδεὶς οὐδέπω 13.69.346. fin. + καὶ προσεκύλισεν λίθον μέγαν
ἐπὶ τὴν θύραν τοῦ μνημείου 13.124.346. 54. + ἡ (ante ἡμέρα)
13.69.346. παρασκευῆς 13.346. ἐπέφωσκεν. 55. αἱ (pro καὶ)
13.69.346. [αὐτῶι]. ἐθεώρουν four. 56. ἀρώματα (not cap.
XXIV. 1).

XXIV. 1. βαθέως 13.124.346. [rest as Scr.]. 3. [as Scr.].
4. ἄνδρες δύο four. [rest as Scr.]. 5. [as Scr.]. 6. [ἀλλ᾽] ἠγέρθη.
[ὡς]. 7. [as Scr.]. 9. – πάντα. 10. – αἱ 69.124. [rest as Scr.:
etiam -ηνῇ]. 11. ὡς εἰ. [αὐτῶν sec.]. 12. Habet [as Scr.].
13. [as Scr.] at ἐξήκοντα. 15. σὺν ζητεῖν. [ὁ ισ]. 17. [as Scr.].
18. – ὁ four. + ἐξ᾽ αὐτῶν (post εἶς) four. [ὡ. ὄν. κλέο]. εἶπεν. εἰς
(pro ἐν prim.) ἱλημ 13.346. 19. [as Scr.]. 20. ὅπως τε αὐτὸν
παρέδωκαν four. 21. ἀλλ᾽ ἄγε (sic). [σήμερον]. 22. [ὄρθριαι].
23. ὀπτασίαν. 24. οὕτως 13.69.346. [καθὼς καὶ]. ἴδον 13.
25. εἶπεν. 27. [μωσέως]. δι᾽ ἑρμήνευεν four. [ἑαυτοῦ]. 28. πρὸς
ἐποιεῖτο αὐτὸς [πορρωτέρω]. 29. [not ἤδη]. εἰσῆλθεν. 30. ηὐλό-
γησεν 13.346. 32. ἐλάλη 346. [rest as Scr.]. 33. [συνηθρ.].
34. [as Scr.]. 36. λεγόντων (pro λαλ-) four. [rest as Scr.].
37. [πτοη-]. 38. διὰ τί. [ταῖς καρδίαις]. 39. ψηλαφήσετε 69.
[rest as Scr.]. 40. [Habet, as Scr.]. 41. [as Scr.]. 42. οἱ δὲ.
ἰχθύος. κηρίον 13.69. [rest as Scr.]. 43. fin. + καὶ τὰ ἐπίλοιπα
ἔδωκεν αὐτοῖς 13.346. 44. [as Scr.]. 46. οὕτως prim. 13.346.

[rest as Scr.]. 47. [as Scr.]. 48. [δὲ ἐ϶ὲ]. 49. [as Scr.]. 50. ἐξήγαγεν. [ἔξω]. [εἰς]. 51, 52. [as Scr.]. 53. διὰ παντὸς [rest as Scr.].

Subscr. Εὐαγγέλιον κατὰ λουκαν (illeg.?) ἐγραφ. ἑλληνιστὶ εἰς ἀλεξανδρίαν 69 τὴν μεγάλην. [μετὰ ιε 69] in modern ink over faded p. m. ἔτει τῆ ι϶̄. τῆς ἀναλήψεως τοῦ κ̄ῡ ⁺ἔχει δὲ ῥήματα κ̄ ω̄γ· στˣˣ β̄ψ̄ν̄ +.

(on same page) Εὐαγγέ κατὰ ἰῶ τὰ κεφά + ᾶ κανᾶ. (Collated with Mill.) γ̄. –καὶ ῑ̄ῡ 69. δ̂ ζήτησις περὶ καθαρισμοῦ 69*. ϛ̄ –τοῦ υἱοῦ (69). ζ̄ –ἔτη ἐτων 69. ἀσθενία αὐτοῦ 69. ἠ –καὶ τῶν δύο ἰχθύων 69. ῑ –ἐκγενετῆς 69. ῑᾱ –τῆς ἐγέρσεως 69. ῑδ̄ τοῦ (pro τῆς) 69. ῑε –καὶ ἐρωτώντων τὸν φίλιππον 69. [Briefer than Mill.] Under slight illumination. + Εὐαγγέλιον κατὰ ἰωαννην.

JOHAN. I. 3. , γέγονεν+. 4. [ἦν]. 6. [νν passim]. 11. ἦλθεν. 12. [ἔλαβον]. 15. ἔμπροσθέ so ver. 27, not ver. 30. 16. [καὶ]. 17. [μωσέως] ἐδώθη 13. 18. [ὁ μονογενὴς υἱὸς]. 19. +πρὸς αὐτὸν (post λευίτας) four. 20. ὡμολόγησεν bis. οὐκ εἰμὶ ἐγώ. 21. ἠρνήσατο. [rest as Scr.]. 22. [εἶπον οὖν]. 23. init. +ὁ δὲ four. 24. [οἱ]. 25. ἠρώτησαν. [rest as Scr.]. 26. +μὲν (post ἐγὼ) four. ἔστηκεν. [rest as Scr.]. 27. ἔμπροσθέ (ver. 4, not ver. 30, but 69) 13. οὐκ εἰμὶ ἐγὼ 13.69. [rest as Scr.]. 28. βηθεβαρᾶ 13.69.346. +τὸ πρῶτον (ante βαπτίζων) 13.346. 29. [ὁ ἰω.]. 30. [περὶ]. +ὑμῖν (post εἶπον) 13.69.124. 31. [as Scr.]. 32. +ὁ (ante ἰω) four. ὡσ εἰ. 33. ἴδεις (ϛ supra). καταβαίνων p. m. (mut.). [οὗτός]. 35. ἱστήκει [ὁ ἰω.] 13. 37. [as Scr.]. 38. [δὲ]. 39. Τίνα (pro Τί) 13.346. [rest as Scr.]. 40. [ἴδετε + ἦλθον]. ἴδων (pro εἶδον). ἐκείνην τὴν ἡμέραν four. – δὲ (post ὥρα) four. 41. + δὲ (post ἦν) 13.346. 42. πρῶτον 13.69.346. μεσίαν 13.69.124. – ὁ four. 43. [καὶ]. [δὲ]. εἶπεν. [ἰωνᾶ]. 44. [ὁ ἰσ̄]. γαλιλεαν modern ink. φίλιπον (mod. ink). +ὁ ῑσ̄ (post αὐτῶι) 13.124.346. 45. – ὁ. φήλιππος (mod. ink). 46. ναζαρέθ 13.124. [rest as Scr.]. 47. [καὶ]. ναζαρέθ four. [no ὁ]. 48. ἰσραηλήτης. δόλως. ἔστιν. 49. [ὁ]. ἴδον 13.346. 50. [as Scr.]. 51. +ὁ (ante ῑσ̄)

four. (After ισ two leaves misplaced cap. IV. 6—52.) + ὅτι
(ante εἶδον) 13.346. ὄψη 13.124. 52. ἀπάρτι 13.69.

II. 1. τῇ τρίτη ἡμέρα four. κανα. 3. ἔχουσιν. [rest as Scr.].
4. init. + καὶ 13.69.346. 5. λέγει 13.346. 6. [ὐδ. λι.]. κείμεναι
ἐξ 346*. 7. γεμήσατε 69.124. [ἐγέμισαν]. 8 or 9. [καὶ]. 10. ὅτ᾽
ἄν. [τότε]. + δὲ (post συ) four. 12. τούτωι 13. [καπερ.]. αὐτοῦ
ter. [ἔμειναν]. 13. – ὁ ἰησοῦς four. 15. [τὸ κέρμα] κατέστρεψεν
13.69** marg. 16. [no + καὶ]. 17. [δὲ]. καταφάγεταί 13.124.
(346). 18. – οὖν 13.69.346. [εἶπον]. 19. [ὁ]. [ἐν]. 20. [as
Scr.]. 22. – αὐτοῖς 13.69.346. Ends with ὧ. εἶπεν αὐτοῖς. Two
leaves lost to cap. IV. 6. ὥρα ἦν ὡσεὶ ἔκτη. 7. [as Scr.].
8. ἀπεληλύθασιν 69. ἀγοράσωσιν. 9. συνχρῶνται. [rest as Scr.].
10. + ὁ (ante ισ) four. 11. [οὖν]. 12. δέδωκεν 69. + τοῦτο (post
φρέαρ) four. ἔπιεν. – οἱ 13. 13. [ὁ ισ]. πί.. mut. 14. – οὐ μὴ
usque ad δώσω αὐτῷ (ὅμοιοτ.) 13. + ζῶντος (ante ἀλλομένου) 13.
15. μὴ δὲ ἔρχομαι 13.69.346. 16, 17. [as Scr.]. 19. fin. +,.
20. τῶ ὄρει τοῦτο four. [δεῖ πρ.]. 21. πίστευέ μοι λέγοντι
13.69.346. προσκυνήσωσι. 23. [ἀλλ᾽]. ἀληθεινοὶ 13, not ver. 37.
προσκυνητὲ. 24. [as Scr.]. 25. οἴδαμεν 13.69.346. μεσίας four.
ὅτ᾽ ἄν. [πάντα]. 27. εἶπεν. [rest as Scr.]. 29. εἶπεν. [ὅσα].
30. [οὖν]. 31. [δὲ]. ἠρώτων not ver. 40. [ῥαββὶ]. 32. ὁ δὲ.
33. πρὸς ἀλλήλους οἱ μαθηταὶ four. 34. [as Scr.]. 35. – ἔτι
13.69.346. τετράμηνος four. ἐστιν. [ἤδη·]. 36. – εἰς ζωὴν.
χαίρει four. [habet καὶ bis]. 37. τοῦτο 13.124. [ὁ]. 38. [ἀπέ-
στειλα]. 39. εἶπέν. [ὅσα]. 40. [as Scr.]. 41. + εἰς αὐτὸν (post
ἐπίστευσαν) four. 42. + παρ᾽ αὐτοῦ (post ἀκηκόαμεν) four. [rest
as Scr.]. 43. – καὶ ἀπῆλθεν 13.69. 44. [ὁ ισ]. 45. [ὅ τε]. ὅσα
(pro ἃ) four. + σημεῖα (post ἐποίησεν) four. 46. πάλιν ὁ ισ 13.69.
κανᾶ. ησ θ error corrected. [rest as Scr.]. 47. ἀπὸ (pro ἐκ) four.
ἦλθεν (pro ἀπῆλθε) 13.69.124. [ἠρώτα αὐτὸν]. 49. τὸν υἱόν
(pro τὸ παιδίον) four. 50. [καὶ]. + ὁ (ante ισ). ἐπορεύθη four.
51. [αὐτοῦ]. ὑπήντησαν 13.124. [ἀπ.]. υἱός (pro παῖς) four.
52. ἐπυνθάνετο four. Ends οὖν τὴν ὤ-. Two leaves lost. Resumes
V. 43. πρσ μου καὶ οὐ λαμβάνετέ με. [λήψεσθε]. 44. [θῦ].
45. [μωσῆς]. 46. [μωσῆ]. ἔγραψε (hiatus) 13. 47. πιστεύσητε
four.

† Hiat Cod. 346 Johan. III. 26 usque ad Johan. VII. 52.

48   JOHN VI. 1—VIII. 21.

VI. 1. + δὲ (post μετὰ) four.   2. ἠκολούθει δὲ (– καὶ) four.
ἐθεώρων (pro ἑώρων) 13.69.   –αὐτοῦ four.   3. ἀνῆλθεν. οὖν (pro
δὲ) 13.69.   [ὁ ἰσ]. ἐκαθέζετο four.   4. – ἡ ἑορτή.   5. – ὁ ἰσ 13.
[τὸν φ.]. ἀγοράσωμεν four.   7. [as Scr.].   9. ἔστιν. – ἐν 13.69. δ'
(' sic p. m.).   10. εἶπεν. [δὲ]. [χ. π.]. ἀνέπεσαν 13.69. ὡσ εἰ.
11. init. καὶ λαβὼν (– δὲ) four. ἤθελον not ver. 21.   [rest as
Scr.].   12. σ (rubricated ω omitted). 14. [as Scr.].   15. Ὁ οὖν
ὁ ἰσ γνοὺς rubro. + οἱ ὄχλοι (post ἔρχεσθαι) 13. -ησεν (– πάλιν)
13.69.   16. εἰς (pro ἐπὶ) four or three.   17. [τὸ πλ.]. + εἰς τὸ
(ante πέραν) 13.69. [καπερ.]. οὔπω (pro οὐκ) three. + εἰς τὸ
πλοῖον (post ἰσ) 13. [rest as Scr.].   18, 19. [as Scr.].   21. ἐγένετο
τὸ πλοῖον ἐπὶ τὴν γῆν three.   22. [ἰδὼν]. ἄλλο πλοιάριον three.
ἀνέβησαν; τοῦ ἰΰ (pro αὐτοῦ prim.) three. αὐτοῦ secund. πλοῖον
(pro πλοιάριον) three.   23. [as Scr.].   24. + ὁ (ante ἰσ) 13.69.
ἔλαβον αὐτοὶ τὰ πλοιάρια (pro ἐνέβησαν καὶ αὐτοὶ εἰς τὰ πλοῖα) three.
[καπερ-].   25. [ῥαββὶ].   26. οὐχ'. ἴδετε 13.   27. δώσει ὑμῖν 13.
τοῦτο (pro -ον) 13.69.   28. ποιήσωμεν 13.   29. ἐστιν. [πιστεύσητε].
30. – σὺ 13.69.   31. ἔφαγον τὸ μάννα three.   δέδωκεν 69.124.
32. [μωσῆς δέδ.].   33. [no ὁ added]. καταβαίνον 13.   [ζ. δ.].
34. εἶπαν 13.   35. εἶπεν οὖν (– δὲ) 13.69. [με]. πεινάσει 13.124.
διψήσει 13.124.   36, 37. [με].   38. ἀπὸ (pro ἐκ) three. [ποιῶ].
39. [πρσ]. ἀλλ'. [ἐν].   40. γάρ (pro δὲ) 13.69.   + πρσ (ante ἵνα)
three. ἔχει three.   + ἐν (post ἐγὼ) three.   41. ὁ ἐκ τοῦ οὐνοῦ
καταβὰς three.   42. [οὐχ']. [οὖν]. [οὗτος]. – ὅτι three.   43. – οὖν
three.   [ὁ ἰσ]. ἵνα τί (pro μὴ) (13).69. [μετ'].   44. + ἐν (ante
τῇ ἐσχ. ἡ) three.   [rest as Scr.].   45. ἔστιν. μ (rubro marg.)
μένον. – τοῦ three.   [rest as Scr.].   46. [ἑωρακεν prim.]. ἑόρακεν
secund. 13. [πρα].   47. [εἰς ἐμὲ].   49. [as Scr.].   50. ἀποθάν...
eras.   51. [as Scr.].   52. οἱ ἰουδαῖοι πρὸς ἀλλήλους 13.69. [rest
as Scr.].   53. σάρκαν not ver. 54, 56. πίετε three.   54. [καὶ ἐγώ].
+ ἐν (ante τῇ ἐσχ.) three.   55. ἀληθής prim. et sec. 13.69. [ἀληθῶς]
ἐστιν.   57. ἀπέσταλκέ 13.69.124. ζήσει 13.124.   58. [ἐκ τοῦ].
[ὑμῶν τὸ μάννα]. [ζήσεται].   59. [καπερ.].   60. [οὗτος ὁ λόγος].
ἀκούειν αὐτοῦ 13.69.   61. ἔγνω (pro εἰδὼς) 13.69. + καὶ (ante
εἶπεν) 124.   62. θεωρεῖτε 13.   63. λελάληκα (pro λαλῶ) three.
64. [ἀλλ']. ἐξαρχῆς.   65. + αὐτοῖς (post ἔλεγεν) 13. [με]. ἤ.
+ ἄνωθεν p. m. (post δεδομένον) ...... p. m. delet. [μου]. 66. + οὖν
(post τούτου) three. τῶν μαθητῶν αὐτοῦ ἀπῆλθον three. οὐκέτι.
67. + μαθηταῖς (post δώδεκα) 13.69.   68. – οὖν three.   69. [as

Scr.]. 71. ἔλεγεν. ἀπὸ καρνώτου (*pro* ἰσκαριώτην) 124.(13.69).
ἔμελλεν παραδιδόναι αὐτὸν three. [ὧν].

VII. 1. μετὰ ταῦτα περιεπάτει ὁ ι̅σ̅ three. 3. [as Scr.].
4. ἐν παρρησία 13.69 αὐτὸς εἰ (part word lost) so 13.124. 5. αὐτοῦ.
6. [οὖν]. 7. – μισεῖ *solus*. ἐστι *hiatus*. 8. [ταύτην· ἐγὼ οὔπω].
– ὅτι. ὁ ἐμὸς καιρὸς three. 9, 10. [as Scr.]. 11. ι (rubric O
omitted). 12. οἱ μὲν. [rest as Scr.]. 14. ᾔδει (ει *eras.*). μεσα-
ζούσης three. [ὁ ι̅σ̅]. ἐδίδασκεν. 15. [as Scr.]. 16. + οὖν (*post*
ἀπεκρίθη) three. [ὁ]. 17. [τοῦ θ̅υ̅]. 18. ἐστιν *bis.* 19. [μωσῆς
δέδωκεν]. 20. [καὶ]. εἶπεν. 21. – ὁ. *fin.* +. 22. μωϋσῆς 13.69.
[μωσέως ver. 23]. [ἐν]. 23. [no ὁ]. – ἄνθρωπον *solus.* 24. [κρί-
νατε]. 25. [-μιτῶν]. 26. *init.* – καὶ 13.69. λέγουσιν. – ἀληθῶς
secund. three. 27. ὅτ᾽ ἂν. ἔρχεται 13. 28. – ὁ ι̅σ̅ (13). 29. – δὲ
three. [ἀπέστειλεν]. 30. + καὶ ἐξῆλθεν ἐκ τῆς χειρὸς αὐτῶν (*post*
πιάσαι) 13.69. [rest as Scr.]. 31. ἐκ τοῦ ὄχλου πολλοὶ (– δὲ)
three. – ὅτι three. ὅτ᾽ ἂν. [μήτι]. – τούτων 13.69. *fin.* ποιεῖ +,
13.69. 32. *init.* + καὶ three. [ταῦτα]. οἱ ἀρχιερεῖς καὶ οἱ φαρισαῖοι
three. ποιάσωσιν not ver. 44. 33. – αὐτοῖς three. χρόνον μικρὸν
three. 34. [no add.], so ver. 36. 35. [as Scr.]. 36. ὁ λόγος
οὗτος 13.69. εἶπεν. [no add.]. – ὑμεῖς 13.69.124. 37. ἱστήκει
13. ἔκραζε 69. [πρός με]. 39. εἶπεν. [οὗ] ἤμελλον three. – ὁ
three. [rest as Scr.]. 40. + αὐτοῦ (*post* λόγον) 13.69. [rest as
Scr.]. 41. – δὲ 13.69.124. [rest as Scr.]. 42. – τοῦ 13.69.124.
δα̅δ̅ *passim.* [rest as Scr.]. 43. [as Scr.]. 44. [ἐπέβαλεν].
45. διὰ τί. ἤγατε (γε *supra p. m.*). 46. [as Scr.]. 47. [οὖν].
– αὐτοῖς 13.69. 48. – ἐκ 13.69.124. 49. εἰσίν. [rest as Scr.].
50. [νυκτὸς]. + τὸ πρότερον (*post* πρὸς αὐτὸν) 13.69.124. 51. παρ᾽
αὐτοῦ πρῶτον 13.69. 52. [εἶπον]. εἶ... (*eras.*). σύ (13) so apparently
here. ἐρεύν..σον (*litera eras.*). οὐκ᾽ ἐγήγερται+αρ (*rubro*).   πάλιν
in same line: *pergit* cap. VIII. 12.

VIII. 12. αὐτοῖς ἐλάλησεν ὁ ι̅σ̅ 13.69.346. [rest as Scr.].
13. σὲ αὐτοῦ. 14. + ὁ (*ante* ι̅σ̅) four. ἐμ᾽ αὐτοῦ so ver. 18, 28,
54, &c. [rest as Scr.]. 15. οὐδ᾽ ἕνα. 16. δὲ κρίνω four.
[rest as Scr.]. 17. [γέγραπται]. 19. + καὶ εἶπεν (*post* ὁ ι̅σ̅) *solus.*
[ᾔδειτε ἂν]. 20. [ὁ ι̅σ̅]. 21. [ὁ ι̅σ̅]. + καὶ (*ante* ὅπου) 13.346.

† Cod. 346 resumed from Johan. III. 26.

S.   4

23. ἔλεγεν (*pro* εἶπεν) 13.69.346. ἔσται *p. m. eras.* τούτου τοῦ κόσμου *secund.* (*non prim.*): *contra* 13.69.124.   24. – οὖν *solus.* + μοι (*post* πιστεύσητέ) four.   25. [*as* Scr.].   26. ἐστιν. λαλῶ (*pro* λέγω) four.   28. [αὐτοῖς]. ὅτ᾽ ἄν. –μου 124.346.   29. ἐστιν + καὶ (*ante* οὐκ) 13.346. ἀφῆκεν. – ὁ πατήρ 13.69.346.   33. + οἱ ἰουδαῖοι (*post* αὐτῷ) four.   34. [ὁ]. ἐστὶν.   36. – οὖν 13. ἐλευθερώσει 13.69.124.   38. *init.* ἐγὼ δὲ four. ἃ ἑόρακα four. [μου]. ἃ ἠκούσατε (*pro* ὃ ἑωράκατε) 13.69.346. *fin.* παρὰ τοῦ πρσ ὑμῶν ποιῆτε 13.346.   39. αὐτῶ καὶ εἶπον four. [ὁ ισ]. [ἦτε]. – ἄν 13.   40. λελάληκα ὑμῖν four. πρσ μου (*pro* Θεοῦ) four.   41. [εἶπον οὖν]. γεγενήμεθα 13.69.124**.   42. ἥκω. ἀπέστειλεν. [rest as Scr.].   43. διὰ τί. τὸν ἐμὸν λόγον 13.69.346.   44. + τοῦ (*post* ἐκ) four. οὐκ᾽ ἔστηκεν (*sic*). ὅτ᾽ ἄν. ἐστὶν· καὶ.   45. ἐγώ δε. + ὑμῖν (*post* λέγω) 13.124.346.   46. – δὲ 13.69.346. διὰ τί. + μὴ (*post* οὐ) *solus.*   47. δια τοῦτο.   48. – οὖν 13.69.346. [εἶπον]. [-είτης]. – σὺ *solus.*   49. + ὁ (*ante* ισ) four. + καὶ εἶπεν (*ante* ἐγώ) four.   51. [*as* Scr.].   52. [εἶπον οὖν] retouch. ἀπέθανεν. γεύσητε 13.69. *fin.* +,.   53. ἀπέθανεν. – σὺ 13.124.346.   54. + ὁ (*ante* ισ) four. δοξάσω four. *fin.* ἡμῶν ἐστιν 69.124*.   55. [καὶ ἐὰν]. ὑμῶν ὅμοιος 13.346. [ἀλλ᾽].   56. τὴν ἡμέραν *bis script., prius eras.* ἴδεν 13.124.346.   57. [*as* Scr.].   58. + οὖν (*post* εἶπεν) four. [ὁ ισ].   59. ἐκρίβη. [*no omiss.*]. οὕτως.

IX. 1. + ὁ ισ (*post* παράγων *init. lect.*) 13.124.346. ἴδεν 13.124.346. γεννητῆς· 13.124.346.   2. ἠρώτησαν *not ver.* 19. [ῥαββὶ].   3. [ὁ].   4. [*as* Scr.].   5. ὅτ᾽ ἄν. ὤ.   6. ἔπτυσεν. ἐπέχρισεν. [rest as Scr.].   7. [νίψαι]. ἦλθεν.   8. [τυφλὸς].   9. + δὲ (*post* ἔλεγεν) four. [rest as Scr.].   10. [*as* Scr.].   11. [no ὁ]. ἐποίησεν. ἐπέχρισεν. εἶπεν. ὕπαγε νίψαι (– καὶ) εἰς τ. κ. 13.69.346. [rest as Scr.].   12. + αὐτοῖς (*post* λέγει) four. [rest as Scr.].   13. ποτὲ.   14. [ὅτε].   15. ἠρώτων. ὁ δὲ. ἐπέθηκε μου ἐπὶ τοὺς ὀφθαλμοὺς four.   16. – τοῦ four. [rest as Scr.]. + δὲ (*post* ἄλλοι) four.   17. λέγουσιν οὖν 13.69.346. [σὺ τί]. ἀνέωξε 13.346.   18. οἱ οουδαῖοι (ι corrected from ο, *p. m.*). [τυφλὸς ἦν].   19. αὐτός (*pro* οὗτός) *solus.* [ἄρτι βλέπει].   20. – αὐτοῖς 13.69.346. [εἶπον]. ὑμῶν altered *p. m.* to ἡμῶν.   21. περὶ ἑαυτοῦ. [rest as Scr.].   22. συνετίθειντο 13.346. ὁμολογήσῃ αὐτὸν four. ἀποσυνάγωγος 13.346.   23. διὰ τοῦτο εἶπον οἱ γονεῖς αὐτοῦ four. [ἐρωτ.].   24, 25, 28. [*as* Scr.].   26. οὖν (*pro* δὲ) four. [πάλιν].

COLLATION OF COD. 556 WITH CODD. 13.69.124.346. 51

ἐποίησέν. ἠνέωξέ 13.346. 27. ἐπιστεύσατε (*pro* ἠκούσατε) four.
29. μωσεῖ four. 30. ἐν γὰρ τοῦτο θ. ἐστιν. [ἀνέωξέ]. 31. ποιεῖ
69*. [rest as Scr.]. 32. ἤνοιξεν. 34. [εἶπον]. 35. ἤκουσεν δὲ ὁ
ισ 13.124.346. [αὐτῶ]. [θῦ]. 36. + καὶ (*post* εἶπεν) four. [κε].
37. [as Scr.]. 39. κσ (*pro* ισ) 13.346. κρῖμα. γενήσονται (*pro*
γένωνται). 40. [as Scr.]. 41. *init.* + καὶ four. – ἀν four. [οὖν].

X. 3. [καλεῖ]. 4. [καὶ ὅταν (*sic*)]. [πρόβατα]. 5. ἀλλωτρίωι
(*prim. tantum*). -σουσιν. 6. ἐγίνωσκον 69.124.346. [ἦν].
7. αὐτοῖς ὁ ισ πάλιν four. [ὅτι]. 8. ἦλθον προεμοῦ 13.69.346.
10. θήσῃ 13.346. 11. αὐτοῦ. 12. ὁ δὲ μισθωτὸς four. ἔστι
13.69.346. [τὰ πρό-]. 13. [ὁ δὲ μισθωτὸς φεύγει]. 14. [as Scr.].
16. δεῖ με four. ἀκούσωσι four. [γενήσεται]. 17. δια τοῦτο. [ὁ
πηρ με]. 18. ἐμ᾿ αὐτοῦ. 19. [οὖν]. 20. [δὲ]. μένεται 69.124.346.
ἀκούεται (ς *supra*). 21. + δὲ (*ante* ἔλεγον) four. ἀνοῖξαι four.
22. – τοῖς four. χιμῶν 13. [rest as Scr.]. 23. σολομῶνος (– τοῦ)
four. 24. [as Scr.]. 25. [αὐτοῖς ὁ]. + μοι (*post* πιστεύετέ) four.
26. ὅτι οὐκ (*pro* οὐ γὰρ) four. [no omiss.]. 27. ἀκούουσιν.
28. [as Scr.]. 29. + αὐτὰ (*post* μοι) four. [μ. π.]. ἐστίν. *fin.*
[μου]. 31. [οὖν]. 32. + γὰρ (*ante* καλὰ ἔργα) *solus.* + καὶ (*post*
μου) 13.69. ἔργων [λιθ. με]. 33. – λέγοντες 13.69.346. ἑαυτὸν
four. 34. [ὁ]. εἶπον four. 35. εἶπεν. [τοῦ θῦ ἐγένετο].
37. μὴ (*pro* οὐ) four. 38. οὐ πιστεύετε (*pro* μὴ πιστεύητε) four.
+ μου (*ante* πιστεύσατε) 13.124.346. [rest as Scr.]. 39. [as
Scr.]. 40. ἀπῆλθεν. [νν]. πρότερον (*pro* πρῶτον) 13.69.346.
[ἔμεινεν]. 41. ἐποίησεν (four) σημεῖον οὐδὲ ἕν 69.124.346. 42. ἐπ.
πολλοὶ εἰς αὐτὸν ἐκεῖ four.

XI. 1. [κώμης μαρ.]. 2. [μαρία]. ἑαυτῆς (*pro* αὐτῆς) 13.
4. ἔστιν. 5. τὴν μαρίαν καὶ τὴν ἀδελφὴν αὐτῆς μάρθαν four.
7. + αὐτοῦ (*post* μαθηταῖς) four. πάλιν εἰς τὴν ἰουδαίαν 13.69.346.
8. [ῥαββὶ]. οἱ ἰουδαῖοι λιθάσαι four. 9. [ὁ]. ὧραι εἰσὶ 13.69.346.
11. εἶπεν. ἐξ ὑπνήσω 13.124. 12. οἱ μαθηταὶ αὐτῶ (– αὐτοῦ) 13.
14. [οὖν]. ἀπέθανεν. [ἀλλ᾿]. 16. [συμμ.]. συναποθάνωμεν 13.346.
17. ἐλθὼν ὁ ισ 13.346 εἰς Βηθανίαν 13.124.346. – οὖν 13.346.
τέσσαρας ἤδη ἤμ. 18. [ἤ]. 19. παραμιθήσονται (69). [rest as
Scr.]. 20. – ὁ four. 21. Leaf lost after εἶπεν οὖν ἡ μάρθα πρὸς
τὸν ιν to ver. 47 Συνήγαγον. + κατὰ τοῦ ιῦ (*post* συνέδριον) four.

4—2

λέγοντες (pro καὶ ἔλεγον) four. [σ. π.]. 48. οὕτως. πιστεύσωσιν four. – οἱ 124.346. 49. οὐδ' ἕν. 50, 51. [as Scr.]. 53. ἐβουλεύσαντο four. 54. [ἰσ οὖν οὐκ ἔτι]. ἐφραὶμ. καὶ ἐκεῖ [διέτριβε] four. [αὐτοῦ]. 56. [ἔλεγον]. ἑστηκῶτες mut. 346 ἐν τῷ ἱερῷ four. 57. – καὶ four. [ἐντολὴν]. ἐστιν.

XII. 1. ὁ οὖν ὁ ἰσ 346. [ὁ τεθ.]. fin. + ὁ ἰσ four. 2. ἐκεῖ δεῖπνον 13.69.346. [no ἐκ]. ἀνακειμένων σὺν four. 3. [μαρία]. ἤλειψε. [τοῦ]. ταῖς θριξὶν αὐτῆς ἐξέμαξεν. αὐτοῦ τοὺς πόδας 13.346. + ὅλη (ante ἐπληρώθη) four. 4. [as Scr.]. 5. διὰ τί. διακοσίων four. 6. εἶπεν. ἔμελλεν four. εἶχεν καὶ. 7. + ὅτι (ante εἰς) 13. [τετήρηκεν]. 9. ἐστιν. 12. ἐπ' αὔριον ὄχλ. [ἔρχεται ὁ ἰσ]. 13. συνάντησιν 13.69.346. [ἔκραζον]. + λέγοντες 13.346. ὡσ ἀννὰ. κῦ. βασιλεὺς (– ὁ) 13.69.124. 15. [θύγατερ]. πώλου 13.346. 16. [δὲ]. [αὐτοῦ]. [ὁ]. 17. [ὅτε]. 18. [καὶ]. ἤκουσαν 13.69.346. 19. [εἶπον]. + ὅλος (post κόσμος) four. 20. + εἰς ἱεροσόλυμα (ante ἵνα) 13.346. [rest as Scr.]. 21. ἠρώτων. 22. [as Scr.]. 23. ἀπεκρίθη (13).69.124.346. λέγων αὐτοῖς 13.69.124. 25. αὐτοῦ bis. ἀπολέσῃ 69. 26. τις ἐμοὶ διακονῇ four. ἔστω (pro ἔσται) 13.346. – καὶ sequens four. fin. + μου ὁ ἐν τοῖς οὐνοῖς 13.346. 27. ταύτης +. 28. + ἅγιε (post περ) 13.346. τὸν υἱὸν (pro τὸ ὄνομα) 13.346. 29. ὁ οὖν ὁ ὄχλος ὁ ἑστηκὼς four. ἔλεγεν 13.346. + ὅτι (ante ἄγγελος) 13.69.346. 30. [as Scr.]. 31. ἐστὶν. 32. καὶ ἐγὼ (69.346 bis). [ἑλκ.]. 33. ἔμελλεν. 34. [no οὖν]. εἰς τὸν αἰῶνα μένει 13.69.346. [σὺ λέγ.]. 35. χρόνον μικρὸν four. ἐν ὑμῖν (pro μεθ' ὑ.) ἐστιν 13.69.346. [ἕως]. σκοτεία semel not ver. 46. οἶδεν. 36. [ἕως]. γένησθαι. [ὁ]. 38. – τοῦ προφήτου 13.69.346. εἶπεν. ἐπίστευσεν. 39. οὐκ ἐδύναντο 13.124.346. [ἠσ-]. 40. ἐπώρωσεν 13.(69).124.346. + καὶ τοῖς ὡσὶν ἀκούσωσι (post ὀφθαλμοῖς) four. ἐπιστρέψωσι 13.69.(124).346. ἰάσομαι four. 41. [ὅτε]. εἶδεν. τοῦ θῦ ver. 43 (pro αὐτοῦ prim.) 13.69.346. 44. ὁ δὲ ἰσ ἔκραζε 13.69.346 καὶ ἔλεγεν four. [ἀλλ']. 45. ἀποστείλαντά (pro πέμψαντά) four. 47. φυλάξῃ (pro πιστεύσῃ) 13.69.346. 48. κρίνει 124.346. 49. ἀπ' ἐμ' αὐτοῦ four. δέδωκεν (13).124.346. 50. ἐστὶν αἰώνιος 13.69.346. ἐγὼ λαλῶ 13.69.346. ἐνετείλατό (pro εἴρηκέ) four. οὕτως.

XIII. 1. ἦλθεν 13.69.346. 2. [γεν.]. – ἰούδα four. [rest as Scr.]. 3. + δὲ (ante ὁ ἰσ) four. init. lect. [δέδ.]. ἐξῆλθεν.

4. τίθησιν. 5. λαβὼν ὕδωρ βάλλει four. 6. νίπτης 13.346. [rest
as Scr.]. 7. +ὁ (ante ἰσ) 13.346. 8. +ὁ (ante πέτρος) four.
μου νίψης τοὺς πόδας 13.69.346. [αὐτῶι ὁ ἰσ]. 9. [σ. π.]. 10. εἰ
μὴ (pro ἢ) 69.346. —ἀλλ᾽ prim. 13.69. ἔστιν. 12. ἔνιψεν αὐτῶν
τοὺς πόδας four. [rest as Scr.]. 13. ὁ κσ καὶ ὁ διδάσκαλος
13.69.346. εἰ μὴ (pro εἰμὶ) 346. 15. δέδωκα four. πεποίηκα four.
ποιεῖτε 13.124.346. 16. αὐτοῦ. 18. +γὰρ (post ἐγὼ) four. [rest as
Scr.]. 19. ἀπάρτι. ὅτ᾽ ἂν γένηται πιστευσητε ὅτι ἐγὼ εἶπον ὑμῖν (pro
ἐγώ εἰμί) 13.346. 20. [ἐάν]. 21. [ὁ ἰσ]. ἐμαρτύρησεν. 22. [οὖν].
+αὐτοῦ (post μαθηταὶ) four. ἀπορούντες 13.69.346. 23. [δὲ]. +ἐκ
(post εἷς) four. 24. πύθεσθε 69* (v s. m. ει p. m.) 13. [rest
as Scr.]. 25. [ἐπιπεσὼν]. οὖν (pro δὲ) 13.69.346. + οὕτως
(ante ἐπὶ) 13.346. 26. +αὐτῶι four. + καὶ λέγει (ante ὁ ἰσ)
13.69.346. ἐμβάψας (pro βάψας) 13.69.346. [ἐπιδώσω]. [ἐμβάψας].
[δίδωσιν ἰούδα]. σίμωνι 13.346 τῶ ἰσκ. 13.69.346. 27. [-νάς]. [ὁ
ἰσ]. 29. —ὁ prim. four. 30. ἐξῆλθεν εὐθέως 13.69.346. νύξ + ὅτε
οὖν ἐξῆλθεν four. 31. [λέγει ὁ ἰσ]. 32. [no omission]. ἑαυτῶ.
33. +χρόνον (post μικρὸν) 13.346. ἐγὼ ὑπάγω four. 34. ἐντοτολὴν
(eras.). δίδομι 13.69. 35. ἔχετε four. 36. +ἐγὼ (ante ὑπάγω)
four. [rest as Scr.]. 37. διὰ τί. [-θῆσαι]. θύσω (ink retouched)
346, not ver. 38. 38. ἀποκρίνεται ὁ ἰσ (— αὐτῷ) four. [φωνήσει].
τρὶς ἀπαρνήσει με 13.69.346.

XIV. 2. +ὅτι (ante πορεύομαι) four. 3. ἑτοιμάσω (— καὶ)
solus. τόπον ὑμῖν 13.69.346. [-λήψομαι]. ἐμ᾽ αὐτόν... [ἐγὼ].
+ἐκεῖ (ante ἦτε) 13.346. 4. —ἐγὼ 13.69.346. [οἴδατε bis]. 5. [as
Scr.]. 6. [ὁ]. 7. καὶ ἀπάρτι. ἑοράκατε. [rest as Scr.]. 9. [as
Scr.]. 10. ἐστιν. [rest as Scr.]. 11. +ἐστιν (ante εἰ δὲ) four.
[μοι]. 12. μείζωνα 13.346. [μου]. 13. [αἰτήσητε]. 14. αἰτήσητέ
με 13. [ἐγὼ]. 15, 16, 17. [as Scr.]. 19. οὐκέτι. [ζήσεσθε].
20. [as Scr.]. 21. [καὶ ἐγὼ]. ἐμφανήσω αὐτῶ 346 ἐμ᾽ αὐτῶ 13.346.
22. +καὶ (ante τί) four. ἑαυτὸν (pro σε-) 13.69*.346. 23. [ὁ].
τηρήσῃ 13.69.346. ποιησόμεθα 69. 24. ῟ους p. m. fin. —πατρός
13.69. 27. μήδε. 28. ἀγαπᾶτέ four. —εἶπον four. +ἐγὼ (ante
πορεύομαι). +μου (post πρα) four. [μου]. ἐστιν. 29. πρὸ τοῦ
(pro πρὶν) four. ὅτ᾽ ἂν. fin. +ὅτι ἐγὼ εἶπον ὑμῖν 13.346.
30. οὐκέτι. ὁ ἄρχων τοῦ κόσμου τούτου 13.346.(69.124). 31. οὕτως.
[rest as Scr.].

XV. 1. ἐστιν. 2. [πλ. καρ.]. φέρη *p. m.* (ει *s. m.*) four.
3. ἤδει (ς *supra*). + καὶ (*ante* ὑμεῖς) 13.346. 4. + γὰρ (*post* καθὼς)
four. [μείνη]. μείνητε ἐν ἐμοί. 5. ὑμῖν (*pro* ἐμοί) 13.346. οὕτως.
6. [μείνη]. ἐκβλήθη (κ *eras.*). αὐτὸ (*pro* αὐτὰ) 13.124.346. + τὸ
(*ante* πῦρ) four. 7. [ἐὰν]. αἰτήσασθε four. 8. πολὺν. [γενήσεσθε].
9. ἠγάπησέν. [rest as Scr.]. 10. [as Scr.]. 11. [μείνη]. 12. + δὲ
(*ante* ἐστιν) four. 13. [τίς]. 14. ποιεῖτε 346. ἃ (*pro* ὅσα)
13.69.346. 15. οὐκ ἔτι. [ὑ. λ.]. ὁ κσ̅ αὐτοῦ 13.124.346.
16. + πολὺν (*ante* καρπὸν) 13.346. καὶ (*pro* ἵνα) four. [αἰτήσητε].
Pro δῶ ὑμῖν *legit* τοῦτο ποιήσω four. ἵνα δοξασθῇ ὁ π̅η̅ρ̅ ἐν τῷ υἱῷ
four. 18. [ὑμῶν]. 20. αὐτοῦ. 21. [ὑμῖν]. 22. [εἶχον] so ver.
24. 24. ἐποίησεν 13.69.124. 25. [as Scr.]. 26. ὅτὰν. [δὲ].
27. ἀπαρχῆς.

XVI. 3. [ὑμῖν]. 4. ὅτ᾽ ἂν. + αὐτῶν (*post* ὥρα) four. μνημο-
νεύσητε 13.346 (– αὐτῶν) 124. 7. + ἐγὼ οὐ *solus* (*ante* μὴ) four.
[οὐκ ἐλεύσεται]. + ἐγώ· (*ante* πορευθῶ) 13.346. 10. [μου]. οὐκέτι.
12. [λ. ὑμ.]. 13. ὅτ᾽ ἂν. λαλήσῃ? *secund.* ει *s. m.* [rest as Scr.].
14. [λήψ.]. 15. λαμβάνει four. 16. – ἐγὼ four. [rest as Scr.].
17. αὐτοῦ. – ἐγὼ four. 18. τί ἐστιν τοῦτο four. – ὃ λέγει four.
[τὸ μ.]. 19. [οὖν ὁ]. 20. – ἀμὴν *semel* 69.346. [rest as Scr.].
21. τίκτει 346. ὅταν *prim.* ὅτ᾽ ἂν *secund.* γεννήσει 346. οὐκέτι
so ver. 25. 22. μὲν οὖν λύπην 69.346. [νῦν]. [ἔχετε]. [αἴρει].
23. [as Scr.]. 24. [λήψ-]. 25. [ἀλλ᾽]. [ἀναγ-]. 27. [τοῦ θῡ].
fin. + καὶ ἥκω three. 28. [παρὰ]. 29. [αὐτῷ]. [no ἐν].
30. ἐγνώκαμεν (*pro* οἴδαμεν) three. ἐλήλυθας (*pro* ἐξῆλθες) three.
31. [ὁ]. 32. [νῦν]. [καὶ ἐμὲ]. + μου (*post* π̅η̅ρ̅) 69.346. ἐστιν.
33. [θλίψιν]. ἕξετε three.

XVII. 1. [ὁ ι̅σ̅]. ἐπάρας three. – καὶ (*ante* εἶπεν) three.
[rest as Scr.]. 2. *init.* + καὶ 346. δώσει *p. m.* [σει *eras.*] three.
3. [-σκωσι]. 4. [ἐτελείωσα]. 6. [δέδωκας]. καὶ ἐμοὶ ἔδωκας
124.346. [-κασι]. 7. ἔγνωσαν three. [rest as Scr.]. 8. [as
Scr.]. 9. εἰσιν. 10. ἐστιν. δεδόξασμε 124.346. + καὶ. Here
7 lines seem illegible, earlier writing? erased at foot of column.
Yet ι̅σ̅ first word? Nοτ N. T. Goes on ver. 11 in next column.
οὐκέτι. [οὗτοι]. εἰσὶν. [ἐγώ]. ᾧ (*pro* οὓς) 13.124.346. [no καὶ].
12. εἰμὶ (*pro* εἰ μὴ) 346. 13. ἐπ᾽ αὐτοῖς (*pro* ἐν αὐτοῖς) 13.69**.346.
16. εἰσὶν. [rest as Scr.]. 17. [σου]. 18. κἀγὼ ἀποστέλλω 13.346.

19. [ἐγὼ]. ἐμ᾽ αὐτόν. ὦσιν καὶ αὐτοὶ four. 20. πιστευόντων four. 21. ὦσιν. [rest as Scr.]. 22. ἔδωκα (13).346. [rest as Scr.]. 23. ὦσιν. [καὶ]. γινώσκει eras. 13.346. 24. δέδωκάς (pro ἔδωκάς) secund. four. 25. [περ].

XVIII. 1. [as Scr.]. 2. Ἤδει. [ὁ ισ̅]. 3. +ὅλην (post λαβὼν) 13.69.346. [καὶ φαρ.]. ὅπλων. 4. ὁ δὲ four ισ̅ ἰδὼν (pro οὖν et εἰδὼς) four. [rest as Scr.]. 5, 6. [as Scr.]. 7. ἐπηρώτησεν αὐτοὺς four. 8. +αὐτοῖς (ante ὁ ισ̅) four. 9. ὁ λόγος πληρωθῇ ὧν 13.346. 10. [ὠτίον]. ὄνομα. μάλχος. 11. [σου]. +αὐτῆς (post θήκην) four. αὐτώ (ὁ supr. ο p. m.). 13. [as Scr.]. 14. ἀποθανεῖν (pro ἀπολέσθαι) four. 15. [as Scr.]. 16. εἰσῆλθεν (pro ἐξῆλθεν) 13.69*.346. ἐκεῖνος (pro ὁ ἄλλος) four. [rest as Scr.]. 17. [as Scr.]. 18. ψῦχος. ἐθερμένοντο 13.124. μετ᾽ αὐτῶν καὶ ὁ πέτρος four. θερμενόμενος 13.124. 20. [αὐτῶ ὁ ισ̅]. [ἐλάλησα] bis. −τῇ four. πάντες (pro πάντοτε): (vid. Beza Elz) four. 21. [ἐπερωτάς]. ἐρώτησον (13). 22. [as Scr.]. 23. ὁ δὲ ισ̅ εἶπεν αὐτῶι (−ἀπεκρίθη) four. 24. +δὲ (post ἀπέστειλεν) four. 25. θερμενόμενος 13.124. +οὖν (post ἠρνήσατο) 13.346. 27. ὁ πέτρος ἠρνήσατο four. ἐφώνησε (hiatus) 13.346. 28. πρωὶ 13.69.346. [ἀλλ᾽ ἵνα].

29. πιλᾶτος hic so XIX. 15, 19, 22, four. +ἔξω (post πιλατος). καιεἶπεν (καὶ above, modern ink). [κατὰ]. 30. [as Scr.]. 31. [as Scr.]. 32. οὐδ᾽ ἕνα. εἶπεν. 33. πάλιν εἰς τὸ πραιτώριον four. 34. εἶπαν 13.346. [rest as Scr.]. 35. ἐποίησα (final letter erased). 36. [ὁ]. οἱ ἐμοὶ ἠγονίζωντο ἂν four. 37. οὐκ οὖν. −ἐγὼ prim. four. 38. ἐξῆλθεν. [rest as Scr.]. 39. Ἔστιν. ἀπολύσω ὑμῖν secund. four. [rest as Scr.]. 40. −πάλιν four. [πάντες].

XIX. 1. ἐμαστίγωσεν. 2. ᾽στέφανον sic. [τῇ κ.]. fin. +καὶ ἤρχοντο πρὸς αὐτὸν four. 3. [ἐδίδουν]. 4. [οὖν]. ὁ πιλάτος ἔξω four. ἐν αὐτῶ οὐχ εὑρίσκω αἰτίαν (−οὐδεμίαν) four. 5. [ὁ]. 6. ἴδον 13.124. 346. +τῶν ἰουδαίων (post ὑπηρέται) four. [λέγοντες]. +αὐτὸν (post ϛρωσον secund.) four. οὐχ᾽. 7. [αὐτῶ]. +καὶ εἶπαν (post οἱ ἰουδαῖοι) four. [ἡμῶν]. υἱὸν θῦ ἑαυτὸν four. 8. τοῦτον τὸν λόγον ὁ πιλάτος four. 10. −οὖν four. [rest as Scr.]. 11. +καὶ εἶπεν αὐτῶ (post ὁ ισ̅) 13.69.346. [rest as Scr.]. 12. οὖν ὁ πιλάτος ἐζήτει four. τὸν ιν̅ (pro αὐτόν) four. ἐκραύγαζον 69.124.346. ἑαυτὸν (13).69.124.346. 13. τούτων τῶν λόγων 13.124. γαβαθά

69**. [rest as Scr.]. 14. ἦν ὡς εἰ (– δὲ) four. 15. + λέγοντες (post οἱ δὲ ἐκραύγασαν) four. – αὐτόν 13. πιλᾶτος (so ver. 19, 22. XVIII. 29). + οὖν (ante οἱ ἀρχιερεῖς) 346. 17. init. οἱ δὲ παραλαβόντες αὐτὸν ἤγαγον· four. καὶ ἐπέθηκαν αὐτῶ τὸν S͞ρον + καὶ βαστάζων αὐτὸν· four. ἐξῆλθεν εἰς τόπον λεγ... [ὃς] 13.124.346 λέγετε 13.346. 19. + ἑβραϊστί + ῥωμαϊστί + ἑλληνιστί (ante ι͞σ) four. 20. [τῆς πόλεως ὁ τόπος]. – καὶ ἦν γεγραμμ. ad fin. vers. four. Cf. ver. 19. 21. εἶπεν. [rest as Scr.]. 23. [τέσσαρα]. τὸν δὲ χιτῶνα (– καὶ) four. ἐπεὶ ἦν (pro ἦν δὲ) four. ἄραφος four. 24. [εἶπον]. – οὖν four. [ἡ λέγουσα]. ἔβαλλον solus. 25, 26. [as Scr.]. 27. ἴδε. ἡμέρας (pro ὥρας) four. [αὐτὴν ὁ μαθ.]. 28. ἰδὼν ὁ ι͞σ four. [πάντα ἤδη]. τετέλεσθαι 13.124.346. πληρωθῇ (pro τελειωθῇ) four. 29. + μετὰ χολῆς (post ὄξους) four. τὸ στόματι 13.346. [rest as Scr.]. 30. ἔλαβεν ὁ ι͞σ τὸ ὄξος four. + μετὰ τῆς χολῆς (ante εἶπεν) four. 31. ἐπεὶ παρασκευὴ ἦν transferunt in locum post ἰουδαῖοι four. [ἐκείνου]. ἠρώτησαν. πιλᾶτον. 32. συνστ. 33. ἴδον 346. [αὐτὸν ἤδη]. 34. ἔνυξεν. εὐθέως ἐξῆλ. four. 35. μεμαρτύρικεν 13.124. + καὶ (ante ὑμεῖς) four. [rest as Scr.]. 38. ἠρώτησε. πιλᾶτον. – ὁ prim. 13.69.124. + αὐτωι (post ὁ πιλατος) 13.346. [rest as Scr.]. 39. ἦλθεν. νυκτὸς πρὸς τὸν ι͞ν 13.124.346. φέρον 69*. [μίγμα]. ὡσ εἰ. 40. αὐτὸν (pro αὐτὸ) 13.346.

XX. 1. [μαρία -ηνὴ]. εἰς τὸ μνημεῖον σκοτίας ἔτι οὔσης 13.69.346. 4. [καὶ ὁ]. προέδραμεν. ἦλθεν. 5. [as Scr.]. 6. [no καὶ ante σίμων]. 8. εἰσῆλθεν. ἴδεν 13.346. 11. [μαρία]. ἱστήκει 124. [τὸ μνημ.]. [ἔξω]. ἔκλαιεν. 13. [καὶ]. 14. [καὶ]. --ὁ four. ἐστίν. 15. [ὁ]. ἐστιν. ἔθηκας αὐτὸν four. 16. ῥαββουνῖ 124. [rest as Scr.]. fin. + καὶ προσέδραμεν ἅψασθαι αὐτοῦ 13.346. 17. + ὅτι (ante ἀναβαίνω) 13.346. [rest as Scr.]. 18. + οὖν (ante μαρία) 124.346. [-ηνὴ]. [ἀπ-]. [ἑώρακε]. 19. [as Scr.]. 20. + καὶ τοὺς πόδας (post χεῖρας) 13.346. 21. [ὁ ι͞σ]. [πέμπω]. 22. ἐνεφύσησεν. 23. ἀφέωνται. ἐάν (pro ἄν secund.) 346. τινον. καὶ κράτηντε. 24. [ὁ]. 25. ὁ δὲ. [rest as Scr.]. 28. – καὶ 13.69. – ὁ four. 29. εἶπεν δὲ (pro λέγει) four. – θωμᾶ four. + με (post ἰδόντες) 346. 30. [αὐτοῦ]. 31. [πιστεύσητε]. – ὁ four. + αἰώνιον (post ζωὴν) four.

XXI. 1.   + αὐτοῦ ἐγερθεὶς ἐκ νεκρῶν (post μαθηταῖς) four.

2. [τοῦ]. 3. [no καὶ]. ἐνέβησαν 13.69.124. – εὐθύς 69. 4. –ἤδη
three. [γεν-]. ἐστίν. [rest as Scr.]. 5. [ὁ ἰσ]. 6. [as Scr.].
οὐκέτι. ἑλκύσαι. 7. + σίμωνι (ς *supra ante* πέτρω) *solus.* ἐστιν
bis. 8. [ἀλλ’]. 10. [ὁ]. 11. τὴν γῆν three. [rest as Scr.].
12. [ὁ]. [δὲ]. 13. [οὖν ὁ]. 14. [ὁ]. [αὐτοῦ]. 15. – σὺ 346.
[rest as Scr.]. 16. σοὶ (*pro* σὺ) 346. ποίμενε. [πρόβατά] so
ver. 17. 17. [as Scr.]. 18. ἤθελες. ὅτ’ ἂν. ζώσοι 346. οἴσοι
69.(346). [rest as Scr.]. 19. εἶπεν. 20. [δὲ]. εἶπεν. 21. [no
οὖν]. 22. [as Scr.]. 23. – αὐτῷ three. [rest as Scr.]. 24. + ὃ
sic (*ante* καὶ γράψας) 346. [rest as Scr.]. 25. ἔστιν. [ὅσα].
γράφητε (modern ink) 69.124. – καθ’ ἕν *habet marg.* in modern
ink. οὐδ’ 69. [χωρήσαι]. [ἀμήν +] * * * * * *rubro*.

Subscr. Εὐαγγέλιον ἐκ τοῦ κατ ιω: ἐγράφη ἑλληνιστὶ εἰς ἔφεσον
μετὰ ἔτη^λ τῆς ἀναλήψεως τοῦ κῡ + ἔχει δὲ ῥήματα ᾱ, π̄ λῆ + ἔχει δὲ
στίχους β̄ κδ̄ + ἐπιδομετι ανοῦ τοῦ βασίλεως * * * * * *. Nearly
as 346.

See p. 15. J. Rendel Harris "The origin of the Leicester
Codex," 1887, pp. 64, 65. He gives the five patriarchates from
Leicester MS. compared with 556, fol. 183 a γνῶσις καὶ ἐπίγνωσις
τῶν πατριαρχῶν θρόνων. Title in 556. I add the following corrections on Harris's collation. τ lost in τέταρτος. ᾱ for πρώτῃ. ³⁴τοῦ
ἀποστόλου καὶ ἀδελφοθέου· γενόμενος. *Habet* 556 τῶν ὁριών. γάλλων
videtur + καὶ (*ante* σπανίας). No καὶ before στύλων. λαγοβαρδων
(so 69). λὶψ (*non* λυψ). 183 b *2nd column: red illumination.*
Αἱ τάξεις τῶν κλιμάτων τῆς ἀφρικῆς | πρῶτον κλῖμα ἡ λιβύη καλουμένη
λούβιε καὶ μαιάδι (*videtur: non* μείρακι with Harris) | Δεύτερον
κλῖμα ἡ μαυρουσία ἤτοι αἰθιοπία. μέλεδι ἐς σε οὐδζ´ | Τρίτον κλῖμα ἡ
μουμέδα· ἤγουν ζέβ | Πέμπτον κλῖμα ἀφρική ἤ... *end of leaf: one
leaf torn out : only a few fragments left.*

† *Explicit* Cod. 13 Johan. xxi. 3.

PROLEGOMENA to B.-C. III. 5. Continued from pp. xx, xxi.

Total variations from Scrivener or Stephen, only now and then
including itacisms = 1693.

13.69.124.346 = (four) 256 + 106 + 61. Johan. 216 + 402
= 1041.

Three in Johan. (where one is missing) = 83.

13.69.346 = 104 + 64 + 14. Johan. 64 = 246.

13.124.346 = 29 + 16. Johan. 25 = 70 + 25 = 95 + 23 = 118.

13.69.124 = 19 + 14 + 6 (much together in peric. adult.) = 39.

13.69 = 35 + 11. Johan. 7 = 53. For all the four Gospels.

13.124 = 5 + 7 + 3 (Matt. I. 16; VII. 9) = 15. * 13 alone :
specially Matt. III. 4, 7; V. 31; IX. 27. Marc. VIII. 38; ix. 11,
21; XIII. 2; XIV. 69. Luc. V. 26 (ἰδ); VII. 33; VIII. 6; IX. 31,
36; X. 35; XII. 13, 29; XVI. 16, 20; XIX. 2; XX. 46 (ταῖς); XXI.
19, 20, 24; XXII. 59. Johan. I. 17, 27, 33; II. 12, 15; IV. 12,
14 (note); V. 46; VII. 13, 28, 52; X. 22; XI. 1, 12; XII. 7, 13; XIII.
24 p. m.; XIV. 13, 21. For a less complete list, see p. xx,
note 1.

13.346 = 37 + 32 + 54 (Jo.) (Luc. VII. 45) = 103. VID. ϛ Luc.
XVI. 13; XVII. 9. Johan. XVIII. 37*.

69.124.346 = 3 + 6 + 4 + 10 = 23.

69.346 = 5 (note Luc. XVI. 13 p. m.). 69.124 = 2. 124.346 = 8.

13 alone 19 * + 14 + Jo. 27 = 60.

69 = 15 + 13 = 28: 124 = 14: 346 (Jo. XII. 1; XIII. 13, 37;
XX. 29; XXI. 16, 18, 24) = 19 + 19 = 38. Solus 558 = 12 + 9 + 15
= 37.

3 or 4 leaves are loose. Slight illuminations stand at head of
books. οὕτω Matth. III. 15 ευσπλ.

8 leaves under illumination, no title. Synaxarion from Easter
Day to ἐν. ἑω ῑα. Johan. XXI. 14—25 σκϛ̄ (imperfect). Then

under illumination τῇ β̄ τοῦ νέου ἔτους [no title]. 7 leaves (one

loose). Then Menology (12 leaves). This κ^ε complete. + ἀκολου^θ

εἰς διαφόρους *rubro* ἤμ. εἰς ἐγκαίνια ναου εισ πανυ^χ *rubro*.

N.B. Ammonian Sections used [unique] in *Syn. Men.* to

facilitate references to Gospels.

On leaf 183 Limits of Five Patriarchates, as in Cod. 69 [refer].

Small piece of one leaf torn out since binding. Slight illumination:

no heading. In 183 b 2nd col. slight illumination. Αἱ τάξεις τῶν

κλιμάτων τῆς ἀφρικῆς.

PART II.

COLLATION OF GOSPELS.

Collation of Scrivener's Editio Major 1887, with *four manuscripts of the Gospels, viz.* Cod. c, Gonville and Caius College (see p. xxviii), Cod. d, Gale (see p. xxxi), Codd. e and f, Wake 12 and Wake 34 (see pp. xxxiv, xxxvi), *together with select readings* from Cod. b (p. xxv) and Cod. j (p. xliii); *and notices of variations of the early editions; viz.* Complutensian 1514 C; Stephen 1546, 1549, 1550 S; S₁, S₂, S₃; Beza 1565—1598 B; Elzevir 1624, 1633 E₁, E₂.

N.B. *This collation is chiefly limited to real various readings: a sufficient general account being given in the Introduction as regards itacisms, the use of ν ἐφελκυστικόν, irregular grammatical forms, ι ascript or postscript, punctuation, and systems of breathings and accents. Transcriptural errors also are not much noticed, unless they are, or may possibly be, connected with various readings.*

S. MATTHÆI. *Titulus* (+ αγιον C) Εὐαγγέλιον κατὰ ματθαῖον bfc. τὸ κατὰ ματθαῖον ἅγιον εὐαγγέλιον cdjB. CAP. I. 1. γεννεσεως f. ἀβρααμ omnes, passim E. 4. ἀμιναδαμ bis be. *Linea erasa in* f *ante* νααссων *prim.* 5. – ἐκ της ραχαβ e, ραχαμ j. 6. – δὲ secund. f. – τὸν βασιλεα b. σολομωνα c s. m. bdefC. – τα c s. m. 8. – ἐγεννησε τον ιωραμ· ιωραμ δὲ (habet marg. s. m.) c. 9. -γεννησε τον ιωαθαμ· ἰωαθαμ δε (habet marg. s. m.) c.

ἄχαζ bis c. 10. μανασση c s. m. f. αμμων bis bf. 11, 12.
μετοικησιας ce. 12. – μετὰ δὲ τὴν μετοικεσίαν βαβυλῶνος
(habet marg. s. m.) c. μετοικησίαν e. ἰἐχωνίας semel.
13, 14. – ἐγεννησε τον αζωρ· αζωρ δε c. 14, 15. ἐλιουδ
bis be. 15. αχιμ bis. – ἐγεννησε τον ματθαν· ματθὰν δὲ c.
17. +ἑως του χριστου (post βαβυλωνος prim.) j. 20. μαρίαν
f. 23. καλέσεις B. 24. – ὁ prim. ce.

CAP. II. 4. +τους (ante γραμματεις) f. 6. – ουδαμως
ελαχ'στη ει (ουδ. εἰ ελαχιστη s. m.). 9. – ὁ (supra p. m.) j.
11. ειδον (pro εὑρον) omnes. 13. – δε ef. των μαγων ef.
18. κλαθμος. ὁδυρμος. ραχιὴλ. 20. πορευου altered.
– τεθνηκασι ad finem versus c s. m. marg. 22. – επι bce.
ναζαρεθ eB.

CAP. III. 4. ὁ (supra, p. m.) c. Ιωννην d. 5. και πασα
και Ἰουδαια (καὶ prim. supra s. m.) c. 6. +ποταμω (ante
ὑπ’) ce. 8. καρπον αξιον bc (non e) djC. 9. +ὅτι (ante
π̅ρ̅α) j. 10. βαλεται e. 11. – και πυρι cdC. 12. – αυτου
(post σιτον) cf.

CAP. IV. 1. ὑπο του π̅ν̅σ̅ εις την ερημον f. 4. +οτι
(ante γεγραπται) bf. εν (pro επι) cf. 8. τουτου (pro του)
s. m. c. 10. +οπισω μου (post υπαγε) cdefjC. 13. κατα-
λειπων c. ναζαρεθ eB. παραθαλασσαν f. Rasura ante
Νεφθαλ. c. 14, 15. Desunt usque ad ὁδον ver. 15 (ὁμοιοτ.) c.
18. – δε f. – ο ι̅σ̅ bcde (non f) C. 20, 22. – ευθεως c.
21. καταρτιζοντες c. 23. ὁ ι̅σ̅ ολην την γαλιλαιαν f.
24. ᵈᵃⁱμονιζομενους (δαι p. m.) d.

CAP. V. 1. – αὐτῶ bc. ρηνοποιοὶ (ει supra p. m.) c.
11. ημων (pro υμων) c. 12. εδιωξας c. 15. ου p. m. ουδε
s. m. d. 16. καλλα d. 17. μὴ νομισητε cC. 19. οὗτος (pro
οὕτω) c. – ος δ’ αν ποιηση ad fin. versus e. 20. ὑμων (ἡμων
c) ἡ δικαιοσυνη bcej (non df). πλεον d. 22. ρακκα c p. m.
ρακκαι f. 23. καὶ ἐκεῖ becdC. 25. +σου (post αντιδικος) c.
– σε παραδω secund. c. 26. οὗ (pro αν) f. 27. ερρηθη (31,

62   COLLATION OF GOSPELS.

33, 38) c (31, 33 c 31 d) cd. —τοις αρχαιοις dfj (*habet* ce) C.
28. εμβλεπων c.   αυτην (*pro* αυτης) bcdjefC.   29. – ὁ c.
+ την (*ante* γεενναν) e.   γεεναν (*sic* 22, 30) C.   30. *Deest ob*
ὁμοιοτ. c.   σκαδαλιζει d *p. m.*   ἐν των μελων σου αποληται e.
απελθη (*pro* βληθη) c.   31. – δε efj.   – οτι be.   αυτην (*pro*
αυτῇ) cef.   32. πας ὁ ἀπολύων (*pro* ος αν απολυση) bej.
36. τριχαν cd.   ποιησαι η μελεναν c.   ποιησαι η μελαιναν ef.
38. οφθαλμον (*pro* οφθαλμος) c.   39. – σου ej.   40. το (*pro*
τῷ) c.   *fin.* + σου f.   41. αγκαρευσει cd.   43. ερρηθη cd.
44. ἡμων (*pro* ὑμων) c.   τοις μισουσιν bcdefj.   – προσευ-
χεσθε ad *fin. vers* (ὁμοιοτ.) c (*habet s. m. at fin.* ἡμας).
45. + τοῖς (*ante* ουρανοις) dej (*non* c) C.   46. φιλους (*pro*
ἀδελφους) bcdefjC.   εθνικοι (*pro* τελωναι) c (εθνηκοι c) d.
48. ως (*pro* ωσπερ) b.   ἡμων (*pro* ὑμων) c   – ὁ *secund.* d.
ουνιος (*pro* ὁ τοις ουνοις) f.

CAP. VI. 1. *init.* + και c.   ἡμων *p. m.* c.   3. ελεμοσυνη d.
4. – αυτος c.   5. ἑστῶτες cfe.   – αν e.   6. ταμειον c.
βλεπω *p. m.* c.   – εν τω κρυπτω c (*non* b).   7. βαττολογειτε
bc.   8. ὁ γαρ π̄η̄ρ ἡμῶν (*sic*) ὁ ουνίος c.   9. ἡμεῖς (*pro* ὑμεῖς) c.
ὄνομ (– σου : *nisi a supra* = σου) d.   13. [*doxol. habet*] befC.
14. – γαρ c.   ἡμῶν (*pro* ὑμων) cd.   15. + ὁ ουρανιος (*ante*
αφησει) C.   18. το εν το κρυπτω *p. m.* c.   – ἐν τω (το c)
φανερω bdefjC.   20. *Deest versus* (ὁμοιοτ.) c.   21. ἡμων (*pro*
ὑμων) *bis* c.   24. μαμωνα bcdefjC   25. ἡμων (*pro* ὑμων)
secund. c.   πλοιον c.   29. + ο (*ante* σολομων) C.   περιεβαλ-
λετο e.   30. ὁλιγοπιστοι cef.   31. αφιεννυσιν *p.m.* e, *p. m.* c.
περιβαλλομεθα f.   32. ἡμων (*pro* ὑμων) c.   34. ἑαυτῇ (*pro*
τὰ ἑαυτης) c (ἑαυτήν) b.   – αρκετον ad *fin. vers.* (ὁμοιοτ.) e.

CAP. VII. 1. κρινατε d.   2. – κριθησεσθε c.   – και εν ω
μετρω μετρειτε (ὁμοιοτ.) c *p. m.*   μετρι(η f)θησεται bcef.
3. καρπος e *p. m.*   τον (*pro* το *secund.*) c.   4. εκβαλλω e.
6. δοτε cdfC.   βαλετε c.   *fin.* ὑμιν d.   9. αν (*pro* εαν *prim.*) f.
αιτησει e.   10. *Deest ob* ὁμοιοτ. *versus* c.   *init.* + ἤ dC.
12. εαν (*pro* αν) bde.   ουτως (*pro* ουτω) cdeC.   ουτως (*pro*
ουτος) eC.   14. *init.* τι bc (οτι c *p. m.*) defjC.   ὁλιγοι ce.

15. – εσωθεν ad fin. vers. c. 16. – αυτων d. σταφϋλλην d.
17. –το δε σαπρον ad fin. vers. (ὁμοιοτ.) c. –δε e. 18. καλλους.
d p. m. 19. + ουν (post παν) d. 21. + τοις (ante ου͞νοις) de.
22. – κ͞ε semel be. 23. ἡμας (pro ὑμας) c. υποχωρετε c.
24. – ουν f. ἀκοῦσῃ c. –μου c. –τουτους be. 25. προσ-
επεσαν bcf [non e] j. τον (pro την) c. 28. ετελεσεν be.
29. fin. + αυτων e.

CAP. VIII. 3. εκαθερισθη f. 4. αλλα ej. 5. αυτω (pro
τω ι͞υ) bcdfjC. fin. αυτης c p. m. 8. λογω bdefj p. m. C
(non c). 10. + μαθηταις αυτου και τοις (ante ακολ.) c.
12. – o prim. C. 13. ἑκατονταρχῃ bf. fin. + και υπο-
στρεψας ο εκατονταρχος εις τον οικον αυτου εν αυτῃ τῃ
ωρα ευρεν τον παιδα αυτου ὑγϊ ἔνοντα (Codex impressus
non habet haec verba nec habet versus Syr.) c recens manus Cj.
14. αυτου (pro πετρου) supra recens manus c. πετρου d
p. m. πενθερα e s. m. 15. fin. αυτω bcdefjC. 16. + το
p. m. (ante λογω). 17. υπο (pro δια) f. ανελαβεν cC.
εβαστασαν c. 20. init. – και d. 21. – αυτον d. – και c.
23. τω ι͞υ (pro αυτω prim.) e. – το ef s. m. 24. κατακα-
λυπτεσθαι + ἦν γὰρ καὶ ὁ ἄνεμος ἐναντίος αὐτοῖς (post
κυματων) c. 25. – αυτου bdej (non c). 27. fin. αυτου (pro
αυτω) c. 28. ελθοντος δε αυτου c. γεργεργεσινων e [non
df]. γαδαρινων c. ισχὺν c. [γεργεσ C Vulg., gerasenorum
Vulg.] 29. – ιησου f. 30. ου s. m. supra μακραν cum Vulg.
31. εκβάλεις ὑμας c. ὑμιν c. 32. + τους χοιρους (pro την
αγελην των χοιρων) c. fin. χεῖρων c. + επετρεψεν αυτοις f.

CAP. IX. 1. αφεονται c. αφαιωνται (sic ver. 5) d. – σοι c.
3. οὕτως τους διαλογισμους (pro τας ενθυμησεις) c. 4. + αὐτοις
(post ειπεν) e. fin. ἡμῶν c. 5. – γαρ e. σου (pro σοι) eC.
6. ιδητε c. – τοτε ce. 8. εφοβηθησαν (pro εθαυμασαν) cf.
9. επι τῶ p. m. c. 11. ελεγον (pro ειπον) f. ἁμαρτωλων d.
+ πινει (post εσθιει) ej. 13. δικαιους καλεσαι f. αλλα acdefC.
15. + χρονον (post οσον) dfj. αι (pro δε, ante ἡμεραι) c.
+ αι supra ημ. d s. m. 16. – δε c. εν (pro επι) f. ερρει c.
17. απολλυνται adf. εισ ασκους βαλλουσι καινους f. κενους

64   COLLATION OF GOSPELS.

c. αμφοτεροι acdef.   18. + τις (ante αρχων) dj.   εισελθων
acf.   + εις (ante ελθων) eC.   + κ̅ε̅ ότη (pro ότι) c.   αλλ' c.
χειραν c.   20. αιμορρουσα c.   — δωδεκα ετη προσελθουσα d
(όμοιοτ.).   22. στραφεις e.   θαρσε c.   24. αυτους p. m. c.
25. ηγειρε f.   27. τω ι̅υ̅ (pro αυτω) c.   + κ̅ε̅ (post ήμας) c.
υίος adefj [non c].   28. — δε.   + αυτω (post δε) cfj.   — o ι̅σ̅ d.
ήμων e.   30. ενεβριμισατο c marg. s. m.   μετ οργης ελαλησεν
d.   33. — οτι acfC.   ουτως εφανη f.   35. fin. + και πολλοι
ηκολουθησαν αυτωι f.   36. επ αυτους (pro περι αυτων) f.
εσκυλμενοι (pro εκλελ.) acej.   ώς cdefjC.   38. θερισμον d
p. m., e p. m.

CAP. X. 1. + ό ι̅σ̅ (post προσκαλ.) f.   2. εισί (pro εστι) cj.
4. + o (ante ισκαριωτης) ae.   — o secund. dC.   ος και
παρεδωκεν f.   παραδιδους c.   fin. αυτων d p. m.   5. — και
εις πολιν ad finem versus (όμοιοτ.) c.   6. πορευεσθαι c
(errat Mill.) d p. m.   7. + μετανοειτε (ante ότι) c p. m. (e
s. m.).   8. — νεκρους εγειρετε acdefjC.   9. κτησεσθε c.   δοται
d p. m.   10. ραβδους cdj s. m. C [non cef].   12. fin. + λεγοντες
ειρηνη τω οικω τουτω cfjC.   13. εισελθετω C.   επ' αυτη c.
14. + εξω (post εξερχεσθε) f.   εκτειναξατε c.   fin. ήμων c.
15. + γαρ (post αμην) c.   γομορων e.   16. αποστελω d.
18. — δε acj.   19. — δε c.   παραδοσουσιν cd (δωσ d).   λαλη-
σειτε prim. cej.   λαλησηται d p.m.   λαλησετε afj.   — δοθησεται
ad fin. vers. c p. m. marg.   20. — το π̅ν̅α̅ c p. m. (habet marg.).
21. αναστησονται c.   23. φευγε d.   εκ της πολεως ταυτης
(pro εν τη π. τ.) c p. m.   24. + αυτου (post διδασκαλον) c.
25. + οι δουλοι (p. m. ό δουλος) f.   απεκαλεσαν deCj s. m.
επικαλεσαντο c.   ποσον e.   26. κεκαλυμενον c p. m.   27. προς
(pro εις) ac.   28. φοβεισθε acdefj.   αποκτενοντων acdjC
(απο των bis scriptum d p. m.) ef.   την ψυχην και το
σωμα ac.   29. ασσαριω c.   της γης c.   fin. + εν τοις
ουνοις c.   30. τριχαις e.   ηριθμηνται f.   31. πολλω dC.
+ γαρ (post πολλων) ef.   33. δε (— αν) f.   αρνησητε cd.
εμπροσθε f p. m.   καγω αυτον e.   + τοις (ante ουνοις) f.
34. της γης f.   37. υπερ εμου bis d.   38. λαμβαννει c.
39. εμων (pro ευρων) c p. m.   — απολεσει usque ad ψυχην

αυτου (ὁμοιοτ.) f. − την f. 42. αν (*pro* ἐαν) ad. των *supra*
p. m. d. των ελαχιστων (*ante* τουτων) e. − μονον c.
ψυχρου· μονον d. απολεσει c.

CAP. XI. 1. + τους λογουσ τουτους (*ante* διατασσων) c.
τους (*pro* τοις) c p. m. − διδασκειν και f. 2. ῑυ (*pro* χῡ) ef.
8. μαλακιοις ce. βασιλειων efjC. 16. παιδιοις acdefCj.
αγορα cdjC. καθεζομενοις εν ταις αγοραις (a) f. ἂ προσφω-
νουνται (*pro* προσφωνουσι) e. ἑτεροις ce. − και (*ante*
λεγουσι) ef. 18. + προς υμας (*ante* ιωαννησ) ef. + ὁ (*ante*
ιωαννης) d. 20. + ὁ ῑσ (*post* ηρξατο) dej. − και λεγουσι
usque ad και (ὁμοιοτ.) c. 21. χωραζειν ce. χωραζιν dfjC.
Βηθσαϊδα cfjC. Βιθσαϊδα d. Βιθσαϊδαν e. − ει cd p. m.
εγενηθησαν f. γινομεναι f. + καθημεναι (*ante* μετενωησαν)
cfj. 23. ἢ (*pro* ἤ) (ἡ a) de. εγενηθησαν f. γινομεναι f.
25. σε (*pro* σοι) c. 27. ὁ εαν βουλεται e. ὁ εαν d p. m. j.
30. − μου *secund.* f.

CAP. XII. 1. επορευετο f p. m. *supra*. καὶ οἱ (*pro* οἱ δε) c.
σταχυας τιλλειν f. 2. + αυτους (*post* ιδοντες) f. + τι (*ante*
ποιουσιν) f. 4. αυτον (*pro* αυτου) c. και διδατε c p. m.
6. μειζον bdfCj. − και bcdeCj. εστιν ὁ υιος του ᾱνου και
του σαββατου f. 10. ην εκει ᾱνοσ c. + εκει (*post* ην) f.
χειραν c p. m. ξηρα c p. m. 11. εστιν (*pro* εσται) f. − ις
(ὁ *supra* s. m.) c. − εις βοθυνον c. αυτῶ (*pro* αυτο) c.
εγειργερται e. 12. μαλλον (*pro* ουν) f. χειραν c p. m. e.
σου την χειρα f. απεκατεσταθη c s. m. C (*non* f). 14. και
εξελθοντες οἱ φαρισαιοι συμβουλιον ελαβον κατ αυτου f.
ἁπαντας d. 16. − μη. ποιησωσιν αυτον f. 17. υπο (*pro*
δια) f. ἠσαϊου c. 18. ἠρετησα ηρετισας d p. m. ἠρετησα
c p. m. 19. κραυγαζει e. 20. [λίνον ce]. εκβαλλη c.
21. − εν τω d. − εν bcejC. το (*pro* τῷ). 22. κωφον και
τυφλον bdf. − και (*ante* λαλειν) fj. 23. λεγοντες (*pro* και
ελεγον) c. + ὁ χῡσ (*post* εστιν) dfjC. 24. δαιμονα f p. m.
αρχον c p. m. καθ ἑαυτην *bis* cf. 26. εκβαλει d. ἑαυτην
(*pro* ἑαυτον) c. 27. εκβαλοῦσι f. κριται εσονται ὑμων f.
28. ει δε (*pro* και) f. εν πνι θῡ εγω bcej. ἆρα d. 29. ἁρπασαι

s. 5

f.   *fin.* διαρπαση bcdej.   ἁρπασει f.   30. + γαρ (*ante* μη
ων) f.   κἂν (*ante* κατ᾿) d.   31. εαν (*pro* αν *prim.*) bdfjC.
— τοις ανοις cf.   τω αιωνι τουτωι c.   τω·νυν αιωνι bcdjC.
33. επιγινωσκεται e.   — και τον καρπον αυτου καλον c *p. m.*
(ὁμοιοτ.).   34. πὸυ *primum* (*pro* πῶς *p. m.*).   — το στομα d.
35. — της καρδιας bcdeCj.   — τα bcefjC.   — του *secund.* C.
+ τα (*ante* πονηρα) dfC.   36. ἀμην δε λεγω ὑμιν f.   ον
(*pro* ὃ) d *p. m.*   37. *fin.* κατακριθησηι bf.   38. — και
φαρισαιων c.   θελωμεν cC.   39. επιζητειται c (ε *p. m.* c).
40. εγενετο (*pro* ἦν) f.   + και (*post* εσται) c.   + ο προφητης
(*post* ιωνας) cf.   41. νινευΐται c.   42. γενεας d *p. m.*
γεεας c *p. m.*   σολομωνος *bis* bcfC.   44. εις τον οικον
μου επιστρεψω f.   υποστρεψω eC.   ελθων be.   ηλθον c.
+ και (*ante* κεκοσμ.) cf.   κεκοσμενον d *p. m.*   45. ελθοντα d.
χειρωνα c.   τη πονηρα ταυτηι bf.   46. παραλαμβαννει c.
εισελθοντα d.   εἰστηκησαν ce.   ἑστηκασιν b.   47. ιδειν (*pro*
σοι λαλησαι) f.   σε (*pro* σοι) c.   εστηκασι bce.   48. λεγοντι
(*pro* ειποντι).   49. τεινας d.   εφη (*pro* ειπεν) ef.   50. — γαρ
d.   + τοις (*ante* ουνοις) d.   ποιησει c(e)(C).   οὗτος (*pro*
αυτος) c.   + και (*ante* αδελφος) bf.   — το d.   σπειραι e.

CAP. XIII. 1. εξελθον d *p. m.*   — απο f.   εκαθιτο ef.
2. — το bd.   καθισθαι c.   ἱστηκει c.   εἱστηκει e.   εν
παραβολαις d.   σπειραι bdefjC.   + εγενετο (*post* και) c.
+ του ουρανου (*post* πετεινα) ef.   5. τα πετρωδες c *p. m.*
ειχεν altered d *p. m.?*   8. ὁ *ter.* cdef.   12. περισευθησεται
e.   13. ου μὴ (*pro* ου) c.   *fin.* συνωσιν ce.   συνῶσι f.
14. πληρωθησεται cf.   — ἐπ᾿ befjC.   αναπληρουνται d *p. m.?*
ἠσαιας bc.   — ἡ *secund.* ef.   ακουσητε c.   *fin.* ιδεται c.
15. — γαρ f.   ιασομαι bcefjC.   16. ακουουσιν bf.   17. — και
prim. c.   18. σπειραντος df.   19. αἱρει (*pro* ἁρπαζει) f.
21. ευθεως c.   23. συνιῶν d.   ὡς δε (*pro* ος δη) c.   ὁ *ter.* cd.
24. ιδε (*post* ἄλλη) c.   σπειραντι d.   25. αυτον (*pro* τους
ανους) f.   27. δουλη c *p. m.*   εσπειρες c.   — σω bcef.   — ουν c.
+ τα bcjC.   28. εχθος c *p. m.* (*sic ver.* 23, 39).   συλλεξομεν
bdefjC.   29. σιτον d.   30. εως (*pro* μεχρι) f.   τω c *p. m.*
ejC.   δεσμους d.   καυσαι e.   — εις *prim.* f.   προς (*pro* εις) f.

31. ελαλησεν (pro παρεθηκεν) f. 32. μειζων cd. 33. + ὁ ισ̅
(post αυτοις) cj. + λεγων (ante ὁμοια) e. εκρυψεν bcdefj.
34. ελαλησεν dej. 35. καὶ κεκρυμμενα c. 36. – αυτω e.
διασαφησον (pro φρασον) f. 37. + αὐτοῖς f. 37, 38. – εστιν
ὁ υιος usque ad το καλον σπερμα (ἐμοιοτ.) e. 39. σπειρων c.
+ οἱ (ante αγγελοι) f. 40. καιεται bcd (non e) jC. 43. init.
ὁτε e. – εκλαμψ̅ e p. m. λαμψουσιν f. + των ουρανων
(post π̅ρ̅σ αυτων) (b)c. – ὁ εχων ad fin. vers. c. 44. – τω
bdefj. 45. – α̅ν̅ω c. 46. fin. ηγορασε τον μαργαριτην εκεινον
(– αυτον) f. 47. ομοιοτ. e. 48. + δε (post ὁτε) f. + αυτην
(post αναβιβασαντες) f. 50. – αυτους c. + την καιομενην
(ante εκει) f. κλαθμος c p. m. 51. – κυριε f. 52. – τη
βασιλεια (– εις) be. προφερει (pro εκβαλλ.) ef. 54. εκ-
πλησσεσθαι cC (non def). + πασα (ante ἡ σοφια) f.
– τουτω c. 55. ελεγετε c. μαρια f. ιωαννης (pro ιωσης)
f. 56. αυτω (pro τουτῳ) d. 57. – αυτου prim. bf.

CAP. XIV. 1. τετράχης (ρ supra s. m.) d. 2. + ὁ (ante
ιωαννης) c. 3. εν τη· φυλακη· απεθετο bf (+ τη ej). 4. – ὁ
c p. m. d. 5. εφοβειτο dj. εφοβητω e. 6. γενεσιοις
δε αγομενοις c. γενομενων (pro αγομενων) f. – της f.
7. αν (pro εαν) d. 8. θελω ἱνα μοι δως (pro δοσ μοι
φησιν) c. + αυτη· (post δοθηναι) f. 11. + το κορασιον (ante
ηνεγκε) f. η κεφαλη αυτου ηνεχθη C. ενεχθη p. m. c. + το
κορασιον (ante ηνεγκεν) e. ηνεγκεν αυτη (ν s. m.) c. 12. ελ-
θοντι c. εξελθοντες C. + αυτου (post σωμα) bc. αυτω c
p. m. – αυτου f. πτωμα f. 13. ακουσας δε (– και) bf.
14. ευσπλαγχνισθη e. επ αυτοις bcdef. 16. υμεις αυτοις cC.
17. – αυτω bc. 19. του χορτου bfj p. m. τοις χορτοις d.
– και secund. bcdefCj. – τους ult. c s. m. supra. fin. ὄχλυς
d p. m. 21. ωσει ανδρες c. 22. fin. τον οχλον c. 24. – ηδη
e. ην μεσον της θαλασσης bf. 25. ηλθε bf. – οισ f.
26. – και οι μαθηται επι την θαλασσαν περιπατουντα f. της
θαλασσης e. 27. – δε c. – αυτω d. σταδιους της γης
απειχεν ἱκανους j. 28. ο δε πετρος ειπεν αυτω c. 31. και
ευθεως (– δε) dC. 32. αναβαντων df. 33. προσελθοντες f.
ελθοντες be. προσεκυνουν cd. αυτον c. 34. την b. γεννη-

68   COLLATION OF GOSPELS.

σαρεθ e. γεννησαρ b. 35. επιγνουντες c. 36. + καν (ante μονον) bfjC.

CAP. XV. 1. αυτωι (pro τω ιυ) f. – οι prim. bdf. φαρισαιοι και γραμματεις f. + τον (ante αρτον) e. 3. διὰ τί passim cef [non d]. 4. – σου bdCj. . + σου (post μρα) ce. 5. ως εαν (pro ος αν) d. αν (pro εαν) c. fin. – αυτου cdf. 7. πρεφητευσεν e (non c). ησαιασ περι υμων ef. + ο προφητης (post ησαιασ) f. 8. – μοι c. αυτου (pro αυτων) c. ο c. – εγγιζει μοι bf. – τω στοματι αυτων και bf. πορω e. 9. διδασκαλιαις c. 10. συνετε f. 13. ορανιος c p. m. 14. τυφλοι εισιν οδηγοι bf. τυφυλων d p. m. Τε (pro δε) c (rubro T). γαρ (pro δε) d. εμπεσουνται bfCj. 15. – αυτω f. των ζιζανιων (pro ταυτην) e. 16. – ο ισ f. 17. ουπω εκπορευεται (pro εκβαλλεται) d. 18. εξερχονται dfj. 19. λογισμοι e. – πορνειαι κλοπαι ψευδομαρτυριαι (ομοιο.) c. 21. – ο f. σιδω e. 22. αυτης (pro εκεινων) f. – αυτω (εκραυγασε) f. 23. προσελθοντες d. ηρωτησαν f. 24. απολολωτα c. 25. προσεκυνησεν d (non c) ej. 26. Transfert λαβειν et βαλειν c p. m. 27. τον κυριον c p. m. 28. – σοι d. 29. εκαθισεν f. 30. πολοι d p. m. κυλους bd. αυτου (pro του ιυ) bdf. κωφους τυφλους e. 31. βλεποτας c. ακουοντας (pro λαλουντας) c. – και τυφλους βλεποντας (ομοιοτ.) | και (ante κυλλους et χωλους) εδοξαζον d(e)fCj. + του (ante ιηλ) fC. 32. ειπεν αυτω ημεραι bd (non Ccfj) e. 35. τοις οχλοις ce. τους οχλους f. προσκαρτερουσι (pro προσμεν.) f. 36. + και (ante ευχαριστησας) f. και λαβων c. 39. ανεβη bcj (non defC). μαγδαλᾶ f.

CAP. XVI. 1. επηρωτων f. επιδειξαι αυτοις εκ του ουρανου c. υποδειξαι C. 2. λεγομενης (pro γενομενης c marg.) c. πειραζει (non ver. 3) c. πυραζει (sic ver. 3) f. 3. – δε d. – υποκριται f (non ce). συνιεται c (pro δυνασθε) ae. 4. μιχαλις cd. απηλθον (λθ) e. 5. λαβειν αρτους f. απελθοντες c. απελαθοντο c. 8. – αυτοις bcf. 11. – πως e. αρτων bc s. m. ef [as Elz.cd]. + προσεχετε δε (post προσεχειν) e. προσεχετε (– δε) f. 12. init. + και f. Deest vers. (ομοιοτ.) c. – της ζυμης f. αλλα f. 14. + αυτωι

(*post* ειπον) f. αλλ (*pro* αλλοι δε) c *p. m.* ηλιαν bcdf.
ερεμιαν c. 16. ὁ πετρος ειπεν (−σιμων) f. 17. −αποκριθεις
δε (− και) f. 18. και εγω λεγω σοι f. 19. − και ὁ ἐαν λυσης
ad fin. vers. (ὁμοιοτ.) c. δωσω δε σοι (−και) f. 20. ταῖς e (ἰσ̄
ὁ χσ̄ ce). διεστειλατο (*at* − ιησους) bdfj. 21. εις ἱεροσυλα
απελθειν bf. 22. − αυτον c. αυτωι επιτιμαν bf. 23. επι-
στραφεις f. 24. − ὁ ἰσ̄ e. 25. δὰν bf. απολεση (*pro* ει) ce.
απολεσει (*pro* η) bcdeC. 26. ωφελησει f. ανταλαγμα de
p. m. 27. εργα (*pro* πραξιν) c (τα *supra* την d *s. m.*).
28. + γαρ (*post* αμην) ef. οδε εστικοτων c. ὧδε ἑστωτες
(− των) dj. + ὁτι (*ante* εστωτων) bf. εστωτες b. των ὦδε
ἑστωτες e. γευσονται cd *p. m.* efC. *fin.* των ουρανων (*pro*
αυτου) c.

Marginal gloss of d ver. 33 σατα μετρον ἑβραικῶς. δηλοῖ
δὲ μόδιον ὑπερ?ληρώμενον. so d ver. 20 διεστείλατο ουκ
αμφιβολως εχρησατο τοις λογοις.

CAP. XVII. 1. *init.* και εγενετο f. παραλαμβαννει c.
− και ιακωβον d *p. m.* (*supra s. m.*). 2. εγενοντο cefj.
3. μωυση cd (μωσεῖ dj ver. 4) ef. 4. υμας (*pro* ἡμασ) c.
ἡλιαν μιαν bf. 5. + δε (*post* ετι) e. εκ (*pro* απο) b *s. m.* cdj.
ειπητε c *p. m.* ειπειτε c *s. m.* δε (*pro* δει) c *p. m.* 10. τις
c *p. m.* 11. − ιησους f. − πρωτον bf. d *note on* αποκατα-
στησει *marg.* αποδωσει. 12. αλλα e. − ουκ c. − εν bcfj
p. m. + παντα (*ante* ὁσα) f. ὁ υιος ὁ του f. 14. αυτον
(*post* αυτω secund.*) bcdefjC. 16. προσηνεγκᾶ c *p. m.* (*a
supra s. m.*). τοις μαθηται d *p. m.* 17. μεθ᾽ ἡμων d.
18. ιαθη (*pro* εθεραπευθη) dj *s. m.* ἄνος (*pro* παις) f.
19. − οι μαθηται d. διὰ τί *passim* cef. 20. − εκει f. μεβησεται
c *p. m.* 21. − και ουδεν αδυνατησει ὑμῖν e. εξερχεται (*pro*
εκπορευεται) c. 22. αναστρεφωμενων c. παραδεδοσθαι d.
fin. + ἁμαρτωλων c. 23. αναστησεται (*pro* εγερθησεται) ce.
24. αυτον c. λαμβανοντες c. διδραγμα bc (τα *supra s. m.*)
bis cefj *p. m.* 25. + και (*ante* λεγει) cf. εισηλθον dj. λαμ-
βαννουσι c. υιον c *p. m.* 26. − λεγει *usque ad* αλλοτριων
(ὁμοιοτ.) c. 27. − δε c. αναβαινοντα c [*non def*] C.

CAP. XVIII. 1. ημερα (*pro* ωρα) bf. προσηλθον αυτω· οι μαθηται αυτου f (– τω ιυ). ᾶρα cd. 2. αυτον (*pro* αυτο) c p. m. γινεσθε f. 4. Deest versus ob ὁμοιοτ. e. ταπεινωσει bdfCj. 5. δεξειται e. – ἐν c. 6. σκαδαλιση d p. m. μυλος ονικος κρεμασθη c. εις (*pro* επι) Ccdej. εις την θαλασσαν (– τω πελαγει) f. 7. init. ἡ (*pro* ει) ce rubro. εισελθειν e. ερχεται b. ερχονται τα σκανδαλα bd. 8. αυτον (*pro* αυτα) f. – η δυο ποδας f (ὁμοιοτ.). 10. διαπαντὸς (c) dC. +τοις (*ante* ουρανοις) f. 11. Habent versum cdef. 12. – αφεις τα εννηκοντα d. ενενικοντα (η ver. 13) cCbj εννέα c. ἐνενηκοντα (ἐ f) εννέα ef: *sic* ver. 13. 14. ημων (μου b) (*pro* υμων) ce p. m. + τοις (*ante* ουνοις) f. 15. ἁμαρτη fCj s. m. – και prim. bcdf. ελλεγξον c. 16. μαρτυρων eras. post δυο prim. d rubro. – ετι f. μαρτυρων δυο f. σταθησεται cd. 17. τη εκκλησια (*pro* της εκκλησιας) e. λοιπω (*pro* σοι) c (λοιπων c s. m.). – ὁ secund. c p. m. 18. και ὁσα ἐὰν λυσητε ad fin. vers. repeated c p. m., eras. c s. m. αν (*pro* εαν) d. 19. + αμην (*post* παλιν) bcdejC. ἀμην (*pro* παλιν) f. αιτησονται cde p. m. + τοις (*ante* ουρανοις) f. 20. ὧ (*pro* οὖ) c p. m. ὁπου (*pro* οὖ) f. 21. ὁ πετρος ειπεν αυτω· f. 22. – λεγει *usque ad* ἑπτακις (ὁμοιοτ.) c. 24. συνερειν c. συναραι ef. προσυνεχθη d p. m. 26. προσεκυνησεν c. αυτον (*pro* αυτω) c. αποδωσω σοι f. πασαν την οφειλην εκεινην (*pro* δανειον) f. 28. ει τι (*pro* ὅ τι) bcdefjC. 29. δουλος d p. m. (συνδουλος s. m.). αποδωσω σοι παντα cj. – παντα bdC. σοι αποδωσω c. 30. ηθελησεν c. ˙+την (*ante* φυλακην) f. 31. γινομενα bis d. εαυτων (*pro* αυτων) cj. 33. και σε d. 34. – οὖ d. – αυτω f. 35. + ουν (*post* οὕτως) cjC [*nil omissum* cdefj] [*habet* b].

CAP. XIX. 1. + της (*ante* γαλιλαιας) cdeC. 2. οικολουθησαν c p. m. 3. ἦ (*pro* ει). – οἱ be. – αυτω secund. be. – ανθρωπω f. πειραζον d p. m. 4. τισας (*pro* ποιησας) bc. ἀπαρχης ce *sic* ver. 8. θυλη c. 5. + αυτου (*post* πρα) djC. προς την γυναικα (*pro* τη γυναικι) d. 6. ουκ (*pro* ουκετι) c. [μωσης] cdf. μωυσης be. εζευξεν f (*sic* ver. 8). 8. εγραψεν (*pro* επετρ.) e. 9. – ὅτι f. οστις (*pro* ὃς) f. – ὁ f. – ει bcd p. m. fjC. γεμησει (*pro* γαμησει) cC. γαμων (*pro*

γαμησας) f. 10. ἢ (pro ει) c p. m. + αυτου (post γυναικος)
f. συμφερε d p. m. 11. init. ὁ δε ισ d : χωρισουσι s. m. c
p. m. for χωρήσουσι (Mill.). 12. + αυτων (post μρσ). – οι-
τινες ευνουχισαν (ὁμοιοτ.) c p. m. (marg. s. m. εὐνουχισαν) e.
13. προσηνεχθησαν cC. τας χειρας αυτοις bf. + αυτου
(post μαθηται) c. επετιμων d. 14. τιουτων d. 15. τας
χειρας αυτοις f. 16. + τις (post εἰς) dj s. m. 17. [as Elz.]
cef. init. ο δε ισ e. λεγεις (pro θελεις) f. 18. – ιησους f.
19. – σου prim. bcd [non C]. fin. ἑαυτον bcd. 20. ταυτα
παντα f. – παντα ταυτα εφυλαξαμην d. 21. θελης c.
θησαυρῶν c p. m. 22. τον λογον ὁ νεανισκος f. 24. – δε be.
καμιλον c. [διελθειν (δ rubro c p. m.) de] at εισελθειν f.
25. – αυτου bd. ἆρα d. 26. fin. – εστι cbdejC [non f].
28. εν τη cf. εν τη παλιγενεσια, d (· c). -αλινγγ c
(sic) f jungit μοι et εν. 29. οικιαν bdej. λιψεται d p. m.
30. + οι (ante εσχατοι secund.) deC.

CAP. XX. 1. ηλθεν c. απο (pro ἅμα) f. 2. και συμφωνησας
(– δε) cdCj. 3. – την bcefCj. ευρεν (pro ειδεν) f. 4. και
εκεινοις cfj. κακεινους e. + μου (post αμπελωνα) c. λωσω
e p. m. (δ s. m.). 5. + την (ante εκτην) ce. ενατην ceC.
6. – εστωτας c. 7. + μου (post αμπελωνα) bc. 8. τον
εσχατων c. πρῶτον d. 10. ενομησαν cd. ενομιζον f. – οτι f
(non ver. 12). – και (ante ελαβον) cj. 12. – ὅτι f. ἴσους ce.
βαστασασοι c. fin. nota interrog. cum cde. 13. δηναριον d.
15. init. ἢ e. ὃ θέλω mutat. c. ει (pro ἢ secund.) bcd p. m.
eC. – ὁ e. 16. c habet ver. 14—19 in marg. rubro. οἱ
πρωτοι εσχατοι και οι εσχατοι πρωτοι f. 17. + αυτου (ante
κατιδιαν d) f. – εν τη ὁδω bf. 18. αναβαινωμεν c. θανατον
bd p. m. 18, 19. – θανατω και παραδωσουσιν Cj. αὐτον
(ὁμοιοτ.) c p. m. 19. εμπεξαι d. αναστηναι (pro αναστησεται) f. 21. θελης c. + σου (post ευωνυμων) bcdefC.
22. το ποτηριον πινειν d. μελλων c. πινειν (pro μελλω
πινειν) ef. ποιειν e. η (pro και) ef. 23. init. – και bc p. m.
+ ὁ ισ (post λεγει) f. – και το βαπτισμα usque ad βαπτισθη-
σεσθε c p. m. (habet marg. c s. m.). η (pro και ante εξ ευων.)
cfC. – μου (post ευων.) cfj. + τουτο (ante δουναι) e. ητοι-

72   COLLATION OF GOSPELS.

μασθαι d *p. m.*   24. – ακουσαντες δε (και) f.   25. – οιδα
c *p. m.* κατακυριευσουσιν c.   26. – δε cj. μεγας γενεσθαι
εν υμιν f.   εσται (*pro* εστω) bdefC.   29. + είναι (*post*
πρωτος*) e.   οχλοι πολλοι f.   ιέριχω bc only.   30. λεησον c
p. m. υιε cbe.   31. αυτους (*pro* αυτοις) c.   υίε ef.   32. ειπεν
αυτοις f.   + ίνα (*ante* ποιησω) e.   33. ανιχθωσιν c.   υμων e
p. m.   34. σπλαχνησθεις? c *p. m.* C.   αυτον d *p. m.* αυτων
d *s. m. fin.* αυτω d.

CAP. XXI. 1. Βηθσφαγὴ cde (-ῇ e) f *p. m.* C.   *fin.* + αυτων
cj.   2. – αυτοις f.   πορευεσθε f.   – την κωμην c (*habet*
marg.). όνον ce.   καὶ πῶλον δεδεμενον μετ αὐτῆς f.   3. –δε
d. ἀποστέλει cj.   αποστέλλει bdCj.   αποστέ e (?).   4. τοτε
(*pro* τουτο) d.   5. βασιλεύσου d.   πραεις d *p. m.* (υ *s. m.*).
7. αυτὸν *pr.* c *p. m.* επεκαθησαν c.   επεκαθισαν df (σεν
s. m. a supra d).   εκαθισεν e.   επεκαθισεν fC.   8. αυτων ef.
αυτων d.   εστρωννυον *prim.* ef.   τον δενδρον c *p. m.*   η. οδω
τα ίματια αυτων bf (b αυτων).   9. ὡσαννᾶ *bis* c.   ωσάννὰ
bis def.   δοξα d *marg.*   – ευλογημενος *ad fin. vers.* e.
11. – ὁ (*ante* ισ) bc.   ναζαρετ cdfC (*s. m.* e).   12. – του
θεοῦ bf.   τῶ (*pro* τῶν) c.   κολυβιστρων και τας καθεδρας
των πωλουντων τὰς καθεδρας κατεστρεψε f.   εποιησατε
αὐτὸν c.   14. χωλοι και τυφλοι cdefC.   – εν τω ίερω cj.
ὡσανα d *s. m.*   16. + ουκ (*ante* ακουεις).   18. επαναγων d
s. m.   19. εν *vel* επ' c (*sic*) cj.   at επ' αυτην d.   επ' αὐτὴ c.
εἰμὶ c.   μονα bcj.   20. και (*pro* κᾶν) c.   21. ὁ (*pro* όν).
ποιήσητε f.   22. εαν (*pro* αν) bdC.   23. διδασκοντα και
προσηλθον αυτω e.   24. ενα λογον d.   ὃ (*pro* ὸν) c.   ἐὰν d
p. m. ερω ὑμιν f.   25. + ἦν (*ante* ἢ εξ) c.   – ουν bdj.
28. δοκῇ e *s. m.*   + τις (*post* ονοσ) cdfCj.   δυο τεκνα c.
fin. –μου be.   30. ἑτερω (*pro* δευτερω) cdf (*non* e).   31. εποιησεν εκ τῶν δυο ce.   + οτι (*ante* εαν) f.   32. ιωαννης προς
ὑμας f.   – οἱ δε τελωναι *usque ad* επιστευσατε αὐτω (ὁμοιοτ.)
.c.   – του f.   – αἱ be.   ε (*pro* αἱ) f.   33. – τις bfj.   πυργον d.
αυτον *s. m.*   ὁ ισ *p. m.?* is this a gloss? [ἐξεδοτο] e.   – ἐν c.
35. εδηραν cd *p. m.* efj.   36. ὡσαύτως f.   37. – δε c.
41. εκδωσεται bdefCj (not c).   42. ἔστη ej.   ὑμων cde.

45. ακουσαντες δε (– και) c. ἔθνη d p. m. f. -ει d s. m.
περι αυτὸ`ν cd p. m.

CAP. XXII. 4. ἠτοιμακα f. 5. ὅς μεν bf. – εις prim. c
p. m. ut επι b (s. m. marg. habet). 7. και ακουσας (– δε) ὁ
βασιλευς εκεινος bcdefCj. απωλεσαν c. αυτον c p. m., ω
s. m. ενεπρησαν c. 8. – ὁ prim. f. – ετοιμος c. 9. πορευ-
θεντες e. εαν (pro αν) bcdCj. 10. – παντας. 11. εχοντα
(pro ενδεδυμενον) f. 12. φιμόομαι το επιστομίζομαι marg.
s. m. 13. +τοις (διακονοις) f. χειρας και ποδας eC. βαλετε
cj. εκβαλατε b (+ αυτὸν b) d. 15. αυτον λογωι (– εν) f.
16. λεγοντας d. μελλει cfj. fin. ἀνου bf. ἀνον d p. m., ω
s. m. 19. επιδειξαται e. τα του κεσαρος κεσαρι c. τω
θυ̅ c p. m. 22. – αυτον c. 23. – οἱ bcCfj. λεγοντι αυτω
και διδασκοντι προσηλθον αυτω e. 24. μωϋσης bc. fin.
αυτω e. 25. – αυτου prim. c. γήμας abc. 26. ὁμοιος c
p. m. 27 et 28. τον p. m. c. 28. αυτην εσχον f. 29. – αυτοις
c. ιδοντες e. 30. γαμιζονται αλλ εισιν ὡς αγγελοι του θυ̅
εν τωι ουρανωι f. – του θυ̅ b. 31. ημιν c p. m. – ὑμιν c.
32. ἀβρααμ ce. ἀβρααμ bdfj. 37. εφη (pro ειπεν) cCj.
39. αὕτη (pro αὐτη) ef. σεαυτον cf. 40. κοσμος (pro νομος) ce.
43. + ὁ ισ (ante πως) f. κν̅ αυτον καλει cj. 46. ἠδυνατο cC.
[οὐκετι] ce.

CAP. XXIII. 2. μωϋσεως f [non bcde]. fin. + λεγοντες c.
3. ἐαν (pro αν) bcdeCj. ημιν c. 4. επιθεασιν d. δε (pro
γαρ) c. αὐτων (pro αὐτων) bj. εαυτων (pro 2nd αυτων) b.
παντα γαρ (not δε). γαρ (post δε secund.) bj. τον ιματιων
c. 6. δε (pro τε) cdj. φυλουσι c. 7. – και τους ασπασμους
εν ταις αγοραις (ὁμοιοτ.) c. ραμβὶ c semel tantum ραβι j
p. m. bis. 8. + ὁ prim. bef. διδασκαλος (pro καθηγγητης)
dj s. m. – παντες ad fin. versus f : habet here ουρανοις ver. 9.
9. ημων (pro υμων secund.) d. 10. εστιν ὑμων d. εστιν ὁ
καθη(ο b)γητης ἡμων ὁ χσ̅ c. 11. – εσται ὑμῶν (ὁμ.) c.
εστω (pro εσται) dj. 13, 14. ordo as Elz.St.defC, at 14, 13 c.
13. – δὲ b. 15. gloss πρόσηλυτοι, in late marg. s. m. προση-
λυτοι οἱ εξ εθνων προσεληλυθοτες. και κατα τους θειους

74 COLLATION OF GOSPELS.

πολιτευομενοι νομους δαδ d. 19. μεῖζων ce. ἁγιαζων cde.
21. – ο supra p. m. c. κατοικησαντι bcdj. κατοικουντι εν
αυτω ef. 23. κοιμηνον c. + δε (post ταυτα) ef. δει (pro
εδει) d s. m. το ελεος ef. ἔδη [no δε] c. 24. κονοπα cf.
κονωπα e. καμῖλον cf. 25. fin. αδικιας (pro ακρασιας)
bcdej (non f)C. 26. εντος (pro εκτος) c. αυτου (pro αυτων)
f. 27. ἡμιν c. 29. μνηματα cf. 30. οτι ει ημεθα C. ἤμεθα
prim. cb (bis). 32. αναπληρωσατε c. ἡμων cf. 33. γενηματα c p. m. 34. – και tert. f. 35. – παν d. ἡμας c.
εκχυνομ. c. ἄβελ ce. – υίου βαραχιου (ὁμοιοτ.?) habet in
calc. marg. s. m. 36. + ὁτι (ante ἡξει) cdej. παντα ταυτα
befC. – μου e. 37. αποκτένουσα cdefCj. νοοσεια f. επι-
συνάγαγεῖν (pro επισυναγει). ορνις επισυναγει b. fin.
ἠθελησα d. 38. – ὑμιν ef. 39. + ὁτι (ante ου μη) e. δε
(pro γαρ) f. + οτι (ante οὐ μη) c. ἀπάρτι fdeCj. απαρτη ce.

CAP. XXIV. 1. του ιυ (pro αυτου) e. απο του ίερου
επορευετο f. + αυτωι (post προσηλθον) dfj3**. 2. ταυτα
παντα bcdefC. – ου prim. c. – μὴ secund. bcdeCj**.
λιθου c. 3. + τουτου cj. 4. επι το ce. 6. μελλησεται d
p. m. ειλλ e. ακουεις c p. m. ορασθε c p. m. ουπου c.
ακαταστασιας (pro ακοας) b. το τελος εστιν f. λιμοι (pro
λοιμοι) c p. m. σισμοι c. 9. τον εθνων cC. – τον f.
14. ἡξει c. 15. [έστος ceCj.] εστως bf. 16. εις (pro επι).
17. + και init. bcj. καταβατω ef. τα (pro τι) bcdeCj.
18. + εισ τα οπισω bf. το ίματιον bfCj. 20. προσευχεσθαι c.
– εν cefj. 21. – εως του νυν bc. – ου fj. 24. σημεια και
τερατα μεγαλα f. 27. – και secund. bcf [not d]. ταμιειοις c.
28. + και (ante οί αετοι) fj. 29. Δ rubro c. σκοτασθησεται
c. 30. επι τον c. 31. αποστελλει bd p. m. c. + και (ante
φωνης) cC. αποστειλει f. αποστελλεῖ d. – φωνης f.
32. μανθανε cf. απεγινωσκεται c. [έκφυη cdej.] ἀπαλος e.
ἀπαλος γενηται f. 33. ταυτα παντα ceC. 34. + δε (post
αμην) e. + ὁτι (ante ου μη) f. + δε (ante λεγω) ce. ταυτη
(pro αυτη) cef. ταυτα παντα cf. – ταυτα cfe. 35. παρελευσεται cefd. 36. – της secund. cdCj. τον ουρανον cf.
37. – και f. σεται d. – τησ sec. e. 38. εκγαμιζοντες c.

40. ὁ *bis* c. − o *bis* b. 41. *Deest versus* (*ob* ὁμοιοτελευτον)
c. μυλωνι b. 42. ἥμων c. 43. ηδη cd. 44. ημεις c.
ετιμοι c. 45. ἆρα c. − επι e. του (του c s. *m.*) δουναι bc.
48. μου ὁ κσ̄ ελθειν be. 49. ἀρξητε d *p. m.* αρξεται c.
τε (*pro* δε) bdj. δουλους (*pro* συνδουλους) c. εσθειη c.
πινη c. 50. ὁ κσ̄ του δου *super ras* c s. *m.* 51. ὁδοντων bc.

Cap. XXV. 2. εξ αυτων ησαν φρονιμοι και πεντε μωραι
(− αἱ *secund.*) bcdefj (*habet* C). 3. αυτων (*pro* ἑαυτων) cdeC.
− εαυτων *prim.* b (ἑαυτων *secund.* e) fCj. 4. ενισταξαν c.
αυτων d. ἑαυτων (*pro* αὐτων *secund.*) ce. − αυτων *prim.* b.
6. εξερχεσθαι f. 8. δος d. 9. αρκεσει cC. υμιν (*pro* ημιν)
bc *p. m.* ef. [*habet* δε ce.] *fin.* αυτοις c *p. m.* 10. ετιμοι
c *p. m.* 11. [και e.] ανηξον c. 14. − αυτοις c. 16. [*habet*
δε e.] εκερδησεν (*pro* εποιησεν) f. επεκερδησα b. 17. − και
αυτος c. 18. − απελθων c. 19. πολυν χρονον bf. λογον
μετ αυτων bC. 20. − ταλαντα *prim.* e. εν (*pro* επ) cf.
23. − αυτω d. 24. λαβων (*pro* ειληφως) cef. διεσκορπησας
c. 25. *fin.* σοι d. 27. καταβαλειν (*pro* βαλειν) fC.
29. δοκει εχειν cdeCj. 30. εκβαλεται d *p. m.* εκβαλετε
cefCj. 31. − δε f. 32. συναχθησονται cdeCj. 34. ευλο-
γημενη c. 35. *fin.* με c *p. m.* 37. εἰ (*pro* η) c. 38. συνη-
γαγωμεν c. *Deest versus* e (same beginning). 40. ειπεν
(*pro* ερει) f. των ελαχιστων των αδελφων μου c. επἴησατε
c *p. m.* 41. ἠτοιμασμενω d *p. m.* 42. με (*pro* μοι) d.
44. − αυτω bcdfCj. 45. ἐμη c.

Cap. XXVI. 1. ελεγεν (*pro* ετελεσεν) c. − παντας d.
2. παραδιδ. d *p. m.* 3. − και οι γραμματεις (ὁμοιοτ.) bcfj.
4. δολω κρατησωσι bcdefCj. *fin.* απολεσωσιν c. 7. πολυτιμου f. 9. εδυνατο f. μῦρον bd (− το f). 10. λεγει (*pro*
ειπεν) c. εποιησεν (*pro* ειργασατο) f. 11. τους πτωχους
γαρ παντοτε bcefj. 12. ενταφιᾶσαι e. πεποιηκεν f. 13. +γαρ
(*post* αμην) c. τοῦτω d *p. m.* εποιισεν e *p. m.* 14. τον
δωδεκα c *p. m.* ἰσκιωτην bcj. 15. και εγω bdCj. παραδοσω
c. 16. ἀπο τότε ce. 17. − αυτω bce. ἑτοιμασομεν dj s. *m.*
18. + αυτοις (*post* ειπεν) ef. 20. + μαθητων f. 22. εἷς (*pro*
αυτω) bf. 23. την χειρα εν τω τρυβλιω bf. τρἴβλιω d.

76 COLLATION OF GOSPELS.

αυτος (pro οὗτος) f. 24. τα σκανδαλα γινονται· καὶ (post
διϊοῦ) c. ἡ (pro εἰ) c p. m. εγενηθη d (ν supra s. m.).
26. −τον c (d habet) bef. εδωκε (pro εδιδου) c. δους (pro
εδιδου) bf. +αυτου (ante και ειπεν) cj. −και (ante ειπε) bf.
27. −τὸ bef. −και secund. e. 28. εκχυνομενον c. 29. ἀπ
αρτι bcdefCj. γενηματος cfj s. m. του τουτου γενηματος be.
πϊω e. 31. −ο ιησους f. 33. −αυτω bf. −και bce. +δε
(post εγω) bc. σκαδαλισ. c prim., et alibi d. 35. απαρνησωμαι cdfCj s. m. +δε (post ὁμοιως) cdefCj. 36. εισερχεται c.
γεθσήμανι ce. γεθσιμανη bj. γεθσημανὴ f. +αυτου (post
μαθηταις) cf. −οὗ bf. 37. ἤρξατο c p. m. +ὁ ῑσ (post
αυτοις) dfj. 39. προσελθων bcde (not f). 40. αγρυπνησαι
(pro γρηγορησαι) d. +και αναστας απο της προσευχης (ante
ερχεται) bc. οὕτως, c at cum nota interrog. bef. In marg. p. m.?
f habet ῡ εις κ^τ λουκά και παλιν αρ^ξ. 42. +ὁ ῑσ (ante λεγων)
ef. το ποτηριον απελθειν απ εμου e. το ποτηριον τουτο b.
43. παλιν ευρεν αυτους bf. ευρεν dej. 45. −αυτου be.
+ἀνων (ante ἁμαρτωλων) f. 46. +εντευθεν (post αγωμεν) cj.
−ηγγικεν d. +ιουδας (post ηγγικεν) e. 47. −ιδου c.
48. αν (pro εαν) dj. 50. εφ ὃ f. εφ ᾧ e. 51. +αυτου (post
χειρα) f. 52. την μαχαιραν σου f. την θηκην (pro τον
τοπον) bf. οι γαρ (pro καὶ γαρ) c. αποθανουνται (pro
απολουνται) deCj. 53. δοκει σοι bf. αρτι ου δυναμαι f.
54. πλρωθωσιν c p. m. δὴ c p. m. 55. verbum eras. post οἱ
δὲ d. με; cd. ἡμας (pro ὑμας) d p. m. −διδασκων f.
56. αφεντες bis script. c p. m. 58. ηκολουθη cd p. m. −απο
c. 59. ὁλον το συνεδριον c. απολεσωσιν (pro θανατωσωσι)
c p. m. θανατωσωσιν αυτον deCj s. m. 60. −και πολλων
usque ad εὑρον (ὁμοιοτ.) c. 63. jungit f αποκρινει et τι.
σοι (pro σου) f. −αποκριθεις f. −ιησους e. fin.+του
ζωντος c. 64. ἀπαρτι defCj. 65. δι'έρρυξε c. 67. ερραπισαν
b. ἐραπησαν (ρ supra e p. m.). εραπησαν c. 70. +αυτων
(ante παντων) dfj. τον ἀνον (pro τι λεγεις) f. ενωπιον (pro
εμπροσθεν) c. 71. αυτοις· εκει και bcdefCj. 73. +παλιν
(post δε) f. 74. καταθεματιζειν bc p. m. def. 75. −του
secund. bde (not f) C.

CAP. XXVII. 1. – *του λαου* d. 2. *δησοντες* d. – *αυτον*
secund. dj. 3. *μεταμελεῖς* c. – *τοις secund.* cj. 6. *κορβονὰν*
f [*non* e]. 8. *την* (*pro της*) d. 9. *ἰέρεμιον* c. *ἰερεμιου* j.
ἰερ- ef. 11. – *ιησους secund.* bc. 12. – *των secund.* cdf.
13. *πιλᾶτος passim* f. 15. *ειωθη* cdf. 17. *βαραβαν* C *sic*
alibi d *p. m.* ver. 16, 20. 20. *αιτησονται* ce. 22. *ποιησωμεν*
c. *λεγουσι* (– *αυτω*) f. 23. – *οἱ δε περισσως* (*ὁμοιοτ.*) c.
26. – *τον prim.* c. *φαγελωσας* c. *φραγγελλώσας* d?
φραγελλωσας f. + *αυτοις* (*ante ἵνα*) f. 27. ἐ*αυτον*^π c *p. m.*
(*π s. m.*). *σπείραν* ef. 29. *ενιπεζον* cj. 30. – *εις prim.* c.
31. *ενεπεξαν* c. – *εις* d (*eras.*). *αυτω* (*pro αυτον prim.*) e
s. m. – *εξεδυσαν αυτον την χλαμυδα και* c. – *αυτον tert.* c.
32. *κηρηναιον* c. *κυρινιναιον* e. Το *ηγγαρ.* d *has gloss ακου-*
σιως ηναγκαζον marg. s. m. 33. *γολγοθὰ* d. ὁ (*pro ὃς*)
bdCj. *λεγομενος* bcfj. *λεγομενον* d. 34. *ποιειν prim.* c.
35. *ταυρωσαντες βαλόντες* cC. *δια* (*pro υπο*) f. *ινα πλ.* ad
fin. vers. bcdeCj [*habet* f]. 37. *αυτο* e *p. m.* (*loco της*) *eras.*

– *ιησους* bcj. 40. *καλυων*^ν d. 41. + *και φαρισσαιων* (*ante*
ελεγον) cdefC (– *πρεσβ.*) f. *fin. σωσαι;* bc *s. m.* defj.
42. *πιστευσομεν* (*-σωμεν* ce) *επ αυτον* cefC. *αυτω* e.
43. – *νυν* cef. *οτι* (*pro ει*) e. 44. *fin. το αυτο δε* fC. *αυτον*
bcjdef. 45. *ενατης* bc *p. m.* Cj *sic* ver. 46 ef. 46. *εβοησεν*
bc. *ἠλι ἠλι λϊμᾶσαβαχθανι* c. *λεμα λιμα σαβαχθανει* b.

λϊμᾶ bd. *λιμά* fC. *ειμι tantum* e. *αβαχθανι* c. *αβαχθανὶ*^ν
(*ν supra p. m.*) f. *ἵνατί* fc. [*-λιπες* cdef.] 47. *ἐστωτων* cde.
– *ὁτι* cfj. 48. *προσδραμων* c. 49. *Deest versus* (*ὁμοιοτ.*) c.
50. – *παλιν* c. 52. *ανεωχθη* ef. *ανεωχθησαν* c *p. m.*
54. *ἑκατοντ*[*αρ s. m.*]*χος* c. 55. + *και* (*post εκει*) bdej *s. m.*
– *απο* c. 56. *μαγδαλϊνή* d (so ver. 61). *ιακωβου* (with
marg. *ἰωσὴφ*) c *s. m.* 58. – *το σωμα secund.* e. *fin. τω*
ιωσηφ f. *ἰωσῆ* e. *fin.*+ *τω ιωσηφ* f. 59. – ὁ c *p. m.* (*supra*
s. m.). *ενετειλιξεν* e. 60. *ωι* (*pro ὃ*) f. *εθετο αυτω* c *p. m.*
(*αυτου* c *s. m.*). *μεγαν λιθον* c. *την θυραν* (*εις marg. s. m.*)
c. 62. *πρεσβυτεροι* (*pro φαρισαιοι*) c. 63. *εγειρομεν* c.
ετι ζων ειπεν f. 64. *κλεψωσι αυτον νυκτος* cj. *τοις*
πρωτης c. *habet νυκτος* C. 65. – *δε* cbe. 66. *ταφον* (*pro*
λιθον) c.

CAP. XXVIII. 1. μαγδαλινη c. τω σαββατων c. 2. μεγας εγενετο d. εγεντο c s. m. – αγγελος γαρ usque ad ουρανου c p. m. 3. – ή d. ειδεα bc. 6. απο των νεκρων (pro γὰρ) f. ἴδετε bis script. d p. m. το σωμα του κ̄ῡ (pro κ̄σ̄) f. 8. init. – και c. 9. – ως δε επορευοντο απαγγειλαι τοις μαθηταις αυτου bcfj. – ὁ bcefCj marg. s. m. εκρατησεν c. 10. κοστουδιας c p. m. απαγγειλλατε c. και εκει d s. m. f. 11. απαγγειλαν f. 14. ποιησωμεν bf. ὑπο (pro επι) d. 15. + τοις (ante ιουδαιοις) c. 19. – ουν bcdefCj. 20. [ἀμην OMNES].

Subscriptiones. Deest in c rubro τελος του κατα ματθαιον ἁγιου ευαγγελίου. rubro στ˟ εις τον ἁγιον μαρκον τον ευαγγελιστην στ˟ β̄ χ̄ εξεδοθη υπ αυτου τουτο μετα χρονους η της χ̄ῡ αναληψεως d. ιστεον οτι το κατα μαρκον ἁγιον ευαγγελιον εγραφει εν αλεξανδρεια ὑπ εαυτου του μαρκου επιτρεψαντος αυτου του αγιου αποστολου και κορυφαιου πετρου. επομοιωματι μοσχου. μετα χρονους ι΄ τῆς χ̄ῡ αναληψεως e rubro. ευαγγελιον κατα μαρκον e rubro. συνεγραφη το κατα ματθαιον αγιον ευαγγελιον μετα χρονους η της χ̄ῡ αναληψεως f. τελος του κατὰ ματθαίον αγίου ευαγγελιου C.

TITLES. Το κατα μαρκον ἁγιον ευαγγελιον c rubro.
† τελος ευαγγελιου κατὰ ματθαιον j.
† ευαγγελιον κατα ματθαιον b.
τελος του κατα ματθαιον ἁγιου ευαγγελιου j.

TITLE : Το κατα μαρκον ἁγιον εὐαγγελιον cdej adding (in e) εγραφει εν αλεξανδρεια ὑπ᾽ αὐτου του μαρκου· επιτρεψαντος αὐτον του ἁγιου αποστολου και κορυφαιου πετρου εν ωμοιωματι μοσχου· μετα χρονους ῑ της χ̄ῡ αναληψεως e. ευαγγελιον κατα μαρκον f. ἁγιον ευαγγελιον κατα μαρκον a Compl.

MARC. I. 1. πρ̊σώπου c p. m. (ο supra s. m.). 5. εξεπορευοντο c. – η c. – οἱ cf. εβαπτιζον c p. m. το s. m. (late)

c. ιορδανι c. εξομολογουμε^{νοι} c (νοι supra c s. m.). 6. + ὁ
(ante ιωαννης) bdeCj. καμιλου ej p. m. Ὀσφὴν c. εσσθιονον
c p. m. (altered s. m.). μελη c. περι? e (pro μελι). 7. ὀπίσω
e. ἱμαντα d. 8. βαπτιζων (pro εβαπτισα) e. 9. ηλθεν ὁ ι̅σ̅
dCj. ναζαρεθ ce [-ετ Cdf]. εις τον ιορδανην ὑπο ιωαννου bf.
10. καταβαινων c. καβαινων d p. m. κα^{τα}βαῖνον d s. m.
11. ηυδοκησα cdj. 12. ευθεως bcdej. ευθεως αυτον το π̅ν̅α f.
13. – εν τη ερημω bef. τεσσαρακοντα ἡμέρας f. – οἱ cf.
14. init. ετὰ c p. m. – ὁ bc. 15. – και λεγων usque ad θ̅υ̅
(ὁμοιοτ.) c. 16. περι (pro παρα) e. θαλασσα d p. m. (ν
supra s. m.). ? σιμονα c. + του σιμωνος (ante βαλλοντας)
(b)cdefC. εις την θαλασσαν f. 16, 17. ἁλιεις cef. 16. δὲ
erased c. ὁ ι̅σ̅ c s. m. 17. – ὁ ι̅σ̅ c. – γενεσθαι bf.
18. αυτων eras. c. – αυτων bf. 19. – εκειθεν f. ὀλιγων c
p. m. (ὀλιγον c s. m.). ζεβεδεου c. δυκτυα c. fin. + αυτων e.
20. ὀπίσω ce passim. αυτον d p. m. αυτων d s. m.
21. + μετ᾽ αυτου (post εσπ.) f. σαββασι c p. m. (mutat.).
+ την (ante συναγ.) cdC vid. Elz. εξεπλισσοντο e. 24. ανε-
κραζε forsan d. συ (pro σου) f. 25. επετημησεν c. απ᾽
(pro εξ) bdf. 26. κραξας c. Deest versus (ὁμοιοτ.) e.
27. συνζητειν e. προσ ἑαυτους bcdefCj. – ἡ (ante καινη) c
p. m. 28. και εξηλθεν (– δε) bf. – ευθυς bc p. m. (marg.
habet) f. – ὁλην f. 29. εξελθων εκ της συναγωγης ηλθεν f.
μετα d (με s. m.) spatium amplius. 30. + του (ante σιμωνος)
bdCj s. m. ευθυς c. 31. – ευθεως bf. 32. ὅτι d p. m. ὁτε
d s. m. εδυσεν f. 33. ην ὁλη η πολις επισυνηγμενη Cbf.
κακακως c p. m. νόσσοις c. 34. παντας τους (pro πολλους)
c. fin. + χ̅ν̅ ειναι dj. + τον χ̅ν̅ αυτον ειναι bf. 35. εννυχιον
c. εννυχον e. + ὁ ι̅σ̅ (ante εις) cC. ειξηλθεν e. 36. init.
αι e (K rubro s. m.). κατεδιωξεν be. + τε (ante σιμων) f.
μαθηται (pro μετ᾽) f. 37. σε ζητουσιν cdefC. 38. + ὁ ι̅σ̅
(ante αγωμεν) f. κωμας και πολεις d s. m. (κωμοπολεις d
p. m.). εκει C. και εκει bd p. m. ej. εληλυθα def. 39. εις
τας συναγωγας f. 40. παρακαλον bc. γονύπετον c. – αυτον
secund. f. θελεις c. 42. ηλεκτρα απηλθεν απ᾽ αυτου f.
εκαθερισθη c. 43. – αυτω prim. f. 44. – μηδεν bC. μηδενι
(pro μηδεν) d. μηδεν c p. m. προσενεγκαι f. προσετεξε d.

80 COLLATION OF GOSPELS.

ὃ (pro ἃ) bf. *fin.* αυτοις (*mutatum*) c. μωϋσῆς f. 45. ελθειν
(pro εξελθειν) d. μὴκέτι d. πάντοθεν f (pro πολλ.).

CAP. II. 1. και εισελθων παλιν b. και εισηλθεν ὁ ι̅σ̅
παλιν c. εισηλθε παλιν de (εισηλθεν e) fCj. δὴ ? (pro δι᾽)
c. 3. ερχεται d p. m. (ονται d s. m.). 4. δυναμενων d s. m.
(-νοι p. m.). την στεγη c. + ὁ ι̅σ̅ (post ην) bf. κραβαττον
(sic ver. 11, 12) bcf. [κραββατον dC.] 5. σου *mutat.* c.
αφέονται e. σου (pro σοι) f. – σου f. 6. γραμματαιων cd
p. m. καθιμενοι e. οὗτως cf. οὗτως bej. 8. το π̅ν̅ι̅ c p. m.
+ αυτοι (ante διαλογιζονται) cdefCj. *fin.* ημων (η *dubium*)
ce. 9. ευκοποτερον c. σου (pro σοι) bcdefC. εγειρε
bce. – και prim. bf. τον κραβαττον σου bf. 10. εχη c.
επι της γης αφιεναι bdf. 11. – και prim. f. εγειρε ce.
12. εναντιων c. εμπροσθεν b. ενωπιον f (pro εναντιον).
ἴδομεν e. 13. *init.* – και e. παλιν᾽ c (ν late). 14. + ὁ ι̅σ̅
(ante ιδεν) c. λευῒ f. – καθημενον c. 15. εν το κατακεισθαι
αυτων c. 16. ελεγων ? c s. m. εσθιετε και πινετε bf.
17. – ὁ. ου γαρ (pro ου) f. – εις μετανοιαν bf (non c).
18. φαρισαιοι (pro των φ.) cj p. m. νηστευωντες d p. m.
(o s. m.). διὰ τί passim ceC. νηστευονται e. – οἱ δὲ σοι
ad fin. vers. (ὁμοιοτ.) f. 19. – ὁ ι̅σ̅ f. – οἱ c. 21. init.
– και be. επιραπτει ce. μηγε (pro μη) be. + απο bf.
+ απ᾽ (ante το πληρωμα) befj. – αυτου f. 22. αλλ᾽ f.
23. σαμβασιν (so ver. 24) c. ποειν c. 24. – εν bce.
25. οτι (pro ότε). επεινασεν και αυτος f. 26. – του cdfj
[habet beC]. *fin.* μετ αυτου ουσιν (b)ej. 27. λεγει (pro
ελεγεν) bf. σαμβατον prim. c. εκτισθη (pro εγενετο) b
(Codd. 1.131.209). 28. και του σαμβατου c.

CAP. III. 1. εισηλθε παλιν c. εξηραμενην ef (sic ver. 3)
d p. m. (μ supra in d s. m.). χειραν e. 2. σάμβασιν c.
κατηγορησουσιν ce. αυτον d p. m. αὐτοῦ d s. m. 3. εγηρε
c. εγειρε be. απολεσαι (pro αποκτειναι) bfj. 5. πορωσει
cf. – σου c. απεκατεσταθη e [not cdf]. 6. ευθυς f. 7. παρα
(pro προς) f. πολλοὶ (πολλυ d p. m.) πληθος cd. ηκολουθησεν bceCj. 8. – απο prim. bej. + καὶ (ante πληθος) c.

+ ηκολουθησαν (*post* πολυ) f. – και περαν *usque ad* τυρον (same beg.) e. 9. προσκαρτερει cC. θλιβοσιν c. 10. αυτον d *p. m.*, ου d *s. m.* αψονται cd *p. m.* (ω d *s. m.*). 11. εθεωρουν cf [*non* j]. προσεπιπτον cfj. προσέπ^{ιπτεν} d (πτεν *supra* d *s. m.*). ʿκραζον c (ε *supra* c *s. m.*) fj. + ὁ χσ (*ante* ο υἱὸς) f. 12. επετιμησεν αυτοις πολλα f *p. m.* φανερον αυτον bcdefCj. 13. προς αυτον (*pro* αυτος) e. 14. – και εποιησε *usque ad* μετ αυτου c. αποστελλει c. 15. θεραπευην c. νοσσους c. 16. πετρω (*pro* πετρον) c. 17. ζεβεδεου c. αυτου (*pro* του ιακωβου) c. βοανεργαις c. βανηρεγεζ b. βοανηργες f. εκβαλβαλλει j. 19. ισκαριωτην cf. Εις (E *rubro*) d. 20. συνερχοντα c. – παλιν f. δυνασθαι d *p. m.*, ε *s. m.* 21. *fin.* έξεστιν c. 23. + ὁ ισ (*post* αυτους) e. 25. Versus deest (ὁμοιοτ.) cej. 26. + το (*ante* τελος) d. 27. ουδεις δυναται (– ου) bcdefCj. ἧς (*pro* εις) c. – εισελθων εις την οικιαν αυτου (ὁμοιοτ.) d. του (– αυτου *prim.*) c. διαρπᾶσαι cd. *fin.* διαρπαση bcdeCj. διαρπασει f. 28. ὁσα (*pro* ὁσας) c. αι (+ αι only b) βλασφημιαι ὁσας ἐαν f. ἂν βλασφημισωσιν e. βλασφησει c. *fin.* κρίματος f (*non* ce). 30. εχη c. 31. και ερχονται f. οὐν e. ἔξω c. οι αδελφοι αυτου και η μηρ αυτου e. ἑστωτες c. 32. – και εκαθητο οχλος περι αυτον (ὁμοιοτ.) c. εκαθιτο ὄχλος περι c. περι αυτον οχλος πολυς bf. αυτον (*pro* αυτω) c. + και αι αδελφαί σου (*ante* εξω) e (*non* b). 33. περι αυτου c. και (*pro* η) f. 35. ποιησει c. + μου (*post* μηρ) cd (*non* b) j.

CAP. IV. 1. θαλασσει c. εν τη θαλλει (*pro* προς την θ.) c. εις πλοιον εμβαντα (– το) f. – επι της γης e. την γην f. 3. ακουσατε f. σπειρε c. 4. – του ουρανου bcdefCj (e *elot.* at κατέ *in loco*). *fin.* αυτο *mutat. in* c. 5. τα πετρωδη f. εχην c. 6. και οτε ανετειλεν ὁ ἥλιος f. μϊ c. 7. συνεπνηξαν ce. αυτω c *mutat.* ανεπνιξαν bf. εδοκεν c *p. m.* e. εποιησεν (*pro* εδωκε) f. 8. αναβαινον e. ἐν *ter.* (εις b) cf. ἐν ej. ἐξικοντα (b)(c)e. ἑκατον ce (*sic ver.* 20). 9. – αυτοις bcdefCj. 10. και ὁτε (– δε) c. κατὰ μόνας c. επηρωτων c. επερωτησαν b. + οι μαθηταὶ αυτου (*ante* οι περι) be. δωδε (d : κα *supra s. m.*). ^{κα} 11. δεδωται d *p. m.* (ο *s. m.*).

τα μυστηρια f. εξωθεν f. — τα ej. λεγεται (pro γινεται) f.
13. — πασας c. 15. ερει c. + αυτου (ante ευθεως) bf.
ακουσι d *p. m.* (ου *supra s. m.*). 16. σπειρωμενοι ce. — ευθεως
e. λαμβαννουσιν c. 17. γινομενης d. 18. ουτοι εισιν
prim. bf, *secund.* ceCj. ακουσαντες· σκαδ̇. (d *p. m.*). 19. βιου
(*pro* του αιωνος τουτου) bf. αἱ ἀπάται f. 20. ουτε εἰσὶν c
mutat. ἐν ter. bc *s. m.* Cj. 21. τεθεῖ (*pro* επιτεθῇ) bc (*non*
f). η ινα υπο την κλινην τεθη f. 22. — τι bcd. ὃ ου μη
(*pro* εαν) e. εαν d *p. m.* αν d *s. m.* 24. αντιμετριθισεται d.
προστεθῆται c. 25. εαν (*pro* ἀν) e. εχη bcde. 26. ουτος c
(*mutat. s. m.*). βαλει c. εν τη γη f. 27. καθευδει cf.
εγειρεται ef. εγηρεται c. ημερα c. βλαστανει f. μη-
κυνεται bf. 28. τον (*ante* σῖτον) bf. επειτα (*pro* ειτα
prim.) c. πληροι c. πρωτον d. 29. αποστελλη e.
30. ομοιωσομεν bcd. παραβαλλωμεν f. -βαλομεν b.
-λουμεν C. 31. κοκκον bcdefCj. σπαρει ce. μικροτερον
bf. τον (*pro* των) *bis* c. μειζον ce. μειζον παντων των
λαχανων bc. 32. κατασκινουν c. 33. — πολλαις bce.
εδυναντο bcdefC. 34. χωρεῖς e. κατηδιαν c. κατιδιαν
defCj. απελυε c. παντα επελυεν e. 35. + δε (*post* οψιας)
cd *s. m.* και τα (— δε) be. 36. παραλαμβαννουσιν c.
πλοια bf. 37. και τα (— δε) e. επεβαλεν cdCj. αυτω
d *p. m.* (ὁ *s. m.*) e. *fin.* + ωστε ηδη γεμιζεσθαι το πλοιον f.
38. εν (*pro* επι *prim.*) be. — το bcfj. πρὸσκεφάλεον c.
-αιον j. πεφήμωσω c. γαλινη cef. μελλει eCj. 40. ουτως
j. ουτος c *p. m.* ω c *s. m.* d. δηλοι c. — ουτω b. 41. ἀρα d.
αρα bd *p. m.* ουτως cd *p. m.* ουτως· πως e. οι ανεμοι bf.

CAP. V. 1. το *supra* d *s. m.* γαδαρινων cC. γεργεσηνων
bCf. 2. υπηντησεν (b)f. κατηκησιν c (οι c *s. m.*).
οικησιν d. μνημασιν bcdeCj. ἀλυσ. (*sic ver.* 4) ce. + ετι
(*ante* εδυν.) f. εδυνατο cef. 4. πεδες c *p. m.*, αι *s. m.* πεδας
d *p. m.* (αι *s. m.*) j. διἐσπάσθαι c. ισχυσε d. ισχυεν αυτον
f. 5. και ην διὰ παντος (διαπαντὸς c) νυκτος και ημερας f.
εν τοις μνημασι και εν τοις ορεσι dfC. κατὰ κόπτον bc.
6. ἀπο μακροθεν d. 7. λεγει (*pro* ειπε) f. ὁρκιζω bce. μϊ

COLLATION OF GOSPELS.

83

c *p. m.* 8. τω ακαθαρτων c *p. m.* απο (*pro* εκ) f. 9. επί-
ρωτα c. επ ηρωτα b. επηρωτησεν f. όνομα *bis* e. όνομα
σοι f. και λεγει αυτω· λεγεὼν (−απεκριθη) f. 10. παρεκαλη
c. ινα μη αποστειλει αυτον e. αγελη χοιρων (χειρων c *sic*
v. 16) μεγαλη πρόσ τω ορει (προσ το ορει c, προς τω ορει Cj,
επι τῶ ορει d, τω ορει b) βοσκομενη f. προσ το ορει e.
βοσκομενη μεγαλη e. 12. παρεκαλουν e. − παντες c.
13. επεμψεν αυτους bc (*pro* επετρεψεν) bc. − ευθεως d.
+ πασα (*post* ὡρμησε) f. κρΐμνου c, κρυμνοῦ ef. εν τη
θαλασσει c. 14. και οἱ βοσκοντες αυτους b. εφυγον f.
απηγγειλαν bcfj. 15. − και *secund.* f. − και *tertium* b.
εσχικοτα c. 16. διηγησαντο δε (− και) bcCj. ιδωντες d.
17. παρεκαλουν (*pro* ηρξαντο παρ.) bf. παρακαλὴν e.
18. εμβαντους c *p. m.* τα c *p. m.* εμβαινοντος f. μετ αυτου
ἢ fj. 19. και (*pro* ο δε ˉισ) f. πεποιηκε cdCj. 21. διαπορ.
d (*o mutatum*). πᾶλιν c. επ᾽ αυτων c *p. m.* (*o s. m.* c).
22. όνομ. bc. ἵάρειρος c *s. m. ut* ἁιρρος *p. m.* αυτων (e : ον
s. m.). αυτου εις τους ποδας f. 23. επιθεις ce. ζησεται cd
p. m., η *s. m.* 24. αυτον e (*mutat.*). 25. ρήσει αίματος c.
γυνῆ d. − τις. 26. − παρ bcf. αυτης (*pro* εαυτης) c *p.*
m. ἑ. (c *s. m.*) dj. − παρ᾽ f. ωφεληθησα c. 27. όπισθεν e.
ἅψομαι e. σωθηναι c. 29. ευθυς f (*sic v.* 30). ἵαται cef.
το σωματι c. 30. τον (*pro* των) c *p. m.* 31. συνθλι-
βοντας σε c. 33. φοβηθησα c. − και τρεμουσα c. επ᾽
αὐτην c (*v eras.*). 34. πιστης ου c *s. m.* ισθη c. 35. και f
marg. s. m. − ετι f. σκυλεις bcfe *p. m.* (λ *supra s. m.*).
36. − ευθεως bf. 38. ερχετε d *p. m.* (ε d *s. m.*). + και
(*ante* κλαιοντας) ef. + κλαυ d *p. m.* f᷉ 39. κλεετε c.
απεθαν *super rasur.* c. καθευδη c. 40. παντας cdefCj.
παραλαμβαννει c. εισπορευετε c. 41. τἁλιθαὶ c. κούμι ef.
μεθερμυνευομενον c. εγειρε b *s. m.* cc. 42. ευθυς f.
43. ειπεν αυτη δοθηναι f.

CAP. VI. 2. ακουσαντες f. σαμβατου c. τουτο c *p. m.*
de (ω c d *s. m.*). δοθησα c. δυναμις c *p. m.* (ει c *s. m.*).
+ αι (*ante* δυναμεις) b (*ut videtur*) f. − οτι cfC. ινα (*pro*
ὅτι) bej. 3. + της (*ante* μαριας) f. και αδελφος (− δε) (b)f.

6—2

84   COLLATION OF GOSPELS.

σιμωνος f (ι refectum). ἠσιν c p. m., ει c s. m.   ὧδε bd.

σκανδαλίζον (το c s. m.). — εν c.   επι (pro εν) f.   fin. αυτω
c p. m. (ε supra c s. m.).   4. + αυτου (post συγγενεσιν) cf (at
συγγενευσιν ce). προφητις c. πρίδη c.   5. εδυνατο ef.
ουκ ἤδυν c super rasuram c.   ουδὲ ἐκῆ ουδε μίαν ειμι c.

ὀλιγοις ce. αρωστοις c p. m. (ρ supra c s. m.).   εθεραπευσεν
(αυτους e supra s. m.).   6. απιστειαν c.   διδασκων d (o
p. m.).   + ὁ ἰσ (post περιηγεν) f.   7. + μαθητας αυτου (post
προσκαλεῖτε) e.   8. παρηγγιλεν c. παραγγελεν C. ερωσιν
c.   την (ante ὁδον) c p. m.   μὲ c p. m.   ζονην c.   9. αλλα
ej.   ενδυσεισθε ce (-σησθε bCd p. m., -σησθαι d s. m.).
ενδεδύσθαι ef.   10. την rasura (ante οικιαν) c.   εξελθητε
c p. m. (ει c s. m.).   11. εαν (pro αν) bdCj. δεξονται cd p.
m. (ω d s. m.) e.   ημων c p. m. (υμων c s. m.).   εκτειναξατε c.   εκτινασαται e.   τον χουν των c.   χου d (ν supra d
s. m.).   υποδηματων (pro ποδων) f.   12. μετανωῆσωσι c.
13. εξεβαλον cefC.   ἤληφον c.   ειληφον e.   πολλους αρρω-
στους ελαιω e.   14. ηρωδης ο βασιλευς be.   την ακοην ἰυ e.
ὄνομα e.   ηγερθη απο των νεκρων f.   αι δυναμεις ενεργουσιν
fj.   15. αλλη prim. c p. m. (ει s. m.).   αλλει c secund. − δε
cef.   − η cdefCj.   16. − ὁ efCj p. m.   απεκεφαλησα cd.
απο (pro εκ) f.   + των (ante νεκρων) cf.   17. − τῇ cdeCj.
18. − ὁ c.   − ὅτι f.   εχην c p. m. (εχειν c s. m.).   19. ενηχεν
c.   αυτον (pro αυτω) c.   εδυνατο f.   20. εφοβητω ce.
εφοβητο d p. m. (ειτο d s. m.).   ακουων (pro ακουσας) d.

21. γενεσιοις d (η supra s. m.).   μεγιστάσιν cde.   Marg. d
s. m. μεγιστανές εισι οἱ του βασιλέως περίβλεπτοι ὑπεξούσιοι.
χηλῐάρχοις c.   πρώτοις c (οις mutat. c).   22. ορχισαμενης c.
συνανακειμενης c.   μοι (pro με) d.   − με eC.   δοσω c.
23. − και ὤμοσεν usque ad δωσω σοι (ὁμοιοτ.) cf.   αιτησεις
d.   24. init. ὁ (pro ἡ) c.   25. μετα σπουδης ευθεως f.

σπουδεις c.   σπουδης d marg. s. m.   εξαιφνης d s. m.
ἐξαύτῆς d p. m.   ἐξαυτῆς c(C).   μη (pro μοι) e.   26. −αυτην
ef.   27. σπεκουλατορα cdefj p. m.   Marg. d s. m. η δορυφορον.

ᵉενχθηναι d (ε supra s. m.). 28. απεκεφαλησεν cd. κεφαλη (pro φυλακη) e prim. το κορασιω c p. m. d. 29. αυτω (pro αυτο) bce. — τῷ befj. 30. απηγγϊλαν c. 31. ανα-παυεσθαι c p. m. (ε c s. m.) e. ολιγον ce. ησαν c p. m. (ει c s. m.). φαγην c. ευκαιρουν bcdefCj. 32 απηλθεν bce. το (mutat.) c. το πλοιον (pro τω πλοιω) e. κατηδίαν c. κατιδιαν·ǀ defCj. το πλοιον d text. p. m. Marg. d s. m.

αναβαντ.·ǀ ·.· εν (pro τω) bf. 33. — οι οχλοι bcdefCj. αυτους (pro αυτον prim.) cef. πεζη d p. m. (οι d s. m.). [προῆλθον c.] προσηλθον de. προς αυτους d. — και συνηλθον προς αυτον bdf. ηλθον C. fin. προσηλθον αυτοις (— προς) f. 34. ο ῑσ ειδεν bef. ῐδεν c. πολλυν d. πολην e. εσπλα-γνησθη c. ευσπλαγνισθη e. ῆσαν (ει s. m.) c. μϊ c. ηρξαντο c. αυτους διδασκειν f. 35. πολη d. 36. αγω-ρασωσιν εαυτοὺς c. φαγουσιν e. 37. αποκριθῆς c. — και prim. c. αγορασομεν bc. δηναριων διακοσιων cdCj. δωσωμεν f. 38. ῐδετε γνώντες c. οι οντες (pro γνοντες) f. ἰχθυας e. 39. χλορῷ cdej. 40. ανεπεσαν bcf. πεντικοντα c. 41. — τους secund. d. κλασας bf. — και quart. f. — αυτου f. 43. κωφινους ce. + περισσευματα (ante κλασματων) f. το περισσευσαν των b. 44. ησαν c (ει c s. m.). — ώσει cdefCj.

ὡς b. πεντακισχηλιοι c. 45. τους τους μαθ e.ᵒ πλοιων c (ο supra s. m. c). προαγην c. + αυτον d marg. s. m. (post προαγειν) b. Βηθσαϊδαν ce. Βηθσαϊδᾶ f. απολυσει bcd. 46. ὄρος ce. προσευξασθε e (αι e s. m.). 47. ὀψιας ce. 48. ἰδων f. εν το ελαυνην c. τεταρτη (ν p. m.?) c. εναντιος ὁ ανεμος [habet και secund.] f. 50. — μετ αυτων bf. φοβεισθη 51. (προς αυτοις b). [εκ περισσοῦ cf.] περίσοῦ e. εθαυ-μαζον· και εξισταντο f. 52. συνηκαν (ν s. m.?) c. αυτων ἡ καρδια bcdef. ἀλλ ῆν (pro ῆν γαρ) f. 53. απηλθον εις (pro ηλθον επι) c. γεννησαρετ bcef (non d) C Lat., C Gk. προσόρμισθησαν c. 54. ἐπιγνώντες c. περὶ δραμῶντες c. fin. + οι ανδρες του τοπου bd supra s. m. 55. init. + και bd. περιεδραμον f. χωραν (pro περίχωρον) f. + και (ante ηρξαντο) f επι τους κραβαττους bf. οις b. κραβατοις c.

86 COLLATION OF GOSPELS.

κραββατοις e. 56. εαν (pro αν prim.) ce. εισε Πορεύοντο c.
+ εις (ante πολεις) c. ἐτίθεσαν f. ἀψονται ce. ἄψωνται d
s. m. ἥπτοντο (η mutat.) c. δἵεσώζοντο bd s. m.

N.B. We have indicated, in this long chapter, all the
variations (some ν εφελκυστικὰ) of Cod. c, by way of justify-
ing our report (see above, p. xxviii) of the general looseness and
want of accuracy in a manuscript otherwise of no slight value.

CAP. VII. 1. γραμματαιων cd (ε d p. m.). 2. + ὅτι (ante
κοιναις) f. τουτεστιν cdef. 3. πυγμὴ ce. νιψονται ce.
– τας cf. 4. – και tert. cf. βαπτισονται ce. χαλκειων bdj.
5. επειτα (ει mutat.) d. διὰτί bcf. ου περιπατουσιν οἱ μαθηταί σου f. παραδωσιν d. 6. προεφυτευσεν c. προεφητευσε περι
ὑμων ἠσαΐας f. ισαϊας C. 7. σεβοντε d p. m. (αι d s. m.).
διδασκαλειαις c. 8. – και ποτηριων (ὁμοιοτ.) c. πολλα
τοιαυτα ποιειται (ε supra s. m.) c. 9. τηρήσεται e. 10.
μωυσης f. 11. + αυτου (post μρι) b. κορβὰν de. ὀφεληθεις
c. 12. οὐκ ἔτι d. οὐκέτι c. – αυτου prim. bf.
13. + ἄλλα (ante παρομοια) f. 14. τον οχλον παντα f.
συνετε f. 15. ἔξωθεν f. κϊνουντα c. – απ᾽ αυτου, εκεινα f.
16. εχη c. 17. επϊρωτων c. 18. οὕτως cdefCj. 19. – τον
bf. αφαιδρονα c. καθαριζων ce. – παντα c. 21. μοιχειαι
c. πορΥειαι c. 22. πονηριαι c rescript? ασέλγειαι cdCf.
ασελγία e. βλασμιαι d (φη supra s. m.). βλασφημίαι cf.
ὑπερηφανεια c. 23. ταυτα παντα bf. εκπορευονται f.
24. εκειθεν δε (– και) f. – την bcdefj. 25. ηχε e. 26. ἡ δε
γυνη (ι b) ην bc. συρα φοινίκισσα bcj. συρα· φοινϊκϊσα d
p. m. (σσ pro σ d s. m.) efC. εκβαλη bceCj. εκβαλλει d
p. m. (η s. m.). 27. γάρ εστι καλὸν bf. κηναριοις c p. m. (υ
s. m.) (sic ver. 28). 28. ψυχϊων d p. m. (ϊ s. m.). εσθιουσιν
bef. 29. ἐξεληλύθη c. 30. ευρεν το παιδιον βεβλημενον
επι της κλινης και το δαιμονιον εξεληλυθος bf. την (της
prim.) θυγατεραν d p. m. 31. + ὁ· ισ (post εξελθων) dej.
παρα (pro προς) f. ἀνα μεσον cde. 32. μογγϊλάλων c p. m.
μογγϊλάλον dCj. 33. επιλαβομενος bC. κατιδιαν dCef.
κατήδίαν c (mutat.). κατιδιαν απο του οχλου e. αυτου

τους δακτυλους f. 34. ἐφφαθᾶ c. 35. γλώττης be. ελαλη
d p. m. (ει s. m.). 36. διεστιλατο c. μηδενὶ ce. τ to
correct ς in διεστ. d. ειπωσιν περι αυτου f. διεστελατο f.
+ αυτοι (ante μαλλον) f. 37. ὑπὲρ περϊσσος cf. ὑπερ εκ
περισσως b.

CAP. VIII. 1. παμπολου bC. — παλιν (d supra ἡμεραις
s. m. habet). παλιν πολλου (pro παμπολλου) cf. πολλου
(— παλιν) e. ο ἰσ bcf. — αυτου c. ειπεν (pro λεγει) c.
2. + τουτον (post επι) f. των οχλον df p. m. (τον df s. m.).
— ἡμερας cC. ἡμεραι bef. φαγουσι cf. 3. ἤκουσιν cj.
[ἤκασι defC.] 4. ὡδε ce. — ωδε f. αρτον ce. επ
ερημια e. 5. επιρωτα c. αρτους εχετε df. 6. την γην c.
+ και (ante ευχαριστησας) dej s. m. — αυτου c. 7. + αυτα
(ante ειπε) c. παραθηναι de. 8. + παντες (ante και ηραν)
e. περισευματα c. 9. — οι φαγοντες f. τετρακησχιλιοι
c. 10. εμβας ευθυς fj. μερι c. ὁρια (pro μερη) f. δαλμα-
νουθᾶ c. 11. fin. αυτω c. 12. στεναξας ef. αυτης (pro
αὕτη) c. αὕτη (pro ταυτη) f. 13. — εμβας f. εις το
πλοιον απηλθε παλιν f. — το prim. de. — εις το περαν f.
14. + και οἱ μαθηταὶ (ante λαβειν) dej s. m. ἑαὐτον c.
15. διεστειλατο ef. + και (supra et post ὁρᾶτε) d s. m.
16. εχωμεν cd p. m. (ο d s. m.). 17. διαλογίζεσθαι c p. m. (ε
c s. m.). ὁ ὕπω e. ὅτι (pro ἔτι) f. πεπορωμενην c.
18. jungit μνημονευετε ὅτε cC (at · ὅτε d) f. 19. + και (ante
ποσους) f. κωφινους e. κλασματων πληρεις bfC. λεγωσιν
f. 20. — δε prim. f. + αρτους (post ἑπτα prim.) cf. σπυρϊδων
mutat. d s. m. + αυτωι (ante ἑπτα secund.) f. 21. λεγει bf.
οὕπω (pro πως ου) de. συνειτε f (ι supra s. m.). 22. Βηθσαϊδα
cfC. 23. — αυτον primum d. 24. βλεψας f. — ὅτι bfCjElz.
— ὁρω bfjElz.1633. 25. πᾶλιν c. απεκατεσταθη c (non ef).
ανεβλεψε Cj. εβλεψεν (pro ενεβλεψεν) e. απαντασ d
(σ eras. bd). 26. — την f. μὴ δὲ εισελθεις c. d habet marg.
s. m. λέγων· ὕπαγε εις τον οἶκον σου, και εαν εις την κωμην
μηδὲνὶ εἴπης εν τη κωμη. 27. κεσαριας c. επιρωτα c.
— αυτοις f. 28. οἱ μεν ιωαννην τον βαπτιστην f. αλλη bis
c p. m. (οι c s. m.). — δε fc s. m. 29. — ὁ prim. d. 30. επε-

τημησεν c(d) so ver. 33.   λεγουσι c.   31. ὑπο (pro απο) f.
+των (ante αρχ. et γραμ. b only) bcdefj.   εγερθηναι (pro
αναστηναι) f.   32. – και παρρησια τον λογον ελαλει c.
33. στραφεις f.   ὀπισω cej.   34. ακολουθειν (pro ελθειν)
bcdefC.   35. εαν (pro αν primum) f.   απολεσει (-ση e) τὴν
ἑαυτοῦ ψυχὴν bceCj.   36. ᾱνος d p. m.   ᾱνον d s. m. or p. m.
κερδησει e.   κερδηση (– εαν) f.   ζημειώθη c.   ζημιωθηναι f.
– ψυχην d p. m. (habet marg. d s. m.).   37. τι γαρ δωσει
(– η) f.   38. ἐὰν (pro ἀν) df.   – αν C.   μ (pro με) c.
μηχαλ. d p. m.   μοιχαλ. d s. m.   e jungit cum cap. IX.

CAP. IX. 1. – ὅτι f.   ὧδε ce.   ὦδε d.   ἑστηκοτων ce (non
f).   γευσονται bcd s. m. e (non f).   εληλυθυια c.   2. – τον
secund. et tert. bc.   – τον ej p. m. secund. or tert. c.   κατιδιαν
d.   κατήδιαν c.   3. εγενοντο ef.   + οἷα κναφευς d.   οἷα
def.   κναφευς dj.   + οὕτως (ante λευκάναι) f.   4. [ἥλιας] f.
ἥλιας j.   ἥλιας ver. 5, 11, 12, 13 f: sic C ver. 5, 11, 12, 13.
μωση bfj.   συνλαλουντες c.   5. μωϋση bfdj.   6. ηδει d p. m.
(ειδ. d s. m.) e.   λαλησει cdefC.   ησαν c p. m. (ει c s. m.).
7. – εγενετο δὲ (– και) f.   αυτοις d p. m. (-τους d s. m.).
– λεγουσα d p. m. (supra d s. m.) fj.   ακουετε αυτου f.   + εν
ᾧ ηυδοκησα (post αγαπητός μου) c.   ακουεται c p. m.   8. εξ-
απεινα c.   Marg. d gloss s. m. ^{γρ -|} ευθεως c.   ει μη (pro αλλα)
fC.   οὐκ ἔτι d.   τὸ ῑν c.   ακουεται c p. m. (ε supra s. m.).
ἐ αὑτων c (at ου? p. m.).   9. διεστηλατο c.   διηγησονται bcd
p. m. (-σωνται d s. m.) e.   10. τουτο c.   εκρατησαν bd p. m.
(a d s. m.).   11. ὅτι d s. m. marg. ^{γρ -|} πως συν λεγουσι. επη-
ρωτησαν e.   δη c p. m. (δεῖ c s. m.).   12. πρωτος f.
13. + και (post αλλα) d.   – και (ante ηλιας) d.   ηλθεν (pro
εληλυθε) e.   περι (pro επ᾽) c.   14. + ὄχλος e.   + αυτου
(post μαθητας) f.   15. ὁ οχλος πας ιδοντες ef.   – αυτον
prim. f.   εξεθαμβηθησαν f.   16. ζητειτε προσ ἑαυτους fC.
αὐτους cde p. m. (αὑτους de s. m.).   17. – εκ (supra s. m.) d.
ἄλαλον e (c mutat.) sic ver. 25 ce.   18. ὅπου c.   καταλαβει e.
ρισσει c.   ρησσει (η d s. m., super rasuram).   ὁδοντας ce.
– αυτου c.   αυτῷ (pro αὐτὸ) c.   εκβαλλωσιν f.   19. αυτοις

(*pro* αυτω) f. 20. ἰδων d *p. m.* (ἰδον d *s. m.*) j. ευθυς f.
την γην f. εκηλυετο c. 21. ἐπἵρωτησεν c. επηρωτισε e.
+ ὁ ισ c. εξου (*pro* ὡς) f. το τουτο c. εκ παιδιοθεν f.
22. + το (*ante* πυρ) cC. αὐτὸν καὶ εις το πυρ εβαλεν c. ἵτι
(*pro* εἴ τι) c. — και *secund.* d. *fin.* ὑμας d. 23. — το (*habet*
ει) d *s. m.* — ει (*habet* το d *s. m.*). 24. απιστεια c. 25. + ὁ
(*ante* οχλος) bcdj. μὴκἔτι c. μὴκέτι e. το αλαλον πνα και
κωφον c. το αλαλον και κωφον πνα bef. εισελθεις d *p. m.*
(ἦς d *s. m.*). 26. + και (*post* πολλα) c. πολλους d. κραξας
e. σπαραξας c. — αυτον ef. απεθν *prim.* d (*sic*). 28. εισ-
ελθοντος αυτου bd *s. m.* κατηδιαν c. κατιδίαν C so
e. επηρωτων αυτου f. υμεις c. [και νηστεια] bcde.
30. κακειθεν b *p. m.* cf. αποκτενοῦσιν e *p. m.* 32. οιγνοουν
c. 33. γενωμενος c. επἵρωτα c. τους μαθητας αυτου
(*pro* αυτους) e. 34. τις αυτων μειζων ειη d *s. m.* μεῖζον c.
35. πρώτος e. 36. — εν d. αὐτῶ *secund.* e. 37. αν (*pro*
εαν) *bis* fj. 38. — δε f. — ὁ cfj. — εν bcdC. ειδαμεν e.
ὀνοματι e. εκβαλλωντα c. εκολυσαμεν c. 39. κολυεται c.
εν (*pro* επι) f. 40. — γαρ bc. καθυμων c. υπερημων bc.
ὑμων *bis* de [*cum* Elz.]. ο f. 41. ποτησει e. — τῷ dj.
εσται d *p. m.* εστε d *s. m.* — αμην λεγω ὑμιν c. 42. εαν
(*pro* ἀν) cjde. + τουτων (*post* μικρων) bd *s. m.* e. η c *p. m.*
(ει c *s. m.*). — αυτω (*ante* μαλλον) d *p. m.* μϋλικὸς *text.* d
marg. s. m. μυλωνϊκος. περίκεται c. 43. σκανδαλισει cd
s. m. σκαδαλϊζη d (ν *non insertum in* d *s. m.*). εις πυρ c
s. m. (*forsan* εκ πυρος c *p. m.*). εισελθειν εις την ζωην
bfj. 45. καλον εστι σε (*pro* σοι) bef. — τους f. 47. ζωην
(*pro* την βασιλειαν του θυ) f. + τους (*ante* δυο) f. επελθειν
(*pro* βληθηναι) f. του θυ *supra* των οὖν c *p. m.* 48. ω
(*pro* ὁ) c. σκοληξ d. — αυτων d (*supra* d *s. m.*). 49. ἀλισ-
θισθησεται c. — ἁλὶ cf. 50. αρτυεται f. εγρηνευεται c.
ἅλας e.

CAP. X. 1. και εκειθεν f. εκειθεν C. δια του *eras.* d *s. m.*
fj. — του *secund.* f. ειωθη ce. 2. — οἱ bdeC. 3, 4. μωϋσης
cf. 3. ενετηλατο c *p. m.* (ει c *s. m.*). 4. εγγραψαι f. 5. — ὁ

ιησους f.   επιστολην (pro εντολην) e.   ηυμων c (both p. m.).

ημιν c.   6. απαρχης e.   αρσε c.   8. ουκετι cef.   ρυκ ετι d.

fin. αλλα και c.   σαρξ μια bcdj.   ο̈ f p. m. (sic).   εζευξεν f.

10. παλιν e.   — του c.   — αυτου prim. f.   επηρωτισαν e.

τουτου (pro του αυτου) j.   επηρωτων f.   11. αν (pro εαν) cf.

γαμησει f.   12. απολυσασα (pro απολυση) f.   — αυτησ f.

— και secund. f.   γαμηθεισα f.   13. αυτων αψηται f.   φερουσιν

f.   14. ηγανατησε d (κ supra s. m.).   αφεται c.   — και (ante

μη) cde.   των ουρανων (pro του θυ) f.   15. — αμην f.   αμην

+ αμην c.   16. ευλεγει bce.   ευλογει, τιθεις τας χειρας επ

αυτοις (— αυτα secund.) f.   17. τις (pro εις) djC.   κληρω-

νομησω d.   ιδού τις πλουσιος προς δραμών (— τις) bc.

18. — αυτώ f.   19. μοιχευσης d p. m. (μηχ. d s. m.).   — μη

αποστερησης bc.   21. αυτων (pro αυτον) d p. m.   + ει

θελεις τελειος ειναι (post υστερει) f.   δώς c.   — τοις bcdefCj.

εξης c.   ακολουθη b.   δευρω c.   fin. + σου f.   23. βασιλεία c

(c s. m. ν).   24. — παλιν c.   ειπεν (pro λεγει) f.   — τοις

secund. bcdefCj.   25. + γαρ (post ευκ.) dC.   εισελθειν (pro

διελθειν) bcd (non ef) C.Elz.   — της bis df.   — της secund. ej.

26. δυνατε d p. m. (αι d s. m.).   27. — τω prim. cdeCj.

— τω̣ bis f.   τουτο αδυνατον εστιν bf.   — εστι secund. bf.

— παντα γαρ ad fin. vers. (ομοιοτ.) d.   28. init. — και bc.

ηρξατο δε (— και) deC.   οικολουθησαμεν c.   29. — δε bcCj.

+ ενεκεν (ante του ευαγγ.) cdCj.   30. + και π̅ρασ (post μ̅ρσ)

cf (post αδελφας) j.   μ̅ρα j.   και π̅ρα και μ̅ρα και γυναικα

και τεκνα f.   + και π̅ρα (post αδελφας) d.   μ̅ρα d.   και π̅ρσ

και μ̅ρσ e.   εκατον ταπλασιωνα c.   31. — οι bdefCj.   32. ησαν

c p. m. (ει c s. m.).   ηξαντο c (ρ supra p. m.).   αυτους (pro

αυτοις) c.   — και ακολουθουντες εφοβουντο (ομοιοτ.) bdj (:)

habet rubro marg. p. m. or s. m.   33. αναβαινωμεν e.   — τοις

secund. cefj.   παραδοσουσιν c.   αυτω (pro αυτον prim.) e, at

αὐτῶ pro αυτον bis f.   34. αὐτον prim. c p. m. (αυτω ce

s. m., forsan p. m.) bis.   εγερθησεται (pro αναστησεται) f.

35. — οι bcdefj.   + αυτωι (post λεγοντες) f.   θελωμεν ce.

+ σε (post εαν) f.   36. + ισ̅ (post ο δε) f.   37. ὑμιν (vero

αυτω eras.) c. 38. – ιησους c. δυνασθαι c. τῶ βαπτισμα
c. η (pro καὶ) f sic ver. 40. 40. – μου secund. ef.
42. κατακυριευσουσιν c. 43. ουτω bcdfC. αν (pro εαν) f.
μεγας γενεσθαι f. ὑμων διακονος bcdefC. εν ὑμιν ειναι (pro
μεγας γενεσθαι) bf. 44. εαν (pro αν) bcdC. 45. – γαρ d
(habet supra s. m.). 46. ἱκανου f. ἱεριχῶ bis c. ἱερϊχῶ d
bis, e prim. + ὁ (ante υιος) e. [βαρτιμαῖος ὁ τ. c.] – ὁ de.
εκαθιτο e. 47. – ὅτι c (insert. supra c s. m. ι̅σ̅ ὁ supra rasur.
c). 48. μᾶλον d. 49. σταθεις f. αυτῶ (pro αυτὸν) bc
p. m. αὐτῶ. φωνηθηναι e. φωνησατε αυτον f. [εγειραι
omnes.] 50. ἱματιον c. αυτον (pro τον ι̅ν̅) d. 51. λεγει
(pro ειπεν) be. θελης ce. τι σοι θελεις ποιησω ef. ινα
ποιησω b. ραμβονὶ (ου pro o s. m.) c. ῥαβουνϊ dC. ραβ-
βουνὶ befj. 52. και ὁ ι̅σ̅ (– δε) f. – και prim. supra rasuram c. ἠκολουθη c. ἠκολούθησε dCj p. m. τω ι̅ν̅ d.
ἠκολούθει e. αυτωι (pro τω ι̅ν̅) bf.

CAP. XI. 1. Βηθσφαγῆ ce (-γὴ bdfCj). + και ηλθε (post
ι̅λημ̅) f. 2. κομην c. – πωλον δεδεμενον e. κεκαθικεν ce.
εκαθισεν οὔπω f (οὔπω e). – αυτον df. 3. αποστελλει
cdfCj. ωδε cde (αποστελει e). 4. – τον bfj. fin. αυτων c
mutat. 5. ἑστηκοτων cej. ἑστωτων df. εστω των C. fin.
πολων c. 6. ειπαν c. καθὼς e. 7. επ αυτον bcf. 8. αλλοι
c p. m.? δενδρον c. fin. εν τη ὁδω d. χιτωνας (pro τα
ἱματια) e. Post ὁδον prim. desunt ad fin. versûs (ὁμοιοτ.) e.
στιβαδας f. εν τη ὁδω primum (pro εις τ. ὁ.) bf. 9. ὡσάννα
c. ὡσαννὰ def (sic ver. 10). ερχωμενος c. 10. init. + και e.
δαυϊδ plenè cC. ὡσανὰ d. 11. – καὶ tert. bfC. – της ωρας
f. fin. + μαθητων e s. m. 12. init. – και e. επινασε c.
13. ἀπὸ μακρόθεν bf. ἰδὸν c. εχουσα ef. ἠ (ει s. m.) ἄρα c.

εν αυτη (pro επ᾽ αυτην) c. ερεν (υ supra s. m.) c. εὕρεν d.
ἀρά τι εὑρήσει f. 14. – ὁ ιησους bj. μὴκέτι ef. μὴδεις
(pro οὐδεις Elz.) cC. φαγη dfCj s. m. φαγει e. ηκουσαν e
(ἡ) f. 15. ηρξαντο c. + παλιν (post ερχονται) f. πολουν-
τας c p. m. πολοῦντων c p. m. πωλ- bis script. d p. m.,
secund. eras. + τους (ante ἀγοραζ.) f. κολυβιστῶν f.

17. – ὅτι e.   αυτον εποιησατε bdf.   18. φαρισαιοι (pro
ἀρχιερεις) ef.   απολεσωσιν bcfC.   απω (o d s. m.) λεσουσιν
d p. m. e.   19. ὄψὲ ce.   20. – πρωι f.   εξηραμενην bcf.
21. ραμβὶ c.   ῥάββί ἴδε e.   εξηρανθη bd mutat. f.   22. + ὁ
(ante ισ̄) bdeCj.   – ιησους f.   ειπεν (pro λεγει) bf.   23. τουτο
c.   πιστευσει ce.   πιστευει f.   ἂν (pro ἐὰν) bc.   24. διατουτο df.   τουτο .. (rasur.) c.   αιτεισθαι ce.   αιτησητε b.
αιτῆσθε dCj.   ἐσται c (mutat. αι).   25. στηκετε bcd.   προσ-
ευχομενος (ος?) d.   26. – ο εν τοις ουρανοις f.   αφισει c.
– αφη υμιν usque ad ουρανοις (ὁμοιοτ.) bd.   27. και ὁ (?)
πρεσβυτεροι και οἱ γραμματεις f.   28. η (pro και secund.) f.
εδωκε την εξουσιαν ταυτην f.   ποιεις cej.   29. και εγω cd
(non e) Cj.   καγω υμιν ερῶ f.   ἔναν c.   30. + ποθεν ἐστιν
(post ιωαννου) cf.   – ην cf.   – αποκρίθητε μοι cdj.   31. διελογιζοντο f.   διὰ τί cef.   – ουν cf.   32. – αλλ' bc.   – εαν
defCj.   δὲ ? eras. post εαν c.   + ὡς (ante ὅτι) c.   ὥστι ὄντως
e.   – ὄντως bf.   οὖνων; def.   οχλον (pro λαον) f.   λεγουσιν
αυτω (– τω ιῡ) c.   33. αποκριθεις ὁ ισ̄ de.   ειπεν (pro λεγει)
f.   εξουσια super rasuram c.

CAP. XII. 1. εν παραβολαις αυτοις λεγειν e.   ανθρωπος
εφυτευσεν f.   εφητευσεν c.   ὤρυξεν c.   πύργον e.   2. δοῦλων
ce p. m. (o ce s. m.).   δουλον τω καιρω e.   – απο c p. m.
(habet marg. s. m.).   τῶν καρπών f.   λαβει e.   3. και (pro
οἱ δὲ) f.   εδηραν cj s. m.   καὶνὸν c.   4. – δουλον c.   + οι δε
(ante κἀκεινον) bf.   λιθοβολισαντες cej.   εκεφαλεωσαν c.
εκεφαλωσαν f.   ἠτιμωμενον e.   5. – αλλους ef.   οὕς μεν f.
δαιροντες dCj s. m.   οὓς δὲ bf.   αποκταινοντες d.   αποκτέν-
(νν b)οντες (b)cfCj.   6. εσχατον προς αυτους f.   init. + θεα-
σαμενος αυτον ερχομενον προς αυτους (ante ειπον) bfC.
– πρὸς ἑαυτους f.   οἱ (pro ἡ) c.   8. απεκτειναν αυτον και
εξεβαλον αυτον f.   9. + εκεινους (post γεωργους) f.   10. ουτως
c p. m. o s. m.   γονιας e.   11. ἔστη bc.   13. προς αυτους c.
λογον c p. m. (ω s. m.).   14. [μέλει cdefj].   + ειπε ουν ἡμιν
bf.   τι σοι δοκει (marg. s. m.: ante ἔξεστιν) f.   κεσαρι c.
οὐ e.   δουναι κηνσον καισαρι· ἢ ου δωμεν (– η μη δωμεν f)
(ὁμοιοτ.).   16. ηνεγκαν (η mutat.) c.   – αυτω bf.   17. κεσαρος

c. κεσαρι c. – ὁ ῑσ f. τα καισαρος (+ ουν b) αποδοτε bf.
18. ἐπὶρώτησαν c. επηρωτων bf. 19. μωϋσης f. [μωσης
cd.] ὅτινος (⁻ˊἐάν τι marg. s. m.) (b)?c. εξαναστησει bcde
(f dubium). 20. – ουν cdeC.Elz. (habet f). 22. ὥσ αὕτως
cef. γυνῆ e. + ουν (post εσχατη) bf. 23. – οὖν fCj.
24. διὰ τοῦτο df. εἰδώτες d p. m. (o s. m.). μηδὲ de.
25. – οἱ bcdefj. 26. εγειρωνται cd. [μωσεως c.] μωϋσεως
bc. του (pro της β.) bcej. ἀβρααμ c. ἀβρ. dj. fin. ; d.
27. θσ̄ bC Latin supra s. m. c inter θσ̄ et νεκρῶν. πολλοι ce.
πλανασθαι c. fin. ; d. 28. γραμματευς (pro των γραμ.) c.
καλος c p. m. (ω c s. m.). απεκριθη αυτοις ποια εντολὴ ἐστι
πρωτη παντων bf. παντων (pro πασων) c. 29. παντων
(– των) c p. m., at πασῶν τῶν c s. m. bdC. – κσ̄ secund. c.
ει (pro εἶς) c p. m. fin. ὑμων d. 30. + παντων (post
εντολη) cf. + και εξ ὁλης της συνεσεως (post καρδιας) e.
– σου (post ψυχης) e. 31. αὐτῆ f. αὐτη b. αυτης (pro
αὕτη) cf. αγαπησης d p. m. (-σεις d s. m.). ἑαὐτὸν de.
32. – θεος cdefCj. 33. + σου (post καρδιας et ψυχης) c.
πλειων c p. m. (o s. m. c). – των secund. bcdeC. και
εξ ολης της ψυχης και εξ ὁλης της συνέσεως f. 34. – ὁ c.
[οὐκέτι cf.] οὐκ᾽ ἔτι cdef. επερωτησαι αυτον f. 35. δαδ̄
εστιν f. 36. – γαρ c. λεγει (pro ειπεν secund.) cdeCj.
– τω prim. et secund. bcdeCj. 37. o (pro ουν) cj?. οὖν
ὁ δαβιδ c. – o C. καλει (pro λεγει) f. ὄχλως c.
ἰδεως c. 38. αυτους (pro αυτοις) f. 39. προτοκαθεδριας
c p. m. (πρω- c s. m.). πρωτοκλησιας fC. 40. κα-
ταισθίοντες c p. m. (ε c s. m.). [κρίμα cdf.] 41. απεναντι cfj. εθεωρη d p. m. (ει s. m.). πας ὁ λαος (pro πῶς ὁ
ὄχλος) d. εβαλον dfC. 42. πτωχοι (pro -η) c. κοδράντῖς
d. 43. ειπεν (pro λεγει) bcfC. + ὁ ῑσ (ante αυτοις ?) c.
43, 44. η πτωχη αὕτη (b) πλειον παντων εβαλε των βαλλοντων bf. βαλλοντων cdCj. 44. περισσευματος αυτων (pro
περισσευοντος αυτοις) f. περισσευματος d. υστερίσεως e.
εβαλλον c. εβαλλεν c.

CAP. XIII. 1. + εκ (*post* εἰς) bcC. — ἴδε c (*habet marg.* ι·
s. m.). ἴδε e. ποδαποι c. ποδαπαι c. -μαι (ν *p. m.*) f.
2. *init.* — και c. αποκριθεὶς ὁ ισ̄ dC. — μεγαλας f. + ὦδε
(*ante* λιθος) bde. επι λιθον ef. 3. ὁρος cde. ἐπίρώτων c.
κατιδιαν def (*non* c) C. 4. — ἡμιν f. — παντα f. ταυτα
παντα bcC. 5. ειπεν αυτοις (*pro* αυτος ηρξατο λεγειν) bf.
απατηση (*pro* πλανηση) f. 6. ὀνοματι c. ἐγὼ υμῖ c
7. — δε c (*supra s. m.* c). θροεῖσθαι ce. θροῆσθε f. οὔπω
cf?. 8. επι εθνος e. βασιλειαν επι βασ. c *p. m.* λοιμοι
(*pro* λιμοι) ce. αρχη ef. ὠδινων e. 9. *junyunt* συναγωγας
et δαρησεσθε cdefC. + δε (*post* ἡγεμονων) e. αχθησεσθε
(*pro* σταθησεσθε) dfj. ἑνεκεν e. *fin.* αυτοις (*mutat.*) c.
10. πρωτον δει cf. 11. αγοσιν b. αγωσιν dej. μεριμνατε
cdj. λαλησετε (*pro* -ητε) defj *s. m.* μὴδὲ cdef. ὑμεῖσ ἐστε
bcdfj. 12. — δε f. 13. — ουτος c *p. m.* (*habet marg.* c *s. m.*).
14. ἑστὼς d. ἑστὼς cej. ἑστως f. ἑστος c. + εν τοπωι
(*ante* ὅπου) f. — οἱ e *mutat.* ὅρη e. 15. δοματος cj.
μῖ c *p. m.* καταβατω *bis script.* e *p. m.* (*eras. s. m.*).
16. — ὦν c (*habet* c *infra s. m.*). ὦν e. ὀπίσω ce. 18. προσευχεσθαι c. *fin.* ἐν χειμῶνος c : *eras.* c *p. m. super* χει
forsan ε .. βα. *in marg.* c *s. m.* μὴδὲ σαβ. Cod. f *p. m. legit*
ἢ ἐν σαββατωι. 19. ἀπαρχῇ c. ἀπαρχῆς ej. εκτη-
σεν c. 20. εξελεξετο d. εκολοβοσε *secund.* c. + εκεινας
(*post* ἡμερας *bis in versu*) f. 21. *init.* — και fd *p. m.* j (*habet*
d *marg. s. m.*). αν (*pro* εαν) f. ἡμιν c. ὦδε bcd. — η bdf.
21, 22. — μη πιστευσητε *usque ad* ψευ. c (*unâ lineâ praeter-
missâ* c : *inserit* c *s. m. marg.*). 22. δοσουσι ce. αποπλα-
νησαν f. 23. ἰδου (so ver. 21) e. 24. [θλίψιν de].
σκοτισθησετε d *p. m.* (-αι d *s. m.*). 25. ἀστέραις c. αἱ
δυνάμεις οἱ c. εσονται εκ του ουρανου (b) πιπτοντες (b)f.
26. ὅψονται c. δυνάμεως καὶ δοξης πολλης bf. 27. ἀπ-
ακρου c. + της (*ante* γης) bcf. ακρων c. + του (*ante* οὐνου)
bf. 28. μαθε ce. — ηδη ef. ἀπαλος bc. εκφύη cdef.
γιγνωσκε c (τ c *s. m.*). -σκεται d. ηδη ὁ κλαδος αὐτης d.
οταν δη ο κλαδος αυτης (— ηδη) c. τα φυλλα εκφυη bf.
29. οὕτως bccfj. ἴδητε ταυτα f. γενομενα c. 30. μεχρης c.
γενηται ταυτα cj. 31. παρελευσεται cdj (-ονται fc *s. m.*).

32. η (pro και) efj. η ωρας (– της) bcc. – της secund. cdCj.
+ τω (ante ουνω) dCj. – ὁ (ante υἱὸς) c (o supra c s. m.) d.
εἰμὶ c p. m. e. οὔτε (pro ουδε) f. των ουρανων f. 33. ἀγρυπνῆτε c. 34. αποδημων f. αφιεις f. ἑκαστω ce. ενετιλατο
c. γρηγορει c. 35. + η (ante οψε) f. ὀψὲ be. – γαρ c.
μεσονυκτιον f. 36. εξεφνης cd p. m. (αι d s. m.) e. 37. ὁ
(pro ἀ) f. λεγω ὑμιν· cfj. πάση c.

CAP. XIV. 1. ἄζημα c. ὅπως (pro πως) f. – αυτον c
p. m. (habet marg. c s. m.). μὴ ποτὲ c. 2. ἵνα μη θορυβος
γενηται f. και εσται θοροβος b. 3. – τῇ bcej. πιστηκῆς c.
πολυτιμου (pro πολυτελους) c. συντρε – (ε mutat.) c. 4. – και
f. 5. ἠδύνατο c. + το μύρον (post τουτο) bcej. πραθην e.
– επανω f. ενεββρημωντο c. ενεβριμουντο f. fin. αυτην f,
at + πολλα c. 6. fin. εν εμοι (pro εις εμε) bcdCj. 7. – και
d. εσχεν bcdefCj. το σωμα μου f. προς (pro εις) c.
9. εαν (pro αν) cdefC. 10. – ὁ prim. bcdef. ίσκαρ. c. – ὁ
secund. (at supra p. m.) f. 11. ακούστες d. εχαρισαν c.
απηγγειλαντο c. αργυρια cdfj. fin. + αυτοις f. εζητη c.
12. θελης c. ετοιμασομεν dj. + σοι (ante ἵνα) c. φάγεις d.
ἑτοιμάσομέν C. σοι φαγεῖν (– ἵνα) f. 13. και sub ακολ. c
p. m. 14. αν (pro εαν) bf. – ὅτι bcef. fin. + μου c.
15. ἡμιν prim. c. ἀνώγεων dj. αναγαιον b. ανωγαιον fC.
fin. ὑμιν c p. m. 16. – αυτου f. καθὼς e. 17. ὀψιας ce.
ηλθε (pro ερχεται) f. ερχετε d. 18. αυτοις (pro ὁ ισ) bcj.
19. λεγε c. καθεις d. καθεῖς ce. λεγει αυτω· εἷς καθεις b.
εἷς καθεις f. + ειμι κε (post εγω prim.) f. 20. τρυβλϋον d.
fin. + αὐτός με παραδώσει f. 21. + οὖν (post μεν) f. η c
p. m. (ει c s. m.). 22. αυτον c p. m. (ω c s. m.). + τον (ante
αρτὸν) c. + και ευχαριστησας (ante ευλογησας) f. + και
Cj (διορθωτής). ευλογήσας (d: ι pro η? p. m.). – φαγετε
bf. 23. – το be (non f). 24. – περι c p. m. (supra c s. m.).
[-υνο-] cdf. 25. ουκετι cf. γενηματος bcfj. αὐτᾶ (αυτων?)
c. 26. εξῆλθων vel ἐξέλθων c p. m. ὅρος de. 27. τα
προβατα διασκορπισθησεται f. διασκορπισκορπήσεσθαι c.
28. μετα δε (– αλλα) d. προσάξω c (σ eras. c s. m.). ὑμῶν
C. 29. και οἱ (pro και εἰ) e, ut κἂν b. σκαδαλισθησονται d

(*non* ver. 27). + εν σοι (*ante* ἀλλ᾽) fC. 30. εφη (*pro* και
λεγει) f. + συ (*ante* σημερον) bcdefCj. – σημερον b. ει?
p. m. (*pro* ἦ) c. 31. + πετρος (*post* ὁ δε) bcde. – μαλλον
bf. δέημε bej. δεημαι c. ὁμοιως (*pro* ὥσαυτως) e. ὡς
αὕτος c *p. m.* σύν σοι αποθανειν cf. απαρνησωμαι cfCj.
32. οὗ το ὄνομα γεθσημανί e. γεθσημανὴ c *s. m.* ει *p. m.*
df. καθησατε c. ὧδε bde. + αν απελθων (*pro* ἕως) c
γρ (c)
(απελθων c *marg. s. m.*) f. προσευξομαι bcd. 33. – τον
secund. et tert. d. – τον *secund.* bcfj. παραλαμβαννει c.
34. περιλυπό d. 35. προσελθὼν bcef. + επι προσωπον
(*post* επεσεν) bcfj. 36. ἀμβᾶ c. ἀββὰ f. προσένεγκαι dj.
σοι παρενεγκεῖν f. τουτο απ᾽ ἐμοῦ bf. 37. ησχυσατε c.
ἴσχϊσας b. 39. εἰπόν c *p. m.* (ω c *s. m.*) e. απελθπροσηύξατο
d. 40. καταβαρυνόμενοι cdefj. εδυναντο (*pro* ἤδεισαν) f.
αποκριθωσιν αυτων bf. 41. – τὸ d?. απεχη? e *p. m.* (ει e
s. m.). ηγγικεν ὁ παραδιδους με f. 43. + ὁ ισκαριωτης (*ante*
εἷς) b *s. m.* cef(j). – ων bdf. ὢν e. + απεσταλμενοι (*post*
ξυλων) c. – των *secund. et tert.* bcf. γραμματαιων c.
44. σήσσημον c *p. m.* συμειον e (συσσ c *s. m.*). ἀπαγαγεται
e. 45. – ελθων (b)cj. + αυτῳ (*post* λεγει) bdej. ραμβὶ
(*pro* ῥαββὶ ῥαββὶ) c. χαιρε (*pro* ραββι *prim.*) Cf. 47. – τις
be. παρεστικότων c. επεσε bc. επαισε (ε *mutat. eras.*) d.
48. ματαμαχ. d. 49. καθημεραν cC. πληρῶσιν d. 50. εφυγον
παντες f. 51. ηκολούθησεν cdfCj. 52. καταλοιπὼν d.
53. ἅπαντες cj. 54. ἀπομακρόθεν cd. ἔσσω c. συγκαθι-
μενος e. θερμενομενος c. – προς το φως c. – c *et* b j. *p. m.*
+ το (*ante* φως) defC. 56. ἴσαι αἱ e. ἴσαι d. κατεμαρτυρουν
(*pro* εψευδομαρτυρουν) f. 58. – αλλον f. 60. – τὸ defC.
επϊρωτησε c. 61. + ισ (*ante* εσιωπα) cj. επϊρωτα c. + και
(*ante* παλιν) d. πᾶλιν e. *fin.* του θυ ευλογητου d *p. m.*
– θυ d *s. m.* 62. εκ δεξιῶν καθιμενον bef d *p. m.* Cj (η? bc
p. m.?) c. ερχωμενον c *p. m.* (ο c *s. m.*). ἐπὶ (*pro* μετα) f.
63. διερρηξε f. λεγων f. – αὑτοῦ c. εχωμεν c. + παντες
(*post* ἤκουσατε) c. 65. αυτου το προσωπον f. προφήτισον
c. + ἡμῖν χε τίς εστιν ὁ παισας σε (*post* προφ.) bf. 66. ὄντως
d *p. m.* (ο d *s. m.*). κάτω εν τῃ αυλη· f. 67. – θερμαινομενος

f. ἐμβλεψας c.   αυτον (pro αὐτῷ) d.   ναζαρινοῦ ῑῡ ῆσθα
(b)e.   68. ηρνισατο e.   ηρνεισατο d.   οὔτε (pro ουδε) bdC.
επισταμαί σοι τί (– συ) f.   ευθεως αλεκτωρ εφωνησεν f.
69. παρεστἴκοσιν c.   + και (ante οὗτος) c.   ηρξατο παλιν
παρεστῶσιν f.   71. ὀμνῦναι bd.   ὀμνῦναι e.   λεγέτε f.
72. τὸ ῥῆμα ὃ c (– ῥῆμα c p. m. c s. m. habet marg.) defCj.
απαρνησει cf.

CAP. XV. 1. γραμματαιων c.   απηγαγον (pro απηνεγκαν)
bf.   – τῷ bf.   2. επεῖρωτησεν ce.   – αυτον c.   πιλᾶτος
f (non e) fere.   3. fin. + αὐτὸς δε οὐδὲν ἀπεκρίνατο fC.
4. – παλιν f.   επἴρωτησεν c.   επηρωτα f.   5. οὐκετι cef.
οὐκ ἔτι d.   θαυμασαι f.   6. βαραβας d (β supra s. m.).
7. οἵτινες e.   πεποιηκεσαν f.   πεποιήκησαν c.   8. ἤρξαντο e.
καθῶς e.   – ἀεὶ fj.   10. παραδωκεισαν e.   παρεδωκαν f.
παραδεδόκησαν c.   οἱ c s. m. (ι c p. m.).   11. απολυσει (απε-
s. m.) c p. m.   12. – παλιν f.   + ινα (ante ποιησω) f.
14. – οἱ δε c.   περισσοτερος d.   περισσως e.   εποιησε
κακον f.   – οἱ δὲ (ad fin. vers.) f (ὁμοιοτ.).   15. ηκανον e.
φραγελωσας ce.   φραγγελλωσας d.   16. ἔσω εις την αὐλην
ej.   σπεῖραν d.   17. περιτιθεασιν αυτωι (pro ενδυουσιν
αυτον) f, bis in versu.   + την (ante πορφυραν) e.   αυτω d
mutat.   + και λεγειν (ante χαιρε) cdCj.   ὁ βασιλευς cdfC.
– αυτον secund. f.   19. την κεφαλην αυτου e.   αυτον d p. m.
(pro αυτω prim. d s. m.).   τυθεντες e.   20. ενεπεξαν c.
αυτω (pro αυτον prim.) c.   – την c (supra c s. m.).   χλαμύδα
(pro πορφυραν) (b)c.   + αυτου (post ιματια) c.   ἴδια e.
σταυρώσον e.   – αυτον ultim. bf.   21. κηρυναιον d.   κυρ?
ef.   22. γολγοθᾶν (ν eras.) bcC.   τον γολγοθὰ fj.   μεθερμηνευομενον (υ c p. m., ι c s. m. pro η) c.   23. εδιδου e.   αυτο
d.   ποιειν c.   ὃς δε (pro ὁ δε) f.   24. διαμεριζονται cdCj.
βαλόντες f.   αρει f.   25. τρήτη d p. m.   27. ἐξευονυμων cd.
[28. habent vers. bcef].   28. γραφῇ e.   29. αυτον super
rasur. (b)?c.   – ουὰ f.   – αυτων c.   καταλύον c.   30. κάτα-
βηθι f.   31. – δε bcdefCj.   αρχϊερεις c.   αρχιαρεις d.   με
(pro μετὰ) c.   λεγων (pro ελεγον) c.   fin. σωσαι bdef.
32. των ιουδαιων (pro του ῑηλ) d.   + αυτω (post πιστευσωμεν)

s.   7

bcdj. +συν (ante αυτω·) f. ονειδιζον d. ὥνειδ. c. 33. γενωμενης c. ἑκτης e. ενατης bceCj. 34. ενατη bceCj. τη
εννατη ωρα f. φονη c p. m. (ω c s. m.). λιμασαβαχθανϊ c.
λιμᾶ σαβ. d. λιμὰ beC. λεμά σαβαχθανὶ f. μεθερμυννευ-
ομεν c. – μεθερμηνευομενον f. – μου prim. cj. εγκατέλιπές
με f. 35. παρεστικοτων c. παρεστωτων f. [ἡλ.] cdj, ἡλ.
ef. 36. – τε bf. και περϊθεις d. ἄφες bc. εἶς· και e.
37. ἀφῆς c. ἀφεῖς e. 38. εσχησθη c. 39. κεντηριων cd.
παρ᾽ εστϊκῶς c. ἐξεναντίας bdef (non c). αυτω (pro αυτου)
c. οὕτως defj at οὕτως (pro οὗτος) bd (non e) [sic c, bis in
versu]. οὗτος ὁ ἀνος b. υισ θυ ἦν c(f). 40. ἀπομακροθεν
cde. – καὶ prim. e. – καὶ secund. cdj s. m. μαγδαληνη d.
-- ἡ τοῦ cef. 41. ηκολουθησαν e. διοίκονουν c. αλαι d
p. m. 42. ὀψιας c. παρασκευη ην d. 43. ἐλθὼν (pro
ἦλθεν) cdj. – ὁ f. ευσχήμον c. ἠτίσατο bc. 44. κεν-
τηριωνα c. 45. κεντηριωνος (υ pro η p. m.) c. εδωρήσατω
d. ιωσὴφ d p. m. (forsan ς pro φ, p. m.). 46. ενιλησε c.
ενείλισσε f. -λισε C. σιδώνι c. προσκυλισας c. εθηκεν
+τον (ante λιθον) f. τη θυρα d. fin.+απηλθεν c. 47. ἠωσῆ
c. τιθετε bc.

CAP. XVI. 1. σαβάτου (super ras.) c. μαγδαλινη e. – ἡ
τοῦ defCj p. m. – του secund. b. αληψωσιν c. ηγωρασαν
dC. fin. τον ϊν (pro αυτον) dCj s. m. 2. τῇ μιᾶ c (σ supra
s. m.) j s. m. εχονται c p. m. mutat. ανατήλαντος c (ει pro
η s. m.). 3. την θυ subscriptum pro τον λί c, both p. m.
μνημεου c p. m. απο (pro εκ) f. 4. μεγα σφοδρα c (σ
supra s. m.). 6. εκθαμβεῖσθαι c. -βησθε bd. ὧδε bcde.
εστρωμένον; bdf. fin. αυτων d p. m. (ο s. m.). 7. +και
(ante ειπατε) f. +ἠγερθη απο των νεκρων cj. και ἰδου
(ante προαγει) c. 8. – ταχὺ bcdefCj. 9. Nulla omissionis
suspicio. +ὁ ισ (ante πρωϊ) dCj. .... c (rubro delet) s. m.
τω καιρω εκεινω αναστας ὁ ισ (– δε) c. Marg. f σλδ αρ^χ
ἑωθιν τ p. m. μαγδαλινῇ e. εκβεβληκη c. 10. απελθουσα
(pro πορευθεισα) f. 11. υπ αυτοις primo c, αὐτῆς e p. m.

13. απηγγίλειλαν c.   14. + δε (post ὕστερον) d.   αννακει-
μενοις (ν eras.) c.   ἔνδεκα bc.   απιστειαν c.   16. απιστισας
c.   18. init. και εν ταις χερσιν j.   ὄφεις ἀροῦσιν f.   βλαψη
cdefCj.   20. [αμην] bcdefC.

Subscriptiones. Desunt in ce Τελος του κατα μαρκον
ἁγιου εὐαγγελιου: στιˣ ωγ´. εξεδοθη μετα χρονους της χυ
αναλ. συνεγραφη τὸ κατα μαρκον ἁγιον ευαγγελιον κατα
χρονους δεκα της χυ αναληψεως.

τελος του κατα μαρκον αγιου ευαγγελιου Compl. † ευαγγελιον κατα μαρκον. τελος του μαρκου ἁγιου ευαγγελιου j.

S. LUCAE EUANGELIUM.

Codd. bcdef (f hiat. ch. II. 15—47 ; V. 42 ad finem libri).
Compl., Er., St., Beza, Elz.

Note. The itacisms, breathings, accents, and transcriptional
errors are less fully recorded in the two last Gospels.

Title. Ευαγγελιον κατα λουκαν b.   το κατα λουκαν
αγιου ευαγγελιου dej.Compl.   το κατα λουκᾶν ευαγγελιον
c.   ευαγγελιον κατα λουκαν f.Erasm.

CAP. I. 2. ἀπαρχῆς def.   5. εξ εφημερίας d marg. d s. m.
εφημερῖα λεγεται ἡ πατρία· λεγεται δὲ ἡ τῆς ἡμερας λει-
τουργία.   7. ἡ f.   8. — δε d (supra d s. m.).   εναντίον be.
9. + δε (post ελαχε) c.   10. ην του λαου bcef.   11. ἑστὼς e.
ἑστῶς b.   — του θυμιαματος c (habet c s. m. ad calcem).
13. καλεσης c.   14. πολλὴ (pro πολλοι) c.   15. θυ (pro κυ)
bdf.   κατασκευασμένον e.   — του cj (supra c s. m.).   σικαιρα
c.   σικερα d, marg. p. m.   σικερα σκευαστὸν πόμα· καὶ παρ'

7—2

ἑβραίοις οὕτω λεγόμενον μέθυσμα οἶνος. ἔτι· e.   17. ἠλϊοῦ
dej. ἠλϊοῦ f.   21. εκδεχόμενος c.   22. *Deest vers. usque ad*
εν τω ναω c (*habet marg. c s. m.*) ὁμοιοτ.   ἐδυνατο f.
25. οὕτως bcdefCj.   ὄνειδος e.   26. [ναζαρετ] cdefC.
27. + και πατριᾶς (*ante* δαδ̄) bfj.   28. + αυτου (*post* ἰδοῦσα)
f.   29. επι τω λογω διεταραχθη (– αυτου) f.   31. συλλήψει
c.   τεξει c.   34. + μοι (*post* εσται) bdefj (*mutat. d marg.*).
35. + εκ σου (*ante* ἅγιον) bfCj.   γεννομενον dj.   36. ἱελισ
– c (i.e. ἱ *pro* ἠ, *eras. c s. m.*).   γηρει def.   37. – παρα e.
38. δούλον c.   39. – δε f.   ὀρεινὴν e.   40. εἰσπάσατο ce.
41. ἤκουσε τὸν ἀσπασμον της μαριας ἡ ἐλισάβετ f.   42. ἀνε-
βοήσε (*pro* ανεφωνησε) cf.   44. εσκι(c η)ρτησε το βρεφος
εν αγαλλιασει cdfCj.   45. λελαμενοις d.   48. ταπινωσιν c.
τοις δουλοις (cf. ver. 38) c.   49. μεγαλεῖα d, *at* d *s. m. marg.*
η ὑψηλα.   50. γενεῶν de, *marg.* d *s. m.* και γενεαν b.
53. καινους c.   55. ἀβραὰμ *interdum* cef.   ἀβρααμ bdj.
ἕως (+ του d) αιωνος (*pro* εις τον αιωνα) bcde, d *marg. s. m.*
58. ὐ περί η και (*pro* οἱ π.) c.   59. + του (*ante* περιτεμειν) c.
αὐτῶ (*pro* αὐτὸ) bcd *p. m.*   61. ὡς (*pro* ὃς) c.   + επι (*ante*
τω ον.) cd.   τουτω *p. m.* d (*forsan mutat.*).   62. θέλει cj.
63. ἐτίσας c.   65. αυτοις (*pro* αυτους) e.   – παντα f.
66. – ην c.   ἆρα f.   67. επληρωθη f.   74. ἀφοβος bc.
ρυσθεντα ef.   75. ὁσιοτητι e.   76. κληθησει c.   προπορευσει e.   77. ἡμων (*pro* αυτων) cef.   79. καθημενης c *p. m.*
(οις c *s. m.*).   ενκαθιμενοις e.   80. λαον (*pro* ἰσραηλ) f.

CAP. II. 1. κεσαρος c.   2. κηρηνιου c.   ἕκαστος e.   ἰδίαν
e.   4. [ναζαρετ] cdefC.   5. εγγυω c.   πριᾶς d *marg. s. m.*
η φυλῆς.   7. εσπ. d *s. m. marg.* σπαργανα τα ιματια ανων·
βρεφους δε τα ρακη.   αυτη (*pro* αυτοις) c.   καταλυ. d *s. m.*
marg. η οἰκία.   8. αγρ. d *marg. s. m.* εν τω αγρω δια
νυκτερευοντες, η αυλιζομενοι.   10. φοβεισθαι c *p. m.* (ε
s. m.) e.   + ὑμεις (*post* φοβ.) f.   11. *Deest versus* c
(*habet s. m. in calce at* be ἡμῖν).   12. εσπαργανομενον
bce.   – τῇ bcdefCj.   13. εξεφνης c.   14. [ευδοκια] bc?d.

15. ver. 15—47 *hiat*. f. ἐπ᾽ *supra* ἀπ᾽ c (both *p. m.*)
(d). – οἱ *secund*. c. ποιμεναις c. + εις (*post* ἑως) eC.
16. – και τον ιωσηφ c (*habet marg*. c *s. m.*). 17. διεγν. d
marg. s. m. ἡ ἱστορησαν. 19. συβαλλουσα d *p. m.* (μ *supra*
s. m.). 20. ὑπεστρεψαν bcdeCj. 21. + αἱ (*ante* ἡμεραι) c.
ὀκτῶ c. αυτον (*pro* το παιδιον) beCj. – και *secund*. (*eras*.)
s. m. 22. *Pro* αὑτῆς C(Beza)d *habet* αὑτῶν (*forsan* αυτων
p.m.). [αυτων] ce. μωυσεως ce. 23. διανοιγων e. 24. το
(*pro* του) δουναι e. 25. εὐλαβὶς c *p. m.* (η c *s. m.*). εὐσεβῆς
(*pro* ευλαβης) be. ην ἁγιον c (*non* d) eC. 26. ἰδειν (*pro*
ἴδη) cd *s. m.* (*non* e). 28. αυτον (*pro* αυτο) c. 30. οἶδον c.
36. προφήτης c *p. m.* (ι *s. m.*) e. αὑτη c. ετϊ cC. με (*pro*
μετα) c. 37. αὑτὴ (*pro* αὑτη) j. και αὑτῆ χεῖρα c. καὶ
αὑτὴ C. χῆρα d. ἢ bd *p. m.* (ἢ d *s. m.*). 38. – αὑτη c *p. m.*
(αὑτη *supra* c *s. m.*). [αὑτη· αὑτῆ] d. ανθομολογειτο cd.
39. ὡς *mutat*. c. ετελεσεν c. – τὰ c. την πολιν ἑαυτων (j)
ναζαρετ cdC. 40. ἐπ᾽ αυτῶ cd (d *s. m. marg.* ἐπ᾽ αὑτὸ).
fin. αυτόν C. 41. πάσχα d *p. m.* 42. ὡς (*pro* ὅτε) c.
43. τελιωσαντων e. ἱερουσαλημ d *s. m.* (-ειμ d *p. m.*).
44. νομησαντες d. συγγενεσιν (ν *s. m. supra, forsan* υ) ce.
45. ὑπέστρεψεν d. μϊ c. 46. ακουωντα d *p. m.* (οντα d
s. m.). 47. *fin*. αυτον c *p. m.* – αυτου· και ἰδόντες c. και
εγω f. 48. ὀδυνομενοι ce (ὁ C). 49. ετι (*pro* ὅτι) c.
51. ναζαρετ cdef. ἡ δε μηρ (– και) f. 52. + ὁ (*ante* Ισ) c.
ἡλικί c. σοφια και ἡλικία και χάριτι· e. + παρα (*ante*
ἀνοισ) e.

CAP. III. 1. – δε *prim*. ce. τηβεριου c. τιβερειου f.
κεσαρος c. τετραρ. *prim*. (*mutat*.) d. τραχωνιδος (τι *supra*
s. m.). ἀβιλινης d. ἀβελινῆς f. 2. ἐπι ἀρχιερεως bcdeCj.
ἅννα c. – τον bcde *p. m.* f. 4. ἠσαιου b. ἠσαιου cdef.
ετοιμασαται cd (ε d). + του (*ante* κυ) c. 5. φαραξ cd
p. m. C. ἐτραχιαι c. λίας c. ὁδους f. 6. ὄψεται c.
7. οὖν e. 8. ἀβρααμ bdfj. ἀβρ. e. τους αξιου c. 9. τῶν
δένδρον c. βάλεται d *p. m.* λ *supra* d *s. m.* 10. επηρωτον c.

αυτων d *p. m.*, ὁ *s. m.* d. [ποιησομεν d, *sic* ver. 12, 14].
ποιησωμεν (*sic* ver. 11, 14) bcefj. 12. +ὑπ ἀυτου (*post*
βαπτισθηναι) cdfj *s. m.* 14. μηδὲν (*pro* μηδὲνα) c. ὁψωνιοις⁻ᐟ
d *s. m. marg.* ὁψωνιον⁻ᐟ παρὰ τῇ θεια γραφῇ ἡ ἀφωρισμένοςⁿ
τροφή. 15. παρα (*pro* περι) c. 16. ἅπασι· λεγων f.
– εγω μεν *usque ad* ὑμας c (*habet marg.* c *s. m.*). +εις
μετανοιαν (*post* ὑμας) f. +εν (*ante* υδατι) d *s. m.* ἱμαντα d.
17. πτοῖον f. ἅλωνα f. ἀχυρον e. 18. εὑηγγελιζοντο c.
19. ἐλλεγχομενος. – φιλιππου bdj (*non* cefC). επιησε c.
20. κατεκλησε c. 22. ηὑδοκησα c. εὑδοκησα bdCj. ηὑδοκησα ef. 23. ἐτῶν, τριάκοντα· αρχομενος e *sine punctis* f.
ὁ ιησους ἦν *eras.* d. – ὁ ιησους C. *etiam* ὡσει‥ αρχομενος^{β   ͧ}
(β a d *s. m.*). ερχομενος ωσει ετων τρι. b. εἶναι.^{γρ} ἠλεί bdj.
24. ματθαν bcde. ματθά f. ἰἁννά c, ἰαννᾶ ef. 25. ματθιου
c. ἐσλί́ d *p. m.* (ι *supra* ε d *s. m.*). εσλει j. ἐσλίν e.
ἐσλείμ f. ἀγγαί d. 26. μααθί c. σεμεεί efj. ἰωσήφ be.
27. ἰωαννάν cd. ἰωναν b. ἰωανναν ef. ιωναν Cj. ρήσᾶ
ef. ροζοβαβελ e. 28. ἦρ f. 29. ἰωσῆ def. ἰωρήμ bf.
ἰωρὶμ ματταθ de. ματθαν c. 30. ἰωνᾶν c. ιωναμ b.
ἰωνάμ f. ἰαραμ j. 31. ματθαν c. μελέα defj. μαινὰν d.
μαϊνά f. ματθά f. 33. ἀμϊναδάμ c. ἀμϊναδαβ fC. ιωράμ
(*pro* ἀράμ) cd. ἐσρώμ cdeC. +του αλμεί του δονει (*ante*
του ἐσρώμ) ce. +του αλμει του αρνει του ιωραμ j. – του
φαρές ce. +του ιωράμ (*ante* ἀράμ) ef (*post* αραμ) b. +του
ιωράμ (*ante* του ἐσρώμ) f. – του φαρὲς e. 34. ἰάκωβου c.
ἀβρααμ bdj. ἀβρααμ ce. θάρρα cdefCj. 35. σερούχ
bcdfCj. ἔβερ dfc *s. m.* (*mutat. ex* ἔρεβ?) d. φάλεκ^{γ} ef
(*supra* f). φαλεγ bj. σαλᾶ e. σαλᾶ f. 37. καϊνάν e.
38. ἐνόσ c.

CAP. IV. 1. – πληρης c *p. m.* πληρης πνσ̅ ἁγιου c *s. m.*
dC. ἡμερ. τεσσακ. *cum sequent.* e (*non* f). ἤγεν c (cf. ver. 9).
εισ στὴν c. 2. συντελεσθησων e. 4. +ὁ (*ante* ισ̅) cf. – ὁ
(*ante* ἀνος̅) bcdefCj. +εκπορευομενω· δια στοματος (*ante*
θυ̅) f. 5. ἀγαγῶν c. – ὁ διαβολος e. ὅρος de. στηγμη c.

6. δοσω c. διδομη c p. *m.* (ι c s. *m.*). 7. προσκυνησεις de. ἐμοῦ bcdC. σοι d p. *m.* (d *marg. s. m.* σου *marg.*). πασα cdeC. σοι πασα bf. 8. ειπεν αυτωι bfj. ὀπισω ce. −γαρ bcd (d s. *m.* *habet supra*) eC. προσκυνησης c. προσκυνησεις‌^β

κ̅ν̅ τὸν θ̅ν̅ σου d (β a d s. *m.*). κ̅ν̅ τον θ̅ν̅ σου προσκυνησεις f. 9. ἤγεν c (γα *supra s. m.*: cf. ver. 1). −εις (*ante* ιλημ) e. ἔστησεν d. λεγει (*pro* ειπεν) f. − το d s. *m.* −o bcdef. 11. −ὅτι bcCj. − και ὅτι d. πόδαν c. −σου e. μήτε (*pro* μηποτε) e. 12. ὁ ι̅σ̅ ειπεν αυτωι f. 13. ἄχρι c. 14. φημει c. καθολην (κατ C) την περι χωρον f. 16. [την ναζαρετ] cdefC. οὗ d p. *m.* (ὅπου d *marg. s. m.*). −ην d (*supra* d s. *m.*). σαμβατων c. αὐτοῦ d p. *m.* (αυτω d s. *m.*). 17. [ἠσαΐ. cdef.] βιβλίον secund. e. 18. εἵνεκεν cd. εἵνεκεν beCj. · ευαγγελισασθαι bcdeCj. αναβλεψεν (ψ *mutat.*) c.

ιασασθε e. τη καρδια e. αποστειλε c. απεσταλκε με! ef. 19. κηρῦξαι d (*non* e *vel* ver. 18). 20. εκαθησεν c. το ὑπηρετη d. *fin.* αυτω d p. *m.* (εις αυτον d s. *m.*). 20. οἱ οφθαλμοι οἱ εν τηι συναγωγη f. 21. και ηρξατο (− δε) f. − αὕτη f. ὥσιν e. 22. χαριτος (ιτ rescript) e. 23. ιατρὶ e. ὧδε cde. 24. − ειπε δε c. − ὑμιν c. 25. − δε eC. + ὅτι (*ante* πολλαι) f. [ἠλιοῦ bcdefj (-οὺ d)]. 26. σαρεπτα c. σαρεφθα f. γυναικ (d s. *m.* a *supra*). 27. εν τωι ιηλ επι ἐλισσαιου του προφητου ef. οἱ μη (*forsan pro* ει μη) c s. *m.* εκαθερισθη e. ναιμαν f. 29. − της secund. bcdefCj. εφ ωι f. εις το d p. *m.* (ὥστε bjd *marg. s. m.*). του ορους rescript e p. *m.* προς (*pro* εις) f. κατακρημνίσαι f. 30. − δε c p. *m.* (*mutat. s. m.*). 31. ὁ ι̅σ̅ (*supra* είς) c s. *m.* σαμβασιν c p. *m.* 32. − εν (*supra*) d s. *m.* ὡς (*pro* εν) e. 34. ἔα e. συ (*pro* σοι) c. 35. ἀπ᾽ (*pro* εξ) ef. − το secund. bdeCj. 36. αληλους d (*supra* d s. *m.*). 37. επορευετο c. τοις (*pro* της) c. ἦχος d (*marg. s. m.* η φημη). ἦχος de. τοις (*pro* της) c. 38. − ή cdeCj. σιμονος secund. c. ἠρωτησεν f. 39. διεικόνει c. 40. ὅσι c. νοσσοις c. ποικιλας

de, -οις j. ἑκάστω de. ἐπὶ θεὶς ef. 41. κραυγαζοντα bcj.
– ὅτι f. λεγειν (pro λαλειν). επετιμων e. ειδεισαν c.
– ὅτι ad fin. vers. e. 42. ἐξελθὸν c p. m. (-ω c s. m.).
επορευετο e. επεζητουν cef. προς αυτον (pro ἑως αυτου) f.
κατηχον c. 43. ἀπέσταλμε. αυτων (pro της γαλιλαιας) ef.
ιουδαιας (pro γαλιλαιας) j.

CAP. V. 1. ὄχλον ce. ἑστῶς bce. ἐσ. f p. m. ἐσ. f s. m.
περι (pro παρα) dj. λιμην d (ν supra d s. m.). γενησαρετ
dfj s. m. (νν cC). 2. πλοιαρια (pro πλοια) f. δεικτυα f.
δύκτυα d p. m. (δι pro δυ s. m.). ἁλιεις ce. 3. ὀλιγον e. εκ
του πλοιου ἐδιδασκε f. 4. το δυον c (ικτ supra s. m.). ἡμων
c p. m. (ὑμων c s. m.). 5. αὑτοι d p. m. (ω d s. m.). – αυτω
b. ελαβωμεν e. 6. πληθος ιχθυων bcdefCj. διέρρυ-
γνητο c. fin. αυτον c p. m. 7. ἐλθόντος bc. αυτους
(pro αυτοις) c (forsan f). 8. γονασι (– του) bcdeCj.
εξελθαι c. εἰμὴ c s. m. 9. ἄγρα d. ἢ (pro ᾗ) cd.
10. πετρω (pro σιμωνι) d. ζογρων c. 11. δεικτυα (pro
πλοια) e. παντα f. 12. ἰδοὺ e. πληρις c. +᾽ ελθὼν (post
λεπρας) f. 14. αυτον (pro αυτω) f. προσένεγκαι d p. m.,
ε d s. m. καθὼς e. fin. αυτης c p. m. αυτοις c s. m.
μωϋσῆς f. 15. ὑπὸ (pro απο) c. 17. εγενετο δε (– και) c.
καθιμενοι e. + οἱ (ante φαρισαιοι) f. οἳ (forsan οὗ s. m.) e.
ελυλυθοτες e. ιασθαι e. 18. θῆναι e. 19. – δια bcC.
+ ὁδον (post ποιας) c s. m. marg. κληνιδιω c. πως (pro δια
ποιας) dfj. – διὰ τον οχλον c. – το (ante μεσον) e.
20. πιστην c. αφεονται c. σου (pro σοι) c. 21. διαλογι-
ζεσθαι d p. m. (-θε d s. m.). – ος λαλει βλασφημιας c (habet
marg. s. m.). εἰμὶ ce p. m. (μη c s. m.). 22. ἡμων c. δια-
λογιζεσθαι d p. m. 23. ευκοποτερον bc. σου αι αμαρτιαι
σου e (cf. ver. 20). εγειρε bce (non df). 24. παραλυτικωι
(pro παραλελυμ.) bf. τον κραββατον (pro το κλινιδιον) f.
25. εφ᾽ ὃ bf. δοξαζον c. 26. ελαβε παντας e. φοβον c.
ειδωμεν e. σιμερον c. 27. επι το de p. m. (ω d s. m.).
– καθημενον b. – επι το τελωνιον bf. 28. κατάλειπὼν c.
καταλιπὼν d(e). – αναστας f. 29. – ὁ bcdefCj. εις την
οικιαν (pro εν τη οικια) f. πολυς τελωνων bf. ἁμαρτωλων

(*pro* αλλων) f. 30. διελογιζοντο p. m. εγγογυζον e. — οἱ
secund. d. φαρισαιοις c. διατί cd. +των (*ante* τελ.) befC.
των τελονων c. πινεται c p. m. (ε *supra* c s. m.). 31. — ειπε
c. ἔχωντες d p. m. (o d s. m.). 33. διὰ τί de *raro.*
διατί c. +δε (*post* ὁμοιως) f. — οἱ (*ante* των φαρ.) d.
φαρσαιων c. 34. νηστευουσιν (*pro* εσθιουσι και πινουσι).
35. —και (*ante* ὁταν) cdefj. +καὶ (*ante* τοτε) cdf. 36. σχισει
c. συμφωνεισει c. + το (*ante* επιβλημα *secund.*) bfj. — ου
c. — επιβλημα *secund.* cC. 37. ο οινος ο νεος fj. οἱ (*pro*
ει) c. 38. νεους (*pro* καινους) f. βλητεων c (-ον c s. m.).

CAP. VI. 1. σαμβατω c p. m. —των bc. τας (*pro* τους) c.
ισθιον c. 2. τοινὲς e. ποειν c. σαμβάσην c p. m. (s. m. ἡ).
3. ειπεν προς αυτους f. ὅτε (*pro* ὁποτε) f. επινασεν c.
4. πῶς (*pro* ως) bf. + ουσιν f. + οντες (*ante* οὓς) c. οἷς
(*pro* οὓς) e. εἰ μῒ c p. m. 5. +ὁ ἰσ (*post* αυτοις) (b)f.
σαμβατου c p. m. 6. —και *prim.* beC. — εν d (*supra* d
s. m.). ἄνος εκει f. ἐκῇ c. 7. +αυτον (*post* θεραπευσει) bC
d *marg. s. m.* παρετηρουντο bf. — αυτον bdeCj. — ἱνα c.
+κατ (*post* κατηγοριαν) ce. 8. ἴδων (*pro* ηδει) c. — και
prim. f. εξηραμενην (*pro* ξηραν) ef. εγειρε bce. και (*pro*
ὁ δε) bf. 9. *jungunt* τί ἔξεστι bcdC. σαμβασιν c. *fin.*
αποκτειναι (*pro* απολεσαι) bcdefCj. 10. ειπεν αυτω (*pro* τω
ἄνω) bcdefC. οὕτως bcdCj p. m. — οὕτω e. απεκατεστάθη
c (*non* df) ej p. m. και ἐξετεινεν (*pro* ὁ δε εποιησεν ουτω) f.
11. ανιας c. ποιήσε ἂν c. ποιησοιεν d s. m. ποιήσειαν
d p. m. 12. διανικτερευων c. ὅρος e. + ὁ ἰσ (*post* ὅρος) f.
13. ὀνομασεν c (*non* ver. 14). 15. — τον του b. 17. το που
c (το c s. m. *forsan* του c p. m.: *sic* f). παιδινοῦ d p. m. (πε.
d s. m.). πασις c. νοσσων c. 18. ὀχλουμενοι *marg.* d s. m.
η ταραττομενοι. 19. ἱᾶτο e. 20. ὀφθαλμους e. ειπεν (*pro*
ἔλεγε) f. + τω πνι (*post* πτωχοὶ) f. των οὔνων (*pro* του
θυ) f. 21. πῒνωντες cd. χορτασθησεσθαι d p. m. (ε s. m.).
κλαιωντες d. γελασεται e. 22. ἔνεκεν eC. 23. χαρητε
bcdCj. τοις ουρανοις f s. m. (ω ου f p. m.). κηρτησατε d.
σκι. d s. m. πολλυς c. ἐπόουν c p. m. (οι s. m.). — γαρ ef.

τους προφητας f. 24. *init.* λην e. 25. +νυν (*post* εμ-
πεπλησμενοι) bcf. 26. −ύμιν bdeCj. ειπωσιν ύμας dC.
− παντες ceC. κατα τα αυτα f. 27. ἀλλὰ bcefCj. καλλως
d. 28. − καὶ cdj. προσευχεσθαι c. επϊρεαζοντων c. ύμας
(*pro* ύμῖν) dej. − εὐλογειτε τους καταρευμενους ὑμιν και
(ὁμοιοτ.) f (*forsan* f *p.m.* ύμας − και). − και dC. 29. +δεξιαν
(*ante* σιαγόνα) f. σοι (*pro* σε) e. 30. απετει c. 31. καθὼς
e. 32. *init.* αι e. ἀγαπόντας e. αγαθοποιηται d *p.m.,* ε
d *s. m.* f. 34. ἐαν δανιζετε bce. απελπιζετε e. − οἱ C.
ἀμαρτωλους cj. ἀμαρτωλους f. απολαβουσι e. ἴσα e
(*non* d). 35. δανίζετε c. οι υιοι C. + εν τοις ουρανοις (*post*
πολυς) f. − του bcdefCj. χσ (*pro* χρηστος) c. 36. καθὼς
e. 37. +και (*ante* μη καταδικ.) c. καταδικαζητε f. 38. διδοται
f *p. m.* (ε *supra* f *s. m.*). + και (*ante* πεπϊεσ.) c. αντιμετρι-
θησεται c. 39. μητοι c. ύδηγει; e. 40. κατϊρτισμενος c.
− ὡς ο διδασκαλος αὐτοῦ f. 41. − δε c. δαι (*pro* δε) f. τω
εν c. κατανωεις f. 42. αδελφαι c. εκβαλλω (*Ad* δϊαβλέψις
ἐκβαλεῖν *in evangeliis explicit egregius hic codex* f, Wake 34).
44. ἑκαστον e. ἰδιον e. σύκα bde. 45. προσφερει *prim.* d
(σ *eras.*). − και ο πονηρος *usque ad* προσφερει το πονηρον
(ὁμοιοτ.) c. εκ γαρ περισσευματος καρδιος (− του *et* της) be.
48. *Repetit* c *ab* πλημμυρας *usque ad fin.* ver. 48, *at* γενωμενης
c, προέρρηξεν *semel* c. 49. + την (*ante* οικιαν) dj. ἢ (*pro*
ἢ) d. ρύγμα c. − εκεινης c.

CAP. VII. 1. επι c. ταυτα (*pro* αυτου) c. 2. ἑκατον-
ταρχου d. εμελλεν bdCj. ἠμελλε e. ὑπαρχων (*pro* κακως
ἔχων) c. 3. αυτους (*pro* αυτον) e. ὅπος c. διασωσει ce.
4. σπουδεως d. ἄξιος e. ὃ (*pro* ᾧ) c. [παρεξει] ceC.
5. συναγωγεῖν c. ὑμων e. 6. αλλ' c. λογον d *p. m.* (ω
d *s. m.* e). λεγον d *s. m.* (ω d *p. m.*). μου υπο την στεγην
bdeCj. 7. ἐμαυτον ἠξιωσα e. αλλ' bcdeCj. 8. − και αλλω
ερχου και ερχεται c (*habet marg.* c *s. m.*) (ὁμοιοτ.). τούτω
c *s. m.* (τουτο jc *p. m.* e). 9. αυτον *eras.* d. ούτε
(*pro* ουδε) ceCj. πιστην c. − λεγω ὑμιν c. 10. ὑπέμφ-
θεντες (*pro* οἱ π.) c. 11. τῷ ἑξῆς c. τη ἑξης d. τῷ ἑξ
ἧς be. της πόλεως (*pro* πολυς) c. − αυτω cde. οἱ

κανοι c. 12. καὶ αὐτὴ χηρα dCj. − καὶ αὕτη χήρα c.
καὶ αυτῆ χηρα be. − ἦν bcdeCj. 13. εὐσπλαγνισθη e
ἐπ᾽ αυτην bde. 14. ἔστησαν d. 15. fin. αὐτης c (mutat.).
16. παντας bcdeC. εγειργερται e. ὑμιν c. + καὶ εν παση
τη ἰούδαια περι αυτου (post περι αυτου) c 19. επεμψαι cC.
20. ἤ (pro ἦ) e. 21. νόσσων c. 22. χολοι c. 23. σκάδα-
λισθη d (ν supra s. m.). 24. μαθητων (pro αγγελων) de.
τοις οχλοις (− προς) ceCj. ἰωανού d semel (ν d s. m.).
ἔρημων d p. m. (o d s. m.). ἐξῆλθετε bc. ἴδου e. διαγοντες
(pro ὑπαρχοντες) e. 28. γεννετοις c. −προφητης ej. μεῖζον
e bis. 29. −πας c. τῷ βάπτησμα d p. m., not d s. m.
30. εἰθετησαν e. ἠθετησαν d. Marg. d s. m. ηγ. ἐξέβαλον.
31. − εἰπε δὲ ο κσ bcdCj (habet d marg. rubro). 32. ὁμιοι c.
αγωρα c. καθιμενοις e. ὠρχησασθαι c. 34. φιλος τελωνων
bcdeCj. λεγεται (sic ver. 33) ce. 35. τεκνον c. 36. φάγει
c (forsan φάγοι d p. m.). μετ᾽ αυτων c. ανεκληθη c.
37. − τη c. + και (ante επιγνουσα) bdej. πολη c. εστιν
(pro ἦν) c. ανακηται c. 38. οπισω cde. τω ἰυ (pro αυτου
prim.) c. θρηξὶ c. 39. φαρῖσαίως c. ἅπτεται e. η ειν
(pro ει ἦν) c p. m. (mutat.). 41. χρεοφειλεται c. δανϊστῆ c.
ὀφειλε c. 42. μϊ c. αὐτὸν (pro αυτων prim.) c. 43. πλοῖον
e. ὑπολαμβαννω c. 44. γυναικαν e. −αυτης c. 45. [εισ-
ηλθον] c. [διελιπε] bc. διέλειπε e. 46. ελεω c. ειληψας
c at ἤληψε c. τους ποδας μου bc. 47. οὖ e. [ἀφέωνται d
passim]. ἀφεονται c. 49. ηρξατο d (ν supra s. m.). 50.
πιστης c.

CAP. VIII. 1. διοδενε bce. + αποστολη (post δωδεκα) c.
καπόλιν e. 2. θεραπευόμεναι e. εκ b. ὑπο (pro απο) c.
ασθενιων c. μαγδαλινὴ c (at -νῆ). ἐξεληλύθη ce. 3. ἐπὶ
τρόπου e. σωσάννα d. αυτοις (pro αυτω) bce, at αυτον d p. m.
4. τὸ (pro των) c. συνιόντως e. 5. κατέφαγον c. ἑαυτου (pro
αὐτου) eC. 6. μϊ c. ηκμαδα c. 7. απεπνηξαν ce. ακαθων
d (ν supra s. m.). 8. εις (pro επι) bcde. 9. επιρωτων d.
− αυτον d (eras.) e. + αυτω (post λέγοντες) e. 10. ακουωντες

108 COLLATION OF GOSPELS.

c. 11. ἔστη cd. 12. αἴρει e. ἔρει c. μι c. αὐτὸν? d p. m.
αυτων d s. m. 13. η (pro οἱ) c p. m. 14. πεσων c(e). ἠσὶν
c p. m. (ει s. m.). ακουοντες e. 15. − οὗτοι c. − καρδια c.
fin. + ταυτα λεγων εφωνη ὁ εχων ὦτα ακουειν ακουετω cdCj.
16. ουδεις (δὲ supra d s. m.). ουδε vel ουδεις d p. m.
τήθησιν c. ἐπὶ τηθησιν c. 17. ἔλθο⸱ c. ὑποκρυφον d.
18. − ουν c. ἀν (pro ἐαν) c secund. bcdC. μι c p. m. ἔχει
d bis secund. e. fin. + ʸᵖκαι προστεθησεται ὑμιν τοις ακουουσιν
d marg. s. m. 19. ἡ (pro οἱ) c. αυτον (pro αυτω d s. m.)
d p. m. συντηχεῖν c. 20. [λεγοντων cd p. m. C.] λεγοντες
d s. m. απηγγειλαν d s. m. απηγγελει c, -λη b. παρηγγειλε
e. ἑστηκασιν ce. 22. ανεβη c. λύμνης d p. m. + το (ante
πλοιον) e. ανιχθησαν c. 23. λελαψ bc. συνεπληρουντω c.
24. init. + και (− δε) d. επετήμησε c. κλυδονι c. γαλινη c.
25. πιστης c p. m. ἀρα bde. 26. γαδαρινων c. γεργεσηιων
b. αντίπερα bcj. 27. εξελθοντα c. ενεδεδύσκετο c. οἰκίω.
28. συ (pro σοι) cd p. m. − ιησου cj. 29. εξεθειν c.
συνηρπάκοι ce. ἀλυσεσι bc. παῖδες (pro πεδαις) c. δια-
ρύσσων c. του δαιμοσ e. 30. επιρωτησε c. επηρωτισε d.
εισηλθον c. 31. ἐπιταξει c. ἄβυσσον e. ἄβυσσων d p. m.
(ο s. m.). 32. χειρων c p. m. (mutat.). − ἱκανων βοσκομενη
d. ὄρει d. επιτρεψει c. απελθειν (pro εισελθειν) c.
33. εισηλθον cde. κρυμνου e. απεπνηγη c. 34. γεγεννημενον c (non d). − απελθοντες bcdej (habet C). 35.
ἐξηλθυ c. γεγονὼς ce. καθιμενον d. σοφρονουντα c.
37. − αυτου c. γαδαρίνων ce. γεργεσηνων b. συνηχοντο
cde. − το b. πλοιων c p. m. (ο s. m.). 38. εξεληλυθη ce.
κσ (pro ισ) e. − ισ b. 40. ὑπὸ στρεφην c. − ο d.
προσδοκωντες αυτον παντες d. 41. ἡς p. m. (pro εις).
43. συνεπνηγον c. + τις (ante γυνη) c. ἰάτροις (− εις)
bcdCj. ὑποδενος (υ s. m.) c. 44. + και (ante προσελθοῦσα)
e. ἔστη d. + δὲ (ante ὄπισθεν) c. 45. − ὁ (ante πετρ.) c.
ἀψαμενος bis bce. 47. αυτου (pro αυτῷ secund.) e. ὡ ἰαθη
e. 48. − θαρσει c. πιστης c. 49. αρχϊσυναγωγον e s. m.
(− ου e p. m.). σκύλου c. σκῦλ. b. 51. init. ελθων bcej.
+ συν αυτω d s. m. supra οὐδένα. ιωαννην και ιακωβον cdeCj.

52. κλαιεται c (ε s. m. c). 53. + το κορασιον (post απεθ.) j. 54. το κορασιον d s. m. supra παῖς. 56. γεγονὼς d¹.

CAP. IX. 1. – μαθητας αυτου bcj (habet marg. s. m.). νόσσους cde. 2. ἰᾶσθε e. 3. ερετε c. ραβδον jd s. m. ῥαβδους ced p. m. πείραν c. μῆτε quart. e. 4. – αν d (supra s. m.). εξερχεσθαι ce. 5. δεξονται bce. – απο c. ἡυμῶν (sic) c. ἐκτειναξατε e. fin. αὐτοῖς (pro ἐπ' αυτους) e. fin. ; d. 7. – δε e. τεταρχης d p. m. (ρ supra d s. m.). γενομενα c. γενωμενα e. διὐπορει c. εγειργερται απο των νεκρων e. 8. ἄλλων e. εφανη (pro ανεστη) e. 9. – ὁ cdeCj (habent). απεκεφαλησα c. 10. κατϊδιαν deC. κατ' ἰδ. c. βηθσαϊδαν be. 11. γνῶντες c. οἰκολ. e p. m. (ἡ. e s. m.). ἐλά. (sic) c. ελαλη d p. m. (ει s. m.). ἰᾶτο ἰασατο d. 12. κλινην c. κωλμας (λ eras.) d. ὧδε bc. ὧδε e. 13. πλειον d p. m. πλειους d s. m. ιχθνες δυο bcdeCj. μητι d p. m. οι d s. m. αγορασομεν d s. m. αγωρασωμεν c(C)j. 14. πεντακησχιλιοι c. κλησιας c. 15. οὕτως dCj. ανεκλιναν d (κατ s. m.). 16. εκατεκλασε c. ἰχθ. e hic. 17. κωφινοι e. 18. κατὰ μόνας c. επηρωτισεν c. ηναι c. 19. init. ὁ δὲ c p. m. οἱ δε c s. m. αλλη c p. m. οι c s. m. ἡλιαν dej. 20. – ὁ dCj. 21. επιτημησας cd p. m. παρηγγἴλε c. 22. γραμματαιων c. 23. ὀπισω cej. απαρνισασθω e. – καθ' ἡμεραν bcdeCj. ακολουθήτω cde. 24. απολεσαι (pro -σει) ce. απολεση (pro -σει) j. οὕτως c p. m. (ο s. m.). 25. – ὅλον c (habet marg. s. m.). 26. δοξει d p. m., η d s. m. τους λογους μου e. επεσχυνθη c. επεσχυνθησεται c. – αυτου και c. 27. τον (των e). ὧδε ἐστωτων bcej. ὧδε e. ὧδε bd. + ὅτι (ante εἰσίν) e. 28. ὡς (pro ὡσεὶ) c. ὀκτῶι και e. – τον bcdeC. ὄρος e. 30. ἥτινες c p. m. οἵτινες c s. m. οἵτες e. μωσης cd. μωϋσης e. ἡλιας cd. 31. οἳ d p. m. οἱ cd s. m. +και

---

¹ The collation of these manuscripts is here tedious enough. The best of them, Cod. f, has left us at Luke vi. 42. The itacisms of the rest are very numerous, while each of them gives us good or novel variations at intervals. The close resemblance of Codd. b and f disappears after S. Mark's Gospel, at least in a great measure.

(*ante* ἔλεγον) d *marg. s. m.* ἠλία d (*ν eras.*). 32. βεβαρημενη
c. βεβαρυμενοι e. 33. (ειπε) – ὁ c. ποιησομεν c. μιαν
μωση bceC. ει C. μίαν ἥλια c. 36. ὥ (? *pro* ὁ) c. 37. τω
ἐξῆς ἡμέρα c. ἐξ ῆς be. 38. δεωμαι c *p. m.* ἐπίβλεψε (-αι
C) e. 39. λαμβαννει c. καταλαμβανει e. ἐξεφνῆς c.
40. ἐκβαλωσιν bcdeCj. αυτον (*pro* αυτο) c. 41. – δε c.
ἄπιστας e. ανεξωμαι c. τον υἱόν σου ὧδε cdeCj. 42. ἰασατο e. 44. ὥτα e. ὖ ἰσ̅ (ο *supra s. m.*) c. παραδίδοσθε c.
45. ἀγνόουν c *p. m.* (η *pro* οι *s. m.*). εσθωνται e. εσθῶται d
p. m. (ν *supra s. m.*). 47. παιδιον ceCd *p. m.* (̅γ̅ρ-ου d *s. m. supra*).
αυτον (*pro* αυτο) c. αυτῶ d *p. m.* – το d *s. m.* ἑαυτῶ e.
48. αποστιλαντα c. ἡμιν c. 49. ἐκβαλλοντα (– τα) bceCj.
50. – γαρ c. αυτον d *p. m.* αυτους d *s. m.* [καθ ἡμων ὑπερ
ἡμων] cd. καθ ὑμων υπερ ὑμων be. 52. σαμαριτων; (*sic*) d.
53. αυτ̅ (i.e. αυτον?) c. 54. ειπομεν c *p. m.*, -ωμεν c *s. m.*
55. επετημησεν c. – και ειπεν *usque ad fin. ver.* 56 σῶσαι c.
ὁ ἰσ̅ (*post* δε) e. ποιου e *s. m.* οἵου *p. m.* ἐστὲ d *marg.*
s. m. ̅γ̅ρεστιν υἱὸς του ανθρωπου· οὐκ ἦλθον d. 56. κωμη (ν
s. m. supra) d. πολιν *p. m.* (*pro* κωμην) c. 57. – αυτων c.
58. κλινει d *p. m.*, ει d *supra s. m.* ἀλωπεκες e. ἀλοπεκος
c. 59. ἄφες e. διαγγελαι (ε C) e. φολεους c. κατασκϊ-
νώσεις c. 61. τοὺς (*pro* τοις) c. ᵃποτάξασθαι d *s. m.*
marg. ᵃ̅ποταξασθαι το χωρις τάξαι τοὺς πρότερον ἀλλήλοις
συντεταγμένους c. 62. ὁ ἰσ̅ προς αυτον ej. αυτου *eras.*
(*post* χειρα) e. ὀπισω e. ευθευς (*pro* εὔθετος) c.

CAP. X. 1. – δε e. ἑβδομίκοντα bc (η *s. m.*) (*sic.* ver. 17).
ανα δυο δυο e (*non* d). ἤμελλεν ej. 2. οὖν e. ὀλιγοι ce.
ὅπος c. εκβαλη cdCj. εκβαλει e. 3. ἄρνας e. 4. βαλ-
λαντιον bceC. μὴδὲ cd. μὴδένα cd. μή (d *supra* τε *s. m.*)
pro μὴ b, *et* μὴδε j. 5. εισερχεσθε d *p. m.* (-ησθε d *s. m.*).
6. – μὲν beC. – ὁ (*ante* υιος) cdeC (so Elz.). επανέπαυσατε
c. ἡμων c. 7. + και (*ante* εσθιοντες) e. – τα c. απο (*pro*
εξ) c. ἄξιος e. 8. – δ' bcej. εἰσερχεσθαι ce. δεχονται cd

p. *m.* (ω d s. *m.*) ce. ἡμας (*pro* ὑμας) c. θεραπευεται c.
9. ἤγγεικεν c. εφ ἡμας c. 10. εἰς ἥ c. εἰσέρχεσθαι ce.
δεξονται c. δέχονται be. 11. κολλυθεντα ἥμων c. ἐφ᾽
ἡμας c. ἤγγικεν ἐφ᾽ ὑμας. 12. – δε bcd (*non* e) j. πολει c
rescript. super ras. ἡ c. 13. χωραζειν (ἰν C) e. χοραζιν
bj. βηθσαϊδαν bc (ν c p. *m. eras.*) d. 13, 14. σϊδονι e.
13. καθήμενοι c. καθιμέναι e. 15. ὑψωθεῖσα c. καταβη-
βασθήσῃ e. 16. ακουων (ν *rubro*) d. αθετων *prim.* d s. *m.*
αθετησας? d p. *m.* 17. ἑβδομικοντα (*sic* ver. 1) ce. ὀνοματι
e. 18. ἑθεόρουν c. 19. διδομοι c. δεδωκα b. – την c.
20. – μαλλον bcdeCj. εγραφ d (η *supra* d s. *m.*). 21. ἠγαλ-
λιασατο e. σοφον c. συνετὸν c (ω c s. *m.*). οὗτος c. – και
στραφεις προσ τους μαθητας ειπε bcC. *Marg.* d s. *m.* πλεο-
νάζει d (*habet* c). μοι παρεδοθη bcdeCj. εἰμὶ *bis* c, *primum* e.
23. κατιδιαν deC. κατ᾽ ἰ. c. 24. – ὑμεις e. 27. ἀγαπησις
c. καρδιασου e p. *m.* (σ *supra* s. *m.*). ἑαυτὸν e (*non* ce).
28. ζησει c. 29. δικαιοῦναι c (αι c p. *m. pro* ε ?). Ἑαυτὼν
c. πλησιων c *mutat.* 30. ὑπολαβων. *Marg.* d s. *m.* ὑπο-
νοήσας ἢ αποκριθεὶς ἢ ἀντειπὼν ἢ ἀντικρούσας. κατεβενεν
e. ἰελημ c. ἱέριχῶ cd. ιερηχω e. ἰλημ e. εκδησαντες c.
– αυτον και πληγας επιθεντες c (ὁμοιοτ.). 31. κασυγκηριαν
c. κατεβενεν e s. *m.* (cf. ver. 30: αι e p. *m.*). 32. *Deest*
versus ὁμοιοτ. 33. σαμαριτης c. σαμαρεῖτις e. εὐσπλαχ-
νίσθη e. εσπλαγχνησθη c. 34. + και (*ante* επιβιβασας δε)
c. επιβηβασας δε d. ἴδιον d. και επεμελήθη αυτου *bis*
scriptum, semel eras. s. *m.* 35. επιμελίθητί c. ὅτι (*pro* ὅ τι)
deC. αὔριον e. 36. + εκ (*post* ουν) e. πλησίον δοκει σοι
cdeCj. 37. σοι (*pro* συ) c. – ποιει c. 39. αδελφοὶ c.
αδελφῇ e. οὖν e. ἢ (*pro* ἡ) be. παρακαθησασα c. ἤκουε
e. των λογων cd. 40. μέλλη c. μελλει dj. σε (*pro* σοι) c.
μη (*pro* μοι) c. 41. ὁ ἰσ ειπεν αὐτῇ de. 42. αφερεθησεται c.

CAP. XI. 1. προσευχομένων c. αυτον *mutat.* c. τὸν ἰν
supra αυτον e. καθῶς e. 2. ὅτ᾽ἀν προσεύχεσθε e. 3.
– το *eras.* d. καθημεραν bcd p. *m.* καθ᾽ η. e. 4. ἄφεσ

e. τα παραπτωματα (pro τας ἁμαρτιας) c. + τω (ante ὀφείλοντι) ej. 5. ἕξει e. πορευεται c. πορευσεται d s. m. πορευετε e. ἐρεῖ (pro ειπη) cde. μεσονυκτιου d p. m. (ω s. m.). αυτου (pro αυτω) c. 6. – μου bdeCj. – ἐξ ὁδου d. 7. παρεχετε c. 8. αυτου (pro αὐτοῦ prim.) c. ἀναίδιαν bc. ὅσον cC. χριζει c. 9. εὑρησεται e. ανογησεται c (supra o s. m.). 10. [λαμβανει; hic C, cf. ver. 26]. 11. + εξ (ante ὑμων) d s. m. ej (ὑμῶν) b. ἢ (pro ει) cdeCj (– και e). 12. init. οἱ (pro ει) bc. αιτησει (-η C) bde. 13. δοματα αγαθα bcdeCj. 14. εκβαλλον c. δαιμονιαν e p. m. (o s. m.). 15. [βεελζεβουλ ce]. + τω (ante ἄρχοντι) bd (non ce). 17. ἰδῶν (pro εἰδὼς) c. ἐρημουτε c. πίπτει c p. m. ἐφ ἑαυτῆς e. 18. ταθησεται c. λεγεται e. 19. – ει δε usque ad δαιμονια c p. m. e, habet c s. m. marg. (ὁμοιοτ.). τίνει d. [δια τοῦτο d]. εκβαλλουσι c. αυτοι κριται ὑμων d (non c). αυτοι ὑμων κριται bj. 20. + του (ante θῦ) c. ἀρα de. ἐφ᾿ ἡμασ c. – ὑμᾶς d. 21. καθοπλησμενος c. καθοπλισμενος be. φυλασσει e. ἑ αὐτοῦ e. 22. ἐπεποιθη c. επεπειθει d p. m. (ποι d s. m.). 24. εξ ελθει c p. m. (η s. m.). τοπον c. εὑρίσκων deC. 25. κοσμημενον d. 26. πονηροτερ c (a supra c s. m.). πονηρωτερα e. ελθοντα (pro εισελ.) cdeC?. 28. μενοῦνγε d marg. s. m. ἡ μᾶλλον μεν ουν· ἀκουωντες d p. m. 29. επαθρηζομενων c. εἰμὶ c. 30. καθῶς de. 31. βασίλησσα νώτου c. σολομώνος prim. c, prim. et sec. dC. σολομῶνος bis e. – και ἰδού...σολ. c ὁμοιοτ. ὧδε bcd. ὧδε e. 32. νινευίται bcej. νινευϊ d (ται supra s. m.). μετενωησαν c. 33. – δε be. κρυπτὴν bcd p. m. (o d s. m.) eCj. ἵν (a supra d s. m.). βλεπωσι το φως c. 34. – ὁ secund. c. ἁπλοῦς ce. – και prim. deC. φωτινον e. εσται cj. σκοτϊνον d. fin. + εσται ce. εστι j. 35. εστί (hiatus) c. 36. ἔχων τί e (– τι b). φωτιζει d p. m. (-ει d s. m.). 37. τὸ λαλησαι be. ἠρωτα e. αριστησει c. ελθών d marg. s. m. και εισελθὼν εις την οικιαν του φαρισαιου ανεκλιθη. 38. πρότερον (pro πρωτον) e. 39. ἔξοθεν c (ver. 40 εξωθεν d s. m., o d p. m.). καθαριζεται ce. ἁρπαγης e.

40. ἄφρονες c.　41. ἐνοντα marg. d s. m. τα ὑπάρχοντα d.
εστι c (hiatus).　42. παρερχεσθαι ce.　+ δε (post ἔδει) e.
43. τας πρωτοκαθέδριας d (την -αν d s. m.).　Marg. d s. m.,
post συναγωγαις· και την πρωτοκλϊσιαν.　αλλα ej.　ἐν τοῖς
δείπνοις d.　ασπαμους d p. m. (σ supra s. m.).　ἀγωραις
cd p. m. (o d s. m.).　44. εστε c (mutat.).　ἄδηλα e.
− οἱ secund. bceCj.　45. ὑβριζων c.　46. προσψάετε d
p. m. (υ supra s. m.).　φορτίζεται c.　49. [δια τοῦτο d].
ἀποστελλῶ c p. m. (-ελῶ c s. m.).　διωξουσιν e.　51.
ἄβελ e.　απολλϋμένου d (o pro υ d p. m.).　52. τον (pro
την) e.　αὐτῆ (pro αυτοι) c.　ησειλθετε c.　53. συνεχειν d
s. m. C.　ενεχειν dj s. m.　αποστομιζειν c.　54. − και
bcdeC.

Cap. XII. 1. επισυναχθησων ce.　+ δε c.　jungunt αυτου
πρωτον bcdeC.　ἑαύτους c.　ζύμεις d (η s. m.).　2. απο-
λυφθησεται c.　3. τϊ σκοτεία bc.　οὖς e.　ταμιοις c.　δοματων
c.　4. φοβηθη prim. (τε added s. m.) d.　αποκτενοντων
(νν b) bcdeCj.　μη c.　φοβηθῆτε cd, at φοβήθητε tert. d.
6. αντι c s. m. (supra ασσαριων) c.　επιλελησμενων d p. m.
(o s. m.).　7. − και d.　τριχαις ce.　μϊ c.　οὖν e.　φοβεισθαι
c.　διεφερεται ce.　fin. + ὑμεις c (non d) Cj.　8. ὁμολογησει
ced p. m.　− εν secund. d (supra d s. m.).　ὁμολογησω κἀγω
(pro ὁ υἱὸς του ανου ὁμολογησει) c.　9. Deest vers. (ὁμοιοτ.) c.
10. βλασφημίσαντι ce.　11. − τας prim. e.　απολογησεσθε
cd p. m. j (η supra ρ in marg. d s. m.) C.　ἢ prim. e (sic ver.
14).　15. − της e.　αὐτῶ (pro αὐτοῦ) e.　18. μειζωνας de
(d s. m. o).　γενηματα Elz.c (non d) C.　19. ετι c.　fin. ποίε
c.　20. αφρον bcdeCj.　απετουσιν d p. m. (αι d s. m.) e.
21. fin. + ταυτα λεγων φωνει· ὁ εχων ὦτα ακοειν ακουετω e.
22. μεριμνάται ce.　δια τουτο d.　λεγω ὑμιν d.　φαγετε d.
+ ἢ τι πιετε (post φαγ.) c.　μὴ δὲ cd.　ενδυσησθε de.

23. + γαρ (ante ψυχη) bc.　25. δυνται d (a supra s. m.).
προσθήναι bce.　26. οὖτε e.　27. − δε bd.　κατανωήσατε c.

s.　8

114 COLLATION OF GOSPELS.

πᾶσι c. περὶ ἐβάλλετο e. 28. + τον (post χορτον) c. ὄντα
e. αὔριον e. ὀλιγοπιστοι e. 29. πιετε c p. m. (η s. m.).
ἢ e. ετεωρίζεσθαι c. 30. − του κοσμου c. χρηζεται e.
31. − πάντα c. 32. μι c. 33. πωλησαται c. ὑπαρχωντα
c. βαλλαντια eC. [βαλαντια bd]. διαφθειρε d mutat.
s. m. 34. καρδι d. εστι d (hiatus, sexies in hoc capite) d.
35. ἕως φύες (pro αἱ οσφυες) c. 36. ἑαὐτὸν c p. m. (ω supra
s. m.). αὐτῶν bd s. m. ἑαυτων d p. m. 37. γρηγορ c (ο
mutat.). fin. αὐτοὺς e. 38. οὕτως bdeCj. 39. τοῦ (το s. m.) c.
γινῶσκεται c. ἤδη d p. m. (-ει d s. m.). την οικιαν (pro τον
οἶκον) cj. 40. γίνεσθαι c. ἔτοιμοι c. 41. ἢ c p. m. et s. m.
42. + αυτω (post ειπε δε) c. φρονημος bc. θεραπιας c.
εσται (pro εστιν) e. σῖμετριον (το supra d s. m.) d p. m.
Marg. d s. m. σῖτομετριον. ἡ σῖτοδοσία· και σῖτομετρειν το
σῖτον παρέχειν. 43. − εὑρησει c. 44. ἀλειθῶς c. − ὅτι c.
45. ἄρξεται e p. m. (-ηται s. m.). 47. − και μη ἑτοιμ. usque
ad αὑτου c ὁμοιοτ. − του κυ c (habet supra c s. m.). αὐτοῦ
(pro ἑαυτοῦ) de. ἑτοιμασας d. μηδὲ e. δαρησεται mut. e.
48. μῖ c. ἄξια e. ὀλιγας ce. ὃ (pro ᾧ secund.) e. παρε-
θετο ce. απαιτησουσιν c. 49. εἰ ηδη d p. m. (εἰ ηδη s. m.)
bd. επι (pro εις) bd. fin. (·) c. 50. συνεχωμαι c p. m. (ο
c s. m.). ἔωσοῦ d. ἕως ὅτου e. 51. [αλλ᾽ ἢ] cd p. m. (αλλα
bd s. m.). − ἢ e. 52. διαμερισμένοι d. διάμερησθησονται c.
53. πενθερα (pro -αν) d. ἐπὶ (pro ἐφ᾽) bcdeCj. − και
υἱος επι πατρι· μητηρ επι θυγατρι και c. + και (ante μηρ) e.
fin. αυτοις (pro αυτης) c. 54. λεγεται e. + ὅτι (ante
ομβρος) c. ουτ (pro ουτω) bcdeCj. 56. ἀνου (pro ουρανου)
c. του ουρανου και της γης dCj s. m. 57. κρινεται e.
58. ἐν τη ὁδω c. μὴ ποτὲ bc. αι (pro σε prim.) de.
πρακτωρ d marg. s. m. πρακτωρ ὁ τὸν ἀδικούμενον εισ-
πραττόμενος. βαλει c. βαλη ej. 59. ἐξελθεις e. τον (pro
το) bcdeC. ἀποδως d p. m. ἀποδωσης d s. m.

CAP. XIII. 1. εν εκεινω (pro εν αυτω) e. απαγγέλοντες
c. [πιλᾶτος de passim]. fin. − αυτων e. 2. δοκειται e.

3. μετανοειτε b. μετανοησετε c. μετανοησητε e. μετα-
νοῄτε d (ση d *s. m. supra*). παντως c. ὡσαύτως ce. απο-
λεισθαι e. 4. ὀκτῶ e. πῦργος e. αὐτοὶ (*pro* οὗτοι) e. 5.
+δε (*post* ουχ) d. μετανοεῖτε c. μετανοησητε ej. 6. τίς ειχεν
e. ζητων καρπον bceCj. ζητων αυτη καρπον d (εν *supra s. m.*).
7. ἰδοὺ e. ἵνα τί cde. καταργη cd *p. m.* (*mut.*). καταργει
και την γην d (β a a d *s. m.*). 8. ἕωσότου d *p. m.* (ὅ d *s. m.*).
καψω c *p. m.* (σ *supra s. m.* c). κοπρια bdeC (*non* c).
9. ποιηση d *p. m.* (-ει d *s. m.*). ποιησει e. εκκοψης e.
10. + ὁ ῑσ (*post* διδασκων) c. σάμβασιν (ν *eras.*) c. 11. ἰδοὺ
e. ασθενειας C. εχουσα c. ὀκτῶ e. 13. ανορθωθη bce.
14. ακρίθεις d *p. m.* (πο *marg.* d *s. m.*). σαμβατ *prim.* c.
το σάββατον d *p. m.* (-ω d *s. m.*). 15. ὑποκριταί bce (*non* d)
Cj. ἕκαστος e. ἢ (*pro* ἧ) e. 16. θυγατεραν ed *p. m.* (ν
eras. d), *non* c. ἀβρααμ ce (ἀβρ. bdj). ὀκτῶ e. 17. ἀντι-
κειμενοι d *p. m.* (-κημ- d *s. m.*). γϊνωμενοις c. 18. τίνη
ὡμοιώσω c. 19. σῖναπνος c. ὃν (*pro* ὃ) ceC. λαβὸν d.
αυτου (*pro* ἑαυτου) bd. ἅνος e. ηὔξανεν e. ὡς (*pro* εις) e.
μεγαν e. κατεσκήνωσαν e. 20. *init.* – και bcdeCj. 21.
εκρυψεν deC (*non* c) Elz. ἀλευρου d. ὀλον e. 23. ὀλιγοι e
(*non* c). εἰ (*pro* εἶπε) c. 24. αγωνίζεσθαι c. 25. *init.* Εφ
οὗ e. Εαν (*pro* αν, E *rubro*) e. εγερθη d. ελθη d *marg.*
s. m. αποκλησει c. ἀρξῆσθαι e. ἐστάναι ce. ἐστᾶναι j.
ἐστᾶναι d. ὑμιν (*pro* ἠμιν) c. – και αποκριθεις ερει ὑμιν c
(ὁμοιοτ.). *fin.* εσται c *p. m.* (ε *s. m.*). 26. εφαγωμεν de.
επιωμεν ce. ὑμων c *p. m.* e. ἠμων c *s. m.* e. 28. ὁδοντων
cd. ὄψεσθε Cjd *mutat.* οψισθε b. ἀβρααμ dj. 29. – απο
secund. bcdeCj. νῶτου c. ανακληθησονται bce. 30. ἰδοὺ e.
– εισι *secund.* c. 31. *init.* ν (*pro* εν) c. θελη c. 32. ἰάσεις
e. 33. αὔριον de (*non* c). ἐχομενη d *s. m.* 34. αποκτεννουσα
cd *s. m.* j. αποσταλμενους c. τα ἑαυτης νοσσία de. 35. ἰδοὺ
e. – ὑμιν c. λεγω δε (– αμην) bcdeCj. ηξει dj. ηξη c.
ηπητε c.

CAP. XIV. 1. εν το d *p. m.* ἐξελθεῖν e. 2. – ἦν e.
ὑδροπικοσ dj. ενωπιον (*pro* εμπροσθεν) d. 3. – ει c.
4. ἰασατο e. απελυ c. 5. – αποκριθεις e. υἱος (*pro* ονος)
cd *s. m.* (*non* e) j. ὁ υἱος (*pro* ονος) b. ονος η ὁ βοὺς e.
ὀνος d *p. m.* εμπεσειτε e. αὐτῶν (*pro* αυτον) c *p. m.* – εν
c. σαμβ c *p. m.* (*mutat.*) *non* ver. 1. 7. προτοκλησιας
(b)c. εξελεγοντο d (οι *supra* d *s. m.*). 8. κατακληθης
d. κατακλιθεις e. προτοκλισιαν c. εντιμωτερος c.
9. ὃς (*pro* ὁ σὲ) cd (*ut videtur*). κακεῖνον (*pro* και αυτον)
e. κατεχην c. τοῦτο e *p. m.* 10. αναπεσε bcdCj.
κεκληκὼς *prim.* e. *fin.* – σοι e. κεκληκόσ *secund.* c. ανακειμενων c. 12. – και *prim.* be. ποιεῖς be. δειπνον (*mutat.*)
d. μὴ δὲ *ter.* de. φωνῇ c. συγγενῆς c. αδελφοῦ σου d
(σ *supra* d *s. m.*). 13. ποῆς d. ποιῆς d *s. m.* 14. "Ο (τι
supra s. m.) d. 15. ταυταν c. αριστον (*pro* αρτον) bcdeCj
p. m. 17. ερχεσθαι c. ἕτοιμα e. 18. ἀπομιᾶς dC. ὑπὸ
(*pro* απο) c. παρετεῖσθαι d. ἰδεῖν e. 19. ζεύγη e. 20. [διὰ
τοῦτο] d. δια τουτο ου *bis script.* c (*semel om.*). 21. παρα-
γενώμενος c. ὀργισθῆς c. και τυφλοὺς και χωλους dCj.
ὧδε cd (*non* e). παντα (*pro* ταῦτα) e. 24. γεύσετε c.
fin. + πολλοι γαρ εισιν κλητοι· ὁλιγοι δε ἐκλεκτοι bce.
25. τῶ ι͡υ (*pro* αὐτῷ) c. 26. αὐτοῦ (*pro* ἑαυτου *prim.*)
bceCj. εἶναι μαθητῆς dC. – και την γυναικα καὶ τα τεκνα
e. 27. ὀπισω ce. λαμβανει (*pro* βασταζει) c. ειναι μου
cd. 28. πύργον cde. + ὁ (*ante* θέλων) bceCj. εις (*pro*
προς) cj. 29. αρξεσθαι c. αρξονται e. ἐμπαιζῆν cd *p. m.*
αυτον (*pro* αυτῳ) c. αυτω j. 30. – ὁ c. 31. *init.* ἢ e.
βουλεύετε c *s. m.* (-αι c *p. m.*) e. επ᾽ αυτον (? ων ?) d
(*mutat.*). ἤκοσι c. ερχωμενω c. ἐπ᾽ αυτων? c. 32. ἔστι
(*pro* ετι) c. πορρω αυτου bcdCj. πορρω αὐτοῦ ὄντως e.
33. οὖν e. τὰς (*pro* πᾶς) c. 34. ἅλας *bis* c. τήνη c.
ἀρτηθησεται c. 35. οὔτε *bis* e. ὦτα e.

CAP. XV. 1. Ἦσαν (H *rubro*) e. – οἱ *secund.* e. 2. δι-
εγόγγιζον e (*sic* c *mutat.*?). ἁμαρτωλους c. 3. ἑκατον c.
καταλήπει c (η *p. m.*, ει *s. m.* c). ἐνενηκοντα ἐννέα ceCj (-τα

εννέα bd). απολολος c. + οὗ (*post* ἕως) bc. *fin.* αὐτῶ cd
p. m. (ο d *s. m.*). 5. επιτήθησιν c. ὅμους c. αυτου (*pro*
ἑαυτου*) cdj *s. m.* 6. συγχάρηται (*sic* ver. 9) c. συγχαρειτε
e. γιτονας c (*non* ver. 9). 7. οὗτος c. – τω c. ενενήκοντα
ἐνέα cCj. οὕτως bd (*sic* ver. 10) eCj. 8. ἀπολέσῃς c.
δραχμας d. σαρει ce. σαιρει d *p. m.* (-ιρει *omiss.*). ἕωσότου
d *p. m.* ἕωσ ὁ d *s. m.* 9. δραγμην c (*non* ver. 8). συγκαλει e.
γειτωνας e. 10. *init.* οὕτω bcj. Οὗτος e. ἐν d *p. m.* ἐνὶ
d *s. m.* 12. επιβαλλων e. 13. του (*pro* μετ ου) c. ἐνὴ c.
ασωτος c (ω *supra s. m.*). 14. δαπανίσαντος c. λοιμος c.
ἤρξατο e. 15. πολητων c. – αυτου e. βοσκην χειρους c.
16. επεθυμη γεμησαι c. γεμεῖσαι e. 17. περισευουσιν c.
19. ούκέτι c (not ver. 21). [οὐκ ἔτι de]. ἄξιος e (*sic* ver.
21). 20. αυτου (*pro* ἑαυτου) cdeC. ευσπλαγχνίσθη e.
εσπλαγχνήσθη c. επεσεν c. κατεφιλη (σεν *om.*) c.
21. – και ουκετι ad *fin. vers.* c (ὁμοιοτ.). 22. χεῖραν c.
23. ἐνεγκαντε c (σ *supra p. m.?*). 24. ἦν e. ἀπολωλος cd
p. m. (ω d *s. m.*). ηυρεθη c. 25. – αυτου beCj. ἐρχωμενος c.
χωρων d *p. m.* (ο d *s. m.*). 26. ἐπινθάνετο c. 27. μουσχον c.
ὑγιένοντα e. 28. ὠργησθη c. οὖν e. 29. ἴδου e. φιλων
(ο *p. m.*) e *s. m.* 30. αυτου (*pro* αυτῶ) c. *fin.* ; c. 32. ἀπολωλος ce. ηὑρεθη c.

CAP. XVI. 1. – καὶ *prim.* ej. οἰκόνομον e *pass.* ὑπαρχωντα c. 2. τοῦτω e. ακουων c. – σου *secund.* δυνησει
ce. ἑαυτοῦ c. σκαπτην c. 4. ὅτ'ἂν cde *fere passim.*
δέξονται ce. 5. χρεοφειλετων c. αυτου (*pro* ἑαυτου) cd
s. m. ειπεν (*pro* ἔλεγε) e. ὀφειλης e. οφφειλεις c.
6. ἑκατὸν c. βαάδους (*pro* βατους) c. – σου bc. 7. ὀγδοη-
κοντα c. 8. επαινεσεν c. φρονίμος d *p. m.* (ω d *s. m.*).
– οἱ c. φρονημοτεροι c. 9. εκληπητε c. εκλειπητε dCj *s. m.*
δεξονται bce. μαμωνα. *Marg.* d *s. m.* μαμωνᾶς γήινος
πλοῦτος περιττὸς καὶ ὑπὲρ τὴν χρείαν. 11. ἐγένεσθαι c.
– το αληθινὸν *usque ad* ἐγένεσθε ver. 12 c (ὁμοιοτ.). 12. ἡ-
μετερον c. 13. – του d. ἢ *prim.* ἢ *secund.* e. μισισει c.
δυνασθαι c. δουλεύην c. 14. ἤκουων c. φιλαργυροι d
mutat. ὑπαρχωντες c. – και *secund.* c. 15. *fin.* – εστιν ej.

118   COLLATION OF GOSPELS.

16. ἀποτότε ce. + ὁ βουλομενος εἰσελθειν (post πᾶς) c.
17. ἤ de. 18. – καὶ πας ὁ ad fin. vers. e (ὁμοιοτ.).
19. καθημεραν bdeC. καθ ἡ. c. βύσσον. Marg. superior
d s. m. βύσσος βαφὴ ἐκ πορφύρας. εὐφραινουμενος d (v eras.).
20. λαμπρος d p. m. (o d s. m.). εκβεβλητο c. εἱλκομενος
d p. m. (ω pro o d s. m.). προ των πυλων (pro προς τον
πυλωνα) e. 21. ψυχίων ce (e + των) mutat. 22. αποθανην
c. – του bcej. ἀβρααμ bcdj ferè. ἀβ. e passim. 23. ἄδει
c p. m. (η d s. m. subs.). απομακροθεν cde. 24. κατὰ
ψύξει c. ὁδυνωμαι e. 25. ὧδε (pro ὅδε) be. ὁδυνᾶσαι e.
26. χάσμα d. ἔνθεν (pro εντευθεν) bcdCj. δύνονται cd
p. m. (ω d s. m.). Post ὅπως pars folii exciditur in e usque
ad finem ver. 30. 28. πέν[τε] d s. m. 29. – εχουσι usque
ad αβρααμ ver. 30 c (ὁμοιοτ.). 30. μετανοησωσιν c.
31. [μωσεως] ce. ἄν c (ε p. m.). πισθησονται c.

CAP. XVII. 1. + αυτου (post μαθητὰς) c. [ανενδ. c].
του eras. (ante μη) d s. m. at habet του cC (non Elz.).
εἰσελθεὶν e. σκάδαλα d p. m. (v insert. d s. m.). 2. λυσιτελῆ
c. μίλος c. μνον. Marg. d s. m. λιθος μυλϊκὸς bj. μετα-
νωηση c p. m. (ο pro ω c s. m.). ἄφες e. 4. ἐπτακις prim. c,
bis e. – της secund. d. επιστρεψει c. – επι σε bcdeCj.
μετανοω (v eras.) c. 5. ἀποστωλοι d p. m. (o s. m.).
6. ἔχετε bd. Cod. e hiat. usque ad fin. ver. 8 (cf. chap. XVI.
18). 7. + αυτου d s. m. (supra et post ἐρεῖ) j. ανάπεσον c.
ανάπεσε bdCj. 8. οὐχι (mutat.) c. ιάκονει c. 9. τα
διδαχθεντα (non ver. 10). – αυτω bcdeCj. 10. οὕτως bcCj.
ουτως de. ἡμεις c. λεγεται e. – ὅτι prim. e, secund. bj
p. m. αχρειοι δουλοι e. ὀφειλομεν ed p. m. C. ωφ. d s. m.
πεηκαμεν d p. m. (ποι supra d s. m.). 11. – αυτον d (habet
marg. s. m.). 12. – αυτου e (at του ιυ init. lectionis). ἔστησαν
c. 13. ἦραν e. επιστα c. 14. αὐτοὺς e (ἐ supra c s. m.).
15. εἷς e. ἰδὼν e. ἄθη e. 16. περὶ (pro παρα) c. fin. τῖς
d p. m. – της d s. m. 17. εκαθερισθησαν c. 18. θῶ; cd.

20. επερωτιθεις c. ^{φαρ}αιων d (φαρ supra s. m.). – απεκριθη usque ad θυ c ὅμοιοτ. παρετηρήσεως c. 21. ὧδε d. ὧδε e (non ver. 23) c. – ἢ cC. ἰδοὺ prim. et secund. at ἰδοὺ tert. e. 22. ἐπιθυμῆτε e. 23. ἰδοὺ et ἰδοὺ e. + εαν (ante ερουσιν) c. – ἢ ceC. μὴ δὲ e. ὀξῇτε c (δ supra c p. m.). 24. αστραπτου c. τον (pro την) dj. οὐνον in marg., non textu, c. λαμπη e. – καὶ bcdeCj. 26. καθὼς hic e. – του prim. bcdeCj.Elz. + του (ante υἱοῦ) cdeC. 27. εγαμιζοντο c. ἀπολεσεν e. 28. εφύτευων c. 31. ὀπίσω e. 33. +αυτην (post σῶσαι) c. απολεση d p. m. (ει s. m.). ὡ b p. m. ὡς d p. m. (ο pro ω d s. m.). εαν d (ε eras.) p. m. απολεσει d p. m. (η d s. m.) j. ζωοποιησει (pro ζωογονησει) ej. 34. δύο εσονται d. – ὁ prim. bcdeCj. – ὁ secund. bj p. m. 35. ἐπι το αυτο c. –ἢ prim. cdC.Elz. παραλαμβανεται c. 36. Deest versus cde habent ver. bC. 37. πτῶμα (pro σωμα) c. +και (ante οἱ) dC. οἱ ἀετοὶ συναχθήσονται e.

CAP. XVIII. 1. ἔλε c. [εκκ. c]. + αυτους (ante προσευχεσθαι) be. 2. κριτῆς d p. m. 3. – τις d (habet j) Elz. χεῖρα c. 4. ηθελεν dj s. m. 5. με (pro μοι, ante κοπον) e s. m. χειρα (pro χηραν) c. ὑποπιαζη cC. ὑπόπιεζη be. 6. δε (mutat.) d. 7. ποιηση bdCj (d mutat.? ει p. m.). βοοντων ce. 8. init.+ ναι cCj. – ἄρα d p. m. (supra d s. m.). ἄρα bcj. εὑρησει e. 9. – καὶ prim. bcdeCj. 11. σταθες, προς c. λιποι e. ἄρπαγες e. ἄδικοι e. 13. ἐστὼς c. νηστεύων c. ἔτυπτε (– εἰς) e. 14. οὗτος e. δεδικαιόμενος c. +γαρ (post ἢ) bcdeCj (γαρ eras. d). ὅ^{τι}d p. m. 15. προ Εφερον d p. m. (σ supra s. m. E rubro). 16. ἄφεται e. 17. ἐὸν d p. m. ἂν d s. m. εισελθει e. 18. επηρώτησεν (b)c. επηρωτοσεν d. αυτον αρχων d (τις^{τις} s. m. ὸς p. m.). 19. εἶς e. 20. fin. – σου e. 22. σοι (mutat.) d. λήπει c. παν^{τα}d (τα supra d s. m.). πώλισον e. ἔχης c. ἔξης c. ἔξεις de. ακολουθη e. 25. ευκοποτερον c. καμιλον c. διατριμαλιὰς e. διελθεὶν (pro εἰσελθειν prim.) e (non cd). – ἢ πλούσιον ad fin. vers. (ὅμοιοτ.) c. 28. – ὁ deCj. ἰδοὺ e.

120 COLLATION OF GOSPELS.

29. + ἀμὴν (post ἀμὴν) e. ἐν...κεν and $\overset{κα}{\text{κα}}$ d s. m. 30. καὶ (pro ὃς) c. πολλαπλασιωνα c. επερχομενω e. 31. ανα-βαινωμεν c. τελεσθ (σθ mutat.) d. $\overset{γε}{\text{γραμμένα}}$ d (γε supra s. m.). τῷ υἱω d p. m. $\overset{περι}{\text{του}}$ υἱου d s. m. 32. εμπεχθησεται c. $\overset{μ}{\text{επ.}}$ d p. m., ut videtur. 32, 33. – καὶ ὑβρισθησεται b huc usque ad fin. vers. c (ὁμοιοτ.). 33. και τη τριτη ἡμερα eCj. εγερθησεται e. 34. συνηκαν (mutat.) e. αλλ' ἦν (pro και ην το ρημα) e. – και secund. j. 35. εγγιζην c. ἱεριχῶ (c)ed p. m. – τις c. εκαθητο d (ι rubro). 36. πορευομενου c. επινθανετο c. 39. επετημων e. 40. επηρωτισεν e. 41. αναβλέψω d (ι pro ε s. m.). 42. ἐνέβλεψε d s. m. αν- d forsan p. m. 41, 42. – ειπε usque ad ὁ ἰσ c (idem clausulæ initium).

CAP. XIX. 1. ἐλθων d. ἱεριχῶ cde. 2. ἰδοὺ d. ὀνοματι d. εστη c. οὗτος πλουσιος (– ην) d. 3. ἰδεὶν e. 4. προ-δραμων c (vel potius προσδρ.). προσδραμων dC (not e). συκομοραῖαν ce (-αίαν) j p. m. συκομορέαν b p. m. ej s. m. ἴδει e. – δι' bcd (habet supra d s. m.) ej. ἤμελλεν (ν eras.) cd (δ pro ν s. m.). ερχεσθαι d p. m. 5. ζαχέε (non ver. 8) c. 6. ὑπεδεξατον (– αυτον) c. 7. παντες bc. 8. εἶ ($\overset{πε}{\text{πε}}$ supra d s. m.) d. $\overline{κν}$ d p. m. ($\overline{ιν}$ d s. m.). ἠμιση e. διδωμοι de. 9. τῷ (mutat.) ce. ἁβρααμ bcd (ἀβ. e) j. 10. ἀπολός c. 11. αυτω (pro αυτον) c. + εἰς (ante ιλημ) ce. αυτοις (pro αυτους) e. ἠ βασιλεῖα του θῦ· μελλει (sic) c. 13. πραγ-ματενεσθε c. πραγματεύσασθαι ed p. m. (-θε d s. m.). 14. ὀπισω ce. ὀπησω d p. m. (ι pro η d s. m.). θέλωμεν e. 15. – και secund. bdj. φωνιθηναι e. εδωκει e. εδεδωκει j. επραγματευσατο e. 16. ἡ μνασ σου bcd (σ eras. d): sic ver. 15, 18, 20. προσηργασατο e. 17. ἴσθη c. δέ[κα] c. 20. ἦν d. 21. αἴρεις e. 22. – δε ej. αἴρων e. εἰμι; c. 23. διά τί c. διὰ τί e. – την bcde. τοις τραπεζιταις C. 24. εχωντι d p. m. (ο d s. m.). 26. init. Ὁ (rubro) δε ειπεν λεγω ὑμῖν e. – γαρ ce. 27. – εκεινους c. θελισαντας d mutat. e. ἀγαγεται e. ὦδε ce. ὦδε d. σφάξατε c.

28. αναβαινον e.   29. – εγενετο c.   βηθσφαγῆ cde (-γὴ)
C. βηθσφαγὴν j.   ὁρος ce.   30. ειπων d p. m. (λεγων supra
d s. m.).   απεναντι e.   εὑρησεται ce (εὑ. e).   εκαθισεν; e.
31. διάτί c.   διατΐ d.   διὰ τί e.   οὕτως (rescript super
rasuram) c.   32. καθὼς e.   35. ἤγαγον e.   επιρρ. ce.
επεβηβασαν be.   36. τα ἱματια ἐν τη ὁδω αυτων e.   αυτου
(mutat.) c p. m.   37. ἤδη e.   ἤρξατο be.   χαιρωντες cd.
38. – βασιλευς c.   39. αυτον (– προς) c.   επετημησον e.
40. σιωπισωσιν e.   41. ω (pro ὡς) c.   επ᾽ αυτην d.
42. – σου prim. c.   σ‿ (οι mut.) d s. m. (σου d p. m.).
43. ἤξουσιν d.   ἐπὶβαλοῦσιν c.   περικυκλωσωσιν (ου pro ω
e p. m.).   44. – και ουκ αφησουσιν εν σοι c (ὁμοιοτ.).
45. ἤρξατο e.   εν αυτω αγοραζοντας εν αυτω και sic d p. m.
46. οἶκος c (secund. tantum).   κληθήσαται (ε pro a s. m.) c.
εποιησαται c p. m.   -τε c s. m.   47. ἦν e.   διδασκον c.   το
eras. (b)dj.   καθημεραν bcdeC.   – οἱ secund. c.   48. ποιησουσιν cdCj.

Cap. XX. 1. – εκεινων e.   διδασκοντος αυτου (mutat.) d.
ευαγγελιζομενον d p. m.   -ου d s. m.   ἱερεῖς (– οἱ) bd p. m.
οἱ αρχ. supra s. m.   ἱρεις cj.   γραμματῖς c.   2. εστι c p. m.
3. λον (pro λογον) e.   αποκρίθητέ (pro εἴπατε) c.   5. διὰ
τί c.   διὰ τί d.   διὰ τί e.   – οὖν bcdeCj s. m.   6. εστι
ιωανν. c.   fin. ειναι c p. m.   ηναι c s. m.   9. – τις bced p. m.
Cj (τις supra s. m.).   10. + τω (ante καιρω) d.   δηραντες
dej s. m.   απεστειλαν c (εξ c s. m. early).   καινον c.
11. ἑτερον πεμψαι c.   τυψαντες (pro δειραντες) cj s. m.
καινόν c.   13. ἴσος c.   ἴσως e.   14. ἰδοντες e.   διελογισαντο
e.   ἑαὑτὸν (pro ἑαυτους) c.   15. – αυτον d p. m. (habet supra
d s. m.).   απελῶνος d (μ supra).   απελῶνα d (μ supra, eras.).
17. + τουτον (ante τουτο) c.   γεγραμενον c.   18. ἐφ᾽ ὧν d.
λικμηση d.   19. – και tert. c.   – τον λαον bdeC.   20. απο-
κρινομενους de p. m.   ὑπ. de s. m.   ἐπὶλαβονται ce.   εγκαθ.
d.   Marg. d s. m. εφεδρους.   λογον d p. m.   λογου s. m.
ἡγεμῶνος bcd.   21. αληθως (pro ορθως) c.   λαμβαννεις c.

23. κατάνωήσας c.   αυτον (pro αυτων) c.   πονηριαν (pro
πανουργιαν) e.   πειράζεται ce.   fin.+ὑποκριταί ce.   24. +οἱ
δε ἐδειξαν και ειπε (post δηναριον) cj.   26. ἤσχυσαν c.
ἐπιλαβέσθε e.   28. μωϋσῆς cC.   εχων erasum (post αποθανη
secund.) c.   ἀδελφος αυτου λαβη d (ὁ supra s. m.).   ἐξανα-
στήσεις d (p. m., -η s. m.) e.   29. ἦσαν e.   31. ὡσαύτως ce.
ὁμοιως (post ὡσαύτως) c.   – δε bc.   – και tert. bcd.Elz.C
(jungit ἑπτα ου dC).   32. – δε bc.   – παντων e.   33. – εν
τη ουν αναστασει usque ad γυνη c (ὁμοιοτ.).   ἔσται (pro
γινεται) e.   γινετε͞ d (αι d s. m.).   34. εκγαμισκωνται d p. m.
εκγαμιζονται d s. m.   35. ουτε bis de.   εκγαμιζονται (non
ver. 34) cdCj.   ουτε e.   ουται c.   της d (οἱ s. m.).   37. δε d
supra (non p. m.).   εκ νεκρων (pro οἱ νεκροι) c.   μωϋσῆς
deCj.   ἀβρααμ cj.   ἀβρααμ bde.   ἱσαακ e.   39. γραμματαιων c p. m. (ε c s. m.).   40. οὐκ ἔτι ce.   οὐκέτι d.
41. + τινες (post λεγουσι) e.   43. ἂν e.   46. προσεχεται c.
γραμματαιων c.   προτοκαθεδριας c (d ρια͞σ s. m. at ν p. m.).
πρωτοκαθεδριαις e.   πρωτοκλησιας cd (κλ̈ι d : ν p. m.
pro σ).   πρωτοκλησιαις e.   47. οἰκιας e.   χειρων c.
χηρων e (η mutat.).   μακρᾶ cd.   κρῖμα bd.

CAP. XXI. 1. – αυτων c.   γαζοφυλακῆον c p. m. (ει s. m.).
πλουσίως c.   2. εἶχε δέ τινα και χείραν c.   ἴδεν δέ τινα και
bCj.   χήρα πενηχρὰν e.   – και dj.   χείραν d (η d s. m.).
εκβαλλουσαν d.   3. χεῖρα c.   – ἡ (ante χῆρα) d (habet marg.
et supra d s. m.) C.   πλοῖον c.   4. ουτοι e.   περισευοντος d.
των περισσευματων αυτων e.   ἔβαλεν (c)e.   5. τινον c.   καὶ
κόσμηται c.   6. λίθον d (non ce) C.   7, 8. – διδασκαλε usque
ad λεγοντες ver. 8 c (ὁμοιοτ.).   7. οὖν e.   γίνεσθε c.
8. πλανησῆται e.   πορεύθηται e.   ὁπίσω cde.   9. ακουσηται
c.   ακουσειτε d p. m.   πτοηθητε c.   δὴ (pro δει) c.   10. οτε
(T omissum) e.   λεγει (pro ελεγεν) ej.   11. λιμοὶ (pro λοιμοὶ)
c.   τρά τε καὶ σημεῖ bis script. c (semel erasum).   12. παντων
bcj.   ἡμας c.   ὀνόματός e (sic ver. 17).   13. προμε Ταν
(T rubro) c.   15. η (pro ουδε) d.   16. παραδοθησεσθαι
d p. m. (ε s. m.).   και συγγενων και φιλων και ἀδελφων

bcdCj.　18. θρὴξ cd s. m.　κτήσεσθε d s. m. (a vel η pro ε
d p. m.).　ὑμων (mutat.) e.　ωληται c.　20. – ὑπο στρατο-
πεδων c.　ερημοσις c.　21. ιουδαία e (mutat.) c.　ἐκχωρήτωσαν
e.　22. ἡμερα c.　εκδηκησεως c.　πλησθηναι e.　24. + εν
(ante στόματι) cd s. m. et marg.　ἄχρι e.　– ἄχρι ad fin.
vers. c ὁμοιοτ,　25. ἄστας e.　ἦχου e.　26. επερχωμενων c.
27. ὄψονται ce.　νεφελαις c.　δοξης c (o mutat.).　28. γενεσθαι
e.　γινεσθε p. m. c (c s. m. ε).　ανακυψψατε (ψ rubro) d.
29. ἴδετε e.　30. προβαλλωσιν d.　– ἤδη secund.　31. οὕτως
bce.　32. – ὅτι c.　γενονται c p. m. (η pro ον c s. m.).
33. παρελευσονται c p. m. c,　παρελευσεται d p. m.
(ον s. m.).　34. – δε c.　μηπωτε d.　βαρηθωσιν bcCj.
βαρῦθωσιν d.　κρεπαλη bc.　εφνιδιος c.　εφ' ἡμας ej p. m.
(υ s. m.).　35. γαρ ελευσεται e,　παρελευσεται d p. m.
(-ονται d s. m.).　καθιμενους e.　36. – ταυτα bcdeCj.
καταξιωθήται c.　– ταυτα γενεσθαι c,　37. εισ τῶ d
p. m. (το d s. m.).　ὅρος e.　38. ὄρθριζε bc.　Hic sequitur
in Codd. a.13.69.124.346 pericopa adulterœ Johan. vii. 53—
viii. 11.

Cap. XXII. 1. ὁρτη d,　2. – οἱ secund. c.　ἀ,,νέλωσιν
(rasur.) dj.　3. – ὁ beCj.　ιουδάν e.　ἐπι καλούμενον d p. m. j
(επι supra d s. m.).　ὄντα c.　4, – τοις secund. bcdj.
5. εχαρισαν e.　συνέθετο d p. m. (v s. m.).　αργυρια d (non
c) j.　6. εξομολογησεν c,　εζητη c.　ἄτερ e.　7. πασχα
(σ fin. eras.) d.　8. ἑτοιμασατε e (non ver. 9).　ὑμῖν d p. m.
ἡμιν d s. m.　10. – δε d (supra s. m.).　θέλης e.　ἑτοιμασομεν
bd p. m. (ο pro ω d s. m.) Cj.　ἰδοὺ e.　εν τη πολει (pro εις
την π.) c.　οἰκίαν e.　οικ ·ʲ marg. d s. m. ηγ οἴκημα.　οῦ e.
11. καταλυμμα c.　με ᵗᵃτων d p. m. (τα supra d s. m.).
12. δειξη ed p. m. (ει d s. m.).　ανωγαιον ceC.　αναγεον b.
αναγαιον dj.　εστρωμμενον c.　13. απελθοντων d.　15. επε-
θυμα d.　16. ουκέτι c.　ουκ ἔτι de.　ἑωσότου d.　18. γενηματος
bceCj.　20. ὡς αὕτος c.　ὡσ αὕτως e,　ἡμων c.　εκχυνομενον
c.　ονοματι (pro αιματι) b.　21. παραδιδοντο c.　22. ὡρισ-
μενον d.　ὁρισμενον e.　23. ἆρα d p. m.　ἄρα d s. m.　ηρξαᵛτο

d *p. m.* (ν *supra s. m.*). εἶν (*pro* εἴη) c. μελλων τουτο bc.
27. μίζων. ουχ᾽ (*pro* οὐχὶ) d. καθῶς (*pro* ὡ;) e. 28. εσται
bc *p. m.* (ὲ dc *s. m.*). τοῖς (*mutat.*) c. 30. πινητε c *s. m.* (ει
pro η c *p. m.*). τοῖς (*pro* της) c. καθίσεσθαι c. καθϊσέσθε
(b)eCd *p. m.* (η *pro* ε *s. m.*). + ιβ (*ante* θρονων) cjd *marg.*
s. m. θρονους δωδεκα. κρινωντες c. – εν τη βασιλεια μου
ej. ἰσραήλ *plenè* c. 32. εκλιπη be (*non* d) j. εκλειπη c
s. m. (η *pro* ει c *p. m.*). ποτὲ ce. 33. ειπε (– αυτω) c.
πορευεσθε e. 34. φωνηση bcdeC. πρινη d *p. m.* -ῖ d *s. m.*
35. ὅτι d *p. m.* ὅτε d *s. m.* βαλλαντιου beC. οὐθ᾽ ἑνὸς ce
(*non* d) j. 36. βαλαντιον c (*supra* λ *p. m.*) bC. πείραν ce
p. m. (η e *s. m.*). , αρατω ὁμοιως και πηραν e. πωλησει
bdej (*non* c) C. αγορασει bcdeCj. 37. – ἔτι c. τελεσθ
(*mutatum*) d. 38. οἱ (*mutat.*) d *p. m.* ἰδοὺ e. ὧδε de.

39. ὅρος ce. – αυτω και e. 40. προσευχεσθαι͏̈ e (αι *et* ε
p. m.?). 41. απεσπασθη (*mutat.*) d. 42. παρενεγκε dej
(-ειν d *p. m.*). *fin.* γενεσθαι c. + καὶ πάλιν ἀπελθὼν
προσηῦξατο c. 43,44. *Nulla omissionis suspicio in* c (σπγ/rubro) e
(σπγ/ι). 43. – αὐτῶ d (*supra p. m. ut videtur*). 44. ἱδρώς d.
υδρώς C. θρομβροι e. *fin.* της γης c. 45. – αυτου c
(cf Elz.) cdC. 46. αυτης (*pro* αυτοις) e. 47. προήρχετο cd.
αυτους, αυτοις d *s. m.* (*pro* αυτων) bced *p. m.* Cj. ἤγγισαι c.
ἤγγισαι e. *fin.* + τουτο γαρ σημειον δεδωκει αυτοις· οτι ον
αν φιλησω αὐτος ἐστιν bcdCj *s. m.* 48. – ῑσ e. 49. ἐπόμενον
e. παταξωμεν c. 50. εἶς e. 51. ἑατε e. ἀψαμενος bce.
52. ελθοντας (*pro* παραγενομενους) c. – ὡς c. ἐξήλθατε c
(*non* de). *fin.* + συλλαβειν με c. 53. καθημεραν bceC.
καθ᾽ ἡμεραν d. – μεθ᾽ ὑμῶν c. ὄντως e. αλλα bdj. + και
(*ante* ουκ εξετ.) e. – εστιν d. – ἡ *secund.* 54. – αὐτὸν
secund. cdeCj *s. m.* οἶκον e. 55. ἀψαντων bc. δε πυρὰν e.
συγκαθησαντων c. εκαθιτο e. 56. ατενησασα c. αυτον
(*pro* αυτω *prim.*) d. καθιμενον e. 57. ἠρνισατο e. – αυτον
prim. ej. 59. ἀλλοτῖ͏σ (*pro* αλλος τις) d (σ *supra insert.* bis
d). ἐπ᾽ αληθειας de. 60. ὃν (*pro* ὃ) c. – ὁ *secund.* bcd
(*non* e) Cj. αλετωρ d. 61. ρηματος (*pro* λογου του) e.
62. – ὁ πετρος cdj. 63. ενεπαιζον (αι *mutat.*) d. δαιροντες

dj. 64. ἑαυτου (pro αυτου) c. επιρωτον c. λεγον (mutat.
super ras.) c p. m. 66. – τε bcd (supra, p. m. videtur). τὲ
e. γραμ^ματεις c p. m. απηγαγον cdCj. fin. αυτων (pro
ἑαυτων) bcdeCj. 67. μῖν d (υ vel η dub.). πιστευσηται cd
(ε pro αι d s. m.). 68. εἰ (pro εαν) c. αποκριθησετε c.
απολυσηται c. 69. καθιμενος e. 70. – εἰ c. –προς αυτους
d. Ὁ τϊ d. μῖ d (ει supra s. m.). 71. αυτω (pro αυτοι) c.
ἠκουσαμεν e.

CAP. XXIII. 1. ἀπ^σ e. ἤγαγον bceCj. – αυτον e.
πηλάτον e. 2. ηρξατο c. κατηγορὴν c. διἀτρέφοντα c.
+ ημων (post εθνος) cd s. m. κολυοντα cd p. m. (ω s. m.).
3. επἰρωτησεν c. εἶπεν (pro εφη) c. 4. πηλάτος e. αἴτιον
e. 5. – της secund. c. ὦδε be. ὦδε c. ὄχλον (pro τον
λαον) d (marg. d s. m. λαον^{γρ -|}). 6. – ὁ d. 7. γνοὺς c. ὄντα
e. ὄτι c s. m. – εκ της c (habet supra c p. m.). – και
secund. c. 8. εξικανου d marg. s. m. + χρονου: at ἐξ
ἱκάνου χρόνου θέλων c(j). – πολλα c. – γινόμενον c.
10. εἱστηκησαν c. εἱστησαν d (marg. d s. m. εἱστηκεισαν^{γρ}
b). – οἱ secund. c. fin. αὐτόν c. 11. – αυτον secund. c.
γραμματεύσιν (pro στρατευμασιν) e. πηλάτω e. 12. – ὁ
secund. cCj. ἐνατῇ (pro ἐν αὐτῇ) c. ἀληλων (λ supra d
s. m.) d. ὄντες e. 14. ἰδοὺ e (sic ver. 15). – ανω τουτω c.
κατηγορειται e. 15. προς αυτον ὑμας c. ανεπεμψα γαρ
αὐτὸν προς ἡμας (sic) e : d marg. s. m. αναπεμψε γαρ αυτον^{γρ -|}
προς ἡμᾶς. ἰδου e. ἄξιον e. 16. πεδευσας c. 17. fin.
+ δεσμιον d supra s. m. 18. – τον bde. ἄραι c. ὑμιν c.
βαραμβαν c. 20. προσεφωνησαι d. 21. σταυροσον secund.
c. 22. αἴτιον ἐν αὐτῶ e. 23. αἰ e. 24. αἴτημα e.
25. – αυτοις bceC. fin. αν αὐτῶν c. 26. + οἱ στρατιωται
(ante επιλαβομενοι) c. κὖριναιου d. κηρ. c p. m. (υ s. m.).
– του prim. bcdeCj. – τέκνα c. Quatuor literæ eras. in e
(post τινος). φερην c. ὄπισθεν e. 27. ἠκολ. e. ἠκολουθη
d p. m. (εἰ d s. m.). 28. ἑαυτους c (forsan -ας). 29. ἔργοντε
c. στῆραι d p. m. (ει d s. m.). 30. ὄρεσιν e. πέσειτε c.

126 COLLATION OF GOSPELS.

καλύψαται e. τό^τε (τε s. m.) d. 31. εἰ d p. m. γίνεται bc.

34. ἄφες e. οἴδασι ce. εἰστηκει e. εβαλον d p. m. (λ supra
d s. m.). 35. +αὐτὸν (inter δε et και) cdj (d s. m. αυτον
supra). 36. ενεπεζον c. αὐτὸν (pro αυτω prim.) c. ὄξος e.
38. ἕλλην e. ἑβραικ e. 39. κρεμμασθεντων c. — εἰ c.
— κακουργων d p. m. (supra d s. m.). 40. –ὁ (ante ἕτερος) c.
ὅτι c p. m. (ε c s. m.). επετημα d. αυτον (pro αυτον αυτῷ^γρ
d s. m.) d p. m. 41. απολαμβανωμεν e. — οὗτος δὲ ad fin.
vers. c. 42. ὅτὰν c. ὅτ'ἂν e. 44. ἕκτη c. ενατης bcC.
47. ἑκατονταρχος c. ὄντος c. 48. γενώμενα c. συμπαρε
(ε p. m. a s. m.) e. 49. εἰστήκησαν ce. εἰστηκεισαν bd.
50. ὀνόματι cd. 51. συγκατατιθεμενος cj. τάξη d p. m.
(ει s. m.) sic. — και (post ὃς) dCj. 53. habet αυτο prim. e.
ενετυλιξε e (– αυτο secund. e). αὐτῷ (pro αυτο tert.) bce.
αυτον (pro αυτο secund.) c. fin. + και προσεκυλισε λιθον
μεγα (– μεγα b) επι την θυραν του μνημειου bc. + καθαρω supra
σινδονι d s. m. ουδέτοτε d. 54. ἡ δε ἡμερα ἦν παρ. c.
— και prim. c. — και secund. bcCd p. m. (supra d s. m.).
+ἡ (ante ἡμερα) d marg. s. m. 55. — και prim. bdeC
at supra γυν.^αι d s. m. j. αἵτινες e. απο (pro εκ) e. 56. μῦρα
d p. m. ἠτοιμασαν e.

CAP. XXIV. 1. T rubro om. c p. m. (ἡ ante δε μιᾶ).
βαθεως ceC. +γυναικες (post ηλθον) e. ἠτήμασαν e.
4. ἰδοὺ e. ανδρες δυο bcdeCj. 5. γενωμενων c. κλινουσῶ
c. των (pro τον) c. 6. ὧδε bcde (" e). μνησθηται d p. m.
(ε d s. m.). ἡμιν c. 9. ἀπηγγιλαν e. παντα ταυτα c.
ἕνδεκα (sic ver. 33) bce. 10. –ἦσαν δὲ ce (eras. e s. m.).
μαγδαλινῆ cd. μαγδαλη b p. m. +ἡ (ante ιακωβου) c.
— αἱ ce (eras. e s. m.). 11. ἠπιστουν e. ἠπίστυν d p. m.
(-ουν? d s. m.). 12. μνημείων c. οθονια ce. ὀθόνεια d.
13. ἴδοὺ e. ἑξήκοντα bcde. κομην d. ιερουσαλειμ d p. m.
(-ήμ d s. m.). ἠ ὀνομα c. 14. ὡμιλυν d s. m. (-ουν d p. m.
cf. ver. 11). 16. ὀφθαλμοι c. 17. τοίνες e. περὶ παντοῦντες.
18. – ὁ cd (eras.) j p. m. εξ αυτων^γρ (post εἷς) d s. m. — ὧ

bc. κλεόπας d *p. m.* κλεώπας d *s. m.* – εν (*ante* ἰλὴμ) bcdeCj *s. m.* 19. ποία de. ὡς (*pro* ὃς) dj. 20. τὲ d. κρίμα bc. κρῖμα d. 21. ηλπιζωμεν c. οὗτος (*pro* αυτος) e. μελλον c. ἄγει e. 22—24. *Sex lineæ excisæ* (*usque ad* σημεῖον ver. 24) e. 22. τϋνὲς d. ὄρθιε c. ἐπὶ τῶ d *p. m.* (*at* τὸ d *s. m.*). μνημιον d *s. m.* (-ειον d *p. m.*). 23. ὀπτασιαν c. 24. οὕτως bcC. οὕτως dej. – και *tert.* d. 25. ῶ e. 27. διερμήνευεν c. διήρ. e. 28. ἤγγισαν e. προσεποιητω πορευετ̅ πορευεσθε e. 29. μεινων c. υμων c. κεκληκεν c. ἑσπεραν e. 30. τω d *p. m.* τὸ d *s. m.* κατακληθήναι bc. κακλϊ̈ d (τα *supra s. m.*). 32. ἐνυμίν c. ελαβη cd *p. m.* (-ει d *s. m.*) e. διήνυγεν ce. 33. συνηθρησμενους c. ἔνδ. bce. 34. ἠγερθη be. ὄντως ὁ κ̅σ̅ dj* (*non s. m.*). ὄντος c. ὄντως e. 36. + και (*ante* αυτος) dC. ἔστη d. 37. πτωῆθέντες c. πτωηθεντες d *p. m.* (*o pro* ω *s. m.*). 38. διάτί ce. 39. ἴδετε e. ὀστέα c. καθῶς e. 40. εδειξεν ce. 41. *init.* ̋τι (*deest rubr.*) e. ἔχετί e. 42. ὀπτοῦ e. ὀπ̂ c. ἀπομελισσιου κηρίον e. μελϊσσειου bdCj *p. m.* 46. οὗτος *bis* c. οὕτως *bis* bdeC. 47. τὸ c. ὀνόματι ce. [αρξαμενον e]. αρξαμενον̅ d *p. m.* (ω *supra* d *s. m.*). 48. ἔσται c. 49. ἰδου e. επαγγελείαν e. ἐφ᾽ ὑμας (ἡ *semiformat.*) e. πολη e. 51. εν το d. 53. διαπαντὸς cd. διὰ παντὸς e. ἱρῶ c. *fin.* [ἀμην cde]. *Desunt subscriptiones* c. *In* e *sex lineæ excisæ ut in* ver. 22, 24.

Sub. τελος e *habet rubro* τῆς ανα[λη̅ψεως?] και του εω̅ τέ[λος] τοῦ κατα λ̅. τελος του κατα λουκαν ευαγγελιου d. τελος συν θεω το κατα λουκαν αγιου ευαγγελιου j. Τελος του κατα λουκαν αγιου ευαγγελιου C.

128 COLLATION OF GOSPELS.

Codd. bcdej Compl.
Cod. e *hiat. usque ad* cap. vii. 39. *hiat.* cap. viii. 31—
ix. 11.
Cod. f *deest.*
Cod. a: *vid.* p. 123, vii. 53—viii. 11.

TITLE. ευαγγελιον κατα ιωαννην b.
Το κατα ιωαννην ευαγγελιον c *rubro.*
Το κατα ιωαννην αγιον ευαγγελιον dCj.

CAP. I. 3. · γεγονεν · bc. 4. — ἡ c *p. m.* (*supra rubro*)
marg. ανθρωπο c *s. m.* 15. εμπροσθε c *s. m.* (*ν eras.*).
— μου *secund.* d. 17. εδοθη (*ν eras.*) c. 18. μονογεννης C.
ὁ μου υιος bcde *recenti manu.* 19. — του c. 21. απεκριθη
(*pro* λεγει) c. ουκ ειμι (*pro* ου) c. 24. οἱ *extra lineam*
j *at* c *p. m.* 26. βαπτιζων c. ἡμων c. 27. — εγω c.
ἱνα *super ras.* λυσω *infra lineam* c *p. m.* 28. βηθανια
bcd *marg.* Cj *marg. at* βηθαβαρᾶ dj *text.* 29. – ὁ
ἰωαννης c. 32. καταβαινων d *p. m.* ὡς (*pro* ὡσει) dj?
34. – και c. 35. ἡστηκει c. εἱστηκει bd *p. m.* 36. *fin.*
+ ὁ αιρων την ἁμαρτιαν του κοσμου c. 37. – αυτου c.
40. – δε bcdCj. 41. – ἦν c. 42. μεσιαν bc *s. m.* (σ *erased*)
dCj. μεθερμηνευομεν (η *s. m.*). – ὁ bcdCj. 43. – δε bc.
ἑρμηνευεται c. 44. – ὁ ιησους bdj. 46. μωϋσεῖς c *rubro.*
– του cdCj. ναζαρεθ bj. ναζαρετ (*sic* ver. 47) cdC. 49. – ὁ
d. 51. μεῖζων cd. 52. *init.* – και c. ἀπάρτι bcdC.

CAP. II. 1. τη τριτη ἡμερα (– τῇ *sec.*) c. γαμο c. εκη
c. 3. ὑστερησαντες c. 4. *init.* + και c. συ (*pro* σοι) dj.
5. λεγει bcd *p. m.* C. ὅτϊ cC. 6. μετριτας c. 9. τῷ ὕδωρ c.
– οινον d *p. m.* του υδατος γεγενημενου d *s. m.* 11. την
αρχην των σημεῖων εποιησεν c. 12. [καπερναουμ bc *passim*
c]. – εκει d. 14, 15. – και τα προβατα *usque ad* βοας
(ὁμοιοτ.) c. 14. κϊρματ d *p. m.,* ε d *s. m.* 15. φραγγελλίον

d. φραγελιον bj. κολΰβιστων c *p. m.* 17. − αυτου c.
καταφαγεται bcd *marg. s. m.* Cj. κατέφαγε d *p. m.*
18. − οἱ c. ἡμιν c. πιεις c. 19. − ὁ bcdCj. εγειρῶ c.
20. ὠκοδομησεν ουτος (− ο ναος) c. 22. ελεγε (− αυτοις)
bcdj. 23. + τοις (*ante* ιεροσ.) bcdCj. πολλη c. 24. αυτον
bd (ε *supra s. m.*) d.

CAP. III. 1. νικόδημος d (not ver. 4, 9). 2. αυτον (*pro* τον
ιν) bcj. 3. − ὁ bcj. 4. − ὁ d. − ανθρωπος d. 5. − ὁ
bdCj. 6, 8. γεγεννημενον *bis* cdC. 10. − ὁ *prim.* bcdCj.
12. *fin.* πιστευσητε d. 15. ἔχει bcd. 20. ελεχθη αυτου τα
εργα cj. 23. σαλημ bcdj. παρεγενοντο dj. 25. ιουδαιου bd
p. m. j. ιουδαιων cd *s. m.* C. 26. ἢ (*pro* ην) c. 27. − ἢ d,
at supra p. m. forsan. 29. ἑστηκῶς c. − του (*post* φωνην)
cC. 31. ἐ c *p. m.* (ανω c *s. m.*). *fin.* ἐστί cdC (εστιν Elz.).
33. λαμβανων c. λαμβὼν d (ν *eras.*). εσφραγησεν c.
34. ὡ (*pro* ὃν) c. 36. ἔχη d *p. m.* ἔχει *marg.* d *s. m.*
+ την (*ante* ζωην) bdj *inserted p. m.* (not c) C. μενεῖ bd *p. m.*
μένει cd *s. m.* μενεί C.

CAP. IV. 1. ισ (*pro* κσ) dCj. 2. αυτος *bis scriptum* c.
3. απηλθον c. − παλιν bcdCj. 5. σαμαριας (*sic* ver. 7) d.
σϋχαρ cdC. οὗ (*pro* ὃ) bdCj. 6. υσ (*pro* ισ) d *p. m.* ουτος
(*pro* ουτως) c. ποιειν (*sic* ver. 9) c. 9. σαμαριτης c.
συχρωνται cd *p. m.* οἱ *supra* d *p. m.?* 12. − οἱ *supra* c
p. m. d *p. m.* 13. − ὁ *prim.* bcdC. αυτω (*pro* αυτη) c *p. m.*
14. δόσω c. − ου μη διψηση *usque ad* δωσω αυτω (ὁμοιοτ.)
c. 15. λεγη d *p. m.* -ει d *s. m.* μηδὲ ἔρχω. c. 16. ανδραν
(*non* ver. 17) c. 17. + αυτω (*post* ειπον) c. 18. Αληθῶς
(A *rubro*) c. 20. τω ορει τουτο bcd (τουτω bd) Cj. 21. ὅ d
p. m. ὅτι *s. m.* (*ante* ἔρχεται) *at* ὅτι d *p. m.* ὅτε d *s. m.* (*ante*
οὔτε). 25. μεσιας bcdC. 27. εθαυμαζον c. 28. τοις a. c
p. m. rescript super ras. 30. − ουν cdj *p. m.* 31. + αυτου
(*post* μαθηται) dCj. 33. ηνεκεν d *p. m.* ηνεγκ. d *s. m.*
35. − ετι d (*non* c) C. τετραμηνός bcdCj. 36. χαιρει cd
p. m. 37. τουτο c. 38. αυτων d *s. m.* (at ο *p. m.*). 42. οὐκ

s.   9

ἔτι cd. 45. εδοξαντο d. ὅσα (*pro* ἃ) d. 46. − ὁ $\overline{\iota\sigma}$ c (not bd). 47. ἤμελλε d *p. m.* 50. + ὁ (*ante* $\overline{\iota\sigma}$ *secundum*) bcdCj. πορευει c. 51. απηντησαν c (ε *s. m.*) *p. m.* 52. + δε (*pro* οὖν) c. κομψον marg. *s. m.* ͺͺ͂ αγαθον ενιοτε d [*abrogat* j *per* ⸗ ver. 46 γαλιλαιας *usque ad* οινον*].

CAP. V. 1. μετα δε ταυτα ην ἑορτῇ c. + ἡ (*ante* εορτη) dCj. 2. επι τη d *erased.* ἑβραιστὴ cd (d *p. m., ι s. m.*). 3, 4. *nullo omissionis vestigio* cd. 4. εταράσσετο το cdC. οὗ δήποτε c *p. m.* εγενετο c. 5. τριακοντα (+ και bcC) bcdC. 6. θελης bcd *p. m.* (-ει d *s. m.*). 7. βαλη bd (*non* c) Cj. μαι̇ c (ε *s. m.*). ερχωμαι c. 8. εγειρε c. κραβαττον (*sic* ver. 9—12) bc. κραμβατον *bis* d (μ *pro* β d *s. m.*). 11. σου *bis* c (*prius eras. non*). 13. ηδη c (ηδει c *s. m.*) d. 14. σοι τί bcd. 15. ἀπηγγειλε c. 18. *init.* + και c. ἴσον cd. 19. βλεπει d *p. m.* (η d *s. m.*). 20. αυτοις d *p. m.* (αυτος d *s. m.*). μειζωνα d. δειξη d *s. m.* (-ει *p. m.*). 21. ουτως bcdCj. θελει d *p. m.* (θελη d *s. m.*). 23. τον $\overline{\pi\rho\alpha}$ *bis script.* c. 25. ἐστὶ (*hiatus*) c. 30. *Habet* $\overline{\pi\rho\sigma}$ d. 34. ἀνῶν c. 35. αγαλλιαθηναι bcdCj. 38. μενον d (τα *s. m.*). 39. ζωην εχην c. − εν αυταις *at* εν αυτο c *s. m. et* αιωνιον cC. ἀικεῖναι d. 41. λαμβαννω (*non* ver. 43) c. 44. ἀνῶν (*pro* αλληλων) d. λαμβαννοντες c. 45. μωσει dC (μωσεῖ bcCj). − γαρ d. 47. *fin.* πιστευετε c.

CAP. VI. 2. ἐποί c. 5. αγορασωμεν c. 6. ηδη d *p. m.* -ει *s. m.* ημελλε bdCj. 7. αρκεσουσιν d. 9. ὀψάρια marg. *note s. m.* ͺͺ͂ ἰχθυδια *sic* ver. 12 d. 10. εν το c. 11. + πεντε (*ante* αρτους) c. 12. επλησθησαν dj. περισσευματα των κλασματων d *p. m.* σαντα *et* γρ κλάσματα d marg. *s. m.* 13. αρτον c *p. m.* (ω *s. m.*). 15. αυτος μονος εις το ὄρος (− παλιν j) c. 18. ὅτε (*pro* ἤ τε) d. διἐγείρετο c. 19. εμηλ. c. − και (*ante* εφοβηθησαν) c. ως d (ει *supra s. m.*)

habet j. 20. $+\overline{\iota\sigma}$ (*ante* λεγει) c. 21. – το *prim*. d. 22. – ὁ
secund. c. ἐστικῶς c. αλλον d. συνῆλθε c p. m. (ση *supra*
s. m.) d. λοῖον c. μονη c. 23. ηλθον cj. 24. – καὶ *prim*.
bcdCj. 26. αυτω (*pro* αυτοις) c. – αμην *semel* c. ἴδετε
cd. 27. ὑμιν (υ *super rasuram*) d *s. m.* ἐσφραγησεν bc.
28. ποιουμεν d p. m. (ω d *s. m.*) C. ποιουμεν j *s. m.* πιῶμεν
c. ποιωμεν bj p. m. εργαζομεθα c. 29. – ὁ bcdCj. εἰς ὧν
(*pro* εις ὁν) c. 30. – συ d. ποεις c. 31. πρε c. αυτους
(*pro* αυτοῖς) c. 33. καταβαίνον b p. m. d p. m. (ω d *s. m.*).
34. ὑμιν c. 35. ζωησ ὁ ερ *fere illegib. in* d. πεινασει c.
πιστεων c. πιστευω d (ν *supra s. m.*). 36. – καὶ *prim*. c.
38. *fin*. με c. 39. – εν bc (j *prius*). 40. ἔχει bcd. – εν
(*supra s. m.*) d : *sic* ver. 54 j. 41. – οἱ c. 45. – του *prim*.
bcdCj. ακουων bcdC. 49. το μαννα εφαγον c. 50. – ἵνα
τις *ad fin. vers*. c. 51. ὁ *secund. mutat. in* d. 52. – προς
αλληλους c. 53. – αμὴν *semel* c. πιητε (πο *s. m.*) c.
58. +μου (*post* τρωγων) cd (d *eras*.) Cj. ζήσει cj ? 64. εἰσὶν
τινὲς εξ ὑμων c. ἢ (*pro* οἱ) c p. m., *at* οἱ (*pro* οἱ) d.
66. – αυτου *prim*. d. οὐκ ἔτι d (*non* c). ὀπίσω c. 68. – ουν
c. 70. – ὁ ἴσ cdCj. εξελαμην d p. m. (εξ *s. m.* d).
71. ἔμελλεν dC. ν (*pro* ων *vel* ον) d p. m. *mutat*. d *s. m.*
ὃν bc.

CAP. VII. 1. – οἱ c. 3. – σου *secund*. d. θεωρη-
σουσι c. 4. παρρ marg. late gloss d. εξουσία ἀδείᾳ.
5. αδελφη c. επιστευσα db *s. m. ut videtur*. 6. ἡμετερος c.
8. – εγω *usque ad* ταυτην (ὁμοιοτ.) d. οὖπω *prim*. οὖπω
secund. c. *In* d *s. m. is inserted marg*. εγω οὖπω αναβαινω
tantum. 9. αυτω (*pro* αυτοις) c. εμειν d (εν *supra* d *s. m.*).
10. – εις την ἑορτην c. 12. – δε bcdC. κοσμον (*pro* οχλον)
d. 13. τὸν ἰούδαιων c. 15. – οἱ. 16. +ουν (*post* απεκριθη)
bcdCj. 17. προτερον c. 18. οὖτως d p. m. (ο *s. m.*).
21. – ὁ bcdCj. 22. σαμβατω c. 24. κρίνεται *prim*. c p. m.
25. – ουν c. 26. – αληθως *prim*. c, *secund*. Cj. 27. ἔρχεται

c (*non* dC). 28. εἴδατε *prim.* 29. – δὲ bcdCj. 30. *Marg.*

d *s. m.* πιασαι⁻ʲ *habet* καὶ⁻ʲ εξηλθεν εκ της χειρος αυτων.

επεβεν^{αλ} d (αλ *supra s. m.*). εληλυθη bd *p. m.* -ει d *s. m.*
31. ὅτι *eras.* d. – τουτων dC. 32. ὑπηρετας οἱ φαρισαιοι
και οἱ αρχιερεῖς bcdCj. 33. – αυτοις bcdCj. 34. ζητησατε

c. In d *s. m.* late marg. ἐγὼ εἰμί⁻ʲ (so ver. 36). 35. ὑμεις d.
+ ὡς (*post* που) c. διἀπορευεσθαι c. 37. [εἰστηκει bc].
39. ὃ ἤμελλον bd. πιστευον^{τες} d (τεσ *supra* d *s. m.*). αγιον⁻ʲ ⁻ʲ
late marg. d *s. m.* – ὁ bcdeCj. [ουδεπω] e. 40. των λογων
bc. τουτων ej. 41, 42. – Οὗτός ἐστιν *ad fin.* ver. 42
(ὁμοιοτ.) c. 41. + ὅτι (*ante* οὗτος) e. – δε bdeCj. 42. βηθλιεμ
d *p. m.* 43. σχῖσμα d. 45. Ἡλ (θον^{θον} *supra* d *s. m.*). 46. – οἱ c.
[διατί] cde. 47. προς αυτους d *p. m.* (αν *eras.* d). 51. ακουσει
e. 52. εγειργερται c. εὑρεννησον e. 53. *Nullum suspicionis*
signum in pericopa adulteræ: omnia uno tenore bcdC. *Rubro*
de υ^{πγ} εἰς την της || *marg.* 53 (viii. 1). απηλθον bj. απηλθεν
(*pro* επορευθη) d *marg. s. m.* be. τον οικον⁻ʲ *marg.* d *s. m.*
τα⁻ʲ ιδια. *Spatium inter* viii. 2 *et* 3 (*Theodora Pelagia*) b.

CAP. VIII. 1 (same as vii. 53). απηλθον bj. απηλθεν d
(*pro* επορευθη ad *s. m. marg.*). ηλθεν ὁ ισ‾ j. viii. 1. + ὁ
(*ante* ισ‾) bcj. 2. + βαθέος (*post* ορθρον) bej. ηλθεν a.
παρεγ^{⁻ʲ γρ} *text.* ad *marg. s. m.* sic Cod. e. 3. *Rubro marg.* εὐ εις
μετανοουντας κατα ιω‾. *Nigro in textu* Τω καιρω εκεινω e.
3. – δε b. ἄγουσιν οἱ γραμματεις και οἱ φαρισαιοι προς [τον
ιν rubro] αυτον be. προσηνεγκαν (– προσ αυτον) a. επι
(*pro* εν) abdeCj. καταλειφθῆσαν c. + τω (*ante* μεσω) abe.
4. ειπον (*pro* λεγουσιν) ae. + πειραζοντες (*ante* διδασκαλε)
ce. ταυτην εὑρωμεν αυτη ἡ γυνη ειληπται a. επαυτοφορω⁻ʲ
(a) μοιχευομενην abdj. *In marg.* d *s. m.* ἐπ᾽ αὐτω τω⁻ʲ
κλεμματι. *At* ταύτην εὕρομεν ἐπαυτοφώρως^{ω C} μοιχευομενην
eC. αὕτη ειληπται a. κατἐλειφθη c. 5. εν δε το (τω a)

νομω ἡμων (ημιν a) μωσης (– ἡμιν a) adC.   μωϋσης (– ημιν
not b) eC.   λιθαζειν abej.   *fin.* + περι αυτης be [not a].
6. επερωτωντες bej.   κατηγοριαν κατ᾽ abdC.   κατεγραφεν c.
fin. + μη προσποιουμενος cdej *s. m.* [not a] C.   7. πρωτον·
ἐπ᾽ αυτην την λιθων c.   ἐπ᾽ αὐτῇ d *p. m.*   επ αυτην d *s. m.*
(πρωτον· c) λιθον (– τον) βαλετω επ αυτην abej.   9. και ὑπο
in d *s. m. marg.* ἐν ἐνιοις ουκ ἔστι.   a (– ακουσαντες και
υπο της συνειδησεως ἐλεγχομενοι ab) habet C.   εξηρχον e
(λ το *s. m.*).   In d εξηρχετο *p. m.*   εξηρχετο *s. m. marg.*
εξηλθον *marg.* a.   εἰς καθεὶς c(de)a.   – ἕως των εσχατων ce
[not a].   κατεληφθη ce.   ὁ ἰσ μονος e.   – ὁ b.   – μονος a.
ουσα (*pro* ἑστωσα) abcdeCj.   10. ιδεν αυτην και ειπεν (– και
μηδενα *usque ad* αυτη) abj.   – η γυνη cdeC.   ειδεν αυτην και
ειπεν e.   γυναι (*pro* ἡ γυνη) abe.   – ἡ γυνη j.   – εκεινοι
(– εκεινος bj) οἱ κατηγοροι σου e (*non* a).   11. – αυτῇ c.   δε
(*pro* αυτη) e.   – δε b.   – και c.   + απο του νυν (*ante* μηκετι)
bdeC [*non* a] j.   In rubro τέ αρ τῆς Ν d.   Rubro Τ τῶν
μετανοουντων e.   12. – αυτοις c.   αυτοις ὁ ἰσ bdeCj.   περι-
πατηση bdeCj.   13. μαρτυρεις bcde.   14. + ὁ (*ante* ἰσ) c.
ελθω (*pro* ηλθον) c.   η που (*pro* και που *secund.*) bcCj.
– ὑμεις δε *ad fin. vers.* e.   15. – δε d.   16. – δε c.   17. το
ὑμετερω c.   19. λεγον c.   – ὁ bcd.   – ει εμε ηδειτε *ad fin.*
vers. (ὁμοιοτ.) c.   20. γαζοφυλακειω c.   γαζο in d *marg. s. m.*
ηγ θησαυρου φυλακίω.   22. – οἱ c.   αποκτενει c.   24. ημιν
c.   – εαν γαρ μη *ad fin. vers.* (ὁμοιοτ.) d.   25. ὅτι cdC.
26. + και (*ante* λαλειν) c.   27. ελαλει (*pro* ελεγεν) be.
29. αυτου (*pro* αυτω) c.   31 [*Hiat* Cod. e *usque ad*
Cap. ix. 11].   μεινη c.   32. – αληθειαν και ἡ αληθεια
c.   33. + και ειπον (*post* απεκριθη) b.   ἀβρααμ c hic (ἀβρ.
ferè).   39. *fin.* – αν d *p. m.* Cj.   40. ἄνοσ d *p. m.* ἄνον
d *s. m.*   *fin.* εποισεν c.   43. τον λογον d *s. m.* τον
εμον b.   44. *init.* υμεις εκ του πρσ ἡμων c. [ἀπάρχης
cd].   εστικεν c.   No stop at end verse c: at ἐστὶ· και d.

48. – οἱ c.   λεγωμεν cd.   52. – οἱ c.   γευσηται bdCj.
θανατω c.   53. ὑμων c.   συ eras. d.   54. δοξασω d.   ἡμων
dj.   56. ηυμων (dubium) d.   εἴδη d.   58. + ουν (post ειπεν)
bc (non j).   γενεσται d p. m., θ s. m.   59. [as Elz.].

CAP. IX. 1. γεννητης c.   2. οι (mut.) γονης c p. m.
3. – ὁ bcdCj.   – οὗτος ἡμαρτεν (same beg.) c p. m. (habet
marg. s. m.).   4. ἦ (pro δει) c.   6. επεχρησε τον πυλον
c p. m.   7. ἑρμυνευεται c.   8. ἔτι (pro ὅτι) c p. m.
– ελεγον c p. m.   9. αλλοι ελεγον ὅτι οὗτος εστι bis script. c
(semel eras.).   10. ηνεωχθησαν bc.   σου (pro σοι) cdC.
11. επεχρησε c.   νηψαμενος (sic ver. 15) c.   14. [ὅτε] e.
15. επεθηκε μου (μοι C) επι τους οφθαλμους bcd p. m. eCj
s. m. (d s. m. επι supra μου τους).   – και prim. d.   16. παρα
θ̄ῡ (– του) e.   σαβτον e.   σχίσμα d p. m.   17. + ουν (post
λεγουσιν) bdCj.   ἤνοιξε e.   18. ἔωσ ὅ d s. m.   20. απεκρισαν
c.   + δε (ante αυτοις) cdCj.   – αυτοις e.   ὑμων d p. m.
21. fin. περι ἑαυτοῦ bceC.   τα περι ͤ αὐτου d (ε p. m.).
22. συνετεθ̇ειντο c.   – οἱ c.   23. εἶπον οἱ γονεις αυτου c.
25. – ουν e.   26. ἀνέωξέ dCj.   28. – ουν bcd s. m. Cj.
29. μωσει λελακεν ο θ̄σ̄ ὁ θ̄σ̄ c p. m. (μωση c p. m.).   μωσει
c s. m. bdeCj.   τουτο c.   30. – αυτοις c.   τουτο c.   ὅ [τι] c
(τι s. m.).   31. ποιεῖ e.   32. γεγεννμενου c p. m.   γεγενη c
s. m.   33. + του (ante θ̄ῡ) bd.   34. – καὶ tert. e.   ἁμαρτιαι
(σ supra s. m.) c.   ὅλως cdj p. m.   35. – ἤκουσεν usque ad
ἔξω (ὁμοιοτ.) c.   αυτω e s. m. (αυτοις p. m.).   36. + και (ante
τις) bcdeCj.   38. προσσεκυνησεν c.   39. ει (pro εις) c.
κρῖμα cj.   γενονται e.   41. + ουν (post εἶπεν) c.   βλεπωμεν e.
ει (pro ἡ) be.

CAP. X. 1. ἀλαχοθεν (λ p. m.?) d.   3. τούτω e.   4. εκβαλλη bdj.   εκβαλει c.   εκβαλλει e.   αυτων (pro αυτῷ) c.
6. παρομιαν c.   7. – ὅτι be.   8. ηλθον προ εμου bcd.
– προεμου eC.   9. εὑρηση e.   10. θυσει c.   περισον c.
[Hiat. Cod. e post απολεση usque ad Cap. xi. 54.]   11. καλλος

secund. d. 12. ὦ[ν] (ν *s. m.*) c. λικος c. 13. φεγ d *p. m.*
μελλει (λ *eras.* d *s. m.*) cd. 18. ελαβα c. 19. σχίσμα d.
21. ανοιγειν. In d *s. m. marg.* ανοῖξαι (νι *s. m.* d).
22. εγκαια d gloss *s. m. marg.* εγκαινϊα καθὼ καινουργηθητϊ
marg. – τοις bcdCj. 23. περιεπατη c. σολομωνος cdC
(– του bcdCj). 25. – απεκριθη αυτοις ὁ ἰσ d *p. m. Habet*
marg. s. m. (ἰησ). 28. απωλονται c. οὐχ᾽ ἁρπαζει d *p. m., σ*
s. m. 29. πάντων d *supra s. m.* μοι μειζων At post ἁρπαζειν d *s. m.*
marg. αὐτα γρ. d. 32. αυτων (ω *mut.*) c. 33. – καὶ (*ante*
ὅτι) d. *Habet supra s. m.* 35. λυθην c. 36. – του c.
38. πιστευσηται c *primum* (ε pro αι) *s. m.* – μη d *p. m.* (ου
supra d *s. m.*). 39. πιᾶσαι c. πιάσαι αυτον d. 41. λεγοντες
(*pro* και ελεγον) c. – μεν c. αὐτοῦ (*pro* τουτου) c.
42. εις αυτον εκει d.

CAP. XI. 2. θρηξιν εαυτης cd *s. m.* (ἑ *supra* d). 5. μάρθα
bc. 8. οἱ ιουδαιοι λιθασαι d. 9. – ὁ bcdCj. ὥραι εἰσὶν
cdCj. 9, 10. περι επατει bc. 10. νυκτη d *p. m.* 12. ει d
p. m. (*pro* εἰπον) (*supra* d *s. m.*). καὶ κοίμηται d *p. m.*
15. πιστευητε d. αλλα bcdCj. 17. – ουν c. 19. ελη-
λυθησαν cd. παραμυθησονται cd (ω d *s. m.*). 20. – ο
cdCj. 21. – ή cdC. ὧδε d (*non* c). 24. + ή (*ante* μαρθα)
cCj. 26. ζῶ c. *fin.* τούτω c. 28. τοῦτο. – απηλθε *usque*
ad ειπουσα *secund.* (ὁμοιοτ.) c. 29. Εκεινη (δὲ *supra s. m.*) d.
εγήρεται c. 30. ή (*pro* ἦν) c. το τοπω c. 31. ιδον d *p. m.*
(τ· d *s. m.*). λεγωντες d *p. m.* αυτης c *mutat.* ὅ (*pro*
ὅτι) c. αυτη c (ω *p. m.*). 32. αυτου εις τους ποδας bdCj.
33. συνεληλυθοτας cj. κλαιΟυσαν c. 34. – κυριε c.
38. επεκητο c. 40. σοι ειπον d. 41. + αυτου *supra* ανω
d *s. m.* 43. δευρο d *marg. s. m.* gloss η ἐλθὲ. 44. κειρίαις d
marg. s. m. (*vel p. m.*). κειρια ειδος ζωνης εκ σχοινιων·
παρεοικὸ ἱμαντι ἤ δεσμοῦσι τας κλίνασ· και κειρια ἤ σπαργα-

νωσις. 45. μαρί^α c (end line). 46. ὅσα (pro ἅ) d (non
ver. 45) C. 48. οὗτος c. οντως bdC. πιστευσωσιν
bcd p. m. 51. αλλ᾽ cj. ημελλε cj. 54. οὐκέτι c. οὐκ ἔτι
d. 56. ἐστικότες c. [Incipit e ἐστηκ.] υμιν δοκει d.
57. δεδωκησαν c. δεδωκεισαν (ε supra s. m.) d. — και
prim. bd (erased) e.

CAP. XII. 1. τεθνηκος e.   2. ἦν των ανακειμενων συν
bcdCj. 3. λητραν cd p. m.   ὁ δε οικια c.   αυτοις (pro
αυτης) e. 4. λέ c. — αυτον c.   5. διἁτί (c)de.   6. ο ὅτι c.

εμελλεν bceCj. γλωσσο Marg. d s. m. θηκην. 9. εκε c.

12. — ὁ secund. bce.   13. βαῖα d marg. s. m. ^{γρ}βαιον ἠ κλαδος

απαντησιν d marg. s. m. ^{γρ}συναντησιν. απαντησιν c.   αυτου

(pro αυτω) c.   εκραζων d p. m.   εκραζον d s. m.   ελεγον
(pro εκραζον) ce. [ὡσαννα cd]. ὡσ ἀννὰ ej. — ὁ ερχομενος
d (habet supra s. m.). — ὁ secund. bdeCj s. m.   14. ἐπ αὐτῶ

cdeCj. ^{rubro}γεγραμενον c. 15. βαCιλευσου c.   σοι supra ερχεται
d s. m.   16. — ὁ bc.   17. ὅτε cdC at ὅτι e.   18. — και c

ηκουσαν cej. 19. ὡφελει d marg. s. m. ^{γρ}   ὥπισω e p. m.
21. ηρωτησαν e. θελωμεν cd p. m.   [22. λεγουσῖ d.]
23. αυτους (pro αυτοις) c. 24. σῖτου e.   πολλὴν d p. m.,
υ s. m. 27. ταύτης; dej. 28. ἦλ d (supra θεν d s. m.).
30. — ὁ bdeCj. 32. ἐλκυσω ce (non d). 34. — ὅτι secund.
cdCj (supra d s. m.). ὑμεις ηκουσαμεν e. 35. ὡς (pro ἕως)
e. +ἡ (ante σκοτία) e. [Post εχετε hiat. e usque ad Cap.
xiii. 27.] απεκρυβη c. 37. επιστευσαν c. — αυτου d p. m.
(inserted supra d s. m. post σημεια). 38. [ἠσαϊου c]. ὑμων
d p. m.   40. ιασωμαι bc.   πεπωρωκεν d marg. s. m.   πωρω
το σκληρῢνω και λῖθοποιω. 41. αυτου p. m. marg. d s. m.
^{γρ}του θεοῦ. ἥπεν c. 43. ηπερ (d marg. s. m., dele περ).
44. πιστεων c. 46. μηνη c. 47. πιστεύσῃ d marg. s. m.

γρ
φυλαξη. 48. αθετων *marg. s. m.* εκβαλλων. κρινεῖ d p. m.
(*mutat.* d *s. m.*). − ο λογος ον *usque ad* κρινει αυτον (ὁμοιοτ.)
c. 50. οὕτως bcdCj.

CAP. XIII. 1. της του πασχα ἑόρτης c. Πᾶσχα d *rubro.*
− αυτου c. μεταλαβη c. 2. − ιουδα c. σημ. c p. m.
3. + δε (*post* ειδως) e. αὐτῶ *mutat.* c. 4. λεντιον (ν *mutat.*) d.
5. + αυτου (*post* μαθητων) c p. m. εἶτα λαβων ὑδωρ βαλλει d.
7. γνωσει c. 8. νιψεις c. εχης c. 10. νηψασθαι c. ὁλως c.
ἢ d p. m. eras. ει μη d s. m. 12. ὁτε c p. m. ὁ c s. m. rubro.
13. ὁ κσ καὶ ὁ διδάσκαλος cj. 15. δεδωκα bcdCj. − εγω d.
ποιεῖτε c. 16. μεῖζων d p. m. 17. ποιειτε ταυτα c. fin.
ταυτα d p. m. (αυτα d s. m.). 18. + δε (*post* παντων) c. επ᾽
c p. m. *mutat.* (*at* μετ *prius*). 19. ἀπάρτι bcdC. 20. λαμ-
βαννων *prim.* c. τον πέμψαντά με λαμβανη c. 22. δε
προς (*pro* ουν εις) d. 23. νακειμενος d p. m. (να d s. m.).
24. ειη (*at* η s. m.) d? 25. ουν (*pro* δε) d s. m. 26. − επι-
δωσω *usque ad* ψωμιον *secund.* (ὁμοιοτ.) c. 27. − ουν c.
εκεινον *mutat.* d? 29. γλωσοκομον e (*Incipit* ver. 27). − ὁ
prim. bce. επει (*mutat.*) d p. m.? ον (*pro* ὧν) c *rubro.*
30, 31. *Jungit* νυξ ὁτε (− ουν) εξηλθεν (ὁμοιοτ.) cd (not e) C.
31. + ουν (*post* λεγει) d s. m. supra. 32. − ει ὁ θσ ἐδοξασθη
εν αυτω (ὁμοιοτ.) d p. m. (*habet supra s. m.*). 33. − οτι c.
εγω ὑπαγω cd (not e) C. 34. και νυν? d p. m. και νην d
s. m. − αγαπατε *prim.* e. − καθως ad fin. vers. (ὁμοιοτ.) ce.
35. τουτο c. εχετε c. 36. + εγω (*ante* υπαγω) bcd, (*post*
ὑπαγω) j. με (*pro* μοι *prim.*) d p. m. Cj. 37. − ὁ bcdeCj.
− ὁ πετρος j. διὰτι bc. διατί e. 38. φωνηση cdeCj.
κ
ἀλέτωρ d (κ supra p. m.) e.

CAP. XIV. 1. ταρασεσθω d. 2. πολλαι μοναι c. πορευ-
ωμαι c. + ὁτι (*supra* and *ante* πορ.) d s. m. [no ὁτι ce.]
ἑτοιμασαι c. 3. − καὶ *secund.* bcej. ἑτοιμασαι (*pro* ἑτοιμασω)
be. παραληψωμαι d p. m., ο d s. m. 4. οἴδατε *prim.* d.
οἴδατε *secund.* e. 7. − εγνωκειτέ με και τον πρα μου (same
σ
beginning) c. απαρτι bcdeC. γινωκετε d p. m. (σ supra

s. m.). αυτον *prim. mutat.* c.   9. φιλιππε; cde.   ὑμιν (*pro*
ἡμιν *sec.*) b *p. m.* d.   10. πιστευεις (εις *mutat.*) c.   − εστι c.
− ὑμιν c.   11. ο (*pro* ὅτι) c.   [εστιν Elz.C *errore, post* εν
εμοι.]   − εστιν cd *p. m.* (*supra* εν εμοι d *s. m.*) (e *habet*).
12. ποιω εγω d.   μειζωνα d.   − και μειζονα *usque ad* ποιησει
(ὁμοιοτ.) c.   13. ὅτι cdeC.   14. *init.* + και bc.   αιτησεετι
d *p. m.?*, η *s. m.*   εν το d *p. m.*, ω *s. m.*   15. μου (*pro* τας
ἐμας) e.   + μου (*ante* τας εμας *sic, ut videtur*) c.   16. + μου
(*post* πρα) d.   δοσει e.   17. *init.* τῶ d *p. m.*   τὸ d *s. m.*
αυτω (*pro* αυτο *secund.*) ω *mutat.* d.   19. [ουκετι cde].   θεό-
ρειτε c.   20. και εγω (*pro* καγω) bc.   21. − ὁ δε αγαπων με
(ὁμοιοτ.) c.   − και εμφανισω αυτω εμαυτον (ὁμοιοτ.) e.
εμφανεισω c.   22. + και (*ante* τϊ) dCj.   23. − ὁ *prim.* bcdeC.
τηρηση c.   ποιησωμεν ej.   24. τηρει; d.   27. − ειρηνην την
εμην διδωμι υμιν (ὁμοιοτ.) c.   ἡμιν (*pro* ὑμιν *tert.*) d.
ταρασσετω d *p. m.* (σθ *pro* τ d *s. m.*).   28. χαριτε e.   πορευ-
σομε c *p. m.*   πορευυμε c *s. m.*   29. γένεσθε d *p. m.* γενεσθαι
d *s. m.*   30. [ουκέτι cd (*non* e)].   − τουτου bcdeCj.   31.
οὕτως bcdeCj.

CAP. XV. 1. αληθηνη c *p. m.* (ϊ c *s. m.*) d *p. m.* (ι d *s. m.*).
2. φερων c *p. m.*, ο c *s. m.*   πλειωνα c.   *fin.* φερει ej.
4. − μεινατε εν εμοι, καγω εν ὑμιν (ὁμοιοτ.) bc.   5. ποιειν
d *s. m.* (d *p. m. non liquet*).   6. αυτο (*pro* αυτα) d *s. m.* ej.
+ το (*ante* πῦρ) bcdCj.   7. εν εμοι *super rasuram* c *s. m.*
αιτησεσθαι c.   8. τουτω (ο *mutat.*) d.   γενησεσθαι c.
γενησησθε d (-σεσθε d *p. m.?*).   [γενησεσθε e.]   *fin.* εμοι e
s. m.   *forsan* η (*pro* οι) e *p. m.*   11. ἡμων c.   14. ποιειτε e.
15. ουκετι c.   ουκ ετι de.   16. ὅτϊ cC.   δωη cd *p. m.* e (δοι
supra d *s. m.*).   δωσει j.   19. − δε cd.   ἡμας c *s. m.* (ἡμας c
p. m.).   20. ἡμετερον c *p. m.* (ὑμετ. c *s. m.*).   22. αυτων
mutat. d (ο d *s. m.*).   24. μη (*mutat.*) d.   25. νομω c (*mutat.*
super ras.).   εμησϊσαν c.   27. [ἀπ' αρχης d.]   ἀπαρχῆς ce.
[ἐξαρχῆς cd Cap. xvi. 4.]

CAP. XVI. 3. − ὑμιν bcdeCj *s. m.*   4. εθη c *p. m.* λ *insert.*
s. m.   6. λελαλυκα c.   − ἡ λυπη *usque ad* συμφερει ὑμιν
ver. 7 (ὁμοιοτ.) c.   7. − εαν γαρ μη απελθω d *p. m.* (d *s. m.*

supra εαν γαρ εγω μη απελθω). + εγω (*ante* μη) bceCj.
— εαν δε πορευθω *ad fin. vers.* (ὁμοιοτ.) c. πωρευθω d (*o*
s. m.). 8. ελλεγξει c. 10. οὐκ ἔτι c (*sic ver.* 21, 25). οὐκ
ἔτι de. 12. δυνασθαι cd *p. m.* (ε *s. m.* d). ακουσει e.
13. ερχομενα c (επ *supra* c *s. m.*). 14. *Deest versus* (ὁμοιοτ.)
ce. 15. λαμβανει bdCj. 16. — εγω bdeCj. 17. ὑμιν d.
18. *fin.* λεγει c *p. m.* λαλει c *s. m.* 19. αληλων d *p. m.* (λ
supra s. m.). ἤθελον e. 20. κλαυσατε c. θρηνήσατε c
(*mut.* ε). χαρησετε d *p. m.* (αι bd *s. m.*). 21. οτη *prim.* c
p. m. (ι c *s. m.*). τικτει ce. γεννησει ce. ὅτι (*pro* ουκ ετι)
d *p. m. supra* d *s. m.* εγενηθη d. 22. ἡμων (*pro* ὑμων *prim.*
et secund., tert. dub.) c. εχετε νυν b. εχετε μεν νυν εχετε
(εχετε *prim. erasum*) d. 23. ὅΤϊ c *s. m.* (*a pro* ι c *p. m. pro*
ὅσα) c. τον τον c. ουκ ητησατε c *bis scriptum, semel eras.*
c *s. m.* αἰτήτε c. ἡμων c. 25. ὅτι οὐκ ἔτι d. 26. *fin.* ημων
c. 27. — και πεπιστευκατε (ὁμοιοτ.) c. 28. — παλιν αφιημι
τον κοσμον (ὁμοιοτ.) c. 29. ουδεμιαν *bis scriptum, semel eras.*
rubro d. 30. οἴδαμεν ὅτι οἶδας e. ταύτω e. 33. ἔξετε e
(Steph.). ἔχετε bcd *p. m.* (*at* ἐξ d *s. m.*) Cj. νενϊκα d *p. m.*
at νενικηκα d *s. m. ad fin. lineæ: etiam* νη d *s. m.*

CAP. XVII. 1. ἐπεῖρε c. επηρε e *nigro* επαρας *rubro* e.
— και (*ante* ειπεν) d *s. m., at* κ *pro* ει *primo* d. δοξασει c
p. m. δοξαση c *s. m.* 2. δωσει bcdeCj. 3. ζωῆ· e. αλη-
θηνον c. 5. ἠ εἰ *super rasuram* c *p. m.* 7. εγνωσαν bd
(εγνωκαν ceC). 8. [δεδ c.]. 10. δεδόξασμε cde. 11. οὐκέτι
bcdej. ὦ Cd *p. m.* j (οὓς d *s. m.*). καθὼς (και *supra* bd
s. m.). [δεδ.] *fin.* + ἐν ἐσμέν c. 12. ὅτι (*pro* ὅτε) c. ετηρων
cd *p. m.* (-ουν c *s. m.*). εἰμι (*pro* ει μη) e. 13. *fin.* αυτοις
cde. 14. μισεῖ (*pro* εμισησεν) e. 15. πονηρου c *super*
rasur. C. 20. πιστευοντων bcdeC. 22. δεδωκας μοι *bis*
scriptum c. 23. *init.* καγω *mutat.* c? (καθῶ *forsan p. m.* c).
σοι (*pro* συ) c. εἴνα c. γινωσκει bce. 24. δεδωκας (*pro*
εδωκας) ceCj. — κοσμου e (*at foot of column*).

Cap. XVIII. 1. χειμαρου bc. [των Κ.] de. 2. + και
(ante ο ισ) c. 3. init. Η rubro (pro ὁ) c. σπείραν (non ver.
12) d. ὅπλων e. 4. επ αυτων d p. m. (ο s. m.). τιναν c.
εἰστήκει ce. 6. ὀπίσω c. 7. – ουν c. αυτοις (pro αυτους)
d (non e). ναζωραιον d s. m., ει or η d p. m.? 8. – ὁ bcdCj.
ειπον (pro ειπεν) e. 10. εἵλκυσεν c. οτιον c. 11. – σου d
p. m. (habet supra d s. m.) eCj (habet c). εδωκε e. πειω c
p. m.? fin. αυτο d s. m. (ω p. m. d). 12. – οἱ c. εδυσαν c.
14. ἕνα c. απολεσθαι d text, marg. d s. m. ͮᵖαποθανειν.
15. συνησῆλθε. 16. εἴστηκη c. την θυραν c. την θυρα e.
εξηλθον c. 17. πεδισκει c. 18. εἰσ(εἰς be)τηκησαν bce.
– οἱ secund. c. ἑστῶς ce (-ὼς e). 20. – τῇ bcej. παντες
(pro πάντοθεν) ce. πάντοτε d p. m. C (marg. s. m. γρ παντες
e s. m. οἱ) e. – οἱ d. 21. επηρωτησεν c. 22. παρεστηκῶς
d. ῥάπησμα d p. m. (ι d s. m.). αποκρινει e. 23. [δερεις]
cd s. m. δαιρεις d p. m. j. 24. πεστειλεν αυτον (A init.
s. m.) e. ἅννας (non ver. 13) c. – ουν cdC (d s. m. ᵈᵉsupra).
αρχιερεαν e. 25. + ουν (post ηρνησατο) cd p. m. (eras. d
s. m.). ου (pro οὐκ εἰμί) c. 26. ὠτίον hic c. 28. πρωι
bcdeCj (πρῶ e). 29. πιλάτος hic de. 31. δε (pro οὖν
secund.) be. 32. θῦ (pro ιησου) c. εμελλεν bcdC. 33. – ουν
d. 34. αλλοις c (-ς c s. m.). 36. – ὁ bcdeCj. εἰ c s. m (η
c p. m.). ἡ ἐμοὶ (pro εἰ ἐμοὶ) c. βασιλεῖ secund. et tert. c.
37. – ὁ secund. cdj. γεγενημαι be. [γεγενν. c.] 38. – παλιν
bdeC. 39. – ὑμιν tert. e. ημιν (pro ὑμιν) d.

Cap. XIX. 1. – ουν c. + αυτον (post εμαστιγωσεν) c.
3. [εδιδουν] e. 4. – ουν c. αυτον ὑμιν ce. ουδεμιαν αιτιαν
εὑρισκω ἐν αυτω c. 6. + αὑτον (post σταυρωσον secund.)
bcdeCj. 7. – οἱ c. εχωμεν c. ἑαυτον θῦ υιον (–του bcdeC)
bc. τον θῦ υιον e. 8. τον λογον τουτον c. 9. πρετωριον c.
11. – ὁ prim. bcd (d s. m. supra) eCj. μείζωνα c. μειζων e.
12. εκραυγασαν be. ἑαυτὸν (pro αὑτον) bcdeCj. 13. τουτων
των λογων ej. βιματος c. λιθυστροτον c. ἑβραϊστι ce.
ἑβραϊστῆ d p. m. (ϊ d s. m.). γαβαθᾶ c. γαβαθά dCj.
γαββαθᾶ e. 14. ἦν (pro δε secund.) cdej. 15. εχωμεν bcd

p. m. (o d s. m.). 16. fin. ἤγαγον cdCj. − και tantum b.
17. εβασταζον c. εἰς τοπον λεγομενον Κρανιου τοπου (− τον)
bc. ἐβραϊστὶ cd. ἐβραϊστη b. γολγοθά de. 20. τίτλων c.
ὁ τοπος της πολεως bcdeCj. ἐβραϊστὶ c(d)e. ἑλληνιστὴ
cd (ι e s. m.). 21. γραφαι c. 23. εποιησεν c. τεσαρα e.
αραφος bce. 25. εἰστήκησαν c. μαγδαλινὴ de. 26, 27. ἴδε
c. ἴδε eC. 27. ὁ μαθητης αυτην bde. + εκεινος (post
μαθητης) cC. 28. ταυτα (pro τουτο) e. ἤδη πάντα d.
− ηδη b. ειδη (pro ηδη) e. πληρωθη (pro τελειωθη) ej.
29. ὄξους bis cde. το στοματι c. 31. σαμβατω c. μεγαλη
ἡμερα (− ἡ) εκεινου bc. [εκεινη dC] cf. Elz. αυτον (pro
αυτων) c. 32. συνσταυρωθεντος c. αυτου (pro αυτω) c.
34. ευθεως bcdeCj. 35. ἀληθηνῇ c. ἐστὶν ἡ μαρτυρία αὐτοῦ
cdCj. εστιν αυτου be. ειδεν (pro οἶδεν) c. + καὶ (post ἱνα)
d s. m. 36. ὁστουν cde. + απ᾽ (ante αυτου) cdCj. 37. − δε
prim. cd (p. m.: supra s. m.) eCj. − o prim. bcdej. δια των
φοβον cd p. m. σωμα prim. rescript. c. τῷ σῶμα d p. m.
(το d s. m.). επεστρεψεν c. αριμαθειας d s. m. − δε secund.
d (supra s. m.). 39. μῖγμα ce. + και (ante σμυρν.) c. ωσ̈
(ει d supra s. m.) dC. 40. εδυσαν ce. αὐτῶ (pro αυτο) c.
+ εν (ante οθονιοις) bcdeCj.

CAP. XX. 1. σαβατων b. σαμβάτων (sic ver. 19) c.
μαγδαλινὴ (non ver. 18 c) ce. πρωία d. βλεπη (sic ver. 5)
c. 2. ἠγαπα (pro εφιλει) e. 4. [και ὁ] e. 6. σίμον hic c.
αὐτῶν (ν eras.) d. 7. εὐθονια d p. m. ὁθόνια ced s. m.
εντετηληγμενον c. εντετὕλι(η d s. m.)γμενον d. 8. ἴδε (pro
ειδεν) c. 9. ηδησαν c. 11. εἰστήκει e. προς τω μνημειω d.
τὸ supra d s. m. Marg. d s. m. γρ. ον. 13. αυτοι (pro αυτη)
cd (mutat. η). ὀπισω e. ἐστωτα e. 14. − ὁ bcdeCj.
15. εθηκας αυτον bcdeCj. 16. λεγη prim. c. ραβουνὶ bcC.
ῥαββουνϊ de. λεγετε e. 17. ἅπτου e. οὔπω e (super ras.
d s. m.). αναβαιβηκα e. fin. ἡμων e p. m., ν s. m.
18. απαγγελουσα bce. ἑωρακά d p. m. (γρ. ε supra d s. m.).
ἑωρακε e. 19. ὀψιας ce. σαμβατων c. και κλυσμενων c.
δια τῶν φόβον cd p. m. e. ἔστη d. εχαρισαν d p. m. (η d
s. m.). 20, 22. τοῦτω c. 21. − ὁ ιϲ e. 22. ενεφυσεισε c.

142   COLLATION OF GOSPELS.

23. τινον c *p. m.*, ω *s. m.*   αφεῖτε c.   αφιενται e.   κρατεῖται
c. καὶ κρατηνται c.   κρατειτε e.   24. εἰς e.   δυδιμος e.
25. – ουν c.   + ὅτι (*ante* ἑωρ.) c.   ἑωράκαμε e.   χεῖραν (*sic*
ver. 27) c.   27. ὧδε de (*non* c).   28. *init.* – και ej**.   – ὁ
prim. bcdeCj.   29. – Θωμᾶ bcdeCj.   πεπιστευκας; bcde.
+ και (*ante* πεπιστευκας) d (*eras. s. m.*).   30. ὅ ἱσ (*pro* ὅτι ο
ἱσ) e.   τούτω d *s. m.*   τοῦτο d *p. m.*   31. – ὁ *prim.* bcdCj.

CAP. XXI. 1. παλιν εφανερωσεν ἑαυτον e.   – παλιν ὁ d.
+ αυτου (*post* μαθηταις) bce.   + αυτου εγερθεις εκ νεκρων
(cf. ver. 14) dj *secunda manus.*   τηβαριᾰδος c.   2. οἱ τοῦ ⁽ᵛⁱᵒⁱ⁾
marg. γρ υιοι *supra* bd *s. m.*   υίοι e.   κανὰ be.   3. ερχώ-
μεθα c.   + ουν (*post* εξηλθον) c.   ἀλιενειν e.   ενεβησαν
bcdeCj.   4. – ηδη c.   ἔστη d.   ἤδησαν ce.   5. – ουν d.
6. οὐκετι c (·) d.   μερει c.   7. επενδυτην gloss *marg.* d *s. m.*
τον εσωτατον ἱματιον ὃ και ὑποκαμϊσον λεγεται.   9. ἐπὶ
κημενον c.   10. + ουν (*post* λεγει) e.   ον (*pro* ὧν) c.
εποιησατε e.   11. Ἤλκυσεν c *rubro.*   δηκτυον c *p. m.*   την
γην d *s. m. forsan* της γης d *p. m.*   12. μα eras. d (*ante* των
μαθητων).   13. λαμβαννη c.   – με d (*habet marg.* d *s. m.*).
πλείων cd *p. m.* (ο d *s. m.*).   16. + ποιμενε b.   ποίμεναι c.
17. οἶδας.   – ελυπηθη *usque ad* φιλεις με c *p. m.* (ὁμοιοτ.)
habet supra c *s. m.*   18. ὅπου *secund.* e.   – και *prim.* c.
19. τουτω c *p. m.* (ο *s. m.*).   σιμαινων c.   δοξασει c *s. m.* (η
p. m.).   20. στιθος e.   22. ερχωμαι c.   23. αποθνήκει d.
24. ειδαμεν c (ο lost *super ras.*).   25. γραφητε bcd *p. m.* (αι
d *s. m.*).   καθεν d *p. m.*   [αμην] ce.

Deest subscriptio bc.   Τελος του κατα ιωαννην αγιου
ευαγγελιου Cj.

Rubro.   τελος του κατα ιω̄ ευ ᵃλ⁸, εξεδοθη κατα χρονους λβ̄'
της του χ̄υ αναληψεως εν πατμω τη νησω· στι β̄ᵡ' ᵞ.   *Cruci-*
form d.

PART III.

COLLATION OF APOCALYPSE.

Authorities quoted (efδCESt.B.Elz.Reuchlin).   e Cod.
26 = Wake 12 (see p. lxxxvii).   f Cod. 27 = Wake 34 (p.
lxxxviii).   δ Cod. 89 = Burdett-Coutts II. 4 (p. lxxxiv).

Ἀποκαλυψις του ἁγιου (– του ἁγιου + αποστολου και
ευαγγελιστου δC) ιωαννου του θεολογου (– του θεολογου δ)
fδCE. Ιῡ χῡ αποκαλυψις, δοθησα τω θεολογω ιωαννη e.
CAP. I. 2. – τε efδC [non E] fin. + και ατινα εισι και α χρη
γενεσθαι μετα ταυτα C tantum. 3. προφητιας C. 4. θῡ
(pro του prim.) efδ [non E]. – του prim. C. ὁς ην E1 tantum. – εστιν e (p. m. ?) fδ. 5. εκ efδ. αγαπωντι efδ. εκ
(pro απο secund.) ESt.1,2. om. ἡμων St.1,2. 6. ποιησαντι
ἡμιν βασιλειον ἱερατευμα (pro ἐποιησεν ἡμ. β. και) f. βασιλειαν (pro βασιλεις και) eδC. – των αιωνιον f. 7. – αυτον
prim. E. εξεκεντισαν E. – ἐπ αυτον E. 8. αλφα ef (τα
αλφα) δC. – αρχη καὶ τελος efδC. κσ̄ ὁ θσ̄ (pro ὁ κσ̄)
efδC. 9. – και prim. efδC. κοινωνος (pro συγκ.) efδC.
εν τη secund. efδC. εν χῶ ιῡ (pro ιῡ χῡ prim.) efδC. – τη
καλουμενη E. – δια secund. E. 10. φωνην οπισω μου efδC.
11. – εγω ειμι usque ad εσχατος· και efδC. βλεπης e. + ἑπτα
(ante εκκλησι.) efδC, at εις ἑπτα εκκλησιας e. – ταις εν
Ασια efδC. σμυρνην E. θυατηρα f. θυατειρας E. φιλα-
δελφιαν eE. 12. + εκει (ante επεστρεψα) efδC. ελαλει fδC,
ελαλη e. 13. – ἑπτα Ev.2 tantum. υἱον fδ [non e, &c.]. μαζοις
C. 14. καὶ ὡς (pro ὡσει) efδ. 16. χειρι αυτου C. οξια E.

— τη *secund.* Ε. — ὁ e. 17. ὅτι (*pro* ὅτε) C. ἔπεσον δ. ἔθηκε
(*pro* ἐπεθ.) efδ. — χειρα efδ. — μοι efδC. 18. — αμην Ε.
κλειδας eδ. του θανατου και του ἀδου efδC. 19. + ουν
(*post* γραψον) efδC. γενεσθαι C. 20. οὕς (*pro* ὤν) ESt.1,2.
αἱ λυχνιαι αἱ ἑπτα efδ (— αἱ *tantum* Ε). — ας ειδες efδ.

CAP. II. 1. της εν εφεσω (*pro* της εφεσινης) efδ. της
εκκλησιας εφεσω C. επι (*pro* εν *secund.*) Ε. 2. κολπον
(*pro* κοπον) e p.m. — σου *secund.* C. επειρασας τους λεγοντας ἑαυτους αποστολους ειναι efδC. 3. και ὑπομονην
εχεις και εβαστασας efδ. εβαπτισας (*pro* εβαστασας) Ε, *ex*
cod. Reuchlini. — και *tert.* efδC. και ουκ εκοπιασας (*pro*
κεκοπιακας και ου κεκμηκας) efδC. 4. αλλα efδC. 5. πεπ-
τωκας efδ. ταχυ efδCSt.2 (*non* St.1) B.Elz. + κατα σου (*post*
κινησω) f. μετανοησεις Ε. 7. — αυτω C. + αυτου (*post*
ζωησ) e. τω παραδεισω (— μεσω) efδ. *fin.* + μου fδC. + σου
e. 8. της εν σμυρνη εκκλησιας efδC. — ὅς efδ. 9. πτωχιαν
Ε. αλλα πλουσιος (— δε) efδC. + εκ (*ante* των λεγοντων)
fδ. 10. παθειν efδ. + δη (*post* ιδου) efδC. ὁ διαβολος εξ
ὑμων efδC. παραθῆτε Εv. 1, πειραθῆτε Εv. 2. ἡμερας efδ.
11. τω (*pro* το) C. 13. σου τα εργα καὶ f [τα εργα σου και
εδ]. — και *quart.* efδC. εμαις (*pro* εν αἱς) Ε, *at* — εν efδ.
ἀντεῖπας fδ. ὁ σατανας κατοικει efδC. 14. αλλα efδ. εδι-
δαξε τον βαλακ efδC, εδιδασκεν εν τω (τον B.Elz) βαλακ
ESB.Elz. + και εδ. + του f (*ante* φαγειν). 15. — των efδ.
ὁμοιως (*pro* ὁ μισω) efδC. 16. + ουν (*post* μετανοησον) efδ.
17. — φαγειν απο efδ. κεκρεμμενου e. κενον C. οιδεν fδC,
ειδεν e (*pro* εγνω). 18. θυατειρη εδ, θυατηρη f, θυατειραις Ε.
19. και την πιστιν και την διακονιαν efδC. — καὶ *sext.* efδC.
20. αλλα efδ. — ολιγα efδC. ὅτι αφεις (αφηκας e) την γυναικα σου (+ την C) ιεζαβελ (ιεζ. δ) ἡ λεγει ἑαυτην efδC, *at*
tantum ιεζαβελ Ε1,2, ιεζαβηλ *erratum* Ε1. προφητην f p.m.
και διδασκει και πλανα τους εμους δ. efδC. φαγειν ειδωλο-
θυτα efδC (ειδολ. e p. m.). 21. *fin.* (*post* μετανοηση) και
ου θελει (— λη e) μετανοησαι εκ της πορνειας αυτης efδC.
22. — εγω efδC. βαλῶ f. μοιχευσαντας δ. αυτης (*pro* αυτων)
efδC. 23. ὁ (*ante* ερευννων) Β. 24. — τοις (*pro* και *prim.*)
efδC. — και *prim.* Β. — και *secund.* efδC. βαθέα efδC (βαθῆ

E). βαλλω efδ. 25. εχω (pro εχετε) e. ανοιξω (pro αν ήξω) fδ [non e, &c.]. 26. και ὁ τηρων και ὁ νικων e. 27. κεραμεικα ef. συντριβησεται efδC.

CAP. III. 1. + ἑπτα (ante πνευματα) efδCElz. [non E.SB]. – το efδC. εχεις ονομα e. και (pro ὅτι secund.) efδ. ζωῆς Er.1 (ex cod. Reuchl.: ζῆς in erratis). 2. στηρισον εδ, στηρηξον Er.1, at τηρησον f. εμελλες (ημ. δ) αποβαλλειν efδ, εμελες αποβαλειν C (pro μελει αποθανειν). εύρικα E. – τα secund. E fin. + μου efδC. 3. – και ηκουσας καὶ τηρει efδ. γνωση efδ. 4. init. + αλλα e, αλλ᾽ fδC. ολιγα εχεις efδC. – και prim. efδC. οἱ (pro ἁ) E. 5. οὕτως (pro οὗτος) ef [non δ]. περιβαλλεῖται C. – εκ της βιβλου κ.τ.λ. usque ad ονομα αυτου f (ὁμοιοτέλευτον: habet marg., forsan p. m., omisso etiam και ενωπιον των αγγελων αυτου). – της prim. ESt.1,2. ὁμολογησω ef marg. C, εξομολογησω δ. 7. φιλαδελφια E. εκκλησια δ. κλειν efδC. δανιδ C. κλεισει (pro κλειει prim.) efδ (κλήσει), C. αυτην, ει μη ὁ ανοιγων (pro και κλειει) efδC fin. ανοιξει efδC. 8. ἡν (pro και prim.) efδC. 9. αυτους (pro ἑαυτους) ESt.1,2. ηξουσι C. – εγω efδC. 11. – Ιδου efδC. 12. στῦλον δ. λαῳ (pro ναῳ) B.Elz. επ αυτου C. ἡ καταβαινει (pro ἡ καταβαινουσα) efδCBElz. [non Eϛ]. απο (pro εκ) fδ [non e]. εκ (pro απο) f. – μου quint. efδ. 14. της εν Λαοδικεια εκκλησιας efδC. – ὁ prim. E. 15. ης (pro ειης) efδC. 16. ου ζεστος ουτε ψυχρος efδC. οὔδε (pro ουτε secund.) E1, correct. in erratis. 17. – ὅτι secund. efδC. εχων e p. m. + ὁ (ante ελεεινος) efδC fin.; e. 18. αγωρασαι ef. χρυσιον παρ εμου efδC. πλουτησεις e. περιβαλλη δ. – και secund. C. κολλυριον efδ. κολουριον C. κουλλουριον E1, correct. in erratis. ινα εγχριση εδ, ινα εγχρησης e p. m. (pro εγχρισον). + επι (ante τους οφθ.) C. 19. ζηλευε (pro ζηλωσον) efδ. 20. + και (ante εισελευσομαι) efδC.

CAP. IV. 1. ανεωγμενη efδC. λεγων (pro λεγουσα) εδ. λεγ ante rasuram f, fin. e, cum sequent. δ. 2. – και prim. efδ. τον θρονον efδ. 3. – και ὁ καθημενος ην fδC. – ην tantum e. + σμαραγδω (ante και σαρδιω) e. σαρδειω fδ p. m. σαρδιω

S.   10

146 COLLATION OF APOCALYPSE.

C. ὅμοια (pro ὅμοιος secund.) CB.Elz. [non Eϛ], at ὁμοίως
efδ. ὅρασις (pro ὁράσει) efC. 3, 4. σκαραγδινων κυκλοθεν
(– και) efδ, at e p. m. σμαραγδω και κυκλωθεν? 4. εικοσιτεσσαρες eC. κ̄δ̄ fδE. – ειδον efδE. – τους secund. E.
εικοσιτεσσαρας eC. κ̄δ̄ fδE. – εσχον efδCEr.1 [habent Er.2.
ϛElz.]. 5. εκπορευοντο E. και φωναι και βρονται efδC.
+ αυτου (post θρονου secund.) efδC. αἱ εισιν ἑπτα (– τα)
efδC. 6. + ὡς (ante θαλασσα) efδC. ὑελινη C tantum.
κρυσταλω e p. m., κρυσταλλου f. ἐμπροσθε Er.2. 7. εχων
(– το sequens) e. – εχον usque ad τεταρτον ζωον (ὁμοιοτελευτον) f. ανθρωπου (– ὡς) εδ. – ζωον quart..εδ. πετο-
μενω efδ. 8. ἐν καθ ἑν (+ αυτων C) εχον efδC. γεμουσιν
efδC. λεγοντες efδE. ἁγιος novies fδC. ὃ ἦν f. 9. δωσι
εδ, δωσει fC (pro δωσουσι). 10. εικοσιτεσσαρες fC, κ̄δ̄ εδE.
προσκυνησουσι efδB.Elz. [non CEϛ]. βαλουσι efδB.Elz. [non
CEϛ]. 11. ὁ κσ̄ και ὁ θσ̄ ἡμων ὁ (– ὁ f) ἁγιος (pro κε) efδ.
την (ante δυναμιν) rescript. f. – τα efδ. ησαν (pro εισι) efδ.

CAP. V. 1. γεγραμμενων e. εξωθεν (pro οπισθεν) efδC.
+ και (ante κατεσφρ.) f. 2. + εν (ante φωνη) efδ. αξιος
εστιν efδ. – εστιν C. 3. εδυνατο efδC. + ανω (post ουνω)
efδ. ουτε (pro ουδε) ter efδ. και (pro ουδε secund.) E.
4. – εγω E. πολυ efδC. και αναγνωναι efδ. 5. – ων efδC.
– εκ E. δαυιδ C. ὁ ανοιγων (pro ανοιξαι) efδ. – λυσαι
efδC. 6. – και ιδου efδ. ἑστηκως δ p. m. εσφαγισμενον C.
εχων e. ἃ (pro οἳ) efδC. – ἑπτα tert. E tantum. πνευματα
του θῡ· efδC. αποστελλο(ω e)μενα (– τα) efδC. 7. ειληφεν
(– το βιβλιον) efδC. fin. + βιβλιον C. 8. κ̄δ̄ omnes. – οἱ C.
επεσαν efE [non δC]. κιθαραν efδ. αἵ εισι (– αἱ) efδ. προσ-
ευχων fδ. 9. εσφραγισας (pro εσφαγης) δ. 10. αυτους
(pro ἡμας) efδC. – τω θῶ E (ex cod. Reuchl.). βασιλευσουσιν
εδ, βασιλευουσιν fC. 11 + ὡς (ante φωνην) efδC. κυκλω
efδC. + και ην ὁ αριθμος αυτων μυριαδες μυριαδων (ante και
χιλιαδες) efδCB.Elz. [omittunt ESt.1ϛ ex cod. Reuchl.]. – των
(ante πρεσβυτερων) St.1,2. 12. εσφαγισμενον C. εστιν
(– το prim.) ESt.1,2. + τον (ante πλουτον) efδ. 13. – εστιν
efδ. επι της γης efδC. – ἁ efδ. παντας (pro παντα) efδC.

λεγοντες E 1 (correct. in erratis). τω θρονω efδ. fin. + αμην
ef[δ]C. 14. – καὶ τὰ τ. usque ad αμην (ὁμοιοτελευτον: supplet
marg. p. m.) δ. λεγοντα το (pro ελεγον) efC. – εικοσιτεσσαρες efδC. επεσον δC [non efEϝB.Elz.]. – ζωντι εις τους
αιωνας των αιωνων efδC.

Cap. VI. 1. ὅτι (pro ὅτε) efC. ἐν (pro μιαν ESt.1, non
St.2: om. μιαν cod. Reuchl.). + ἑπτα (ante σφραγιδων) efδC.
φωνην e, φωνη fδC. – και βλεπε C. ιδε (pro βλεπε) efδ.
2. – και ειδον efδ. αυτον (pro αυτω prim.) efδC. εχον e.
– και (ante ἱνα) e. 3. οτι (pro ὅτε) C. την σφραγιδα την
δευτεραν ESt.1,2 (ex cod. Reuchl.). – και βλεπε efδC.
4. πυρος ef. αυτον (pro αυτω prim.) efδC, at e primo
αυτων. εκ (pro απο) efδC. – και (ante ἱνα) efδC. 5. την
σφραγιδα την τριτην efδC. – και βλεπε C. ιδε (pro βλεπε)
efδ. και ειδον efδ. αυτον (pro αυτω) efδC. εχον C.
6. – και τρεις χ. κρ. δηναριου (ὁμοιοτελευτον) f. χοίνες (pro
χοινικες) e. + ου (ante μη) f. 7. την τεταρτην σφραγιδα C.
+ και (ante ηκουσα) f. – φωνην efδC. του τεταρτου λεγοντος ζωου f p. m. λεγοντος (pro λεγουσαν) εδC. – και
βλεπε C. ιδε (pro βλεπε) efδ. 8. – Και ειδον efδ. – αυτου
prim. E (ex cod. Reuchl., sic etiam ακουλουθει sequens). – ὁ
secund. C. ηκολουθει αυτω (– μετ’) efδ. αυτω (pro αυτοις)
efδC. επι το τεταρτον· αποκτειναι efδC. – εν (ante θανατω)
e. – καὶ (ante ὑπο) E ex cod. Reuchl. 9. εσφρ μενων e. των
ανθρωπων των εσφαγισμενων C. + του αρνιου (ante ἤν) efδC.
10. εκραξαν efδC. φωνην μεγαλην efδ. – ὁ tert. efδC. εκ-
δικης δ p. m. εκ (pro απο) efδC. 11. εδοθη αυτοις στολη
λευκη efδ. ἑκασταις ESt.1 (non St.2). – και εδοθ. usque ad
λευκ. C, εδοθη pro ερρεθη posito. αναπαυσονται δ, αναπαυ-
σωντο E. – ετι f [non εδ]. – μικρον efδC. – οὗ efδ.
πληρωσωσι efδ cod. Reuchl., πληρωθωσι C [πληρωσονται
EϝB.Elz.]. + και (ante οἱ μελλοντες) efδ. αποκτενεσθαι e,
αποκτεννεσθαι fδ. 12. + και (ante ὅτε) eC. – ιδου efδC.
μελας εγενετο efδC. σακος f. + ὁλη (post σεληνη) efδ.
13. επεσον εδC [non fEϝB.Elz.]. βαλουσα efδ. ανεμου
μεγαλου efδ. 14. + ὁ (ante οὖνοσ) efδC. ἑλισσομενον e (sic)
C (ελ.), ἑλισσομενος fδ, εἱλισσομενον ESt.1. – αυτων e.

10—2

εκηνηθησαν e p. m.   15. και οι χιλιαρχοι και οι πλουσιοι
και οι ισχυροι (non δυνατοι) efδC.   – πας secund. efδ.
16. τω θρονω efδ.   17. – ἡ μεγαλη f.

CAP. VII. 1.   τουτο (pro ταυτα) efδC.   κρατουντες E.
+ ὁ (ante ανεμος) e.   τι ef, τη δ p. m. (pro παν).   2. αγγελον
αλλον f.   αναβαινοντα efδC.   + του (ante θῦ) f.   ἀδικῆναι
E.   3. αδικησατε C.   αχρι (– οὗ) ESt.1,2 ex cod. Reuchl.
σφραγισωμεν efδCSt.1,2EB.Elz. [– ζωμεν Eς], μετοπων eC.
4. των αριθμων C.   ἑκατον και τεσσαρακοντα τεσσαρες fδC
[ρμδ e].   εσφαγμενων (sic) f, εσφραγισμενων εδ (pro εσφρα-
γισμενοι).   5. εσφραγισμεναι (pro -νοι prim.) ef [non δC].
5—8. Post εσφρ. prim. deest hoc verbum decies in efδC.
ρουβημ e, ρουβειν C, ρουβιμ ESt.1 (non St.2) ex cod. Reuchl.
6. φυλην prim. e p. m.   νεφθαλημ f, νεφθαλιμ ESt.1 (non
St.2).   μανασση C.   7. ισασχαρ Elz. tantum.   8. Βενιαμην e
fin. εσφραγισμεναι efδ [non C].   9. – αυτον efδC.   εδυνατο
efδC.   – και φυλων E ex cod. Reuchl.   – και (ante γλωσσων)
εδ.   ἑστωτας e, ἑστωτας fδ.   περιβεβλημενους efδ.   φοινικας
efδ.   10. κραζουσι efδC.   τω θῶ ἡμων τω καθημενω επι τω
θρονω (του θρονου CElz.) efδCB.Elz. [non Eς].   11. ἑστηκεσαν
e, εἱστηκεισαν fδCSt.2 (non St.1).   επεσαν fE [non εδ].
+ αυτου (post θρονου) efδ.   τα προσωπα efδC.   12. και ἡ
σοφια και ἡ δοξα e.   – ἡ sept. C.   13. αποκριθη E.   τινες;
(– εισι) E ex cod. Reuchl.   14. ειπον (pro ειρηκα) efδC.
+ μου (post κε) efδC.   επλατυναν fESt.1,2 (επλατειναν cod.
Reuchl.), at επλυναν eC.   – στολας αυτων secund. efδ, at
αυτας C.   15. επι τω θρονω efδC.   16. πιναουσιν eC.
– ετι secund. E ex cod. Reuchl.   ουδ᾽ ου (pro ουδε secund.)
efδC.   πεσει E.   17. ποιμαινει efδ.   ὁδηγει efδ.   ζωησ (pro
ζωσας) efδC.   εκ (pro απο) εδC.   – και εξαλειψει ad fin.
Er.1 ex cod. Reuchl.

CAP. VIII. 2.   – τους ἑπτα E ex cod. Reuchl.   – ἑπτα
prim. e.   ἑστηκασι e, ἑστηκεσαν f.   3. του θυσιαστηριου
prim. efδC.   δωσει ef [non δ].   4. – ὁ e.   5. τον (pro το)
et αυτον (pro αυτο) efδCElz. [non EςB].   βρονται και φωναι
και αστραπαι efδ.   6. – οἱ E ex cod. Reuchl.   + οἱ (ante

εχοντες) εδC [non f]. 7. – αγγελος εfδC. χαλατα E1
(correct. in erratis). + εν (ante αἱματι) εfδC. + και το
τριτον της γης κατεκαη (post γην) εfδC. – και το τριτον
των δενδρων κατεκαη C. 8. πυρι εfδC. 9. – των εν τη
θαλασση E ex cod. Reuchl. – των secund. εfδC. διεφθα-
ρησαν C, διεφθαρησεν E. 10. του (pro το) e. + των (ante
ὑδατων) εfδC. 11. + ὁ (ante αψινθος) εfδC. εγενετο (pro
γινεται) εfδC. + των ὑδατων (post το τριτον) εfδCB.Elz.
[om. Es]. + των (ante ανων) εfδC. απεθανεν E. 12. και
το τριτον αυτης μη φανη· ἡ ἡμερα (pro και ἡ ἡμ. μη φαινη
το τρ. αυτης) εfδ. 13. αετου πετομενου (pro αγγελου πετω-
μενου) εfδC. μεσουρανισματι E ex cod. Reuchl. + τρις
(post μεγαλη) C. οὐαι bis tantum E ex cod. Reuchl. τους
κανοικουντας εfδ. τρειων E.

CAP. IX. 2. – και ηνοιξε το φρεαρ της αβυσσου εfδ.
– εκ του φρεατος ὡς καπνος (ὁμοιοτελευτον) fE ex cod. Reuchl.
καιομενης (pro μεγαλης) εfδC. 3. εξηλθεν? e p. m. 4. αυτοις (pro αυταις) C. – μονους εfδE ex cod. Reuchl. – ουκ
E1 (correct. in erratis). – του θῦ E ex cod. Reuchl. μετοπων
e. – αυτων E ex cod. Reuchl. 5. αυτοις (pro αυταις) E ex
cod. Reuchl. βασανισωσι C, βασανισθησωνται ESt.1,2.
πληξη (pro παίση) e. 6. ζητουσιν fδC. ου μη εfδC, ουκ E
(pro ουχ). εὑρησωσιν fδ [non eC], ευρισουσιν E2 (correct.
in errat.). φευγει E ex cod. Reuchl. (E.2 correct. in errat.).
απ αυτων ὁ θανατος εfδC. 7. ὁμοιματα E. ητοιμασμενα C.
χρυσοι (pro ὁμοιοι χρυσω) εfδC. 9. ἁρματων e. – ἱππων f.
10. και (pro ην) εfδC. εξουσιαν εχουσι του (pro και ἡ
εξουσια αυτων) εfδC. 11. init. εχουσαι βασιλεα επ αυτων
αγγελον (– και et τον) εfδC, etiam E επ αυτων. ἑαυτω (pro
αυτω) E. αβααδδων εδ, αββααδδων f, αββαδων CE. – και
(ante εν τη Ελ.) e, εν τη Ελληνικη δε (– και) f, εν δε τη Ελλ.
(– και) δC. + ὁ (ante απολλυων) C. 12. ερχεται fδC [non
e]. – ετι E ex cod. Reuchl. Μετα ταυτα cum sequentibus εδ.
13. – του tert. E. 14. λεγοντος fδ [non e]. ὁ εχων (pro ὁς
ειχε) εfδC. εφρατη e. 15. + εις την (ante ἡμεραν) εfδ.
– και ἡμεραν C. 16. + των (ante στρατευματων) εfδC.
ἱππου εfδC. – δυο εfδC. – και secund. εfδC. των (pro

150   COLLATION OF APOCALYPSE.

τον) εδ. 17. ωρασει C. ιακισνινους C. 18. απο (pro ὑπο)
efδC. + πληγων (ante τουτων) efδC. απο (pro εκ prim.)
efδ. – εκ secund. et tert. efδC. 19. init. ἡ γαρ εξουσια των
ἱππων εν τω στοματι αυτων εστιν (εστι eC) και εν ταις
ουραις αυτων· αἱ γαρ ουραι efδC. ὁμοιοι CE ex cod. Reuchl.
St.1 (non St.2). οφεων efδ. 20. ου κατεκαυθησαν (pro ουκ
απεκτανθησαν) e. ου (pro ουτε prim.) efδ. + τα (ante
ειδωλα) efδCE ex cod. Reuchl. St.1,2. – και τα χαλκα ef.
21. φώνων f. – ουτε εκ των φαρμακειων αυτων (ὁμοιοτ.) e.
φαρμακων fδ, φαρμακιων C.

CAP. X. 1. – αλλον efδC. +ἡ (ante ιρις) efδC. +αυτου
(post κεφαλης) efC. στῦλοι δ. 2. εχων (pro ειχεν) efδ.
βιβλιον efδ, βιβλιδαριον C. + το (post βιβλαριδιον) E3
[ανεωγμενον efδ]. της θαλασσης efδC. και τον ευωνυμον
(– δε) e. της γης efδC. 3. φωνας? e p. m. – αἱ E ex cod.
Reuchl. St.1,2. 4. – αἱ prim. E ex cod. Reuchl. St.1,2. τα
φωνας E. – τας φωνας ἑαυτων efδC. ημελλον δ. – μοι
efδC. ελαλησεν secund. E. αυτα (pro ταυτα) efδ, at και
μετα ταυτα γραφεις C fin. γραφης ESt.1,2. 5. ἑστωτα e.
+την δεξιαν (post αυτου) efδC. 6. ωμοσε (– εν prim.) efδ.
– και την γην και τα εν αυτη E ex cod. Reuchl. την θαλασσα
e. fin. ουκ ετι εσται ef (ουκετι) δC. 7. αλλ efδC. μελλει E.
– και C. ετελεσθη efδ. ο ευηγγελισατο (pro ὡς ευηγγελισε) C.
τους δουλους αυτου τους προφητας efδC. 8. βιβλιδαριον efδC.
ανεωγμενον efδC. +του (ante αγγελου) efδC. 9. απηλθα f.
δουναι (pro Δος) efδ. – το E4,5. βιβλιδαριον efδC. – τω
E. 10. βιβλιον efδ, βιβλιδαριον C. ἦν (pro ἦν) efδ. – εν
E ex cod. Reuchl. St.1,2. 11. λεγουσι efδ (– ιν). σαι (pro
σε) e. +επι (ante εθνεσι) fδ (– ιν) C [non e]. γλωτταις E
ex cod. Reuchl. St.1,2.

CAP. XI. 1. + εἱστηκει ὁ αγγελος (post ραβδω) C, και ὁ
αγγελος εἱστηκει B.Elz. [non efδEϛ]. 2. εξωθεν (pro εσωθεν)
efδCB.Elz. [non Eϛ]. εξωθεν (pro εξω) eCE [non fδ]. με-
τρησεις C. και (pro ὁτι) E. + και (post τεσσαρακοντα) efδ.
3. ἑξηκοντα e. 4. οἱ (pro αἱ) e. + αἱ (ante δυο secund.) efδC.
κῦ (pro θῦ) efδC. ἑστωτες fδ, ἑστωτες e, ἑστωσαι E. 5. θελει

prim. efδC. θελει αυτους *secund.* efδC. − αυτους *secund.* E.

ούτως efδCE. 6. εχουσι τον ουνον εξουσιαν κλεισαι efδ.

ύατος El (*correct. in erratis*). ύετος βρεχη τας ήμερας της.

προφητειας αυτων efδC. + ταις (*ante ήμεραις*) E *ex cod.*

Reuchl. St.1,2. − αυτα E *ex cod. Reuchl.* + εν (*ante παση*

πληγη) CE *ex cod. Reuchl.* όσάκισ εαν θελησωσιν εν παση

πληγη efδ. 7. ότε τελεσουσι E *ex cod. Reuchl.* − το *secund.*

ESt.1,2. μετ αυτων πολεμον efδC. αποκτανει ESt.1,2.

8. το πτωμα efδ. + της (*ante πολεως*) efδC. σωδομα C.

− και *secund.* E *ex cod. Reuchl.* αυτων (*pro ήμων*) efδC.

9. βλεπουσιν efδC. φιλών e *p. m.* γλωττων ESt.1,2.

− και εθνων E *ex cod. Reuchl.* το πτωμα *prim.* efδ. − και

(*ante ήμισυ*) efδC. ουχ C. μνημα efδC. *Post* αυτων *prim.*

pergit E (*ferè cum cod. Reuchl.*). και οί εκ των εθνων ήμ.

τρ. και ήμισυ,...αφιουσι (αφησουσι E.2 *in erratis*)...μνηματα.

10. χαιρουσιν efδC, χαρουσι E. ευφρανουνται ESt.1,2.

δωσωσιν e, δωσουσιν fδ (*pro πεμψουσιν*). αλληλους e.

11. − τας CE *ex cod. Reuchl.* St.1,2. εις (*pro* επ *prim.*) fδ

[*non* e]. αυτοις (− επ) E *ex cod. Reuchl.* έστησαν δ. επε-

πεσεν fC [*non* εδ]. 12. ηκουσα efδC. φωνης μεγαλης C.

λεγουσης C. αναβατε ώδε e. 13. *init.* − και efδ. ήμερα

(*pro ώρα*) efδC (*cum antecedentibus jungit* δ). 14. − ή *prim.*

E. ή ουαι ή τριτη ιδου efδC [*habet* ιδου E not St.1]. 15. λε-

γοντες efδ (*marg. p. m.* λεγουσαι δ). εγενετο ή βασιλεια efδC.

+ ιῦ χῦ (*post* ήμων) f *p. m.* βασιλευει f. 16. − και *secund.*

eC [οί κδ fδE]. − οί *secund.* E *ex cod. Reuchl.* οί ενωπιον

του θρονου (θῦ *p. m.* e), οί καθηνται efδ. επεσον δC [*non*

ef Eς B.Elz.]. 17. παντοκρατορ e. − και ό ερχομενος efδ.

− την *prim.* ESt.1,2. 18. φθειροντας E *ex cod. Reuchl.*

19. ηνοιχθη efδ. του κυ (*pro* αυτου *prim.*) efδC. − και

σεισμος efδC.

CAP. XII. 1. − ή E *ex cod. Reuchl.* 2. εκραξεν e, εκραζεν

fδC. 3. πυρος μεγας εδ, πυρρος μεγας f. εχον e *p. m.* έπτα

διαδηματα efδC *fin.* − έπτα E *ex cod. Reuchl.* (E2 *corr. in*

erratis). 4. − αυτου E *ex cod. Reuchl.* τριτων e *p. m.* − του

ουνου El *ex cod. Reuchl.* έστηκεν e. μελουσης τικτειν C.

152   COLLATION OF APOCALYPSE.

φαγη E *ex cod. Reuchl.*   5. ετεκεν δ.   ποιμανειν C, ποιμενειν
E.   − εν E *ex cod. Reuchl.* St.1,2.   ηρπαγη C.   + προς *(ante*
τον θρονον)* efδC.   6. + εκει *(post* εχει)* efδC.   υπο *(pro* απο)*
ef.   − του f.   εκτρεφωσιν efδC.   εξηκοντα e.   7. (+ του C)
πολεμησαι μετα του δρ. efδC.   μετα *(pro* κατα)* St.1,2.
8. ισχυσεν efδC.   ουδε *(pro* ουτε)* efδC.   αυτω *(pro* αυτων)*
efδC.   9. − ὁ *tert.* E *ex cod. Reuchl.* St.1,2.   − ὁ *sext.* efδC.
− μετ αυτου eE *ex cod. Reuchl.*   − εβληθησαν e.   10. εν τω
ουνω λεγουσαν fδC.   − εν τω ουνω e.   εβληθη efδ.   − ὁ κατη-
γορος των αδελφων ἡμων E *ex cod. Reuchl.*   αυτους *(pro*
αυτων)* E *ex cod. Reuchl.*   − ἡμων *tert.* E *ex cod. Reuchl.*
11. αυτων δια? e *p. m.*   μεχρι *(pro* αχρι)* f.   12. ευφραινεσθαι
e *p. m.*   − οἱ *prim.* efδ.   κατοικουντες *(pro* σκηνουντες)* e.
− τοις κατοικουσι efδC.   τη γη και τη θαλασση efδC.   + ὁ
(ante εχων)* E *cum cod. Reuchl.* St.1,2.   13. ειδον E.   − την
prim. C.   εδιωξα E.   + τον υιον *(ante* τον αρρ.)* e.   14. πτε-
ρυγες e *p. m.*   πεταται E *ex cod. Reuchl.*   οπως τρεφηται
(pro οπου τρεφεται)* ef *(sic)* δC.   15. εκ του στοματος αυτου
οπισω *(ὀπ.* e)* της γυναικος efδC.   αυτην *(pro* ταυτην)* efδC,
− ταυτην E (E2 *correct. in errat.*).   ποταμοφόρον e.   16. ἡ
γυναικη *(pro* ἡ γη *prim.*), etiam κατεπιεν ὁ, etiam ὁ δρα *(pro*
ὁν), etiam ver.* 17 λ *(pro* ὁ) e *p. m., errore.*   17. οργισθη C.
− του *(ante* ιυ) efδ.   − χυ efδC.

CAP. XIII. 1.   αναβαινων f *p. m.*   κερατα δεκα και
κεφαλας ἑπτα efδC.   ἑπτα *(pro* δέκα *prim.)* E1.   ονοματα
efδC.   2. − ην E *ex cod. Reuchl.*   ἦν e.   αρκου e *(sic)* fδ [*non*
CE*].*   θρονων? e *p. m.*   3. − ειδον fδC.   + εκ *(post* μιαν)*
efδC.   ὡσει *(pro* ὡς) efδC.   εσφραγισμενην δ *p. m. (cf. Cap.*
V. 9).   εθαυμασεν ὁλη ἡ γη (− εν) efδCB.Elz. [*non* Eϛ *cum*
cod. Reuchl.].   4. τω δρακοντι τω δεδωκοτι την εξουσιαν
(− δς) efδC.   τω θηριω *(pro* το θηριον)* efδC.   + και *(ante*
τις *secund.)* C.   δυνατος *(pro* δυναται)* efδC.   5. λαλον E.
βλασφημιαν ef (− ια) δC.   + πολεμον *(ante* ποιησαι)* efδCElz.
[*non* EϛB *ex cod. Reuchl.*].   6. − το *prim.* δ.   − και *tert.* efδ.
7. πόλμον E1.   ποιησαι πολεμον efδC.   + και λαον *(post*
φυλην)* efδ.   8. αυτον *(pro* αυτω)* efδ.   ουτε *(pro* ου)* fδ [*non*
e].   το ονομα εν τω βιβλιω efδC.   + του *(ante* εσφαγμ.)* efδC.

COLLATION OF APOCALYPSE. 153

εσφαγισμενου E (E2 correct. in erratis). 10. init. ειτις εχει
αιχμαλωσιαν υπαγει· (– αιχμ. συναγει εις) efδC [ει τις
αιχμαλωσιαν συναγει, om. εις αιχμ. υπαγει cod. Reuchl.
EϛElz.]. αποκτενει e, – αποκτενεῖ δ. – εν μαχαιρα
secund. fδ [non e]. 11. – δυο efδ. αρνιου E ex cod. Reuchl.
St.1,2. 12. εποιει (pro ποιει secund.) efδC. εν αυτη κατοικουντας efδC. 13. init. και πυρ ινα εκ του ουνου καταβαινη
(– ποιη) efδC. επι (pro εις) efδC. 14. + τους εμους (post
πλανα) efδC. οικονα C. ειχε (pro εχει) C, at in fine ὃ ειχε
πληγην και εζησεν (– σε e) απο της μαχαιρας efδ. 15. πνευμα
δουναι efδC. και ινα (pro ινα και) C. – ἡ fC. + ινα (ante
ὁσοι) f. εαν (pro αν) efδ. τη εικονι (pro την εικονα) efδ, at
ποιει τους μη προσκυνουντας τη εικονι (– ὁσοι αν) C. – ινα
(ante αποκτ.) efδ. και ποιει (pro αποκτ.) e primὸ. 16. + ινα
λαβωσι το χαραγμα αυτου και (post δουλους) e. δωσωσιν
ef p. m. δ, δωσουσιν f s. m., δωσιν C. αυτους· (pro αυτοις) e.
χαραγματα efδC. – της prim. fδ. το μετωπον fδ, το μετοπον
e, των μετοπων C. 17. δυναται fδE ex cod. Reuchl. St.1 [non
eSt.2]. αγωρᾶσαι e. – η secund. efδ. 18. – τον prim. efδC.
– τον secund. E2,3. – και (post ανου εστι) e?fδC. εξακοσιοι
εξηκοντα εξ C.

CAP. XIV. 1. + το (ante αρνιον) efδ. ἑστηκος e, ἑστος
E1, ἑστως E2, ἑστος St.1,2. ορος e. + αριθμος (ante ρμδ)
efδ?. – ἑκατον E1. + αυτου, και το ονομα (post ονομα) efδC.
καιομενον (pro γεγρ.) E ex cod. Reuchl. γεγραμμενων e p. m.
μετοπων eδ. 2. ἡ φωνη ἥν ηκουσα (pro φωνην ηκουσα) efδC.
+ ὡς (ante κιθαρωδων) efδC. κιθαραζοντων E1. 3. – ὡς
efδC. ουδε εις fδ [non e]. εδυνατο efC [non δ]. ρμδ efδ.
ἡγορασμενα δ. 4. οἱ (pro οἰ) e. – εισιν tert. E ex cod.
Reuchl. St.1,2. + γαρ (post ὁπου) C. εαν (pro αν) efδ.
απερχη (pro υπαγη) e p. m. + ὑπο ιυ (ante ηγορασθησαν)
efδC. om. τω (ante αρνιω) St.1,2. 5. και ουχ ευρεθη εν τω
στοματι αυτων ψευδος (non δολος) efδ. ουκ E. ψευδος (pro
δολος) C. – ενωπιον του θρονου του θυ efδC. 6. – αλλον
fδE ex cod. Reuchl. [non e]. πετομενον efδC. μεσουρανισματι
E (– ησματι E2 correct.). ευαγγελισασθαι C. + τους

καθημενους (ante τους κατοικουντας) E ex cod. Reuchl. καθημενους (pro κατοικουντας) efδC. + επι (ante παν) efδC. 7. λεγων efδC. φοβηθητε E. κν (pro θν) efδ. προσκυνησετε E. αυτον τον ποιησαντα (pro τω ποιησαντι) efδ. + την (ante θαλασσαν) efδC. 8. + δευτερος (ante αγγελος) efδ. ηκολουθησεν δ. – επεσεν usque ad τριτος αγγελος ver. 9 (ὁμοιοτελ.) f. – επεσεν εδ. βαβουλων Elz. (1624). – ἡ πολις εδC. ἢ (pro ὁτι) e. – ὁτι δC. – του θυμου E ex cod. Reuchl. ταυτης (pro αυτης) δ. + τα (ante εθνη) εδC. 9. αλλος αγγελος τριτος εδC. ειτι δ. προσκυνει το θηριον efδC. τω θηριω (θυριω E2) E. μετοπου e. 10. κεκεραμενου E in annotationibus. – ἁγνων e [non fδ]. αγγελων των ἁγιων ESt.1,2. 11. εις αιωνας (– να e) αιωνων αναβαινει efδC. αιωνα E ex cod. Reuchl. St.1,2. τω θηριω E. – το secund. E ex cod. Reuchl. St.1,2. 12. init. jungit cum praeced. δ. + ἡ (ante ὑπομονη) efδ. – ὡδε secund. efδ. – του θῡ E ex cod. Reuchl. + του (ante ιυ) C. 13. – μοι efδ. απαρτι λεγει (· δ) ναι fδC [non ESᵋElz.]. αναπαυσονται E ex cod. Reuchl. γαρ (pro δε) e. – αυτων secund. E ex cod. Reuchl. ακολουθειν e p. m. 14. καθημενον ὁμοιον efδ. υιν efδ, υιος E1 ex cod. Reuchl. εχοντα ef. την κεφαλης e p. m. 15. φωνη μεγαλη efδC. + τη (ante φωνη) E ex cod. Reuchl. ηλθεν (– σοι) efδC. – του secund. fδE ex cod. Reuchl. [non e]. 16. τη νεφελη efδ. 17. αγγελος αλλος e, at transfert αγγελος E in locum post ουνιο cum cod. Reuchl., sequentibus St.1,2. 18. + εν (ante κραυγη) δ [non ef]. + της αμπελου (post βοτρυας) efδCB.Elz. [non ESᵋ ex cod. Reuchl.]. fin. ηκμασεν ἡ σταφυλη της γης (– αυτης) efδ. 19. εξεβαλεν (pro εβαλεν prim.) efδ. λῖνον e p. m. ελαβεν (pro εβαλεν secund.) E1. fin. τον μεγαν efδC. 20. εξωθεν (pro εξω) efδC. χαλενων e p. m. αχ fδ, at διακοσιων e, εν αλλω β f marg. p. m.

CAP. XV. 1. αυτοις (pro αυταις) E. 2. ὑελινην bis. πυρι μεμιγμενην C. εκ της εικονος και εκ του θηριου αυτου efδ. – εκ του χαραγματος αυτου efδC. ἑστωτας eE (ἑστωτα E2 correct. in- errat.). + τας (ante κιθαρας) efδ. 3. μωυσεως efδ, μωυσεος C. + του (ante δουλου) C. κυριος ESt.1,2.

παντοκρατορ e. εθνων (pro ἁγιων) efδC. 4. – σε E ex cod.
Reuchl. σε φοβηθη δ. δοξασει ef [non δ]. ἁγιος (pro ὁσιος)
efδC (+ ει C) E in annot. παντες (pro παντα τα εθνη) efδ.
ἠξουσι e. 5. – ιδου efδC. 6. οἱ αγγελοι οἱ ἑπτα f. + οἱ
(ante εχοντες) efδC. – εκ του ναου efδ. ουρανου (pro ναου)
C. + οἳ ησαν (ante ενδεδ.) efδC. + και (ante καθαρον) C.
– και secund. efδE ex cod. Reuchl. περιεσζωσμενοι C, περι-
ζωσμενοι ESt.1,2. – περι E ex cod. Reuchl. 7. – εκ ESt.1,2.
– γεμουσας f. τον αιωνα τω e. 8. + εκ του (ante καπνου)
efδ. εδυνατο efδ. εν τω ναω (pro εις τον ν.) E ex cod. Reuchl.
– ἑπτα secund. E.

CAP. XVI. 1. μεγαλης φωνης fδ [non e]. – εκ του ναου
efδ. – και secund. eCE ex cod. Reuchl. St.1,2. εκχεετε
St.1,2, etiam – του θῡ E ex cod. Reuchl. + ἑπτα (ante
φιαλας) efδ. 2. – ὁ E. εις (pro επι), etiam επι (pro εις)
efδ. προσκυνουντας τη εικονι αυτου efδC, την εικονα προσκυνουντας αυτου E ex cod. Reuchl. St.1,2. 3. – ζωσα efδ.
4. – αγγελος efδ. εζεχεε C. – εις secund C. 5. – των
ὑδατων E ex cod. Reuchl. – Κυριε efδC. ὁς, ἠν (sic) e.
– και tert. C. – και ὁ (ante ὁσιος) efδ. εσομενος (pro ὁσιος)
Elz. 1633. 6. εξεχεον ESt.1,2. αυτης (pro – οις) e p. m.
– γαρ efδC. 7. – αλλου C. – αλλου εκ efδ. παντοκρατορ
e. 8. ὁτε (pro ὁ) E1. – αγγελος ef [non δ]. εν πυρι τους
ανουσ efδ. 9. + οἱ ανοι (post εβλασφημησαν) efδC. + την
(ante εξουσιαν) C. 10. πεμΠτος super rasur. e p. m.
– αγγελος efδ. εμασωντο eδE ex cod. Reuchl. [non f].
11. ἑλκεων E1. 12. ς e. – αγγελος efδE1 ex cod. Reuchl.
εξεχεεν αυτου την φιαλην fδ. – τον tert. efδC. – αυτου
secund. E ex cod. Reuchl. ανατολης efδ. 13. – εκ του
στοματος του δρακοντος και f. ακαθαρτα τρια efδ. ὡς
βατραχοι (pro ὁμοια βατραχοις) efδC. 14. δαιμονιων efδ.
ἁ εκπορευεται efδCB.Elz. [E�horz ex cod. Reuchl.]. – της γης
και efδC. + τον (ante πολεμον) efδC. – του secund. δ.
παντοκρατωρος C. 16. – τον prim. C. μαγεδων efδ, αρμα-
γεδων CE (ἀρ. E: αρμαχεδδων St.1,2, hermageddon E1 Lat.,
armadeddon E2). 17. – αγγελος efδ. επι (pro εις) efδ. εκ
(pro μεγαλη απο του ναου) E ex cod. Reuchl. 18. αστραπαι

και φωναι και βρονται e, αστραπαι και βρονται και φωναι fδC. — εγενετο prim. efδ. ουνοι (pro ανοι) e. +και (ante επι) E. τιλικουτος e. ούτως E. 19. επεσαν f [non εδ]. +ή (ante βαβυλων) e. 20. — και prim. E ex cod. Reuchl. όρη e. ουκ E. ˙ 21. οἱ E. αὕτη (pro αυτης) fδ [non e].

CAP. XVII. 1. — μοι efδC. κρῖμα E tantum. επι ὑδατων πολλων E ex cod. Reuchl. 2. οἱ κατοικουντες την γην εκ του οινου της πορνειας αυτης efδC. 3. — εν εδ. +το (ante κοκκινον) fδ. ονοματα efδ. — κεφαλας έπτα και E ex cod. Reuchl. 4. ἦν (pro ἡ secund.) efδC. πορφυρουν efδ, πορφυραν C. κοκκινον efδC. — και tert. efδC. χρυσιω efδ. τημιω δ. ποτηριον χρυσουν efδ. τα ακαθαρτα της (pro ακαθαρτητος) efδC cod. Reuchl. [non EʔElz.]. της γης (pro αυτης) efδ. 5. μετοπον e. πορνων eC. τη γης Ev.1. 6. μεθνουσαν e p. m. — εκ prim. efδ. — και secund. εδ. — και εκ του αἱματος των (post ἁγιων: ὁμοιοτ.) f. 7. διὰ τί efE. ερω σοι efδ. +και (ante του εχοντος) E ex cod. Reuchl. 8. init. +το efδC. ἦν (pro ἦν) e. ὑπαγει ESt.1,2. την γην (pro επι της γης) efδ. το ονομα efδ. του βιβλιου efδ. βλεποντων ὁτι ην (ἦν e) το θηριον efδ. ὁτι CE1 [ʔ τι E2]. fin. και παρεσται fC. και παρεστειν cod. Reuchl. [καίπερ ἔστι E, καίπερ ἐστιν St.1,2,3]. 8, 9. και παρεσται ωδε εδ. 9. έπτα ορη (όρη e) εισιν efδC. 10. init. — και f. εισιν ἑπτα ef. επεσον C tantum. — και secund. efδC. δει αυτον efδ. 11. ὁ ἦν e. ούτος (pro ἁυτος) efδ. +ὁ (ante ὁγδοος) e. 12. ούπω e, at ουκ E. 13. εχουσι γνωμην efδ. — την secund. efδ. αυτων (pro ἑαυτων) efδC. διδοασιν efδC (διασιν cod. Reuchl. p. m.). 16. και (pro επι) efδC. ηριμωμενην f, ερημωμενην E ex cod. Reuchl. +ποιησουσιν αυτην (post γυμνην) efδC. αυτοι (pro αυτην ultim.) e. καυσουσιν E ex cod. Reuchl. 17. γνωμην μιαν efδC. τεθωσιν e, τελεσθωσιν fδ, τελεσθησονται C. οἱ λογοι (pro τα ῥηματα) efδC. 18. το eras. post πολις e. +επι (ante της γης) efδ.

CAP. XVIII. 1. init. — Και efδ. +αλλον (ante αγγελον) efδCE [non cod. Reuchl. ʔElz.]. 2. ισχυρα φωνη (— εν et μεγαλη) efδ s. m., εν ισχυρα φωνη (— μεγαλη) δ p. m. C.

ισχυει E. – επεσεν ef. – επεσε δ. – φυλακη παντος secund. δ. ορνιου E (E2 correct. in erratis). 3. του θυμου του οινου C. πεπωκασι e, πεπτωκασι fδ, πεποτικε C. αυτης (pro της γης secund.) E ex cod. Reuchl. στρηνου E. 4. εξελθε efδ. – εξ αυτης E ex cod. Reuchl. (E2 correct. in erratis). – και secund. E ex cod. Reuchl. p. m. εκ των πληγων αυτης ινα μη λαβητε efδC. 5. εκολληθησαν (pro ηκολ.) efδC cum cod. Reuchl. + αυτης (ante ὁ θσ) eδC. 6. αὐτῇ ἀπέδωκε (– ὑμιν) e. – ὑμιν eδ. – αυτη secund. efδ. + τα (ante διπλα) efδ. + ὡς και αυτη· και (ante κατα) efδ. + αυτης (post ποτηριω) eδ. αυτην (pro αυτη ultim.) e. 7. εδοξεν αυτη (pro εδοξ. ἑαυτ.) e. αυτην (pro ἑαυτην) fδ. κερασατε (pro τοσουτον δοτε) E ex cod. Reuchl. [E2 correct. in erratis]. – και πενθος prim. C. + ὅτι (ante καθημαι) C. ὅτι καθως (pro καθημαι) efδ. 8. – και prim. efδ. κανθησεται e. κρινας efδC, κρινῶν E. 9. κλαυσουσι (– αυτην) efδC. αυτην (pro αυτη) efδC. 10. – τον E. μεγαλης e. – εν efδC. 11. κλαυσουσιν efδ. πενθησουσιν efδ. εν ἑαυτοις (pro επ αυτη) E ex cod. Reuchl. ουκετι cum sequent. efδ. 12. γωμον e p. m. γομος E. ουτε (pro και tert.) E ex cod. Reuchl. βυσσινου efδ. πορφυρου efδCE (E2 correct. in erratis). – και σηρικου E ex cod. Reuchl. σιρικου e. – και μαρμαρου E ex cod. Reuchl. 13. κινναμωμου efδ. θυμιαμα E ex cod. Reuchl. μυρον eδESt.1. – και οινον efδ. και προβατα και κτηνη efδ. ῥαιδων efδC. 14. ἡ ὀπωραι E1. ὀπωρα f. απηλθον (prim.) E. απωλετο (pro απηλθεν secund.) efδ, at απωλοντο C. ουκετι f. αυτα ου μη εὑρης efδ. εὑρησεις (pro εὑρης) CE ex cod. Reuchl. 15. αυπ (pro απ) e p. m. + και (ante κλαιοντες) efδ. 16. – και (ante λεγοντες) e (λεγουσιν e) fδ. – ουαι semel efδ. βυσσον eδ. – βυσσινον usque ad κεχρυσωμενη (ὁμοιοτελ.) f. κεχρυσω-μενοι Elz. χρυσιω (– εν) efδ. 17. ὁ επι τοπον πλεων efδ, ὁ επι των πλοιων πλεων C (pro επι των πλοιων ὁ ὁμιλος). – και ὁσοι E. εργαζοντες E. 18. ἑστησαν δ. εκραυγαζον f. βλεποντες (pro ὁρωντες) efδC. πολη e. 19. εβαλλον f s. m. χνουν E (cf. Mark VI. 11) St.1 (non St.2). + και (ante λεγοντες) eδC, at λεγοντες. και πενθουντες και κλαι-οντες f. – ουαι semel eδ, ουαι, ουαι E1. + τα (ante πλοια)

efδC. αυτου (pro αυτης) e p. m. 20. αυτη (pro αυτην) efδC.
+ και οἱ (ante αποστολοι) efδC. 21. μεγα E. ὁρμηματι E1.
22. αυληστων e. 23. – και φως λυχνου ου μη φανη εν σοι
ετι (ὁμοιοτ.) eE. – ὁτι prim. efδ. – σου prim. f. μεγιστάνες
efδ p. m. E. 24. αἱματα efδC.

CAP. XIX. 1. init. – Και efδ. + ὡς efδCEIz. [non EϚB.
ex cod. Reuchl.]. – μεγαλην E ex cod. Reuchl., at μεγαλην
οχλου πολλου efδ. λεγοντων efδC. + το (ante αλληλουια)
E ex cod. Reuchl. και ἡ δυναμις και ἡ δοξα (– και ἡ τιμη et
κ͞ω) του θ͞υ ἡμων efδC. 2. αἱτινες (pro ὁτι prim.) e. αλη-
θειναι e. διεφθειρε efδC. – της efδC. 3. ειρηκεν efδC.
– αυτης E ex cod. Reuchl. 4. επεσον εδC.EIz. [non EϚB].
οἱ prim. E. – και secund. fδC. κ͞δ eE. τω θρονω efδ.
5. + ἡ (ante φωνη) e. απο (pro εκ) efδ. εξηλθεν (– λεγουσα)
E ex cod. Reuchl. τω θ͞ω (pro τον θ͞ν) f. δουλοι εδ. – και
tert. efδC. 6. – ὡς prim. E ex cod. Reuchl. p. m. λεγοντες
efδ, λεγοντων CEIz. [– τας EϚB. ex cod. Reuchl.]. εβασι-
λευσεν (– κ͞σ) E ex cod. Reuchl. + ἡμων (post θ͞σ) efδC.
7. [ὁτι f sic: ὁτε Wetstein]. – αυτου E ex cod. Reuchl.
8. περιβαλληται δ. λαμπρον και καθαρον efδC. των ἁγιων
εστι(ν fδ) efδC. 9. – γραψον et – του γαμου E ex cod.
Reuchl. τον (pro το) e cf. ver. 17. του θ͞υ εισιν efδ.
10. επεσα efδ p. m. (non marg.) E2 ex cod. Reuchl., εμπεσα
E1. ὡρα δ: cf. ch. XXII. 9. + και (ante των εχοντων) E
ex cod. Reuchl. – του prim. efδC. – του secund. E eᴪ cod.
Reuchl. 11. θημ in καθημενος e s. m. – καλουμενος E ex
cod. Reuchl. κρινει e. 12. – ὡς efδC. εχον e. ονοματα
γεγραμμενα ἁ (pro ονομα γεγραμμενον ὁ) f, at + ονοματα
γεγραμμενα και (post εχων) εδC. ειδεν (pro οιδεν) B.
13. κεκληται efδ. 14. + τα (post στρατευματα) εδCEIz.
[non f et EϚB ex cod. Reuchl.]. ηκολουθουν E ex cod. Reuchl.
επι (pro εφ) efδC. ενδεδομενος e. – και secund. efC [non δ].
15. + διστομος (ante οξεια) efδC. παταξη δC, παταξει e,
παραταξη f (pro πατασση). – κὰι ult. efδC. – του ult. E
ex cod. Reuchl. 16. – το secund. efδC. 17. – ἑνα efδ.
– ἑστωτα E1. – τω E. + εν (post εκραξεν) efδ. ορνιοις

E1, ορνοϊοις E2. πετομενοις efC [non δ]. μεσουρανισματι
E (−ησματι E2 in erratis) cf. ch. VIII. 13. συναχθητε
(−και) efδC fin. τον δειπον τον μεγαν του θῦ e. το δ. το
μεγα του θῦ fδC. 18. − σαρκας secund. E (−και σαρκ. χιλιαρ.
cod. Reuchl.). ἱππων δ. επ αυτω E. + τε (post ελευθερων
et μικρων) efδC. − και septim. C. 19. − της γης e. + τον
(ante πολεμον) efδ. 20. ὁ μετ αυτου efδ, μετ αυτου ὁ C (pro
μετα τουτου ὁ). βληθησονται E ex cod. Reuchl. − τω (ante
θειω) efδC. 21. − του prim. E. εξελθουση (pro εκπορευομενω)
efδC. − τα E.

CAP. XX. 1. κλειν efδC. ἀλυσιν e. 2. + ὁ (ante σατανας)
fδC [non e]. + ὁ πλανων την οικουμενην ὁλην (post σατανας)
efδC. εδυσεν e. 3. εδησεν (pro εκλεισεν) E ex cod. Reuchl.
εκλεισε (− αυτον secund.) efδC. πλανα ετι τα εθνη efδC.
− τα secund. E ex cod. Reuchl. St.1,2. − και ult. efδ. λυθηναι
αυτον efδ. 4. εκαθησαν e. επανω (pro επ') e. πεπλεκισμενων
E. το θηριον ουδε την εικονα efδ. τη εικονι CElz. [non EϚB.
ex cod. Reuchl.]. ελαβε e. μετοπον e. − αυτων (post μετ.) efδ.
αυτου (pro αυτων ult.) e. + τον (ante χῦ) efδCElz. [non EϚB.
ex cod. Reuchl.]. − τα E ex cod. Reuchl. St.1,2. 5. − οἱ δε
λοιποι usque ad τα χιλια ετη (ὁμοιοτ.) fδ. και οἱ λοιποι
(− δε) eC. εζησαν eC. αχρι (pro ἑως) eC, etiam cod. Reuchl.
+ αχρι, (post ετη) E. αὑτη E1. 6. ὁ δευτερος θανατος efδC.
μετα ταυτα (pro μετ αυτου) efδ. 7. ὁτε ετελεσθησαν E ex
cod. Reuchl. St.1,2. at μετα (pro ὁταν τελεσθη) efδ. 8. − ταις
ESt.1,2. − τον secund. E (ex cod. Reuchl.). + τον (ante
πολεμον) efδC. + αυτων (post αριθμος) efδ. ὡσει (pro ὡς
ἡ) fδ [non e]. αμμως δ p. m. 9. εκυκλευσαν fδC [non e].
εκ του ουνου απο του θῦ efδC. 10. − ὁ prim. E ex cod.
Reuchl. + του (ante θειου) ef. + και (post ὁπου) efδC.
11. μεγαν λευκον fδC. − μεγαν e. επ αυτον efδC. ὁ ουνος
και ἡ γη C. ουκ E. 12. ἑστωτας τους μικρους και τους
μεγαλους e. τους μεγαλους και τους μικρους C. − μικρους
και μεγαλους fδ. ἑστωτας E. θρονου (pro θῦ) efδC. ηνοιξαν
eδ, ηνοιξεν f, ανεωχθησαν C, ηνοιχθησαν E ex cod. Reuchl.
(pro ηνεωχθησαν). αλλο (ν e) βιβλιον efδC. ανεωχθη C,
ηνοιχθη E. εν τοις βιβλοις (sic) e. τοσι E1. 13. αυτοις

(*pro αυτη*) E1 *ex cod. Reuchl.* τους νεκρους τους εν αυτη efδ.
− ὁ *prim.* f. τους νεκρους τους εν αυτοις efδ. ἑαυτων (*pro*
εν αυτοις) C. *fin.* αυτου (*pro* αυτων) δ. 14. ὁ θανατος ὁ
δευτερος εστιν ἡ λιμνη του πυρος efδC (εστιν ὁ θαν. κ.τ.λ. C).
15. − και f. εισ (*pro* ει) e. τω βιβλιω efδ.

CAP. XXI. 1. απηλθεν (*pro* παρηλθε) efδ. 2. − εγω
ιωαννης efδC. ειδον transferunt *in locum post* καινην efδC.
εκ του ουνου απο του θῦ efδ. 3. λαος efδC. μετ αυτων
εσται efδ. − θ̅σ̅ αυτων efδC. 4. απ αυτων (*pro* ὁ θ̅σ̅) efδ.
− ὁ θ̅σ̅ C. οφθαλμον et ετη *prim.* e *p. m.* − ετι *prim.* E *ex*
cod. Reuchl. απηλθεν (-ε f) efδ. 5. *init.* − και fδ [*non* e].
τω θρονω efδ. ιδου bis e. παντα καινα ποιω efδ, καινα
ποιω παντα C. − μοι fδ [*non* e]. *fin.* πιστοι και αληθινοι
του θῦ εισι (-ν f) efδ. 6. γεγονα εγω (− ειμι) e, γεγονα (− εγω
ειμι) fδCE *in annot. ex cod. Reuchl., at in textu* γεγονε, εγω
ειμι. αλφα ef. + και (*post* ὦ) δ. − ἡ eC. − το *tert.* eC.
+ αυτω (*post* δωσω) efδ. − του E. − της ζωης δ. 7. δωσω
αυτω ταυτα (*pro* κληρονομησει παντα) efδ. ταυτα (*pro*
παντα) C. − ὁ *secund.* eC. μου υἱος (*pro* μοι ὁ υἱός) fδ.
λαος (*pro* υἱός) e *p. m.* 8. *init.* τοις δε δειλοις efδC. + και
ἁμαρτωλοις (*post* απιστοις) efδC. φαρμακοῖς efE1 *ex cod.*
Reuchl., -άκοις δ, -ακοίς C. εστι θανατος ὁ δευτερος e,
εστιν ὁ θανατος ὁ (− ὁ f *primo*) δευτερος fδC. 9. ηλθεν
(− προς με) e (οἱ λοιποὶ *p. m.*) fδC. + εκ (*post* εἰς) efδC.
− τας *secund.* efδC. − των *tert.* efδ. την γυναικα την νυμφην
του αρνιου efδC. 10. με (*pro* μοι) f. − την μεγαλην efδ.
− την (*ante* ἁγιαν) C. εκ (*pro* απο) efδ. 11. − και efδC.
− ὡς λιθω E *ex cod. Reuchl.* κρυσταλιζοντι C (κρισ- E1 *in*
annot.). 12. εχουσα bis efδE *ex cod. Reuchl.* St.1,2. − τε
efδC. πυλεωσι E. δεκαδυο (*pro* δωδεκα *secund.*) fδ. εστιν
ονοματα (*pro* εστι) efδ. − των *ultim.* εδ. − των υἱων f.
13. *init.* + και e. απο ανατολων efδC. + και (*ante* απο β.)
efδC. βορα E *ex cod. Reuchl.* (E2 *correct. in erratis*). + και
(*ante* απο ν.) fδC. − απο νοτου *usque ad fin. versûs* e.
μεσημβριας (*pro* νοτου) E *ex cod. Reuchl.* + και (*ante* απο
δ.) fδC. 14. − το E, *forsan ex cod. Reuchl.* επ αυτων (*pro*
εν αυτοις) efδC. + δωδεκα (*ante* ονοματα) efδC. ι̅β̅ αποστ. f.

COLLATION OF APOCALYPSE. 161

15. +μετρον (*post* ειχε) efδC. +και το τειχος αυτης fδC.
16. τεταγ? (*pro* τετραγ) e *p. m.* αυτου (*pro* αυτης) E,
correct. E2 *in erratis.* – τοσουτον εστιν efδC. ὁσον e, ὁσου-
τον E. – και tert. efδC. + εν (*ante* τω καλαμω) E *ex cod.*
Reuchl. St.1,2. σταδιους efδCElz. [*non* EϚB. *ex cod. Reuchl.*].
δεκαδυο efδ. +δωδεκα (*ante* το μηκος *secund.*) efδC. ἴσα δ,
ἴσα E. 17. – εμετρησε efδ. ρμδ efδ. 18. ἦν e. ἴασπις
(sic ver. 19) δ. ὁμοιον efδC. ὑελω efC [*non* δ]. 19. *init.*
– και efδ. καλκϊδῶν E. 20. σαρδωνυξ eC. σαρδιον efδ.
βηριλλιος E1,2.3 *ex cod. Reuchl.,* βηριλλος E4,5. εννατος
eESt.1,2B.Elz. [ενατος fδCϚ]. παζιον δ, τὸ πάζιον f, τοπαζιος
E2 (*correct. in erratis*). χρυσοπρασινος f, χρυσοπασος δ.
ἑνδεκατος e. ὑακίνθινος C. αμεθυσος eE3,4,5 *cum cod.*
Reuchl., αμεθησος E1,2. 21. ὑελος ef [*non* δ] C. διαυγης
(*pro* διαφανης) efδC. 22. – κσ ὁ e. 23. φαινουσιν e *p. m.*
– εν efδE *ex cod. Reuchl.* αὐτὴ γαρ ἡ (*pro* αὐτὴ· ἡ γὰρ) efδ
(αὐτῆ). αὐτη (*pro* αυτην) E. 24. περιπατησουσι τα εθνη
δια του φωτος αυτης (– των σωζομενων) efδC. φερουσιν
αυτω δοξαν και τιμην των εθνων (– την bis, et αυτων) efδ.
– και την τιμην E *ex cod. Reuchl.* 25. – οἱ ESt.1,2. 26. *fin.*
+ ἱνα εισελθωσιν (-σι, e) efδ: *omittit versum* E, *propter*
comment. in cod. Reuchlini. 27. κοινον efδC. ὁ ποιων (*pro*
ποιουν) fδ [*non* e]. τω βιβλω (sic) f.

CAP. XXII. 1. ποταμον καθαρον eC. – καθαρον fδ.
και του αρνιου *cum sequent.* fδ. 2. εκειθεν (*pro* εντευθεν
secund.) efδ. – ἑνα efδC. αποδιδους ἑκαστον e, αποδιδους
ἑκαστος fδ. αποδιδους C, αποδιδοντα E *ex cod. Reuchl.*
– τον E *ex cod. Reuchl.* των καρπων e. 3. καταθεμα efδC.
εκει (*pro* ετι) C. + εκει (*post* θϋ) e. λατρευουσιν δ.
4. μετοπων e. 5. – εκει efδ. ου χρεια (– εχουσι) efδ.
– ἡλιου efδ. φωτιει efδC. ὁ E1. 6. λεγει (*pro* ειπε) efδC.
πνων των (*pro* ἁγιων) efδC. + με (*post* απεστειλε) e.
– δειξαι τοις δουλοις αυτου efδ. 7. *init.* + και efδ. 8. καγω
efδC. ιωαννες E1. ὁ ακουων και βλεπων ταυτα efδC. ὁτε
ειδον (*pro* εβλεψα) efδ. επεσον efδCElz. [επεσα EϚB. *ex*
cod. Reuchl.]. δεικνυντος efδ, δειγνυντος C. 9. – μοι f.
ὡρα δ: cf. ch. XIX. 10. – γαρ efδC. – των *secund.* E *ex*

S.   11

cod. Reuchl. St.1,2. *– και (ante των τηρ.)* C. 10. *– ὅτι* efδ.
– ὁ E. *+ γαρ (post καιρος)* εδ *fin. εστι* C. 11. *ετῇ prim.* e
p. m. ρυπαρος ρυπαρευθητω ef *(sine ρυπαρος, errore)* δC.
δικαιοσυνην ποιησατω (pro δικαιωθητω) efδC. 12. *init.*
– και efδC. *– το* f. *εσται αυτου* efδC. 13. *– ειμι* efδC.
αλφα efδC. *ὁ πρωτος και ὁ εσχατος· ἡ αρχη και το τελος*
efδ. *– ὁ secund.* E. 14. *πυλεωσιν* E *ex cod. Reuchl.* [*cœtera
cum* ϛ *omnes*]. 15. *– δε* efδC. *– οἱ tert.* E *ex cod. Reuchl.*
*St.1,2. *– ὁ* efδC. 16. *– επι* E *ex cod. Reuchl.* *– ἡ* E.
$\overline{δαδ}$ *(– του)* efδ. *δαυιδ* C. *– ὁ secund.* E. *ὁ πρωϊνος (pro
και ορθρινος)* efδC. 17. *ερχου (pro ελθε)* bis efδC. *ερχεσθω
(pro ελθετω)* efδC. *– και quint.* efδC. *λαβετω (pro λαμ-
βανετω το)* efδC. 18. *μαρτυρω εγω (pro Συμμαρτυρουμαι
γαρ)* efδC. *+ τω (ante ακουοντι)* efδ. *– της* ESt.1,2. *– του*
ESt.1,2. *ει (pro εαν)* E, *at ἐὰν εἴ* St.1 *(non St.2).* *επιθη επ
αυτα (pro επιτιθη προς ταυτα)* ef *(sic)* δC. *επιθῆσαι* e,
επιθήσαι fδC *(pro επιθησει).* *επ αυτον ὁ $\overline{θσ}$* C. *+ ἑπτα
(ante πληγας)* C. *+ τω (ante βιβλιω)* efδC. 19. *ει (pro
εαν)* E, *at ἐὰν εἴ* St.1 *(non St.2).* *αφελη* efδC. *των βιβλἰων?*
e *p. m., του βιβλἰου* e *s. m.* fδC *(pro βιβλου prim.).* *αφελη*
e *p. m., αφελοι* e *s. m.* δC, *αφελαι* f *(sic),* *αφελει* E2 *(pro
αφαιρησει* E1). *του ξυλου (pro βιβλου secund.)* efδ *(– του)*
C. *– της secund.* E. *– εκ της* E. *– της quart.* ESt.1,2.
– και ultim. efδC. *+ τω (ante βιβλιω)* efδC. 20. *και (pro
ναι secund.)* B. 21. *– ἡμων* efδC. *– $\overline{χυ}$* e. *των ἁγιων (pro
ὑμων)* efδC.

Subscriptiones. Αποκαλυψις του ἁγιου $\overline{ιω}$ του θεολογου
f. Τελος της αποκαλυψεως C. *Desunt in* εδ.

---

* *Hic explicit cod. Reuchlini.* "Quanquam in calce hujus libri nonnulla
verba reperi apud nostros, quæ aberant in Græcis exemplaribus, ea tamen ex
latini adjecimus." Annotationes, E1.

PART IV.

COLLATION OF PALIMPSEST B.-C. III. 46.

Fol. 206 a 1.

Isai. ıx. 17—x. 24.

φρανθησεται κ̅σ̅
και τουσ ορφανουσ
αυτων και τασ χῆ
ρασ αυτων ουκ ελε
ησει· ὅτι παντεσ
ανομοι και πονηροι
και παν στομα λα
λει αδικα· επι πα
σιν τουτοισ ουκ απε
στραφη ο θυμοσ αυ
.... χειρ
αυτου υψηλη· και
καυθησεται ωσ πυρ
η ανομια και ωσ
αγρωστισ ξηρα βρω
θησεται ὑπο πυροσ
και κατακαυθη῎῎
σεται εν τοισ δα
σεσι … δρυμου· ϛ
συγκαταφαγεται τα
κυκλω των βουνων

Fol. 206 a 2.

παν̇τα· δια θυ

μον οργησ κ̅υ̅ σα
βαωθ συγκεκαυ
ται η γη ολη και
εσται ο λαοσ ωσ ὑ
πο πυροσ κατα
κεκαυμενοσ.
ανοσ τον αδελ
φον αυτου ουκ ελε?
ησει? αλλα εκκλινει?
εισ τα δεξια οτι …
πεινασει και φα
γεται εκ των αρι
στερων· καὶ οὐ μὴ
εμπλησθη α̅ν̅ο̅σ̅
εσθιων τασ σαρκασ
του βραχιονοσ αὐ
του· φαγεται γαρ ..
ἐφραιμ του μα
νασση και μανασ
σησ τον εφραιμ

Fol. 206 b 1.

ὅτι ἅμα πολιορκι
σουσιν τον ιουδα
Ἐπι τούτοισ πᾶσιν
᾽ουκ απεστραφη ὁ

θυμοσ αὐτοῦ ἀλ
λ ἔτι ἡ χεὶρ αὐτοῦ
ὑψηλη οὐαι τοῖσ
γραφουσι πονηρι
αν γραφοντ…
……… γρα
φουσιν· εκλινον
τεσ γαρ κρισιν πτω
χων αρπαζοντεσ
κριμα πενητων
του λαου μου ωσ
τε ειναι αυτοισ χη
ραν ἐισ αρπαγην
και ορφανον εισ
προνομην και
τι ποιησουσιν τη
ημερα τησ επισκο

Fol. 206 b 2.

πησ + ἡ γαρ θλ…σ
αὐτων πορρωθεν
ἥξει και προσ τι
να καταφευξεσθε
του βοηθηθηναι
και …………
ψετε …………

μων του ἐμ..
εισ απαγωγην
και υποκατω α
νηρη ... ων πε..
ται επι πασι του
τοισ ουκ απεστρ
αφη ο θυμοσ αυτου
αλλ ετι η χειρ αυ
του υψηλη
(one blank line)
4 lines of other matter
follow: quite illegible.

Fol. 207 a 1.

Genesis XXVII. 1—11.

κ   ο θ̅σ̅
κ̅υ̅ και
ενωπιον τοῦ θ̅υ̅ μου
(blank line)
κσ ο̇ θσ
ζωη
(Two blank lines)
[Ε]ιπατωσαν οἱ λελυτρω
μενοι οὐ
(One blank line)

[Κ]αὶ ἐγένετο μετὰ τὸ γη
ρᾶσαι τὸν ἰσαὰκ
καὶ ημβλύνθη
σαν οι οφθαλμοι
αὐτοῦ τοῦ μη
οραν καὶ ἐκάλε
σεν ἰσαὰκ τὸν

Fol. 207 a 2.

υἱὸν αὐτοῦ τον
πρεσβυτερον
καὶ ἔιπεν αὐτῶ
υἱὲ καὶ ἔιπεν
ἰδὼ ἐγω· ἔιπεν
δε αὐτῶ ἰσαακ
ἰδοὺ ἐγω γεγήρακα
καὶ ὀυ γιγνώσκω
τὴν ἡμέραν τῆσ
τελευτῆσ μου νῦν
ὀῦν λάβε το σκευ
οσ σου τήν τε φά?
ρετραν καὶ τὸ τό
ξον και ἔξελθε
εισ το πεδιον? ϛ
θήρευσόν μοι θή
ραν· και ποίησον
μοι ἐδεσματα
ὡσ φιλῶ ἐγω· καὶ
ενεγκον μοι ἵνα
φαγω ὁπωσ ἐυλο

Fol. 207 b 1.

γήσῃ σε η ψυχή μου
πρινὴ αποθανεῖν
με + ῥεβέκκα
δὲ ἤκουσεν λα
λοῦντοσ ἰσαακ·
πρὸσ ἠσαῦ τὸν ὑι
ον αυτοῦ Ἐπορεύ
θη δὲ ἠσαῦ εἰσ τὸ
πέδιον θηρευσαι
θηραν τῶ π̅ρ̅ι αὐ
του ῥεβέκκα δὲ
..ἶπεν πρὸσ ἰακὼβ
τὸν υἱὸν αὐτῆσ
τον νεώτερον

ἰδε ἐγὼ ἤκουσα
λαλοῦντοσ τοῦ
π̅ρ̅σ̅ σου προσ ἠ
σαῦ λέγοντοσ
ἔνεγκέ μοι θήραν
καὶ ποίησον μοι
ἐδέσματα καὶ

Fol. 207 b 2.

φαγῶν ἐυλογήσω
σε εναντίον κ̅υ̅
πρὸ τοῦ με ἀπο
θανεῖν νῦν ὀῦν
'υἱὲ· ἄκουσόν μου
καθα εγώ σοι ἐντέλ
λομαι καὶ πορευ
θεισ εἰσ τὰ πρό
βατα λάβε μοι
εκεῖθεν δυο ἐρι
φουσ ἀπαλουσ
καὶ καλοὺσ . αι
ποιήσω ἀ . τοὺσ
ἐδέσματα τῶ π̅ρ̅ι
σου ὡσ φιλεῖ και
εἰσ ... τῶ π̅ρ̅ι σου
καὶ φάγεται ὅπωσ
'ευλογήσῃ σε ὁ π̅α̅ρ̅
σου πρὸ τοῦ ἀπο
θανεῖν ἔιπεν δὲ
ιακὼβ πρὸσ ῥε
Continued Fol. 211.

Fol. 208 a 1.

Prov. XIX. 16—25.

τῶν ἑαυτου ...
απ?..ολεῖται· ὁ ελε

ων πτωχον δανί
ζει θῶ· κατὰ
δε τὸ δομα αὐτοῦ
ανταποδωσει
αὐτῶ· παίδενε
υἱόν σου. οὕτως
γὰρ εσται ἐλπίσ
εἰσ δὲ ὕβριν μὴ ἐ
πο..ροῦ τῇ ψυχῇ σου
κακοφρων ανηρ
πολλὰ ζημιωθη
σεται ἐὰν δὲ λυ?
μενηται και τὴν
ψυχην προσθησει
ἄκουε υἱὲ παιδεί
αν πρσ σου· ινα
σοφοσ γενη επι γῇ
ρουσ. πολλοὶ λο
γισμοι ἐν καρδία

Fol. 208 a 2.

Prov. xix. 21—25.

ανδροσ ἡ δὲ βου
λὴ τοῦ θῦ κρατή
σει εἰσ τὸν αιωνα
καρπὸσ ἀνδρὸσ
ἐλεημοσύνη κρεισ
σον δε. πτωχοσ δί
καιοσ· ἢ πλουσιοσ
ψεύστησ φοβοσ κῦ
εἰσ πνοην ανδρι
ὁ δὲ πλανώμενοσ
ἐν πύλαισ αὐλι
σθησεται ἐν τόποισ
οἷσ ουκ ἐπισκοπεῖ

ται ὁ αἰωνιοσ· ὁ ἐν
κρυπτων εἰσ τὸν κολ
πον αὐτου· χειρασ
ἀδίκωσ· 'Ουδὲ τῶ
στόματι 'ου μὴ προ
σάγει αὐτάσ λοι
μοῦ μαστιγουμε
νου ἄφρων πα

Fol. 208 b 1.

νουργότεροσ γίνε
ται· ἐαν δὲ ἐλέγχησ
ανδρα φρόνιμον.
νοησει αισθησιν
(Two lines blank.)
καταμαχητον τεῖχοσ ἔ
δωκασ τῇ πολει ημων
την τεκουσαν σε παρθε
νον· δι αὐτῆσ σερ απο
τῶν κύκλω συν επιτι
θεμενων? κακῶν, ἐξε
λου δεόμεθα τὰς ψυχασ
ἡμων
(One line blank.)
[B].ηθησον μοι κε ὁ θσ μου
και σωσον με κατα τὸ
ελεοσ σου + 5ι
εισ την αινεσιν μου
μη παρασκοπησισ

Fol. 208 b 2.

Isai. xlix. 6, 7.

...ε λεγει κσ· I
δου δέδωκα σε· εισ
διαθηκην γενουσ

εισ φωσ εθνων· τοῦ
εἶναί σε εισ σριαν
ἑωσ ἐσχάτου τῆσ
γῆσ· ουτωσ λεγει κσ
ὁ ρυσαμενοσ σε. ὁ
θσ ιηλ ἁγιάσατε
τὸν φαυλίζοντα
εαυτην· ἁγιάσατε
τὸν φαυλίζοντα τὴν
ψυχὴν αὐτου· τὸν
βδελυσσόμενον ὑ
πο τῶν ἐθνῶν· τῶν
δουλων τῶν αρχόν
των βασιλεῖσ ο
ψονται αὐτον· καὶ ἀ
ναστήσονται ἄρχον
τεσ· καὶ προσκυνη
σουσιν αὐτὸν ἔνεκεν

Continued Fol. 212.

Fol. 209 a 1.

Gen. vi. 17—22.

τελευτησει· και
στησω? την δια
θηκην μου μετα
σου εισελευση
δε εισ την κιβω
του συ και οι υι
οι σου· και η γυνη
σου και αι γυναι
κεσ των υἱῶν σου
και απο παν
των των κτηνω
και απο παντων
των θηριων. 5

In Bodl. Laud. 36, a lectionary of the Old Test. Gen. vi. 9—22 is appointed for τῇ β̄ τῆς γ̄ εβδ. ἑσπερ [Lent]. p. 66ᵇ.

απο πασησ σαρ
κοσ· δυο δυο
απο παντων
εισαξεισ εισ
την κιβωτον
ἱνα τρεφεισ με
τα σεαυτου
αρσεν και θηλυ

Fol. 209 a 2.

εσονται· απο
παντων των
ορνεων και των
πετεινων του ου
ρανου κατα
γενοσ· και απο
παντων των κτη
νων κατα γενοσ
και απο παντῶ
των ερπετων τῶ
ερποντων επι
τησ γησ κατα
γενοσ αυτων
δυο δυο απο
παντων εισελευ
σονται προσ σε
τρεφεσθαι μετα σου
αρσεν και θηλυ
συ δε ληψει με
τα σεαυτου α
πο παντων των

Fol. 209 b 1.

βρωματων α ἐ
δεσθε· καὶ συνά
ξεισ προσ σεαυ
τόν + καὶ ἔσται συ
και ἐκεῖνοισ φα
γειν· καὶ ἐποίη

σεν νῶε πάντα
ὅσα ἐνετείλατο
αὐτῶ ὁ θσ οὕτως
ἐποίησεν
2 lines blank.
μνησθησομαι του ονο
ματοσ σου· εν πλα
... κρε το. η καρδ.

(Prov. VIII. 1—7.)
ιε. συ τὴν σοφί
αν κηρυξον. ἵνα
φρονησισ σοι
ὑπακουσῃ· Ἐπι
γὰρ τῶν ὑψηλῶν
ἄκρων· ἔστιν

Fol. 209 b 2.

ἀναμεσον δὲ
τῶν τρίβων
ἔστηκεν παρὰ
γὰρ πύλαισ δυ
νατῶν παρεδ
ρεύει εν δε ει
σόδοισ υμνειται
ὑμᾶσ ῶ ἄνοι πα
ρακαλῶ καὶ
προιεμαι εμην
φωνην υιουσ
ἄνων νοησα
τε ακακοι πα
νουργιαν οἱ δὲ
απαιδευτοι ἔν
θεσθε καρδίαν.
εἰσακούσατε
μου· σεμνὰ γὰρ
ἐρῶ· και ανοι
σω απο χειλε
ων ἀγαθά ὅτι

Fol. 210 a 1.

Prov. VIII. 21.

σαυροὺσ αὐτῶν
ἐμπλησω ἀ
γαθῶν
....
.... επαρ?
χον κυ και υ...
...ρ ...λλ......
ἐλέησον ἡμᾶσ
κατὰ τὸ μέγα
σου ελεοσ· ὡσ φιλα:
One line blank.
[Κ]σ των δυναμεων
μεθήμ· ἂν ληπτω:
θσ ἡμῶν καταφυ
γὴ καὶ Δη βοηθ:
One line blank.

Isai. IX. 9—17.

[Τ]άδε λέγει κσ
γνώσονται πᾶσ

Fol. 210 a 2.

ὁ λαὸσ τοῦ ἐφραιμ
καὶ οἱ καθημε
νοι ἐν σαμαρεί
α· ἐφ' ὕβρει και
ὑψηλῇ καρδία
λέγοντεσ πλίν
θοι πεπτωκασιν
ἀλλὰ δεῦτε· λα
ξεύσωμεν λίθουσ·
καὶ κόψωμεν
συκαμίνουσ καὶ
κέδρουσ· καὶ οἱ
κοδομήσωμεν

ἑαυτοῖσ πύργουσ
καὶ ῥάξει ὁ θσ̄
τοὺσ ἐπανιστα
μένουσ ἐπὶ ὄροσ
σιῶν καὶ ἐξ ὧν??? ?
ἐπαυτοὺσ κυκλω??
'ς τοὺσ εχθρουσ ἰ
οὐδα διασκεδάσει

Fol. 210 b 1.

Isai. ix. 9—14.

συρίαν ἀφ' ἠλί
ου ἀνατολῶν·
καὶ τοὺσ ἔλλη
νασ ἀφ ἡλίου
δυσμῶν· τοὺσ κα
τεσθίοντασ τον
?ισραηλ??? ὅλον
τῶ στοματι
ἐπὶ πασι τούτοισ
οὐκ ἀπεστράφη
ὁ θυμὸσ ἀυτοῦ·
ἀλλ' ἔτι ἡ χεὶρ
ἀυτοῦ ὑψηλή·
καὶ ὁ λαὸσ ου
κ απεστραφη· ε̇
ωσ ἐπλήγγη· και
κν̄ τῶν δυνά
μεων οὐκ ἐξε
ζήτησαν· καὶ
αφεῖλεν κσ̄ ἀ
πὸ ιηλ κεφαλην

Fol. 210 b 2.

καὶ ουραν· μεγαν
καὶ μικρὸν 'εν
μιᾶ ἡμερα +

πρεσβύτην ς̄
τουσ τὰ πρό
σωπα θαυμα
ζοντασ ἀυτη
η αρχη + και προ
φητην διδά
σκοντα ἀνομα
ὁῦτοσ ἡ ουρα
καὶ ἔσονται οἱ
μακαρίζοντεσ
τὸν λαὸν τουτο̂
πλανιοντεσ
καὶ πλανῶσιν,
ὅπωσ καταπί
ωσιν αυτουσ
διατουτο επι
τοὺσ νεανίσκοισ
ἀυτῶν 'ουκ ἐν
Continued Fol. 206.

Fol. 211 a 1.

Gen. xxvii. 11—23.

Continued from Fol.
207.

Β...............
αυτ............
δελφ... ου...
δασυσ εγω δε α
νηρλ...... μήπο
τε ψηλαφησ... με
ὁ πηρ̄ και εσομαι
ἐναντιον αυτου
ὡσ καταφρονῶ͡
και ἐπάξω ἐπέ
μαυτον κατα
ραν και ου ευλο
γιαν εῖπεν δὲ
ἀυτῶ ἡ μηρ̄· επε

με η καταρα σου
τεκνον· μονον ἐ
πακουσον τησ
φωνῆσ μου. και
πορευθεισ ἔνεγκαι
μοι + πορευθεὶσ δὲ
ἔλαβεν· και ην...

Fol. 211 a 2.

...κεν τῇ μρ̄ι ἀυ
του· καὶ ἐποιησεν
ἡ μηρ ἀυτου ἐδέσ
ματα· καθὰ ἐ
φίλει ὁ πηρ̄ ἀυτου
και λαβοῦσα ρεβεκ
κα την στολὴν ἡ
σαυ τοῦ υἱοῦ ἀυ
τῆσ τοῦ πρεσβυ
τέρου την καλην
ἣ ἦν παρ' ἀυτῆ
ἐν τῶι οἴκ... ἐνέ
δυσεν ἴακωβ τον
υἱὸν ἀυτῆσ τὸν νε
ώτερον + καὶ τα
δέρματα τῶν
ἐρίφων περιέθη
κεν περὶ τουσ βρα
χίονασ ἀυτοῦ· ς̄
ἐπὶ τὰ γυμνα του
τραχήλου αυτου

Fol. 211 b 1.

και εδωκεν τα...
δεσματα και το...
ἄρτουσ· οὓσ ἐπόι
ησεν. εἰσ τασ χεῖ

ρασ ἰακωβ τοῦ
υιου αὐτῆσ· καὶ
ἐισήνεγκεν τῶι
π̅ρι αὐτοῦ καὶ
ἐῖπεν περ· ὁ δὲ
ἐῖπεν ἰδοὺ ἐγώ
τίσ ἐῖ σὺ τέκνον
Καὶ ἐῖπεν ιακωβ
τῶ π̅ρι αὐτοῦ
...ω ἦσαν ὁ πρω
τοτοκοσ σου ἐποί
ησα καθὰ ἐλα
λησασ μοι ανα
στασ· καθησον
καὶ φάγε· ὅπωσ
ἐυλογηση με η ψυ
χῆ σου. ἐῖπεν δε

Fol. 211 b 2.

....
............υ
...αχυ.....ρεσ
ὦ τέκνον καὶ ἐῖ
πεν· ὁ παρεδω
κεν κσ̅ ο θσ̅· εναν
τιον ἐμοῦ· ἐῖπεν
δε· ισαακ τω ια
κωβ εγγισον μοι
και ψηλαφησω σε
τεκνον ει συ ἐῖ ὁ
ὑιος μου ησαῦ. ἠ
ου· ἤγγισεν δε ἰα
κωβ πρὸς ισα
ακ τὸν π̅ρα αυτου
καὶ ἐψηλαφησεν
αὐτὸν καὶ ἐῖπεν
ἡ μεν φωνὴ φωνὴ

ἰακωβ + αι δε χεῖ
ρες χειρες ἤσαυ
καὶ ὀυκ ἐπεγνω
Continued on Fol. 213.

Fol. 212 a 1.
Isai. XLIX. 7—10.
(Continued from Fol. 208.)

κ̅υ̅ + ὅτι πιστός ἐστι
ὁ ἅγιοσ τ̅ου ἰη̅λ καὶ
ἐξελεξατό σε + ου
τωσ λεγει κσ̅· και
ρω δεκτωι ἐπήκου
σά σου καὶ ἐν ἡμέ
ρα σριασ εβοήθη
σά σοι· καὶ ἔπλα
σά σε· καὶ ἔδωκά
σε· καὶ ἔθηκα σε
εἰσ διαθήκην ἐ
θνων τοῦ κατα
5̅ῆσαι την γῆν
και κατακληρονο
μῆσαι κληρονομί
αν ερημον λεγον
τα τοῖσ ἐν δεσμοισ
ἐξελθετε ?. και τοῖσ
ἐν τῶ σκοτει ανα
καλύφθητε και ἐν
πασαισ ταῖσ ο

Fol. 212 a 2.
δοισ βοσκηθησον
ται και ἐν πάσαισ
ταῖσ τρίβοισ ἡ νομὴ
ἀυτῶν + ου πεινά
σουσιν ὀυδε διψη
σουσιν ουδε πα

ταξει αυτουσ ο
καυσιον ουδε ὁ η
λιοσ + αλλ ο ἐλε
ων αυτουσ πα
ρακαλεσει αυτουσ
(one blank line)
[Ο]υκ ερευσεισ τον λαον
κατα την ταξιν βελ. ?
ειπεν ὁ κσ̅ τῶ κω̅ μου
(two lines blank)
ὅλη σοφία φοβοσ κ̅υ̅
συ ει .... θ̅σ̅
ομολογουμαι σοι κ̅ε̅
ἐν ὅλη καρ^δ μῦ ἐν βου

Fol. 212 b 1.
Gen. XXXI. 3—10.

κ̅ν̅........
[Ε]ιπεν κσ̅ πρὸσ
ἰακωβ αποστρέ
φου εἰσ τὸν ὀῖκον
τοῦ π̅ρ̅σ̅ σου. 5̅
εἰσ την γενεαν
σου αποστειλασ
δὲ ἰακωβ· ἐκά
λεσε λιαν και ῥα
χηλ εισ το πεδιον
ὁυ τα ποίμνια·
και ειπεν αυταισ
ὁρῶ ἐγω το προ
σωπον τοῦ π̅ρ̅σ̅
υμων· ὅτι ουκ εστι
προσ ἐμὲ ὥσ
εχθεσ και τρίτην
ημεραν ὁ δε
θ̅σ̅ του π̅ρ̅σ̅ μου
ἦν μετ ἐμου + και
αυται δὲ οιδατε

Fol. 212 *b* 2.

ὅτι εν παση τῆ
ἰσχύϊ μου δεδού
λευκα τῶ πρι ὺ
μῶν· ὁ δε πηρ ὺ
μων παρεκρου
σατο με· καὶ ἤλλα
ξε τὸν μισθον μου
τῶν δεκα ἀμνῶν
καὶ ου δέδωκεν
αὐτῶ ὁ θσ κακο
ποιῆσαί με ἐὰν
ουτωσ ειπη τὰ
ποικιλα ἐσται σοι
μισθοσ και τεξε?
ται παντα τα
προβατά σου λευκά
Καὶ ἀφειλατο ὁ θσ
πάντα τὰ κτή
νη τοῦ πρσ ὑμῶν
και ἔδωκεν μοι
αὐτα + καὶ ἐγένετο
(Laud. 36. τη γ των
βαίων Gen. XXXI. 3—
16 : ends ὁ θσ σου
ποιει).

Fol. 213 *a* 1.

Gen. XXVII. 23—33.

....
αἰ..........ωσ
αι χει... του αδελ
φὸυ αυτου δασειαι
και ευλογησεν αυ
τον· καὶ ειπεν
συ ει ὁ? υιοσ μου η?
s.

σαυ· ο δε ειπεν
εγω· καὶ εἶπεν
προσάγαγέ μοι καὶ
φάγομαι ἀπὸ τῆσ
θήρασ σου τέκνον.
και ἐυλογήσει σε
η ψυχή μου· καὶ
προσήνεγκεν αὐτῶ
και εφαγεν καὶ εἰ
σηνεγκεν αὐτῶ οἶ
νον· καὶ ἔπιεν·
καὶ εἶπεν αὐτῶ·
ἰσαὰκ ὁ πηρ αυ
του εγγισον μοι.

Fol. 213 *a* 2.

...ιλησον με
τεκνον και .γγ.
σασ εφιλησεν
αὐτον και ω??
σφράνθη την ο?
σμην των ιματι
ων αὐτου και ευ?
λογησεν αυτον 5
εἶπεν· ἰδοὺ ὁ?σμη
τοῦ υιου...μου ωσ
ὁ?σμη ἀγροῦ πλη?
ρουσ ον ευλογη
σεν κσ και δωη
σοι ο θσ ἀπο τῆσ
δρόσου τοῦ ουνου
και απὸ τῆσ πι
ότητοσ τῆσ γῆσ
καὶ πλῆθος σίτου
και οινου· καὶ δου
λευσατωσάν σοι
ἔθνη. καὶ προσκύ

Fol. 213 *b* 1.

Cont. from Fol. 211.

νησουσίν σοι...
τεσ· και γίνου κ...
οσ τοῦ αδελφοῦ
σου. καὶ προσκυ
νησουσιν σοι οἱ υἱ
οἱ τοῦ πρσ σου
ὁ καταρωμενοσ
σε επικαταρατοσ
ὅ δε ευλογων σε ευ
λογημένοσ.
Και εγενετο μετὰ τὸ
πάυσασθαι ἰσα
ἀκ· ἐυλογουντα
ιακωβ τον υιον αυ
τοῦ· καὶ ἐγένετο· ὅ
σον ἐξῆλθεν ἰακὼβ
ἀπὸ προσώπου ἰ
σαὰκ τοῦ πρσ αυ
τοῦ + και ἠσαῦ ὁ ἀ
δελφοσ αυτου ἠλ
θεν απο τῆς θή

Fol. 213 *b* 2.

.................εν
και...........μα
τα κα...σήνεγκε
τῶ πρι αυτοῦ καὶ
ἐιπεν· ἀναστή
τω ὁ πηρ μου· καὶ
φαγέτω ἀπὸ τῆσ
θήρασ τοῦ υἱου
αὐτοῦ· ὅπωσ ἐυ
λογήση με ἡ ψυχή
σου. κὸι εἶπεν αυ
τω ἰσαὰκ ὁ πηρ

12

αὐτοῦ τίσ εἶ σύ·
ὁ δὲ εἶπεν + ἐγώ ειμι
ὁ ὑ͞σ σου ὁ πρωτο
τοκοσ ησᾶν ἐξέ
στη δε ισαακ εκ
στασιν μεγαλην σφο
δρα· καὶ εἶπεν
και τίσ᾽ εστιν ᾽ο θη
ρευσασ μοι θηραν
Continued Fol. 216.

Fol. 214 α 1.

Prov. xxiii. 24—
xxiv. 4.

Επι νιωι δὲ ......
ευφρανθήσε ......
καρδία αὐτοῦ
ἐυφραινέσθω ὁ π͞η͞ρ
σου καὶ ἡ μ͞η͞ρ σου
επι σοι· καὶ χαιρέ
δω ἡ τεκουσα σε
δόσ μοι υἱὲ σην
καρδιαν· οἱ δὲ σοι
ὀφθαλμοι· ἐμασ
ὁ δουσ τηρ...ωσαν
πιθοσ γὰρ τετριμ
μενοσ εστιν· ἀλλό
τριοσ ὅικοσ· καὶ
φρέαρ στενὸν ἀλλό
τριον· ουτωσ γὰρ
συντομωσ ἀπο
λεῖται καὶ πᾶσ
παράνομοσ ἀνα
λωθησεται· τί
νι ὀναι· τινι θο

Fol. 214 α 2.

....
...............δί
...ι κὰι λ.χαι τί
νι συντριμματ ͣ
διακενησ· τίνοσ
πελιδνοὶ οἱ οφθαλ
μοι ὀυ τῶν ἐγχρο
νιζοντων ἐν ὀι
νοισ· και τῶν κα
τασκοπουμένων
ποῦ πότοι γίνον
ται μη μεθύσκεσ
θε ὀίνω· ἀλλ? ο
μιλείτε ανοισ
δικαίοισ· κὰι ὀμι
λειτε ἐν περιπά
τοισ· ἐὰν γὰρ εἰσ
τασ φιάλασ και
τὸ ποτήριον δῶσ
τοὺσ ὀφθαλμουσ
σου· ὕστερον περι

Fol. 214 b 1.

....
περ?...........
τὸ δε ε.χατον· ω...
περ ὑπὸ ὄφεωσ·
πεπληγὼσ ἐκτεί
νεται· και ωσπερ
ὑπο κεραστου δια
χειται αυτωι ο ιοσ
οἱ ὀφθαλμοι σου ὄ
ταν ἴδωσιν ἀλλο
τρίαν· τὸ στόμα
σου τότε λαλήσει
σκολιὰ· καὶ κα
(sic) τατακησῃ· ωσ

περ ἐν καρδία
θαλάσσησ· καὶ
ὥσπερ κυβερ
νητησ ἐν πολλω
κλυδωνι· ᾽ἰδου
ερεισ? ετυπτον με
και ουκ επονεσα?

Fol. 214 b 2.

......αιξαν μοι·
...᾽ ουκ ἤδειν πο
τε ἔσται ὄρθροσ· ἵνα
ἐλθὼν ζητησω·
μεθ ὧν συνελεύσο
μαι· υἱὲ μη ζηλω
σησ ἄνδρασ κά
κουσ μηδε επι
θυμησησ ἔιναι
μετ αὐτῶν· ψευ
δῆ γαρ μελετα· ἡ
καρδία αὐτῶν
καὶ πόνουσ τα
χειλη αυτων λαλει
μετα σοφιασ· οικο
δομειται ὅικοσ ͼ
μετα συνεσεωσ
ἀνορθοῦται· και
μετα αισθησεωσ
ἐμπιπλαται τα
ταμιεια παντοσ

FINIS.

CAMBRIDGE : PRINTED BY C. J. CLAY, M.A. AND SONS, AT THE UNIVERSITY PRESS.

For EU product safety concerns, contact us at Calle de José Abascal, 56–1°,
28003 Madrid, Spain or eugpsr@cambridge.org.

www.ingramcontent.com/pod-product-compliance
Ingram Content Group UK Ltd.
Pitfield, Milton Keynes, MK11 3LW, UK
UKHW010345140625
459647UK00010B/832